Language in Literature

Jakobson, age twenty-three, summer 1920, Prague

ROMAN JAKOBSON

Language in Literature

EDITED BY KRYSTYNA POMORSKA
AND STEPHEN RUDY

THE BELKNAP PRESS OF
HARVARD UNIVERSITY PRESS
CAMBRIDGE, MASSACHUSETTS
LONDON, ENGLAND

Library of Congress Cataloging-in-Publication Data

Jakobson, Roman, 1896–
    Language in literature.

    Bibliography: p.
    Includes index.
    1. Literature. 2. Poetics. 3. Semiotics.
I. Pomorska, Krystyna. II. Rudy, Stephen. III. Title.
PN54.J35   1987   809   86-19465
ISBN 0-674-51027-5 (alk. paper) (cloth)
ISBN 0-674-51028-3 (paper)

CONTENTS

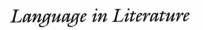

Language in Literature

Editors' Note

The texts of previously published essays are reprinted here with minimal editorial change. Publication and translation information is given at the beginning of the notes to each chapter.

For the transliteration of Russian we have decided to maintain the "linguistic" system throughout the book, since that is what Roman Jakobson would have preferred.

We are grateful to Natalia Glazman and John MacDougall for their invaluable assistance in the production of this book.

Introduction

by Krystyna Pomorska

Roman Jakobson was a thinker who approached every domain of human endeavor in a dynamic, integrated way. Any activity of man is organically connected with language: the life work of Jakobson exemplifies this truth to the fullest. The title of his last book, *Verbal Art, Verbal Sign, Verbal Time,* itself bears out that fact.[1] Even if language, in some cases, is not directly involved in the act of creation, it still remains a model for such an act. Consequently, the methods of modern linguistics, elaborated by Jakobson and his fellow scholars in the Moscow and Prague Linguistic Circles, serve as a basis for the scientific analysis of any language or artistic code. On the other hand, Jakobson's paraphrase of Terence—"Linguista sum; linguistici nihil a me alienum esse puto"—not only reflects his belief that linguistics is central to the scholar, but also that the sphere of linguistics is tied into a feedback system with man's other activities and endeavors.

When speaking about poetry and artistic prose, Jakobson consistently used the term "verbal art"—his apt translation of the Russian term *slovesnost'* or *slovesnoe iskusstvo.* There is, however, a deeper sense to the term. In Russian scholarship there has always been a close connection between the study of language, written literature, and the oral folk tradition. The three branches were considered and studied as one domain, integrated by language as the basic object of investigation. Jakobson's alma mater, Moscow University, was the center of this method. The ties between art and linguistics, however, became far more important in the theory that Jakobson himself developed. The necessity to draw conclusions from the language of poetry for the science of language and, conversely, to apply methods elaborated in linguistics to the study of poetry became clear for Jakobson during his high-school years at the Lazarev Institute of Oriental Languages in Moscow. The milieu in which Jakobson lived during his youth helped him to form this conviction. In *Dialogues,* his scholarly autobiography, he says: "I grew up among artists." [2] As early as 1913 he was a friend of leading painters and poets of the time: Kazimir Malevič, Pavel Filonov, Velimir Xlebnikov, and Aleksej Kručenyx. Jakobson himself became an ardent Futurist and wrote experimental "supraconscious" poems. In his correspondence of these years with Kručenyx and Xlebnikov he developed ideas bolder than those of Kručenyx and Xlebnikov themselves. He proposed poetry made of consonants only and experimented with "visual poetry," graphic puzzles composed of "interlaced letters" (*splety bukv*). Under the pen name Aljagrov, Jakobson's supraconscious poetry was published, jointly with Kručenyx, in a booklet *Zaumnaja gniga* (1915), illustrated by the renowned painter Olga Rozanova. *Zaumnaja gniga* was shown at the 1979 Paris exhibition "Paris—Moscow 1900–1930," at the Centre George Pompidou, and it figures as one of the most important items in the catalogue of the exhibition.

The scientific laboratories in which linguists and poets exchanged experiences and knowledge were the Moscow Linguistic Circle, founded in 1915, and the Prague Linguistic Circle, which initiated its activities in 1926. Jakobson was the cofounder of both circles, and the president and vice-president of each, respectively. In 1916, a group of Petersburg literary scholars, later labeled the Formalists, founded the Society for the Study of Poetic Language (OPOJAZ), with the Moscow Circle as their model. Jakobson became an active member and supporter. As one of the more brilliant members of OPOJAZ, Jurij Tynjanov, later said, without Jakobson "OPOJAZ would not exist." Jakobson declares in the acknowledgments to his *Selected Writings,* vol. II: "I still feel particularly attached to both congenial circles, two unusual workshops of vigorous and ardent research in the science of lan-

2

guage—*Moskovskij Lingvističeskij Kružok* and *Pražský Linguistický Krouzek.* A recent issue of an American journal names them 'two of the century's most imaginative and productive intellectual groups' . . . The proclaimed and achieved cooperation of the inquirers into the realm of the word with its creative masters seems to me an invaluable asset in the activities of both circles. We learned from poets. In particular, ties to the poetic experiments of Velimir Xlebnikov and to their author were the first and most powerful spur to my pondering on the complex anatomy of the word [*slovo kak takovoe* (the word as such)]."[3]

Jakobson's friendship with and admiration for Xlebnikov resulted in his first lengthy work on poetic language, which applied some principles from the new science of language: the appreciation of phonemes as the units most responsible for differentiating meanings. This was *The Newest Russian Poetry: First Sketch, Approaches to Xlebnikov,* written in 1919 as a preface for a planned edition of Xlebnikov's collected works, to be edited jointly by the young scholar and the poet. The edition did not materialize, but Jakobson presented his work at the Moscow Linguistic Circle in 1919, and its second version, partially reconstructed by the author in Prague, was published there in 1921.

His friendship with another great poet, Vladimir Majakovskij, started in 1916 and lasted until the poet's suicide in 1930. Jakobson devoted to Majakovskij's poetry a part of his second book, *On Czech Verse Primarily Compared to Russian* (1922), as well as a number of essays, the most important of which is included in this volume, "On a Generation That Squandered Its Poets." It is a penetrating analysis of the poet's essential myth, which another Russian poet, Mandelštam, later called "a thing of biblical power." Majakovskij's participation in Moscow Linguistic Circle debates is described in Jakobson's well-known essay "Linguistics and Poetics," which is also included here.

In another autobiographical document, the "Retrospect" in *SW* I, Jakobson emphasizes the importance of avant-garde painting for his theories. He writes:

> Perhaps the strongest impulse toward a shift in the approach to language and linguistics, however, was—for me, at least—the turbulent artistic movement of the early twentieth century. The great men of art born in the 1880's—Picasso (1881–1973), Joyce (1882–1941), Braque (1882–1963), Stravinsky (1882–1971), Xlebnikov (1885–1922), Le Corbusier (1887–1965)—were able to complete a thorough and comprehensive schooling in one of the most placid

spans of world history, before that "last hour of universal calm" (*Poslednij čas vsemirnoj tišiny*) was shattered by a train of cataclysms. The leading artists of that generation keenly anticipated the upheavals that were to come and met them while still young and dynamic enough to test their own creative power in this crucible. The extraordinary capacity of these discoverers to overcome again and again the faded habits of their own yesterdays, together with an unprecedented gift for seizing and shaping anew every older tradition or foreign model without sacrificing the stamp of their own permanent individuality in the amazing polyphony of ever new creations, is intimately allied to their unique feeling for the dialectic tension between the parts and the uniting whole, and between the conjugated parts, primarily between the two aspects of any artistic sign, its *signans* and its *signatum*. Stravinsky with his "search for the *One* out of the *Many*" reveals the core of his work when he reminds us that "the one precedes the many" and that "the coexistence of the two is constantly necessary." As he realized, all the problems of art (and, we may add, of language too) "revolve ineluctably about this question."

Those of us who were concerned with language learned to apply the principle of relativity in linguistic operations; we were consistently drawn in this direction by the spectacular development of modern physics and by the pictorial theory and practice of cubism, where everything "is based on relationship" and interaction between parts and wholes, between color and shape, between the representation and the represented. "I do not believe in things," Braque declared, "I believe only in their relationship." The mode in which the *signatum* stands relatively to the *signans,* on the one hand, and to the *denotatum,* on the other, had never been laid bare so plainly, nor the semantic problems of art brought forward so provocatively as in cubist pictures, which delay recognition of the transformed and obscured object or even reduce it to zero.[4]

Thus poetry and visual art became for Jakobson the fundamental spheres for observing how verbal phenomena work and for studying how to approach them. Poetry as a system not belonging to ordinary communication informed Jakobson's linguistic theory, especially his view on the problem of meaning, in a way similar to that of language pathology, to which he turned in later years. The extraordinary nature of poetic language lies in its primarily semiotic aspect. Of the two indissoluble parts of the language which constitute a sign—signifier and signified—it is the first that becomes most important in poetry. In a way, the signifier plays an independent, self-sufficient role: for example, the sound, as such—a signifier in relation to meaning—creates new semiotic relations as it carries inner motifs and themes, discernible on the level of a special sound pattern for which Jakobson used the old rhetorical term "paronomasia." The best analysis of this function of sound in poetry is offered in two works, "Language in Operation" and "Linguistics and Poetics."

Similar to the self-sufficiency of sound, grammatical categories in a poetic context also acquire a special significance and act as poetic tropes. Here also the grammatical signifier—for example, gender—governs the poetic universe and imposes its own, arbitrary as it is, signified upon the context. For instance, in his "Bronze Horseman" Puškin can oppose *Moscow* to a new *capital* (Petersburg) as an old *widow* to a young *princess,* and thus populate the passage with feminine "personalities." This is possible because in Russian both the proper place name *Moskva* and the noun *stolica* (capital) are of feminine gender. The gender in any grammar is arbitrary: in French death is feminine (*la mort*), while in German it is masculine (*der Tod*). Even in English, where gender is not immediately, morphologically marked or, as Jakobson says, is not obligatory, its arbitrary character comes to mind in cases where feminine gender is attributed to inanimate objects (ships). Thanks to its specific properties, grammar in poetry is not only just grammar but becomes a grammatical trope, endowed with a new, previously unrealized function and meaning.

As experimental poetry, especially Futurism, nourished Jakobson's new ideas of meaning, so modern painting, especially Cubism, informed his principle of relativity and, as he testifies in the "Retrospect" quoted above, helped to develop his phonological theory. According to phonology, the basic unit of speech, the phoneme, can be further dissolved into a set of specific properties or *distinctive features*. These properties work only in relation to each other and form *binary oppositions* that make up the phonemic system of language. Most important, it was disclosed that in the phonological system a distinctive feature is a unit that helps to differentiate meaning. For example, in a pair *bit* and *pit*, /b/ differs from its counterpart /p/ by the feature of voicedness. Thus it was shown how meaning is indissoluble from sound on every level of language.

Jakobson further applied the principle of relative, binary relations to the other components of language and verbal art. In poetry, the binary relations become an all-encompassing principle: a set of sequences themselves that provide the basic verse structure—parallelism. Following the ingenious anticipation of Gerard Manley Hopkins, Jakobson formulated the essential principle of poetry as that of *parallelism*. His classic study, "Grammatical Parallelism and Its Russian Facet," analyzes various types of parallelism in poetry, ranging from the canonical biblical type through folk poetry of various nations to Chinese verbal art. In *Dialogues* Jakobson characterizes parallelism succinctly: "There is a system of steady correspondences in composition and order of elements on many different levels: syntactic constructions, grammatical forms and grammatical categories, lexical synonyms . . . and finally combinations of sounds and prosodic schemes. This system confers upon the lines connected through parallelism both clear uniformity and great diversity. Against the background of the integral matrix, the effect of the variations of phonic, grammatical and lexical forms and meanings appear particularly eloquent."[5]

Jakobson emphasized that parallelism does not consist of identity but of *equivalence;* the equivalent pairs are, in turn, juxtaposed according to the principle of simlarity or contrast. Parallelism thus conceived creates variations amid the invariant: variations, since every combination of a pair is different; the invariant, since parallelism is inherent to poetic work.

Furthermore, artistic prose is also based on the same principle, although there is a hierarchical difference between the parallelism of verse and that of prose. "In poetry, it is the verse itself that dictates the structure of parallelism. The prosodic structure of the verse as a whole, the melodic unity and the repetition of the line and its metrical constituents determine the parallel distribution of elements of grammatical and lexical semantics, and, inevitably, the sound organizes the meaning. Inversely, in prose semantic units differing in extent play the primary role in organizing parallel structures. In this case, the parallelism of units connected by similarity, contrast or contiguity actively influences the composition of the plot, the characterization of the subjects of the action, and the sequence of themes in the narrative."[6]

According to Jakobson's theory, parallelism occurs wherever art itself occurs. In the 1930s he went beyond the limits of art as a "text" and sought the parallelistic, rather than causal, relation between poetry and the biography of a poet. Jakobson was able to discover the dialectical tension between the two realms, largely thanks to his intimate ties with the artists of his time, ties he maintained throughout his life. In Russia he was close to Xlebnikov, Majakovskij, and other poets and painters of his time or generation; in 1920 he went to Czechoslovakia, where he lived until the beginning of World War II, and the milieu was similar. Here again he found friends among the Czech avant-garde poets, to whom he always felt closer than to academic people.

Along with poetry and poets, folklore remained throughout Jakobson's life a subject of both admiration and study. From his freshman year, he engaged in fieldwork in dialectology, together with his university colleague and great friend, Petr Bogatyrev. In his "Retrospect" to *SW* IV, devoted to Slavic epic studies, he vividly describes the adventure in which the two researchers were involved in the Vereja district near Moscow, during the first year of World War I. They were taken by the local people for German spies and almost lost their lives as victims of a spontaneous revenge. In his typical way, Jakobson describes this incident not only as a fascinating anecdote but as an example of a myth *in statu nascendi:* "Rumors were growing: we were 'heard' talking German to each other, we were 'seen' poisoning wells . . . Our documents were declared to be fake and our glasses were considered evidence of our Germanity . . . We were witnessing a drastic example of the rise, multiplication and diffusion of formulaic responses to the burning topics. As it was stated in our report, 'something sprang up that probably might be called collective creation.'"[7] This experience did not discourage the researcher; Jakobson kept gathering folklore in various forms, using it as a subject and a tool of research. All his life he remained an ardent admirer of folk art. His collection of Russian *lubki*, along with paintings on glass and Slavic, Mexican, and Brazilian naive figurines, filled his study and his house. He inspired and encouraged people to study folk cuisine and medicine.

Jakobson regarded mythology and myth not only as an oral tradition worthy of investigation but as an omnipresent factor underlying all our activities. Among various types of myths he underlined the significance of national historical consciousness, with its specific interpretations of facts and occurrences. Most eloquent examples in this respect are the famous manuscript forgeries of the Romantic era, such as James Macpherson's *Works of Ossian* in Scotland or V. V. Hanka's skillful fabrication of Czech epics. As Jakobson shows, these myths, especially in Bohemia, were necessary for the nation's self-determination and thus should be treated as a positive part of its history.

Jakobson's pioneering thoughts on phonology, compatible with myth and mythology, influenced and thus found support and confirmation in modern anthropology, especially in the school of Claude Lévi-Strauss. The two men met for the first time in 1942, at the École Libre des Hautes Études, founded in New York by French and Belgian scholars in exile. Between 1942 and 1946, during Jakobson's professorship at the École Libre, the linguist and the ethnologist attended each other's lectures and shared their thoughts. In a recent interview for *Le Nouvel Observateur*, Lévi-Strauss said: "at the time I was a structuralist without knowing about it. Like Monsieur Jourdan, who spoke in prose. It was Jakobson, his lectures, which revealed to me that what I tried to do myself . . . had existed already in another discipline as a school of thought."[8] In recent years this school of thought influenced not only anthropology and psychoanalysis but history, conceived as "metahistory," according to the eloquent title of a book by Hayden White.[9]

The historical perspective is intrinsic to Jakobson's theory, according to which the time factor is omnipresent in language phenomena. The acknowledgment of ever-present temporal processes, in its turn, abolishes the absolute and endows any system under investigation with particular dynamism. Jakobson was concerned with these questions since at least 1919, when he wrote his article "Futurism," originally published in the Moscow journal *Iskusstvo* (Art). In later years he tested principles of temporality and dynamism against the vast material of linguistic phenomena, especially in the area of phonological systems. In particular he argued with the theories of Ferdinand de Saussure, who automatically divided phenomena of the past (diachrony), which he considered dynamic, and those he called systemic (synchrony), which he considered nondynamic.

Jakobson's scholarly environment, especially the Prague Circle, was for him a natural support. The year 1928 became a culmination point in Jakobson's and the Circle's efforts to introduce a historical perspective into linguistics and verbal art. Here is the scholar's personal account of those times and works, from the perspective of half a century:

> It is worth noting that the problem of a historical approach was concentrated on with special attention by the scholarship at the end of the 1920s. I believed it appropriate that the questions involved in the application of this method to different spheres of human activity and creation should be formulated and presented for discussion in the form of a few succinct theses. In the fall of

1927 I prepared a text on the treatment of the phonological systems and their historical changes, with the intention of presenting it to the First International Congress of Linguists that was to take place in The Hague in April, 1928. After securing the written approval of my friends and close collaborators, the linguists N. S. Trubetzkoy and Sergej Josifovič Karcevskij (1884–1955), I sent my theses to the Committee of the Congress. Both Trubetzkoy and I were amazed at the positive reaction of the Congress, and especially of W. Meyer-Lübke (1861–1936), the celebrated representative of the older generation of linguists who chaired the meeting that sympathetically discussed the principles we advanced. My collaborators and I were particularly delighted that our proposals immediately brought the international avant-garde of our science together as a group outside the official meeting halls of the Congress.

It was this success that inspired the manifesto "Problemy izučenija literatury i jazyka" (*Problems in the study of literature and language*), which I wrote at the end of the same year in close collaboration with Jurij Tynjanov (1894–1943), who was visiting me in Prague at that time. The short article was published in *Novyj Lef* upon Tynjanov's return to Leningrad and provoked a number of reactions from members of the OPOJAZ. The commentary that accompanies the new (1977) collection of Tynjanov's articles on the history of literature gives some details of this intense discussion. However, none of these reactions was published at the time, because the independent positions of the society became an object of official sanctions that soon led to the total suppression of this historic association.

In our manifesto we asserted that the immanent character of changes within literature and their close ties to the system of literary values necessarily implied a coordination between synchrony and diachrony in literature: the isolation of the notion of system from that of its transformation lost significance, since there does not and cannot exist an immobile system; evolution possesses a systemic character. This manifesto of ours remained sealed in silence in Russia for more than half a century. It was published only recently, in the collection of Tynjanov's writings mentioned above, long after it had often been quoted in the West, had been translated into a number of languages and had been the subject of an international debate. Our comparative study of language and of literature was important not only for insisting on the commonality of problems, but also for drawing attention to the mutual relation existing between literature (as well as language) and the different contiguous levels of the cultural context. And this relationship called for a wider structural elaboration, based on the new and fruitful semiotic concept of the "system of systems," in order to explain the link that united the different cultural levels without appeal to the confusing idea of a mechanistic sequence of cause and effect.[10]

Among elements whose *relations* constitute the dynamic system of language and art, some are more steady than others, and they play a specific role in the stabilization and balance of a system. The components of language do not constantly change but remain steady for longer periods, or else two components, the new and the old one, may coexist for some time; one finds the same process in the history of art. Jakobson attaches the most important role to the *generation* as a mechanism for producing, retaining, and conveying artistic and, by the same token, spiritual values. Moreover, he sees definite distributional regularities in specific types of art produced by different generations. In his preface to the anthology *La Poésie Russe* (1965), Jakobson offers a "table of generations," using the traditional Russian term as well as examples from his native Russia's art of the nineteenth and twentieth centuries.[11] The table of generations demonstrates how some decades were dominated by poets, for example, the 1880s, when Blok, Belyj, Axmatova, and Xlebnikov (to mention names of primary importance) were born; other periods favored prose writers. One finds a similar regularity in the birthdates of great musicians as opposed to painters. Focusing on a dynamic group rather than on approximately dated trends, Jakobson points toward a clearer, more realistic, and more functional historical mechanism.

V. V. Ivanov, a leading contemporary scholar, said in 1983: "Jakobson belongs to that powerful trend in our culture that is larger than just linguistics and literary studies, one to which the names of Baxtin and Vygotskij also belong. This trend—at a time when no one even thought about it—interpreted culture in a completely new way . . . The Futurism and avant-gardism of Jakobson's beginnings remained forever an essential part of him. But not in the sense that he would remain for long in the same place. He very quickly departed from his own self. This was a special manifestation of his Futurism. He once said that he was like the Baron von Münchhausen, who pulled himself up by his own hair. He always wanted to be unidentical with himself." Unerringly, Ivanov pointed to the core: "Roman Jakobson . . . always thought about the most general matters in concrete terms, with reference to particular examples, and always spoke about this clearly and understandably. We shall always remember Jakobson as the man who proved that one can do scientific work with joy, without pedantry or routine, that one can do it as something great and meaningful, under any circumstances, even in the face of catastrophes—and success- fully."[12]

Publisher's note: Krystyna Pomorska Jakobson was able to complete the reading of galley proofs before she died on December 19, 1986.

PART I

Questions of Literary Theory

The chief characteristic of Roman Jakobson's literary theory is his integrated and interdisciplinary approach to the work of art. His starting point is the interdependence between verbal art and language. In the early essay "On Realism in Art" (1921), Jakobson shows that realistic fiction, like any other style, depends on the medium of language and the conventions it implies. "Realism" does not represent the extraliterary world as it really is; rather, it follows certain rules whose goal is to create a particular illusion of reality. Jakobson's articles on "Futurism" (1919) and "Dada" (1921) are akin to his study of realism. The author links Cubism and Futurism in painting to the latest findings in science that clarify the discrepancy between the nature of a physical object and our perception of it. Thus in avant-garde art the "deformation" of an object is induced by a dynamic perception of its physical shape, whereas the naive illusionism of traditional painting, with its perspectival conventions, limited the reality it depicted. Moreover, in modern art an object is not only mediated by a set of pictorial devices, but the devices themselves are laid bare. Cubism and Futurism led to the realization that, to paraphrase Braque, not things but the relations between them constitute reality. Dada, in Jakobson's interpretation, is an even more radical type of relativism: the understanding of past art as both conventional and temporally conditioned leads Dada to assume an antiaesthetic and nihilistic stance.

"Problems in the Study of Language and Literature," written in 1928 in collaboration with the Leningrad literary critic Jurij Tynjanov (1894–1943), and "The Dominant," a lecture from Jakobson's course on Russian Formalism at Brno University in 1935, both address questions of literary evolution. As opposed to scholars who insist on separating the history of literature (diachronic studies) from the description of a literary system as a static pattern (synchronic studies), Jakobson and Tynjanov argue that any evolution possesses a systemic character and that any system is dynamic in nature. Moreover, as a hierarchical structure, a work of art must have a focal component—a "dominant"—that specifies it. For example, medieval Slavic verse was specified by the obligatory presence of rhyme, whereas for later types of verse an equal number of syllables per line was required and rhyme became optional. Similarly, an entire epoch viewed as a system has a dominant: for Romanticism it was music; for the Renaissance, visual art. The dominant is thus changeable as a specifier of the system and accounts for its historical dynamism.

"Language in Operation" (written in 1949 but first published only in 1964) and especially "Linguistics and Poetics" (1960) are among Jakobson's most comprehensive and renowned studies. "Language in Operation" examines the close interconnection between sound and meaning that is integral to a poetic work. An analysis of Edgar Allan Poe's "The Raven" reveals the importance of the refrain *nevermore* in determining its sound texture and thematics, which is supported by the poet's own account of its creation. In "Linguistics and Poetics" Jakobson constructs a model of language in operation, utilizing the insights of communication theory. The six factors involved in any speech event are shown to have corresponding linguistic functions. This model makes it possible to integrate the poetic function into any speech event and to define poetic usage as a focus on the linguistic material itself. Poetry thus proves to be one of the most semioticized subcodes of the linguistic system.

The last essay in this section, "Two Aspects of Language and Two Types of Aphasic Disturbances" (1956), integrates linguistic theory with poetics and neurolinguistics in a profound and suggestive way. It provides rigorous proof for Jakobson's theory of poetic language, in particular his conception of metaphor and metonymy. Our entire linguistic activity gravitates around the axes of selection and combination, which are connected respectively to the metaphoric and metonymic poles in language: the process of selection underlies the metaphoric operation of comparison, while combinatorial procedures are related to the metonymic operation of contiguity. Neurolinguistically, the primacy of these two processes is evident from the role they play in the two polar aphasic syndromes, which Jakobson labels "similarity" and "contiguity" disorders. They are related, in turn, to the two basic types of discourse, poetry and prose.

CHAPTER 1

On Realism in Art

Until recently, the history of art, particularly that of literature, has had more in common with causerie than with scholarship. It obeyed all the laws of causerie, skipping blithely from topic to topic, from lyrical effusions on the elegance of forms to anecdotes from the artist's life, from psychological truisms to questions concerning philosophical significance and social environment. It is a gratifying and easy task to chat about life and times using literary work as a basis, just as it is more gratifying and easier to copy from a plaster cast than to draw a living body. In causerie we are slipshod with our terminology; in fact, variations in terms and equivocations so apt to punning often lend considerable charm to the conversation. The history of art has been equally slipshod with respect to scholarly terminology. It has employed the current vocabulary without screening the words critically, without defining them precisely, and without considering the multiplicity of their meanings. For example, historians of literature unconscionably confused the idealism denoting a specific philosophical doctrine with a looser idealism denoting behavior motivated by other than narrow considerations of material gain. Still more hopeless was the web of confusion surrounding the term "form," brilliantly exposed by Anton Marty in his works on general grammar. It was the term "realism," however, which fared especially badly. The uncritical use of this word, so very elusive in meaning, has had fateful consequences.

What is realism as understood by the theoretician of art? It is an artistic trend which aims at conveying reality as closely as possible and strives for maximum verisimilitude. We call realistic those works which we feel accurately depict life by displaying verisimilitude. Right off we are faced with an ambiguity, namely:

> 1. *Realism may refer to the aspiration and intent of the author; i.e., a work is understood to be realistic if it is conceived by its author as a display of verisimilitude, as true to life* (meaning *A*).
> 2. *A work may be called realistic if I, the person judging it, perceive it as true to life* (meaning *B*).

In the first case, we are forced to evaluate on an intrinsic basis; in the second case, the reader's individual impression is the decisive criterion. The history of art has hopelessly confused these two interpretations of the term "realism." An objective and irrefutable validity is ascribed to individual, private local points of view. The question as to whether a given work is realistic or not is covertly reduced to the question of what attitude I take toward it. Thus meaning *B* imperceptibly replaces meaning *A*.

Classicists, sentimentalists, the romanticists to a certain extent, even the "realists" of the nineteenth century, the modernists to a large degree, and finally the futurists, expressionists, and their like, have more than once steadfastly proclaimed faithfulness to reality, maximum verisimilitude—in other words, realism—as the guiding motto of their artistic program. In the nineteenth century, this motto gave rise to an artistic movement. It was primarily the late copiers of that trend who outlined the currently recognized history of art, in particular, the history of literature. Hence one specific case, one separate artistic movement, was identified as the ultimate manifestation of realism in art and was made the standard by which to measure the degree of realism in preceding and succeeding artistic movements. Thus a new covert identification has occurred, a third meaning of the word "realism" has crept in (meaning *C*), *one which comprehends the sum total of the features characteristic of one specific artistic current of the nineteenth century.*

In other words, to the literary historians the realistic works of the last century represent the highest degree of verisimilitude, the maximum faithfulness to life.

Let us now analyze the concept of verisimilitude in art. While in painting and in the other visual arts the illusion of an objective and absolute faithfulness to reality is conceivable, "natural" (in Plato's terminology), verisimilitude in a verbal expression or in a literary description obviously makes no sense whatever. Can the question be raised about a higher degree of verisimilitude of this or that poetic trope? Can one say that one metaphor or metonymy is conventional or, so to say, figurative? The methods of projecting three-dimensional space onto a flat surface are established by convention; the use of color, the abstracting, the simplification, of the object depicted, and the choice of reproducible features are all based on convention. It is necessary to learn the conventional language of painting in order to "see" a picture, just as it is impossible to understand what is said without knowing the language. This conventional, traditional aspect of painting to a great extent conditions the very act of our visual perception. As tradition accumulates, the painted image becomes an ideogram, a formula, to which the object portrayed is linked by contiguity. Recognition becomes instantaneous. We no longer see a picture. The ideogram needs to be deformed. The artist-innovator must impose a new form upon our perceptions, if we are to detect in a given thing those traits which went unnoticed the day before. He may present the object in an unusual perspective; he may violate the rules of composition canonized by his predecessors. Thus Kramskoj, one of the founders of the so-called realist school of Russian painting, recounts in his memoirs his efforts to deform to the utmost the principles of composition as advocated by the Academy. The motivation behind this "disorder" was the desire for a closer approximation of reality. The urge to deform an ideogram usually underlies the Sturm und Drang stage of new artistic currents.

Everyday language uses a number of euphemisms, including polite formulas, circumlocutions, allusions, and stock phrases. However, when we want our speech to be candid, natural, and expressive, we discard the usual polite etiquette and call things by their real names. They have a fresh ring, and we feel that they are "the right words." But as soon as the name has merged with the object it designates, we must, conversely, resort to metaphor, allusion, or allegory if we wish a more expressive term. It will sound more impressive, it will be *more striking*.

To put it in another way, when searching for a word which will revitalize an object, we pick a farfetched word, unusual at least in its given application, a word which is forced into service. Such an unexpected word may, depending on current usage, be either a figurative or a direct reference to the object. Examples of this sort are numerous, particularly in the history of obscene vocabulary. To call the sex act by its own name sounds brazen, but if in certain circles strong language is the rule, a trope or euphemism is more forceful and effective. Such is the verb *utilizirovat'* (to utilize) of the Russian hussar. Foreign words are accordingly more insulting and are readily picked up for such purposes. A Russian may use the absurd epithets *gollandskij* (Dutch) or *moržovyj* (walruslike) as abusive modifiers of an object which has nothing to do with either Holland or walruses; the impact of his swearing is greatly heightened as a result. Instead of the infamous oath involving copulation with the addressee's mother, the Russian peasant prefers the fantastic image of copulating with the addressee's soul—and, for further emphasis, uses the negative parallelism: *tvoju dušu ne mat'* (your soul not your mother).

The same applies to revolutionary realism in literature. The words of yesterday's narrative grow stale; now the item is described by features that were yesterday held to be the least descriptive, the least worth representing, features which were scarcely noticed. "He is fond of dwelling on unessential details" is the classic judgment passed on the innovators by conservative critics of every era. I leave it to the lover of quotations to collect similar judgments pronounced on Puškin, Gogol', Tolstoj, Andrej Belyj, and others by their contemporaries. To the followers of a new movement, a description based on unessential details seems more real than the petrified tradition of their predecessors. But the perception of those of a more conservative persuasion continues to be determined by the old canons; they will accordingly interpret any deformation of these canons by a new movement as a rejection of the principle of verisimilitude, as a deviation from realism. They will therefore uphold the old canons as the only realistic ones. Thus, in discussing meaning *A* of the term "realism" (the artistic intent to render life as it is), we see that the definition leaves room for ambiguity:

> *A₁. The tendency to deform given artistic norms conceived as an approximation of reality.*
>
> *A₂. The conservative tendency to remain within the limits of a given artistic tradition, conceived as faithfulness to reality.*

Meaning *B* presupposes that my subjective evaluation will pronounce a given artistic fact faithful to reality; thus, factoring in the results obtained, we find:

> B_1. *I rebel against a given artistic code and view its deformation as a more accurate rendition of reality.*
> B_2. *I am conservative and view the deformation of the artistic code, to which I subscribe, as a distortion of reality.*

In the latter case, only those artistic facts which do not contradict my artistic values may be called realistic. But inasmuch as I hold my own values (the tradition to which I belong) to be the most realistic, and because I feel that within the framework of other traditions my code cannot be fully realized even if the tradition in question does not contradict it, I find in these traditions only a partial, embryonic, immature, or decadent realism. I declare that the only genuine realism is the one on which I was brought up. Conversely, in the case of B_1, my attitude to all artistic formulas contradicting a particular set of artistic values unacceptable to me would be similar to my attitude in the case of B_2 toward forms which are *not* in opposition. I can readily ascribe a realistic tendency (realistic as understood by A_1) to forms which were never conceived as such. In the same way, the Primitives were often interpreted from the point of view of B_1. While their incompatibility with the norms on which we were raised was immediately evident, their faithful adherence to their own norms and tradition was lost from view (A_2 was interpreted as A_1). Similarly, certain writings may be felt and interpreted as poetry, although not at all meant as such. Consider Gogol''s pronouncement about the poetic qualities of an inventory of the Muscovite crown jewels, Novalis' observation about the poetic nature of the alphabet, the statement of the Futurist Kručenyx about the poetic sound of a laundry list, or that of the poet Xlebnikov claiming that at times a misprint can be an artistically valid distortion of a word.

The concrete content of A_1, A_2, B_1, and B_2 is extremely relative. Thus a contemporary critic might detect realism in Delacroix, but not in Delaroche; in El Greco and Andrej Rublev, but not in Guido Reni; in a Scythian idol, but not in the Laocoön. A directly opposite judgment, however, would have been characteristic of a pupil of the Academy in the previous century. Whoever senses faithfulness to life in Racine does not find it in Shakespeare, and vice versa.

In the second half of the nineteenth century, a group of painters struggled in Russia on behalf of realism (the first phase of C, i.e., a special case of A_1). One of them, Repin, painted a picture, "Ivan the Terrible Kills His Son." Repin's supporters greeted it as realistic (C, a special case of B_1). Repin's teacher at the Academy, however, was appalled by the lack of realism in the painting, and he carefully itemized all the instances of Repin's distortion of verisimilitude by comparison with the academic canon which was for him the only guarantee of verisimilitude (from the standpoint of B_2). But the Academy tradition soon faded, and the canons of the "realist" Itinerants (*peredvižniki*) were adopted and became social fact. Then new tendencies arose in painting, a new Sturm und Drang began; translated into the language of manifestos, a new truth was being sought.

To the artist of today, therefore, Repin's painting seems unnatural and untrue to life (from the standpoint of B_2). In turn, Repin failed to see anything in Degas and Cézanne except grimace and distortion (from the standpoint of B_2). These examples bring the extreme relativity of the concept of "realism" into sharp relief. Meanwhile, those art historians who, as we have already indicated, were primarily associated with the later imitators of "realism" by virtue of their aesthetic code (the second phase of C), arbitrarily equated C and B_2, even though C is in fact simply a special case of B. As we know, meaning B covertly replaces A, so that the whole difference between A_1 and A_2 is lost, and the destruction of ideographs is understood only as a means of creating new ones. The conservative, of course, fails to recognize the self-sufficient aesthetic value of deformation. Thus, supposedly having A in mind (actually A_2), the historian of art addresses himself to C. Therefore, when a literary historian brilliantly declares that "Russian literature is typically realistic," his statement is tantamount to saying, "Man is typically twenty years old."

As the tradition equating realism with C became established, new realist artists (in the A_1 sense) were compelled to call themselves neorealists, realists in the higher sense of the word, or naturalists, and they drew a line between quasi- or pseudo-realism (C) and what they conceived to be genuine realism (i.e., their own). "I am a realist, but only in the higher sense of the word," Dostoevskij declared. And an almost identical declaration has been made in turn by the Symbolists, by Italian and Russian Futurists, by German Expressionists, and so on. These neorealists have at various times completely identified their aesthetic platforms with realism in general, and, therefore, in evaluating the representatives of *C,* they had to expel them from the ranks of realism. Thus posthumous criticism has periodically questioned the realism of Gogol', Dostoevskij, Tolstoj, Turgenev, and Ostrovskij.

The manner in which *C* itself is characterized by historians of art, especially historians of literature, is very vague and approximate. We must not forget that the imitators were those who decided which characteristics typified realism. A closer analysis will no doubt replace *C* with a number of more precise values and will reveal that certain devices which we indiscriminately associate with *C* are by no means typical of all the representatives of the so-called realist school; the same devices are in fact also found outside the realist school.

We have already mentioned the characterization of progressive realism in terms of unessential details. One such device—cultivated, incidentally, by a number of the representatives of the *C* school (in Russia, the so-called Gogolian school) and for that reason sometimes incorrectly identified with *C*—is *the condensation of the narrative by means of images based on contiguity, that is, avoidance of the normal designative term in favor of metonymy or synecdoche.* This "condensation" is realized either in spite of the plot or by eliminating the plot entirely. Let us take a crude example from Russian literature, that of the suicides of Poor Liza and Anna Karenina. Describing Anna's suicide, Tolstoj primarily writes about her handbag. Such an unessential detail would have made no sense to Karamzin, although Karamzin's own tale (in comparison with the eighteenth-century adventure novel) would likewise seem but a series of unessential details. If the hero of an eighteenth-century adventure novel encounters a passer-by, it may be taken for granted that the latter is of importance either to the hero or, at least, to the plot. But it is obligatory in Gogol' or Tolstoj or Dostoevskij that the hero first meet an unimportant and (from the point of view of the story) superfluous passer-by, and that their resulting conversation should have no bearing on the story. Since such a device is frequently thought to be realistic, we will denote it by *D,* stressing that this *D* is often found within *C.*

A pupil is asked to solve a problem: "A bird flew out of its cage; how soon will it reach the forest, if it flies at such and such a speed per minute, and the distance between the cage and the forest is such and such?" "What color is the cage?" asks the child. This child is a typical realist in the *D* sense of the word.

Or an anecdote of the type known as the Armenian riddle: "It hangs in the drawing room and is green; what is it?" The answer: "A herring."—"Why in a drawing room?"—"Well, why couldn't they hang it there?" "Why green?"—"It was painted green."—"But why?"—"To make it harder to guess." This desire to conceal the answer, this deliberate effort to delay recognition, brings out a new feature, the newly improvised epithet. Exaggeration in art is unavoidable, wrote Dostoevskij; in order to show an object, it is necessary to deform the shape it used to have; it must be tinted, just as slides to be viewed under the microscope are tinted. You color your object in an original way and think that it has become more palpable, *clearer,* more real (A_1). In a Cubist's picture, a single object is multiplied and shown from several points of view; thus it is made more palpable. This is a device used in painting. But it is also possible to motivate and justify this device in the painting itself; an object is doubled when reflected in a mirror. The same is true of literature. The herring is green because it has been painted; a startling epithet results, and the trope becomes an epic motif. "Why did you paint it?" The author will always have an answer, but, in fact, there is only one right answer: "To make it harder to guess."

Thus a strange term may be foisted on an object or asserted as a particular aspect of it. Negative parallelism explicitly rejects metaphorical substitution for its proper term: "I am not a tree, I am a woman," says the girl in a poem by the Czech poet Šrámek. This literary construction can be justified; from a special narrative feature, it can become a detail of plot development: "Some said, 'These are the footprints of an ermine'; others reported, 'No, these are not the footprints of an ermine; it was Čurila Plenkovič passing by.'" Inverted negative parallelism rejects a normally used term and employs a metaphor (in the Šrámek poem quoted earlier: "I am not a woman, I am a tree," or the following from a play by another Czech poet, Čapek: "What is this?—A handkerchief.—But it is not a handkerchief. It is a beautiful woman standing by the window. She's dressed all in white and is dreaming of love").

In Russian erotic tales, copulation is frequently stated in terms of inverted parallelism; the same is true of wedding songs, with the difference that in the latter, the constructions using metaphors are not usually justified, while in the former these metaphors find motivation as the means by which the cunning hero can seduce the fair maid, or as an interpretation of human copulation by an animal incapable of comprehending it. From time to time, the consistent motivation and justification of poetic constructions have also been called realism. Thus the Czech novelist Čapek-Chod in his tale, "The Westernmost Slav," slyly calls the first chapter, in which "romantic" fantasy is motivated by typhoid delirium, a "realistic chapter."

Let us use E to designate such realism, i.e., *the requirement of consistent motivation and realization of poetic devices*. This E is often confused with C, B, and so on. By failing to distinguish among the variety of concepts latent in the term "realism," theoreticians and historians of art—in particular, of literature—are acting as if the term were a bottomless sack into which everything and anything could be conveniently thrown.

This objection may be made: No, not everything. No one will call Hoffmann's fantastic tales realistic. But does this not indicate that there is somehow a single meaning in the word "realism," that there is, after all, some common denominator?

My answer is: No one will call a "key" a "lock," but this does not mean that the word "lock" has only one meaning. We cannot equate with impunity the various meanings of the word "realism" just as we cannot, unless we wish to be called mad, equate a hair lock with a padlock. It is true that the various meanings of some words (for example, "bill") are far more distinct from one another than they are in the case of the word "realism," where we can imagine a set of facts about which we could simultaneously say, "this is realism in the meaning C, B, or A_1 of the word." Nevertheless, it is inexcusable to confuse C, B, A_1, and so on. A term once used in American slang to denote a socially inept person was "turkey." There are probably "turkeys" in Turkey, and there are doubtless men named Harry who are blessed with great amounts of hair. But we should not jump to conclusions concerning the social aptitudes of the Turks or the hairiness of men named Harry. This "commandment" is self-evident to the point of imbecility, yet those who speak of artistic realism continually sin against it.

CHAPTER 2

Futurism

It was in the twentieth century that painting first consistently broke off with the tendencies of naive realism. In the last century the picture was obliged to convey perception; the artist was a slave to routine, and he consciously ignored both everyday and scientific experience. As if what we know about an object were one thing, and the direct content of a presentation of objects were an entirely different thing—and the two completely unrelated. As if we knew an object only from one side, from one point of view, as if, upon seeing a forehead, we forget that the nape of the neck exists, as if the neck were the dark side of the moon, unknown and unseen. Similar to the way in which in old novels the events are presented to us only so far as they are known to the hero. One can find attempts at doubling points of view on an object even in the old painting, motivated by the reflection of a landscape or of a body in the water or in a mirror. Compare likewise the device in Old Russian painting of depicting a martyr in one and the same picture twice or three times in contiguous stages of an action in the process of unfolding. But it was Cubism that first canonized multiple points of view. Deformation was realized in earlier pictorial art on an insignificant scale: for example, hyperbole was tolerated, or the deformation was motivated by an application that was humorous (caricature), ornamental (teratology), or finally by the data of nature itself (chiaroscuro). Freed from motivational motifs by the acts of Cézanne, deformation was canonized by Cubism.

The Impressionists, applying the experience of science, had decomposed color into its component parts. Color ceased to be subjugated to the sensation of the nature depicted. There appeared blotches of color, even chromatic combinations, which copied nothing, which were not imposed upon the picture from without. The creative mastery of color naturally led to a realization of the following law: any increase in form is accompanied by a change in color, and any change in color generates new forms (a formulation of Gleizes and Metzinger).[1]

In science this law was first advanced, it seems, by Stumpf, one of the pioneers of the new psychology, who spoke about the correlation between color and colored spatial form: quality shares in changes of extension. When extension is changed, quality is also transformed. Quality and extension are by nature inseparable and cannot be imagined independently of one another. This obligatory connection may be opposed to the empirical connectedness of two parts lacking such an obligatory character, e.g., a head and torso. Such parts can be imagined separately.[2]

The set (*ustanovka*)[3] toward nature created for painting an obligatory connection precisely of such parts which are in essence disconnected, whereas the mutual dependence of form and color was not recognized. On the contrary, a set toward pictorial expression resulted in the creative realization of the necessity of the latter connection, where the object is freely interpenetrated by other forms (so-called Divisionism). Line and surface attract the artist's attention; they cannot exclusively copy the boundaries of nature; the Cubist consciously cuts nature up with surfaces, introduces arbitrary lines.

The emancipation of painting from elementary illusionism entails an intensive elaboration of various areas of pictorial expression. The correlations of volumes, constructive asymmetry, chromatic contrast, and texture enter the foreground of the artist's consciousness.

The results of this realization are the following: (1) the canonization of a series of devices, which thus also allows one to speak of Cubism as a school; (2) the laying bare of the device. Thus the realized texture no longer seeks any sort of justification for itself; it becomes autonomous, demands for itself new methods of formulation, new material. Pieces of paper begin to be pasted on the picture, sand is thrown on it. Finally, cardboard, wood, tin, and so on, are used.

Futurism brings with it practically no new pictorial devices; instead, it widely utilizes Cubist methods. It is not a new school of painting, but rather a new aesthetics. The very approach to the picture, to painting, to art, changes. Futurism offers picture-slogans, pictorial demonstrations. It has no fixed, crystallized canons. Futurism is the antipode of classicism.

Without a set, to use a psychological term, without a style, to use a term from art criticism, there can be no presentation of an object. For the nineteenth century, what is characteristic is a striving to see things as they were seen in the past, as it is customary to see: to see like Raphael, like Botticelli. The present was projected into the past, and the past dictated the future, all according to the famous formula: "Another day has gone by, praise the Lord. Lord grant tomorrow be the same."

What art, if not representational art, could serve so successfully the basic tendency of fixing the instant of movement, of breaking down a movement into a series of separate static elements? But static perception is a fiction. As a matter of fact, "everything is moving, everything is quickly being transformed. A profile never remains motionless before one's eyes; it continuously appears and disappears. As a result of the stability of the image on the retina, objects multiply, are deformed, follow one another, like hurried vibrations in the space one is running through. So it is that running horses have not four legs but twenty, and their movements are triangular" (from a manifesto of Futurist artists).[4]

Static, one-sided, isolated perception—a pictorial anachronism—is something in the nature of the classical muses, gods, and lyres. But we are no longer shooting out of a harquebus or traveling in a heavy carriage. The new art has put an end to static forms; it has even put an end to the last fetish of the static: beauty. In painting nothing is absolute. What was true for the artists of yesterday is today a lie, as one Futurist manifesto puts it.

The overcoming of *statics*, the discarding of the absolute, is the main thrust of modern times, the order of the day. A negative philosophy and tanks, scientific experiment and deputies of Soviets, the principle of relativity and the Futurist "Down With!" are destroying the garden hedges of the old culture. The unity of the fronts of attack is astonishing.

"At the present time we are again experiencing a period in which the old scientific edifice is crumbling, but the crumbling is so complete that it is unprecedented in the history of science. But even that is not all. Among the truths being destroyed are ones which were never even uttered by anyone, which were never emphasized, so self-apparent did they seem, so unconsciously were they used and posited as the basis for every sort of reasoning." A particularly characteristic feature of the new doctrine is the unprecedented paradoxical nature of many of even its simplest propositions: they clearly contradict what is usually called "common sense."

The last sign of substance is vanishing from the physical world. "How do we picture time to ourselves? As something flowing continuously and homogeneously, with an eternal, identical speed everywhere. One and the same time flows in the entire world; it is quite obvious that there cannot be two times which flow in different parts of the universe at different speeds. Closely connected with this are our conceptions of the simultaneity of two events, of 'before' and of 'after,' for these three most elementary notions are accessible even to an infant; they have an identical sense, by whomever or wherever they are used. The concept of time conceals for us something absolute, something completely unrelative. But the new doctrine rejects the absolute character of time, and therefore the existence of 'world' time as well. Every identical self-moving system has its own time; the speed of time-flow is not identical in each such system." Does absolute peace of mind exist, even if only in the form of an abstract concept which has no real existence in nature? From the principle of relativity it follows that absolute peace of mind does not exist.

"Time gets involved in all spatial dimensions. We cannot define the geometrical form of a body which is in motion in relation to us. We define always its kinetic form. Thus our spatial dimensions occur in reality not in a three-dimensional, but in a four-dimensional variety."

"These pictures in the field of philosophical thought should produce a revolution greater than Copernicus' displacement of the earth from the center of the universe . . . Does not the power of the natural sciences make itself felt in the transition from an undisputed experimental fact—the impossibility of determining the absolute motion of the earth—to questions of the psyche? The contemporary philosopher cries out in embarrassment: There is nothing but deceit on that side of the truth."

"The newly discovered offers a sufficient quantity of images for the construction of the world, but they break its former architecture, so familiar to us, and can be fit only within the boundaries of a new style, one which far out-distances in its free lines the borders not only of the old external world, but also of the basic forms of our thinking."

(Direct quotations in this and the preceding four paragraphs are from O. D. Xvol'son, *The Principle of Relativity,* and N. A. Umov, *The Characteristic Features of Contemporary Natural-Scientific Thought.*)

The basic tendencies of collectivist thought: the destruction of abstract fetishism, the destruction of the remnants of statics (Bogdanov, *The Sciences of Social Consciousness*). And so the main lines of the moment are obvious in all domains of culture.

If Cubism, following Cézanne's behests, constructed a picture by starting from the simplest volumes—the cube, cone, sphere—offering its own sort of primitiveness in painting, then the Futurists in search of kinetic forms introduced into the picture the curved cone, the curved cylinder, collisions of cones with sharp, curved ellipsoids, and so on, in a word, destroying the mountings of volumes (see Carrà's manifesto).[5]

Perceptions, in multiplying, become mechanized; objects, not being perceived, are taken on faith. Painting battles against the automatization of perception; it signals the object. But, having become antiquated, artistic forms are also perceived on faith. Cubism and Futurism widely use the device of impeded perception, which corresponds in poetry to the step-ladder construction discovered by contemporary theoreticians.

In the fact that even the most discerning eye is able only with difficulty to make sense of objects that have been totally transubstantiated, there is a particular charm. A picture that gives itself with such reserve expects precisely that it will be questioned again and again. Let us take Leonardo da Vinci's words as a defense of Cubism in this respect:

> We know well that our sight, by rapid observations, discovers in one point an infinity of forms: nevertheless it only understands one thing at a time. Suppose that you, reader, were to see the whole of this page at a glance, and concluded instantly that it is full of various letters; you would not at the same moment know

what letters they are, nor what they would mean. You would have to go from one word to another and from line to line if you would wish to know these letters, just as you would have to climb step by step to reach the top of a building, or else never reach the top. (Cited by Gleizes and Metzinger.)[6]

A particular instance of impeded recognition in painting, i.e., a construction of the type—this is a lion, not a dog—is like a riddle which deliberately leads us to a false solution; compare the so-called "false recognition" of classical poetics or the negative parallelism of the Slavic epic. Aristotle: "For men delight in seeing likenesses because in contemplating them it happens that they are learning and reasoning out what each thing is, e.g. that this man [in the painting] is that [sort of man]; for if by fortune one has not previously seen what is imitated, the likeness will not produce pleasure as an imitation, but because of its execution, or surface coloring, or some other cause of this sort."[7] In other words, it was already clear to Aristotle that, alongside a type of painting that signals the perception of nature, there exists a type of painting that signals our direct chromatic and spatial perception (it does not matter whether the object is unknown or whether it has simply dropped out of the picture).

When a critic looking at such pictures is at a loss and asks: "What in the world does this mean, I don't understand"—and what precisely does he want to understand?—he is like the metaphysician of the fable: they want to pull him out of the hole in the ground he's in and all he can do is ask: "What sort of thing is rope?" More briefly: for him, perception that is valuable in and of itself does not exist. He prefers paper currency to gold: currency, with its conventionally assigned value, seems to him more "literary."

CHAPTER 3

Dada

Dada means nothing.
Dada 3, 1918

Dilettantes, rise up against art!
Poster at Dada exhibition, Berlin, June 1920

In these days of petty affairs and stable values, social thought is subjugated to the laws of bell-ringing patriotism. Just as, for a child, the world does not extend beyond the nursery, and everything outside that realm is thought of by analogy, so the petty bourgeois evaluates all cities in comparison to his native city. Citizens of a somewhat higher order lay everything that relates, if not to a different city, then to a foreign country, on the Procrustean bed of the *homely* and dance according to the tune of their native culture. One's own little world and all that is "translatable" into one's own dialect versus the incomprehensible barbarians—such is the usual scheme. Is this not the reason for the fact that sailors are revolutionary, that they lack that very "stove," that hearth, that little house of their own, and are everywhere equally *chez soi?* Limitation in time corresponds to limitation in space; the past is normally depicted by a series of metaphors whose material is the present. But at the moment, despite the fact that Europe has been turned into a multiplicity of isolated points by visas, currencies, cordons of all sorts, space is being reduced in gigantic strides—by radio, the telephone, aeroplanes. Even if the books and pictures do not get through today, beleaguered as they are by chauvinism and the "hard currency" of state national borders, nevertheless the questions that are being decided today somewhere in Versailles are questions of self-interest for the Silesian worker, and if the price of bread rises, the hungry citydweller begins to "feel" world politics. The appeal to one's countrymen loses its conviction. Even the humorists are crying that there is no longer an established order of things (*byt*).[1] Values are not in demand.

What corresponds in scientific thought to this sudden "swing"? Replacing the science of the "thousand and first example," inescapable in days when the formula "So it was, so it shall be" ruled, when tomorrow put itself under the obligation of resembling today, and when every respectable man had his own *chez soi,* there suddenly appears the science of relativity. For yesterday's physicist, if not our earth, then at least our space and our time were the only possible ones and imposed themselves on all worlds; now they are proclaimed to be merely particular instances. Not a single trace of the old physics has remained. The old physicists have three arguments: "He's a Jew," "He's a Bolshevik," "It contradicts 'common sense.'" The great historian Spengler, in his outspoken book *The Decline of the West* (1920), says that history never existed and is not possible as a science, and above all that there was never a sense of proportions. Thus the African divides the world into his village and "the rest"—and the moon seems smaller to him than the cloud covering it. According to Spengler, when Kant philosophizes about norms, he is sure of the actuality of his propositions for people of all times and nations, but he does not state this outright, since he and his readers take it for granted. But in the meanwhile the norms he established are obligatory only for Western modes of thought.

It is characteristic that ten years ago Velimir Xlebnikov wrote: "Kant, thinking to establish the boundaries of human reason, determined only the boundaries of the German mind. The slight absent-mindedness of a scholar."[2] Spengler compares his strictly relativistic system to Copernicus' discoveries. It would be more correct to compare it to Einstein's; the Copernican system corresponds rather to the transition from the history of Christianity to the history of mankind. Spengler's book has caused a good deal of noise in the press. The *Vossische Zeitung* concluded: "Ah, relativism! Why say such sad things?" There appeared a voluminous reproof that succeeded in finding a true antidote to Spengler's system. This rebuke resounded from the church pulpit. This is no personal whim—the power of the Vatican is growing; the pope has not had so many nuncios for a long time. It is not without reason that the French government, rejoicing that France has finally disengaged itself from its revolutionary past, is in such a hurry to stress its piousness.

In all domains of science there is the same total rout of the old, the rejection of the local point of view, and new giddy perspectives. One's most elementary premises, which were unshakeable not so long ago, now clearly reveal their provisional character. Thus Buxarin, in his *The Economics of the Transitional Period,* discloses the meaninglessness of the Marxist concepts of "value," "goods," and so on, in application to our time, the fact that they are connected to certain already crystallized forms, the fact that they are particular instances.

Relevant here too is the aesthetics of Futurism, which refused to write beauty and art with capital letters. But Western Futurism is two-faced. On the one hand, it was the first to become aware of the tautological nature of the old formula—"In the name of beauty we are destroying all laws"—from which it follows that the history of every new current in comparison to its predecessor is a legalization of illegality; hence it would seem that there can be no punitive sanctions on what is possible in art, since instead of a decreed new beauty there is a consciousness of the particularity, the episodic nature of each artistic manifestation. It would seem that the scientific, historically minded Futurists, who rejected the past point-blank precisely because of their historicity, are the first who cannot create a new canon. On the other hand, Western Futurism in all of its variants endeavors to become an artistic movement (the thousand and first). "Classics of Futurism" is an oxymoron if you take as your starting point the original conception of Futurism; nevertheless, it has come to "classics," or to a need for them. "One of the innumerable isms," said the critics, and found Futurism's Achilles' heel. The demand arose for a new differentiation, "a manifestation parallel to the relativistic philosophies of the current moment—a 'nonaxiom,'" as one of the literary pioneers, Huelsenbeck, announced.[3] "I'm against systems; the most acceptable system is to have absolutely no system at all," added another pioneer, the Romanian Tristan Tzara. There follow battle cries repeating Marinetti: "Down with all that is like a mummy and sits solidly!" Hence "anticultural propaganda," "Bolshevism in art." "The gilding is crumbling off,

off the French, like any other. If you tremble, gentlemen, for the morals of your wives, for the tranquility of your cooks and the faithfulness of your mistresses, for the solidity of your rockingchairs and your nightpots, for the security of your government, you are right. But what will you do about it? You are rotting, and the fire has already begun" (Ribemont-Dessaignes). "I smash," exclaims Tzara somewhat in the tone of Leonid Andreev, "skull cases and the social organization: all must be demoralized."

There was a need to christen this "systemless" aesthetic rebellion, "this Fronde of great international artistic currents," as Huelsenbeck put it. In 1916 "Dada" was named. The name, along with the commentaries that followed, at once knocked out of the hands of critics their main weapon—the accusation of charlatanism and trickery. "Futurism sings of . . ." Marinetti used to write—and then came columns of objects celebrated by Futurism. The critic would pick up a Futurist almanac, leaf through its pages, and conclude: "I don't see it." "Futurism concludes," "Futurism bears with it," "Futurism conceals," wrote the ideologists who had become infected with the exoterica of Symbolism. "I don't see it! Ah, the frauds!" answered the critic. "'Futurism is the art of the future,' they say," he would reflect, "why, it's a lie!" "'Expressionism is expressive art'—they lie!" But "Dada," what does "Dada" mean? "Dada means nothing," the Dadaists hastened to reply, running interference as it were. "It doesn't smell of anything, it doesn't mean anything," says the Dada artist Picabia, bending the old Armenian riddle. A Dada manifesto invites the bourgeoisie to create myths about the essence of Dada. "Dada—now there's a word that sets off ideas; each bourgeois is a little playwright, inventing different dialogues." The manifesto informs lovers of etymology that certain blacks call the tail of a holy cow "dada"; in one part of Italy "dada" means mother; in Russian "da" is an affirmation. But "Dada" is connected neither with the one nor the other nor the third. It is simply a meaningless little word thrown into circulation in Europe, a little word with which one can juggle *à l'aise,* thinking up meanings, adjoining suffixes, coining complex words which create the illusion that they refer to objects: dadasopher, dadapit.

"The word *dada* expresses the internationality of the movement," Huelsenbeck writes. The very question "What is Dada?" is itself undadaistic and sophomoric, he also notes. "What does Dada want?"— Dada doesn't want anything. "I am writing a manifesto and I don't want anything . . . and I am on principle against manifestoes, as I am also against principles," Tzara declares.

No matter what you accuse Dada of, you can't accuse it of being dishonest, of concealment, of hedging its bets. Dada honorably perceives the "limitedness of its existence in time"; it relativizes itself historically, in its own words. Meanwhile, the first result of establishing a scientific view of artistic expression, that is, the laying bare of the device, is the cry: "The old art is dead" or "Art is dead," depending on the temperament of the person doing the yelling. The first call was issued by the Futurists, hence "Vive le futur!" The second, not without some stipulations, was issued by Dada—what business of theirs, of artists, is the future?—"A bas le futur!" So the improviser from Odoevskij's story, having received the gift of a clarity of vision which laid everything bare, ends his life as a fool in a cap scrawling transrational verses.[4] The laying bare of the device is sharp; it is precisely a laying bare; the already laid-bare device—no longer in sharp confrontation with the code (à la langue)—is vapid, it lacks flavor. The initially laid-bare device is usually justified and regulated by so-called constructive laws, but, for example, the path from rhyme to assonance to a set toward any relationship between sounds leads to the announcement that a laundry list is a poetic work. Then letters in arbitrary order, randomly struck on a typewriter, are considered verses; dabs on a canvas made by a donkey's tail dipped in paint are considered a painting. With Dada's appeal, "Dilettantes, rise up against art," we have gone from yesterday's cult of "made things" (say, refined assonance) to the poetics of the first word let slip (a laundry list). What is Dada by profession? To use an expression from Moscow artistic jargon, the Dadaists are "painters of the word." They have more declarations than poems and pictures. And actually in their poems and pictures there is nothing new, even if only in comparison to Italian and Russian Futurism. Tatlin's "Maschinenkunst," universal poems made up of vowels, round verses (simultaneism), the music of noise (bruitism), primitivism—a sort of poetic Berlitz:

> Meine Mutter sagte mir verjage die Hühner
> ich aber kann nicht fortjagen die Hühner. (Tzara)

Finally, paroxysms of naive realism: "Dada has common sense and in a chair sees a chair, in a plum—a plum."

But the crux of the matter lies elsewhere, and the Dadaists understand this. "Dada is not an artistic movement," they say. "In Switzerland Dada is for abstract (nonobjective) art, in Berlin—against." What is important is that, having finished once and for all with the principle of the legendary coalition of form and content, through a realization of the violence of artistic form, the toning down of pictorial and poetic semantics, through the color and texture *as such* of the nonobjective picture, through the fanatic word of transrational verses *as such,* we come in Russia to the blue grass of the first celebrations of October[5] and in the West to the unambiguous Dadaist formula: "Nous voulons nous voulons nous voulons pisser en couleurs diverses." Coloring *as such*! Only the canvas is removed, like an act in a sideshow one has grown tired of.

Poetry and painting became for Dada one of the acts of the sideshow. Let us be frank: poetry and painting occupy in our consciousness an excessively high position only because of tradition. "The English are so sure of the genius of Shakespeare that they don't consider it necessary even to read him," as Aubrey Beardsley puts it. We are prepared to respect the classics but for reading prefer literature written for train rides: detective stories, novels about adultery, that whole area of "belles-lettres" in which the *word* makes itself least heard. Dostoevskij, if one reads him inattentively, quickly becomes a cheap best seller, and it is hardly by chance that in the West they prefer to see his works in the movies. If the theaters are full, then it is more a matter of tradition than of interest on the part of the public. The theater is dying; the movies are blossoming. The screen ceases bit by bit to be the equivalent of the stage; it frees itself of the theatrical unities, of the theatrical mise en scène. The aphorism of the Dadaist Mehring is timely: "The popularity of an idea springs from the possibility of transferring onto film its anecdotal content." For variety's sake the Western reader is willing to accept a peppering of self-valuable words.[6] The Parisian newspaper *Le Siècle* states: "We need a literature which the mind can savor like a cocktail." During the last decade, no one has brought to the artistic market so much varied junk of all times and places as the very people who reject the past. It should be understood that the Dadaists are also eclectics, though theirs is not the museum-bound eclecticism of respectful veneration, but a motley café *chantant* program (not by chance was Dada born in a cabaret in Zurich). A little song of the Maoris takes turns with a Parisian music-hall number, a sentimental lyric—with the above-mentioned color effect. "I like an old work for its novelty. Only contrast links us to the past," Tzara explains.

One should take into account the background against which Dada is frolicking in order to understand certain of its manifestations. For example, the infantile anti-French attacks of the French Dadaists and the anti-German attacks of the Germans ten years ago might sound naive and purposeless. But today, in the countries of the Entente there rages an almost zoological nationalism, while in response to it in Germany there grows the hypertrophied national pride of an oppressed people. The Royal British Society contemplates refusing Einstein a medal so as not to export gold to Germany, while the French newspapers are outraged by the fact that Hamsun, who according to rumor was a Germanophile during the war, was given a Nobel Prize. The politically innocent Dada arouses terrible suspicion on the part of those same papers that it is some sort of German machination, while those papers print advertisements for "nationalistic double beds." Against this background, the Dadaist Fronde is quite understandable. At the present moment, when even scientific ties have been severed, Dada is one of the few truly international societies of the bourgeois intelligentsia.

By the way, it is a unique Internationale; the Dadaist Bauman lays his cards on the table when he says that "Dada is the product of international hotels." The environment in which Dada was reared was that of the adventuristic bourgeoisie of the war—the profiteers, the nouveaux riches, the Schieberen, the black-marketeers, or whatever else they were called. Dada's sociopsychological twins in old Spain gave birth to the so-called picaresque novel. They know no traditions ("je ne veux même pas savoir s'il y a eu des hommes avant moi"); their future is doubtful ("à bas le futur"); they are in a hurry to take what is theirs ("give and take, live and die"). They are exceptionally supple and adaptable ("one can perform contrary actions at the same time, in a single, fresh breath"); they are artists at what they do ("advertising and business are also poetic elements"). They do not object to the war ("still today for war"); yet they are the first to proclaim the cause of erasing the boundaries between yesterday's warring powers ("me, I'm of many nationalities"). When it comes right down to it, they are satisfied and therefore prefer bars ("he holds war and peace in his toga, but decides in favor of a cherry brandy flip"). Here, amid the "cosmopolitan mixture of god and the bordello," in Tzara's testimonial, Dada is born.

"The time is Dada-ripe," Huelsenbeck assures us. "With Dada it will ascend, and with Dada it will vanish."

CHAPTER 4

The Dominant

The first three stages of Formalist research have been briefly characterized as follows: (1) analysis of the sound aspects of a literary work; (2) problems of meaning within the framework of poetics; (3) integration of sound and meaning into an inseparable whole. During this latter stage, the concept of the *dominant* was particularly fruitful; it was one of the most crucial, elaborated, and productive concepts in Russian Formalist theory. The dominant may be defined as the focusing component of a work of art: it rules, determines, and transforms the remaining components. It is the dominant which guarantees the integrity of the structure.

The dominant specifies the work. The specific trait of bound language is obviously its prosodic pattern, its verse form. It might seem that this is simply a tautology: verse is verse. However, we must constantly bear in mind that the element which specifies a given variety of language dominates the entire structure and thus acts as its mandatory and inalienable constituent, dominating all the remaining elements and exerting direct influence upon them. Verse in turn is not a simple concept and not an indivisible unit. Verse itself is a system of values; as with any value system, it possesses its own hierarchy of superior and inferior values and one leading value, the dominant, without which (within the framework of a given literary period and a given artistic trend) verse cannot be conceived and evaluated as verse. For example, in Czech poetry of the fourteenth century the inalienable mark of verse was not the syllabic scheme but rhyme, since there existed poems with unequal numbers of syllables per line (termed "measureless" verses) which nevertheless were conceived as verses, whereas unrhymed verses were not tolerated during that period. On the other hand, in Czech Realist poetry of the second half of the nineteenth century, rhyme was a dispensable device, whereas the syllabic scheme was a mandatory, inalienable component, without which verse was not verse; from the point of view of that school, free verse was judged as unacceptable *arrhythmia*. For the present-day Czech brought up on modern free verse, neither rhyme nor a syllabic pattern is mandatory for verse; instead, the mandatory component consists of intonational integrity—intonation becomes the dominant of verse. If we were to compare the measured regular verse of the Old Czech *Alexandreis,* the rhymed verse of the Realist period, and the rhymed measured verse of the present epoch, we would observe in all three cases the same elements—rhyme, a syllabic scheme, and intonational unity—but a different hierarchy of values, different specific mandatory, indispensable elements; it is precisely these specific elements which determine the role and the structure of the other components.

We may seek a dominant not only in the poetic work of an individual artist and not only in the poetic canon, the set of norms of a given poetic school, but also in the art of a given epoch, viewed as a particular whole. For example, it is evident that in Renaissance art such a dominant, such an acme of the aesthetic criteria of the time, was represented by the visual arts. Other arts oriented themselves toward the visual arts and were valued according to the degree of their closeness to the latter. On the other hand, in Romantic art the supreme value was assigned to music. Thus, Romantic poetry oriented itself toward music: its verse is musically focused; its verse intonation imitates musical melody. This focusing on a dominant which is in fact external to the poetic work substantially changes the poem's structure with regard to sound texture, syntactic structure, and imagery; it alters the poem's metrical and strophical criteria and its composition. In Realist aesthetics the dominant was verbal art, and the hierarchy of poetic values was modified accordingly.

Moreover, the definition of an artistic work as compared to other sets of cultural values substantially changes as soon as the concept of the dominant becomes our point of departure. For example, the relationship between a poetic work and other verbal messages acquires a more exact determination. Equating a poetic work with an aesthetic, or more precisely with a poetic, function, as far as we deal with verbal material, is characteristic of those epochs which proclaim self-sufficient, pure art, *l'art pour l'art*. In the early steps of the Formalist school, it was still possible to observe distinct traces of such an equation. However, this equation is unquestionably erroneous: a poetic work is not confined to aesthetic function alone, but has in addition many other functions. Actually, the intentions of a poetic work are often closely related to philosophy, social didactics, and so on. Just as a poetic work is not exhausted by its aesthetic function, similarly the aesthetic function is not limited to poetic works; an orator's address, everyday conversation, newspaper articles, advertisements, a scientific treatise—all may employ aesthetic considerations, give expression to the aesthetic function, and often use words in and for themselves, not merely as a referential device.

In direct opposition to the straight monistic point of view is the mechanistic standpoint, which recognizes the multiplicity of functions of a poetic work and judges that work, either knowingly or unintentionally, as a mechanical agglomeration of functions. Because a poetic work also has a referential function, it is sometimes considered by adherents of the latter point of view as a straightforward document of cultural history, social relations, or biography. In contrast to one-sided monism and one-sided pluralism, there exists a point of view which combines an awareness of the multiple functions of a poetic work with a comprehension of its integrity, that is to say, that function which unites and determines the poetic work. From this point of view, a poetic work cannot be defined as a work fulfilling neither an exclusively aesthetic function nor an aesthetic function along with other functions; rather, a poetic work is defined as a verbal message whose aesthetic function is its dominant. Of course, the marks disclosing the implementation of the aesthetic function are not unchangeable or always uniform. Each concrete poetic canon, every set of temporal poetic norms, however, comprises indispensable, distinctive elements without which the work cannot be identified as poetic.

The definition of the aesthetic function as the dominant of a poetic work permits us to determine the hierarchy of diverse linguistic functions within the poetic work. In the referential function, the sign has a minimal internal connection with the designated object, and therefore the sign in itself carries only a minimal importance; on the other hand, the expressive function demands a more direct, intimate relationship between the sign and the object, and therefore a greater attention to the internal structure of the sign. In comparison with referential language, emotive language, which primarily fulfills an expressive function, is as a rule closer to poetic language (which is directed precisely toward the sign as such). Poetic language and emotive language often overlap each other, and therefore these two varieties of language are often quite erroneously identified. If the aesthetic function is the dominant in a verbal message, then this message may certainly use many devices of expressive language; but these components are then subject to the decisive function of the work, and they are transformed by its dominant.

Inquiry into the dominant had important consequences for Formalist views of literary evolution. In the evolution of poetic form it is not so much a question of the disappearance of certain elements and the emergence of others as it is a question of shifts in the mutual relationship among the diverse components of the system, in other words, a question of the shifting dominant. Within a given complex of poetic norms in general, or especially within the set of poetic norms valid for a given poetic genre, elements which were originally secondary become essential and primary. On the other hand, the elements which were originally the dominant ones become subsidiary and optional. In the early works of Šklovskij, a poetic work was defined as a mere sum of its artistic devices, while poetic evolution appeared nothing more than a substitution of certain devices. With the further development of Formalism, there arose the accurate conception of a poetic work as a structured system, a regularly ordered hierarchical set of artistic devices. Poetic evolution is a shift in this hierarchy. The hierarchy of artistic devices changes within the framework of a given poetic genre; the change, moreover, affects the hierarchy of poetic genres and, simultaneously, the distribution of artistic devices among the individual genres. Genres which were originally secondary paths, subsidiary variants, now come to the fore, whereas the canonical genres are pushed toward the rear. Various Formalist works deal with the individual periods of Russian literary history from this point of view. Gukovskij analyzes the evolution of poetry in the eighteenth century; Tynjanov and Èjxenbaum, followed by a number of their disciples, investigate the evolution of Russian poetry and prose during the first half of the nineteenth century; Viktor Vinogradov studies the evolution of Russian prose beginning with Gogol'; Èjxenbaum treats the development of Tolstoj's prose against the background of contemporaneous Russian and European prose. The image of Russian literary history substantially changes; it becomes incomparably richer and at the same time more monolithic, more synthetic and ordered, than were the *membra disjecta* of previous literary scholarship.

However, the problems of evolution are not limited to literary history. Questions concerning changes in the mutual relationship between the individual arts also arise, and here the scrutiny of transitional regions is particularly fruitful; for example, an analysis of a transitional region between painting and poetry, such as illustration, or an analysis of a border region between music and poetry, such as the romance.

Finally, the problem of changes in the mutual relationship between the arts and other closely related cultural domains arises, especially with respect to the mutual relationship between literature and other kinds of verbal messages. Here the instability of boundaries, the change in the content and extent of the individual domains, is particularly illuminating. Of special interest for investigators are the transitional genres. In certain periods such genres are evaluated as extraliterary and extrapoetical, while in other periods they may fulfill an important literary function because they comprise those elements which are about to be emphasized by belles lettres, whereas the canonical literary forms are deprived of these elements. Such transitional genres are, for example, the various forms of *littérature intime*—letters, diaries, notebooks, travelogues—which in certain periods (for example, in Russian literature of the first half of the nineteenth century) serve an important function within the total complex of literary values.

In other words, continual shifts in the system of artistic values imply continual shifts in the evaluation of different phenomena of art. That which, from the point of view of the old system, was slighted or judged to be imperfect, dilettantish, aberrant, or simply wrong or that which was considered heretical, decadent, and worthless may appear and, from the perspective of a new system, be adopted as a positive value. The verses of the Russian late-Romantic lyricists Tjutčev and Fet were criticized by the Realist critics for their errors, their alleged carelessness, and so on. Turgenev, who published these poems, thoroughly corrected their rhythm and style in order to improve them and adjust them to the extant norm. Turgenev's editing of these poems became the canonical version, and not until modern times have the original texts been reinstated, rehabilitated, and recognized as an initial step toward a new concept of poetic form. The Czech philologist J. Král rejected the verse of Erben and Čelakovský as erroneous and shabby from the viewpoint of the Realistic school of poetry, whereas the modern era praises these verses precisely for those features which had been condemned in the name of the Realist canon. The works of the great Russian composer Musorgskij did not correspond to the requirements of musical instrumentation current in the late nineteenth century, and the contemporaneous master of compositional technique, Rimskij-Korsakov, refashioned them in accordance with the prevalent taste of his epoch; however, the new generation has promoted the pathbreaking values saved by Musorgskij's "unsophisticatedness" but temporarily suppressed Rimskij-Korsakov's corrections and has naturally removed those retouchings from such compositions as *Boris Godunov.*

The shifting, the transformation, of the relationship between individual artistic components became the central issue in Formalist investigations. This aspect of Formalist analysis in the field of poetic language had a pioneering significance for linguistic research in general, since it provided important impulses toward overcoming and bridging the gap between the diachronic historical method and the synchronic method of chronological cross section. It was the Formalist research which clearly demonstrated that shifting and change are not only historical statements (first there was A, and then A_1 arose in place of A) but that shift is also a directly experienced synchronic phenomenon, a relevant artistic value. The reader of a poem or the viewer of a painting has a vivid awareness of two orders: the traditional canon and the artistic novelty as a deviation from that canon. It is precisely against the background of the tradition that innovation is conceived. The Formalist studies brought to light that this simultaneous preservation of tradition and breaking away from tradition form the essence of every new work of art.

CHAPTER 5

Problems in the Study of Language and Literature

With Jurij Tynjanov

1. The immediate problems facing Russian literary and linguistic science demand a precise theoretical platform. They require a firm dissociation from the increasing mechanistic tendency to paste together mechanically the new methodology and old obsolete methods; they necessitate a determined refusal of the contraband offer of naive psychologism and other methodological hand-me-downs in the guise of new terminology.

Furthermore, academic eclecticism and pedantic "formalism"—which replaces analysis by terminology and the classification of phenomena—and the repeated attempts to shift literary and linguistic studies from a systematic science to episodic and anecdotal genres should be rejected.

2. The history of literature (art), being simultaneous with other historical series, is characterized, as is each of these series, by a complex network of specific structural laws. Without an elucidation of these laws, it is impossible to establish in a scientific manner the correlation between the literary series and other historical series.

3. The evolution of literature cannot be understood until the evolu-

tionary problem ceases to be obscured by questions about episodic, nonsystemic genesis, whether literary (for example, so-called "literary influences") or extraliterary. The literary and extraliterary material used in literature may be introduced into the orbit of scientific investigation only when it is considered from a functional point of view.

4. The sharp opposition of synchronic (static) and diachronic cross-sections has recently become a fruitful working hypothesis, both for linguistics and for history of literature, inasmuch as it has demonstrated that language, as well as literature, has a systemic character at each individual moment of its existence. At the present time, the achievements of the synchronic concept force us to reconsider the principles of diachrony as well. The idea of a mechanical agglomeration of material, having been replaced by the concept of a system or structure in the realm of synchronic study, underwent a corresponding replacement in the realm of diachronic study as well. The history of a system is in turn a system. Pure synchronism now proves to be an illusion: every synchronic system has its past and its future as inseparable structural elements of the system: (a) archaism as a fact of style, the linguistic and literary background recognized as the rejected old-fashioned style; (b) the tendency toward innovation in language and literature recognized as a renewal of the system.

The opposition between synchrony and diachrony was an opposition between the concept of system and the concept of evolution; thus it loses its importance in principle as soon as we recognize that every system necessarily exists as an evolution, whereas, on the other hand, evolution is inescapably of a systemic nature.

5. The concept of a synchronic literary system does not coincide with the naively envisaged concept of a chronological epoch, since the former embraces not only works of art which are close to each other in time but also works which are drawn into the orbit of the system from foreign literatures or previous epochs. An indifferent cataloguing of coexisting phenomena is not sufficient; what is important is their hierarchical significance for the given epoch.

6. The assertion of two differing concepts—*la langue* and *la parole*—and the analysis of the relationship between them (the Geneva School) has been exceedingly fruitful for linguistic science. The principles involved in relating these two categories (the existing norm and individual utterances) as applied to literature must be elaborated. In the latter case, the individual utterance cannot be considered without reference

48

to the existing complex of norms. (The investigator, in isolating the former from the latter, inescapably deforms the system of artistic values under consideration, thus losing the possibility of establishing its immanent laws.)

7. An analysis of the structural laws of language and literature and their evolution inevitably leads to the establishment of a limited series of actually existing structural types (and, correspondingly, of types of structural evolution).

8. A disclosure of the immanent laws of the history of literature (and language) allows us to determine the character of each specific change in literary (and linguistic) systems. However, these laws do not allow us to explain the tempo of evolution or the chosen path of evolution when several theoretically possible evolutionary paths are given. This is owing to the fact that the immanent laws of literary (and, correspondingly, linguistic) evolution form an indeterminate equation: although they admit only a limited number of possible solutions, they do not necessarily specify a unique solution. The question of a specific choice of path, or at least of the dominant, can be solved only through an analysis of the correlation between the literary series and other historical series. This correlation (a system of systems) has its own structural laws, which must be submitted to investigation. It would be methodologically fatal to consider the correlation of systems without taking into account the immanent laws of each system.

CHAPTER 6

Language in Operation

Then the bird said "Nevermore."
Edgar Allan Poe

Recently, aboard a train, I overheard a scrap of conversation. A man said to a young lady, "They were playing 'The Raven' on the radio. An old record of a London actor dead for years. I wish you had heard his *Nevermore*." Although I was not the addressee of the stranger's oral message, I received it nevertheless and later transposed this utterance first into handwritten and then into printed symbols; now it has become a part of a new framework—my message to the prospective reader of these pages.

The stranger had resorted to a literary quotation, which apparently alluded to an emotional experience shared with his female interlocutor. He referred to a performance allegedly transmitted by broadcast. A dead British actor was the original sender of a message addressed "to whom it may concern." He, in turn, had merely reproduced Edgar Allan Poe's literary message of 1845. Furthermore, the American poet himself was ostensibly only transmitting the confession of a "lover lamenting his deceased mistress"[1]—perhaps the poet himself, perhaps some other man, real or imaginary. Within this monologue, the word *nevermore* is attributed to a talking bird, with the further implication that *that one word* uttered by the Raven had been *caught from some unhappy master,* as the *melancholy burden* of his customary laments.

Thus the same single word was successively set in motion by the hypothetical "master," the Raven, the lover, the poet, the actor, the radio station, the stranger on the train, and finally by the present author. The "master" repeatedly exteriorized the elliptic one-word sentence of his inner speech, *nevermore;* the bird mimicked its sound sequence; the lover retained it in his memory and reported the Raven's part with reference to its probable provenience; the poet wrote and published the lover's story, actually inventing the lover's, Raven's, and master's roles; the actor read and recited for a recording the piece assigned by the poet to the lover with its *nevermore* attributed by the lover to the Raven; the radio station selected the record and put it on the air; the stranger listened, remembered, and quoted this message with reference to its sources, and the linguist noted his quotation, reconstituting the whole sequence of transmitters and perhaps even making up the roles of the stranger, the broadcaster, and the actor.

This is a chain of actual and fictitious senders and receivers, most of whom merely relay and to a large extent intentionally quote one and the same message, which, at least to a few of them, was familiar beforehand. Some of the participants in this one-way communication are widely separated from each other in time and/or space, and these gaps are bridged through various means of recording and transmission. The whole sequence offers a typical example of an intricate process of communication. It is very different from the trivial pattern of the speech circuit graphically presented in textbooks: *A* and *B* talk face to face so that an imaginary thread goes from *A*'s brain through his mouth to the ear and brain of *B* and through his mouth back to *A*'s ear and brain.

"The Raven" is a poem written for mass consumption or, to use Poe's own phrase, a poem created "for the express purpose of running"; and it did indeed have a great "run."[2] In this mass-oriented poetic utterance, as the author well understood, the reported speech of the avian title-hero is the "pivot upon which the whole structure might turn" (p. 37). Actually, this message within a message "produced a sensation," and readers were reportedly "haunted by the *Nevermore.*" The key, afterwards revealed by the writer himself, lies in his bold experimentation with the procedures of communication and with its underlying duality: "the great element of unexpectedness" combined with its very opposite. "As evil cannot exist without good, so unexpectedness must arise from expectedness."[3]

When the unusual visitor first entered his chamber, the host did not know what the intruder would say, if anything. He had no expectations whatever: thus he put his question "in jest and without looking for a reply" (p. 45). He was therefore *startled at the stillness broken by reply so aptly spoken*. The bird's "continuous use of the one word 'Nevermore'" (p. 38) indicates, however, that *what it utters is its only stock and store*. This, once known, inverts the situation from one of total uncertainty to one of complete predictability. Similarly, there is no freedom of choice when an officer of the Fourth Hussars is commissioned to perform a task: "Sir" is the only admissible answer. However, as Churchill notes in his memoirs,[4] this reply can carry a wide range of emotional modulations; whereas the "*non*-reasoning creature capable of speech" (p. 38), having presumably learned its word by rote, monotonously repeats it without any variation. Thus its utterance lacks both cognitive and emotive information. The automatic speech of the *ungainly fowl* and the speaker itself are intentionally deprived of any individuality: it even appears sexless. To show this is the purpose of the formulas *Sir or Madam* and *with mien of lord or lady*, which some critics call mere padding. On the other hand, each time the *nevermore* is ascribed not to the indifferent pronouncements of the Raven but to the passionate ravings of the lover, an exclamation mark, symbolizing an emotive intonation, is substituted for the customary period.

The word itself "should involve the utmost conceivable amount of sorrow and despair" (p. 40), yet the sensory sameness of the message dispatched by both creatures, man and bird, arouses a peculiar satisfaction of relieved, "broken" loneliness. The pleasure increases, inasmuch as this *equalization* ties together the most dissimilar of all imaginable interlocutors—two talking bipeds, one featherless and the other feathered. As the author relates, "a parrot, in the first instance, suggested itself, but was superseded forthwith by a Raven . . . infinitely more in keeping with the intended *tone*" (pp. 38–39). The surprise that an exchange should occur at all is counteracted by the likeness of the *grim, ungainly, ghastly, gaunt,* and *ominous* character of the utterer to its obsessive utterance.

With each repetition of the bird's stereotyped rejoinder, the bereaved lover more surely anticipates it, so that he adapts his questions to what Poe defines as "the *expected* 'Nevermore.'" In an amazing grasp of the multiple functions performed simultaneously by verbal communication, Poe says that these queries are propounded "half in superstition and half in that species of despair which delights in self-torture" (p. 40). For talking birds, however, as their student Mowrer noted,[5] vocalization is primarily a means of getting their human partner to continue communication with them and to give in fact no *sign of parting.*

In this peculiar variety of interlocution, here carried to its extreme limit, each question is predetermined by the answer that follows: the answer is the stimulus and the question, the response. Incidentally, these echoing queries are inversely analogous to the interpretation of the echo as a reply to the questioner, and Poe, who was most sensitive to punctuation in verse, persistently inserted the question mark in the proof sheet of this stanza:

> And the only word there spoken was the whispered word,
>   "Lenore?"
> This I whispered, and an echo murmured back the word,
>   "Lenore!"[6]

The inverted answer and question game is typical of inner speech, where the subject knows beforehand the reply to the question he will put to himself. Poe leaves an opening for this optional interpretation of the quasi-dialogue with the Raven: toward the end of the poem "the intention of making him emblematical of *Mournful and Never-ending Remembrance* is permitted distinctly to be seen" (p. 46). Perhaps the bird and its replies are only imagined by the lover. A vacillation between the factual and the metaphorical levels is facilitated by a recurrent allusion to dozing (*While I nodded, nearly napping . . . dreaming dreams*) and by "transferring the point itself into the realm of Memory"[7] (*Ah, distinctly I remember*).

All the traits typical of verbal hallucination—as listed, for example, in Lagache's monograph[8]—appear in the confession of Poe's lover: diminution of vigilance, anguish, *alienation* of one's own speech and its attribution to an *alter,* accompanied by "a close *circumscription of space*" (p. 42). Poe's skill in suggesting the empirical plausibility of an unnatural event was admired and praised by Dostoevskij,[9] who recaptured it in Ivan Karamazov's nightmare. Here the delirious hero alternately interprets his experience as a hallucinatory monologue of his own or as an intrusion by an "unexpected visitor." The stranger is addressed as "devil" by Ivan, as *bird or devil* by Poe's hero; both men are uncertain whether they are asleep or awake. "No, you are not someone apart, you are myself," Ivan insists; "it's I, I myself speaking, not you"; and the intruder agrees: "I am only your hallucination." The intermittent use of the first- and second-person pronouns by both "speakers" reveals, however, the ambiguity of the theme. In Poe's view, without such a tension between the "upper" and the "under current" of meaning, "there is always a certain hardness or nakedness, which repels the artistical eye" (pp. 45–46). The two cardinal and complementary traits of verbal behavior are brought out here: that inner speech is in essence a dialogue and that any reported speech is *appropriated* and remolded by the quoter, whether it is a quotation from an alter or from an earlier phase of the ego (*said I*). Poe is right: it is the tension between these two aspects of verbal behavior which imparts to "The Raven"—and, let us add, to the climax of *The Brothers Karamazov*—so much of its poetic richness. This antinomy reinforces another, analogous tension— the tension between the poet's ego and the I of the fictitious storyteller: *I betook myself to linking fancy unto fancy.*

If in a sequence a prior moment depends upon a later one, linguists speak about a *regressive action*. For instance, when Spanish and English changed the first /l/ of the word *colonel* into /r/ in anticipation of the final /l/, this change exhibits a regressive dissimilation. R. G. Kent reports a typical slip by a radio announcer, in which "the convention was in session" became "the confession was in session": the final word had exerted a regressive assimilative influence upon the proper "convention."[10] Likewise, in "The Raven" the question is dependent on the reply. Moreover, the imaginary respondent is retrospectively deduced from its response *Nevermore*. The utterance is inhuman, both in its persistent cruelty and in its automatic, repetitive monotony. Hence an articulate but subhuman creature is suggested as speaker, and in particular a corvine bird, not only because of its gloomy appearance and "ominous reputation" (p. 40) but also because in most of its phonemes the noun *raven* is simply an inversion of the sinister *never*. Poe signals this connection by adjoining the two words: *Quoth the Raven "Nevermore."* The juxtaposition becomes particularly telling in the final stanza:

> And the Raven, never flitting, still is sitting; *still* is sitting
> On the pallid bust of Pallas just above my chamber door;
> And his eyes have all the seeming of a demon's that is dreaming,

> And the lamp-light o'er him streaming throws his shadow on the
> floor;
> And my soul from out that shadow that lies floating on the floor
> Shall be lifted—nevermore!

Here the pair *Raven, never* is enhanced by a series of other mutually corresponding sound sequences, matched to create an affinity between certain key words and to underscore their semantic association. The introductory clause, concluded with the series *still—sit—still—sit,* is linked with the final clause by the chain *flit—float—floor—lift,* and both pivots are manifestly juxtaposed: *never flitting, still is sitting.* The play upon the words *pallid* and *Pallas* is reinforced by the whimsical rhyme *pallid bust—Pallas just.* The initial dentals /s,d/ of the corresponding sequences *seeming* and *demon* (trochaic feet with the same vocalic segment followed by an /m/ and in both cases with a final nasal) are with a slight variation blended in the groups *is dreaming* /zd/ and *streaming* /st/. In the prefatory note to the first publication of this poem, written by the poet himself or at his instigation, "the studious use of similar sounds in unusual places"[11] is singled out as its chief device. Against the background of equidistant and regularly recurring rhymes, Poe deliberately introduces rhymes displaced to achieve the "whole effect of unexpectedness."[12] Regularly repeated sound sequences in such customary rhymes as *remember—December—ember* or *morrow—borrow—sorrow* are supplemented by "reversals" (to use Edmund Wilson's term): *lonely* /lóunli/—*only* /óunli/—*soul in* /sóulɪn/. The regressive aspect of the speech-sequence is under focus, and this variation serves to interlock the "never = ending" theme of *the Raven, sitting lonely,* with the opposite theme of *the lost Lenore* /linór/.

Not only the questions propounded by the desperate lover but in fact the whole poem are predetermined by the final rejoinder *nevermore* and are composed in distinct anticipation of the dénouement, as the author disclosed in "The Philosophy of Composition" (1846), his own commentary to "The Raven": "the poem may be said to have its beginning—at the end" (p. 40). It is indeed difficult to understand now the continuous repudiations of Poe's piece of self-analysis, called a misleading mystification, a premeditated farce, unparalleled effrontery, and one of his mischievous caprices to catch the critics. Although Poe's letter of August 9, 1846, to his friend Cooke recommended this commentary as the "best specimen of analysis,"[13] an alleged oral statement by the writer was quoted posthumously: a supposed confession that he had never intended this article to be received seriously. French poets, however, admiring both Poe's poetry and his essays on poetry, have wondered in which instance he was jesting: whether in writing this marvelous commentary or in disavowing it to soothe a sentimental female interviewer.

In point of fact, the author of "The Raven" formulated perfectly the relationship between poetic language and its translation into what now would be called the metalanguage of scientific analysis. In his *Marginalia,* Poe recognized that the two aspects stand in complementary relation to each other: he said that we are able "to see distinctly the machinery" of any work of art and at the same time to enjoy this ability, but "only just in proportion as we do *not* enjoy the legitimate effect designed by the artist." Moreover, in order to counter past and future objections to his analysis of "The Raven," he added that "to reflect analytically upon Art, is to reflect after the fashion of the mirrors in the temple of Smyrna, which represent the fairest images as deformed" (1849).[14] Truth, in Poe's opinion, demands a precision absolutely antagonistic to the predominant aim of poetic fiction; but when he translated the language of art into the language of precision, the critics apprehended his attempt as a mere fiction defying truth.

The author's account of the poem's composition, which critics of the past pronounced a juggling trick or grand hoax upon its readers, has recently been described by Denis Marion as an act of self-deception.[15] Yet with equal justice it might be set against the intimate story of Poe's own life with Virginia Clemm in "hourly anticipation of her loss."

The alternation between the illusory glimmer of hope in the lover's queries and the finality of the "anticipated answer" *Nevermore* is utilized to "bring him . . . the most of the luxury of sorrow," until the Raven's inevitable reply to "the lover's final demand" proclaims the irrevocability of his loss and provides him with the "indulgence . . . of this self-torture" (p. 45). A few months after Virginia's death Poe wrote to George Eveleth:

> Six years ago, a wife, whom I loved as no man ever loved before [in "The Raven" we read of *terrors never felt before*], ruptured a blood-vessel in singing. Her life was despaired of. I took leave of her forever and underwent all the agonies of her death. She recovered partially and I again hoped. At the end of a year the vessel broke again—I went through precisely the same scene. Again in

about a year afterward. Then again—again—again and even once again at varying intervals. Each time I felt all the agonies of her death—and at each accession of the disorder I loved her more dearly and clung to her life with more desperate pertinacity . . . I became insane, with long intervals of horrible sanity . . . I had indeed nearly abandoned all hope of a permanent cure when I found one in the *death* of my wife. This I can and do endure as becomes a man—it was the horrible, never-ending oscillation between hope and despair which I could *not* longer have endured without the total loss of reason.[16]

In both cases, in "The Raven" and in the epistolary confession, the anticipated denouement is everlasting bereavement: Virginia's death after years of protracted agony and the lover's despair of meeting Lenore even in another world. "The Raven" appeared on January 29, 1845; "The Philosophy of Composition" was published in April 1846; Poe's wife died on January 30, 1847. Thus "the *expected* 'Nevermore,'" revealed in the essay as the central motif of the poem, is in tune with the biographical background as well.

Poe's critical essay, however, dismisses the circumstances which stimulate the poet as irrelevant to a consideration of the poem itself. The theme of the 'bereaved lover" (p. 39) antedates Virginia's illness and in fact haunts all Poe's poetry and prose. In "The Raven" this theme displays a particular "force of contrast" (p. 43), expressed in a pointedly romantic oxymoron: the colloquy between the lover and the bird is an anomalous communication about the severance of all communication. This pseudo-dialogue is tragically one-sided: there is no real interchange of any kind. To his desperate queries and appeals the hero receives only seeming answers—from the bird, from the echo, and from the volumes of *forgotten lore;* his own lips are "best suited" (p. 39) for vain soliloquy. Here a further oxymoron, a new contradiction, is advanced by the poet: he assigns to this solitary speech the widest radius of overt communication, but realizes at once that this exhibitionistic widening of the appeal may "endanger the psychological reality of the image of the enlarged self confronting the notself," as it was later to be formulated by Edward Sapir.[17]

It may be recalled once more that the supreme effect of "The Raven" lies in its daring experimentation with intricate problems of communication. The dominant motif of the poem is the lover's irrevocable loss of contact with the *rare and radiant maiden;* henceforth no common context with her is conceivable, either on this earth or *within the distant Aidenn* (the fanciful spelling is needed as an echo for *maiden*). In Poe's poetic creed, it is a mere "array of incident," irrelevant to the "machinery" of his work, whether the lover's loss is due to the maiden's death or to a more homely and prosaic, but nonetheless inexorable, message of the variety *I will not see you again,* transmitted to that gloomy room in upper New York which was allegedly depicted in "The Raven." Nothing about the heroine except her absence and her namelessness forevermore is of any significance for the poet's purpose: his poem "will be poetic in the exact ratio of its dispassion."[18] But to suit the "popular taste" (p. 34) and perhaps to allay repressed fears and desires of his own, the poet chose to have the maiden dead—death was "the most melancholy of topics" (p. 39)—and to borrow for her the sonorous name *Lenore* from the famous ballad about the living bride of the dead.

Poe's insight into "the wheels and pinions" (p. 33) of verbal art and of verbal structure in general, the insight of an artist and analyst combined, is startling indeed. His skilled employment in verse and his linguistic examination of the refrain *Nevermore* are especially pertinent, for it is here that "the sense of identity" (p. 37) is directly challenged, both as to sound and to meaning. The inevitable *Nevermore* is always the same and always different: on the one hand, expressive modulations diversify the sound and, on the other, "the *variation of application*" (p. 39), that is, the multiformity of contexts, imparts a different connotation to the meaning of the word on its every recurrence.

A word out of context allows an indeterminate number of solutions, and the listener is *engaged in guessing* what is meant by the isolated *Nevermore*. But within the context of the dialogue it signifies by turns: nevermore will you forget her; nevermore will you take comfort; nevermore will you embrace her; nevermore will I leave you. Moreover, the same word can function as a proper name, an emblematic noun which the lover attributes to his nocturnal visitor: *a bird above his chamber door . . . with such name as "Nevermore."* Poe rendered this variation of usage particularly effective "by adhering, in general, to the monotone of sound"—that is to say, by favoring a deliberate suppression of emotive modulations.

On the other hand, however great the variety of contextual meanings, the word *nevermore,* like any other word, retains the same general meaning through all its varied applications. The tension between this intrinsic unity and the diversity of contextual or situational meanings is the pivotal problem of the linguistic discipline labeled *semantics,* while the discipline termed *phonemics* is primarily concerned with the tension between identity and variation on the sound level of language. The compound *nevermore* denotes a negation, a denial forever in the future as opposed to the past. Even the transposition of this temporal adverb into a proper name retains a metaphorical tie with this general semantic value.

An everlasting disavowal seems inconceivable, and popular wisdom strives to charm it away by such witty contradictions as "a neverday when the owl bares its rump," and "when Hell freezes over," or other similar locutions studied by Archer Taylor.[19] Curiously enough, in the same year "The Raven" was written, a scholarly interest in locutions for "never" and "nevermore" was manifested for the first time, by the German poet Uhland. More than anyone, Baudelaire, in his notes to Poe's poem, vividly conceived the particular conceptual and emotive tensity of this "profound and mysterious" word.[20] It fuses end with endlessness. It contrasts the prospective with the foregone, the eternal with the transient, negation with assertion, and in itself it contrasts sharply with the animal nature of the utterer, who is inescapably bound to the tangible present of time and space. Poe's challenging oxymoron became a cliché, and in a popular hit of prerevolutionary Russia "a parrot cries *jamais, jamais,* always *jamais.*"

To anticipate the final refrain and to enhance its import, Poe employs a species of etymological figure. Semantically, the author prepares us for the unlimited negation *nevermore* by repeating the restrictive negation *merely this and nothing more;* the negation of *balm* in the future is foreshadowed by the negation of comparable *fantastic* terrors in the past; and the negated assertion *will be . . . nevermore* is preceded by the despair of the asserted negation *nameless here for evermore.* Externally, the poem breaks up the unit *nevermore* into its grammatical constituents by separating *more, ever,* and *no* (with its alternant *n-,* the latter figuring before a vowel: *n-ever, n-aught, n-ay, n-either, n-or*), and setting them in new contexts, most of which correspond in meter and rhyme: *Only this and nothing more; Nameless here for evermore; terrors never felt before; ever dared to dream before; and the stillness gave no token.* Further, the unit *more* is susceptible of dissociation into root and suffix, when it is confronted with *most* and with the degrees of comparison from other adjectives, as in *somewhat louder than before.*

The components we obtain by dissecting all these units into smaller fractions are themselves devoid of meaning. These components of the sound texture are laid bare through the equality and diversity of the phonemes in the pervasive Byronesque rhyme: *bore—door—core—shore—wore—yore—o'er,* with *more* at the close of each stanza. In addition to the rhymes, internal groups of phonemes in the preceding lines also prompt the concluding *nevermore.* Thus the hemistich *from thy memories of Lenore* (as well as *take thy form from off my door*) rehearses the close, with its accumulation of nasals /m, n/, labial continuants /f,v/, and the phoneme represented by the letter *r: Quoth the Raven: 'Nevermore.'* The sound texture accentuates the confrontation between the relics of the past and the omen of the future.

Such punlike, pseudo-etymological figures, by involving words similar in sound, stress their semantic affinity. Thus in the line *Whether Tempter sent, or whether tempest tossed thee here ashore,* both like-sounding nouns act as derivatives of the same root, denoting two varieties of evil power. *Pallid* as an epithet of the sculptured *Pallas* figures as quasi-related to the goddess' name. In the line about *the Raven, sitting lonely on that placid bust,* the sound shape of the adjective *placid* evokes the missing reference to Pallas. The expression *beast upon the sculptured bust* suggests a puzzling connection between the sitter and the seat, both named by two alternants of the "same" root. This propensity to infer a connection in meaning from similarity in sound illustrates the poetic function of language.

At the beginning of this essay, when I mentioned a young lady I met on a train, the word *lady* was used simply to signal the thing meant; but in the sentence, "'Lady' is a dissyllabic noun," the same word is employed to signal itself. The poetic function entangles the word in both of these uses at once. In "The Raven," the vocable *lady* denotes a female of distinction, as opposed both to *lord,* male of distinction, and to females without distinction. At the same time, it partakes a playful rhyme and signals the close of a hemistich (*But, with mien of lord or lady*), exhibiting a partial sound identity with its counterparts *made he* and *stayed he,* besides, in contradistinction to these, a syntactical indivisibility: /méid-i/—/stéid-i/—/léidi/. A sound or sound sequence striking enough to be set in relief by repetitive use in the key word and surrounding vocables may even determine the choice of such a word, as Poe himself acknowledged. Thus his reference to the poet's selection of words "embodying" (p. 38) certain intended sounds is fully justified.

Before proceeding to a systematic study of sound and meaning in their interrelation, we have attempted an exploratory sally into the very core of verbal communication. For this purpose it seems most appropriate to choose a specimen like "The Raven," which approaches this process in all its amazing complexity and nakedness. "That mysterious affinity which binds together the sound and the sense," an affinity distinctly palpable in poetic language and ardently professed by Edgar Allan Poe, has determined our choice, because "objects," as he said, "should be attained through means best adapted for their attainment."

CHAPTER 7

Linguistics and Poetics

Fortunately, scholarly and political conferences have nothing in common. The success of a political convention depends on the general agreement of the majority or totality of its participants. The use of votes and vetoes, however, is alien to scholarly discussion, where disagreement generally proves to be more productive than agreement. Disagreement discloses antinomies and tensions within the field discussed and calls for novel exploration. Not political conferences but rather exploratory activities in Antarctica present an analogy to scholarly meetings: international experts in various disciplines attempt to map an unknown region and find out where the greatest obstacles for the explorer are, the insurmountable peaks and precipices. Such a mapping seems to have been the chief task of our conference, and in this respect its work has been quite successful. Have we not realized what problems are the most crucial and the most controversial? Have we not also learned how to switch our codes, what terms to expound or even to avoid in order to prevent misunderstandings with people using different departmental jargon? Such questions, I believe, for most of the members of this conference, if not for all of them, are somewhat clearer today than they were three days ago.

I have been asked for summary remarks about poetics in its relation to linguistics. Poetics deals primarily with the question, "What makes a verbal message a work of art?" Because the main subject of poetics is the *differentia specifica* of verbal art in relation to other arts and in relation to other kinds of verbal behavior, poetics is entitled to the leading place in literary studies.

Poetics deals with problems of verbal structure, just as the analysis of painting is concerned with pictorial structure. Since linguistics is the global science of verbal structure, poetics may be regarded as an integral part of linguistics.

Arguments against such a claim must be thoroughly discussed. It is evident that many devices studied by poetics are not confined to verbal art. We can refer to the possibility of transposing *Wuthering Heights* into a motion picture, medieval legends into frescoes and miniatures, or *L'Après-midi d'un faune* into music, ballet, and graphic art. However ludicrous the idea of the *Iliad* and *Odyssey* in comics may seem, certain structural features of their plot are preserved despite the disappearance of their verbal shape. The question of whether W. B. Yeats was right in affirming that William Blake was "the one perfectly fit illustrator for the *Inferno* and the *Purgatorio*" is a proof that different arts are comparable. The problems of the baroque or any other historical style transgress the frame of a single art. When handling the surrealistic metaphor, we could hardly pass by Max Ernst's pictures or Luis Buñuel's films, *The Andalusian Dog* and *The Golden Age*. In short, many poetic features belong not only to the science of language but to the whole theory of signs, that is, to general semiotics. This statement, however, is valid not only for verbal art but also for all varieties of language, since language shares many properties with certain other systems of signs or even with all of them (pansemiotic features).

Likewise, a second objection contains nothing that would be specific for literature: the question of relations between the word and the world concerns not only verbal art but actually all kinds of discourse. Linguistics is likely to explore all possible problems of relation between discourse and the "universe of discourse": what of this universe is verbalized by a given discourse and how it is verbalized. The truth values, however, as far as they are—to say with the logicians—"extralinguistic entities," obviously exceed the bounds of poetics and of linguistics in general.

Sometimes we hear that poetics in contradistinction to linguistics, is concerned with evaluation. This separation of the two fields from each other is based on a current but erroneous interpretation of the contrast between the structure of poetry and other types of verbal structure: the latter are said to be opposed by their "casual," designless nature to the "noncasual," purposeful character of poetic language. In point of fact, any verbal behavior is goal-directed, but the aims are different and the conformity of the means used to the effect aimed at is a problem that evermore preoccupies inquirers into the diverse kinds of verbal communication. There is a close correspondence, much closer than critics believe, between the question of linguistic phenomena expanding in space and time and the spatial and temporal spread of literary models. Even such discontinuous expansion as the resurrection of neglected or forgotten poets—for instance, the posthumous discovery and subsequent canonization of Emily Dickinson (d. 1886) and Gerard Manley Hopkins (d. 1889), the tardy fame of Lautréamont (d. 1870) among surrealist poets, and the salient influence of the hitherto ignored Cyprian Norwid (d. 1883) on Polish modern poetry—finds a parallel in the history of standard languages that tend to revive outdated models, sometimes long forgotten, as was the case in literary Czech, which toward the beginning of the nineteenth century leaned toward sixteenth-century models.

Unfortunately, the terminological confusion of "literary studies" with "criticism" tempts the student of literature to replace the description of the intrinsic values of a literary work with a subjective, censorious verdict. The label "literary critic" applied to an investigator of literature is as erroneous as "grammatical (or lexical) critic" would be applied to a linguist. Syntactic and morphologic research cannot be supplanted by a normative grammar, and likewise no manifesto, foisting a critic's own tastes and opinions on creative literature, can serve as a substitute for an objective scholarly analysis of verbal art. This statement should not be mistaken for the quietist principle of laissez faire; any verbal culture involves programmatic, planning, normative endeavors. Yet why is a clear-cut discrimination made between pure and applied linguistics or between phonetics and orthoepy, but not between literary studies and criticism?

Literary studies, with poetics as their focal point, consist like linguistics of two sets of problems: synchrony and diachrony. The synchronic description envisages not only the literary production of any given stage but also that part of the literary tradition which for the stage in question has remained vital or has been revived. Thus, for instance, Shakespeare, on the one hand, and Donne, Marvell, Keats, and Emily Dickinson, on the other, are experienced by the present English poetic world, whereas the works of James Thomson and Longfellow, for the time being, do not belong to viable artistic values. The selection of classics and their reinterpretation by a novel trend is a substantial problem of synchronic literary studies. Synchronic poetics, like synchronic linguistics, is not to be confused with statics; any stage discriminates between more conservative and more innovative forms. Any contemporary stage is experienced in its temporal dynamics, and, on the other hand, the historical approach both in poetics and in linguistics is concerned not only with changes but also with continuous, enduring, static factors. A thoroughly comprehensive historical poetics or history of language is a superstructure to be built on a series of successive synchronic descriptions.

Insistence on keeping poetics apart from linguistics is warranted only when the field of linguistics appears to be illicitly restricted, for example, when the sentence is viewed by some linguists as the highest analyzable construction, or when the scope of linguistics is confined to grammar alone or uniquely to nonsemantic questions of external form or to the inventory of denotative devices with no reference to free variations. Voegelin has clearly pointed out the two most important and related problems that face structural linguistics, namely, a revision of "the monolithic hypothesis about language" and a concern with "the interdependence of diverse structures within one language."[1] No doubt, for any speech community, for any speaker, there exists a unity of language, but this over-all code represents a system of interconnected subcodes; every language encompasses several concurrent patterns, each characterized by different functions.

Obviously we must agree with Sapir that, on the whole, "ideation reigns supreme in language,"[2] but this supremacy does not authorize linguistics to disregard the "secondary factors." The emotive elements of speech, which, as Joos is prone to believe, cannot be described "with a finite number of absolute categories," are classified by him "as nonlinguistic elements of the real world." Hence, "for us they remain vague, protean, fluctuating phenomena," he concludes, "which we refuse to tolerate in our science."[3] Joos is indeed a brilliant expert in reduction experiments, and his emphatic demand for the "expulsion" of emotive elements "from linguistic science" is a radical experiment in reduction—*reductio ad absurdum*.

Language must be investigated in all the variety of its functions. Before discussing the poetic function we must define its place among the other functions of language. An outline of these functions demands a concise survey of the constitutive factors in any speech event, in any act of verbal communication. The ADDRESSER sends a MESSAGE to the ADDRESSEE. To be operative the message requires a CONTEXT referred to (the "referent" in another, somewhat ambiguous, nomenclature), graspable by the addressee, and either verbal or capable of being verbalized; a CODE fully, or at least partially, common to the addresser and addressee (or in other words, to the encoder and decoder of the message); and, finally, a CONTACT, a physical channel and psychological connection between the addresser and the addressee, enabling both of them to enter and stay in communication. All these factors inalienably involved in verbal communication may be schematized as follows:

	CONTEXT	
ADDRESSER	MESSAGE	ADDRESSEE
	CONTACT	
	CODE	

Each of these six factors determines a different function of language. Although we distinguish six basic aspects of language, we could, however, hardly find verbal messages that would fulfill only one function. The diversity lies not in a monopoly of some one of these several functions but in a different hierarchical order of functions. The verbal structure of a message depends primarily on the predominant function. But even though a set (*Einstellung*) toward the referent, an orientation toward the context—briefly, the so-called REFERENTIAL, "denotative," "cognitive" function—is the leading task of numerous messages, the accessory participation of the other functions in such messages must be taken into account by the observant linguist.

The so-called EMOTIVE or "expressive" function, focused on the addresser, aims a direct expression of the speaker's attitude toward what he is speaking about. It tends to produce an impression of a certain emotion, whether true or feigned; therefore, the term "emotive," launched and advocated by Marty,[4] has proved to be preferable to "emotional." The purely emotive stratum in language is presented by the interjections. They differ from the means of referential language both by their sound pattern (peculiar sound sequences or even sounds elsewhere unusual) and by their syntactic role (they are not components but equivalents of sentences). *"Tut! Tut!* said McGinty": the complete utterance of Conan Doyle's character consists of two suction clicks. The emotive function, laid bare in the interjections, flavors to some extent all our utterances, on their phonic, grammatical, and lexical level. If we analyze language from the standpoint of the information it carries, we cannot restrict the notion of information to the cognitive aspect of language. A man, using expressive features to indicate his angry or ironic attitude, conveys ostensible information, and evidently this verbal behavior cannot be likened to such nonsemiotic, nutritive activities as "eating grapefruit" (despite Chatman's bold simile). The difference between [bɪg] and the emphatic prolongation of the vowel [bɪ:g] is a conventional, coded linguistic feature like the difference between the short and long vowel in such Czech pairs as [vi] "you" and [vi:] "knows," but in the latter pair the differential information is phonemic and in the former emotive. As long as we are interested in phonemic invariants, the English /i/ and /i:/ appear to be mere variants of one and the same phoneme, but if we are concerned with emotive units, the relation between the invariants and variants is reversed: length and shortness are invariants implemented by variable phonemes. Saporta's surmise that emotive difference is a nonlinguistic feature, "attributable to the delivery of the message and not to the message,"[5] arbitrarily reduces the informational capacity of messages.

A former actor of Stanislavskij's Moscow Theater told me how at his audition he was asked by the famous director to make forty different messages from the phrase *Segodnja večerom* (This evening), by diversifying its expressive tint. He made a list of some forty emotional situations, then emitted the given phrase in accordance with each of these situations, which his audience had to recognize only from the changes in the sound shape of the same two words. For our research work in the description and analysis of contemporary Standard Russian (under the auspices of the Rockefeller Foundation) this actor was asked to repeat Stanislavskij's test. He wrote down some fifty situations framing the same elliptic sentence and made of it fifty corresponding messages for a tape recording. Most of the messages were correctly and circumstantially decoded by Moscovite listeners. May I add that all such emotive cues easily undergo linguistic analysis.

Orientation toward the addressee, the CONATIVE function, finds its purest grammatical expression in the vocative and imperative, which syntactically, morphologically, and often even phonemically deviate from other nominal and verbal categories. The imperative sentences cardinally differ from declarative sentences: the latter are and the former are not liable to a truth test. When in O'Neill's play *The Fountain*, Nano "(in a fierce tone of command)" says "Drink!"—the imperative cannot be challenged by the question "is it true or not?" which may be, however, perfectly well asked after such sentences as "one drank," "one will drink," "one would drink." In contradistinction to the imperative sentences, the declarative sentences are convertible into interrogative sentences: "did one drink?," "will one drink?," "would one drink?"

The traditional model of language as elucidated particularly by Bühler[6] was confined to these three functions—emotive, conative, and referential—and the three apexes of this model—the first person of the addresser, the second person of the addressee, and the "third person" properly (someone or something spoken of). Certain additional verbal functions can be easily inferred from this triadic model. Thus the magic, incantatory function is chiefly some kind of conversion of an absent or inanimate "third person" into an addressee of a conative message. "May this sty dry up, *tfu, tfu, tfu, tfu*" (Lithuanian spell).[7] "Water, queen river, daybreak! Send grief beyond the blue sea, to the sea bottom, like a gray stone never to rise from the sea bottom, may grief never come to burden the light heart of God's servant, may grief be removed and sink away" (North Russian incantation).[8] "Sun, stand thou still upon Gibeon; and thou, Moon, in the valley of Aj-a-lon. And the sun stood still, and the moon stayed" (Joshua 10.12). We observe, however, three further constitutive factors of verbal communication and three corresponding functions of language.

There are messages primarily serving to establish, to prolong, or to discontinue communication, to check whether the channel works ("Hello, do you hear me?"), to attract the attention of the interlocutor or to confirm his continued attention ("Are you listening?" or in Shakespearean diction, "Lend me your ears!"—and on the other end of the wire "Um-hum!"). This set for contact, or in Malinowski's terms PHATIC function,[9] may be displayed by a profuse exchange of ritualized formulas, by entire dialogues with the mere purport of prolonging communication. Dorothy Parker caught eloquent examples: "'Well!' the young man said. 'Well!' she said. 'Well, here we are,' he said. 'Here we are,' she said, 'Aren't we?' 'I should say we were,' he said,

'Eeyop! Here we are.' 'Well!' she said. 'Well!' he said, 'well.'" The endeavor to start and sustain communication is typical of talking birds; thus the phatic function of language is the only one they share with human beings. It is also the first verbal function acquired by infants; they are prone to communicate before being able to send or receive informative communication.

A distinction has been made in modern logic between two levels of language: "object language" speaking of objects and "metalanguage" speaking of language.[10] But metalanguage is not only a necessary scientific tool utilized by logicians and linguists; it plays also an important role in our everyday language. Like Molière's Jourdain who used prose without knowing it, we practice metalanguage without realizing the metalingual character of our operations. Whenever the addresser and/or the addressee need to check up whether they use the same code, speech is focused on the code: it performs a METALINGUAL (i.e., glossing) function. "I don't follow you—what do you mean?" asks the addressee, or in Shakespearean diction, "What is't thou say'st?" And the addresser in anticipation of such recapturing question inquires: "Do you know what I mean?" Imagine such an exasperating dialogue: "The sophomore was plucked." 'But what is *plucked?*" "*Plucked* means the same as *flunked.*" "And *flunked?*" "*To be flunked* is *to fail an exam.*" "And what is *sophomore?*" persists the interrogator innocent of school vocabulary. "*A sophomore* is (or means) a *second-year student.*" All these equational sentences convey information merely about the lexical code of English; their function is strictly metalingual. Any process of language learning, in particular child acquisition of the mother tongue, makes wide use of such metalingual operations; and aphasia may often be defined as a loss of ability for metalingual operations.

I have brought up all the six factors involved in verbal communication except the message itself. The set (*Einstellung*) toward the message as such, focus on the message for its own sake, is the POETIC function of language. This function cannot be productively studied out of touch with the general problems of language, and, on the other hand, the scrutiny of language requires a thorough consideration of its poetic function. Any attempt to reduce the sphere of the poetic function to poetry or to confine poetry to the poetic function would be a delusive oversimplification. The poetic function is not the sole function of verbal art but only its dominant, determining function, whereas in all other verbal activities it acts as a subsidiary, accessory constituent. This function, by promoting the palpability of signs, deepens the fundamental dichotomy of signs and objects. Hence, when dealing with the poetic function, linguistics cannot limit itself to the field of poetry.

'Why do you always say *Joan and Margery,* yet never *Margery and Joan?* Do you prefer Joan to her twin sister?" "Not at all, it just sounds smoother." In a sequence of two coordinate names, so far as no problems of rank interfere, the precedence of the shorter name suits the speaker, unaccountably for him, as a well-ordered shape for the message.

A girl used to talk about "the horrible Harry." "Why horrible?" "Because I hate him." "But why not *dreadful, terrible, frightful, disgusting?"* "I don't know why, but *horrible* fits him better." Without realizing it, she clung to the poetic device of paronomasia.

The political slogan "I like Ike" /ay layk ayk/, succinctly structured, consists of three monosyllables and counts three diphthongs /ay/, each of them symmetrically followed by one consonantal phoneme, / ..l.. k..k /. The makeup of the three words presents a variation: no consonantal phonemes in the first word, two around the diphthong in the second, and one final consonant in the third. A similar dominant nucleus /ay/ was noticed by Hymes in some of the sonnets of Keats.[11] Both cola of the trisyllabic formula "I like / Ike" rhyme with each other, and the second of the two rhyming words is fully included in the first one (echo rhyme), /layk/—/ayk/, a paronomastic image of a feeling which totally envelops its object. Both cola alliterate with each other, and the first of the two alliterating words is included in the second: /ay/—/ayk/, a paronomastic image of the loving subject enveloped by the beloved object. The secondary, poetic function of this campaign slogan reinforces its impressiveness and efficacy.

As I said, the linguistic study of the poetic function must overstep the limits of poetry, and, on the other hand, the linguistic scrutiny of poetry cannot limit itself to the poetic function. The particularities of diverse poetic genres imply a differently ranked participation of the other verbal functions along with the dominant poetic function. Epic poetry, focused on the third person, strongly involves the referential function of language; the lyric, oriented toward the first person, is intimately linked with the emotive function; poetry of the second person is imbued with the conative function and is either supplicatory or exhortative, depending on whether the first person is subordinated to the second one or the second to the first.

Now that our cursory description of the six basic functions of verbal communication is more or less complete, we may complement our scheme of the fundamental factors with a corresponding scheme of the functions:

REFERENTIAL

EMOTIVE   POETIC   CONATIVE

PHATIC

METALINGUAL

What is the empirical linguistic criterion of the poetic function? In particular, what is the indispensable feature inherent in any piece of poetry? To answer this question we must recall the two basic modes of arrangement used in verbal behavior, *selection* and *combination*. If "child" is the topic of the message, the speaker selects one among the extant, more or less similar nouns like child, kid, youngster, tot, all of them equivalent in a certain respect, and then, to comment on this topic, he may select one of the semantically cognate verbs—sleeps, dozes, nods, naps. Both chosen words combine in the speech chain. The selection is produced on the basis of equivalence, similarity and dissimilarity, synonymy and antonymy, while the combination, the build-up of the sequence, is based on contiguity. *The poetic function projects the principle of equivalence from the axis of selection into the axis of combination.* Equivalence is promoted to the constitutive device of the sequence. In poetry one syllable is equalized with any other syllable of the same sequence; word stress is assumed to equal word stress, as unstress equals unstress; prosodic long is matched with long, and short with short; word boundary equals word boundary, no boundary equals no boundary; syntactic pause equals syntactic pause, no pause equals no pause. Syllables are converted into units of measure, and so are morae or stresses.

It may be objected that metalanguage also makes a sequential use of equivalent units when combining synonymic expressions into an equational sentence: $A = A$ ("*Mare* is *the female of the horse*"). Poetry and metalanguage, however, are in diametrical opposition to each other: in metalanguage the sequence is used to build an equation, whereas in poetry the equation is used to build a sequence.

In poetry, and to a certain extent in latent manifestations of the poetic function, sequences delimited by word boundaries become commensurable whether they are sensed as isochronic or graded. "Joan and Margery" showed us the poetic principle of syllable gradation, the same principle that in the closes of Serbian folk epics has been raised to a compulsory law.[12] Without its two dactylic words the combination "*in*nocent *by*stander" would hardly have become a hackneyed phrase. The symmetry of three disyllabic verbs with an identical initial consonant and identical final vowel added splendor to the laconic victory message of Caesar: "Veni, vidi, vici."

Measure of sequences is a device that, outside of the poetic function, finds no application in language. Only in poetry with its regular reiteration of equivalent units is the time of the speech flow experienced, as it is—to cite another semiotic pattern—with musical time. Gerard Manley Hopkins, an outstanding searcher in the science of poetic language, defined verse as "speech wholly or partially repeating the same figure of sound."[13] Hopkins' subsequent question, "but is all verse poetry?" can be definitely answered as soon as the poetic function ceases to be arbitrarily confined to the domain of poetry. Mnemonic lines cited by Hopkins (like "Thirty days hath September"), modern advertising jingles, and versified medieval laws, mentioned by Lotz,[14] or finally Sanskrit scientific treatises in verse which in Indic tradition are strictly distinguished from true poetry (*kāvya*)—all these metrical texts make use of the poetic function without, however, assigning to this function the coercing, determining role it carries in poetry. Thus verse actually exceeds the limits of poetry, but at the same time verse always implies the poetic function. And apparently no human culture ignores verse making, whereas there are many cultural patterns without "applied" verse; and even in such cultures as possess both pure and applied verses, the latter appear to be a secondary, unquestionably derived phenomenon. The adaptation of poetic means for some heterogeneous purpose does not conceal their primary essence, just as elements of emotive language, when utilized in poetry, still maintain their emotive tinge. A filibusterer may recite *Hiawatha* because it is long, yet poeticalness still remains the primary intent of this text itself. Self-evidently, the existence of versified, musical, and pictorial commercials does not separate the questions of verse or of musical and pictorial form from the study of poetry, music, and fine arts.

To sum up, the analysis of verse is entirely within the competence of poetics, and the latter may be defined as that part of linguistics which treats the poetic function in its relationship to the other functions of language. Poetics in the wider sense of the word deals with the poetic function not only in poetry, where this function is superimposed upon the other functions of language, but also outside poetry, when some other function is superimposed upon the poetic function.

The reiterative "figure of sound," which Hopkins saw as the constitutive principle of verse, can be further specified. Such a figure always utilizes at least one (or more than one) binary contrast of a relatively high and relatively low prominence effected by the different sections of the phonemic sequence.

Within a syllable the more prominent, nuclear, syllabic part, constituting the peak of the syllable, is opposed to the less prominent, marginal, nonsyllabic phonemes. Any syllable contains a syllabic phoneme, and the interval between two successive syllabics is, in some languages, always and, in others, overwhelmingly carried out by marginal, nonsyllabic phonemes. In so-called syllabic versification the number of syllabics in a metrically delimited chain (time series) is a constant, whereas the presence of a nonsyllabic phoneme or cluster between every two syllabics of a metrical chain is a constant only in languages with an indispensable occurrence of nonsyllabics between syllabics and, furthermore, in those verse systems where hiatus is prohibited. Another manifestation of a tendency toward a uniform syllabic model is the avoidance of closed syllables at the end of the line, observable, for instance, in Serbian epic songs. Italian syllabic verse shows a tendency to treat a sequence of vowels unseparated by consonantal phonemes as one single metrical syllable.[15]

In some patterns of versification the syllable is the only constant unit of verse measure, and a grammatical limit is the only constant line of demarcation between measured sequences, whereas in other patterns syllables in turn are dichotomized into more and less prominent, or two levels of grammatical limits are distinguished in their metrical function: word boundaries and syntactic pauses.

Except the varieties of the so-called vers libre that are based on conjugate intonations and pauses only, any meter uses the syllable as a unit of measure at least in certain sections of the verse. Thus in purely accentual verse ("sprung rhythm" in Hopkins' vocabulary), the number of syllables in the upbeat (called "slack" by Hopkins[16]) may vary, but the downbeat (ictus) constantly contains one single syllable.

In any accentual verse the contrast between higher and lower prominence is achieved by syllables under stress versus unstressed syllables.

Most accentual patterns operate primarily with the contrast of syllables with and without word stress, but some varieties of accentual verse deal with syntactic, phrasal stresses, those which Wimsatt and Beardsley cite as "the major stresses of the major words"[17] and which are opposed as prominent to syllables without such major, syntactic stress.

In quantitative ("chronemic") verse, long and short syllables are mutually opposed as more and less prominent. This contrast is usually carried out by syllable nuclei, phonemically long and short. But in metrical patterns like Ancient Greek and Arabic, which equalize length "by position" with length "by nature," the minimal syllables consisting of a consonantal phoneme and one mora vowel are opposed to syllables with a surplus (a second mora or a closing consonant) as simpler and less prominent syllables opposed to those that are more complex and prominent.

The question still remains open whether, besides accentual and chronemic verse, there exists a "tonemic" type of versification in languages where differences of syllabic intonations are used to distinguish word meanings.[18] In classical Chinese poetry,[19] syllables with modulations (in Chinese *tsê*, deflected tones) are opposed to the nonmodulated syllabes (*p'ing*, level tones), but apparently a chronemic principle underlies this opposition, as was suspected by Polivanov[20] and keenly interpreted by Wang Li;[21] in the Chinese metrical tradition the level tones prove to be opposed to the deflected tones as long tonal peaks of syllables to short ones, so that verse is based on the opposition of length and shortness.

Joseph Greenberg brought to my attention another variety of tonemic versification—the verse of Efik riddles based on the level feature.[22] In the sample cited by Simmons,[23] the query and the response form two octosyllables with an alike distribution of *h*(igh)- and *l*(ow)-tone syllabics; in each hemistich, moreover, the last three of the four syllables present an identical tonemic pattern: *lhhl/hhhl/lhhl/hhhl/*. Whereas Chinese versification appears as a peculiar variety of quantitative verse, the verse of the Efik riddles is linked with the usual accentual verse by an opposition of two degrees of prominence (strength or height) of the vocal tone. Thus a metrical system of versification can be based only on the opposition of syllabic peaks and slopes (syllabic verse), on the relative level of the peaks (accentual verse), and on the relative length of the syllabic peaks or entire syllables (quantitative verse).

74

In textbooks of literature we sometimes encounter a superstitious contraposition of syllabism as a mere mechanical count of syllables to the lively pulsation of accentual verse. If we examine, however, the binary meters of strictly syllabic and at the same time accentual versification, we observe two homogeneous successions of wavelike peaks and valleys. Of these two undulatory curves, the syllabic one carries nuclear phonemes in the crest and usually marginal phonemes in the bottom. As a rule the accentual curve superimposed upon the syllabic curve alternates stressed and unstressed syllables in the crests and bottoms respectively.

For comparison with the English meters that we have discussed at length, I bring to your attention the similar Russian binary verse forms which for the last fifty years have undergone an exhaustive investigation.[24] The structure of the verse can be very thoroughly described and interpreted in terms of enchained probabilities. Besides the compulsory word boundary between the lines, which is an invariant throughout all Russian meters, in the classic pattern of Russian syllabic accentual verse ("syllabotonic" in native nomenclature) we observe the following constants: (1) the number of syllables in the line from its beginning to the last downbeat is stable; (2) this very last downbeat always carries a word stress; (3) a stressed syllable cannot fall on the upbeat if the downbeat is fulfilled by an unstressed syllable of the same word unit (so that a word stress can coincide with an upbeat only as far as it belongs to a monosyllabic word unit).

Along with these characteristics compulsory for any line composed in a given meter, there are features that show a high probability of occurrence without being constantly present. Besides signals certain to occur ("probability one"), signals likely to occur ("probabilities less than one") enter into the notion of meter. Using Cherry's description of human communication,[25] we could say that the reader of poetry obviously "may be unable to attach numerical frequencies" to the constituents of the meter, but as far as he conceives the verse shape, he unwittingly gets an inkling of their "rank order."

In the Russian binary meters, all odd syllables counting back from the last downbeat—briefly, all the upbeats—are usually fulfilled by unstressed syllables, except some very low percentage of stressed monosyllables. All even syllables, again counting back from the last downbeat, show a sizable preference for syllables under word stress, but the probabilities of their occurrence are unequally distributed among the successive downbeats of the line. The higher the relative frequency of word stresses in a given downbeat, the lower the ratio shown by the preceding downbeat. Since the last downbeat is constantly stressed, the next to last has the lowest percentages of word stresses; in the preceding downbeat their amount is again higher, without attaining the maximum, displayed by the final downbeat; one downbeat further toward the beginning of the line, the amount of the stresses sinks once more, without reaching the minimum of the next-to-last downbeat; and so on. Thus the distribution of word stresses among the downbeats within the line, the split into strong and weak downbeats, creates a *regressive undulatory curve* superimposed upon the wavy alternation of downbeats and upbeats. Incidentally, there is also the captivating question of the relationship between the strong downbeats and phrasal stresses.

The Russian binary meters reveal a stratified arrangement of three undulatory curves: (I) alternation of syllabic nuclei and margins; (II) division of syllabic nuclei into alternating downbeats and upbeats; and (III) alternation of strong and weak downbeats. For example, the Russian masculine iambic tetrameter of the nineteenth and present centuries may be represented as in the figure below, and a similar triadic pattern appears in the corresponding English forms.

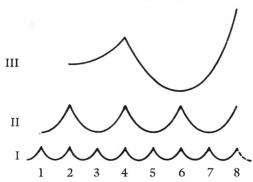

Three out of five downbeats are deprived of word stress in Shelley's iambic line "Laugh with an inextinguishable laughter." Seven out of sixteen downbeats are stressless in the following quatrain from Pasternak's late iambic tetrameter "Zemlja" (Earth):

I úlica za panibráta
S okónnicej podslepovátoj,

I béloj nóči i zakátu
Ne razminút'sja u rekí.

Since the overwhelming majority of downbeats concur with word stresses, the listener or reader of Russian verses is prepared with a high degree of probability to meet a word stress in any even syllable of iambic lines, but at the very beginning of Pasternak's quatrain the fourth and, one foot further, the sixth syllable, both in the first and in the following line, present him with a *frustrated expectation*. The degree of such a "frustration" is higher when the stress is lacking in a strong downbeat and becomes particularly outstanding when two successive downbeats carry unstressed syllables. The stresslessness of two adjacent downbeats is the less probable and the most striking when it embraces a whole hemistich, as in a later line of the same poem: "Čtoby za gorodskóju grán'ju" [štəbyzəgərackóju grán'ju]. The expectation depends on the treatment of a given downbeat in the poem and more generally in the whole extant metrical tradition. In the last downbeat but one, unstress may, however, outweigh the stress. Thus in this poem only 17 of 41 lines have a word stress on their sixth syllable. Yet in such a case the inertia of the stressed even syllables alternating with the unstressed odd syllables prompts some expectancy of stress also for the sixth syllable of the iambic tetrameter.

Quite naturally it was Edgar Allan Poe, the poet and theoretician of defeated anticipation, who metrically and psychologically appraised the human sense of gratification from the unexpected which arises from expectedness, each unthinkable without its opposite, "as evil cannot exist without good."[26] Here we could easily apply Robert Frost's formula from "The Figure a Poem Makes": "The figure is the same as for love."

The so-called shifts of word stress in polysyllabic words from the downbeat to the upbeat ("reversed feet"), which are unknown to the standard forms of Russian verse, appear quite usually in English poetry after a metrical and/or syntactic pause. A notable example is the rhythmical variation of the same adjective in Milton's "Infinite wrath and infinite despair." In the line "Nearer, my God, to Thee, nearer to Thee," the stressed syllable of one and the same word occurs twice in the upbeat, first at the beginning of the line and a second time at the beginning of a phrase. This license, discussed by Jespersen[27] and current in many languages, is entirely explainable by the particular import of the relation between an upbeat and the immediately preceding downbeat. Where such an immediate precedence is impeded by an inserted pause, the upbeat becomes a kind of *syllaba anceps*.

Besides the rules that underlie the compulsory features of verse, the rules governing its optional traits also pertain to meter. We are inclined to designate such phenomena as unstress in the downbeats and stress in upbeats as deviations, but it must be remembered that these are allowed oscillations, departures within the limits of the law. In British parliamentary terms, it is not an opposition to its majesty the meter but an opposition of its majesty. As to the actual infringements of metrical laws, the discussion of such violations recalls Osip Brik, perhaps the keenest of the Russian Formalists, who used to say that political conspirators are tried and condemned only for unsuccessful attempts at a forcible upheaval, because in the case of a successful coup it is the conspirators who assume the role of judges and prosecutors. If the violences against the meter take root, they themselves become metrical rules.

Far from being an abstract, theoretical scheme, meter—or in more explicit terms, *verse design*—underlies the structure of any single line— or, in logical terminology, any single *verse instance*. Design and instance are correlative concepts. The verse design determines the invariant features of the verse instances and sets up the limits of variations. A Serbian peasant reciter of epic poetry memorizes, performs, and, to a high extent, improvises thousands, sometimes tens of thousands of lines, and their meter is alive in his mind. Unable to abstract its rules, he nonetheless notices and repudiates even the slightest infringement of these rules. Any line of Serbian epics contains precisely ten syllables and is followed by a syntactic pause. There is furthermore a compulsory word boundary before the fifth syllable and a compulsory absence of word boundary before the fourth and the tenth syllable. The verse has, moreover, significant quantitative and accentual characteristics.[28]

This Serbian epic break, along with many similar examples presented by comparative metrics, is a persuasive warning against the erroneous identification of a break with a syntactic pause. The obligatory word boundary must not be combined with a pause and is not even meant to be audible to the ear. The analysis of Serbian epic songs phonographically recorded proves that there are no compulsory audible clues to the break, and yet any attempt to abolish the word boundary before the fifth syllable by a mere insignificant change in word order is immediately condemned by the narrator. The grammatical fact that the

fourth and fifth syllables pertain to two different word units is sufficient for the appraisal of the break. Thus verse design goes far beyond
the questions of sheer song shape; it is a much wider linguistic phenomenon, and it yields to no isolating phonetic treatment.

I say "linguistic phenomenon" even though Chatman states that
"the meter exists as a system outside the language."[29] Yes, meter appears also in other arts dealing with time sequence. There are many
linguistic problems—for instance, syntax—which likewise overstep the
limit of language and are common to different semiotic systems. We
may speak even about the grammar of traffic signals. There exists a
signal code, where a yellow light when combined with green warns
that free passage is close to being stopped and when combined with
red announces the approaching cessation of the stoppage; such a yellow signal offers a close analogue to the verbal completive aspect. Poetic meter, however, has so many intrinsically linguistic particularities
that it is most convenient to describe it from a purely linguistic point
of view.

Let us add that no linguistic property of the verse design should be
disregarded. Thus, for example, it would be an unfortunate mistake to
deny the constitutive value of intonation in English meters. Not to
mention its fundamental role in the meters of such a master of English
free verse as Whitman, it is hardly possible to ignore the metrical significance of pausal intonation ("final juncture"), whether "cadence" or
"anticadence"[30] in poems like "The Rape of the Lock" with its intentional avoidance of enjambments. Yet even a vehement accumulation
of enjambments never hides their digressive, variational status; they
always set off the normal coincidence of syntactic pause and pausal
intonation with the metrical limit. Whatever is the reciter's way of
reading, the intonational constraint of the poem remains valid. The
intonational contour specific to a poem, to a poet, to a poetic school is
one of the most notable topics brought to discussion by the Russian
Formalists.[31]

The verse design is embodied in verse instances. Usually the free
variation of these instances is denoted by the somewhat equivocal label
"rhythm." A variation of *verse instances* within a given poem must be
strictly distinguished from the variable *delivery instances*. The intention
"to describe the verse line as it is actually performed" is of lesser use
for the synchronic and historical analysis of poetry than it is for the
study of its recitation in the present and the past. Meanwhile the truth

is simple and clear: "There are many performances of the same poem—differing among themselves in many ways. A performance is an event, but the poem itself, if there *is* any poem, must be some kind of enduring object."[32] This sage memento of Wimsatt and Beardsley belongs indeed to the essentials of modern metrics.

In Shakespeare's verses the second, stressed syllable of the word "absurd" usually falls on the downbeat, but once in the third act of *Hamlet* it falls on the upbeat: "No, let the candied tongue lick absurd pomp." The reciter may scan the word "absurd" in this line with an initial stress on the first syllable or observe the final word stress in accordance with the standard accentuation. He may also subordinate the word stress of the adjective in favor of the strong syntactic stress of the following head word, as suggested by Hill: "Nó, lèt thĕ cândĭed tóngue lĭck ăb-sùrd pómp,"[33] as in Hopkins' conception of English antispasts—"regrét néver."[34] There is, finally, the possibility of emphatic modifications either through a "fluctuating accentuation" (*schwebende Betonung*) embracing both syllables or through an exclamatory reinforcement of the first syllable [àb-súrd]. But whatever solution the reciter chooses, the shift of the word stress from the downbeat to the upbeat with no antecedent pause is still arresting, and the moment of frustrated expectation stays viable. Wherever the reciter puts the accent, the discrepancy between the English word stress on the second syllable of "absurd" and the downbeat attached to the first syllable persists as a constitutive feature of the verse instance. The tension between the ictus and the usual word stress is inherent in this line independently of its different implementations by various actors and readers. As Hopkins observes, in the preface to his poems, "two rhythms are in some manner running at once."[35] His description of such a contrapuntal run can be reinterpreted. The superinducing of the equivalence principle upon the word sequence or, in other terms, the *mounting* of the metrical form upon the usual speech form necessarily gives the experience of a double, ambiguous shape to anyone who is familiar with the given language and with verse. Both the convergences and the divergences between the two forms, both the warranted and the frustrated expectations, supply this experience.

How the given verse instance is implemented in the given delivery instance depends on the *delivery design* of the reciter; he may cling to a scanning style or tend toward proselike prosody or freely oscillate between these two poles. We must be on guard against simplistic binarism which reduces two couples into one single opposition either by suppressing the cardinal distinction between verse design and verse instance (as well as between delivery design and delivery instance) or by an erroneous identification of delivery instance and delivery design with the verse instance and verse design.

> "But tell me, child, your choice; what shall I buy
> You?"—"Father, what you buy me I like best."

These two lines from "The Handsome Heart" by Hopkins contain a heavy enjambment which puts a verse boundary before the concluding monosyllable of a phrase, of a sentence, of an utterance. The recitation of these pentameters may be strictly metrical with a manifest pause between "buy" and "you" and a suppressed pause after the pronoun. Or, on the contrary, there may be displayed a prose-oriented manner without any separation of the words "buy you" and with a marked pausal intonation at the end of the question. None of these ways of recitation can, however, hide the intentional discrepancy between the metrical and syntactic division. The verse shape of a poem remains completely independent of its variable delivery, whereby I do not intend to nullify the alluring question of *Autorenleser* and *Selbstleser* launched by Sievers.[36]

No doubt, verse is primarily a recurrent "figure of sound." Primarily, always, but never uniquely. Any attempts to confine such poetic conventions as meters, alliteration, or rhyme to the sound level are speculative reasonings without any empirical justification. The projection of the equational principle into the sequence has a much deeper and wider significance. Valéry's view of poetry as "hesitation between the sound and the sense" is much more realistic and scientific than any bias of phonetic isolationism.[37]

Although rhyme by definition is based on a regular recurrence of equivalent phonemes or phonemic groups, it would be an unsound oversimplification to treat rhyme merely from the standpoint of sound. Rhyme necessarily involves a semantic relationship between rhyming units ("rhyme-fellows" in Hopkins' nomenclature).[38] In scrutinizing a rhyme we are faced with the question of whether or not it is a homoioteleuton, which confronts similar derivational and/or inflexional suffixes (congratulations-decorations), or whether the rhyming words belong to the same or to different grammatical categories. Thus, for example, Hopkins' fourfold rhyme is an agreement of two nouns—

"kind" and "mind"—both contrasting with the adjective "blind" and with the verb "find." Is there a semantic propinquity, a sort of simile between rhyming lexical units, as in dove-love, light-bright, place-space, name-fame? Do the rhyming members carry the same syntactic function? The difference between the morphological class and the syntactic application may be pointed out in rhyme. Thus in Poe's lines, "While I nodded, nearly *napping,* suddenly there came a *tapping.* As of someone gently *rapping,*" the three rhyming words, morphologically alike, are all three syntactically different. Are totally or partly homonymic rhymes prohibited, tolerated, or favored? Such full homonyms as son-sun, I-eye, eve-eave, and on the other hand, echo rhymes like December-ember, infinite-night, swarm-warm, smiles-miles? What about compound rhymes (such as Hopkins' "enjoyment—toy meant" or "began some—ransom"), where a word unit accords with a word group?

A poet or poetic school may be oriented toward or against grammatical rhyme; rhymes must be either grammatical or antigrammatical; an agrammatical rhyme, indifferent to the relation between sound and grammatical structure, would, like any agrammatism, belong to verbal pathology. If a poet tends to avoid grammatical rhymes, for him, as Hopkins said, "There are two elements in the beauty rhyme has to the mind, the likeness or sameness of sound and the unlikeness or difference of meaning."[39] Whatever the relation between sound and meaning in different rhyme techniques, both spheres are necessarily involved. After Wimsatt's illuminating observations about the meaningfulness of rhyme[40] and the shrewd modern studies of Slavic rhyme patterns, a student in poetics can hardly maintain that rhymes signify merely in a very vague way.

Rhyme is only a particular, condensed case of a much more general, we may even say the fundamental, problem of poetry, namely *parallelism.* Here again Hopkins, in his student papers of 1865, displayed a prodigious insight into the structure of poetry:

> The artificial part of poetry, perhaps we shall be right to say all artifice, reduces itself to the principle of parallelism. The structure of poetry is that of continuous parallelism, ranging from the technical so-called Parallelisms of Hebrew poetry and the antiphons of Church music up to the intricacy of Greek or Italian or English verse. But parallelism is of two kinds necessarily—where the opposition is clearly marked, and where it is transitional rather or

chromatic. Only the first kind, that of marked parallelism, is concerned with the structure of verse—in rhythm, the recurrence of a certain sequence of syllables, in metre, the recurrence of a certain sequence of rhythm, in alliteration, in assonance and in rhyme. Now the force of this recurrence is to beget a recurrence or parallelism answering to it in the words or thought and, speaking roughly and rather for the tendency than the invariable result, the more marked parallelism in structure whether of elaboration or of emphasis begets more marked parallelism in the words and sense . . . To the marked or abrupt kind of parallelism belong metaphor, simile, parable, and so on, where the effect is sought in likeness of things, and antithesis, contrast, and so on, where it is sought in unlikeness.[41]

Briefly, equivalence in sound, projected into the sequence as its constitutive principle, inevitably involves semantic equivalence, and on any linguistic level any constituent of such a sequence prompts one of the two correlative experiences which Hopkins neatly defines as "comparison for likeness' sake" and "comparison for unlikeness' sake."[42]

Folklore offers the most clear-cut and stereotyped forms of poetry, particularly suitable for structural scrutiny (as Sebeok illustrated with Cheremis samples).[43] Those oral traditions that use grammatical parallelism to connect consecutive lines, for example, Finno-Ugric patterns of verse[44] and to a high degree also Russian folk poetry, can be fruitfully analyzed on all linguistic levels—phonological, morphological, syntactic, and lexical: we learn what elements are conceived as equivalent and how likeness on certain levels is tempered by conspicuous difference on other ones. Such forms enable us to verify Ransom's wise suggestion that "the meter-and-meaning process is the organic art of poetry, and involves all its important characters."[45] These clear-cut traditional structures may dispel Wimsatt's doubts about the possibility of writing a grammar of the meter's interaction with the sense, as well as a grammar of the arrangement of metaphors.[46] As soon as parallelism is promoted to canon, the interaction between meter and meaning and the arrangement of tropes cease to be "the free and individual and unpredictable parts of the poetry."

Let me translate a few typical lines from Russian wedding songs about the appearance of the bridegroom:

A brave fellow was going to the porch,
Vasilij was walking to the manor.

The translation is literal; the verbs, however, take the final position in both Russian clauses (*Dobroj mólodec k séníčkam privoráčival, / Vasílij k téremu prixážival*). The lines wholly correspond to each other syntactically and morphologically. Both predicative verbs have the same prefixes and suffixes and the same vocalic alternant in the stem; they are alike in aspect, tense, number, and gender; and, moreover, they are synonymous. Both subjects, the common noun and the proper name, refer to the same person and form an appositional group. The two modifiers of place are expressed by identical prepositional constructions, and the first one stands in a synechdochic relation to the second.

These verses may occur preceded by another line of similar grammatical (syntactic and morphologic) makeup: "Not a bright falcon was flying beyond the hills" or "Not a fierce horse was coming at gallop to the court." The "bright falcon" and the "fierce horse" of these variants are put in metaphorical relation with the "brave fellow." This a traditional Slavic negative parallelism—the refutation of the metaphorical state (vehicle) in favor of the factual state (tenor). The negation *ne* may, however, be omitted: *Jasjón sokol zá gory zaljótyval* (A bright falcon was flying beyond the hills) or *Retív kon' kó dvoru priskákival* (A fierce horse was coming at a gallop to the court). In the first of the two examples the *metaphorical* relation is maintained: a brave fellow appeared at the porch like a bright falcon from behind the hills. In the other instance, however, the semantic connection becomes ambiguous. A comparison between the appearing bridegroom and the galloping horse suggests itself, but at the same time the halt of the horse at the court actually anticipates the approach of the hero to the house. Thus, before introducing the rider and the manor of his fiancée, the song evokes the contiguous, *metonymical* images of the horse and of the courtyard: possession instead of possessor, and outdoors instead of inside. The exposition of the groom may be broken up into two consecutive moments even without substituting the horse for the horseman: "A brave fellow was coming at a gallop to the court, / Vasilij was walking to the porch." Thus the "fierce horse," emerging in the preceding line at a similar metrical and syntactic place as the "brave fellow," figures simultaneously as a likeness to and as a representative possession of this fellow, properly speaking—*pars pro toto* for the horseman. The horse image is on the border line between metonymy and synecdoche. From these suggestive connotations of the "fierce horse" there ensues a metaphorical synecdoche: in the wedding songs and other varieties of Russian erotic lore, the masculine *retiv kon'* becomes a latent or even patent phallic symbol.

As early as the 1880s, Potebnja, a remarkable inquirer into Slavic poetics, pointed out that in folk poetry symbols are, as it were, materialized (*oveščestvlen*), converted into an accessory of the ambiance.[47] Still a symbol, it is put, however, in a connection with the action. Thus a simile is presented in the shape of a temporal sequence. In Potebnja's examples from Slavic folklore, the willow, under which a girl passes, serves at the same time as her image; the tree and the girl are both present in the same verbal simulacrum of the willow. Quite similarly, the horse of the love songs remains a symbol of virility not only when the maid is asked by the lad to feed his steed but even when being saddled or put into the stable or tied to a tree.

In poetry not only the phonological sequence but, in the same way, any sequence of semantic units strives to build an equation. Similarity superimposed on contiguity imparts to poetry its thoroughgoing symbolic, multiplex, polysemantic essence, which is beautifully suggested by Goethe's "Alles Vergängliche ist nur ein Gleichnis" (Anything transient is but a likeness). Said more technically, anything sequent is a simile. In poetry, where similarity is superinduced upon contiguity, any metonymy is slightly metaphoric and any metaphor has a metonymic tint.

Ambiguity is an intrinsic, inalienable character of any self-focused message, briefly, a corollary feature of poetry. Let us repeat with Empson: "The machinations of ambiguity are among the very roots of poetry."[48] Not only the message itself but also its addresser and addressee become ambiguous. Besides the author and the reader, there is the "I" of the lyrical hero or of the fictitious storyteller and the "you" or "thou" of the alleged addressee of dramatic monologues, supplications, and epistles. For example the poem "Wrestling Jacob" is addressed by its title hero to the Saviour and simultaneously acts as a subjective message of the poet Charles Wesley (1707–1788) to his readers. Virtually any poetic message is a quasi-quoted discourse with all those peculiar, intricate problems which "speech within speech" offers to the linguist.

The supremacy of the poetic function over the referential function does not obliterate the reference but makes it ambiguous. The double-sensed message finds correspondence in a split addresser, in a split addressee, as well as in a split reference, as is cogently exposed in the preambles to fairy tales of various peoples, for instance, in the usual exordium of the Majorca storytellers: "Aixo era y no era" (It was and it was not).[49] The repetitiveness effected by imparting the equivalence principle to the sequence makes reiterable not only the constituent sequences of the poetic messages but the whole message as well. This capacity for reiteration whether immediate or delayed, this reification of a poetic message and its constituents, this conversion of a message into an enduring thing, indeed all this represents an inherent and effective property of poetry.

In a sequence in which similarity is superimposed on contiguity, two similar phonemic sequences near to each other are prone to assume a paronomastic function. Words similar in sound are drawn together in meaning. It is true that the first line of the final stanza in Poe's "Raven" makes wide use of repetitive alliterations, as noted by Valéry,[50] but "the overwhelming effect" of this line and of the whole stanza is due primarily to the sway of poetic etymology.

> And the Raven, never flitting, still is sitting, *still* is sitting
> On the pallid bust of Pallas just above my chamber door;
> And his eyes have all the seeming of a demon's that is dreaming,
> And the lamp-light o'er him streaming throws his shadow on the
> floor:
> And my soul from out that shadow that lies floating on the floor
> Shall be lifted—nevermore!

The perch of the raven, "the pallid bust of Pallas," is merged through the "sonorous" paronomasia /pǽləd/—/pǽləs/ into one organic whole (similar to Shelley's molded line "Sculptured on alabaster obelisk" /sk.lp/—/l.b.st/—/b.l.sk/). Both confronted words were blended earlier in another epithet of the same bust—*placid* /plǽsɪd/—a poetic portmanteau, and the bond between the sitter and the seat was in turn fastened by a paronomasia: "*bird* or *beast* upon the . . . *bust*." The bird "is sitting / On the pallid bust of Pallas just above my chamber door," and the raven on his perch, despite the lover's imperative "take thy form from off my door," is nailed into place by the words /ʒʌst əbʌv/, both of them blended in /bʌst/.

The never-ending stay of the grim guest is expressed by a chain of ingenious paronomasias, partly inversive, as we would expect from such a deliberate experimenter in anticipatory, regressive modus operandi, such a master in "writing backwards" as Edgar Allan Poe. In the introductory line of this concluding stanza, "raven," contiguous to the bleak refrain word "never," appears once more as an embodied mirror image of this "never": /n.v.r/—/r.v.n/. Salient paronomasias interconnect both emblems of the everlasting despair, first "the Raven, never flitting," at the beginning of the very last stanza, and second, in its very last lines the "shadow that lies floating on the floor," and "shall be lifted—nevermore": /névər flítíŋ/—/flótíŋ/. . ./flɔ́r/. . ./líftəd névər/. The alliterations that struck Valéry build a paronomastic string: /stí . . ./—/sít . . ./—/stí . . ./—/sít . . ./. The invariance of the group is particularly stressed by the variation in its order. The two luminous effects in the chiaroscuro—the "fiery eyes" of the black fowl and the lamplight throwing "his shadow on the floor"—are evoked to add to the gloom of the whole picture and are again bound by the "vivid effect" of paronomasias: /ɔ́lðə símɪŋ/ . . . /dímənz/ . . . / ɪz drímɪŋ/—/ɔrɪm strímɪŋ/. "That shadow that lies /láyz/" pairs with the raven's "eyes" /áyz/ in an impressively misplaced echo rhyme.

In poetry, any conspicuous similarity in sound is evaluated in respect to similarity and/or dissimilarity in meaning. But Pope's alliterative precept to poets—"the sound must seem an echo of the sense"—has a wider application. In referential language the connection between *signans* and *signatum* is overwhelmingly based on their codified contiguity, which is often confusingly labeled "arbitrariness of the verbal sign." The relevance of the sound-meaning nexus is a simple corollary of the superposition of similarity upon contiguity. Sound symbolism is an undeniably objective relation founded on a phenomenal connection between different sensory modes, in particular between the visual and the auditory experience. If the results of research in this area have sometimes been vague or controversial, it is primarily due to an insufficient care for the methods of psychological and linguistic inquiry. Particularly from the linguistic point of view the picture has often been distorted by lack of attention to the phonological aspect of speech sounds or by inevitably vain operations with complex phonemic units instead of with their ultimate components. But when on testing, for example, such phonemic oppositions as grave versus acute we ask whether /i/ or /u/ is darker, some of the subjects may respond that this question makes no sense to them, but hardly one will state that /i/ is the darker of the two.

Poetry is not the only area where sound symbolism makes itself felt, but it is a province where the internal nexus between sound and meaning changes from latent into patent and manifests itself most palpably and intensely, as was noted in Hymes's stimulating paper.[51] The super-average accumulation of a certain class of phonemes or a contrastive assemblage of two opposite classes in the sound texture of a line, of a stanza, of a poem acts like an "undercurrent of meaning," to use Poe's picturesque expression.[52] In two polar words phonemic relationship may be in agreement with their semantic opposition, as in Russian /d'en'/'day' and /noč/ 'night,' with acute vowels and consonants in the diurnal name of the corresponding grave vowel in the nocturnal name. A reinforcement of this contrast by surrounding the first word with acute phonemes, in contradistinction to the grave phonemic neighborhood of the second word, makes the sound into a thorough echo of the sense. But in the French *jour* 'day' and *nuit* 'night' the distribution of grave and acute vowels is inverted, so that Mallarmé's *Divagations* accuse his mother tongue of a deceitful perversity in assigning to day a dark timbre and to night a light one.[53] Whorf states that when in its sound shape "a word has an acoustic similarity to its own meaning, we can notice it . . . But when the opposite occurs, nobody notices it." Poetic language, however, and particularly French poetry in the collision between sound and meaning detected by Mallarmé, either seeks a phonological alternation of such a discrepancy and drowns the "converse" distribution of vocalic features by surrounding *nuit* with grave and *jour* with acute phonemes; or it resorts to a semantic shift and its imagery of day and night replaces the imagery of light and dark by other synesthetic correlates of the phonemic opposition grave/acute and, for instance, puts the heavy, warm day in contrast to the airy, cool night—because "human subjects seem to associate the experiences of bright, sharp, hard, high, light (in weight), quick, high-pitched, narrow, and so on in a long series, with each other; and conversely the experiences of dark, warm, yielding, soft, blunt, heavy, slow, low-pitched, wide, etc., in another long series."[54]

However effective is the emphasis on repetition in poetry, the sound texture is still far from being confined to numerical contrivances, and a phoneme that appears only once, but in a key word, in a pertinent position, against a contrastive background, may acquire striking significance. As painters used to say, "Un kilo de vert n'est pas plus vert qu'un demi kilo."

Any analysis of poetic sound texture must consistently take into account the phonological structure of the given language and, beside the overall code, the hierarchy of phonological distinctions in the given poetic convention as well. Thus the approximate rhymes used by Slavic peoples in oral and in some stages of written tradition admit unlike consonants in the rhyming members (e.g., Czech *boty, boky, stopy, kosy, sochy*) but, as Nitch noticed, no mutual correspondence between voiced and voiceless consonants is allowed,[55] so that the quoted Czech words cannot rhyme with *body, doby, kozy, rohy*. In the songs of some American Indian peoples such as the Pima-Papago and Tepecano, according to Herzog's observations—only partly communicated in print[56]—the phonemic distinction between voiced and voiceless plosives and between them and nasals is replaced by a free variation, whereas the distinction between labials, dentals, velars, and palatals is rigorously maintained. Thus in the poetry of these languages consonants lose two of the four distinctive features, voiced/voiceless and nasal/oral, and preserve the other two, grave/acute and compact/diffuse. The selection and hierarchic stratification of valid categories is a factor of primary importance for poetics both on the phonological and on the grammatical level.

Old Indic and medieval Latin literary theory keenly distinguished two poles of verbal art, labeled in Sanskrit *Pāñcālī* and *Vaidarbhī* and correspondingly in Latin *ornatus difficilis* and *ornatus facilis*,[57] the latter style evidently being much more difficult to analyze linguistically because in such literary forms verbal devices are unostentatious and language seems a nearly transparent garment. But one must say with Charles Sanders Peirce: "This clothing never can be completely stripped off; it is only changed for something more diaphanous."[58] "Verseless composition," as Hopkins calls the prosaic variety of verbal art—where parallelisms are not so strictly marked and strictly regular as "continuous parallelism" and where there is no dominant figure of sound[59]—present more entangled problems for poetics, as does any transitional linguistic area. In this case the transition is between strictly poetic and strictly referential language. But Propp's pioneering monograph on the structure of the fairy tale[60] shows us how a consistently syntactic approach can be of paramount help even in classifying the traditional plots and in tracing the puzzling laws that underlie their composition and selection. The studies of Lévi-Strauss[61] display a much deeper but essentially similar approach to the same constructional problem.

It is no mere chance that metonymic structures are less explored than the field of metaphor. Allow me to repeat my old observation that the study of poetic tropes has been directed mainly toward metaphor and that so-called realistic literature, intimately tied to the metonymic principle, still defies interpretation, although the same linguistic methodology that poetics uses when analyzing the metaphorical style of romantic poetry is entirely applicable to the metonymical texture of realistic prose.[62]

Textbooks believe in the occurrence of poems devoid of imagery, but actually a scarcity of lexical tropes is counterbalanced by gorgeous grammatical tropes and figures. The poetic resources concealed in the morphological and syntactic structure of language—briefly, the poetry of grammar and its literary product, the grammar of poetry—have been seldom known to critics and mostly disregarded by linguists but skillfully mastered by creative writers.

The main dramatic force of Antony's exordium to the funeral oration for Caesar is achieved by Shakespeare's playing on grammatical categories and constructions. Mark Antony lampoons Brutus' speech by changing the alleged reasons for Caesar's assassination into plain linguistic fictions. Brutus' accusation of Caesar, "as he was ambitious, I slew him," undergoes successive transformations. First Antony reduces it to a mere quotation which puts the responsibility for the statement on the speaker quoted: "The noble Brutus / Hath told you." When repeated, this reference to Brutus is put into opposition to Antony's own assertions by an adversative "but" and further degraded by a concessive "yet." The reference to the alleger's honor ceases to justify the allegation when repeated with a substitution of the merely copulative "and" instead of the previous causal "for," and when finally put into question through the malicious insertion of a modal "sure":

> The noble Brutus
> Hath told you Caesar was ambitious;
> For Brutus is an honourable man,
> But Brutus says he was ambitious,
> And Brutus is an honourable man.
> Yet Brutus says he was ambitious,
> And Brutus is an honourable man.
> Yet Brutus says he was ambitious,
> And, sure, he is an honourable man.

The following polyptoton—"I speak . . . Brutus spoke . . . I am to speak"—presents the repeated allegation as mere reported speech instead of reported facts. The effect lies, modal logic would say, in the oblique context of the arguments adduced, which makes them into unprovable belief sentences:

> I speak not to disprove what Brutus spoke,
> But here I am to speak what I do know.

The most effective device of Antony's irony is the *modus obliquus* of Brutus' abstracts changed into a *modus rectus* to disclose that these reified attributes are nothing but linguistic fictions. To Brutus' saying "he was ambitious," Antony first replies by transferring the adjective from the agent to the action ("Did this in Caesar seem ambitious?"), then by eliciting the abstract noun "ambition" and converting it into the subject of a concrete passive construction "Ambition should be made of sterner stuff" and subsequently to the predicate noun of an interrogative sentence, "Was this ambition?"—Brutus' appeal "hear me for my cause" is answered by the same noun *in recto,* the hypostatized subject of an interrogative, active construction: "What cause withholds you?" While Brutus calls "awake your senses, that you may the better judge," the abstract substantive derived from "judge" becomes an apostrophized agent in Antony's report: "O judgment, thou art fled to brutish beasts." Incidentally, this apostrophe with its murderous paronomasia *Brutus-brutish* is reminiscent of Caesar's parting exclamation "Et tu, Brute!" Properties and activities are exhibited *in recto,* whereas their carriers appear either *in obliquo* ("withholds you," "to brutish beasts," "back to me") or as subjects of negative actions ("men have lost," "I must pause"):

> You all did love him once, not without cause;
> What cause withholds you then to mourn for him?
> O judgment, thou art fled to brutish beasts,
> And men have lost their reason!

The last two lines of Antony's exordium display the ostensible independence of these grammatical metonymies. The stereotyped "I mourn for so-and-so" and the figurative but still stereotyped "so-and-so is in the coffin and my heart is with him" or "goes out to him" give place in Antony's speech to a daringly realized metonymy; the trope becomes a part of poetic reality:

> My heart is in the coffin there with Caesar,
> And I must pause till it come back to me.

In poetry the internal form of a name, that is, the semantic load of its constituents, regains its pertinence. "Cocktails" may resume their obliterated kinship with plumage. Their colors are vivified in Mac Hammond's lines, "The ghost of a Bronx pink lady / With orange blossoms afloat in her hair," and the etymological metaphor attains its realization: "O, Bloody Mary, / The cocktails have crowed not the cocks!" ("At an Old Fashion Bar in Manhattan"). In T. S. Eliot's comedy *The Cocktail Party,* the evocation of cocktails is interwoven with sinister zoological motifs. The play begins with Alex's exclamation:

> You've missed the point completely, Julia:
> There *were* no tigers. *That* was the point.

Julia recollects the only man she ever met "who could hear the cry of bats." A moment later she announces: "Now I want to relax. Are there any more cocktails?" And in the last act of the play Julia once more asks Alex, "You were shooting tigers?" And Alex answers:

> There are no tigers, Julia,
> In Kinkanja . . .
> Though whether the monkeys are the core of the problem
> Or merely a symptom, I am not so sure . . .
> The majority of the natives are heathen:
> They hold these monkeys in peculiar veneration . . .
> Some of the tribes are Christian converts . . .
> They trap the monkeys. And they eat them.
> The young monkeys are extremely palatable . . .
> I invented for the natives several new recipes.

As to the heathens, "instead of eating monkeys, / They are eating Christians. / Julia: Who have eaten monkeys." All of a sudden she exclaims:

> Somebody must have walked over my grave:
> I'm feeling so chilly. Give me some gin.
> . Not a cocktail. I'm freezing—in July!

Wallace Stevens' poem "An Ordinary Evening in New Haven" revives the head word of the city name first through a discreet allusion to heaven and then through a direct punlike confrontation similar to Hopkins' "Heaven-Haven."

> The dry eucalyptus *seeks god in the rainy cloud.*
> Professor Eucalyptus of New Haven *seeks him in New Haven* . . .

The instinct *for heaven* had its counterpart:
The instinct for earth, *for New Haven,* for his room . . .

The adjective "New" of the city name is laid bare through the concatenation of opposites:

The oldest-newest day is the newest alone.
The oldest-newest night does not creak by . . .

When in 1919 the Moscow Linguistic Circle discussed how to define and delimit the range of *epitheta ornantia,* the poet Majakovskij rebuked us by saying that for him any adjective appearing in a poem was thereby a poetic epithet, even "great" in the Great Bear or "big" and "little" in such names of Moscow streets as Bol'šaja (big) Presnja and Malaja (little) Presnja. Compare Majakovskij's poem of 1915, "I and Napoleon," which begins with the words *Ja živu na Bol'šoj Presne,/ 34, 24* . . . : "I live on the Big Presnja, 34, 24. Apparently it's not my business that somewhere in the stormy world people went and invented war." And the poem ends: "The war has killed one more, the poet from the Big Presnja" (*poèta s Bol'šoj Presni*). Briefly, poeticalness is not a supplementation of discourse with rhetorical adornment but a total reevaluation of the discourse and of all its components whatsoever.

A missionary blamed his African flock for walking around with no clothes on. "And what about yourself?" they pointed to his visage, "are not you, too, somewhere naked?" "Well, but that is my face." "Yet in us," retorted the natives, "everywhere it is face." So in poetry any verbal element is converted into a figure of poetic speech.

My attempt to vindicate the right and duty of linguistics to direct the investigation of verbal art in all its compass and extent can come to a conclusion with the same burden which summarized my report to the 1953 conference here at Indiana University: "Linguista sum; linguistici nihil a me alienum puto."[63] If the poet Ransom is right (and he is right) that "poetry is a kind of language,"[64] the linguist whose field is any kind of language may and must include poetry in his study. Let us not forget the wise precept of Paul Valéry: "literature is and cannot be anything but a sort of extension and application of certain properties of language."[65] The present conference has clearly shown that the time when both linguists and literary historians eluded questions of poetic structure is now safely behind us. Indeed, as Hollander stated, "there seems to be no reason for trying to separate the literary from the overall linguistic."[66] If there are some critics who still doubt the competence of linguistics to embrace the field of poetics, I believe that the poetic incompetence of some bigoted linguists has been mistaken for an inadequacy of the linguistic science itself. All of us here, however, definitely realize that a linguist deaf to the poetic function of language and a literary scholar indifferent to linguistic problems and unconversant with linguistic methods are equally flagrant anachronisms.

CHAPTER 8

Two Aspects of Language and Two Types of Aphasic Disturbances

I. The Linguistic Problems of Aphasia

If aphasia is a language disturbance, as the term itself suggests, then any description and classification of aphasic syndromes must begin with the question of what aspects of language are impaired in the various species of such a disorder. This problem, which was approached long ago by Hughlings Jackson,[1] cannot be solved without the participation of professional linguists familiar with the patterning and functioning of language.

To study adequately any breakdown in communications we must first understand the nature and structure of the particular mode of communication that has ceased to function. Linguistics is concerned with language in all its aspects—language in operation, language in drift,[2] language in the nascent state, and language in dissolution.

There are psychopathologists who assign a high importance to the linguistic problems involved in the study of language disturbances;[3] some of these questions have been touched upon in the best treatises on aphasia.[4] Yet, in most cases, this valid insistence on the linguist's contribution to the investigation of aphasia has been ignored. For instance, one book, dealing to a great extent with the complex and intricate problems of infantile aphasia, calls for a coordination of various disciplines and appeals for cooperation to otolaryngologists, pediatricians, audiologists, psychiatrists, and educators; but the science of language is passed over in silence, as if disorders in speech perception had nothing whatever to do with language.[5]

Linguists are also responsible for the delay in undertaking a joint inquiry into aphasia. Nothing comparable to the minute linguistic observations of infants of various countries has been performed with respect to aphasics. Nor has there been any attempt to reinterpret and systematize from the point of view of linguistics the multifarious clinical data on diverse types of aphasia. That this should be true is all the more surprising in view of the fact that, on the one hand, the amazing progress of structural linguistics has endowed the investigator with efficient tools and methods for the study of verbal regression and, on the other, the aphasic disintegration of the verbal pattern may provide the linguist with new insights into the general laws of language.

The application of purely linguistic criteria to the interpretation and classification of aphasic facts can substantially contribute to the science of language and language disturbances, provided that linguists remain as careful and cautious when dealing with psychological and neurological data as they have been in their traditional field. First of all, they should be familiar with the technical terms and devices of the medical disciplines dealing with aphasia; then, they must submit the clinical case reports to thorough linguistic analysis; and, further, they should themselves work with aphasic patients in order to approach the cases directly and not only through a reinterpretation of prepared records which have been quite differently conceived and elaborated.

There is one level of aphasic phenomena where amazing agreement has been achieved between those psychiatrists and linguists who have tackled these problems, namely the disintegration of the sound pattern.[6] This dissolution exhibits a time order of great regularity. Aphasic regression has proved to be a mirror of the child's acquisition of speech sounds: it shows the child's development in reverse. Furthermore, comparison of child language and aphasia enables us to establish several *laws of implication*. The search for this order of acquisitions and losses and for the general laws of implication cannot be confined to the phonemic pattern but must be extended also to the grammatical system.[7]

II. The Twofold Character of Language

Speech implies a selection of certain linguistic entities and their combination into linguistic units of a higher degree of complexity. At the lexical level this is readily apparent: the speaker selects words and combines them into sentences according to the syntactic system of the language he is using; sentences in their turn are combined into utterances. But the speaker is by no means a completely free agent in his choice of words: his selection (except for the rare case of actual neology) must be made from the lexical storehouse which he and his addressee possess in common. The communication engineer most properly approaches the essence of the speech event when he assumes that in the optimal exchange of information the speaker and the listener have at their disposal more or less the same "filing cabinet of *prefabricated* representations": the addresser of a verbal message selects one of these "preconceived possibilities," and the addressee is supposed to make an identical choice from the same assembly of "possibilities already foreseen and provided for."[8] Thus the efficiency of a speech event demands the use of a common code by its participants.

"'Did you say *pig* or *fig?*' said the Cat. 'I said *pig,*' replied Alice."[9] In this peculiar utterance the feline addressee attempts to recapture a linguistic choice made by the addresser. In the common code of the Cat and Alice (spoken English), the difference between a stop and a continuant, other things being equal, may change the meaning of the message. Alice had used the distinctive feature stop versus continuant, rejecting the latter and choosing the former of the two opposites; and in the same act of speech she combined this solution with certain other simultaneous features, using the gravity and the tenseness of /p/ in contradistinction to the acuteness of /t/ and to the laxness of /b/. Thus all these attributes have been combined into a bundle of distinctive features, the so-called phoneme. The phoneme /p/ was then followed by the phonemes /i/ and /g/, themselves bundles of simultaneously produced distinctive features. Hence the *concurrence* of simultaneous entities and the *concatenation* of successive entities are the two ways in which we speakers combine linguistic constituents.

Neither such bundles as /p/ or /f/ nor such sequences of bundles as /pig/ or /fig/ are invented by the speaker who uses them. Neither can the distinctive feature stop versus continuant nor the phoneme /p/ occur out of context. The stop feature appears in combination with certain other concurrent features, and the repertory of combinations of these features into phonemes such as /p/, /b/, /t/, /d/, /k/, /g/ is limited by the code of the given language. The code sets limitations on the possible combinations of the phoneme /p/ with other following and/ or preceding phonemes; and only part of the permissible phoneme sequences are actually utilized in the lexical stock of a given language. Even when other combinations of phonemes are theoretically possible, the speaker, as a rule, is only a word user, not a word coiner. When faced with individual words, we expect them to be coded units. In order to grasp the word *nylon* one must know the meaning assigned to this vocable in the lexical code of modern English.

In any language there exist also coded word groups called *phrase words*. The meaning of the idiom *how do you do* cannot be derived by adding together the meanings of its lexical constituents; the whole is not equal to the sum of its parts. Word groups which in this respect behave like single words are a common but nonetheless only marginal case. In order to comprehend the overwhelming majority of word groups, we need be familiar only with the constituent words and with the syntactical rules of their combination. Within these limitations we are free to put words in new contexts. Of course, this freedom is relative, and the pressure of current clichés upon our choice of combinations is considerable. But the freedom to compose quite new contexts is undeniable, despite the relatively low statistical probability of their occurrence.

Thus, in the combination of linguistic units, there is an ascending scale of freedom. In the combination of distinctive features into phonemes, the freedom of the individual speaker is zero: the code has already established all the possibilities which may be utilized in the given language. Freedom to combine phonemes into words is circumscribed; it is limited to the marginal situation of word coinage. In forming sentences with words, the speaker is less constrained. And finally, in the combination of sentences into utterances, the action of compulsory syntactical rules ceases, and the freedom of any individual speaker to create novel contexts increases substantially, although again the numerous stereotyped utterances are not to be overlooked.

Any linguistic sign involves two modes of arrangement:

(1) *Combination.* Any sign is made up of constituent signs and/or occurs only in combination with other signs. This means that any linguistic unit at one and the same time serves as a context for simpler

units and/or finds its own context in a more complex linguistic unit. Hence any actual grouping of linguistic units binds them into a superior unit: combination and contexture are two faces of the same operation.

(2) *Selection.* A selection between alternatives implies the possibility of substituting one for the other, equivalent in one respect and different in another. Actually, selection and substitution are two faces of the same operation.

The fundamental role which these two operations play in language was clearly realized by Ferdinand de Saussure. Yet of the two varieties of combination—concurrence and concatenation—it was only the latter, the temporal sequence, which was recognized by the Geneva linguist. Despite his own insight into the phoneme as a set of concurrent distinctive features (*éléments différentiels des phonèmes*), the scholar succumbed to the traditional belief in the linear character of language "which excludes the possibility of pronouncing two elements at the same time."[10]

In order to delimit the two modes of arrangement we have described as combination and selection, de Saussure states that the former "is *in presentia:* it is based on two or several terms jointly present in an actual series," whereas the latter "connects terms *in absentia* as members of a virtual mnemonic series." That is to say, selection (and, correspondingly, substitution) deals with entities conjoined in the code but not in the given message, whereas, in the case of combination, the entities are conjoined in both or only in the actual message. The addressee perceives that the given utterance (message) is a *combination* of constituent parts (sentences, words, phonemes) *selected* from the repository of all possible constituent parts (the code). The constituents of a context are in a state of *contiguity,* while in a substitution set signs are linked by various degrees of *similarity* which fluctuate between the equivalence of synonyms and the common core of antonyms.

These two operations provide each linguistic sign with two sets of *interpretants,* to utilize the effective concept introduced by Charles Sanders Peirce.[11] There are two references which serve to interpret the sign—one to the code and the other to the context, whether coded or free, and in each of these ways the sign is related to another set of linguistic signs, through an *alternation* in the former case and through an *alignment* in the latter. A given significative unit may be replaced by other, more explicit signs of the same code, whereby its general mean-

99

ing is revealed, while its contextual meaning is determined by its connection with other signs within the same sequence.

The constituents of any message are necessarily linked with the code by an internal relation and with the message by an external relation. Language in its various aspects deals with both modes of relation. Whether messages are exchanged or communication proceeds unilaterally from the addresser to the addressee, there must be some kind of contiguity between the participants of any speech event to assure the transmission of the message. The separation in space, and often in time, between two individuals, the addresser and the addressee, is bridged by an internal relation: there must be a certain equivalence between the symbols used by the addresser and those known and interpreted by the addressee. Without such an equivalence the message is fruitless: even when it reaches the receiver it does not affect him.

III. The Similarity Disorder

It is clear that speech disturbances may affect in varying degrees the individual's capacity for combination and selection of linguistic units, and indeed the question of which of these two operations is chiefly impaired proves to be of far-reaching significance in describing, analyzing, and classifying the diverse forms of aphasia. This dichotomy is perhaps even more suggestive than the classical distinction between *emissive* and *receptive* aphasia, indicating which of the two functions in speech exchange, the encoding or the decoding of verbal messages, is particularly affected.

Head attempted to classify cases of aphasia into definite groups, and to each of these varieties he assigned "a name chosen to signify the most salient defect in the management and comprehension of words and phrases."[12] Following this device, we distinguish two basic types of aphasia—depending on whether the major deficiency lies in selection and substitution, with relative stability of combination and contexture; or conversely, in combination and contexture, with relative retention of normal selection and substitution. In outlining these two opposite patterns of aphasia, I shall utilize mainly Goldstein's data.

For aphasics of the first type (selection deficiency), the context is the indispensable and decisive factor. When presented with scraps of words or sentences, such a patient readily completes them. His speech is merely reactive: he easily carries on conversation but has difficulties in starting a dialogue; he is able to reply to a real or imaginary addresser when he is, or imagines himself to be, the addressee of the message. It is particularly hard for him to perform, or even to understand, such a closed discourse as the monologue. The more his utterances are dependent on the context, the better he copes with his verbal task. He feels unable to utter a sentence which responds neither to the cue of his interlocutor nor to the actual situation. The sentence "it rains" cannot be produced unless the utterer sees that it is actually raining. The deeper the utterance is embedded in the verbal or nonverbalized context, the higher are the chances of its successful performance by this class of patients.

Likewise, the more a word is dependent on the other words of the same sentence and the more it refers to the syntactical context, the less it is affected by the speech disturbance. Therefore words syntactically subordinated by grammatical agreement or government are more tenacious, whereas the main subordinating agent of the sentence, namely the subject, tends to be omitted. As long as beginning is the patient's main difficulty, it is obvious that he will fail precisely at the starting point, the cornerstone of the sentence pattern. In this type of language disturbance, sentences are conceived as elliptical sequels to be supplied from antecedent sentences uttered, if not imagined, by the aphasic himself or received by him from the other partner in the colloquy, actual if not imaginary. Key words may be dropped or superseded by abstract anaphoric substitutes.[13] A specific noun, as Freud noticed, is replaced by a very general one, for instance *machin* or *chose* in the speech of French aphasics.[14] In a dialectal German sample of "amnesic aphasia" observed by Goldstein, *Ding* (thing) or *Stückel* (piece) was substituted for all inanimate nouns, and *überfahren* (perform) for verbs which were identifiable from the context or situation and therefore appeared superfluous to the patient.

Words with an inherent reference to the context, such as pronouns and pronominal adverbs, and words serving merely to construct the context, such as connectives and auxiliaries, are particularly prone to survive. A typical utterance of a German patient, recorded by Quensel and quoted by Goldstein, will serve as illustration: "Ich bin doch hier unten, na wenn ich gewesen bin ich weess nicht, we das, nu wenn ich, ob das nun doch, noch, ja. Was Sie her, wenn ich, och ich weess nicht, we das hier war ja." Thus only the framework, the connecting links of communication, is spared by this type of aphasia at its critical stage.

In the theory of language, since the early Middle Ages, it has repeatedly been asserted that the word out of context has no meaning. The validity of this statement is, however, confined to aphasia or, more exactly, to one type of aphasia. In the pathological cases under discussion, an isolated word means actually nothing but "blab." As numerous tests have disclosed, for such patients two occurrences of the same word in two different contexts are mere homonyms. Since distinctive vocables carry a higher amount of information than homonyms, some aphasics of this type tend to supplant the contextual variants of one word by different terms, each of them specific for the given environment. Thus Goldstein's patient never uttered the word *knife* alone but, according to its use and surroundings, alternately called the knife *pencil-sharpener, apple-parer, bread-knife, knife-and-fork;* so the word *knife* was changed from a free form, capable of occurring alone, into a bound form.

"I have a good apartment, entrance hall, bedroom, kitchen," Goldstein's patient says. "There are also big apartments, only in the rear live bachelors." A more explicit form, the word group *unmarried people,* could have been substituted for *bachelors,* but this univerbal term was selected by the speaker. When repeatedly asked what a bachelor was, the patient did not answer and was "apparently in distress." A reply like "a bachelor is an unmarried man" or "an unmarried man is a bachelor" would present an equational predication and thus a projection of a substitution set from the lexical code of the English language into the context of the given message. The equivalent terms become two correlated parts of the sentence and consequently are tied by contiguity. The patient was able to select the appropriate term *bachelor* when it was supported by the context of a customary conversation about "bachelor apartments," but was incapable of utilizing the substitution set *bachelor = unmarried man* as the topic of a sentence because the ability for autonomous selection and substitution had been affected. The equational sentence vainly demanded from the patient carries as its sole information: "*bachelor* means an unmarried man" or "an unmarried man is called a *bachelor.*"

The same difficulty arises when the patient is asked to name an object pointed to or handled by the examiner. The aphasic with a defect in substitution will not supplement the pointing or handling gesture of the examiner with the name of the object pointed to. Instead of saying "this is [called] a pencil," he will merely add an elliptical note about its use: "To write." If one of the synonymic signs is present (for instance, the word *bachelor* or the pointing to the pencil) then the other sign (such as the phrase *unmarried man* or the word *pencil*) becomes redundant and consequently superfluous. For the aphasic, both signs are in complementary distribution: if one is performed by the examiner, the patient will avoid its synonym: "I understand everything" or "Ich weiss es schon" will be his typical reaction. Likewise, the picture of an object will cause suppression of its name: a verbal sign is supplanted by a pictorial sign. When the picture of a compass was presented to a patient of Lotmar's, he responded: "Yes, it's a . . . I know what it belongs to, but I cannot recall the technical expression . . . Yes . . . direction . . . to show direction . . . a magnet points to the north."[15] Such patients fail to shift, as Peirce would say, from an index or icon to a corresponding verbal symbol.[16]

Even simple repetition of a word uttered by the examiner seems to the patient unnecessarily redundant, and despite instructions received he is unable to repeat it. Told to repeat the word "no," Head's patient replied "No, I don't know how to do it." While spontaneously using the word in the context of his answer ("No, I don't . . ."), he could not produce the purest form of equational predication, the tautology $a = a$: /no/ is /no/.

One of the important contributions of symbolic logic to the science of language is its emphasis on the distinction between *object language* and *metalanguage*. As Carnap states, "in order to speak *about* any *object language,* we need a *metalanguage.*"[17] On these two different levels of language the same linguistic stock may be used; thus we may speak in English (as metalanguage) about English (as object language) and interpret English words and sentences by means of English synonyms, circumlocutions, and paraphrases. Obviously such operations, labeled *metalinguistic* by the logicians, are not their invention: far from being confined to the sphere of science, they prove to be an integral part of our customary linguistic activities. The participants in a dialogue often check whether they are using the same code. "Do you follow me? Do you see what I mean?" the speaker asks, or the listener himself breaks in with "What do you mean?" Then, by replacing the questionable sign with another sign from the same linguistic code or with a whole group of code signs, the sender of the message seeks to make it more accessible to the decoder.

The interpretation of one linguistic sign through other, in some respect homogeneous, signs of the same language is a metalinguistic operation which also plays an essential role in children's language learning. Observations have disclosed what a considerable place talk about language occupies in the verbal behavior of preschool children.[18] Recourse to metalanguage is necessary both for the acquisition of language and for its normal functioning. The aphasic defect in the "capacity of naming" is properly a loss of metalanguage. As a matter of fact, the examples of equational predication sought in vain from the patients cited above are metalinguistic propositions referring to the English language. Their explicit wording would be: "In the code we use, the name of the indicated object is *pencil*"; or "In the code we use, the word '*bachelor*' and the circumlocution '*unmarried man*' are equivalent."

Such an aphasic can switch neither from a word to its synonyms or circumlocutions nor to its *heteronyms* (equivalent expressions in other languages). Loss of bilingualism and confinement to a single dialectal variety of a single language is a symptomatic manifestation of this disorder.

According to an old but recurrent bias, a single individual's way of speaking at a given time, labeled *idiolect,* has been viewed as the only concrete linguistic reality. In one discussion of this concept the following objections were raised:

> Everyone, when speaking to another person, tries, deliberately or involuntarily, to hit upon a common vocabulary: either to please or simply to be understood or, finally, to bring him out, he uses the terms of his addressee. There is no such thing as private property in language: everything is socialized. Verbal exchange, like any form of intercourse, requires at least two communicators, and idiolect proves to be a somewhat perverse fiction.[19]

This statement needs, however, one reservation: for an aphasic who has lost the capacity for code switching, the idiolect indeed becomes the sole linguistic reality. As long as he does not regard another's speech as a message addressed to him in his own verbal pattern, he feels, as a patient of Hemphil and Stengel expressed it: "I can hear you dead plain but I cannot get what you say . . . I hear your voice but not the words . . . It does not pronounce itself."[20] He considers the other's utterance to be either gibberish or at least in an unknown language.

As noted above, it is the external relation of contiguity which unites the constituents of a context, and the internal relation of similarity which underlies the substitution set. Hence, for an aphasic with impaired substitution and intact contexture, operations involving similarity yield to those based on contiguity. It could be predicted that under these conditions any semantic grouping would be guided by spatial or temporal contiguity rather than by similarity. Actually Goldstein's tests justify such an expectation: a female patient of this type, when asked to list a few names of animals, disposed them in the same order in which she had seen them in the zoo; similarly, despite instructions to arrange certain objects according to color, size, and shape, she classified them on the basis of their spatial contiguity as home things, office materials, etc., and justified this grouping by a reference to a display window where "it does not matter what the things are" (they do not have to be similar). The same patient was willing to name the primary hues—red, yellow, green, and blue—but declined to extend these names to the transitional varieties since, for her, words had no capacity to assume additional, shifted meanings associated by similarity with their primary meaning.

One must agree with Goldstein's observation that patients of this type "grasped the words in their literal meaning but could not be brought to understand the metaphoric character of the same words" (p. 270). It would, however, be an unwarranted generalization to assume that figurative speech is altogether incomprehensible to them. Of the two polar figures of speech, metaphor and metonymy, the latter, based on contiguity, is widely employed by aphasics whose selective capacities have been affected. *Fork* is substituted for *knife, table* for *lamp, smoke* for *pipe, eat* for *toaster.* A typical case is reported by Head: "When he failed to recall the name for 'black,' he described it as 'What you do for the dead'; this he shortened to 'dead.'" Such metonymies may be characterized as projections from the line of a habitual context into the line of substitution and selection: a sign (*fork*) which usually occurs together with another sign (*knife*) may be used instead of this sign. Phrases like "knife and fork," "table lamp," "to smoke a pipe," induced the metonymies *fork, table, smoke;* the relation between the use of an object (toast) and the means of its production underlies the metonymy *eat* for *toaster.* "When does one wear black?"—"When mourning the dead": in place of naming the color, the cause of its traditional use is designated. The escape from sameness to contiguity is particularly striking in such cases as Goldstein's patient who would answer with a metonymy when asked to repeat a given word and, for instance, would say *glass* for *window* and *heaven* for *God.*

When the selective capacity is strongly impaired and the gift for combination at least partly preserved, then contiguity determines the patient's whole verbal behavior, and we may designate this type of aphasia *similarity disorder.*

IV. The Contiguity Disorder

From 1864 on it was repeatedly pointed out in Hughlings Jackson's pioneer contributions to the modern study of language and language disturbances:

> It is not enough to say that speech consists of words. It consists of words referring to one another in a particular manner; and, without a proper interrelation of its parts, a verbal utterance would be a mere succession of names embodying no proposition.[21]

> Loss of speech is the loss of power to propositionize . . . Speechlessness does not mean entire wordlessness.[22]

Impairment of the ability to propositionize or, generally speaking, to combine simpler linguistic entities into more complex units, is actually confined to one type of aphasia, the opposite of the type discussed in the preceding section. There is no wordlessness, since the entity preserved in most of such cases is the word, which can be defined as the highest among the linguistic units compulsorily coded—we compose our own sentences and utterances out of the word stock supplied by the code.

This contexture-deficient aphasia, which could be termed the *contiguity disorder,* diminishes the extent and variety of sentences. The syntactical rules organizing words into higher units are lost; this loss, called *agrammatism,* causes the degeneration of the sentence into a mere "word heap," to use Jackson's image.[23] Word order becomes chaotic; the ties of grammatical coordination and subordination, whether concord or government, are dissolved. As might be expected, words endowed with purely grammatical functions, like conjunctions, prepositions, pronouns, and articles, disappear first, giving rise to the so-called "telegraphic style," whereas in the case of a similarity disorder they are the most resistant. The less a word depends grammatically on the context, the stronger is its tenacity in the speech of aphasics with a contiguity disorder and the earlier it is dropped by patients with a similarity disorder. Thus the "kernel subject word" is the first to fall out of the sentence in cases of similarity disorder and, conversely, it is the least destructible in the opposite type of aphasia.

The type of aphasia affecting contexture tends to give rise to infantile one-sentence utterances and one-word sentences. Only a few longer, stereotyped, ready-made sentences manage to survive. In advanced cases of this disease, each utterance is reduced to a single one-word sentence. While contexture disintegrates, the selective operation goes on. "To say what a thing is, is to say what it is like," Jackson notes. The patient confined to the substitution set (once contexture is deficient) deals with similarities, and his approximate identifications are of a metaphoric nature, contrary to the metonymic ones familiar to the opposite type of aphasics. *Spyglass* for *microscope* or *fire* for *gaslight* are typical examples of such quasi-metaphoric expressions, as Jackson termed them, since, in contradistinction to rhetoric or poetic metaphors, they present no deliberate transfer of meaning.

In a normal language pattern, the word is at the same time both a constituent part of a superimposed context, the sentence, and itself a context superimposed on ever smaller constituents, morphemes (minimum units endowed with meaning) and phonemes. We have discussed the effect of contiguity disorder on the combination of words into higher units. The relationship between the word and its constituents reflects the same impairment, yet in a somewhat different way. A typical feature of agrammatism is the abolition of inflection: there appear such *unmarked* categories as the infinitive in the place of diverse finite verbal forms and, in languages with declension, the nominative instead of all the oblique cases. These defects are due partly to the elimination of government and concord, partly to the loss of ability to dissolve words into stem and desinence. Finally, a paradigm (in particular a set of grammatical cases such as *he–his–him* or of tenses such as *he votes–he voted*) present the same semantic content from different points of view associated with each other by contiguity; so there is one more impetus for aphasics with a contiguity disorder to dismiss such sets.

Also, as a rule, words derived from the same root, such as *grant–grantor–grantee* are semantically related by contiguity. The patients under discussion are either inclined to drop the derivative words, or the combination of a root with a derivational suffix, and even a compound of two words become irresolvable for them. Patients who understood and uttered such compounds as *Thanksgiving* or *Battersea*, but were unable to grasp or say *thanks* and *giving* or *batter* and *sea,* have often been cited. As long as the sense of derivation is still alive, so that this process is still used for creating innovations in the code, one can observe a tendency toward oversimplification and automatism: if the derivative word constitutes a semantic unit which cannot be entirely inferred from the meaning of its components, the Gestalt is misunderstood. Thus the Russian word *mokr-íca* signifies "wood-louse," but a Russian aphasic interpreted it as "something humid," especially "humid weather," since the root *mokr-* means "humid" and the suffix *-ica* designates a carrier of the given property, as in *nelépica* (something absurd), *svetlíca* (light room), *temníca* (dungeon, literally dark room).

When, before World War II, phonemics was the most controversial area in the science of language, doubts were expressed by some linguists as to whether phonemes really play an autonomous part in our verbal behavior. It was even suggested that the meaningful (*significative*) units of the linguistic code, such as morphemes or rather words, are the minimal entities with which we actually deal in a speech event, whereas the merely *distinctive* units, such as phonemes, are an artificial construct to facilitate the scientific description and analysis of a language. This view, which was stigmatized by Sapir as "the reverse of realistic,"[24] remains, however, perfectly valid with respect to a certain pathological type: in one variety of aphasia, which sometimes has been labeled "atactic," the word is the sole linguistic unity preserved. The patient has only an integral, indissolvable image of any familiar word, and all other sound-sequences are either alien and inscrutable to him, or he merges them into familiar words by disregarding their phonetic deviations. One of Goldstein's patients "perceived some words, but . . . the vowels and consonants of which they consisted were not perceived" (p. 218). A French aphasic recognized, understood, repeated, and spontaneously produced the word *café* (coffee) or *pavé* (roadway) but was unable to grasp, discern, or repeat such nonsensical sequences as *fĕca, fakĕ, kĕfa, pafĕ.* None of these difficulties exists for a normal French-speaking listener as long as the sound sequences and their components fit the French phonemic pattern. Such a listener may even apprehend these sequences as words unknown to him but plausibly belonging to the French vocabulary and presumably different in meaning, since they differ from each other either in the order of their phonemes or in the phonemes themselves.

If an aphasic becomes unable to resolve the word into its phonemic constituents, his control over its construction weakens, and perceptible damage to phonemes and their combinations easily follows. The gradual regression of the sound pattern in aphasics regularly reverses the order of children's phonemic acquisitions. This regression involves an inflation of homonyms and a decrease of vocabulary. If this twofold—phonemic and lexical—disablement progresses further, the last residues of speech are one-phoneme, one-word, one-sentence utterances: the patient relapses into the initial phases of an infant's linguistic development or even to the prelingual stage: he faces *aphasia universalis,* the total loss of the power to use or apprehend speech.

The separateness of the two functions—one distinctive and the other significative—is a peculiar feature of language as compared to other semiotic systems. There arises a conflict between these two levels of language when the aphasic deficient in contexture exhibits a tendency to abolish the hierarchy of linguistic units and to reduce their scale to a single level. The last level to remain is either a class of significative values, the word, as in the cases touched upon, or a class of distinctive values, the phoneme. In the latter case the patient is still able to identify, distinguish, and reproduce phonemes, but loses the capacity to do the same with words. In an intermediate case, words are identified, distinguished, and reproduced; according to Goldstein's acute formulation, they "may be grasped as known but not understood" (p. 90). Here the word loses its normal significative function and assumes the purely distinctive function which normally pertains to the phoneme.

V. The Metaphoric and Metonymic Poles

The varieties of aphasia are numerous and diverse, but all of them lie between the two polar types just described. Every form of aphasic disturbance consists in some impairment, more or less severe, of the faculty either for selection and substitution or for combination and contexture. The former affliction involves a deterioration of metalinguistic operations, while the latter damages the capacity for maintaining the hierarchy of linguistic units. The relation of similarity is suppressed in the former, the relation of contiguity in the latter type of aphasia. Metaphor is alien to the similarity disorder, and metonymy to the contiguity disorder.

The development of a discourse may take place along two different semantic lines: one topic may lead to another either through their similarity or through their contiguity. The metaphoric way would be the most appropriate term for the first case and the metonymic way for the second, since they find their most condensed expression in metaphor and metonymy respectively. In aphasia one or the other of these two processes is restricted or totally blocked—an effect which makes the study of aphasia particularly illuminating for the linguist. In normal verbal behavior both processes are continually operative, but careful observation will reveal that under the influence of a cultural pattern, personality, and verbal style, preference is given to one of the two processes over the other.

In a well-known psychological test, children are confronted with some noun and told to utter the first verbal response that comes into their heads. In this experiment two opposite linguistic predilections are invariably exhibited: the response is intended either as a substitute for or as a complement to the stimulus. In the latter case the stimulus and the response together form a proper syntactic construction, most usually a sentence. These two types of reaction have been labeled *substitutive* and *predicative*.

To the stimulus *hut* one response was *burnt out;* another, *is a poor little house.* Both reactions are predicative; but the first creates a purely narrative context, while in the second there is a double connection with the subject *hut:* on the one hand, a positional (namely, syntactic) contiguity and, on the other, a semantic similarity.

The same stimulus produced the following substitutive reactions: the tautology *hut;* the synonyms *cabin* and *hovel;* the antonym *palace;* and the metaphors *den* and *burrow.* The capacity of two words to replace one another is an instance of positional similarity, and, in addition, all these responses are linked to the stimulus by semantic similarity (or contrast). Metonymical responses to the same stimulus, such as *thatch, litter,* or *poverty,* combine and contrast the positional similarity with semantic contiguity.

In manipulating these two kinds of connection (similarity and contiguity) in both their aspects (positional and semantic)—selecting, combining, and ranking them—an individual exhibits his personal style, his verbal predilections and preferences.

In verbal art the interaction of these two elements is especially pronounced. Rich material for the study of this relationship is to be found in verse patterns which require a compulsory *parallelism* between adjacent lines, for example in biblical poetry or in the Finnic and, to some extent, the Russian oral traditions. This provides an objective criterion of what in the given speech community acts as a correspondence. Since on any verbal level—morphemic, lexical, syntactic, and phraseological—either of these two relations (similarity and contiguity) can appear—and each in either of two aspects, an impressive range of possible configurations is created. Either of the two gravitational poles may prevail. In Russian lyrical songs, for example, metaphoric constructions predominate, while in the heroic epics the metonymic way is preponderant.

In poetry there are various motives which determine the choice between these alternants. The primacy of the metaphoric process in the literary schools of Romanticism and Symbolism has been repeatedly acknowledged, but it is still insufficiently realized that it is the predominance of metonymy which underlies and actually predetermines the so-called Realist trend, which belongs to an intermediary stage between the decline of Romanticism and the rise of Symbolism and is opposed to both. Following the path of contiguous relationships, the Realist author metonymically digresses from the plot to the atmosphere and from the characters to the setting in space and time. He is fond of synecdochic details. In the scene of Anna Karenina's suicide Tolstoj's artistic attention is focused on the heroine's handbag; and in *War and Peace* the synecdoches "hair on the upper lip" and "bare shoulders" are used by the same writer to stand for the female characters to whom these features belong.

The alternative predominance of one or the other of these two processes is by no means confined to verbal art. The same oscillation occurs in sign systems other than language.[25] A salient example from the history of painting is the manifestly metonymical orientation of Cubism, where the object is transformed into a set of synecdoches; the Surrealist painters responded with a patently metaphorical attitude. Ever since the productions of D. W. Griffith, the art of the cinema, with its highly developed capacity for changing the angle, perspective, and focus of shots, has broken with the tradition of the theater and ranged an unprecedented variety of synecdochic close-ups and metonymic set-ups in general. In such motion pictures as those of Charlie Chaplin and Eisenstein,[26] these devices in turn were overlayed by a novel, metaphoric montage with its lap dissolves—the filmic similes.[27]

The bipolar structure of language (or other semiotic systems) and, in aphasia, the fixation on one of these poles to the exclusion of the other require systematic comparative study. The retention of either of these alternatives in the two types of aphasia must be confronted with the predominance of the same pole in certain styles, personal habits, current fashions, etc. A careful analysis and comparison of these phenomena with the whole syndrome of the corresponding type of aphasia is an imperative task for joint research by experts in psychopathology, psychology, linguistics, poetics, and semiotics, the general science of signs. The dichotomy discussed here appears to be of primal significance and consequence for all verbal behavior and for human behavior in general.[28]

To indicate the possibilities of the projected comparative research, I choose an example from a Russian folktale which employs parallelism as a comic device: "Thomas is a bachelor; Jeremiah is unmarried" (*Fomá xólost; Erjóma neženát*). Here the predicates in the two parallel clauses are associated by similarity: they are in fact synonymous. The subjects of both clauses are masculine proper names and hence morphologically similar, while on the other hand they denote two contiguous heroes of the same tale, created to perform identical actions and thus to justify the use of synonymous pairs of predicates. A somewhat modified version of the same construction occurs in a familiar wedding song in which each of the wedding guests is addressed in turn by his first name and patronymic: "Gleb is a bachelor; Ivanovič is unmarried." While both predicates here are again synonyms, the relationship between the two subjects is changed: both are proper names denoting the same man and are normally used contiguously as a mode of polite address.

In the quotation from the folktale, the two parallel clauses refer to two separate facts, the marital status of Thomas and the similar status of Jeremiah. In the verse from the wedding song, however, the two clauses are synonymous: they redundantly reiterate the celibacy of the same hero, splitting him into two verbal hypostases.

The Russian novelist Gleb Ivanovič Uspenskij (1840–1902) in the last years of his life suffered from a mental illness involving a speech disorder. His first name and patronymic, *Gleb Ivanovič,* traditionally combined in polite intercourse, for him split into two distinct names designating two separate beings: Gleb was endowed with all his virtues, while Ivanovič, the name relating a son to his father, became the incarnation of all Uspenskij's vices. The linguistic aspect of this split personality is the patient's inability to use two symbols for the same thing, and it is thus a similarity disorder. Since the similarity disorder is bound up with the metonymical bent, an examination of the literary manner Uspenskij had employed as a young writer takes on particular interest. And the study of Anatolij Kamegulov, who analyzed Uspenskij's style, bears out our theoretical expectations. He shows that Uspenskij had a particular penchant for metonymy, and especially for synecdoche, and that he carried it so far that "the reader is crushed by the multiplicity of detail unloaded on him in a limited verbal space, and is physically unable to grasp the whole, so that the portrait is often lost."[29]

To be sure, the metonymical style in Uspenskij is obviously prompted by the prevailing literary canon of his time, late nineteenth-century "realism"; but the personal stamp of Gleb Ivanovič made his pen particularly suitable for this artistic trend in its extreme manifestations and finally left its mark upon the verbal aspect of his mental illness.

A competition between both devices, metonymic and metaphoric, is manifest in any symbolic process, be it intrapersonal or social. Thus in an inquiry into the structure of dreams, the decisive question is whether the symbols and the temporal sequences used are based on contiguity (Freud's metonymic "displacement" and synecdochic "condensation") or on similarity (Freud's "identification and symbolism"). The principles underlying magic rites have been resolved by Frazer into two types: charms based on the law of similarity and those founded on association by contiguity. The first of these two great branches of sympathetic magic has been called "homoeopathic" or "imitative," and the second, "contagious" magic.[30] This bipartition is indeed illuminating. Nonetheless, for the most part, the question of the two poles is still neglected, despite its wide scope and importance for the study of any symbolic behavior, especially verbal, and of its impairments. What is the main reason for this neglect?

Similarity in meaning connects the symbols of a metalanguage with the symbols of the language referred to. Similarity connects a metaphorical term with the term for which it is substituted. Consequently, when constructing a metalanguage to interpret tropes, the researcher possesses more homogeneous means to handle metaphor, whereas metonymy, based on a different principle, easily defies interpretation. Therefore nothing comparable to the rich literature on metaphor[31] can be cited for the theory of metonymy. For the same reason, it is generally realized that Romanticism is closely linked with metaphor, whereas the equally intimate ties of Realism with metonymy usually remain unnoticed. Not only the tool of the observer but also the object of observation are responsible for the preponderance of metaphor over metonymy in scholarship. Since poetry is focused upon the sign, and pragmatical prose primarily upon the referent, tropes and figures were studied mainly as poetic devices. The principle of similarity underlies poetry; the metrical parallelism of lines or the phonic equivalence of rhyming words prompts the question of semantic similarity and contrast; there exist, for instance, grammatical and antigrammatical but never agrammatical rhymes. Prose, on the contrary, is forwarded essentially by contiguity. Thus for poetry, metaphor—and for prose, metonymy—is the line of least resistance and consequently the study of poetical tropes is directed chiefly toward metaphor. The actual bipolarity has been artificially replaced in these studies by an amputated, unipolar scheme which, strikingly enough, coincides with one of the two aphasic patterns, namely with the contiguity disorder.

PART II

Grammar
in Poetry

The nature of poetry in Jakobson's view lies in the repetition of equivalent units: "on every level of language the essence of poetic artifice consists in recurrent returns." Although this is obvious in the case of meter or rhyme, it is less so when one turns from repeated "figures of sound" to repeated "figures of grammar." In the 1960s and '70s Jakobson concentrated his study of verse on what he termed the poetry of grammar and the grammar of poetry. His investigation into this new domain resulted in rigorous linguistic analyses of some forty poems written in over a dozen different languages (see *Selected Writings* III).

The broader perspectives and tasks to be confronted in this type of analysis were announced in Jakobson's programmatic essay "Poetry of Grammar and Grammar of Poetry" (1960). As the study of rhetoric vividly illustrates, identical referential concepts can be conveyed in language by a wide variety of expressive devices that radically affect a statement's nuances of meaning. In poetry, the most formalized use of language, the suggestive possibilities of grammar are exploited fully, and linguistic means become a vital component of poetic mythology. This is particularly evident from Jakobson's analysis of such "imageless" poems as Puškin's "I Loved You," where in the absence of the traditional tropes and figures it is the play of grammatical concepts that creates the poetic effect. More usual, however, is the interplay of imagery and grammar, as demonstrated by Jakobson's analysis of Puškin's album verses, "What is there for you in my name?"

In his essay "Grammatical Parallelism and Its Russian Facet" (1966) Jakobson presents in detail the history of scholarly investigations into the marked types of canonic parallelism found in biblical verse, the Vedas, and Chinese poetry. Parallelistic construction is almost universal in the folk poetry of the world and is far from being a merely formal feature of such verse. Jakobson subjects a Russian folksong to minute analysis, arriving at the conclusion that "any word or clause when entering into a poem built on pervasive parallelism is, under the constraint of this system, immediately incorporated into the tenacious array of cohesive grammatical forms and semantic values."

Grammar is never treated in isolation in Jakobson's structuralist analyses of poetry: instead it is shown to be one of numerous elements, including meter, rhyme, sound figures, lexicon, and imagery, that enter into mutual relations across the span of the text to give it its unique meaning. The complex interplay of elements that constitutes a poem is exemplified by two of Jakobson's best-known analyses of the sonnet form: "Baudelaire's 'Les Chats'" (1961), written in collaboration with Claude Lévi-Strauss, and "Shakespeare's Verbal Art in 'Th'Expence of Spirit'" (1968), coauthored by L. G. Jones. In "Yeats' 'Sorrow of Love' through the Years" (1977), written jointly with Stephen Rudy, the insights that structural analysis provides in approaching individual texts are extended to the historical dimension: the variables and invariants of Yeats' poetic system are deduced from an analysis of two versions of the same poem written some thirty years apart.

The question of whether the structures a linguist establishes through painstaking analysis are conscious poetic devices was one that Jakobson's critics and readers often raised. In "Subliminal Verbal Patterning in Poetry" (1970) he replies that poetic devices are always purposive, even if they remain totally unconscious on the poet's part. As the example of Velimir Xlebnikov's "The Grasshopper" demonstrates, poets themselves may later be astounded by the complex structuration of even their most spontaneous creations. In "Supraconscious Turgenev" (1979) Jakobson analyzes a seven-word formula that the Russian writer uttered out of exasperation when confronted by the alien and cold atmosphere of a London private club. Not only is Turgenev's "impromptu" structured to an amazing degree, it also reveals certain essential traits of his poetics as well as the powerful influence of his native culinary system as a symbolic code.

CHAPTER 9

Poetry of Grammar and Grammar of Poetry

> And the bell of verbal endings
> Shows me the distant path.
> *Osip Mandel'štam*

I. Grammatical Parallelism

During the late 1930s, while editing Puškin's works in Czech translation, I was struck by the way in which poems that seemed to approximate closely the Russian text, its images and sound structure, often produced the distressing impression of a complete rift with the original because of the inability or impossibility of reproducing their grammatical structure. Gradually, it became clear: in Puškin's poetry the guiding significance of the morphological and syntactic fabric is interwoven with and rivals the artistic role of verbal tropes. Indeed, at times it takes over and becomes the primary, even exclusive, vehicle of the poems' innermost symbolism. Accordingly, in the afterword to the Czech volume of Puškin's lyric poetry, I noted that "in Puškin a striking actualization of grammatical oppositions, especially in verbal and pronominal forms, is connected with a keen regard for meaning. Often contrasts, affinities, and contiguities of tense and number, of verbal aspect and voice, acquire a directly leading role in the composition of particular poems. Emphasized by an opposition of grammatical category, they function like poetic images, and, for instance, a masterful alternation of grammatical categories of person becomes a means of intense dramatization. There can hardly be an example of a more skillful poetic exploitation of morphological possibilities."[1]

In particular, the experience gained during a seminar on Puškin's *The Bronze Horseman* and its translation into other Slavic languages allowed me to characterize an example of a consistent opposition of the imperfective and perfective aspects. In the "Petersburg Tale" it serves as a grammatically expressive projection of the tragic conflict between the limitless and seemingly eternal power of Peter the Great, "ruler of half the world," and the fatal limitedness of all the actions performed by the characterless clerk Eugene, who dared with his incantatory formula *Užó tebé!* (Just you wait!) to proclaim the limit of the miracle-working tsar and builder.[2] Both these experiences convinced me that the question of the interrelations between grammar and poetry demanded a systematic and detailed clarification.

According to Edward Sapir, the juxtaposition of such sequences as *the farmer kills the duckling* and *the man takes the chick* makes us "feel instinctively, without the slightest attempt at conscious analysis, that the two sentences fit precisely the same pattern, that they are really the same fundamental sentence, differing only in their material trappings. In other words, they express identical relational concepts in an identical manner." Conversely, we may modify the sentence or its single words "in some purely relational, nonmaterial regard" without altering any of the material concepts expressed.[3] When assigning to certain terms of the sentence a different position in its syntactic pattern and replacing, for instance, the word order "*A* kills *B*" by the inverse sequence "*B* kills *A*," we do not vary the material concepts involved but uniquely their mutual relationship. Likewise a substitution of *farmers* for *farmer* or *killed* for *kills* alters only the relational concepts of the sentence, while there are no changes in the "concrete wherewithal of speech"; its "material trappings" remain invariable.

Despite some borderline, transitional formations, there is in language a definite, clear-cut discrimination between these two classes of expressed concepts—material and relational—or, in more technical terms, between the lexical and grammatical aspects of language. The linguist must faithfully follow this objective structural dichotomy and thoroughly translate the grammatical concepts actually present in a given language into his technical metalanguage, without any imposition of arbitrary or outlandish categories upon the language observed. The categories described are intrinsic constituents of the verbal code, manipulated by language users, and not at all "grammarian's conveniences," as even such attentive inquirers into poets' grammar as, for example, Donald Davie were inclined to believe.[4]

A difference in grammatical concepts does not necessarily represent a difference in the state of affairs referred to. If one witness asserts that "the farmer killed the duckling," while the other affirms that "the duckling was killed by the farmer," the two men cannot be accused of presenting discrepant testimonies, in spite of the polar difference between the grammatical concepts expressed by active and passive constructions. One and the same state of affairs is presented by the sentences: *A lie* (or *lying* or *to lie*) *is a sin* (or *is sinful*). *To lie is to sin, Liars sin* (or *are sinful* or *are sinners*), or with a generalizing singular *The liar sins* (or *is sinful, is a sinner*). Only the way of presentation differs. Fundamentally the same equational proposition may be expressed in terms of actors (*liars, sinners*) or actions (*to lie, to sin*) and we may present these actions "as if" abstracted (*lying*) and reified (*lie, sin*) or ascribe them to the subject as its properties (*sinful*). The part of speech is one of the grammatical categories which reflect, according to Sapir's manual, "not so much our intuitive analysis of reality as our ability to compose that reality into a variety of formal patterns."[5] Later, in his preliminary notes to the planned *Foundations of Language*, Sapir outlined the fundamental types of referents which serve as "a natural basis for parts of speech," namely *existents* and their linguistic expression, the *noun; occurrents* expressed by the *verb;* and finally *modes of existence and occurrence* represented in language by the *adjective* and the *adverb* respectively.[6]

Jeremy Bentham, who was perhaps the first to disclose the manifold "linguistic fictions" which underlie the grammatical structure and which are used throughout the whole field of language as a "necessary resource," arrived in his *Theory of Fictions* at a challenging conclusion: "to language, then—to language alone—it is that fictitious entities owe their existence: their impossible, yet indispensable existence."[7] Linguistic fictions should neither be "mistaken for realities" nor be ascribed to the creative fancy of linguists: they "owe their existence" actually "to language alone" and particularly to the "grammatical form of the discourse," in Bentham's terms.[8]

The indispensable, mandatory role played by the grammatical con-

cepts confronts us with the intricate problem of the relationship between referential, cognitive value and linguistic fiction. Is the significance of grammatical concepts really questionable or are perhaps some
subliminal verisimilar assumptions attached to them? How far can
scientific thought overcome the pressure of grammatical patterns?
Whatever the solution of these still controversial questions is, certainly
there is one domain of verbal activities where "the classificatory rules
of the game"[9] acquire their highest significance; *in fiction,* in verbal art,
linguistic fictions are fully realized. It is quite evident that grammatical concepts—or in Fortunatov's pointed nomenclature, "formal
meanings"[10]—find their widest applications in poetry as the most formalized manifestation of language. There, where the poetic function
dominates over the strictly cognitive function, the latter is more or less
dimmed, or as Sir Philip Sidney declared in his *Defence of Poesie,* "Now
for the Poet, he nothing affirmeth, and therefore never lieth." Consequently, in Bentham's succinct formulation, "the Fictions of the poet
are pure of insincerity."[11]

When in the finale of Majakovskij's poem *Xorošo* we read—"i žizn' /
xorošá, // i žít' / xorošó//" (literally, both life is good and it is good to
live)—one will hardly look for a cognitive difference between these
two coordinate clauses, but in poetic mythology the linguistic fiction
of the substantivized and hence hypostatized process grows into a metonymic image of life as such, taken by itself and substituted for living
people, *abstractum pro concreto,* as Galfredus de Vino Salvo, the cunning English scholar of the early thirteenth century, explains in his
Poetria nova.[12] In contradistinction to the first clause with its predicative adjective of the same personifiable, feminine gender as the subject,
the second clause with its imperfective infinitive and with a neuter,
subjectless form of the predicate, represents a pure process without any
limitation or transposition and with an open place for the dative of
agent.

The recurrent "figure of grammar," which along with the "figure of
sound" Gerard Manley Hopkins[13] saw to be the constitutive principle
of verse, is particularly palpable in those poetic forms where contiguous metrical units are more or less consistently combined through
grammatical parallelism into pairs or, optionally, triplets. Sapir's definition quoted above is perfectly applicable to such neighbor sequences: "they are really the same fundamental sentence, differing only
in their material trappings."

There are several tentative outlines devoted to different specimens of such canonical or nearly canonical parallelism, labeled carmen style by J. Gonda in his monograph,[14] full of interesting remarks about "balanced binary word groups" in the Veda and also in the Nias ballads and priestly litanies. Particular attention has been paid by scholars to the biblical *parallelismus membrorum* rooted in an archaic Canaanite tradition and to the pervasive, continuous role of parallelism in Chinese verse and poetic prose.[15] A similar pattern proves to underlie the oral poetry of Finno-Ugric, Turkic, and Mongolian peoples.[16] The same devices play a cardinal role in Russian folk songs and recitatives.[17] Compare this typical preamble of Russian heroic epics (*byliny*):

Kak vo stól'nom górode vo Kíeve,	How in the capital city, in Kiev,
A u láskova knjázja u Vladímira,	Under the gracious prince, under Vladimir,
A i býlo stolován'e počótnyj stól,	There was banqueting, an honorable banquet,
A i býlo pirován'e počéstnyj pír,	There was feasting, an honorary feast,
A i vsé na pirú da napiválisja,	Everyone at the feast was drunk,
A i vsé na pirú da porasxvástalis',	Everyone at the feast was boasting,
Úmnyj xvástaet zolotój kaznój,	The clever one boasts of his golden stock,
Glúpyj xvástaet molodój ženój.	The stupid one boasts of his young wife.

Parallelistic systems of verbal art give us a direct insight into the speakers' own conception of the grammatical equivalences. The analysis of various kinds of poetic license in the domain of parallelism, like the examination of rhyming conventions, may provide us with important clues for interpreting the makeup of a given language and the hierarchical order of its constituents (e.g., the current equation between the Finnish allative and illative or between the preterit and present against the background of unpairable cases or verbal categories, according to Steinitz's observations in his path-breaking inquiry into parallelism in Karelian folklore).[18] The interaction between syntactic, morphologic and lexical equivalences and discrepancies, the diverse kinds of semantic contiguities, similarities, synonymies and antonymies, finally the different types of functions of allegedly "isolated lines," all such phenomena call for a systematic analysis indispensable for the comprehension and interpretation of the various grammatical contrivances in poetry. Such a crucial linguistic and poetic problem as parallelism can hardly be mastered by a scrutiny automatically restricted to the external form and excluding any discussion of grammatical and lexical meanings.

In the endless travel songs of the Kola Lapps[19] two juxtaposed persons, performing identical actions, are the uniform topic, impelling an automatic concatenation of verses of such a pattern: "*A* is sitting on the right side of the boat; *B* is sitting on the left side. *A* has a paddle in the right hand; *B* has a paddle in the left hand," and so on.

In the Russian sung or narrated folk stories of Foma and Erema (Thomas and Jeremy), both unlucky brothers are used as a comic motivation for a chain of parallel clauses, parodying the carmen style, typical of Russian folk poetry and presenting quasi-differential characteristics of the two brothers by a juxtaposition of synonymous expressions or closely coincident images: "They uncovered Erema and they found Foma; They beat Erema and they did not pardon Foma; Erema ran away into a birch wood, and Foma into an oak wood," and so on.[20]

In the North Russian ballad "Vasilij and Sofija"[21] the binary grammatical parallelism becomes the pivot of the plot and carries the whole dramatic development of this beautiful and concise *bylina*. In terms of antithetical parallelism the initial church scene contrasts the pious invocation "Father God!" of the parishioners and Sofia's incestuous call "My brother Vasilij!" The subsequent malicious intervention of the mother introduces a chain of distichs tying together both heroes through a strict correspondence between any line devoted to the brother and its counterpart speaking of his sister. Some of these pairs of parallel members in their stereotyped construction resemble the mentioned clichés of the songs of the Lapps: "Vasilij was buried on the right hand, And Sofija was buried on the left hand." The interlacement of the lovers' fates is reinforced by chiasmic constructions: "Vasilij, drink, but don't give to Sofija, And Sofija, drink, don't give to Vasilij! Yet Vasilij drank and feasted Sofija, yet Sofija drank and feasted Vasilij." The same function is performed by the images of a *kiparis* (cypress) tree, with masculine name, on Sofija's grave, and of a *verba* (willow), with feminine name, on the adjacent grave of Vasilij: "They wove together with their heads, / and they stuck together with their leaves.//" The parallel destruction of both trees by the mother echoes the violent death of both siblings. I doubt that efforts of such scholars as Christine Brooke-Rose[22] to draw a rigorous line of demarcation between tropes and poetic scenery are applicable to this ballad, and in general the range of poems and poetic trends for which such a boundary actually exists is very limited.

According to one of Hopkins' brightest contributions to poetics, his paper of 1865 "On the Origin of Beauty," such canonical structures as Hebrew poetry "paired off in parallelisms" are well-known, "but the important part played by parallelism of expression in our poetry is not so well-known: I think it will surprise anyone when first pointed out."[23] Notwithstanding some isolated exceptions such as Berry's recent reconnaissance,[24] the role performed by the "figure of grammar" in world poetry from antiquity up to the present time is still surprising for students of literature a whole century after it was first pointed out by Hopkins. The ancient and medieval theory of poetry had an inkling of poetic grammar and was prone to discriminate between lexical tropes and grammatical figures (*figurae verborum*), but these sound rudiments were later lost.

One may state that in poetry similarity is superimposed on contiguity, and hence "equivalence is promoted to the constitutive device of the sequence."[25] Here any noticeable reiteration of the same grammatical concept becomes an effective poetic device. Any unbiased, attentive, exhaustive, total description of the selection, distribution and interrelation of diverse morphological classes and syntactic constructions in a given poem surprises the examiner himself by unexpected, striking symmetries and antisymmetries, balanced structures, efficient accumulation of equivalent forms and salient contrasts, finally by rigid restrictions in the repertory of morphological and syntactic constituents used in the poem, eliminations which, on the other hand, permit us to follow the masterly interplay of the actualized constituents. Let us insist on the strikingness of these devices; any sensitive reader, as Sapir would say, feels instinctively the poetic effect and the semantic load of these grammatical appliances, "without the slightest attempt at conscious analysis," and in many cases the poet himself in this respect is similar to such a reader. In the same way, both the traditional listener and the performer of folk poetry, which is based on a nearly constant parallelism, catches the deviations without, however, being capable of analyzing them, as the Serbian guslars and their audience notice and

127

often condemn any deviation from the syllabic patterns of the epic songs from the regular location of the break but do not know how to define such a slip.

Often contrasts in the grammatical makeup support the metrical division of a poem into strophes and smaller sections, as for instance, in the double trichotomy of the Hussite battle song of the early fifteenth century,[26] or, even, they underlie and build such a stratified composition, as we observe in Marvell's poem "To His Coy Mistress," with its three tripartite paragraphs, grammatically delimited and subdivided.[27]

The juxtaposition of contrasting grammatical concepts may be compared with the so-called dynamic cutting in film montage, a type of cutting which, as in Spottiswoode's definition,[28] uses the juxtaposition of contrasting shots or sequences to generate in the mind of the spectator ideas that these constituent shots or sequences by themselves do not carry.

Among grammatical categories utilized for parallelisms and contrasts we actually find all the parts of speech, both mutable and immutable: numbers, genders, cases, grades, tenses, aspects, moods, voices, classes of abstract and concrete words, animates and inanimates, appellatives and proper names, affirmatives and negatives, finite and infinite verbal forms, definite and indefinite pronouns or articles, and diverse syntactic elements and constructions.

II. Poetry without Images

The Russian writer Veresaev confessed in his intimate notes that sometimes he felt as if imagery were "a mere counterfeit of genuine poetry."[29] As a rule, in imageless poems it is the "figure of grammar" which dominates and which supplants the tropes. Both the Hussite battle song and such lyrics of Puškin as "Ja vas ljubil" are eloquent examples of such a monopoly of grammatical devices. Much more usual, however, is an intensive interplay of both elements, as for instance, in Puškin's stanzas "Čto v imeni tebe moëm," manifestly contrasting with his cited composition "without images," both written in the same year and probably dedicated to the same addressee, Karolina Sobańska.[30] The imaginative, metaphoric vehicles of a poem may be opposed to its matter-of-fact level by a sharp concomitant contrast of their grammatical constituents, as we observe, for example, in the Polish concise meditations of Cyprian Norwid, one of the greatest world poets of the later nineteenth century.[31]

Puškin's poem "I Loved You" has been cited repeatedly by literary critics as a striking example of imageless poetry. Its vocabulary does not include a single live trope, the one seeming exception, *ljubov' ugasla* (love has died out), being merely a dead lexicalized metaphor. On the other hand, this eight-line poem is saturated with grammatical figures, even if this essential feature of its texture has not been hitherto accorded proper attention.

> ₁Ja vas ljubil: ljubov' ešče, byt' možet,
> ₂V duše moej ugasla ne sovsem;
> ₃No pust' ona vas bol'še ne trevožit;
> ₄Ja ne xoču pečalit' vas ničem.
>
> ₅Ja vas ljubil bezmolvno, beznadežno,
> ₆To robost'ju, to revnost'ju tomim;
> ₇Ja vas ljubil tak iskrenno, tak nežno,
> ₈Kak daj vam Bog ljubimoj byt' drugim.

> ₁I loved you: love has not yet, it may be,
> ₂Died out completely in my soul;
> ₃But let it not trouble you any more;
> ₄I do not wish to sadden you in any way.
>
> ₅I loved you silently, hopelessly,
> ₆Tormented now by shyness, now by jealousy;
> ₇I loved you so truly, so tenderly
> ₈As God grant you to be loved by another.

The very selection of grammatical forms in the poem is striking. It contains forty-seven words, including a total of twenty-nine inflectional forms. Of the latter, fourteen, or almost half, are pronouns, ten are verbs, and only five are nouns—moreover, nouns of an abstract, speculative character. In the entire work there is not a single adjective, whereas the number of adverbs is as high as ten. Pronouns—being thoroughly grammatical, purely relational words deprived of a properly lexical, material meaning—are clearly opposed to the remaining inflected parts of speech. All three dramatis personae are designated in the poem exclusively by pronouns: *ja* (I) *in recto; vy* (you) and *drugoj* (another) *in obliquo*. The poem consists of two quatrains with alternating rhymes. The first-person pronoun, which always occupies the first syllable of a line, is encountered four times, once in each couplet—in the first and fourth line of the first quatrain, and in the first and third of the second. *Ja* (I) occurs here only in the nominative case, only as the subject of the proposition, and, moreover, only in combination with the accusative form *vas* (you). The second-person pronoun, which occurs exclusively in the accusative and dative (in the so-called directional cases), figures in the poem six times, once in each line, except for the second line of each quatrain, being, moreover, combined with some other pronoun each time it occurs. The form *vas* (you), a direct object, is always dependent (directly or indirectly) on a pronominal subject. In four instances that subject is *ja;* in another it is the anaphoric *ona* (she), referring to *ljubov'* (love) on the part of the first-person subject. In contrast, the dative *vam* (you), which appears in the final, syntactically subordinated, line in place of the direct object *vas,* is coupled with a new pronominal form, *drugim* (another). The latter word, in a peripheral case, the "instrumental of the perpetrator of an action,"[32] together with the equally peripheral dative, introduces at the end of the concluding line the third participant in the lyric drama, who is opposed to the nominative *ja* with which the introductory line began.

The author of this eight-line verse epistle addresses the heroine six times. Three times he repeats the key formula *ja vas ljubil* (I loved you), which opens first the initial quatrain and then the first and second couplets of the final quatrain, thus introducing into the two-stanza monologue a traditional ternary division: 4 + 2 + 2. The ternary construction unfolds each time in a different way. The first quatrain develops the theme of the *predicate:* an etymological figure replaces the verb *ljubil* (loved) with the abstract noun *ljubov'* (love), lending it the appearance of an independent, unconditional being. Despite the orientation toward the past tense, nothing in the development of the lyric theme is shown as being in a state of completion. Here Puškin, an unsurpassed master at utilizing the dramatic collision between verbal aspects, avoids indicative forms of the perfective aspect. The sole exception—₁*ljubov' ešče, byt' možet,* ₂*V duše moej ugasla ne sovsem* (love has not yet, it may be, Died out completely in my soul)—actually supports the rule, since the surrounding accessory words—*ešče* (yet), *byt' možet* (it may be, perhaps), *ne sovsem* (not completely)—bring to naught the fictitious theme of the end. Nothing is completed, but the placing into question of the completion implied by the perfective aspect is answered, on the other hand, after the adversative *no* (but), by a negation of the present tense both in and of itself (*ja ne xoču,* I do not want) and in the composition of the descriptive imperative (₃*No pust' ona vas bol'še ne trevožit*, But let it not trouble you any more). In general, there are no positive turns of phrase with finite present tense forms throughout the poem.

The beginning of the second quatrain repeats the key formula and then goes on to develop the theme of the *subject*. Both the adverbal adverbs and the instrumental forms with accessory passive predicates relating to the same subject "I" extend even into the past the overtly or latently negative terms that in the first quatrain painted the present in a tone of inactive self-denial.

Finally, following the third repetition of the initial formula, the last line of the poem is devoted to its *object*: ₇*Ja vas ljubil . . .*₈*Kak daj vam Bog ljubimoj byt' drugim* (I loved you . . . As God grant you to be loved by another), with a pronominal polyptoton *vas—vam*. Here for the first time there is a genuine contrast between the two moments of the dramatic development: the two rhyming lines are similar syntactically—each contains a combination of the passive voice with an instrumental (₆*revnost'ju tomim*, tormented by jealousy—₈*ljubimoj byt' drugim*, to be loved by another)—but the authorial recognition of the "other" contradicts the earlier tormenting jealousy. The absence of articles in Russian makes it possible not to specify whether it is to a different, vague "other" or to one and the same "other" that the jealousy in the past and the present blessing relate. The two imperative constructions—₃*No pust' ona vas bol'še ne trevožit* (But let it not trouble you any more) and ₈*Kak daj vam Bog ljubimoj byt' drugim* (As God grant you to be loved by another)—complement one another, as it were. In the meantime, the epistle intentionally leaves open the possibility for completely different interpretations of the last verse. On the one hand, it may be understood as an incantatory dénouement to the poem. On the other, the frozen expression *daj vam Bog* (God grant you), notwithstanding the imperative, which is whimsically shifted into a subordinate clause,[33] may be interpreted as a kind of "non-real mood," signifying that without supernatural interference the heroine will almost certainly never again encounter another such love. In the latter case the final sentence of the quatrain may be considered a kind of "understood negation" in Jespersen's terms[34] and becomes yet another of the diverse examples of negation in the poem. Apart from several negative constructions, the entire repertoire of finite forms in the poem is composed of the past tense of the verb *ljubit'* (to love).

To repeat, among the inflected words in Puškin's "I loved you," pronouns dominate. There are few nouns, and all of them belong to the speculative sphere characterizing—except for the concluding appeal to God—the psychic world of the first-person speaker. The word in the text that occurs most frequently and that is distributed with the greatest regularity is the pronoun *vy* (you): it alone appears in the accusative and dative cases and, moreover, exclusively in those cases. Closely linked with it, and second in frequency, is the pronoun *ja* (I), which is used exclusively as a subject and exclusively at the beginning of a line. The share of the predicates that combine with this subject is allotted to adverbs, whereas the accessory, nonpersonal verbal forms are accompanied by complements in the instrumental case: ₄*pečalit' vas ničem* (sadden you in any way, lit. with anything); ₆*To robost'ju, to revnost'ju tomim* (Tormented now by shyness, now by jealousy); ₈*ljubimoj byt' drugim* (to be loved by another). Adjectives, and adnominal forms in general, do not appear in these quatrains. Constructions with prepositions are almost completely absent. The significance of the poetic redistributions of the makeup, frequency, mutual interrelation, and arrangement of the various grammatical categories of the Russian language in this poem is so distinct that it hardly needs a detailed semantic commentary. It is enough to read Julian Tuwim's Polish translation of these verses—"kochałem panią—i miłości mojej/ Może się jeszcze resztki w duszy tlą"[35]—to be immediately convinced that even such a poetic virtuoso, the minute he failed to render the grammatical structure of Puškin's quatrains, could not help but reduce to nil their artistic strength.

III. Grammar and Geometry

The obligatory character of the grammatical processes and concepts constrains the poet to reckon with them; either he strives for symmetry and sticks to these simple, repeatable, diaphanous patterns, based on a binary principle, or he may cope with them, while longing for an "organic chaos." I have stated repeatedly that the rhyme technique is "either grammatical or antigrammatical" but never agrammatical, and the same may be applied as well to poets' grammar in general. There is in this respect a remarkable analogy between the role of grammar in poetry and the painter's composition, based on a latent or patent geometrical order or on a revulsion against geometrical arrangements. For the figurative arts geometrical principles represent a "beautiful necessity,"[36] according to the designation taken over by Bragdon from Emerson. It is the same necessity that in language marks out the grammatical meanings.[37] The correspondence between the two fields which already in the thirteenth century was pointed out by Robert Kilwardby[38] and which prompted Spinoza to treat grammar *more geometrico,* has emerged in a linguistic study by Benjamin Lee Whorf, "Language, Mind and Reality" (1942), published shortly after his death. The author discusses the abstract "designs of sentence structure" as opposed to "individual sentences" and to the vocabulary, which is a "somewhat rudimentary and not self-sufficient part" of the linguistic order, and envisages "a 'geometry' of form principles characteristic of each language."[39] A further comparison between grammar and geometry was outlined in Stalin's polemics of 1950 against Marr's linguistic bias: the distinctive property of grammar lies in its abstractive power; "abstracting itself from anything that is particular and concrete in words and sentences, grammar treats only the general patterns, underlying the word changes and the combination of words into sentences, and builds in such a way grammatical rules and laws. In this respect grammar bears a resemblance to geometry, which, when giving its laws, abstracts itself from concrete objects, treats objects as bodies deprived of concreteness and defines their mutual relations not as concrete relations of certain concrete objects but as relations of bodies in general, namely, relations deprived of any concreteness."[40] The abstractive power of human thought, underlying—in the views of the two quoted authors—both geometrical relations and grammar, superimposes simple geometrical and grammatical figures upon the pictorial world of particular objects and upon the concrete lexical "wherewithal" of verbal art, as was shrewdly realized in the thirteenth century by Villard de Honnecourt for graphic arts and by Galfredus for poetry.

The pivotal role performed in the grammatical texture of poetry by diverse kinds of pronouns is due to the fact that pronouns, in contradistinction to all other autonomous words, are purely grammatical, relational units, and besides substantival and adjectival pronouns we must include in this class also adverbial pronouns and the so-called substantive (rather pronominal) verbs such as *to be* and *to have.* The relation of pronouns to nonpronominal words has been repeatedly compared with the relation between geometrical and physical bodies.[41]

Beside common or widespread devices the grammatical texture of poetry offers many salient differential features, typical of a given national literature or of a limited period, a specific trend, an individual poet or even one single work. The thirteenth-century students of the arts whose names we have quoted remind us of the extraordinary compositional sense and skill of the Gothic epoch and help us to interpret the impressive structure of the Hussite battle song "Ktož jsú boží bojovníci." We deliberately dwell on this incentive revolutionary poem almost free of tropes, far from decorativeness and mannerism. The grammatical structure of this work reveals a particularly elaborate articulation.

As shown by the analysis of the song,[42] its three strophes in turn display a trinitarian form: they are divided into three smaller strophic units—*membra*. Each of the three strophes exhibits its specific grammatical features which we labeled "vertical similarities." Each of the three membra throughout the three strophes has its particular properties, termed "horizontal similarities" and distinguishing any given membrum in the strophe from its two other membra. The initial and the final membra of the song are linked together with its central membrum (the second membrum of the second strophe) and differ from the rest of the membra by special features, enabling us to connect these three membra through a "falling diagonal," in contradistinction to the "rising diagonal" linking the central membrum of the song with the final membrum of the initial strophe and with the initial membrum of the final strophe. Furthermore, noticeable similarities bring together (and separate from the rest of the song) the central membra of the first and third strophes with the initial membrum of the second strophe, and, on the other hand, the final membra of the first and third strophes with the central membrum of the second strophe. The former disposition may be labeled "higher upright arc," while the latter will be called "lower upright arc." There appear, moreover, the "inverted arcs," likewise grammatically delimited, a "higher" one, uniting the initial membra of the first and last strophes with the central membrum of the second strophe, and a "lower inverted arc," tying the central membra of the first and last strophes with the final membrum of the second strophe.

This steadfast "membrification" and congruous geometricity must be viewed against the background of Gothic art and scholasticism, convincingly compared by Erwin Panofsky. In its shape the Czech song of the early fifteenth century approximates the authoritative precepts of the "classic *Summa* with its three requirements of (1) totality (sufficient enumeration), (2) arrangement according to a system of homologous parts and parts of parts (sufficient articulation), and (3) distinctness and deductive cogency (sufficient interrelation)."[43] However immense the difference is between Thomism and the ideology of the anonymous author of *Zisskiana cantio,* the shape of this song totally satisfies the artistic request of Thomas Aquinas: "the senses delight in things duly proportioned as in something akin to them; for, the sense, too, is a kind of reason as is every cognitive power." The grammatical texture of the Hussite chorale corresponds to the compositional principles of Czech contemporaneous painting. In his monograph about the pictorial art of the Hussite epoch,[44] Kropáček analyzes the style of the early fifteenth century and points out a congruous and systematic articulation of the surface, a strict subordination of the individual parts to the total compositional tasks, and a deliberate use of contrasts.

The Czech example helps us to glance into the intricacy of correspondences between the functions of grammar in poetry and of relational geometry in painting. We are faced with the phenomenological problem of an intrinsic kinship between both factors and with a concrete historical search for the convergent development and for the interaction between verbal and representational art. Furthermore, in the quest for a delineation of artistic trends and traditions, the analysis of grammatical texture provides us with important clues, and, finally, we approach the vital question of how a poetic work exploits the extant inventory of masterly devices for a new end and re-evaluates them in the light of their novel tasks. Thus, for instance, the masterpiece of Hussite revolutionary poetry has inherited from the opulent Gothic stock both kinds of grammatical parallelism, in Hopkins' parlance "comparison for likeness" and "comparison for unlikeness,"[45] and we have to investigate how the combination of these two, mainly grammatical, ways of proceeding enabled the poet to achieve a coherent, convincing, effective transition from the initial spiritual through the belligerent argumentation of the second strophe to the military orders and battle cries of the finale, or—in other words—how the poetic delight in verbal structures duly proportioned grows into a preceptive power leading to direct action.

IV. Grammatical Originality

The essential literary-critical question of the individuality and comparative characteristics of poems, poets, and poetic schools can and should be posed in the realm of grammar. Despite the common grammatical pattern of Puškin's poetry, each of his poems is unique and unrepeatable in its artistic choice and use of grammatical material. Thus, for example, the quatrains "What is there for you in my name?", though close in time and circumstances to the eight-line "I Loved You," reveal quite a few distinguishing features. We will attempt, on the basis of a few examples, to show the essence of Puškin's "uncommon expression" and, on the other hand, to compare his album verse, inseparably linked with the poetic quests of Russian and Western Romanticism, to the quite disparate and distinct Gothic canon, visible in the song of Jan Žižka's comrades-in-arms.

$_1$Čto v imeni tebe moëm?
$_2$Ono umrët, kak šum pečal'nyj
$_3$Volny, plesnuvšej v bereg dal'nyj,
$_4$Kak zvuk nočnoj v lesu gluxom.

$_5$Ono na pamjatnom listke
$_6$Ostavit mërtvyj sled, podobnyj
$_7$Uzoru nadpisi nadgrobnoj
$_8$Na neponjatnom jazyke.

$_9$Čto v nëm? Zabytoe davno
$_{10}$V volnen'jax novyx i mjatežnyx,
$_{11}$Tvoej duše ne dast ono
$_{12}$Vospominanij čistyx, nežnyx.

$_{13}$No v den' pečali, v tišine,
$_{14}$Proiznesi ego toskuja,
$_{14}$Skaži: est' pamjat' obo mne,
$_{16}$Est' v mire serdce, gde živu ja.

$_1$What is there for you in my name?
$_2$It will die, like the sad noise
$_3$Of a wave that has splashed against a distant shore,
$_4$Like a nocturnal sound in a dense woods.

$_5$On the memorial page it
$_6$Will leave a dead trace akin
$_7$To the pattern of a tombstone inscription
$_8$In an incomprehensible language.

$_9$What is in it? Long forgotten
$_{10}$In new and stormy agitations,
$_{11}$It will not give your soul
$_{12}$Pure, tender memories.

$_{13}$But on a day of sadness, in silence,
$_{14}$Pronounce it while languishing,

₁₅Say: there is memory of me,
₁₆There is in the world a heart in which I live.

In this poem, in distinction to the lines of "I Loved You," the pronouns, twelve in all, yield in quantity both to nouns (twenty) and adjectives (thirteen), but still continue to play a capital role. They constitute three of the four independent words of the first line: *Čto v imeni tebe moëm?* (*What* is there for *you* in *my* name?). In the authorial speech encompassing all but the last two lines of the poem, all the subjects of the main clauses are purely grammatical, consisting as they do of pronouns: ₁*Čto* (what), ₂*Ono* (it), ₅*Ono*, ₉*Čto*. However, in place of the personal pronouns of "I Loved You" interrogative and anaphoric forms predominate here, whereas the second-person pronoun in the first and third quatrains of the poem—whether personal or possessive—occurs exclusively in the dative case, thus remaining merely an addressee, and not the direct theme of the epistle (₁*tebe,* for [lit. to] you, ₁₁*Tvoej duše,* to your soul). Only in the last quatrain does the category of the second person emerge in the verbs, and then it is precisely in the two paired forms of the imperative mood: ₁₄*Proiznesi* (pronounce), ₁₅*Skaži* (say).

Both poems begin and end with pronouns, but in contrast to "I Loved You," the addresser of this epistle is designated neither by a personal pronoun nor by first-person verbs, but only by a possessive pronoun, which relates exclusively to the author's *name,* and that, moreover, in order to put into doubt any possible meaning the name might have for the poem's addressee: ₁"What is there for you in my name?" True, a first-person pronoun does appear in the penultimate line of the poem, first in an indirect, mediated form: ₁₅*est' pamjat' obo mne* (there is memory of me). Finally, in the last, hypercatalectic syllable of the final line, the unexpected first-person subject with a corresponding verbal predicate—so sharply opposed to the preceding inanimate and indirect subjects ("what" and "it")—appears for the first time: ₁₆*Est' v mire serdce, gde živu ja* (There is in the world a heart in which live I). (Note that "I Loved You," on the contrary, begins with the pronoun "I.") Yet even this final self-assertion by no means belongs to the author but is thrust upon the addressee by him: the concluding "I" is spoken by the heroine of the epistle at the author's prompting, while the author himself is conveyed throughout in impersonal terms either of a metonymic (₁*v imeni moëm,* in my name) or synecdochic nature (₁₆*est' v mire serdce,* there is in the world a heart),

137

or in repeated anaphoric references to the discarded metonymy ($_{5,\,11}$*ono,* it), or in secondary metonymic reflections (not the name itself but its $_6$*mërtvyj sled* $_5$*na pamjatnom listke,* dead trace on the memorial page), or, finally, in metaphoric replies to metonymic images, developed into complex comparisons ($_2$*kak* . . .$_4$*kak* . . .$_6$*podobnyj,* like . . . like . . . akin to . . .). In its abundance of tropes this verse epistle essentially differs, to repeat, from the poem "I Loved You." If in the latter grammatical figures carry the entire weight, here the artistic roles are divided between poetic grammar and lexicon.

The principle of a proportional section is apparent here, however complex and capricious its embodiment. The text divides into two eight-line units, each with the same introductory question, as if reacting to an invitation to write a name in a guest book or keepsake album ($_1$"What is there for you in my name?"—$_9$"What is in it?"), and with an answer to its own question. The second pair of quatrains changes the embracing rhyme scheme of the first two in favor of alternating rhymes, giving rise to the unusual collision of two differently rhyming masculine lines at the center of the poem ($_8$*jazyké,* language, and $_9$*davnó,* long ago). Discarding the metaphoric plan of the first two quatrains, the last two transfer the development of the lyrical theme onto the level of literal, direct meanings, and, correspondingly, the negative construction $_{11}$*ne dast ono* $_{12}$*Vospominanij* (it will not give . . . memories) takes the place of the affirmative constructions of a metaphorical order. It is noteworthy that the initial quatrain, which compared the poet's name to the dying "noise of a wave," finds an echo in the third stanza in the related but dead lexical metaphor "new and stormy agitations" (the Russian word for agitations, *volnenija,* is derived from *volna,* wave), in which, it would seem, the senseless name is fated to be engulfed.

At the same time, however, the poem as a whole is subject to another sort of division, in its turn of a dichotomous nature: the entire grammatical composition of the terminal quatrain is strikingly opposed to the initial three quatrains. To the indicative mood of the mournful perfective verbs in the non-past tense (semantically, future tense)—$_2$*umrët* (will die), $_6$*Ostavit mërtvyj sled* (will leave a dead trace), $_{11}$*ne dast* . . .$_{12}$*Vospominanij* (will not give . . . memories)—the final quatrain opposes the imperative of two perfective verbs of speaking ($_{14}$*Proiznesi,* pronounce, $_{15}$*Skaži,* say) which enjoin the addressee's direct speech. That speech removes all the imagined losses through a final affirmation of continued life, which counters the authorial tirade directed at the poem's heroine in the first three quatrains by introducing the first verbal form in the imperfective aspect in the poem $_{16}$*živu ja* (I live). The entire lexicon of the poem changes accordingly: the heroine is called upon to answer the previous terms *umrët* (will die), *mërtvyj* (dead), *nadgrobnaja nadpis'* (tombstone inscription) with the statement: $_{16}$*Est' v mire serdce, gde živu ja* (There is in the world a heart in which I live), with its hint of the traditional paronomasia *neu*MIR*á-juščij* MIR (undying world). The fourth quatrain negates the first three: for you my name is dead, but let it serve you as a sign of my unchanging memory of you. Or, as it is formulated in a later poem by Puškin: *I šlëš' otvet/ Tebe ž net otzyva* (And you send an answer/ But there is no response to you; "Echo," 1831).

The first quatrain had predicted that the poet's name would "die, like the sad noise of a wave," "like a nocturnal sound," and it is precisely to these images that the last stanza returns. There the forgotten name is called upon to resound not at night, vanishing "in a dense woods" ($_4$*v lesu gluxom*—in the bookish metaphor resuscitated by Puškin), but "on a day of sadness," and not in tune to the "sad noise of a wave" but "in silence" ($_{13}$*v tišine*). In the last quatrain the replacement of night by day and of noise by silence is clearly symbolic, as is the grammatical shift. It is hardly fortuitous that in place of the adjectives of the first stanza—"sad" and "nocturnal"—nouns figure in the last quatrain—"in a day of sadness," "in silence." In general, in contradistinction to the abundance of attributive adjectives and adverbs characteristic of the first three stanzas (five in each), in the fourth quatrain such forms are entirely lacking, just as they were lacking in "I Loved You," where, on the other hand, there are plenty of adverbs, which are almost completely absent in the poem under analysis. The final quatrain of "What is there for you in my name?" breaks with the spectacular, decorative style of the first three stanzas, a style that is entirely alien to the text of "I Loved You."

Thus the antithesis of the epistle, its last quatrain, which opens with the adversative *no* (but), the sole copulative conjunction in the poem, differs essentially in its grammatical makeup from the rest of the poem. Unique to it are the repeated imperative forms, in opposition to the indicative mood used invariably throughout the first three quatrains, and an adverbial gerund, contrasting with the previous nominal participles; in distinction to the preceding part of the text, this quatrain introduces quoted speech, the twice repeated predicate *est'* (there is), a first-person subject and object, a complete subordinate clause, and, finally, the imperfective aspect of the verb following a string of perfective forms.

Despite the quantitative disproportion of the first, indicative, and the second, imperative parts (twelve initial lines against the final four), both identically form three further degrees of subdivisions into paratactic pairs of independent syntactic groups. The first three-stanza part embraces two syntactically parallel question-answer constructions, once again of unequal length (eight initial lines versus the four lines of the third quatrain). Correspondingly, the second half of the poem, its final quatrain, contains two parallel sentences, which are closely related thematically. The question-answer constructions of the first part both consist of an identical interrogative sentence and of an answer with one and the same anaphoric subject. To this secondary division of the first part there corresponds in the second part the binary character of the second imperative sentence, which includes direct speech and thus breaks down into the introductory demand (*skaži*, say) and the quote itself (*est'*, there is). Finally, the first of the answers breaks down into two parallel sentences of a metaphoric stamp and closely related thematically, both with an enjambement in the middle of the stanza (I *Ono umrët, kak šum pečal'nyj/Volny . . .* II *Ono . . . Ostavit mërtvyj sled, podobnyj/Uzoru . . .*). This is the last of the three concentric forms of parataxis to be found in the first part of the poem, which is matched in the second part by a division of the quoted speech into parallel, thematically similar sentences (*Est' pamjat'*, There is memory; *Est' . . . serdce*, There is a heart).

If the last quatrain includes just as many independent paratactical pairs as do the three preceding quatrains taken together, then—to the contrary—of six dependent groups (three conjunctive circumstantial clauses and three "attributive-predicative adjuncts," as Šaxmatov calls them),[46] three groups belong to the first quatrain, the richest in metaphoric constructions ($_2$*kak* . . . 'like', $_3$*plesnuvšej*, splashed against, $_4$*kak*, like), while in the three remaining quatrains there is but one example of hypotaxis per quatrain (II *podobnyj*, akin to; III *Zabytoe*, forgotten; IV *gde*, where).

The most striking fact that emerges from all these delimitations is the sharp and many-sided contrast between the first and last quatrains, that is, the opening and dénouement of the lyric theme, not withstanding the simultaneous presence of shared features. Both the contrast and communality find their expression in the sound texture as well. Among the stressed vowels in downbeats, dark (labialized) vowels predominate in the first quatrain, and their number consistently falls in subsequent quatrains, reaching a minimum in the fourth quatrain (I: 8, II: 5, III: 4, IV: 3). Moreover, the maximum number of stressed diffuse (narrow) vowels (*u* and *i*) occur in the two extreme quatrains—the first (6) and fourth (5)—and oppose them to the two internal quatrains (II: o, III: 2).

Let us briefly recapitulate the movement of the theme from the opening to the dénouement, which is clearly articulated in the treatment of grammatical categories, especially case forms. As the initial quatrains make clear, the poet has been asked to inscribe his name in a keepsake album. An interior dialogue, consisting of alternating questions and answers, serves as a rebuke to this implied proposition.

The name will be heard no more. It will vanish without a trace, "will die," according to the intransitive construction of the first quatrain, where only in the metaphoric image of a "wave that has splashed against a distant shore" does the prepositional accusative give a hint of questing after an object. The second quatrain, replacing the name with its written reflection, introduces a transitive form ("it will leave . . . a trace"), but the epithet "dead" as a direct object returns us to the theme of aimlessness developed in the first quatrain. The metaphoric plan of the second quatrain opens with a dative of comparison ("akin to the pattern") and prepares, as it were, for the appearance of a dative in its basic function: the third quatrain introduces a noun ($_{11}$ *Tvoej duše,* to your soul) with a dative of advantage (*dativus commodi*), but again the context, in this case the negated "it will not give," reduces the advantage to null.

The sound texture of the last quatrain has something in common with the diffuse vowels of the initial quatrain, and the thematics of the fourth stanza again concentrate on the spoken name of the first quatrain rather than on its written reflection. The lyric plot began with the sound of the name having faded away; it ends with its sound being pronounced "in silence." In the poem's sound texture the muted, neutral diffuse vowels of the two extreme quatrains accordingly echo each other. However, the dénouement changes the role of the name in an essential way. In response to the invitation—clear from the context though not directly specified—to write his name in an album, the poet answers the album's owner with an appeal: $_{14}$*Proiznesi ego toskuja* (Pronounce it while languishing). In place of the nominative *ono* (it), which refers to the "name" in each of the first three quatrains (I_2, II_1, III_3), one finds the accusative of the same anaphoric pronoun (IV_2) as the object of a second-person imperative addressed to the heroine, who thus turns at the author's will from an inactive addressee ($_1$*tebe,* for [lit. to] you) into a persona dramatis or, more accurately, a persona who is called upon to act.

Echoing the triple *ono* of the first three quatrains and the phonic variations on this pronoun in the third quatrain—a fourfold combination of *n* with *o* and with a preceding or following *v*—the fourth quatrain, which eliminates this subject pronoun, opens in a punning way with precisely the same combination:

> Čto v NËm? Zabytoe davNO
> V volnen'jax NOVyx i mjatežnyx,
> Tvoej duše ne dast ONO
> Vospominanij čistyx, nežnyx.
>
> NO v den' pečali, v tišine . . .

The name, given throughout the first three quatrains as completely divorced from the insensible surroundings, is ascribed to the heroine in a speech that, though merely emblematic, nevertheless for the first time contains a reference to the possessor of the name: "There is in the world a *heart*." It is noteworthy that the authorial "I" is not named in the poem, and when the last lines of the final quatrain finally have recourse to a first-person pronoun, it enters into the direct speech thrust upon the heroine by the authorial imperatives and designates not the author but the heroine. The loss of memories of "me" (the author) is here opposed, in an autonomous framework, to the unshakeable memory of "me" (the forgetful owner of the "memorial page").

The heroine's self-affirmation by means of an appeal to the author's name that is enjoined on her by the author himself is prepared for by the same play on the variations and shifts in the meanings of case forms that the entire poem utilized so intensively. To its numerous case constructions one should apply the searching remarks of Jeremy Bentham[47] about the close contact and mutual interpenetration of two linguistic spheres—the material and the abstract—which appears, for example, in the vacillation of such prepositions as *v* (in) between its proper, material, locational meaning, on the one hand, and an incorporeal, abstract meaning, on the other. The conflict between the two functions of combinations of the locative case with the prepositions *v* and *na* (in) in each of the first three quatrains is given by Puškin in a deliberately sharpened form. In the first quatrain the lines ₁*Čto v imeni tebe moëm?* (What is there for you *in* my name?) and ₃*Kak zvuk nočnoj v lesu gluxom* (Like a nocturnal sound *in* a dense woods) are linked by a grammatical rhyme (the masculine adjectives in the locative *moëm*, my—*gluxóm*, dense). One and the same preposition is endowed with an abstract meaning in the first case and a concretely localized meaning in the second. The extrinsic preposition *na* (on, in, at)—opposed in Russian to the embracing preposition *v* (in, on)—in accordance with the transition from the resounding name to its written form, in turn enters in two parallel lines in the second quatrain, linked by a grammatical rhyme—the first time in a localized sense (*na pamjatnom listké*, *on* the memorial page), the second time in an abstract sense (*na neponjatnom jazyké*, *in* an incomprehensible language). Moreover, the semantic opposition of these two rhyming lines is sharpened by means of a punning paronomasia: Ono na Pamjatnom—na nePonjatnom. In the third quatrain the juxtaposition of two phrases with the preposition *v* follows in general outlines the first quatrain, but the elliptical repetition of the question ₉*Čto v nëm?* (What's in it?) allows for a double interpretation along abstract (What does it mean to you?) as well as genuinely localized lines (What does it contain?). In line with this shift the fourth quatrain leans toward the proper meaning of the same preposition (₁₃*v tišine*, in silence; ₁₆*Est' v mire*, There is in the world). In response to the question posed in the poem's initial line—"What is there for you in my name?"—the heroine is urged to give an answer prompted by the author himself, an answer that contains the embracing preposition *v* three times in its primary, material meaning: *in* the name signed for her and pronounced by her in answer to the poet's appeal, there is contained evidence that there is a person *in* the world *in* whose heart it continues to live. The shift from the nocturnal ₂*Ono umrët* (It will die) to the diurnal ₁₆*živu ja* (I live) echoes the gradual replacement of dark vowels by light ones.

It is curious that both Puškin's quatrains and the Hussite battle song identically end with a double imperative calling for a double reply on the part of the second-person addressee. This reply is a synthetic answer, in the case of Puškin's epistle to the initial interrogative *Čto*

(What)—*Proiznesi* . . . , *Skaži* . . . , *est'* . . . , *est'* . . . (Pronounce [it], Say [it], there is, there is)—in the case of the Czech song to the relative interrogative *Ktož* (Who):

> A s tiem vesele křikněte
> řkúc: "Na ně, hr na ně!"
> braň svú rukama chutnajte,
> "Bóh pán naš!" křikněte!

> Then gaily shout across the land,
> "Against them now, hurrah!"
> Clutching your weapon in your hand
> Cry out, "Our Lord and God!"

However, it is precisely against the background of this common feature that the differences in fundamentals of poetic grammar become evident, in particular, Puškin's sliding between juxtaposed grammatical categories, for example, different cases or different combinatory meanings of one and the same case—in a word, his continual change of focus. The analysis of such exploitations of grammar hardly eliminates the problem of grammatical parallelism in poetry, but posits it in a new, dynamic dimension.

CHAPTER 10

Grammatical Parallelism and Its Russian Facet

When approaching the linguistic problem of grammatical parallelism one is irresistibly impelled to quote again and again the pathbreaking study written exactly one hundred years ago by the juvenile Gerard Manley Hopkins:

> The artificial part of poetry, perhaps we shall be right to say all artifice, reduces itself to the principle of parallelism. The structure of poetry is that of continuous parallelism, ranging from the technical so-called Parallelisms of Hebrew poetry and the antiphons of Church music to the intricacy of Greek or Italian or English verse.[1]

We have learned the suggestive etymology of the terms *prose* and *verse*—the former, *oratio prosa* < *prorsa* < *proversa* (speech turned straightforward), and the latter, *versus* (return). Hence we must consistently draw all inferences from the obvious fact that on every level of language the essence of poetic artifice consists in recurrent returns. Phonemic features and sequences, both morphologic and lexical, syntactic and phraseological units, when occurring in metrically or strophically corresponding positions, are necessarily subject to the conscious or subconscious questions of whether, how far, and in what respect the positionally corresponding entities are mutually similar.

Those poetic patterns where certain similarities between successive verbal sequences are compulsory or enjoy a high preference appear to be widespread in the languages of the world, and they are particularly gratifying both for the study of poetic language and for linguistic analysis in general. Such traditional types of canonic parallelism offer us an insight into the various forms of relationship among the different aspects of language and answer the pertinent question: what kindred grammatical or phonological categories may function as equivalent within the given pattern? We can infer that such categories share a common denominator in the linguistic code of the respective speech community.

Of these systems the biblical *parallelismus membrorum* was the first to attract the attention of Western scholars. In "The Preliminary Dissertation" to his translation of Isaiah, first published in 1778, Robert Lowth laid down the foundations of a systematic inquiry into the verbal texture of ancient Hebrew poetry, and adopted the term "parallelism" for poetics:

> The correspondence of one Verse, or Line, with another, I call Parallelism. When a proposition is delivered, and a second is subjoined to it, or drawn under it, equivalent, or contrasted with it, in Sense; or familiar to it in the form of Grammatical Construction; these I call Parallel Lines; and the words or phrases answering one to another in the corresponding Lines, Parallel Terms.
>
> Parallel Lines may be reduced to Three sorts; Parallels Synonymous, Parallels Antithetic, and Parallels Synthetic. . . . It is to be observed that the several sorts of Parallels are perpetually mixed with one another; and this mixture gives a variety and beauty to the composition.[2]

"Of the three different sorts of Parallels" viewed by Lowth, "every one hath its peculiar character and proper effect" (XXVII). Synonymous lines "correspond one to another by expressing the same sense in different, but equivalent terms; when a Proposition is delivered, and it is immediately repeated, in the whole or in part, the expression being varied, but the sense entirely, or nearly the same" (XI). Two antithetic lines "correspond with one another by an Opposition . . . sometimes in expressions, sometimes in sense only. Accordingly the degrees of Antithesis are various; from an exact contraposition of word to word through the whole sentence, down to a general disparity, with something of a contrariety, in the two propositions" (XIX). To these two types the author opposes purely grammatical congruences, which he calls "Synthetic or Constructive" and "where the Parallelism consists only in the similar form of Construction." The verses are bound by a mere "correspondence between different propositions, in respect of the shape and turn of the whole sentence, and of the constructive parts; such as noun answering to noun, verb to verb, member to member, negative to negative, interrogative to interrogative" (XXI).

Newman's and Popper's painstaking critical survey[3] paved the way for the recent cardinal revision of pivotal questions bound up with biblical parallelism, its essence and history.[4] The last decades of intensive investigation have thrown new light on the close relationship between the metrico-strophic form of Hebrew and Ugaritic poetic writings and their "repetitive parallelism" (the term used in current Semitic studies). The prosodic and verbal organization which appears chiefly in the most archaic biblical poems and the Canaanite epics proves to go back to an ancient Canaanite tradition with certain Akkadian connections. The reconstruction and philological interpretation of early biblical poetic remains is a spectacular achievement of modern research. Now, in the light of the work done, the structure of parallelism underlying biblical and Ugaritic poetry requires a rigorous linguistic analysis, and the seemingly infinite variety of extant parallels must yield to a precise and comprehensive typology. Lowth's bold yet premature effort demands to be resumed on a new level.

His example served as a model for the first Western attempt to examine another ancient literary tradition that has never abandoned parallelism as its cardinal poetic artifice. A paper "On the Poetry of the Chinese" read by J. F. Davis in 1829 at a meeting of the Royal Asiatic Society declared parallelism to be the most interesting feature in the construction of Chinese verse, "as it presents a striking correspondence with what has been remarked of Hebrew poetry."[5] Davis quoted extensively the dissertation of Bishop Lowth, closely followed the latter's way of outlining three different kinds of correspondence, and observed that the third sort of parallel—which Lowth denominates as the synthetic or constructive—"is by far the most common species of parallelism with the Chinese." Both other sorts "are generally accompanied by this last—the correpsondence of sense, whether it consists in equivalency or opposition, is almost always attended by correspondence of construction: the latter is often found without the former, while the converse seldom takes place. It pervades Chinese poetry universally, forms its chief characteristic feature, and is the source of a great deal of its artificial beauty" (pp. 414–415).[6]

These definitions and classificatory criteria underlie a number of later studies which aimed primarily at an adequate translation of Chinese poetic works.[7] Today a need for more precise and minute description has become obvious. Hightower has translated two Chinese pieces from the fifth and sixth centuries which are composed in the so-called "parallel prose" or, strictly speaking, in verses of a fluid, sliding meter, and studied their organizing principle.[8] Aware of the necessity for discerning all the varieties of parallelism, the scholar consults the native Chinese tradition of studies in this field, which surpass the foreign observations in both age and acuity. In particular he cites Kūkai's ninth-century compilation from older Chinese sources, *Bunkyō hifuron*, a treatise on literary theory which enumerates twenty-nine modes of parallelism.[9] Hightower himself operates with six types of Simple Parallelism—reiteration, synonymy, antonymy, "likes" (lexical and grammatical similitude),[10] "unlikes" (grammatical without lexical similitude), and "formal pairs" ("far-fetched linkages" in lexical semantics without grammatical similitude). He also broaches the problems of Complex Parallelism and the metrical, grammatical, and phonic parallels.

P. A. Boodberg's Sinological "Cedules" dealing with diverse aspects of parallelism—grammatical, lexical, prosodic—and with the polysemantic load of the matched words and lines, especially in connection with the intricacies of translating Chinese verse, are penetrating prolegomena to a still missing systematic linguistic inquiry into the framework of this magnificent poetic tradition. Boodberg has shown that a function of the second line of a couplet is "to give us the clue for the construction of the first" and to bring out the dormant primary meaning of the confronted words; he has made clear that "parallelism is not merely a stylistic device of formularistic syntactical duplication; it is intended to achieve a result reminiscent of binocular vision, the superimposition of two syntactical images in order to endow them with solidity and depth, the repetition of the pattern having the effect of binding together syntagms that appear at first rather loosely aligned."[11]

This is basically tantamount to the evaluation of biblical parallelism propounded by Herder in his famed response to Lowth's Latin volume: "Both limbs strengthen, elevate, support each other."[12] Norden's attempt to disunite both poetic canons and to oppose the Chinese "parallelism of form" to the Hebrew "parallelism of thought," though frequently cited, is hardly tenable.[13] The grammatical and lexical congruences of Chinese verses are not inferior to biblical parallelism in their semantic charge. As demonstrated by Chmielewski, China's linguistic parallelism may be "matched by that of the logical structure" and assumes a "potentially positive role in spontaneous logical thinking."[14] According to another noted Polish Sinologist, Jabłoński, the variform parallelism that is the most salient feature of Chinese verbal style displays a harmonious, intimate relationship "with the Chinese conception of the world, considered as a play of two principles alternating in time and opposed in space. One should say sexes rather than principles, since [the Chinese] believe more in viewing the world as divided into pairs of objects, of attributes, of aspects that are at the same time coupled and opposed."[15] Norden had based his division on an impression of a predominantly metaphoric parallelism in biblical poetry and on the familiar prejudice that the metonymic correspondences—such as partition and enumeration of particulars—which link "constructively parallel" lines (Lowth, XXIII; Jabłoński, pp. 27ff) are merely cumulative and not integrative.[16]

The symmetrical "carmen-style" akin to the *parallelismus membrorum* is attested by numerous instances in the Veda, and Gonda's comprehensive monograph scrupulously examines the typical repetitive devices connected with this mode of expression.[17] The ancient Indic tendency toward symmetric correspondences, however, cannot be equated with the above-cited patterns of canonical, pervasive parallelism.

I

Grammatical parallelism belongs to the poetic canon of numerous folk patterns. Gonda (pp. 28ff) referred to divers countries in different parts of the world with prevalently "binary structures" of grammatically and lexically corresponding lines in traditional prayers, exorcisms, magic songs, and other forms of oral verse, and in particular brought to the reader's attention the litanies and ballads of Nias (west of Sumatra), "expressed in the form of a pair of parallel, highly synonymic members."[18] But our information about the distribution of parallelism in the folklore of the world and its character in various languages is still sparse and fragmentary, and hence, for the time being, we must remain confined primarily to the results of inquiry into the parallelistic songs of the Ural-Altaic area.

In his fundamental monograph about parallelism in Finnish-Karelian folk poetry, Steinitz has traced the beginnings of scholarly interest in this problem.[19] It is noteworthy indeed that the earliest references to Finnish poetic parallelism proceeded from a comparison with biblical poetry and that the first statements about the similarity of these two patterns by Cajanus and Juslenius appeared long before Lowth's *Hebraica*.[20] Despite the growing enthusiasm for Finland's folklore, from the beginning to the middle of the nineteenth century, its verbal structure usually dropped out of the scope of local and Western scholarly interests, whereas the poet Longfellow, through Anton Schiefner's German translation of the *Kalevala* (1852), grasped the parallelistic style of the original and applied it in his *Song of Hiawatha* (1855).

In the sixties the essence of the Finnish poetic language reentered the field of investigation. The grammatical composition of the *Kalevala*'s parallelistic distichs was plotted in Ahlqvist's dissertation "Finnish Poetics from the Linguistic Standpoint," at a time when no other system of parallelism had undergone a similar treatment.[21] But Steinitz was the first to succeed, seventy years later, in completing a thoroughly scientific "grammar of parallelism," as the author himself defined the task of his inquiry into the epic, lyric, and magic songs of the famed Finnish-Karelian singer Arhippa Perttunen. This is a pioneer work not only in the Finno-Ugric field but also, and foremost, in the method of approach to the structural analysis of grammatical parallelism. The syntactic and morphologic aspects of this poetic pattern are succinctly outlined in Steinitz's monograph, whereas their interconnections and the diverse semantic associations between the parallelled lines and their components are only glimpsed. The investigator revealed the variety of grammatical relations between the parallelled verses, but the interconnection of these structurally different distichs and their characteristic functions within a broader context calls for a self-contained and integral treatment of a given song in its entirety, as a consequence of which the presumably unpaired, isolated lines would also obtain a new and more nuanced interpretation as to their place and role.

Stimulated by Steinitz's research,[22] Austerlitz, in his careful study of

Ostyak and Vogul metrics, pays chief attention to "parallel structures," but where Steinitz's work of 1934 left questions open, Austerlitz's analysis of Ob-Ugrian parallelism was, as he says, "automatically restricted to the formal features of the material," and ergo not supposed to "include semantics or any domain beyond grammar."[23] The likewise automatic confinement of the analysis to the immediate contextual vicinity creates an artificial chasm between the cohesive and allegedly isolated lines, which could have been avoided "if the ordering of lines within the structure of a poem as a whole had dominated the presentation," according to a reviewer's sound suggestion.[24] Austerlitz's remarks on the Hungarian vestiges of poetic parallelism (p. 125) and Steinitz's references to a similar pattern in Western Finnic and Mordvinian oral poetry (§ 3) allow a surmise of a common Finno-Ugric or even Uralic tradition, as Lotz suggests in his analysis of a Sayan-Samoyed song.[25]

Oral poetry of diverse Turkic peoples displays a rigorous parallelistic canon which is probably of common origin, as Kowalski's and Žirmunskij's broad surveys persuasively testify.[26] The earliest record of these folk epics, the Oghuz "Kitab-i Dede Qorkut," belongs to the sixteenth century.[27] The older the features we observe in the cultural pattern of a Turkic people, the more sustained is the parallelistic groundwork of the native oral poetry, especially the epic. Although this Turkic compulsory matrix has much in common with the Finno-Ugric systems, the differences are equally striking. An intensive structural analysis of parallelism as it functions in the folklore of single Turkic peoples is a pressing linguistic task.

In an account illustrated by numerous examples and modeled upon Steinitz' classification of the Finnish-Karelian material, Poppe has shown that parallelism is common likewise to the oral poetry of all Mongolian peoples,[28] although this feature has generally been ignored by students of Mongolian literature and folklore. Thus most of the vast Ural-Altaic area displays an oral tradition founded on grammatical parallelism, and both the convergent and the divergent traits must be singled out by a deep comparative study of its regional variants.

II

The only living oral tradition in the Indo-European world that uses grammatical parallelism as its basic mode of concatenating successive verses is Russian folk poetry, both songs and recitatives.[29] This constructive principle of Russian folklore was first pointed out in a paper devoted to the *Kalevala* and published anonymously as an item of "Miscellany" in a popular Petersburg periodical of 1842 with an eloquent subtitle: "The identity of foundations in Hebrew, Chinese, Scandinavian, and Finnish versification, as well as in the verse art of Russian folklore—Parallelism."[30] The Finnish *Kanteletar* is declared (p. 59) to bear a close resemblance to Russian folksongs "in rhythm and constitution" (*ladom i skladom*).

> The *constitution* of the verse is quite the same as in archaic Russian songs. . . . Apparently hitherto nobody has taken notice of the extremely interesting fact that the *constitution* of our folk songs belongs to the primeval human inventions in verbal music and is intimately connected, on the one hand, with the poetics of the Scandinavian skalds and Finnic rhapsodes (*bjarmskix bajanov*) and, on the other, with the versification of the ancient Hebrews and of the contemporary Chinese. Until the learned verbal music, i.e. the tact measure, was introduced, . . . two natural harmonic principles, *parallelism* and *alliteration,* were perhaps the universal basis of songcraft.[31] The term "parallelism" was first applied to the peculiar feature observed by commentators of the Bible in Hebrew versification and meant that the second or third line of a strophe almost always presents an interpretation or a paraphrase or a simple repetition of a thought, figure, metaphor contained in the preceding verse or verses. Nowhere else could one find such splendid and opulent examples of this method as in our Russian songs, whose entire constitution is based on parallelism (pp. 60–61).

The author adduces a few examples and comments on their partly metaphorical, partly synonymic aspect; he adds that such constructions, which might be drawn by the thousand from Russian folk poetry, form its very essence. "It is neither vagary nor barbarism but a spirited observance of an inner, indissoluble bond between thought and sound, or perhaps rather an unconscious, instinctive, spontaneous sense of a musical logic of thoughts and of a corresponding musical logic of sounds." This paper is particularly memorable, since it belongs to an epoch of general inattention toward Finnish parallelism, which in 1835 remained omitted even in Elias Lönnrot's preface to his first edition of the *Kalevala* (cf. Steinitz, p. 17).

Thirty years later, Olesnickij, writing on rhythm and meter in the Old Testament, while discussing Lowth's theory of the *parallelismus membrorum,* referred to other oriental instances of the same architectonic design, observable in Egyptian inscriptions, in many Vedic passages, and with particular consistency in Chinese poetry. He concluded his survey with a cursory remark on "the very rich parallelism encountered in each of our folk songs and byliny," exemplified by two lengthy quotations from Russian historical songs.[32]

In his detailed studies on the constitution of the language of Russian folksongs, Šafranov[33] attacked Olesnickij's view that parallelism does not pertain to poetic forms (CCII, pp. 233ff) and returned to the anonym's distinction between the rhythm (*lad*) and the constitution (*sklad*) of the Russian song, assigning to the latter rhetorical and to the former musical foundations (pp. 256ff), and insisting on the relative autonomy of each factor (CCV, p. 99). In Russian musical folklore he found two joint constitutive features—repetition and parallelism, the latter almost as pertinent as in ancient Hebrew lyrics (CCV, pp. 84ff)—and drafted a brief and approximate linguistic enumeration of diverse parallelistic patterns (pp. 101–104). Štokmar's objection that in some genres of Russian folk songs, particularly in the byliny, "repetitions and parallelism do not play such a considerable part" is mistaken, since precisely in the structure of the epics and in the concatenation of their verses the role of parallelism is dominant.[34]

Strange as it may seem, during the more than eighty-five years that separate us from Šafranov's draft, no systematic effort has been made to fathom the system of Russian grammatical parallelism. In Žirmunskij's monograph on the history and theory of rhyme the chapter "Rhyme in the Bylina" surveys the homoioteleuton, a typical byproduct of morphologic, particularly epiphoric, parallelism, without considering the over-all problems of parallelistic texture in Russian epic folklore, although it is only in this context that terminal phonemic correspondences receive a thorough explication.[35] The statistics of rhymed lines (p. 264) are hardly informative without numerical data about all forms of parallelism in the byliny. I have demonstrated the diverse semantic interrelations between two parallel clauses from Russian wedding songs.[36] Synonymy in parallel verses was touched upon in Evgen'eva's recent book on the language of oral poetry.[37] But as a rule current writing on Russian folklore still underrates or disregards the functions performed by grammatical parallelism in the semantic and formal structure of oral epics and lyrics. Before attempting a methodical treatise on the whole of this subject, with particular reference to the specific aspects it acquires in different poetic genres, one must examine the complex parallelistic texture of a single song in order to observe the concrete interplay of the multiform devices, each with its proper task and aim.

III

The famous eighteenth-century collection of Russian folk songs, chiefly epics, written down somewhere in Western Siberia by or from an otherwise unknown Kirša Danilov, includes a succinct musical text "Ox v gore žit' nekručinnu byt'" (Oh, to live in grief, to be unchagrined) which is transliterated here, without the spelling vacillations of the manuscript, and provided with a translation that is as literal as possible.[38]

1	A i góre góre— gorevánʹice!	And grief grief—little grieving!
2	A v góre žítʹ—nekručínnu býtʹ,	And to live in grief—to be unchagrined,
3	Nagómu xodítʹ—ne stydítisja,	To walk naked—to be unashamed.
4	A i déneg nétu—pered dénʹgami,	And (if) there is no money— (it is) before money,
5	Pojavílasʹ grívna—pered zlými dní.	(If) a coin has appeared—(it is) before penury.
6	Ne byvátʹ plešátomu kudrjávomu,	No way for a bald one to be curly,
7	Ne byvátʹ guljáščemu bogátomu,	No way for an idle one to be rich.
8	Ne otróstitʹ déreva suxovérxogo,	No way to grow a dry-topped tree,
9	Ne otkórmitʹ kónja suxopárogo,	No way to fatten a withered horse,
10	Ne utéšiti ditjá bez máteri,	No way to console a child without a mother,
11	Ne skroítʹ atlásu bez mástera.	No way to cut satin without a master.
12	A góre, góre— gorevánʹice!	And grief, grief—little grieving!
13	A i lýkom góre podpojásalosʹ,	And grief girded itself with bark,
14	Močalámi nógi izopútany.	The feet wound with bast.
15	A já ot górja v temný lesá,	And I (ran) from grief to the dark forests,

$_{16}$ A góre < . . .> prežde vék zašël;		And grief came there beforehand;
$_{17}$ A já ot górja v počéstnoj pír,		And I (ran) from grief to an honorable feast,
$_{18}$ A góre zašël—vperedi sidít;		And grief came there—in front (he) sits;
$_{19}$ A já ot górja na carëv kabák,		And I (ran) from grief to a tsar's drinking house,
$_{20}$ A góre vstrečáet—píva taščít;		And grief meets (me)—(he) is drawing beer.
21 Kák ja nág to stál, nasmejálsja ón.		When I became naked, he jeered.

The story of an ill-fated lad (or girl) persecuted by a personified, myth-icized Grief is recounted in numerous Russian lyrico-epic songs, some predominantly epic and others lyric, like Kirša's version. Russian literature of the seventeenth century tried to efface the boundary that divided written literature from oral. Poetic texts, customarily transmitted only by mouth, were put on paper, and several hybrid works arose on the borderline between folklore and written literature, particularly the long "Tale of Grief and Misfortune" (*Povest' o Gore i Zločastii*), preserved in a single manuscript of the very late seventeenth century.[39] One can only agree with the students of this remarkable poem composed in the verse form of oral epics, and particularly with Ržiga, who compared in detail its text with folksongs about Grief,[40] that this *Povest'* takes over from oral poetry the ancient motif of everlasting grief and transforms it into a complex artistic synthesis of bookmanship and folklore. It is possible that the written *Tale* of the seventeenth century in turn produced a certain effect on the folksongs of this cycle, although all the properties which the *Povest'* shares with some of these songs are typical of folklore poetics, and none of the bookish elements inherent in the manuscript of the seventeenth century is reflected in the oral epics or lyrics. Thus the supposition of the mighty influence exerted by folk poetry on the written tale is incomparably better founded than are surmises of any reverse infiltration.

In particular, Ržiga's assumption that Kirša's variant was a lyrical composition prompted by the *Povest'* (p. 313) is quite improbable. One can hardly agree that when this song coincides with the *Povest'* the former proves to be "an obvious derivative" of the latter. On the contrary, in the song the features shared with the *Povest'* are organically linked with the entire context and based on traditional principles of oral poetics, whereas in the *Tale* they are much more sporadic and inconsistent, and the common passages are adapted to an alien context. The folklore formulas in question must have been borrowed by seventeenth-century literati from the oral tradition. Some of these epigrammatic formulas entered also into the repertory of folk proverbs. Compare verses 1 and 2 of the song with the proverb adduced by Dal': *V gore žit' —nekručinnu byt'; nagomu xodit' —ne soromit'sja.*[41] Furthermore, Kirša's variant exhibits certain motifs shared with other folksongs on the same theme, yet missing in the *Povest'*. The parallelistic canon rigorously followed in these specimens of the grief folklore obviously suffers from the transfer of oral tradition into the frame of the written tale, and shows many gaps, heterogeneous retouches, and deviations from the customary forms of verses and their concatenation.[42]

Hightower's delineation of Chinese parallelism may be applied to Russian folk poetry as well. In both languages the distich is the basic structural unit, and "the first effect of the other varieties of parallelism is to reinforce the repeated pattern. It is on this underlying pattern or series of patterns that the more subtle forms of grammatical and phonic parallelism introduce their counterpoint, a series of stresses and strains" (pp. 61, 69). The typical feature of Chinese parallelistic texts analyzed by the quoted Sinologist—the occasional "isolated single lines" which chiefly signal the beginning and end of an entire text or of its paragraphs—is likewise shared by Russian folk poetry, and by Kirša's song in particular. Hightower designates as a paragraph a larger structural unit "which is significant both by marking stages in the development of a theme and also by determining to some extent the form of the couplets [distichs] which go to make it up." Similar observations on pairless verses in the Finnish-Karelian runes at the beginning of songs or of their autonomous parts were made by Ahlqvist (p. 177). According to Steinitz (§ 11), ten of nineteen epic *Kalevala* songs recorded in the 1830s from the foremost Karelian rhapsodist Arhippa Perttunen begin with a nonparallel line. In biblical poetry, particularly in the Psalms, "single lines, or *monostichs,*" as Driver states, "are found but rarely, being generally used to express a thought with some emphasis at the beginning, or occasionally at the end, of a poem."[43]

Kirša's song contains 21 lines, three of which have no adjacent mate. Of these three lines, 1 begins the song and 21 ends it, while 12 opens the second paragraph, which is quite different from the first in both theme and grammatical texture. Actually, lines 1 and 12, which carry the burden of the song, vary while still adhering to the parallelistic pattern of the entire composition: the introductory verse of the first paragraph does not cohere with any other line of the same paragraph, but is matched by the nearly identical opening of the next paragraph.

Moreover, these two lines display an internal grammatical parallelism of their hemistichs, a device shared by the intermediate lines, i.e. by all the lines of the first paragraph. The repeated apostrophe is similar to the predominant type of monostichs observed by Steinitz (§§ 12, 14), which consist of a noun in the nominative with its apposition. Most frequently such substantives are "proper names, personal or mythological," and *góre gorevánʹice* approaches the latter category.[44] The syntactic independence of lines 1 and 2 focuses attention on the internal structure of the verse and primarily on the parallelism of its hemistichs. The evocation of Grief, destined to become the chief actor in the song, opens its first line, and the internal parallelism is reinforced by the reduplication *góre góre* and by the etymological figure (paregmenon) which links the apposition *gorevánʹice* to its head word *góre*.[45] Tautological variations of this noun are usual in Russian emotive speech: *góre górʹkoe, góre gorjúčee, góre górjuško,* etc.; *Povestʹ 296: Govorít sero góre gorínskoe*. The denominative verb *gorevátʹ* (to grieve) from *góre* (grief) gave in turn a deverbative noun *gorevánʹe* (grieving), used here in its diminutive form *gorevánʹice*, which opposes to the virtual nomen agentis a somewhat softened or even caressing nomen actionis. Thus the tinge of oxymoron evidenced by the following verses is prompted from the beginning. Anyone who knows Sergej Esenin's poetry can immediately grasp why this self-contradictory phrase was to become his favorite catchword (*eseninskoe slovco*).[46]

The nominative *góre*, linked by a paregmenon with the derived, likewise nominative form *gorevánʹice* of the same line, is on the other hand connected by a polyptoton with the locative *v góre*, which occupies the same metrical position in the second line as the initial *góre* in the first line. Grief, to be portrayed as an invincible evil power in the finale of the song, is rather minimized in its opening lines, which turn this apparition (*góre góre*) first into a mere process (*gorevánʹice*) and then into a simple adverbial modifier of manner (*v góre*). This gradual weakening of the sorrowful topic is used to justify the oxymoron ₂*v góre žitʹ* — *nekručinnu býtʹ* (to live in grief—to be unchagrined).

Gore-kručina, s górja—s kručíny frequently occur in Russian as coupled synonyms (*Povestʹ 358: u górja u kručíny*). The confrontation of

antonyms is a salient device of parallelism. These "straightforward parallels" in Kūkai's nomenclature occupy the first place among his 29
types of parallelism and are recommended by him for beginners' practice before trying other kinds.

Antonymy connects both hemistichs in lines 2, 3 and 6, 7 and
is represented in this pair of distichs by two different kinds of opposition.[47] The hemistichs within 2 and 3 juxtapose contradictories,
whereas antonymy of the hemistichs in 6 and 7 is built on contraries:
$_6$*plešátomu: kudrjávomu,* $_7$*guljáščemu: bogátomu.*[48] As Harkins pointed
out, *góre* "represents a physical condition," while *kručina* is the corresponding psychological state" (p. 202). The possibility or even necessity of subjective indifference toward a disappointing reality is deliberately proclaimed in lines 2 and 3 as a unity of contradictories in sharp
contradistinction to the incompatibility of contraries advanced in 6
and 7. *Nekručínnu* could easily be replaced by *véselu* 'cheerful' or *rá-
dostnu* 'joyous' (*Povest'* 194: *kručinovat, skórben, nerádosten*), but the
gradual, smooth transition from the initial bravado to the theme of
inevitable doom requires single negative terms, and the litotes which
concludes both 2 and 3 and takes an intermediate place between the
attenuating *gorevánʹice* (a typical "minution," or "meiosis," in the
terms of Latin and Greek rhetoric) and the increasingly negative wording of the further maxims.[49]

Lines 4 and, in reverse order, 5 play with two opposites: absence and
presence of money. The lack of means is treated as a contradictory in
the first line of this distich and as a contrary in the second: $_4$ *déneg nétu*
(no money) and $_5$ *zlými dní* (penury)—compare the two parallel antitheses of contradictories jointed in the proverb *Dénʹgi k bogátomu,
zlýdni k ubógomu.* Thus line 4 joins the preceding verses built on contradictories, while line 5 shares its use of contraries with the next distich. The constant alternation of opposites enunciated in the distich 4–
5 is an intermediate link between 2 and 3, with their comforting unity
of opposites, and the gloomy, irreconcilable contrariness of hemistichs
within 6 and 7. The second hemistich of 4—*pered dénʹgami*—is akin to
the cheerful ends of 2 and 3, whereas the dismal portent—*pered zlými
dní*—ties line 5 to the subsequent pessimistic propositions.

In the distich 2–3 both lines, and within each line both hemistichs,
are syntactically and morphologically parallel. All four hemistichs finish with (or consist of) an infinitive in a similar syntactic function. In
Russian the traditional juxtaposition *žítʹ da býtʹ* is brought about by

the semantic affinity of the verbs, by their homoioteleuton, and by the formula *žíl býl,* which is a reinterpreted vestige of the pluperfect. A certain contrast of parallel forms is introduced by the copulative use of ₂*být'* in contrast to the strictly lexical, notional verbs ₂*žít'* and ₃*stydítisja.* The reflexive voice of the last of these is another variational element. The parallelism is supported (1) by the negation *ne,* which opens the second hemistich in both lines, (2) by phonemic similarity between the beginnings of these lines: /ʌ√GÓr'e ~ /nʌGÓmu/, and (3) by the /i/ in all five of the other stressed syllables and the same sequence /d'it'/ in both hemistichs of 3 (/xoD'íT'/ ~ /stiD'íT'isa/). In the proverb cited by Dal' this sound figure is replaced by the correspondence /nagómu/ ~ /soɾóM'itca/. The positionally congruent and phonemically identical stressed syllables of ₂ *v góre* and ₃ *nagómu* belong to syntactically equivalent terms; both of them are adverbial modifiers in infinitive clauses. The grief imagery employed by the first line of the distich is matched in the second by the similar and contiguous motif of poverty (cf. the proverb *Líxo žit' v núže, a v góre i togó xúže*) and particularly by a synecdochic image of nakedness. The semantically significant correspondence between *góre* and *nagómu* receives an analogous paronomastic treatment in the *Povest'* 311: /zʌNAGím TO GÓr'e n'epoGÓN' itca/; 312:/da n'iKTÓ kNAGÓmu n'epr'iv'áżetca/.

The distich 2–3 exhibits, as Hightower terms it, a "double parallelism" in combining the mutual symmetry of lines with the internal symmetry of their hemistichs. These two forms of parallelism are complemented by a third and even wider correspondence between the second hemistich in the first line of this distich and the first hemistich in its second line: ₂ *nekručínnu být'* and ₃ *nagómu xodít'* form a close morphologic anadiplosis, whereas on this grammatical level the congruence of both hemistichs within each line and of the corresponding hemistichs within the distich is chiefly epiphoric (₃ *nagómu* finds no morphologic equivalent either in the second hemistich of the same line or in the first hemistich of 2).

The anadiplosis (*styk* in Russian terminology), customary in the byliny and other kinds of Russian folk poetry, turns the second half of the couplet into a sort of sequel to its first half: the man who appears lighthearted in grief can afford to stroll in rags without any embarrassment.[50] The corresponding line 366 of the *Povest'* —*a v góre žit'* —*nekručínnu být', a krúčinnu v góre—pogínuti* (And [if one is] to live in grief—[he has] to be unchagrined, And [if] chagrined in grief—[one has] to perish)—constructed on chiastic antonyms (*žít'* ~ *pogínuti;* *nekručínnu* ~ *kručínnu*), rationalizes the antecedent line by a causal motivation: "because otherwise one would perish."

In the distich 4–5 the second hemistich of both lines consists of the same proposition *pered* followed by an instrumental plural form. This morphologic and phonemic correspondence—/D'EN'*ga*M'I/ ~ /zlíM'I DN'I/—/ is reinforced by the paronomasia /D'EN'*gi*/ ~ /D'EN'/, DN'*i*/.[51] Both hemistichs of 4 are tied together by the polyptoton *déneg* —*dén'gami*. The first, mutually antithetic hemistichs of 4 and 5 contain the synonyms *dén'gi* and *grívna* (pars pro toto). The metathetic sound figures within these hemistichs—₄ /d'ÉN'ek N'Étu/, ₅ /pojaV'ílas gr'ívna/ —conform to the chiastic character of the whole distich.[52] Among the first seven lines of the song the fifth is the only one devoid of internal parallelism. This deficiency is compensated for by the exceptional cohesion of both hemistichs through two pairs of identical stressed vowels: two /í/ ~ two /í/. The sameness of all vowel phonemes under stress characterizes also the surrounding lines—4, 6, and 7—but in these the number of stressed vowels is limited to three: two /é/ + one /é/ in 4; two /á/ + one /á/ in both 6 and 7.

In the distich 6–7 the second line fully matches the first in syntax and morphology. Each contains the negation *ne* and the infinitive *byvát'* followed by two masculine adjectives in the dative case. The grammatical parallelism of both hemistichs is built on these adjectives, which are morphologically equivalent but have dissimilar syntactic functions. The four dative forms are interconnected by chiastic rhymes, ₆ *plešátomu* ~ ₇ *bogátomu* and ₆ *kudrjávomu* ~ ₇ *guljáščemu;* in the second pair the pretonic /u/ is preceded by an initial velar stop and the stressed /á/ is preceded by a palatalized liquid. The semantic interconnection of both lines consists in the parallel reference to the incompatibility of two contraries, and while the contrariness of "bald" and "curly" appears self-evident, the more oblique antithesis of "idle" and "rich" is corroborated by the formal parallelism with the antecedent line. The corresponding passage in the *Povest'* impairs the formal parallelism and the typical folkloric play on antonyms, and changes the distich into a moralizing lesson: ₄₁₀ *ne byváti brážniku bogátu,* ₄₁₁ *ne byváti kostarjú v sláve dóbroj* (No way for a reveler to be rich, No way for a dice player to have a good name).

Both lines of the distichs 8–9 and 10–11 exhibit an identical syntactic combination of the same morphologic categories. Genders are the only admitted variables, and this variation is constantly utilized: inanim. neut. *déreva* ~ anim. masc. *kónja;* the exceptional anim. neut. *ditjá* ~ inanim. masc. *atlásu;* anim. fem. *máteri* ~ anim. masc. *mástera.*

Each distich alternates two grammatical objects, one of which refers to the animate and one to the inanimate world, and all four metaphoric images play up the theme of the hero's gloomy destiny: 8 and 9 deal with the incurability of morbid organisms, both characterized by compound adjectives with the same first component *suxo-* (dry); 10 and 11 equate the child deprived of a mother with a precious cloth left without any master, and the sound texture underscores the intimacy of both absent ties by a childishly tinged accumulation of palatalized dentals—/n'e ut'ešit'i d'it'á be'z mát'er'i/[53]—and by the paronomastic makeup of the second line: 11 /n'eskRoŕt' αtlásu b'ezmást'eRα/. Most probably, the wording of line 408 in the *Povest'* —/što n'e klást'i skarlátu b'ez mást'eRα/ (that there is no way to cut scarlet without a master)— reflects the original wording of the verse in question. Ržiga claims that these two lines in Kirša's song "by themselves are startling, because it is incomprehensible why they refer to the child, to the mother, and to satin" (p. 313). He believes to have found the explanation in the *Povest'*, where the lad introduces this distich by recollecting how in childhood he had been dressed up and admired by his mother. Yet this psychological justification of the two typical metaphorical lines, which are firmly parallel on the grammatical, semantic, and phonemic levels (/d'it'á b'ezmát'er'i/ ~ /atlásu b'ezmást'eRα/) and which appear inseparably linked with the entire context of Kirša's song, obviously presents a secondary contrivance alien to the oral tradition and apparently inserted by the seventeenth-century writer and reader.

The parallelism of contiguous hemistichs is particularly distinct in the distich 2–3, with its double infinitives in each line. The second pair of conditional sentences, with its chiastic composition, underlies the inner symmetry of the distich 4–5. Within the next three distichs each of the six lines contains only one clause, but distributes two morphologically equivalent forms between its two hemistichs: the two adjectival datives in 6 and 7, the genitives of the object and of the "predicative attribute" in 8 and 9 (*déreva suxovérxogo, kónja suxopárogo*),[54] and the genitives—one with and the other without a preposition—in 10 and 11 (*ditjá bez máteri, atlásu bez mástera*).

The two paragraphs of the song differ manifestly in their grammatical composition. The first paragraph (lines 1–11) contains ten infinitives and only one finite verb (the preterit $_5$ *pojavílas'*) against nine finite forms and no infinitives in the second paragraph (12–21). There are no pronouns in §I, and five personal pronouns in §II. Aside from the three nominatives in the "anacrustic" introductory line to each of the two paragraphs (1 and 12), ten nominatives—five substantival and five pronominal—occur in §II and only one in §I: $_5$ *pojavílas' grívna* (a coin appeared). Throughout the five couplets of §I this is the only clause which is not ostensively negative. The negative character of the discourse gradually intensifies. The negated adjective at the end of 2 is followed by the negated verb at the end of 3 (a special negation by a nexal negative, in Otto Jespersen's terms). In the first hemistich of 4 the negation *nétu* functions as predicate, and 5, as mentioned earlier, may be defined as implied negation. All the sentences of lines 6–11 begin with the negation *ne;* moreover lines 10 and 11 introduce their second hemistich with the negative preposition *bez* (without).

In §I eight adjectives are used; six of them appear without any substantive and two act as postposed predicative attributes, whereas all three adjectives of §II are prepositive epithets.

In §I all seven verbs of the first three distichs are intransitive, in contradistinction to the four transitive verbs of the other two distichs. The four infinitives of the latter distichs are perfective, while all six infinitives of the former distichs are imperfective. Each line of the five distichs designates the relation between a certain condition and its result, either patently, in the asyndetic conditional sentences of the first two distichs, or latently, in the three further distichs marked by six anaphoric negations (if one is bald, then . . .; if the tree is dry-topped, then . . .; if the child has no mother, then . . .). While all the lines of the three initial distichs put the protasis into their first hemistich and the apodosis into the second, the last two distichs invert this order. The infinitive constructions of these two distichs omit the agent but consistently designate the patient by the genitive case of substantives. No substantives but only dative forms of adjectives are combined with the intransitive infinitives of the preceding distichs.

Besides the nominative, the marked cases are differently distributed in the two paragraphs of Kirša's song. The accusative, absent from §I, is represented in §II by three prepositional constructions with nouns and their adjectival attributes. There is no dative in §II, while in §I this case appears six times and is monopolized by independent adjectives, which in turn occur solely in the dative case. The instrumental figures in each paragraph only with a preposition in §I, and only without one in §II. The genitive takes part in negative constructions of §I five times without and twice with a preposition, whereas in §II—aside from the adverbialized *prežde vék*—this case figures once in partitive meaning and three times with the preposition *ot* (from). The only instance of the locative in the song, $_2$ *v góre,* confronted with the nominative $_1$ *góre-góre,* carries the syntactic and morphologic contrast between these two cases, one compulsorily prepositional and the other always prepositionless.

No events are reported in §I; its sole topic lies in explicitly negative situations perpetually returning (4–5) or necessarily inferred from unhappy premises. The independent infinitives, either directly negated or accompanied by negatives, assert intolerability, inconceivability, impossibility.[55] The person involved in these infinitive constructions is introduced by the multiple dative forms as a mere addressee of the verdicts pronounced; he remains unnamed and merely qualified by adjectives. When, in the last two distichs of this pararaph, genuine transitive actions are introduced, no actor is revealed; only their goal is designated by metaphorical nouns. The virtual completion of these perfectivized actions is negated, and their goals bear the severe genitive of negation, which, in general, dominates the nouns throughout all the distichs of §I; the accidental, ephemeral *grívna* is the only exception among the nouns individualized by the singular number, whereas plurals emerge in the marginal instrumental case with the anticipatory preposition *pered.* The grammatical imagery of grim devastation here reaches its culmination.

In contradistinction to the sententious style of §I, the first distich of §II immediately starts a new, narrative tone. Each of the parallelled clauses contains a noun in the nominative as its subject and a verbal predicate with a modifier in the instrumental case. Number serves as an expressive variable: the plural of all three words in line 14 (*močalámi nógi izopútany*) is opposed to the singular of the corresponding forms in 13 (*lýkom góre podpojásalos'*), and this variation is supplemented by the difference between two kindred verbal voices—the reflexive and the passive. Both synecdochic expressions of misery (*nagotá i bosotá bezmérnaja,* an infinite want of apparel and footgear) are linked by contiguity and similarity. The traditional association between both instrumentals is attested by the folk proverb *Lýki da močály, a tudá ž pomčáli.* The symmetrical imagery of this distich reappears in the various songs of the same cycle surveyed by Ržiga, whereas *Povest' 361–362* violates the grammatical and lexical parallelism and weakens the portrayal of the *góre* by substituting a negative clause for the suggestive features which serve in folk poetry to achieve the personification of grief: *bóso, nágo, nét na góre ni nítočki, / ešče lýčkom góre podpojásano.*

Both paragraphs of Kirša's song begin with the same monostich and present an obvious correspondence between their initial distichs. In particular, the merging of grief and poverty stressed in lines 2–3 inspires the images of 13–14, where the misery of the griever is transferred, however, by a metonymical trope from the griever to the grief itself. Puškin, an attentive reader of Kirša's songs, singled out the figurative expression *lýkom góre podpojásalos'* as a "striking representation of misery."

The second line of this distich says, ambiguously, *nógi* without any possessive; "grief's feet" would create a violent catachresis, while "griever's feet" would hamper the gradual introduction of "fictio personae." The personification actually proceeds step by step. Line 13 is the first to present grief as an actor by providing *góre* with a predicate, but this preterit of neuter gender underscores the neuter—a preeminently inanimate gender—of the subject. This gender is focused on by all three words of this line, including the neuter modifier *lýkom,* against the background of the pervading feminine in $_{14}$ *močalámi nógi izopútany.* Only the further sentences with the subject *góre* will replace the neuter reflexive $_{13}$ *podpojásalos'* by the masculine active $_{16,\ 18}$ *zašél;* as a further step in this activation, the predicates to *góre* will be expressed by transitive verbs, $_{20}$ *vstrečáet* (meets) and *taščít* (draws). The climax is attained with the substitution of the masculine pronoun *ón* for *góre* at the very end of the final line.

The relation between lines 12 and 13 demands closer examination. In the reduplicated *góre góre* which opens the introductory line to both paragraphs, the first of the two identical words, $_1$ /GÓR'E *gór'e*/ stands in positional correspondence to $_2$ /v GÓR'E/, whereas it is the second occurrence in line 12 that corresponds to $_{13}$ /*lýkom* GÓR'E/. This divergence prompts a different phrasing of lines 1 and 12. In 1 and the subsequent lines, the boundary (|) between the two "speech measures"[56] lies between the second and third of the three main accents, and thus coincides with the boundary (|) of the two hemistichs: $_1$ *a i góre góre || gorevánʹice! ||* $_2$ *a v góre žít' || nekručínnu být', ||* $_3$ *nagómu xodít' || ne stydítisja. ||,* etc. In 13 and 14, on the other hand, the boundary between the two speech measures does not coincide with the boundary between the two hemistichs. In these lines the modifiers $_{13}$ *lýkom* and $_{14}$ *močalámi* are placed before the subjects $_{13}$ *góre* and $_{14}$ *nógi* and thus are separated from the predicates $_{13}$ *podpojásalos'* and $_{14}$ *izopútany*. This hyperbaton (separation of two syntactically connected words) means that the speech-measure boundary falls between the modifier and the subject, i.e. between the first and the second of the three principal accents. Such phrasing then spreads to the introductory line as well: $_{12}$ *a góre,* | *góre* | *gorevánꞌice,* ‖ $_{13}$ *a i lýkom* | *góre* | *podpojásalos',* ‖ $_{14}$ *močalámi* | *nógi* | *izopútany.* ‖

The root of *góre* or the whole word thrice repeated, either literally or with synonymous variations, is customarily tied to the same context within folk songs of like tenor. For instance, Sreznevskij's record of the grief song states: *K emu górjuško, góre górꞌkoe,* ‖ *iz-pod móstičku góre, s-pod kalínovogo,* ‖ *iz-pod kústyšku, s-pod rakítovogo,* ‖ *vo otópočkax góre vo lozóvenꞌkix,* ‖ *vo obóročkax góre vo močálꞌnenꞌkix;* ‖ *močáloj góre priopútavši,* ‖ *ono lýkom góre opojásavši.*[57] In one variant from the Saratov region the corresponding passage reads: *Oj ty, góre moe, góre, góre séroe,* ‖ *lýčkom svjázannoe, podpojásannoe,* and in a different Saratov variant: *Ox ti, góre, toská-pečálꞌ.*[58] Compare the traditional formula: *Ax ja bédnaja gorjúša gore—górꞌkaja.*[59]

While at the beginning of Kirša's song the threefold evocation of *góre* acts as a syntactically separate apostrophe, in §II the same sequence reappears as an anticipatory, repetitive subject in respect to the clause $_{13}$ *góre podpojásalos'*. Whatever might have been the original wording of line 11, Kirša's variant displays a paronomastic bond between $_{11}$ /ATLÁsu/ and $_{13}$ /potpojÁSALos/; bark supersedes the precious satin.

Góre of line 1 was responded to by the degrading $_2$ *v góre* and remained unnamed in the further lines of §I, whereas in §II almost every line is permeated with this noun. The metrical place of the nominative *góre*, which line 13 shares with the second *góre* in 12, is maintained by the genitive *górja* in 15, 17, 19, while the nominative *góre* in 16, 18, 20 in turn shares its position with the initial *góre* in 12.

A far-reaching symmetry interconnects both paragraphs. Their initial distichs, in conformity with the terminal diminutive *gorevánꞌice* of the introductory line, attempt to minimize the grief. The griever and pauper seems to disregard his grief and misery which are subject to raillery (2–3), and poverty is said to be just as transitory as wealthiness

(4–5). It is not the griever but grief itself which turns out to be miserable (13–14). These endeavors to dismiss the tragic topic yield in both paragraphs to six-line groups with desperate avowals of ubiquitous and perpetual damnation. An anaphoric constant fastens together all the lines of each hexastich; in the string 6–11 every line begins with the negation *ne* attached to an infinitive, and in the string 15–20 with the repetitive conjunction *a* succeeded by a nominative.[60] The same connective *a*, alone or combined with *i*, opens the monostich of both paragraphs and also each separate distich outside these serried hexastichs, whereas the second line of every separate distich is devoid of connectives. The double connective *a i* and the single *a* display a regular alternation: $_1$ *a i*, $_2$ *a*, $_4$ *a i*, $_{12}$ *a*, $_{13}$ *a i*, $_{15-20}$ *a*.

The hexastich 15–20 is built on the parallelism of three entire distichs. "Parallel terms in alternate lines" occupy the second position in Kūkai's classification. All three odd lines of the hexastich share their initial hemistich *a já ot górja* and the grammatical pattern of the second hemistich—the locational preposition $_{15, 17}$ *v* or $_{19}$ *na* with a noun in the accusative preceded by its epithet. All three even lines of the hexastich begin with *a góre* and end with a finite verb: $_{16}$ *zašël* ~ $_{18}$ *sidít* ~ $_{20}$ *taščit*. Thus the three odd lines of the hexastisch on the one hand and its three even lines on the other are tied together by two kinds of correspondences: the anaphoric parallelism is literally repetitive, whereas the epiphoric parallelism is based on mere similarity of grammatical and lexical meanings.

Lines 18 and 20 have a finite form at the end of both hemistichs and thus display an internal parallelism; in 16 the end of the first hemistich is apparently missing, and one may guess that here, as in the two other even lines, the hemistich contained a complete clause, e.g., *a góre* [*už tám*].[61]

This hexastich explicitly disjoins the griever and the grief. The first, repeated hemistich of the odd lines—*a já ot górja*—suggests an interplay of two different semantic interpretations: "afflicted by" and "away from" grief. In the proverb *Ot górja bežál, da v bedú popál* (ran away from grief but got into trouble) the abstract meaning of grief is supported by its juxtaposition with trouble, and the concrete predicates function here as verbal metaphors. The directional modifiers "into forests," "to a feast," "into a tavern" would still allow the conception of grief as the griever's status, but the even lines definitely impute personality to *góre*. The polyptotic confrontation of the genitivus separationis ₁₅,₁₇,₁₉ *ot górja* and of the nominative ₁₆,₁₈,₂₀ *góre* introduces a shrill semantic antithesis of the flight from grief and into the arms of the omnipresent grief. Line 18, *a góre zašël—vperedí sidít*, is particularly characteristic in its "bifunctionalism": *vperedí* means simultaneously priority in time and in rank (*mestničestvo*).[62] The vicious circle traced in each of the three distichs is preluded by the grammatical antonymy between the hemistichs of each odd line, which oppose the genitive *ot górja* in its ablative function to the allative function of the accusatives *v lesá, na pír, v kabák*. In §I the parallelism of hemistichs is antonymic in contradistinction to the synonymic parallelism of lines; in the hexastich of §II the correspondence between alternating lines is synonymic while between adjacent lines it is antonymic. As to the parallelism of hemistichs in this hexastich, it is synonymic within the even lines and antonymic within the odd lines.[63]

The organic parts of this threefold parallel structure, with their increasing intensity and the image of the tavern as the last attempted refuge, appear to be scattered and disparate throughout the *Povest'*; cf. *170: prišël molodéc na césten pír* and *305: Ty pojdí, molodéc, na carëv kabák;* also *353: Ino kínus' ja mólodec v bystrú rekú.*

The scene of action is determined and delimited by three ablative prepositional constructions with genitives and by three allative, likewise prepositional constructions with accusatives that are additionally characterized by epitheta ornantia. The paragraph is rich in grammatical subjects and, after having introduced two nouns with verbal predicates, it inaugurates the hexastich with the nominative *já* (I) in a reiterative verbless phrase—the first instance of a pronoun in the song. The predicates of *góre* in §II progressively enlarge the designated sphere and effect of action; from the reflexive (13) they pass to the active voice (16–20) and from the perfective preterit (13, first half of 18) to the imperfective present, which denotes actions of limitless unfolding (second half of 18, 20). The intransitive verbs (13–18) yield to two transitive verbs (20), the first of which appears without any object (*vstrečáet*), while the second governs a partitive genitive (*píva taščít*). No direct accusative object finds a place in the song, whereas the image of grief's complete dominance over the lad is familiar to the *Povest'*. *349: Axti mné, zločástie gorínskoe! 350: do bedý menja mólodca domýkalo, 351: umorílo menja mólodca smért'ju golódnoju.* The shift from intransitive to transitive verbs again draws together the ends of both paragraphs.

The middle one of the three main accents falls on /o/ in all verses from lines 12 to 19 except the defective 16: $_{12, 13}$ *góre* $\sim _{14}$ *nógi* $\sim _{15, 17}$ *górja* $\sim _{18}$ *zašël* $\sim _{19}$ *górja*. A relation of mirror symmetry ties together the first line of the hexastich with the first line of the separate distich in their sound texture—$_{13}$ /Líkom GÓR'e potpojÁsalos/ $\sim _{15}$ /JÁ odGÓR'a ft'emni/. The last word of 13, paronomastically linked with 11 (as shown above), is echoed by the final words of the two following lines—$_{13}$ /POTPOJÁSLos/ $\sim _{14}$/izOPÚTani/ $\sim _{15}$/LSÁ/.

The consistent gradation of grief's activity finds eloquent expression in the lexical and phonemic distribution thoughout the hexastich. The two margins of line 16—*a góre . . . zašël*—are reiterated and condensed in the first hemistich of 18—*a góre zašël*—while the second hemistich, united by the repetition of its stressed syllable—/ft'er'eD'i s'iD'it/—is echoed by the double /i/ in the corresponding hemistich of 20—/p'íva taščít/. The stressed vowels of the thrice repeated hemistich *a já ot górja* are reversed in the second half of $_{19}$ *na carëv kabák* and again in the adjacent hemistich of $_{20}$ *a góre vstrečáet*: /áó/ $\sim$ /óá/ $\sim$ /óá/.

The concluding monostich of the song, $_{21}$ *kák ja nág to stál, nasme-jálsja ón*, differs grammatically and (see below) also metrically from the rest of the text; namely, it encompasses two different subjects with two different predicates, which are the only hypotactic clauses in the song, and the final word of this line is the sole anaphoric pronoun. This pairless line exhibits an internal chiastic parallelism: in the first hemistich the subject is followed and in the second one preceded by a perfective masculine preterit.

The sound texture ties the finale with the initial line of the adjacent distich: $_{19}$/kabák/ $\sim _{21}$ /kák já nák/; and both hemistichs of the terminal line are manifestly interconnected: /JÁ NÁk to stÁL/ $\sim$ /NASm'eJÁLsa/. In general the confrontation of the two hemistichs is particularly prominent in this independent line. For the first time the subjects designating both heroes appear in close juxtaposition. Their inequality is apparent. *Ja*, in contradistinction to *ón*, fills an upbeat and belongs to a subordinate clause. Only here does *ja* serve as part of a verbal clause, but this verb in turn is a mere copula which endows the subject with a new predicate adjective, whereas seven autonomous notional verbs relate as predicates to "grief." No verbs of action and no nouns are assigned in the song to its sole human hero, whose lyric ego finds its peculiar expression in the impersonal gnomic distichs of §I and then in the epic, self-effacing story of persecution. Simple finite forms of notional verbs all have third-person-singular subjects: 5, 13, 16, 18, 20, 21.

The motif of nakedness reappears for the third time: $_3$ *nagómu xodit'* (to walk naked); the imagery of undress in 13–14; and now $_{21}$ *kák ja nág to stál* (when I became naked). Whereas originally the naked griever was compelled to deride his own grief and misery, and then later claimed that actually grief was wretched and stripped, now finally grief ('qui rira le dernier') jeers at the divestiture of the miserable griever with a transparent paronomastic reminiscence of the bark girdle: $_{14}$ /*potpo*JÁSAL*os*/ $\sim$ $_{21}$ /*nasm'e*JÁLSA/. The circle, opened with the triple apostrophe to *góre*, is closed by the pronoun $_{21}$ *ón*, referring to the same fatal apparition.

IV

The verse of Kirša's song implements the oral epic meter with its traditional trochaic tendency and six downbeats interlaid with five up-beats.[64] The initial downbeat with the following upbeat forms the on-set (anacrusis) of the line, the final downbeat with the preceding up-beat builds the offset (coda), and the sequence from the first internal downbeat to the last internal downbeat has been termed the verse stem. The weak, external downbeats, that is, the final beat of the offset, and especially the initial syllable of the onset, are for the most part filled by unstressed or weakly stressed syllables. Of the internal (stem) downbeats the heaviest are the first and the last, both of which are almost constantly implemented by strongly stressed syllables. The regressive undulatory curve inherent in Russian verses regulates the distribution of stresses among the internal downbeats, weakens the next to last and reinforces the second from last, so that the third of the internal downbeats very rarely carries a stressed syllable, and the second of these downbeats is predominantly supplied with a word stress. Hence the first, the second, and the fourth internal downbeats carry the three leading accents of the verse.

Line 1 of Kirša's song—*A i {góre góre gorevàn'}ice* (with the verse stem enclosed in braces)—strictly follows the outlined metrical design. Of the twenty-one lines, ten maintain the hendecasyllabic pattern, six are reduced to ten syllables, and three to nine: in line 8 a twelfth syllable is inserted, while the octosyllabic line 16 is apparently defective. In the overwhelming majority of lines (14 of 21) the third of the four internal downbeats is immediately preceded by a word boundary; these lines correspondingly terminate with a five-syllable segment (e.g. *gorevàn'ice*).

The variations of the metrical design are closely linked with the composition of the song and its division into parallelistic groups of lines. As soon as *grief* is introduced by the first line, every new mention of *góre* or of *ja* in the close neighborhood of *góre* at the beginning of the verse stem emphatically reduces the onset to one syllable: $_2$ *a v góre*, $_{12, 16, 18, 19}$ *a góre*, $_{15, 17, 19}$ *a já ot górja*. The same reduction in $_3$ *nagómu* is engendered by its phonemic parallelism with $_2$ *a v góre*. The rest of the lines preserve the disyllabic onset. In this connection a peculiarity of Russian verse is to be noted, frequent cases where the syllabic scheme is retained but the stresses deviate from the metrical pattern: $_3$*nagómu xodit'*, $_8$ *ne otrostít'*, $_9$ *ne otkormít' konjá;* here, to be sure, the dialectal accents *otróstit'*, *otkórmit'*, and *kónja* may be assumed,[65] but a contrived discrepancy between the ictuses and verbal accents must be admitted in such instances as $_{18}$ *a góre zašel* or the hendecasyllable $_{20}$ *a góre vstrečáet, píva taščít*, where a scanning would require *góre* and *pivá*.

The three opening distichs of the song are internally cemented and differentiated by dissimilar endings of the initial hemistich. The entire verse pattern of the introductory model line (1) is strictly followed by the second of these three distichs (4–5); the preceding two lines curtail their first hemistich by a masculine close—$_2$ *žít'* ~ $_3$ *xodít'* —and correspondingly in the verse end $_2$ *být'*. Conversely, the last of the three distichs expands in the first hemistich of both lines to seven syllables by a dactylic close encompassing the third, prefinal downbeat of the verse stem, and correspondingly shortens the second hemistich to four syllables. The following distich returns to the pentasyllabic pattern of the final hemistich, but in 8 nonetheless it maintains the heptasyllabic scheme of the initial hemistich, as prompted by lines 6 and 7, while restoring its hexasyllabic measure in 9. Possibly the first hemistichs in both lines of this distich display also a shift of stresses. In the last distich of the first paragraph (10–11) the even hemistich assumes the same tetrasyllabic shape as in the second from last distich (6–7), whereas the next to last (8–9) and third from last (4–5) distichs use the pentasyllabic form. The rhythmic novelty of the distich 10–11 lies in the end of the odd hemistich, which in 10 is the only one throughout the entire song to shift the word stress from the second internal downbeat to the third (*Ne utéšiti ditjá*), whereas in 11 the syllable to carry the third internal downbeat is omitted.

The initial, epically tinged distich of the second paragraph (13–14)

with its narrative preterit construction— *A i lýkom góre podpojásalos'* —
follows the standard epic form of the tone-setting line 1 and of the
distich 4–5, the only distich in the first paragraph with a verb in the
past tense, and develops precisely the closing motif of that distich:
the theme of imminent penury. These two cognate distichs and the
expository line 1 are the only ones in the entire song that begin with
the anacrusis *a i* (Kirša's manuscript writes *ai*) typical of the byliny.

The hexastich 15–20 differs sharply from the preceding text. The final syllable of each of the six lines carries a syntactically relevant word
stress, which in five cases falls on disyllabic words, and only once on a
monosyllable ($_{17}$ *pír*). The two examples of final stress in the earlier
lines belong to weak monosyllables, virtual enclitics: the copula in
$_2$ *nekručinnu byt'* and the second part of the loose compound *zlýdni*
(penury), which allows a declensional inflection of both components—
$_5$ *pered zlými dnì*.

The reduced onset of these lines and the peculiar tension between
the syllabic and accentual pattern were discussed above. The omission
of a border syllable between the hemistichs is apparent in lines 15 and
17–19. The high ratio of stressed syllables singles out this hexastich
and, even more strikingly, the concluding monostich of the song. Both
external downbeats—*kák* and *ón*—are implemented by stressed monosyllables. Three of the eleven syllables carry stressed downbeats in the
first line of the song, and five of the ten in its last line. Here Slavic and
particularly Russian epic verse, based on internal asymmetry, yields to
a perfect metrical parallelism of pentasyllabic hemistichs.[66] The odd
hemistich, consisting exclusively of monosyllables in both downbeats
and upbeats—*Kàk ja nág to stál* (all five written separately in Kirša's
manuscript, where proclitics are always joined to the adjacent word)—
signals the denouement of the rhythmic development. The moving
force is ebbing, the powerful contrast between tops and slacks is fading. The startling dramatism and picturesque variety of rhythmic figures come abruptly to an end under the murderous raillery of the
omnipresent persecutor.

These cursory remarks on the metrical parallelism in Kirša's song
could be concluded with a repeated reminder of Hightower's observations on Chinese poetics: "It is on this underlying pattern or series
of patterns that the more subtle forms of grammatical and phonic parallelism introduce their counterpoint, a series of stresses and strains."

V

Hightower introduces his tentative translation of Chinese parallelistic compositions by qualifying their reading as an "exercise in verbal polyphony" (p. 69). "The extraordinary exuberance in both quantity and variety of the repetitive parallelism of the Song of Deborah" was pointed out in Albright's paper "The Psalm of Habakkuk" and suspected of going back to a "Canaanite rococo . . . which we may suppose to have been popular about the first half of the twelfth century B.C." The "excessiveness of parallelism and terminal sound correspondences" in the verbal mastery of the narrator (*skazitel'*) Kalinin, whose byliny were recorded by Hilferding, suggested to Žirmunskij an association with the baroque style (p. 337). Such examples could be easily multiplied, and they clash with the fictitious but still indelible view of parallelism as a survival of a primevally helpless, tongue-tied means of expression. Even Miklosich explained the repetitive, parallelistic devices in the Slavic epic tradition by the incapacity of the singer of the "nature epic" to disengage himself immediately from an idea and by the consequent necessity to utter "a thought or a series of thoughts more than once" and referred to the Finnish parallelism as a typical example.[67]

The search for the origin of parallelism in the antiphonal performance of the paired lines is perplexed by the overwhelming majority of parallelistic systems which show no trace of any amoebean technique. The repeated attempts to derive parallelism from a mental automatism which underlies any oral style and from mnemotechnical processes upon which the oral performer is forced to rely[68] are invalidated on the one hand by the abundance both of entire folk traditions totally unfamiliar with pervasive parallelism and of different poetic genres that within one folklore system are opposed to each other by the presence or absence of this device; on the other hand, such thousands-of-years-old written poetry as that of China adheres to the parallelistic rules which are somewhat relaxed in the native folklore (Jabłoński, p. 22).

Herder, "the great advocate of parallelism" according to his own expression (p. 24), resolutely attacked the afterward repeatedly enunciated bias that "parallelism is monotonous and presents a perpetual tautology" (p. 6) and that "if everything has to be said twice, then the first saying must have been only half achieved and defective" (p. 21). Herder's succinct reply—"Haven't you ever seen a dance before?"—followed by a comparison of Hebrew poetry with such a dance, transfers grammatical parallelism from the class of genetic debilities and their remedies into the proper category of purposive poetic devices. Or, to quote another master and theoretician of poetic language, Hopkins, the artifice of poetry "reduces itself to the principle of parallelism": equivalent entities confront one another by appearing in equivalent positions.

Any form of parallelism is an apportionment of invariants and variables. The stricter the distribution of the former, the greater the discernibility and effectiveness of the variations. Pervasive parallelism inevitably activates all the levels of language: the distinctive features, inherent and prosodic, the morphologic and syntactic categories and forms, the lexical units and their semantic classes in both their convergences and divergences acquire an autonomous poetic value. This focusing upon phonological, grammatical, and semantic structures in their multiform interplay does not remain confined to the limits of parallel lines but expands throughout their distribution within the entire context; therefore the grammar of parallelistic pieces becomes particularly significant. The symmetries of the paired lines in turn vivify the question of congruences in the narrower margins of paired hemistichs and in the broader frame of successive distichs. The dichotomous principle underlying the distich may develop into a symmetrical dichotomy of much longer strings, like the two paragraphs of Kirša's song.

The pervasive parallelism of oral poetry attains such a refinement in "verbal polyphony" and its semantic tension that the myth of primitive poverty and paucity of creativeness once more betrays its unfitness.[69] Gonda is right when stating that in all these symmetrical compositions "there is abundant scope for variety" (p. 49). The choice and hierarchy of more bound and of more variable linguistic elements differ from system to system. Conjectural schemes of a gradual decomposition of canonical parallelism on the path from primitivism to highly developed forms are nothing but arbitrary constructs.

The pervasive parallelism used to build up line sequences must be accurately distinguished from single similes carrying the theme of lyric songs. Veselovskij[70] trenchantly separated the former device, labeled "rhythmic parallelism" and "familiar to Hebrew, Chinese, and Finnish poetry," from the latter, which he termed "psychological" or "sense imbued" (*soderžatel'nyj*) "parallelism" (p. 142). There are, however, inconsistencies in Veselovskij's delimination of the different modes of parallelism. Although similes bringing together natural scenery and human life are quite familiar to pervasively parallelistic patterns of poetry, Veselovskij considers any such parallel as a typical specimen of "sense imbued" parallelism, while any "slackening of intelligible correlations between the components of parallels" is branded as a decadence and decomposition of the originally sense imbued parallelism. The claimed result is "a set of rhythmic sequences without any meaningful correspondence instead of an alternation of internally connected images" (pp. 142, 163). Objections inevitably arise against the preconceived idea of a genetic filiation between the two varieties of parallelism, and against Veselovskij's examples of a mere "rhythmico-musical" balancing, in particular the Chuvash song adduced by him as the chief illustration: "The billows swell to attain the shore, the girl dresses up to attract the fiancé; the forest grows to become high, the girl friend grows up to be mature, she dresses her hair to be pretty." Verbs of growth and improvement are presented as goal-directed toward the highest aim. These lines would turn out to be a clear-cut instance of sense imbued, metaphoric parallelism if Veselovskij had applied here his sagacious criterion which later on revealed its pertinence in Propp's inquiry into the structural laws of traditional fairy tales.[71] "What matters is not the *identification* of human and natural life, and not the *comparison* which presupposes a dwelling upon the separateness of things compared, but a *juxtaposition* made on the basis of action . . . The parallelism of folk songs reposes first and foremost in the category of action" (pp. 131, 157). The parallelistic simile is determined not so much by the participants of the process as by their syntactically expressed interrelation. The Chuvash song discussed is a warning against a disregard for latent congruences; invariants hidden from the observer behind the surface variables occupy a significant place in the topology of parallelistic transformations.

With all its intricacy, the structure of parallelistic poetry appears diaphanous as soon as it is submitted to a close linguistic analysis, both of the parallel distichs and of their relationship within a broader context. The hexastich 4:8 in the Song of Solomon, discussed by Bertholet[72] and Albright,[73] is said to contain "allusions of unmistakably Canaanite mythological origin" and to belong to the most archaic poetic texts of the Bible. The following transcription is accompanied by a translation which nearly coincides with Albright's wording.

ʔittī millǝbānōn kallāh	With me from Lebanon, bride,
ʔittī millǝbānōn tābōʔī	with me from Lebanon come!
tāšūrī mērōʔš ʔǎmānāh	depart from the peak of Amanah,
mērōʔš śǝnīr wǝḥermōn	from the peak of Senir and Hermon,
mimmǝʕōnōt ʔǎrāyōt	from the lairs of lions,
mēharǝrēy nǝmērīm	from the mountains of leopards!

The whole hexastich is cemented by the six occurrences of the preposition "from" and by a noun as the second word unit of every line. Each of the three distichs has its own conspicuous structural properties. The first is the only one which repeats words in identical metrical positions. The first word pair is echoed in 2, and while the third words of the two lines belong to different parts of speech, they still follow the parallelistic pattern, since both the vocative function of the final noun in 1 and the imperative function of the final verb in 2 represent one and the same conative level of language.[74] Thus the first distich, alone in this fragment, fulfills the leading scheme of ancient Hebrew parallelism: *abc—abc* (or more exactly *abc¹—abc²*). In a similar way the Russian folksong treats imperatives as parallels to vocative terms: *Solovéj ty mój solovéjuško! ‖ Ne vzvivájsja ty vysokóxon'ko!*[75] "Nightingale!" and "Don't soar!", "Uncle!" and "Come!", "Brother!" and "Ride!" figure in binary formulas of Russian wedding songs.

All of the next four lines are syntactically united and differ from the first distich by the presence of nouns in the construct state. The second distich displays characteristic shifts in word position. The two verbs of the hexastich stand out vividly against the background of its twelve nouns; both are similar morphologically and syntactically and polar within the same semantic class—"come" with allative meaning and "depart" with ablative. Together they build an anadiplosis: the first distich is closed by one verb, and the second opens with the other verb; the former verb is preceded, and the latter followed by a prepositional construction. The medial *mērōʔš* of line 3 is repeated at the beginning of 4. In this shift the central place occupied by the second distich within the hexastich finds its clear-cut expression: in an interplay of dichotomy with trichotomy the same preposition "from" which introduces the three final, heptasyllabic, pervasively nominal lines is prefixed to the central word in the three initial, longer lines.

This shift is connected with a significant stylistic feature which Bharata's *Nāṭyaśāstra,* going back to the second century A.D., names *dīpaka* (condensed expression) and ranks together with three other figures of speech—simile, metaphor, and repetition. While discussing typical examples of such sentence contraction skillfully employed in Vedic poetics, Gonda notes that "if the verbal idea of two successive units is identical, the verb is very often omitted" (pp. 397 ff, 66, 226).[76] Precisely such an abbreviated repetition constitutes the biblical "incomplete parallelisms" in distichs quoted by Neuman (p. 152) from Amos, as for instance "And-I-raised-up some-of-your-sons for-prophets, ‖ and-some of-your-youths for-Nazarites." Obviously, this variety of parallels may be labeled "incomplete" (*abc-bc*), but only if the elliptic zero-verb (a^0) of lines 4, 5, 6 is not reckoned among the matched terms.[77] Of course, from the metrical point of view line 4 in its relation to 3 would become defective without the "compensation" provided by the divarication of one noun into two coordinate forms (with the only conjunction in the entire hexastich: $abc^1\text{-}bc^2c^3$), whereas the lines of the third distich remain metrically binomial but syntactically trinomial, including the zero verb: (*tāšûrī*) *mimmǝʕōnōt ʔărāyōt* etc. In just this cleavage between the metrical binomial and the virtual grammatical trinomial lies the particularity of the last distich, which, moreover, opposes its four plurals to the twelve singular forms (five of them proper names) of the first two distichs. The formally identical connection between the head noun and its nominal modifier in the medial and final distichs differs semantically: to the part-whole relation in 3 and 4 the lines 5 and 6 oppose a difference between dwelling and dwellers.

Finally, each line contains exactly two contiguous constituents which have isosyllabic correspondents in the parallel line, but both their position in the line and their number of syllables change from distich to distich:

I	II	III
$2\,4\tfrac{2}{3}$	$\tfrac{3}{2}\,2\,3$	$4\,3$

Both syllabic asymmetries—two against three in the first distich, and three against two in the second—rest upon a confrontation of trisyllabic verbs with disyllabic nominal forms.

The striking trait of the sound texture is the profusion of nasals (21) and their symmetrical distribution: three in each of the first three lines, four in each of the three following lines.

Rhyme has been repeatedly characterized as a condensed parallelism, but rigorous comparison of rhyme and pervasive parallelism shows that there is a fundamental difference. The *phonemic* equivalence of rhyming words is compulsory, whereas the linguistic level of any correspondence between two parallelled terms is subject to a free choice. The fluctuating distribution of different linguistic levels between variables and invariants imparts a highly diversified character to parallelistic poetry and provides it with ample opportunities to individualize the parts and to group them with respect to the wholes. Against a background of totally congruent lines, the sporadic concurrence of equivalence on one linguistic level with disagreement on another level acts as a forceful device. In the popular distich of a Russian folksong (Šejn, nos. 1510, 2128), negative parallelism supplants the image of the trumpet which sounds early in the morning (*ne trúbon'ka trúbit ráno pó utru*) or after the early dew (*ráno pó rose*) by the image of a girl who weeps for her braid (*pláčet ráno pó kose*). Both *po utru* or *po rose* and *po kose* are dative constructions with the same preposition *po*, but their syntactic function is quite different. With another preceding line the same second line appears in a distich quoted by Veselovskij: *Plávala vútica pó rose,* ‖ *plákala Mášin'ka pó kose* (The duckling swam after the early dew, Mašin'ka wept for her braid, p. 166). The syntactic parallelism stops at the last word, while there is a complete correspondence in morphologic structure, in the number of syllables, in the distribution of stresses and word boundaries, and, moreover, a striking phonemic likeness of the two marginal words: *plávala* ~ *plákala, pó rose* ~ *pó kose*. Both lines reiterate the consonants /v/ and /k/ which differentiate their initial words: *plávala* ~ *vútica; plákala* ~ *Mášin'ка* ~ *pó kose*. The imagery of the former variant, a contrast between auditory images—blowing and weeping—yields here to a customary chain of fluid images: water alluded to by the evocation of the swimming duck, dew, and the girl's tears.

A consistent linguistic analysis of pervasive parallelism cuts down the number of unmatched terms within the distichs; moreover, many of the quasi-unpaired lines prove to correspond one with another. The two terms of syntactic agreement obviously form a cohesive pair. This kind of parallelism, observed by Gevirtz in biblical poetry and termed "epithetic" (pp. 26, 49), is very frequent in Russian folksongs. Evgen'eva cites a typical example: *Záin'ka, popytájsja u vorót,* ‖ *Séren'koj, popytájsja u novýx,* literally 'Hare, try at the gate, Gray, try at the new'.

Likewise, the governing and governed terms appear to function as symmetrical forms "when firmly embedded in an otherwise impeccably parallel context," if one may apply Hightower's suitable expression (p. 63) also to such occurrences. Driver's remark about the second line which "in different ways supplements or completes" the first line of the distich applies to the relation of headwords and their modifiers, but the label "synthetic or constructive parallelism" that he attaches to this definition figures here in a sense which has nothing in common with the original meaning assigned to the same double term by Lowth and his followers.[78]

A line of two synonymous predicates matched by a line of two nearly synonymous accusatives—a direct object and its apposition—in a distich of a North Russian bride's lament is a typical example of a parallelism based on syntactic government: *Ugljadíla, uprimítila* || *Svoegó kormil'cja bátjuška* (I saw, I sighted My guardian father).[79] Another distich with a direct object in its second line does not, however, belong to this type: *Tut sidéla krásna dévica* || *I česála rúsy kóson'ki* (There was sitting a pretty girl And combing her russet tresses). Both nouns and their epithets function as morphologic parallels, with a notable equivalence of their two direct cases—the nominative and the accusative.

Not only agreement or government but also the relation between subject and predicate occasionally underlies parallel lines: *K tebé idút da žálujut* || *Tvoi mílye podrúžen'ki* (Here come and honor you Your dear bridesmaids; Šejn, no. 1470). On the semantic level, we observed that parallels may be either metaphoric or metonymic, based on similarity and contiguity respectively. Likewise, the syntactic aspect of parallelism offers two types of pairs: either the second line presents a pattern *similar* to the preceding one, or the lines complement each other as two *contiguous* constituents of one grammatical construction.

Finally, on closer examination an isolated line surrounded by paralleled distichs may turn out to be a "monomial parallel," according to Veselovskij's seemingly paradoxical designation (p. 205). Such a monostich may reflect either a simile reduced to a bare metaphoric expression with the complete omission of its guessable, usually familiar clue, or a double formula which is reiterated with an elliptic suppression of one of its members. The lamenting bride first addresses her father *Podojdú ja, molodëšen'ka,* || *Ja sprošú, gorjúxa bénnaja* (I shall come, I the juvenile, I shall ask, I the poor griever), then turns to her mother with a further lament, *Ja eščó, gorjúxa bénnaja,* ‖ *Pogljažú da, molodёšen'ka* (Now I shall, I the poor griever, look about, I the juvenile); but later, when appealing to her brothers and thereafter to her sisters, she contrasts the same formula to a single line: *Ja eščó pojdú, molodёšen'ka* (Now I shall go, I the juvenile; Sokolov, nos. 73–76). Such monostichs, which depend on a contiguity association with their total context, are the utmost abridgements of Bharata's *dīpaka* (condensed expression).

When listening to a discussion of philologists as to what kind of attributes may in poetry be considered as epithets, Vladimir Majakovskij interjected that for him any attribute whatsoever when appearing in poetry spontaneously becomes an epithet.[80] In a similar way, any word or clause when entering into a poem built on pervasive parallelism is, under the constraint of this system, immediately incorporated into the tenacious array of cohesive grammatical forms and semantic values. The metaphoric image of "orphan lines" is a contrivance of a detached onlooker to whom the verbal art of continuous correspondences remains aesthetically alien. Orphan lines in poetry of pervasive parallels are a contradiction in terms, since whatever the status of a line, all its structure and functions are indissolubly interlaced with the near and distant verbal environment, and the task of linguistic analysis is to disclose the levels of this coaction. When seen from the inside of the parallelistic system, the supposed orphanhood, like any other componential status, turns into a network of multifarious compelling affinities.[81]

CHAPTER 11

Baudelaire's "Les Chats"

With Claude Lévi-Strauss

1 Les amoureux fervents et les savants austères
2 Aiment également, dans leur mûre saison,
3 Les chats puissants et doux, orgueil de la maison,
4 Qui comme eux sont frileux et comme eux sédentaires.

5 Amis de la science et de la volupté,
6 Ils cherchent le silence et l'horreur des ténèbres;
7 L'Érèbe les eût pris pour ses coursiers funèbres,
8 S'ils pouvaient au servage incliner leur fierté.

9 Ils prennent en songeant les nobles attitudes
10 Des grands sphinx allongés au fond des solitudes,
11 Qui semblent s'endormir dans un rêve sans fin;

12 Leurs reins féconds sont pleins d'étincelles magiques,
13 Et des parcelles d'or, ainsi qu'un sable fin,
14 Étoilent vaguement leurs prunelles mystiques.

Fervent lovers and austere scholars
Love equally, in their ripe season,
Powerful and gentle cats, the pride of the house,
Who like them are sensitive to cold and like them
   sedentary.

Friends of learning and of voluptuousness,
They seek silence and the horror of the shadows;
Erebus would have taken them as his gloomy coursers,
If they were able to incline their pride to servitude.

They assume in dozing the majestic poses
Of grand sphinxes reclining in the depths of solitudes
Who seem to be asleep in a dream without end;

Their fertile loins are full of magic sparks,
And particles of gold, like fine grains of sand,
Vaguely fleck their mystic pupils with stars.

If one can give credence to the feuilleton "Le Chat Trott" by Champfleury, where this sonnet of Baudelaire was first published (*Le Corsaire,* November 14, 1847), it must already have been written by March 1840, and—contrary to the claims of certain exegetes—the early text in *Le Corsaire* and that in *Les Fleurs du mal* (1857) correspond word for word.

In the organization of the rhymes, the poet follows the scheme: aBBa CddC eeFgFg (upper-case letters being used to denote the lines ending in masculine rhymes and lower-case letters for the lines ending in feminine rhymes). This chain of rhymes is divided into three strophic units, namely, two quatrains and one sestet composed of two tercets, which form a certain whole since the disposition of the rhymes within this sestet is controlled in sonnets, as Grammont has shown, "by the same rules as in any strophe of six lines."[1]

The rhyme scheme of the sonnet in question is the corollary of three dissimilative rules:

1. Two plain (couplet) rhymes cannot follow one another.

2. If two contiguous lines belong to different rhymes, one of them must be feminine and the other masculine.

3. At the end of contiguous stanzas feminine lines and masculine lines alternate: $_4$*sédentaires*—$_8$*fierté*—$_{14}$*mystiques*.

Following the classical pattern, the so-called feminine rhymes always end in a mute syllable and the masculine rhymes in a fully sounded syllable. The difference between the two classes of rhymes persists equally in the current pronunciation which suppresses the "mute *e*" of the final syllable, the last fully sounded vowel being followed by consonants in all the feminine rhymes of the sonnet (*austères—sédentaires, ténèbres—funèbres, attitudes—solitudes, magiques—mystiques*), whereas all its masculine rhymes end in a vowel (*saison—maison, volupté—fierté, fin—fin*). The relation between the classification of rhymes and the choice of grammatical categories emphasizes the importance of the role played by grammar as well as by rhyme in the structure of this sonnet.

All the lines end with nominal forms, either substantive (8) or adjectival (6). All the substantives are feminine. The final noun is plural in the eight lines with a feminine rhyme, which are all longer, either by a syllable in the traditional manner or by a postvocalic consonant in present-day pronunciation, whereas the shorter lines, those with a masculine rhyme, end in all six cases with a singular noun.

In the two quatrains, the masculine rhymes are constituted by substantives and the feminine rhymes by adjectives, with the exception of the key word $_6$*ténèbres,* which rhymes with $_7$*funèbres.* We shall return later to the whole question of the relationship between these two particular lines. As far as the tercets are concerned, the three lines of the first tercet all end with substantives, and those of the second with adjectives. Thus the rhyme which links the two tercets—the only instance in this poem of a homonymous rhyme ($_{11}$*sans fin*—$_{13}$*sable fin*)—places a masculine adjective in opposition to a feminine substantive—and it is the only adjective, and the only example of the masculine gender, among the masculine rhymes in the sonnet.

The sonnet is made up of three complex sentences delimited by periods, that is, each of the two quatrains and the sestet. These three sentences display an arithmetical progression according to the number of independent clause and of the finite verbal forms: (1) one single finite (*aiment*); (2) two finites (*cherchent, eût pris*); (3) three finites (*prennent, sont, étoilent*). On the other hand, the subordinate clause in each of the three sentences has but one finite: (1) *qui . . . sont;* (2) *s'ils pouvaient;* (3) *qui semblent.*

This ternary division of the sonnet implies an antinomy between both two-rhyme sentences and the final three-rhyme sentence. It is counterbalanced by a dichotomy which divides the work into two coupled stanzas, that is, into two pairs of quatrains and two pairs of tercets. This binary principle, supported in turn by the grammatical organization of the text, also implies an antinomy, this time between the two initial subdivisions or stanzas of four lines and the two last stanzas of three lines. It is on the tension between these two modes of arrangement and between their symmetrical and dissymetrical constituents that the composition of the whole work is based.

There is a clear-cut syntactical parallel between the pair of quatrains on the one hand and the pair of tercets on the other. Both the first quatrain and the first tercet consist of two clauses, of which the second is relative, and introduced in both cases by the same pronoun, *qui.* This clause comprises the last line of its stanza and is dependent on a masculine plural substantive, which serves as accessory in the principal clause ($_3$*Les chats,* $_{10}$*Des . . . sphinx*). The second quatrain (and equally the second tercet) contains two coordinate clauses, of which the last, complex in its turn, comprises the two final lines of the stanza (7–8 and 13–14) and includes a subordinate clause which is linked to the main clause by a conjunction. In the quatrain this clause is conditional

($_8$*S'ils pouvaient*); that of the tercet is comparative ($_{13}$*ainsi qu'un*). The first is postpositive, whereas the second, incomplete, is an interpolated clause.

In the 1847 *Le Corsaire* text, the punctuation of the sonnet corresponds to this division. The first tercet ends with a period, as does the first quatrain. In the second tercet and in the second quatrain, the last two lines are preceded by a semicolon.

The semantic aspect of the grammatical subjects reinforces this parallelism between the two quatrains on the one hand and the two tercets on the other:

(I) Quatrains	*(II) Tercets*
(1) First	(1) First
(2) Second	(2) Second

The subjects of the first quatrain and of the first tercet designate only animate beings, whereas one of the two subjects of the second quatrain and all the grammatical subjects of the second tercet are inanimate substantives: $_7$*L'Érèbe*, $_{12}$*Leurs reins*, $_{13}$*des parcelles*, $_{13}$*un sable*. In addition to these so-called horizontal correspondences, there is a correspondence that could be called vertical, one which opposes the totality of the two quatrains to the totality of the two tercets. While all the direct objects in the two tercets are inanimate substantives ($_9$*les nobles attitudes*, $_{14}$*leurs prunelles*), the sole direct object of the first quatrain is an animate substantive ($_3$*les chats*). The objects of the second quatrain include, in addition to the inanimate substantives ($_6$*le silence et l'horreur*), the pronoun *les* which refers to *les chats* of the preceding sentence. If we look at the relationship between subject and object, the sonnet presents two correspondences which could be called diagonal. One descending diagonal links the two exterior stanzas (the first quatrain and the last tercet) and puts them in opposition to an ascending diagonal which links the two interior stanzas. In the exterior stanzas subject and object form part of the same semantic category: animate in the first quatrain (*amoureux, savants—chats*) and inanimate in the second tercet (*reins, parcelles—prunelles*). Conversely, in the interior stanzas, object and subject are in opposing categories: in the first tercet the inanimate object is opposed to the animate subject (*ils [chats]—attitudes*), whereas in the second quatrain the same relationship (*ils [chats]—silence, horreur*) alternates with that of the animate object and inanimate subject (*Érèbe—les [chats]*).

Thus, each of the four stanzas retains its own individuality: the animate class, which is common to both subject and object in the first quatrain, is peculiar to the subject only in the first tercet; in the second quatrain this class characterizes either subject or object, whereas in the second tercet, neither the one nor the other.

There are several striking correspondences in the grammatical structure both of the beginning and of the end of the sonnet. At the end as well as at the beginning, but nowhere else, there are two subjects with only one predicate and only one direct object. Each of these subjects, as well as their objects, has a modifier (*Les amoureux fervents, les savants austères—Les chats puissants et doux; des parcelles d'or, un sable fin—leurs prunelles mystiques*). The two predicates, the first and last in the sonnet, are the only ones accompanied by adverbs, both of them derived from adjectives and linked to one another by a deep rhyme: $_2$*Aiment également*—$_{14}$*Étoilent vaguement*. The second and penultimate predicates are the only ones that comprise a copula and a predicative adjective, the latter being emphasized in both cases by an internal rhyme: $_4$Qui comme *eux* sont fril*eux*; $_{12}$ Leurs *reins* féconds sont p*leins*. Generally speaking, only the two exterior stanzas are rich in adjectives: nine in the quatrain and five in the tercet; whereas the two interior stanzas have only three adjectives in all (*funèbres, nobles, grands*).

As we have already noted, it is only at the beginning and at the end of the poem that the subjects are of the same class as the objects: each one belongs to the animate class in the first quatrain and to the inanimate in the second tercet. Animate beings, their functions and their activities, dominate the initial stanza. The first line contains nothing but adjectives. Of these, the two substantival forms which act as subjects—*les amoureux* and *les savants*—display verbal roots: the text is inaugurated by "those who love" and by "those who know." In the last line of the poem, the opposite occurs: the transitive verb *étoilent*, which serves as a predicate, is derived from a substantive. The latter is related to the series of inanimate and concrete appellatives which dominate this tercet and distinguish it from the three anterior stanzas. A clear homophony can be heard between this verb and the members of the series in question: /etɛsɛlə/—/e de parsɛlə/—/etwalə/. Finally, the subordinate clauses contained in the last lines of these two medial stanzas each include an adverbial infinitive, these two object-complements being the only infinitives in the entire poem: $_8$*S'ils pouvaient . . . incliner*; $_{11}$*Qui semblent s'endormir.*

As we have seen, neither the dichotomous partition of the sonnet nor the division into three stanzas results in an equilibrium of the isometric constituents. But if one were to divide the fourteen lines into two equal parts, the seventh line would end the first half of the poem, and the eighth line would mark the beginning of the second half. It is, therefore, significant that just these two middle lines stand out most obviously in their grammatical makeup from the rest of the poem. Actually, in more than one respect, the poem falls into three parts: in this case into the middle pair of lines and two isometric groups, that is to say, the six lines which precede this pair and the six which follow it. Hence there emerges a kind of couplet inserted between two sestets.

All personal verb forms and pronouns and all the subjects of verbal clauses are plural throughout the sonnet, except in line 7, *L'Érèbe les eût pris pour ses coursiers funèbres,* which contains the only proper noun in the poem and is the only instance of both the finite verb and its subject being in the singular. Furthermore, it is the only line in which the possessive pronoun (*ses*) refers to a singular. Only the third person is used in the sonnet. The only verbal tense used is the present, except in lines 7 and 8, where the poet envisages an imaginary action ($_7$*eût pris*) arising out of an unreal premise ($_8$*S'ils pouvaient*).

The sonnet shows a pronounced tendency to provide every verb and every substantive with a modifier. Each verbal form is accompanied by a governed modifier (substantive, pronoun, infinitive) or by a predicative adjective. All transitive verbs govern only substantives ($_{2-3}$*Aiment . . . Les chats;* $_6$*cherchent le silence et l'horreur;* $_9$*prennent . . . les . . . attitudes;* $_{14}$*Étoilent . . . leurs prunelles*). The pronoun which serves as the object in the seventh line is the sole deviation: *les eût pris.*

With the exception of adnominal adjuncts which are never accompanied by any modifier in the sonnet, the substantives (including the substantivized adjectives) are always modified by attributes (for example, $_3$*chats puissants et doux*) or by adjuncts ($_5$*Amis de la science et de la volupté*); line 7 again provides the only exception *L'Érèbe les eût pris.*

All five attributes in the first quatrain ($_1$*fervents,* $_1$*austères,* $_2$*mûre,* $_3$*puissants,* $_3$*doux*) and all six in the two tercets ($_9$*nobles,* $_{10}$*grands,* $_{12}$*féconds,* $_{12}$*magiques,* $_{13}$*fin,* $_{14}$*mystiques*) are qualitative epithets, whereas the second quatrain has no adjectives other than the determinative attribute in the seventh line (*coursiers funèbres*). It is also this line which inverts the animate/inanimate order underlying the relation between subject and object in the other lines of this quatrain and which is, in fact, the only one in the entire sonnet to adopt this inanimate/animate order.

Several striking peculiarities clearly distinguish line 7 only, or the last two lines of the second quatrain, from the rest of the sonnet. However, it must be noted that the tendency for the medial distich to stand out agrees with the principle of an asymmetrical trichotomy, which puts the whole of the second quatrain in opposition to the first quatrain on the one hand and in opposition to the final sestet on the other, thus creating a kind of central strophe distinct in several respects from the marginal strophic units. We have already shown that only in line 7 are subject and predicate in the singular, but this observation can be extended: only in the second quatrain do we find either subject or object in the singular and whereas in line 7 the singularity of the subject (*L'Érèbe*) is opposed to the plurality of the object (*les*), the adjoining lines invert this relation, having a plural subject and a singular object (₆*Ils cherchent le silence et l'horreur;* ₈*S'ils pouvaient . . . incliner leur fierté*).

In the other stanzas, both object and subject are plural (₁₋₃*les amoureux . . . et les savants . . . Aiment . . . Les chats;* ₉*Ils prennent . . . les . . . attitudes;* ₁₃₋₁₄*Et des parcelles . . . Étoilent . . . leurs prunelles*). It is notable that in the second quatrain singularity of subject and object coincides with the inanimate and plurality with the animate class. The importance of grammatical number to Baudelaire becomes particularly noteworthy by virtue of the role it plays in opposition relations in the rhymes of the sonnet.

It must be added that the rhymes in the second quatrain are distinguishable by their structure from all other rhymes in the poem. The feminine rhyme *ténèbres—funèbres* in the second quatrain is the only one which brings together two different parts of speech. Moreover, all the rhymes in the sonnet, except those in the quatrain in question, comprise one or more identical phonemes, either immediately preceding or some distance in front of the stressed syllable, usually reinforced by a supportive consonant: ₁*savants austères*—₄*sédentaires,* ₂*mûre saison*—₃*maison,* ₉*attitudes*—*solitudes,* ₁₁*un rêve sans fin*—₁₃*un sable fin,* ₁₂*étincelles magiques*— ₁₄ *prunelles mystiques.* In the second quatrain, neither the pair ₅*volupté*—₈ *fierté,* nor ₆*ténèbres*—₇ *funèbres,* offer any correspondence in the syllable anterior to the rhyme itself. On the other hand, the final words in the seventh and eighth lines are alliterative, ₇*funèbres*—₈*fierté,* and the sixth and fifth lines are linked by the repetition of the final syllable of ₅volup*té* in ₆*té*nèbres and by the internal rhyme $_5$*science*—$_6$*silence,* which reinforces the affinity between the two lines. Thus the rhymes themselves exhibit a certain relaxation of the ties between the two halves of the second quatrain.

A salient role in the phonic texture of the sonnet is played by the nasal vowels. These phonemes, "as though veiled by nasality," as Grammont aptly puts it,[2] occur very frequently in the first quatrain (9 nasals, from 2 to 3 per line) but most particularly in the final sestet (22 nasals with increasing frequency throughout the first tercet, $_9$3—$_{10}$4—$_{11}$6: Qui s*em*blent s'*en*dormir d*ans un* rêve s*ans* f*in*; and with decreasing frequency throughout the second tercet, $_{12}$5—$_{13}$3—$_{14}$1). In contrast, the second quatrain contains only three: one per line, excepting the seventh, the sole line in the sonnet without a nasal vowel; this quatrain is also the only stanza where the masculine rhyme does not contain a nasal vowel. Then, again, it is in the second quatrain that the role of phonic dominant passes from vowels to consonantal phonemes, in particular to liquids. The second quatrain is the only one which shows an excessive number of these liquid phonemes, 24 in all, as compared to 15 in the first quatrain, 11 in the first tercet, and 14 in the second. The total number of /r/'s is slightly lower than the number of /l/'s (31 versus 33), but the seventh line, which has only two /l/'s, contains five /r/'s, that is to say, more than any other line in the sonnet: L'É*r*èbe les eût p*r*is pou*r* ses cou*r*siers funèb*r*es. According to Grammont, it is by opposition to /r/ that /l/ "gives the impression of a sound that is neither grating, rasping, nor rough but, on the contrary, that glides and flows, that is limpid."[3] The abrupt nature of every /r/, and particularly the French /r/, in comparison with the glissando of the /l/ is clearly illustrated in Durand's accoustical analysis of the two liquids.[4] The agglomeration of the /r/'s eloquently echoes the delusive association of the cats with Erebus, followed by the antithetic ascent of the empirical felines to their miraculous transfigurations.

The first six lines of the sonnet are linked by a characteristic reiteration: a symmetrical pair of coordinate phrases linked by the same conjunction *et*: $_1$*Les amoureux fervents et les savants austères;* $_3$*Les chats puissants et doux;* $_4$*Qui comme eux sont frileux et comme eux sédentaires;* $_5$*Amis de la science et de la volupté.* The binarism of the determinants thus forms a chiasmus with the binarism of the determined in the next line—$_6$*le silence et l'horreur des ténèbres*—which puts an end to these binary constructions. This construction, common to all the lines of this "sestet," does not recur in the remainder of the poem. The juxtapositions without a conjunction are a variation of the same scheme:

₂*Aiment également, dans leur mûre saison* (parallel circumstantial complements); ₃*Les chats . . . orgueil* (a substantive in apposition to another).

These pairs of coordinate phrases and their rhymes (not only those which are exterior and underline the semantic links such as ₁*austères—*₄*sédentaires,* ₂*saison—* ₃*maison,* but also and especially the internal rhymes) serve to draw the lines of this introduction closer together: ₁*amoureux—*₄*comme eux—*₄*frileux—*₄*comme eux;* ₁*fervents—*₁*savants—*₂*également—*₂*dans—*₃*puissants;* ₅*science—*₆*silence.* Thus all the adjectives characterizing the persons in the first quatrain are rhyme words, with the one exception ₃*doux.* A double etymological figure links the openings of three of the lines, ₁*Les amoureux—*₃*Aiment—*₅*Amis,* in accordance with the unity of this crypto-stanza of six lines, which starts and ends with a couplet, each of whose first hemistichs rhyme: ₁*fervents—*₂*également;* ₅*science—*₆*silence.*

Les chats, who are the direct object of the clause comprising the first three lines of the sonnet, become the implicit subject of the clauses in the following three lines (₄*Qui comme eux sont frileux;* ₆*Ils cherchent le silence*), revealing the outline of a division of this quasi-sestet into two quasi-tercets. The middle "distich" recapitulates the metamorphosis of the cats: from an implicit object (₇*L'Érèbe les eût pris*) into an equally implicit grammatical subject (₈*S'ils pouvaient*). In this respect the eighth line coincides with the following sentence (₉*Ils prennent*).

In general, the postpositive subordinate clauses form a kind of transition between the subordinating clause and the sentence which follows it. Thus, the implicit subject "chats" of the ninth and tenth lines changes into a reference to the metaphor "sphinx" in the relative clause of the eleventh line (*Qui semblent s'endormir dans un rêve sans fin*) and, as a result, links this line to the tropes serving as grammatical subjects in the final tercet. The indefinite article, entirely alien to the first ten lines with their fourteen definite articles, is the only one admitted in the four concluding lines of the sonnet.

Thus, thanks to the ambiguous references in the two relative clauses, in the eleventh and the fourth lines, the four concluding lines allow us to glimpse at the contour of an imaginary quatrain which somehow corresponds to the initial quatrain of the sonnet. On the other hand, the final tercet has a formal structure which seems reflected in the first three lines of the sonnet.

Animate subjects are never expressed by substantives, but either by substantivized adjectives, in the first line of the sonnet (*les amoureux, les savants*), or by personal and relative pronouns, in the further clauses. Human beings appear only in the first clause, in the form of a double subject supported by substantivized verbal adjectives.

The cats, named in the title of the sonnet, are called by name only once in the text, as the direct object in the first clause: $_1$*Les amoureux . . . et les savants . . .*$_2$*Aiment . . .*$_3$*Les chats.* Not only is the word *chats* avoided in the further lines of the poem, but even the initial hushing phoneme /ʃ/ recurs only in a single word: $_6$/ilʃɛrʃɛ/. It denotes, with reduplication, the first reported action of the felines. This voiceless sibilant, linked to the name of the poem's heroes, is carefully avoided throughout the remainder of the sonnet.

From the third line, the cats become an implicit subject, which proves to be the last animate subject in the sonnet. The substantive *chats,* in the roles of subject, object, and adnominal adjunct, is replaced by the anaphoric pronouns $_{6,8,9}$*ils,* $_7$*les,* $_{8,12,14}$*leur(s),* and it is only to *les chats* that the substantive pronouns *ils* and *les* refer. These accessory (adverbal) forms occur solely in the two interior stanzas, that is, in the second quatrain and in the first tercet. The corresponding autonomous form $_4$*eux* is used twice in the initial quatrain and refers only to the human characters of the sonnet, whereas no substantive pronouns occur in the final tercet.

The two subjects of the initial clause of the sonnet have one single predicate and one single object. Thus $_1$*Les amoureux fervents et les savants austères* end up $_2$*dans leur mûre saison* by finding their identity in an intermediary being, an animal which encompasses the antinomic traits of two human but mutually opposed conditions. The two human categories, sensual/intellectual, oppose each other, and the mediation is achieved by means of the cats. Hence the role of subject is latently assumed by the cats, who are at one and the same time scholars and lovers.

The two quatrains objectively present the personage of the cat, whereas the two tercets carry out his transfiguration. However, the second quatrain differs fundamentally from the first and, in general, from all the other stanzas. The equivocal formulation, *ils cherchent le silence et l'horreur des ténèbres,* gives rise to a misunderstanding summoned up in the seventh line of the sonnet and denounced in the following line. The aberrant character of this quatrain, especially the perplexity of its last half, and more particularly of line 7, is thoroughly marked by the peculiarities of its grammatical and phonic texture.

The semantic affinity between *L'Érèbe* ("dark region bordering on

Hell," metonymic substitute for "the powers of darkness" and particularly for Erebus, "brother of Night") and the cats' predilection for *l'horreur des ténèbres,* corroborated by the phonic similarity between /tenɛbrə/ and /erɛbə/, all but harness the cats, heroes of the poem, to the grisly task of *coursiers funèbres.* Does the line which insinuates that *L'Érèbe les eût pris pour ses coursiers* raise a question of frustrated desire or one of false recognition? The meaning of this passage, long puzzled over by the critics,[5] remains purposely ambiguous.

Each of the quatrains, as well as each of the tercets, tries to give the cats a new identity. While the first quatrain linked the cats to two types of human condition, thanks to their pride they succeed in rejecting the new identity put forward in the second quatrain, which would associate them with an animal condition: that of coursers placed in a mythological context. It is the only identification that is rejected in the course of the whole poem. The grammatical composition of this passage, which contrasts expressly with that of the other stanzas, betrays its peculiar character: unreal conditional, lack of qualitative attributes, and an inanimate singular subject devoid of any modifier and governing an animate plural object.

Allusive oxymorons unite the stanzas. $_8$*S'ils "pouvaient" au servage incliner leur fierté*—but they cannot do so (*ils ne "peuvent" pas*) because they are truly $_3$*puissants.* They cannot be passively taken ($_7$*pris*) to play an active role, and hence they themselves actively take ($_9$*prennent*) a passive role because they are obstinately *sédentaires.*

Leur fierté predestines them for the $_9$*nobles attitudes* $_{10}$*Des grands sphinx.* The $_{10}$*sphinx allongés* and the cats that mime them $_9$*en songeant* are united by a paranomastic link between the only two participial forms in the sonnet: /ãsɔ̃ʒã/ and /alɔ̃ʒe/. The cats seem to identify themselves with the sphinxes, who in their turn $_{11}$*semblent s'endormir,* but the illusory comparison, assimilating the sedentary cats (and by implication all who are $_4$*comme eux*), to the immobility of the supernatural beings, achieves the status of a metamorphosis. The cats and the human beings who are identified with them are reunited in the mythical beasts with human heads and animal bodies. Thus the rejected identification appears to be replaced by a new, equally mythological identification.

En songeant, the cats manage to identify themselves with the $_{10}$*grands sphinx.* A chain of paronomasias, linked to these key words and combining nasal vowels with continuant dentals and labials, reinforces the metamorphosis: $_9$*en songeant* /ãsɔ̃../—$_{10}$*grands sphinx*

/...āsfɛ̃../—$_{10}$*fond* /fõ/—$_{11}$*semblent* /sã.../—$_{11}$*s'endormir* /sã....../—$_{11}$*dans un* /.ãzœ̃/—$_{11}$*sans fin* /sãfɛ̃/. The acute nasal /ɛ̃/ and the other phonemes of the word $_{10}$*sphinx* /sfɛ̃ks/ recur in the last tercet: $_{12}$*reins* /.ɛ̃/—$_{12}$*pleins* /..ɛ̃/—$_{13}$*étincelles* /.. ɛ̃s... /—$_{13}$*ainsi* /ɛ̃s/—$_{13}$ *qu'un sable* /kœ̃s... /—$_{13}$*fin* /fɛ̃/.

We read in the first quatrain: $_3$*Les chats puissants et doux, orgueil de la maison.* Does this mean that the cats, proud of their home, are the incarnation of that pride, or that the house, proud of its feline inhabitants, tries, like Erebus, to domesticate them? Whichever it may be, the $_3$*maison* which circumscribes the cats in the first quatrain is transformed into a spacious desert, $_{10}$*fond des solitudes.* And the fear of cold, bringing together the cats, $_4$*frileux,* and the lovers, $_1$*fervents* (note the paronomasia /fɛrvã/—/frilø/), is dispelled by the appropriate climate of the austere solitudes (as austere as the scholars) of the desert (torrid like the fervent lovers) which surrounds the sphinxes. On the temporal level, the $_2$*mûre saison,* which rhymed with $_3$*la maison* in the first quatrain and approached it in meaning, has a clear counterpart in the first tercet. These two visibly parallel groups of words ($_2$*dans leur mûre saison* and $_{11}$*dans un rêve sans fin*) mutually oppose each other, the one evoking numbered days and the other, eternity. No constructions with *dans* or with any other adverbial preposition occur elsewhere in the sonnet.

The miraculous quality of the cats pervades the two tercets. The metamorphosis unfolds right to the end of the sonnet. In the first tercet the image of the sphinxes stretched out in the desert already vacillates between the creature and its simulacrum, and in the following tercet the animate beings disappear behind particles of matter. Synecdoche substitutes for the cat-sphinxes various parts of their bodies: $_{12}$*leurs reins* (the loins of the cats), $_{14}$*leurs prunelles* (the pupils of their eyes). In the final tercet, the implicit subject of the interior stanzas again becomes an accessory part of the sentence. The cats appear first as an implicit adjunct of the subject—$_{12}$*Leurs reins féconds sont pleins*—then, in the poem's last clause, they function as a mere implicit adjunct of the object: $_{14}$*Étoilent vaguement leurs prunelles.* Thus the cats appear to be linked to the object of the transitive verb in the last clause of the sonnet and to the subject in the penultimate, antecedent clause, thereby establishing a double correspondence on the one hand with the cats as direct object in the first clause of the sonnet and, on the other, with the cats as subject of its second clause.

Whereas at the beginning of the sonnet both subject and object were of the animate class, the two similar parts of the final clause both belong to the inanimate class. In general, all the substantives in the last tercet are concrete nouns of the same class: $_{12}$*reins*, $_{12}$*étincelles*, $_{13}$*parcelles*, $_{13}$*or*, $_{13}$*sable*, $_{14}$*prunelles*, while in all previous stanzas the inanimate appellatives, except for the adnominal ones, were abstract nouns: $_2$*saison*, $_3$*orgueil*, $_6$*silence*, $_6$*horreur*, $_8$*servage*, $_8$*fierté*, $_9$*attitudes*, $_{11}$*rêve*. The inanimate feminine gender, common to the subject and to the object of the final clause—$_{13-14}$*des parcelles d'or . . .Étoilent . . . leurs prunelles*—counterbalances the subject and object of the initial clause, which both belong to the animate masculine gender—$_{1-3}$*Les amoureux . . . et les savants . . . Aiment . . . Les chats. Parcelles* in line 13 is the only feminine subject in the whole sonnet, and it contrasts with the masculine *sable fin* at the end of the same line, which in turn is the only example of the masculine gender among the sonnet's masculine rhymes. In the last tercet, the ultimate particles of matter serve in turns as object and subject. A new identification, the last within the sonnet, associates these incandescent particles with *sable fin* and transforms them into stars.

The remarkable rhyme which links the two tercets is the only homonymous rhyme in the whole sonnet and the only one among its masculine rhymes which juxtaposes different parts of speech. There is also a certain syntactic symmetry between the two rhyme words, since both end subordinate clauses, one of which is complete and the other, elliptical. The correspondence, far from being confined to the final syllable, closely brings the whole of both lines together: $_{11}$/sãblə sãdɔrmir dãnzœ̃ rɛvə sã fɛ̃/—$_{13}$/parsɛlə dɔr ɛ̃si kœ̃ sablə fɛ̃/. It is not by chance that precisely the rhyme that links the two tercets evokes *un sable fin*, thus taking the desert motif up again, in the same position as *un rêve sans fin* of the *grands sphinx* appears in the first tercet.

La maison, which circumscribes the cats in the first quatrain, is abolished in the first tercet with its realm of desert solitudes, true unfolded house of the cat-sphinxes. In its turn, this "nonhouse" yields to the cosmic innumerability of the cats (these, like all the personae of the sonnet, are treated as *pluralia tantum*). They become, so to speak, the house of the nonhouse, since within the irises of their eyes they enclose the sand of the deserts and the light of the stars.

The epilogue takes up again the initial theme of lovers and scholars united in *Les chats puissants et doux*. The first line of the second tercet seems to answer the first line of the second quatrain; the cats being

$_5$*Amis . . . de la volupté,* $_{12}$*Leurs reins féconds sont pleins.* One is tempted to believe that this has to do with the procreative force, but Baudelaire's works easily invite ambiguous solutions. Is it a matter of a power particular to the loins or of electric sparks in the animal's fur? Whatever it may be, it is a "magic" power that is attributed to them. But the second quatrain opened with two collateral adjuncts: $_5$*Amis de la science et de la volupté,* and the final tercet alludes not only to the $_1$*amoureux fervents* but to the $_1$*savants austères* as well.

In the last tercet, the rhyming suffixes emphasize the strong semantic link between the $_{12}$*éti*ncelles, $_{13}$*par*celles *d'or* and $_{14}$*prun*elles of the cat-sphinxes on the one hand and, on the other, between the sparks $_{12}$*Mag*iques emanating from the animal and its pupils $_{14}$*Myst*iques illuminated by an inner light and open to a hidden meaning. This is the only rhyme in the sonnet which is stripped of its supporting consonant, as if to lay bare the equivalence of the morphemes, and the alliteration of the initial /m/'s ties the two adjectives even closer together. $_6$*L'horreur des ténèbres* vanishes before this double luminance, which is reflected on the phonic level by the predominance of phonemes of light timbre (acute tonality) among the nasal vowels of the final stanza (6 front versus 3 back vowels), whereas there was a far greater number of nasal vowels of grave tonality in the preceding stanzas (9 versus o in the first quatrain, 2 versus 1 in the second, and 10 versus 3 in the first tercet).

Due to the preponderance of synecdochic tropes at the end of the sonnet, where parts of the animal are substituted for the whole and, on the other hand, the animal itself is substituted for the universe of which it is a part, the images seek, as if by design, to lose themselves in imprecision. The definite article gives way to the indefinite article and the adverb which accompanies the verbal metaphor—$_{14}$*Étoilent vaguement*—brilliantly reflects the poetics of the epilogue. The conformity between the tercets and the corresponding quatrains (horizontal parallelism) is striking. The narrow limits of space ($_3$*maison*) and of time ($_2$*mûre saison*) imposed in the first quatrain are opposed in the first tercet by the removal or suppression of boundaries ($_{10}$*fond des solitudes,* $_{11}$*rêve sans fin*). Similarly, in the second tercet, the magic of the light radiating from the cats triumphs over $_6$*l'horreur des ténèbres,* which nearly wrought such deception in the second quatrain.

Now, in drawing together the parts of our analysis, we shall try to show how all these different levels blend, complement each other, or combine to give the poem the value of an absolute object.

To begin with, the divisions of the text: Several can be distinguished which are perfectly clear, as much from the grammatical point of view as from the semantic relations between different parts of the poem. As we have already pointed out, there is a primary division corresponding to the three parts, each of which ends with a period, namely, the two quatrains and the ensemble of the two tercets. The first quatrain presents, in the form of an objective and static picture, a factual situation or one that purports to be so. The second quatrain attributes to the cats a purpose that is interpreted by the powers of Erebus, and to the powers of Erebus, a purpose in regard to the cats, which the latter reject. Thus, in these two sections, the cats are seen from without, first through the passivity to which lovers and scholars are especially susceptible and, second, through the activity perceived by the powers of Erebus. By contrast, in the last part of the sonnet this opposition is overcome by acknowledging a passivity actively assumed by the cats, no longer interpreted from without but from within.

A second division enabled us to oppose the ensemble of the two tercets to the ensemble of the two quatrains, at the same time revealing a close connection between the first quatrain and the first tercet and between the second quatrain and the second tercet. As a matter of fact:

1. The ensemble of the two quatrains is opposed to the ensemble of the two tercets in the sense that the latter dispenses with the point of view of the observer (*amoureux, savants,* powers of Erebus) and places the being of the cats outside all spatial and temporal limits.

2. The first quatrain introduces these spatial-temporal limits (*maison, saison*), and the first tercet abolishes them (*au fond des solitudes, rêve sans fin*).

3. The second quatrain defines the cats in terms of the darkness in which they place themselves, the second tercet in terms of the light they radiate (*étincelles, étoiles*).

Finally, a third division is superimposed upon the preceding one by regrouping, this time in chiasmus, the initial quatrain and the final tercet on the one hand and, on the other, the interior stanzas: the second quatrain and the first tercet. In the former couple, the independent clauses assign to the cats the role of syntactical modifiers, whereas from the outset the latter two stanzas assign to the cats the function of subject.

These phenomena of formal distribution obviously have a semantic foundation. The point of departure of the first quatrain is furnished by the proximity, within the same house, of the cats with the scholars or lovers. A double resemblance arises out of this contiguity (*comme eux, comme eux*). Similarly, a relation of contiguity in the final tercet also evolves to the point of resemblance, but whereas, in the first quatrain, the metonymical relation of the feline and human inhabitants of the house underlies their metaphorical relation, in the final tercet this situation is interiorized: the link of contiguity rests upon the synecdoche rather than upon the metonymy proper. The parts of the cat's body (*reins, prunelles*) provide a metaphorical evocation of the astral, cosmic cat, with a concomitant transition from precision to vagueness (*également—vaguement*). The analogy between the interior stanzas is based on connections of equivalence, the one turned down in the second quatrain (cats and *coursiers funèbres*), the other accepted in the first tercet (cats and *grands sphinx*). In the former case, this leads to a rejection of contiguity (between the cats and *l'Érèbe*) and, in the latter case, to the settlement of the cats *au fond des solitudes*. Contrary to the former case, the transition is made from a relation of equivalence, a reinforced form of resemblance (thus a metaphorical move), to relations of contiguity (thus metonymical), either negative or positive.

Up to this point, the poem has appeared to consist of systems of equivalences which fit inside one another and which offer, in their totality, the appearance of a closed system. There is, however, yet another way of looking at it, whereby the poem takes on the appearance of an open system in dynamic progression from beginning to end.

In the first part of this study we elucidated a division of the poem into two sestets separated by a distich whose structure contrasted vigorously with the rest. In the course of our recapitulation, we provisionally set this division to one side, because we felt that, unlike the others, it marks the stages of a progression from the order of the real (the first sestet) to that of the surreal (the second sestet). This transition operates via the distich, which by the accumulation of semantic and formal devices lures the reader for a brief moment into a doubly unreal uni-

1 to 6	7 and 8	9 to 14
extrinsic		intrinsic
empirical	mythological	
real	*unreal*	*surreal*

verse, since, while sharing with the first sestet the standpoint of exteriority, it anticipates the mythological tone of the second sestet. By this sudden oscillation both of tone and of theme, the distich fulfils a function somewhat resembling that of modulation in a musical composition.

The purpose of this modulation is to resolve the opposition, implicit or explicit from the beginning of the poem, between the metaphorical and metonymical procedures. The solution provided by the final sestet is achieved by transferring this opposition to the very heart of the metonymy, while expressing it by metaphorical means. In effect, each of the tercets puts forward an inverse image of the cats. In the first tercet, the cats originally enclosed in the house are, so to speak, extravasated from it in order to expand spatially and temporally in the infinite deserts and the dream without end. The movement is from the inside to the outside, from cats in seclusion to cats at liberty. In the second tercet, the breaking down of barriers is interiorized by the cats' attaining cosmic proportions, since they conceal in certain parts of their bodies (*reins* and *prunelles*) the sands of the desert and the stars of the sky. In both cases the transformation occurs via metaphorical devices, but there is no thorough equilibrium between the two transformations: the first still owes something to semblance (*prennent . . . les . . . attitudes . . . qui semblent s'endormir*) and to dream (*en songeant . . . dans un rêve*), whereas in the second case the transformation is declared and affirmed as truly achieved (*sont pleins . . . Étoilent*). In the first the cats close their eyes to sleep, in the second they keep them open.

Nevertheless, these ample metaphors of the final sestet simply transpose to the scale of the universe an opposition that was already implicitly formulated in the first line of the poem. Around the "lovers" and "scholar" terms are assembled which unite them respectively in a contracted or dilated relation: the man in love is joined to the woman as the scholar is to the universe: two types of conjunction, the one close and the other remote.[6] It is the same rapport that the final transfigurations evoke: dilation of the cats in time and space—constriction of time and space within the beings of the cats. But, here again, just as noted earlier, the symmetry between the two formulas is not complete. The latter contains within it a collection of all the oppositions: the *reins féconds* recall the *volupté* of the *amoureux,* as do the *prunelles* the *science* of the *savants; magiques* refers to the active fervor of the one, *mystiques* to the contemplative attitude of the other.

Two final points: The fact that all the grammatical subjects in the sonnet (with the exception of the proper noun *l'Érèbe*) are plural, and that all feminine rhymes are formed with plurals (including the substantive *solitudes*), is curiously illuminated by a few passages from Baudelaire's *Foules* which, moreover, seem to throw light upon the whole of the sonnet: "Multitude, solitude: terms equal and interchangeable by the active and fertile poet . . . The poet enjoys that incomparable privilege, that he can, at will, be both himself and another . . . What men call love is very small, very restricted and very weak compared to that ineffable orgy, that blessed prostitution of the soul which gives itself in its entirety, its poetry and charity, to the unforeseen which emerges, to the unknown one who passes."[7]

In the poet's sonnet, the cats are initially qualified as *puissants et doux* and in the final line their pupils are likened to the stars. Crépet and Blin[8] compare this to a line in Sainte-Beuve: "l'astre puissant et doux" (1829) and find the same epithets in a poem by Brizeux (1832) in which women are thus apostrophized: "Êtres deux fois doués! Êtres puissants et doux!"

This would confirm, were there any need to do so, that for Baudelaire the image of the cat is closely linked to that of the woman, as is shown explicitly in two other poems entitled "Le Chat" and pertaining to the same collection. Thus the sonnet—"Viens, mon beau chat, sur mon cœur amoureux"—contains the revealing line: "Je vois ma femme en esprit." The second of these poems—"Dans ma cervelle se promène . . . Un beau chat, fort, doux"—squarely asks the question: "est-il fée, est-il dieu?" This motif of vacillation between male and female is subjacent in "Les Chats," where it shows through from beneath intentional ambiguities (*Les amoureux . . . Aiment . . . Les chats puissants et doux; Leurs reins féconds*). Michel Butor notes with reason that for Baudelaire "these two aspects: femininity and supervirility, far from being mutually exclusive, are in fact bound together."[9] All the characters in the sonnet are of masculine gender, but *les chats* and their alter ego, *les grands sphinx,* share an androgynous nature. This very ambiguity is emphasized throughout the sonnet by the paradoxical choice of feminine substantives for so-called masculine rhymes.[10] The cats, by their mediation, permit the removal of woman from the initial assemblage formed by lovers and scholars. "Le poète des Chats," liberated from love "bien petit, bien restreint," meets face to face and perhaps even blends with the universe, delivered from the scholar's austerity.

CHAPTER 12

Shakespeare's Verbal Art in "Th' Expence of Spirit"

With L. G. Jones

"What is the figure? What is the figure?"
Love's Labor's Lost, 5.1.63

The hundred-twenty-ninth of the 154 sonnets composed by Shakespeare toward the threshold of the seventeenth century and printed in the 1609 Quarto may be read as follows:

I ₁Th' expence of Spirit | in a waste of shame
    ₂Is lust in action, | and till action, lust
    ₃Is perjurd, murdrous, | blouddy full of blame,
    ₄Savage, extreame, rude, | cruel, not to trust,
II ₁Injoyd no sooner | but dispised straight,
    ₂Past reason hunted, | and no sooner had
    ₃Past reason hated | as a swollowed bayt,
    ₄On purpose layd | to make | the taker mad.
III ₁Mad[e] In pursut | and in possession so,
    ₂Had, having, and in quest, | to have extreame,
    ₃A blisse in proofe | and provd | a[nd] very wo,
    ₄Before a joy proposd | behind a dreame,
IV   ₁All this the world | well knowes | yet none knowes well,
    ₂To shun the heaven | that leads | men to this hell.

I. Constituents: Rhymes, Strophes, Lines

This English sonnet contains three quatrains, each of them with its own alternate masculine rhymes, and a terminal couplet with a plain masculine rhyme. Of the seven rhymes only the first, juxtaposing two nouns with the same preposition (*of shame*—*of blame*), is grammatical. The second rhyme again begins with a noun, but confronts it with a different part of speech. The third rhyme and the last three rhymes invert this order: a non-noun is followed by a noun, whereas the fourth, the central of the seven rhymes, has no noun at all and consists of the participle *had* and the adjective *mad*. The first rhyming word within the second or only rhyme of each strophe is duplicated elsewhere in the sonnet: II_2 *lust*—*lust*; II_2 *had*—III_2 *Had*; III_2 *extreame*—I_4 *extreame*; IV_1 *well*—*well*. In the second strophe the second rhyme word is also repeated: II_4 *mad*—III_1 *Mad*.

The four strophic units exhibit three kinds of binary correspondences to which the current classification of rhyme patterns may be extended and applied: 1) alternation (a b a b), which ties together the two *odd* strophes (I, III) and opposes them to the *even* strophes which are tied in turn to each other (II, IV); 2) framing (a b b a), which brings together the enclosing *outer* strophes (I, IV) and opposes them to the two enclosed, mutually related *inner* strophes (II, III); 3) neighborhood (a a b b), which builds pairs of *anterior* (I, II) and *posterior* (III, IV) strophes opposed to one another. To these three symmetrical interconnections virtually inherent in any four-strophe composition, Shakespearean sonnets join an effective asymmetrical contrast between the *terminal* couplet and the three quatrains viewed as *nonterminal* strophes (a a a b).

Sonnet 129 shows clearly how, in addition to the structural convergences of entire strophes, the lines themselves can display their own lucid binary correspondences. The iambic pentameters of this fourteen-line poem present a striking difference between the phrasing of the first seven, *centripetal*, afferent lines, moving in a direction toward the center of the entire poem, and the further seven, *centrifugal*, efferent lines, proceeding in a direction away from its center. In the centripetal lines the third foot of the iambic pentameter is cut by a break, an obligatory word boundary, which falls here precisely in the middle of the line, after the fifth syllable. To this feminine, caesural break between the upbeat and the downbeat of the third, middle, foot the seven centrifugal lines oppose a masculine, diaretic break marking the beginning and/or the end of the middle foot: both limits in five instances and only one of these limits in two cases. This break falls after the fourth, downbeat, syllable and/or the sixth, likewise downbeat, syllable. (See above, our text of the sonnet with those breaks marked by vertical lines.)

II. Spelling and Punctuation

In our reading of the sonnet we follow the editio princeps but discard its confusing use of *i* for both *i* and *j* (*periurd, inioyd, ioy*) and of *u* for a noninitial *v* (*sauage, hauing, haue, proud, heauen*), a use which even gave rise to the ludicrous question whether the *i* in words like *ioy* was not pronounced as it was written. We preserve the orthographic oscillations of the Elizabethan period because in certain cases they reveal peculiarities of the early pronunciation or offer visual support to Shakespeare's rhymes: in III *so—extreame—wo—dreame*. We only use angle brackets [] to indicate that III$_3$ *and very wo* instead of *a very wo* is an obvious misprint under the assimilative influence of the antecedent *and* in the same line and in the first two lines of the same quatrain, and that the adjective *mad* and not the participle *made* is evidently meant in III$_1$. Kökeritz points to the episodic spelling *made* for *mad* and *mad* for *made* in Shakespeare's plays and to the poet's puns on these two words.[1]

The spreading syncope of the participial *e* in English of the sixteenth and seventeenth centuries is shown in the first edition of the sonnet by the omission of the *e*. It is only after *ow* that this *e* is conventionally preserved in spelling. II$_3$ *swollowed*, cf. also IV$_1$ *knowes* (twice), and one could hardly follow those critics who say that this participle, occupying precisely two beats of the line, "must have been meant as a three-syllabled word." Only the form *dispised* in II$_1$ is written and evidently meant to be preserved in pronunciation as elsewhere in Shakespeare's verse (*Othello*, 1.1.162: *And what's to come of my despised* time). A possible reason for this conservative form in the sonnet is the tendency towards a dissimilatory alternation of the endings -*d* and -*ed* within the lines of the second quatrain, rich in participles: $_1$ *injoyd—dispised*, $_2$ *hunted—had*, $_3$ *hated—swollowed* (*swollow'd*).

One can but agree with George Wyndham's plea for the structural justification of the deviant punctuation in the 1609 Quarto and especially in "the magnificent 129."[2] Thus the peculiar distribution of commas within the lines is explainable by the hybrid function which so often in the use of poets proves to be a compromise between syntactic division and rhythmic phrasing; hence in the centrifugal lines the syntactically motivated comma is omitted as unnecessary when the syntactic pauses coincide with the breaks so that the rhythmic phrasing prompts the desirable segmentation of the lines. On the other hand, the seemingly unexpected comma in III$_2$ *Had, having, and in quest, | to have extreame* is needed to point out the break at the end of the middle foot since a) the break at the beginning of this foot is lacking, while b) the break in the preceding line marks only the beginning but not the end of the middle foot: *Mad In pursut | and in possession so,* and since c) the break signaled by the comma is only lexically but not syntactically motivated. The two lines in question are the sole centrifugal lines with a break which marks only the beginning or the end of the middle foot, whereas in the other lines of the same rhythmic group both the beginning and the end of the middle foot are marked by a break. As to the centripetal lines, the absence of the comma after *blouddy* in the sequence of four collateral adjectives *Is perjurd, murdrous, | blouddy full of blame,* emphasizes the higher relevance of the preceding word boundary, which carried the compulsory break throughout the first half of the sonnet.

III. Interpretation

An insight into the peculiar use of commas in the first edition of the sonnet and a consistently comparative analysis of its four stanzas lead us to their tentative explanatory rewording, literal as far as possible:

I   In action, lust is the expenditure of vital power (mind and semen) in a wasting of shame (chastity and genitalia), and until action, lust is deliberately treacherous, murderous, bloody, culpable, savage, intemperate, brutal, cruel, perfidious;

II   no sooner enjoyed than at once despised, no sooner crazily sought than crazily hated as a swallowed bait that has been purposely laid (for fornication and trapping) to make the taker mad.

III   Mad, both in pursuit and in possession, intemperate after having had, when having, and in the quest to have a bliss while being tried and a real woe after having been tried, beforehand a proposed joy, afterwards a phantom;

IV   all this is well-known to the world but nobody knows well enough to shun the heaven that leads men to this hell.

Among the far-sighted predictions made by Charles Sanders Peirce one may quote his early note that "by showing in many places puns hitherto unnoticed" the study of Shakespearean pronunciation will give us "an understanding of lines hitherto unintelligible."[3] At present, investigators such as Kökeritz and Mahood have disclosed the abundance and relevance of word play, lexical ambiguities, and puns in Shakespeare's works.[4] These devices must be and have been interpreted against the background of Elizabethan rhetoric and ars poetica (especially in the stimulating monograph by Sister Miriam Joseph),[5] though their creative power infinitely transcends any bookish recipes and rubrics. A kind of semantic counterpoint of a sublime and a crude meaning within the same word, similar to that which Kökeritz detects in *As You Like It*,[6] is observable also in Sonnet 129. *Spirit*, in the vocabulary of Shakespeare's era, meant a life-giving, vital power manifested in mind and in semen as well; correspondingly, *shame* carried the meaning of chastity and genitalia as parts of shame. The rapprochement of both words is not confined in the poet's use to this sonnet (*Cymbeline*, 5.3.35f: *guilded pale lookes: Part shame, part spirit renew'd*); also both nearly synonymous negative characteristics of *lust in action— expence* and *waste*—are bound together in his dramatic diction (*Lear*, 2.1.100: *To have th' expense and waste of his revenues*). The intimate connection of blood and sperm in English Renaissance physiology and belles-lettres was noted by Hilton Landry,[7] and the coappearance of *blood* with *lust* is quite common in Shakespeare's phraseology. The double entendre in the author's lexicon does not interfere, however, with the essentially homogeneous and firm thematic construction of his poems and of this sonnet in particular.

IV. Pervasive Features

The numerous variables which form a salient network of binary oppositions between the four strophic units are most effective against the background of pervasive features common to all four strophes. Thus every strophe presents its specific selection of verbal categories, but on the other hand, each strophe is endowed with one instance of the infinitive which belongs to one of its even lines, the fourth line of I and II and the second of III and IV. All these infinitive forms of transitive verbs differ in their syntactic function and the first and last of them seem even to transgress the grammatical standard of Elizabethan times:

I$_3$ *Is . . . $_4$not to trust*
II$_4$ *layd to make the taker mad*
III$_2$ *in quest to have*
IV$_1$ *none knowes well,* [how] IV$_2$ *To shun the heaven,* in an elliptic
    clause described by Puttenham as "the figure of default"[8]

A characteristic pervasive feature is the manifest lack of certain grammatical categories throughout the whole poem. It is the only one among the 154 sonnets of the 1609 Quarto which contains no personal or corresponding possessive pronouns. In Sonnets 5, 68, and 94 only third-person pronouns occur, while the rest of the sonnets make wide use of the first- and second-person pronouns. Sonnet 129 avoids epithets: with the exception of the assertoric rather than qualitative modifier in III$_3$ *very wo,* adjectives are not used as attributes but only in a predicative function and once—in II$_4$ *to make the taker mad*—as a complement. Except for the word *men* in the final line, only singular forms occur in the sonnet. The poem admits no other finites than the third-person singular of the present tense.

Each line displays a conspicuous alliteration or repetition of sound sequences and entire morphemes or words:

1   *expence of Spirit* (sp— sp)
2   *lust in action—action, lust*
3   *blouddy—blame*
4   *extreame—trust* (str— tr.st)
5   *sooner—straight*
6   *hunted—had*
7   *hated—bayt* /eyt/—/eyt/
8   *make—mad*
9   *pursut—possession*
10 *had, having—had*
11 *proof—provd*
12 *before a—behind a*

The widely repetitive texture of the two final lines will be analyzed below in Section VIII, devoted to the terminal couplet.

The poem, which begins with a characteristic contraction of two contiguous vowels, *Th' expence,* is entirely devoid of hiatus. The initial vowels of words with a tense or lax onset (*h* or #) are symmetrically distributed in the sonnet. One of the two parts of each distich begins with such an onset which in the odd strophes opens their inner lines and in the even strophes opens the first line, as well as the fourth when it is a quatrain:

2 *Is*
3 *Is*
5 *Injoyd*
8 *On*
10 *Had*
11 *A*
13 *All*

In its downbeats each quatrain includes three, and the terminal couplet two, vocalic onsets; in eight instances the vowel is /æ/; and in all four strophes the second downbeat appears to be endowed with such an onset: I_2 *in action, and till action* (/æ/ – /æ/ – /æ/); II_2 *hunted, and no sooner had* (/hʌ/ – /æ/ – /æ/); III_2 *having and in quest to have* (/hæ/ – /æ/ – /hæ/); IV_2 *heaven . . . hell* /hɛ/ – /hɛ/).

The semantic leitmotif of each strophe is one of tragic predestination: *lust . . . is perjurd* ($I_{2, 3}$), or deliberately treacherous. It is a murderous bait laid on purpose (II) and proposing a seemingly joyful and heavenly bliss, only to change it into a very woe. The terminology of this plot is closely linked with the vocabulary of Shakespeare's dramas:

O passing traitor, perjurd and unjust! (*3 Henry VI,* 5.1.106)
There's no trust [cf. 129: I_4 *not to trust*], No faith, no honesty
  in men; all perjurd (*Romeo and Juliet,* 3.2.85f)
Perjurie, in the high'st Degree; Murther, stern murther [cf. 129:
  I_3 *perjurd, murdrous*] (*Richard III,* 5.3.228f)
What to ourselves in passion we *propose*
The passion ending, doth the purpose lose [cf. 129: II_4 On
  purpose layd—III_4 Before a joy *proposd*] (*Hamlet,* 3.2.204)

The phonic affinity of *perjurd* with *purpose* is supplemented by the confrontation of the latter word with *proposd* in the final lines of II and III, and the etymological kinship of these two words is revived by the poet. If the first centrifugal line of the sonnet introduces the hero, *the taker,* however, still not as an agent but as a victim, the final centrifugal line brings the exposure of the malevolent culprit, *the heaven that leads*

men to this hell, and thus discloses by what perjurer the joy was proposed and the lure laid. As Douglas Bush judiciously notes, "the sen-
sual lover's *heaven* and *hell* are grimly ironic reminders of their religious counterparts," while the surmise launched by Riding and Graves
that in this sonnet "*Heaven* to Shakespeare is the longing for a temporary stability" finds no support in the poet's text.[9]

V. Odd against Even

The manifold correspondences between the odd strophes, on the
one hand, and those between the even strophes, on the other hand, as
well as their mutual contrast, display the most elaborate symmetries in
the sonnet, and it is precisely the hierarchy of the three interstrophic
correlations that individualizes and diversifies the four-strophe poems
of any verbal artist. The presentation of the theme in the odd strophes
of 129 is an intensely abstractive confrontation of the different stages
of lust (*before, in action, behind*), whereas the even strophes are centered
upon the metamorphosis itself (II_2 *hunted, and no sooner had* $_3$*Past reason hated;* and in IV the way from *heaven to hell*). One could compare
the even strophes with a motion picture of a merely straightforward
development, whereas the odd strophes introduce a retrospective and
generalizing approach: I_2 *In action, and till action;* III_2 *Had, having,
and in quest, to have extreame.* These quatrains look for the inalterable
essence of the depicted passion: III_1 *Mad In pursut and in possession so.*

The odd strophes in contradistinction to the even ones abound in
substantives and adjectives: seventeen (9 + 8) substantives versus six
(2 + 4), as well as ten adjectives (8 + 2) versus one (1 + #). Strophe
I concentrates eight of the substantives in its first distich and all eight
adjectives in the second distich, while III confines its adjectives to the
first distich and most of its substantives to the second one. All seventeen substantives of the odd strophes are abstract, all six substantives
of the even strophes are concrete, if from the list of substantives we
exclude those three abstracts of II which form part of adverbial expressions (II_2, $_3$ *Past reason;* $_4$ *On purpose*). The abstracts fall into two categories: a) verbal nexus words: five substantives in I and four in III (I:
expence, waste, action, action, blame; III: *pursut, possession, quest, proofe*);
b) feelings, states, faculties: four in I and equally in III (I: *Spirit, shame,
lust, lust;* III: *blisse, wo, joy, dreame*). The symmetry between I and III
appears to be total if we confront III only with the first, purely sub-

stantival distich of the first strophe. This distich contains precisely four verbal nexus words while the only substantive of the second distich, endowed with eight adjectives, functions as a mere modifier of its last adjective: *full of blame* (blameful).

Only in the odd strophes do substantives occur as modifiers of other substantives or of adjectives (6 + 4). In the odd strophes verbal forms (3 + 5) are devoid of modifiers. In the even strophes verbal forms (7 + 4) require modifiers with only one exception (II_3 *a swollowed bayt*). All these rules exhibit the sharp difference between the odd and even strophes, the latter dynamic, oriented toward verbs or verbals and superimposing them upon other parts of speech, whereas the odd strophes deploy a much more static and synthesizing tendency and hence focus upon abstract substantives and upon adjectives. The verbal orientation of the even strophes may be exemplified both by the terminal couplet built on the only three concrete finites of the poem, and by the second quatrain a) with its participles which their modifiers distinctly separate from adjectives and b) with the two concrete deverbative nouns *taker* and *bayt*. Compare, as to Shakespeare's feeling for the verbal cognates of the latter noun, his sentence "Bait the hook well; this fish will bite" (*Much Ado about Nothing*, 2.3.114).

Both animates of the sonnet, the two which pertain to the personal (human) gender, function as direct objects in the last line of the even strophes: II *taker* and IV *men*. In common usage the unmarked agent of the verb is an animate, primarily of personal gender, and the unmarked goal is an inanimate. But in both cited constructions with transitive verbs the sonnet inverts this nuclear order. Both personal nouns of the poem characterize human beings as passive goals of extrinsic nonhuman and inhuman actions. It is significant that the deverbative noun, II_4 *taker*, provided with an agentive, personal suffix, and subordinate to the verb *to make*, characterizes this human being as an undergoer of action. The phonic and semantic correspondence between the verbs *make* and *take* is underscored by the first rhyme *make—take* of Sonnet 81 and by the terminal rhyme *take—make* of 91.

Conjunctions are only copulative in the odd strophes (1 + 3); chiefly adversative in the even strophes (1 + 1). The neighborhood of conjunctions and negatives is alien to the odd strophes but regular in the even strophes: II_1 *no sooner . . . but;* $_2$*and no sooner;* IV_1 *yet none*. These differences between the conjunctions and their use in the two pairs of strophic units characterize the higher dramatic tension of the even strophes.

Only the even strophes display hypotaxis and end in multileveled "progressive" structures, i.e. constructions with several degrees of subordinates, each of them postposed to the subordinating constituent (Yngve and Halliday):[10]

> II A. *hated* B. *as a swollowed bayt* C. *on purpose layd* D. *to make* E. *the taker* F. *mad.*
>
> IV A. *none knowes well* B. *to shun* C. *the heaven* D. *that leads* E. *men* F. *to this hell*

The penultimate constituents of both progressive structures are the only animate nouns of the sonnet (II_4 *the taker*, IV_2 *men*), and both constructions finish with the only substantival tropes: *bayt* and *taker; heaven* and *hell* instead of heaven's sovereign and hellish torment.

There is a close connection between the final lines of both strophes in their consonantal texture:

> II *layd* (l.d) *to* (t) *make* (m) *the* (ð) *taker* (t) *mad* (m.d)
> IV *that* (ð.t) *leads* (l.d) *men* (m) *to* (t) *this* (ð) *hell* (l)

Also the next-to-last line reveals a similar texture in both strophes: II *swollowed*—IV *knows well.*

The intimate rapport between I and III is manifested by their rhymes. The first rhyme of I and the last rhyme of III end in *m,* and the rhyming word units are disyllabic in both cases: *of shame—of blame, extreame—a dreame,* whereas the other rhyme of I confronts imparisyllabic word units, *lust—to trust,* and the rest of the rhyming units are all monosyllabic. Likewise the first sonnet to the Dark Lady, No. 127, has one rhyme ending in *m* within both odd quatrains: I_2 *name*—and again $_4$*shame*, III_2 *seeme*—$_4$*esteeme;* moreover, the rhyme III $_1$*so*—$_3$*wo* of 129 is present but inverted in the terminal couplet of 127 (and also of 90). In the interval between the two lines with an *m*-rhyme, both odd strophes exhibit mutual symmetric correspondences: the first hemistich and the beginning of the second one in I_2 agree with the analogous parts of III_3:

> $\quad\quad$ 2 $\quad\quad\quad\quad\quad\quad$ 3 $\quad\quad$ 1
> I_2 *Is lust* (l.s) [when lust is] *in action,* | *and*
> $\quad\quad$ 2 $\quad\quad\quad\quad\quad\quad$ 3 $\quad\quad$ 1
> III_3 *A blisse* (l.s.) [when lust is] *in proofe* | *and*

Thus *lust* in I_2 acts as substance and *bliss* in III_3 as an accident. By the way, the preposition *in* appears only in the odd strophes: twice in I and four times in III. The rhyme word *extreame* of III_2 is anticipated in I_4 where the pair of collateral adjectives—*Savage, extreame*—builds a quasi-choriambic commencement of the iambic line (cf. Jespersen's initiatory discussion)[11] and corresponds rhythmically to the only other 'choriambic' start: III_1 *Mad In pursut*, followed in turn by the collateral adjective *extreame,* the former adjective beginning and the latter ending in *m.* In the first line of the third strophe the preposition *in* is twice tied to the metrical downbeat, and perhaps the capitalized *In* of the editio princeps is meant to signal the regular downbeat of the metrical scheme. The clusters of I_4 *extreame* (kstr) . . . *not to trust* (tt.tr.st) and III_2 *in quest, to have* (k.stt.) *extreame* (kstr) are each concatenated with an infinitive. The emphatic adjectival distich concluding the first strophe particularly abounds in expressive reiterations of complex clusters:

> *Is perjurd, murdrous, blouddy full of blame,* (rdm.rdr bl bl.m)
> *Savage, extreame, rude, cruel, not to trust* (kstr.mr.d kr tr.st).

In the initial lines of I and III the last upbeat with both adjacent downbeats exhibits two similar chains of consonantal phonemes: I_1 *Spirit* (sp.r.t) *in*—III_1 *in pursut* (p.rs.t).

VI. Outer against Inner

As shown by many four-strophe poems in world literature, the outer strophes carry a higher syntactic rank than the inner ones. The inner strophes are devoid of finites, but comprise (6 + 4) participles. On the other hand, the outer strophes are deprived of participles, but each of these strophes contains one finite which occurs twice in the coordinate clauses linked by a conjunction: I_1 *Th' expence* . . . $_2$*Is lust* . . . *and* . . . *lust* $_3$*Is perjurd;* IV_1 *the world well knowes yet none knowes well.* In each of these instances both clauses display a metathesis: I_2 *Is lust in action—till action lust* $_3$*Is;* IV_1 *well knowes—knowes well.* In the first strophe *lust* occurs in two different syntactic functions. In the fourth strophe the adverb *well* when preposed and postposed displays two distinct semantic nuances: "widely knows" in the former case and "knows enough" in the final position. The finites of the two outer strophes differ both morphologically and syntactically; to the two copulas of the first strophe the fourth contraposes three transitives: twice *knowes* in the first line and *leads* in the second. In the main clauses each of these strophes presents two subjects and two finite predicates; the fourth strophe, moreover, includes a subordinate clause with one subject and one finite predicate, whereas no subjects and, as mentioned, no finite predicates occur in the inner strophes. Rhythmically, the last half of the last line of the last strophe (*léads mén to this héll*: $\acute{-}\,\acute{-}\,-\,-\,\acute{-}$) stands in relations of mirror symmetry to the first half of the last line of the first strophe (*sávage, extréame, rúde*: $\acute{-}\,-\,-\,\acute{-}\,\acute{-}$); these are the only two occurrences of a stressed monosyllable under an internal upbeat.

The typical features of the inner strophes are, in the terms of Sister Miriam Joseph, "grammatical figures that work by defect and so represent short-cuts in expression."[12] These strophes are constructed of minor clauses deprived of finites and acting effectively in an independent function: compare Barbara Strang's pertinent remarks on "disjunctive grammar";[13] and the occasional objections against the "inappropriate" period put in the 1609 Quarto at the end of the second strophe are hardly vindicable.[14] The effacement of the functional limit between adjectives and adverbs may be noted as a specific property of the inner strophes: II_1 *dispised straight* (adverbialized adjective); III_1 *in possession so* (adjectivized adverb). Both inner strophes excell in what Shakespeare's *Timon* calls "confounding contraries": II_1 *injoyd—dispised*, $_2$*hunted—*$_3$*hated*, III_1 *pursut—possession*, $_3$*blisse—wo*.

Puttenham's figure of "redouble" (a word which terminates one line and is repeated at the beginning of the next line) is typical of the close ties between the inner strophes: II finishes and III begins with the adjective *mad* used in the former instance as a grammatical modifier specifying the final phase of lust, and in the latter case as a head word applied to all stages of this evil obsession. The participle *had* (once in final and once in initial rhyme with *mad*) concludes II_2 and opens III_2. The construction II_4 *on purpose*, anterior to the final *mad*, and the construction III_1 *in pursut*, following after the initial *mad*, correspond to each other by the nasal of the preposition and by the same prefix. The use of "translacer," as Puttenham called the repetition of the same root with different affixes, is customary in the inner strophes: *Injoyd* in the initial line of II and *joy* in the final line of III; *Had, having* and *to have* in III_2; *proofe and provd* in III_3; II_4 *purpose—*III_4 *proposd*. The figures mentioned build up a complex correspondence between the inner strophes: II_1 *Injoyd*, $_2$*had*, $_4$*On purpose* . . . *mad—*III_1 *Mad*, $_2$*Had*, $_4$*joy proposd*. Each of these two corresponding sets contain two participles, one substantive and one adjective. The inner strophes are further linked by a paronomastic chain: II_1 *dispised straight* (d.sp.z.d str.t),

II$_{2,\ 3}$ *Past reason* (p.str.z.n), $_4$*On purpose* (np.rp.s), III$_1$ *In pursut* (np.rs.t), $_4$*proposd* (pr.p.zd).

VII. Anterior against Posterior

The two first and likewise the two last strophes manifest a noticeably small number of specific correspondences, and among the three types of interstrophic correlations the opposition of the anterior to the posterior strophes plays a subaltern, third-rate role in Sonnet 129. The anterior strophes show an internal alternation of definite and indefinite articles, one *the* followed by one *a* in I and one *a* followed by one *the* in II, whereas the posterior strophes contain either only indefinite articles (four in III) or only definite (two in IV). However, the most relevant feature in the distribution of definite and indefinite articles is rather the absence of indefinite articles, which opposes the terminal couplet to all three quatrains.

Besides the *m*-rhymes shared by both odd strophes, the other three rhymes of the anterior strophes end in a dental stop, while the rhymes of the posterior strophes lack obstruents. To the nine identical diphthongs of the first two strophes—I *waste, shame, blame;* II *straight, hated, bayt, layd, make, taker*—no similar dipthong corresponds in the posterior strophes.

Within each of the two contiguous strophic pairs, anterior/posterior grammatical contrasts between neighboring strophes play an incomparably wider role (odd versus even and outer versus inner) than specific similarities in their grammatical structure.

Despite the relative independence of the inner strophes from the adjacent outer strophes, the latter occupy an elevated position in the grammatical texture of the poem. Accordingly, both pairs of contiguous strophes present two opposite types of grading: the first, outer odd strophe towering above the subsequent even strophe heralds the immutably murderous essence of lust, whereas the terminal, outer even strophe imposes upon the posterior strophic pair the concluding, strenuous theme of the inescapable, infernal end.

VIII. Couplet against Quatrains

The terminal couplet exhibits a considerable number of features alien to the three quatrains. This couplet is devoid of adjectives, parti-

ciples, indefinite articles (against the fifteen adjectives, eleven participles, and six indefinite articles of the quatrains), and of relational
(grammatical) verbs. It is the only strophe with a plural substantive,
notional (lexical) finites, substantival and adjectival pronouns and with
a relative clause. The four nouns of IV are pure substantives, whereas
in the quatrains most of the substantives are deeply related to verbs: I
expence, Spirit (whose relation with the Latin *spirare* and with such
prefixed verbs as *respire, inspire, expire,* could hardly have escaped the
attention of the poet), *waste, action, blame;* II *bayt, taker;* III *pursut,
possession, quest, proofe.* The nouns of the couplet are the so-called
"uniques."[15] In the universe of discourse referred to by the poem there
is only one world, one heaven, and one hell; such a contextual parti-
cularization assigns a definite article to *the world* and to *the heaven that
leads men to this hell;* the latter, viewed "in a close affinity to proper
names," is devoid of any article but supplied with an anaphoric deter-
miner. The definite articles of the couplet as a specific variety of their
"particularizing uses" differ visibly from the same articles in the quatrains where they fulfill a "nonparticularizing" function: a noun used
generically in I_1 *Th' expence of Spirit* or figuring as a type of its class
when II_4 *the taker* represents the entire class of takers lured by a bait.[16]
In the couplet its nouns of ample semantic scope are akin to the pronominal totalizers, according to Sapir's formulation,[17] IV_1 *all, none.*

The terminal couplet opposes concrete and primary nouns to the
abstract and/or deverbative nouns of the quatrains. In a similar way the
concrete finites of the terminal couplet differ from the abstract *is* of I
and from the derived, participial forms of II and III. It is worth notice
that in one "of the most wonderful of the generalizing sonnets," as
Barber justly defines this "great poem,"[18] glorified by some critics as
even "the greatest in the world,"[19] the deepest semantic effects of its
quatrains are achieved by a nearly exclusive use of constituents which,
since Bentham and Brentano,[20] have been labeled mere "linguistic fictions" and which are relegated to "surface" structures by linguists of
today. The path from the quatrains to the couplet would be, in terms
of Jeremy Bentham and his reistic heirs, a transition from "names of
fictitious entities" to "names of fabulous entities."

The sonnet has two topics—the lust and the luster—and omits the
designation of the former in the final strophe and the designation of
the latter in the initial strophe. The abstract appellation of the first
topic attracts a string of further abstract nouns. The first strophe char-

acterizes lust in itself; the second launches a set of passive participles with a hint of the yet unnamed dramatis personae and finishes by referring to the *taker* of the *bayt;* the third strophe uses active participles to depict the taker's behavior and brings forward images of lust as objects of his strivings. The adjective *extreame* applied to lust in the first strophe is transferred to the luster in the third. Mere anaphoric pronouns refer in the terminal couplet to the previous representation of lust, and the notion of the luster grows into a generalized idea of *men* and their damnation. The final line seems to allude to the ultimate persona, the celestial condemner of mankind.

The entire couplet consists solely of monosyllables, partly stressable, partly proclitic; but note Puttenham: "In words monosyllable . . . the accent is indifferent and may be used for sharp or flat and heavy at our pleasure"![21] We observe a similar lapidary makeup of the terminal couplet in several other of Shakespeare's sonnets, such as 2, 18, and 43. This structure favors a clear-cut duple phrasing of the lines in question:

> *All this | the world | well knowes | yet none | knowes well,*
> *To shun | the heaven | that leads | men to this hell.*

This metrical phrasing is prepared for by the oxytones which fill the preceding two lines, so that eight of ten feet are expressly signaled within each of the two final distichs:

> III$_3$ *A blisse | in proofe | and provd | a very wo,*
> *Before | a joy | proposd | behind | a dreame . . .*

The sound texture of the couplet is particularly dense: in initial position we observe five instances of /ð/, three of /w/ (against two /ð/ and two /w/ throughout the twelve lines of the quatrains). In stressed words initial and final /n/ occur seven times and /l/ without following vowel five times (whereas the twelve lines of the first three strophes show no /n/ and no /l/ in the same positions). Among the vowels the six /ɛ/ of the couplet (3 + 3) are the most apparent. The sequence of three monosyllables with an internal /ɛ/, *heaven* /hɛvn/—*men* /mɛn/—*hell* /hɛl/, follows the vertical iconographic disposition and developmental order of the story; the affinity of the first noun with the second is underlined by the final /n/ and with the third one by the initial /h/. Various types of repeated groups with or without inversion emerge in the couplet: *well knowes—none knowes well* (cf. Kökeritz, on the identical pronunciation of "known" and "none" [noːn]);[22] $_1$*All this the—*

$_2the$ . . . *this hell* (lŏ.ð—ð.ð.l); $_1well$, $_2To$—$_2that$ *leads* (lt—tl); $_2shun$ *the—heaven that* (nð—nð).

IX. Center against Marginals

It is worth noting that the last two lines of the second quatrain differ from the six preceding lines as well as from the six following lines and build a sui generis central distich which encompasses the seventh centripetal line and the first of the seven centrifugal lines. Each of the six initial lines displays a grammatical parallelism of its two hemistichs: words of the same grammatical category appear twice in the same syntactic function (I_1 *of Spirit, of shame;* $_2in$ *action, till action;* $_3$, $_4$sequences of collateral adjectives; II_1 *Injoyd, dispised;* $_2hunted, had$). The central lines are devoid of such an intralinear parallelism and especially II_4 is built of five totally unlike grammatical forms. This distich, moreover, carries the only simile and thereby the only syntactic instance of a comparative construction (*as* . . .). The six final lines of the sonnet return to the grammatical (morphologic and, save III_2 and IV_2, syntactic) parallelism of hemistichs which was typical of the six initial lines: III_1 *in pursut, in possession;* $_2having, to have$ (!); $_3A$ *blisse, a wo;* $_4a$ *joy, a dream;* IV_1 *knowes, knowes;* $_2the$ *heaven, to this hell* (!). In each of these twelve marginal lines a semantic similarity connects the paralleled vocables and sharpens the divergence between these intralinear conformities and the whimsical bilinear simile of the central distich.

The unequal number of lines in the four strophes—3·4 + 1·2—called forth two kinds of counteraction in the grammatical organization of the sonnet: on the one hand, a manifold contrast between the couplet and the quatrains and, on the other hand, a semblance of a central distich symmetrically fringed with marginal sextets. Significant thematic, morphologic, syntactic, and paronomastic congruities link together these two-line keynotes of the whole poem.

X. Anagrams?

In a few of Shakespeare's sonnets (134–136) his name Will is inserted in a punning way and suggests the tentative question whether his signature is not anagrammatized in 129 so that the poet's remark—"every word doth almost tell my name" (Sonnet 76)—might be applied in its literal meaning to the poem under discussion. Especially the letters and sounds of the first line seem to disclose the family name of the poet, written in his own and contemporaneous spellings as *Shakspere, Shakspeare, Shackspeare, Shaxpere:*[23] I₁ *expence* (xp) *of Spirit* (sp.r) *shame* (sha), while the terminal couplet with its thrice iterated /w/ and particularly with the words *well* (w.ll) *yet* (y) *men* (m) could carry a latent allusion to *William.* Since in wordplays Shakespeare was prone to equate the vocables *will* and *well,*[24] the entire concluding couplet could—perhaps!—conceal a second, facetious autobiographical reading: "All this [is] the world Will knows, yet none knows Will to shun the heaven that leads men to this hell." The omission of the copulative verb would be consistent with the ellipses used in the rest of the sonnet; moreover, the contraction of "this is" to "this" was current during the Shakespearean era.[25]

XI. *Concluding Questions*

After an attentive inquiry into Shakespeare's Sonnet 129 with its amazing external and internal structuration palpable to any responsive and unprejudiced reader, one may ask whether it is possible to affirm with John Crowe Ransom that far from being a true sonnet this is only a fourteen-line poem, "with no logical organization at all" except that it has a little couplet conclusion.[26] Or can one accept J. M. Robertson's allegation of "verbal impotence" and "violence without regard to psychic fitness yet collapsing to the damage of the argument as in *past reason hated*"? And is it believable that "collapse recurs when a *very wo* fades into *a dreame* for the rhyme's sake"?[27] Furthermore, how could a thorough student of Shakespearean poetics, grammatical schemes, and rhyme technique agree with Edward Hubler that "the anticlimactic position of *not to trust* is owing entirely to the need for a rhyme" or that this poem, in spite of its rhyme pattern, "is not written in quatrains"?[28] Would not a careful insight into the sonnet rise up against C. W. M. Johnson's surmise that the image of *a swollowed bayt* suggests "an hostility and mutual distrust between partners in lust" (although "she" is neither mentioned nor intimated in the sonnet) and that these lines allude "to the effects of 'the great pox'"?[29] Finally, is it possible for a reader attentive to Shakespeare's poetry and to his "figures of grammatical construction," as Puttenham labels them, to admit Richard Levin's explication of this work and, namely, to gloss its sequence of strophes as a successive recovery from a "bitter disgust to a recent sexual encounter," gradually "fading out in the speaker's memory" and leading him towards a more "favorable view of lust"? [30]

A sound reaction against such forced, oversimplified, and diluting interpretations of Shakespeare's very words and particularly against an excessive modernization of his punctuation led Laura Riding and Robert Graves to the opposite extreme. If more than once the Elizabethan was subliminally adapted by editors and commentators to a Victorian poetics, the authors of the essay "William Shakespeare and E. E. Cummings" are in turn prone to close the chasm between these two poets of dissimilar quests and strivings. The research of the last decades has shown the significant role of fanciful ambiguities in the work of Shakespeare, but there is a far-reaching distance from his puns and double meanings to the surmise of the free and infinite multiplicity of semantic load attributed to Sonnet 129 by the critics named. An objective scrutiny of Shakespeare's language and verbal art, with particular reference to this poem, reveals the cogent and mandatory unity of its thematic and compositional framework. The perspicuous confrontation of a joy proposed beforehand with a phantom lingering afterwards (III_4) cannot be arbitrarily recast into a joy "to be desired through the dream by which lust leads itself on" or into such accessory "legitimate" meanings as "before a joy can be proposed there must be a dream behind, a joy lost by waking" or "before a joy can be proposed it must be put behind as a dream," and so on.[31] That none of these alleged meanings has the slightest substantiation in Shakespeare's verse, "so far from variation or quick change" (Sonnet 76), can and must be corroborated by a structural analysis of his text and poetic texture in all its interlaced facets.

CHAPTER 13

Yeats' "Sorrow of Love" through the Years

With Stephen Rudy

Why, what could she have done being what she is?
Was there another Troy for her to burn?
  "No Second Troy," 1910

Paul Valéry, both a poet and an inquisitive theoretician of poetry as an "art of language," recalls the story of the painter Degas, who loved to write poems, yet once complained to Mallarmé that he felt unable to achieve what he wanted in poetry despite being "full of ideas." Mallarmé's apt reply was: "It is hardly with ideas, my dear Degas, that one makes poetry. It is with words."[1] In Valéry's view Mallarmé was right, for the essence of poetry lies precisely in the poetic transformation of verbal material and in the coupling of its phonetic and semantic aspects.[2]

William Butler Yeats, in a paper written in 1898 in favor of "art that is not mere story-telling," defended the notion that "pattern and rhythm are the road to open symbolism." According to Yeats, "the arts have already become full of pattern and rhythm. Subject pictures no longer interest us." In this context he refers precisely to Degas, in Yeats' opinion an artist whose excessive and obstinate desire to 'picture' life— "and life at its most vivid and vigorous"—had harmed his work.[3] The poet's emphasis on pattern reminds one of Benjamin Lee Whorf, the penetrating linguist who realized that "the 'patternment' aspect of language always overrides and controls the 'lexation' or name-giving aspect,"[4] and an inquiry into the role of "pattern" in Yeats' own poetry becomes particularly attractive, especially when one is confronted with his constant and careful modifications of his own works.

Text and Variants

As early as 1899 Yeats stated that he "revised, and, to a great extent, rewrote . . . certain lyrics."[5] His epigraph to *Collected Works in Verse and Prose* (Stratford-on-Avon, 1908) reads:

> The friends that have it I do wrong
> When ever I remake a song,
> Should know what issue is at stake:
> It is myself that I remake.[6]

And in January, 1927 he mentions "new revisions on which my heart is greatly set" and adds, characteristically, "one is always cutting out the dead wood."[7] For the 1925 edition of his *Early Poems and Stories* he "altered considerably" several of his poems, among them "The Sorrow of Love," "till they are altogether new poems. Whatever changes I have made are but an attempt to express better what I thought and felt when I was a very young man."[8]

"The Sorrow of Love," which we will henceforth refer to as *SL,* is preserved in the poet's manuscript of October 1891 (*SL 1891*), then in two variants of 1892 differing slightly from each other, one published in the volume *The Countess Kathleen and Various Legends and Lyrics* (*SL 1892*) and the other in the weekly *The Independent* of October 20, 1892 (*SL 1892 Ind*). Later single changes appeared in Yeats' *Poems* (1895) and in their revised edition (1899). The radically reshaped text appeared first in Yeats' *Early Poems and Stories* (*SL 1925*), the notes to which, expressly mentioning *SL,* were quoted above.[9]

The poet's "Sorrow of Love," which may be traced in its textual changes through over three decades, proved to be fruitful material for investigation. The comparative reproduction of *SL 1925* and the first version included in one of Yeats' volumes, *SL 1892,* with all other relevant textual variants, follows:

The Sorrow of Love
(final version, 1925)

₁The brawling of a sparrow in the eaves,
₂The brilliant moon and all the milky sky,

I   ₃And all that famous harmony of leaves,
    ₄Had blotted out man's image and his cry.

    ₁A girl arose that had red mournful lips
    ₂And seemed the greatness of the world in tears,
II ₃Doomed like Odysseus and the labouring ships
    ₄And proud as Priam murdered with his peers;

    ₁Arose, and on the instant clamorous eaves,
    ₂A climbing moon upon an empty sky,
III ₃And all that lamentation of the leaves,
    ₄Could but compose man's image and his cry.

The Sorrow of Love [a]

(first book version, 1892)

    ₁The quarrel [b] of the sparrows in the eaves,
    ₂The full round moon and the star-laden sky,
I   ₃And the loud song of the ever-singing leaves [c]
    ₄Had hid [d] away earth's old and weary [e] cry.

    ₁And then you came with those red mournful lips,
    ₂And with you came the whole of the world's tears,
II ₃And all the sorrows [f] of her labouring ships
    ₄And all the burden [g] of her myriad [h] years.

    ₁And now the sparrows warring [i] in the eaves,
    ₂The crumbling [j] moon, the white [k] stars in the sky,
III ₃And the loud chaunting of the unquiet leaves, [l]
    ₄Are shaken with earth's old and weary [e] cry.

[a] *1892 Ind:* the World [b] *1892 Ind:* quarreling [c] *1895:* leaves, [d] *1891:* hushed [e] *1892 Ind:* bitter [f] *1892 Ind:* sorrow; *1895:* trouble [g] *1895:* trouble [h] *1891:* million [i] *1891:* angry sparrows; *1892 Ind:* warring sparrows [j] *1891* and *1892 Ind:* withered; *1895:* curd-pale [k] *1892 Ind:* pale [l] *1891:* The wearisome loud chaunting of the leaves.

Actually, the poem offers two profoundly different texts, the early version of 1892, with a series of variants from the manuscript of 1891 to the final retouchings of 1895, and, on the other hand, the last, radically revised version of 1925. The final revision was so extensive that the vocabulary of the two versions has in common only: 1) the rhyme-words—in a few cases with their antecedent auxiliary words (I ₁*in the eaves,* ₂*and . . . the . . . sky,* ₃*of . . . leaves,* ₄*and . . . cry;* III ₃*of the . . . leaves,* ₄*and . . . cry*) and with the exception of one substitution (*1925:*II ₄*peers* for *1892: years*)—or with their attributes in the inner quatrain (II ₁*red mournful,* ₃*labouring*); 2) seven initial accessory monosyllables (five *and,* two *the,* one *had*); 3) one noun inside the second line of each quatrain (I ₂*moon,* II ₂*world,* III ₂*moon*).

Composition

The poem consists of three quatrains which in their structure display two patent binary oppositions: the two outer quatrains (I and III) exhibit common properties distinct from those of the inner quatrain (II), while at the same time they differ essentially in their internal structure from each other.

Both in the early and final version the poem confronts two opposite levels of subject matter, the upper and lower respectively. Six lines are devoted to each of them. The upper sphere, which may be labeled the "overground" level, is treated in the first three lines of each outer quatrain. The lower level is focused upon in the four lines of the inner quatrain and in the fourth line of each outer quatrain. The last line of these two quatrains (I_4 and III_4) designates its topic as *earth* in the early version of the poem and as *man* in the late version, and the lower level may thus be defined as 'terrestrial' in respect to *SL 1892* and as specifically 'human' in *SL 1925*.

Only the outer quatrains expressly designate the two different levels and bring them into conflict. In both versions of the poem the initial quatrain portrays the outcome of this combat as a victory, and the final quatrain—as a defeat, of the overground level. Yet the extent of these outcomes varies significantly in the two versions of the poem. In the early version (*SL 1892*) the two rival levels continue to coexist, and only their hierarchy undergoes a change: at the beginning the overground I $_4$*Had hid away earth's old and weary cry,* but at the end it is the characters of the overground who III $_4$*Are shaken with earth's . . . cry.* To this preserved contiguity of the adversary spheres the late version of the poem (*SL 1925*) replies first by the obliteration of the human level (the overground I $_4$*Had blotted out man's image and his cry*) and then, conversely, by the dissolution of the overground in the human level (the characters of the upper level III $_4$*Could but compose man's image and his cry*). In the parlance of the French translator Yves Bonnefoy, "Ne purent être qu'à l'image de l'homme et son cri d'angoisse," and in R. Exner's German translation, "Verdichten sich zu Menschenruf und Menschenbild."[10] As indicated by *A Concordance to the Poems of W. B. Yeats,* the verb *compose* appears in Yeats' poetry but once, in the final line of *SL 1925.*[11]

The mere contiguity, definable in metonymic terms, which characterized the two spheres in the outer quatrains of *SL 1892,* in *SL 1925* turns into a mutual metamorphosis of two contrastive sets of givens. The alternation of auditory and visual phenomena which delineate the upper sphere remains valid in both versions (the noise of the sparrow, the celestial view, the sound of leaves). In the early version, however, the lower sphere is merely audible, whereas in *SL 1925* it incorporates the visual dimension as well (*image* and *cry*) and thus corresponds in its deployment to the overground level.

In the inner quatrain of *SL 1925,* the heroine who suddenly emerges (II ₁*A girl arose*) is identified—through a chain of similes (II ₂*seemed,* ₃*like,* ₄*as*)—with the tragic and heroic human world. The system of metaphors underlying the inner quatrain of *SL 1925* differs patently from the whimsical metathetic confrontation of the two sociative prepositions *with* (II ₁*And then you came with.* . . . , ₂*And with you came* . . .) in *SL 1892* and from the series of summarizing totalizers (II ₂*the whole of* . . . , ₃*And all the* . . . *of* . . . , ₄*And all the* . . . *of* . . .) in the early version. The first of these totalizers (II ₂*the whole of the world's tears*) was transformed in SL 1925 into II ₂*the greatness of the world in tears,* which is in rough semantic contrast with I ₂*The brawling of a sparrow in the eaves,* while at the same time demonstrating an expressive formal parallelism that further emphasizes the irreconcilable divergences between the two levels.

To the simultaneous concord and discord between the parts of each of the integral poems, Yeats' creed as poet and creative visionary adds a different fusion of stability and variability, namely his view of development as "a temporal image of that which remains in itself," to quote Hegel as cited by the poet.[12] The two kinds of continual conflict between being and its opposite encompass both "coexistence" and "succession" according to Yeats, and in the case under discussion this applies to the dramatic tension both between the inner and outer or initial and final stanzas within one version of the poem and between the poem in its two different versions, the latter of which is seen by the author on the one hand as an "altogether new" poem and on the other hand as still belonging "to the time when [it was] first written."[13] Like the individual stanzas of *SL 1892* or *1925,* which find their antithesis within the given version, these two versions in turn stand next to each other in an antithetical struggle and harmonious complementarity.

In the Dedication to his *Early Poems and Stories* (1925) Yeats concludes his comments on the new versions of some poems "written before his seven-and-twentieth year" with the conviction: "I have found a more appropriate simplicity."[14] Critics, with rare exceptions,[15] have repudiated the alteration of *SL* with such statements as: "the new version as a whole is both ill-digested and obscure";[16] "the poem has been emptied of its vital content";[17] the earlier versions of *SL* "were inherently more logical and less pretentious and hence more charming."[18] It seems necessary to replace such unsubstantiated polemical replies to the poet's own view by a detailed and objective comparison of Yeats' poem in its two phases.

Grammar

It is against the background of the manifest grammatical symmetry underlying and uniting the three quatrains—and this symmetry is indeed supreme in *SL 1925*—that the significant individuality of each stanza in the dramatic composition of the entire poem gains a particular potency and eloquence. The distinct and thematically related features which differentiate single quatrains, their distichs, and single lines are achieved either through appreciable deviations from the predominant morphological and syntactic matrices or through the filling of these matrices with semantically divergent lexical and phraseological constituents. Robert Frost's metaphor, a favorite of I. A. Richards, on poets' preference for playing tennis with a net is valid not only for meter and rhyme but for the grammatical pattern of a poem as well.

-Ing Forms

1925

Before focusing on the two basic grammatical opposites—noun and verb—let us mention the intermediate morphological entity which is, according to Strang, "best labeled non-committally the *-ing form*."[19] Such forms appear once in every stanza of *SL 1925*, each time introducing the motif of movement into the nominal part of the three sentences: the first, in a substantival function, I $_1$*The brawling,* and the other two in an adjectival use, II $_3$*the labouring ships* and III $_2$*A climbing moon.*

1891–92

Like *SL 1925*, the manuscript of 1891 contained one *-ing* form in each quatrain, two of the three in adjectival and one in substantival function (I ₃*ever-singing*, II ₃*labouring*, III ₃*the . . . chaunting*). Their salient pattern in *SL 1891* was their location in the third line of each quatrain. *SL 1892* displays a greater tendency toward dynamism in the third quatrain, in which, besides the already-mentioned substantival III ₃*the . . . chaunting*, one finds the two attributes, ₁*warring* and ₂*crumbling*.

Nouns

1925

The poem contains twenty-seven (3^3) nouns, nine (3^2) in each quatrain, of which three in each quatrain occur with prepositions:

    I ₁(of) *sparrow*, (in) *eaves*; ₂*moon, sky*; ₃*harmony*, (of) *leaves*; ₄*man's image, cry*

    II ₁*girl, lips*; ₂*greatness*, (of) *world*, (in) *tears*; ₃*Odysseus, ships*; ₄*Priam*, (with) *peers*

    III ₁(on) *instant, eaves*; ₂*moon*, (upon) *sky*; ₃*lamentation*, (of) *leaves*; ₄*man's, image, cry*

One even line of each quatrain has three nouns (I₄, II₂, III₄), and any other line—two nouns. This rule can be further specified. In the outer (odd) quatrains the even line of the even distich contains an odd number of nouns (3), whereas in the inner (even) quatrains this odd number of nouns (3) is found in the even line of the odd distich. Any other line of the poem contains an even number of nouns (2).

Each quatrain has only one abstract noun, each of more than one syllable and each followed by the same preposition: I ₃*harmony* (of); II ₂*greatness* (of); III ₃*lamentation* (of).

The poem contains six personal (human, belonging to the *who*-gender) nouns, of which two common (II ₁*girl*, ₄*peers*) and two proper names (₃*Odysseus*, ₄*Priam*) appear in the inner quatrain, whereas each of the outer quatrains has only one personal noun, the possessive *man's* in I₄ and III₄. Of these six personal nouns only one (II ₁*girl*) belongs to the feminine (*she*-) gender, while the other five are of the masculine (*he*-) gender.

Only nouns function as rhyme fellows, and the plural occurs solely in rhymes: eight of the twelve rhyme fellows are plural nouns. Might not this propensity of the rhyming line-ends for the plural perhaps underscore a contrast between the frame of the lines and their inside? Is not the inside of the line the actual arena in which the individual actors of the drama perform, such as "the brawling sparrow" and "the brilliant moon," "a girl" and "man," "Odysseus" and "Priam"? The distinctness of the rhymes is highlighted not only by their grammatical peculiarities, but also by the consistent use of monosyllabic words in all the rhymes of the poem and by the common vocalic properties that all of them share: the rhymes of the first quatrain, all repeated in the third, are built on the phoneme /i/ alone or as the asyllabic end of the dipthong /ai/, while all four lines of the second quatrain use /ɪ/, the lax (short) opposite of the tense /i/. The two constituents of each of the six rhymes are morphologically homogeneous but syntactically heterogeneous. In each quatrain one line ends in a grammatical subject (I $_2$*sky*, II $_3$*ships*, III $_1$*eaves*), one in a direct object (I $_4$*cry*, II $_1$*lips*, III $_4$*cry*), and two in prepositional constructions (I $_1$*in the eaves*, $_3$*of leaves*; II $_2$*in tears*, $_4$*with his peers*; III $_2$*upon an empty sky*, $_3$*of the leaves*). The variety in the syntactic use of the rhyming nouns achieved in *SL 1925* is lacking in the early version, where ten of the rhyme-fellows belong to prepositional constructions. The only exception in *SL 1892* is the rhyming of the subject I $_2$*sky* with the direct object I $_4$*cry*, which grammatically underlines the striking opposition of the overground and terrestrial levels.

1892

The distribution of nouns is here less symmetrical than in the final version. There is a total of 25 nouns in *SL 1892*, the number per quatrain oscillating between nine (I) and eight (II and III). One line of each quatrain contains three nouns; two lines—two nouns each; and one line—two or one.

All three abstract nouns of *SL 1925* are innovations of the final version; the early version is completely devoid of abstracts. There are no properly personal nouns, but *SL 1892* contains three possessive forms, each in an even line of a different quatrain and each pertaining to a noun which exhibits, in Jespersen's terms,[20] "some approach to personification": II $_2$*the world's tears* and I$_4$, III$_4$ *earth's cry*, the latter in positional correspondence to the possessive form of the properly personal noun in *SL 1925*, I$_4$, III $_4$*man's*. (As regards the personalization of the possessives of *SL 1892*, cf. such lines in Yeats' works as "The wandering earth *herself* . . ." or "before earth took him to her stony care."[21] It is noteworthy that in both versions the possessive always falls on the metrical upbeat. The increase of personalization among the nouns of *SL 1925* is also witnessed by the replacement of the personal pronoun *you* in II $_{1-2}$ of *SL 1892* by the noun II $_1$*girl*.)

The number of plurals in the rhyme-fellows remains constant in both versions, but *SL 1892* has, in addition, four plural nouns *inside* the line, one in quatrains I and II, and two in quatrain III; I $_1$*sparrows;* II $_3$*sorrows,* III $_1$*sparrows,* $_2$*stars*. All four interior plurals are framed by hissing sibilants, an initial /s/ and a final /z/, and have a stressed vowel followed by /r/. Thus the grammatical differentiation between the inside and the end of the lines achieved in *SL 1925* by the restriction of plural nouns to the latter is missing in *SL 1892*.

The word *sorrows* of II$_3$ was apparently discarded in the final version to avoid the repetition of the words of the title within the text, as in a similar way the tentative title of *SL 1892 Ind,* "The Sorrow of the World" was cancelled because *world,* not *love,* occurs in the text. The pun-like confrontation of II $_3$*sorrows* and I$_1$, III $_1$*sparrows* became confined in *SL 1925* to the title and opening line, where *sparrows* imitate the singular form of *Sorrow*. This change from plural to singular, effective not only in grammatical meaning but also in sound— I $_1$*The brawling of a sparrow*—met with the objections of the critic Parkinson, for whom "*brawling* is not perfectly right; can one sparrow brawl?"[22] Cf., however, such usages of this word in Yeats' poetry as "big brawling lout" or "I took you for a brawling ghost."[23]

Prenominal Attributes

1925

The phrases built of nouns and prenominal attributes (adjectives proper and -*ing* forms) in the three quatrains of *SL 1925* display a remarkably symmetrical patterning:

	LINE: 1.	2.	3.	4.		TOTAL
I:	—	2	1	—	=	3
QUATRAIN II:	2	—	1	—	=	3
III:	1	2	—	—	=	3
						9

224

Each quatrain contains two lines with and two lines without prenominal attributes. There are no prenominal attributes in the fourth line of any quatrain. Of the first three lines in each quatrain, one line contains two, one line—one, and one line—no prenominal attributes. The third line contains no more than one prenominal attribute (I $_3$*famous*, II $_3$*labouring*, III$_3$———). If one of the first three lines contains no prenominal attributes, a neighboring line will have two of them: I $_1$———, $_2$*brilliant, milky*; II $_1$*red, mournful,* $_2$———; III $_2$*climbing, empty*, $_3$———). In contradistinction to the outer quatrains, with prenominal attributes in contiguous lines, the inner quatrain has such attributes in its odd lines only. The line without prenominal attributes advances from one quatrain to the next, so that its distribution forms a descending curve. The distribution of prenominal attributes in the first three lines of the final quatrain displays a mirror symmetry to that of the initial quatrain ($1, 2, — \leftrightarrow —, 2, 1$).

<hr>

1892

The early version of *SL* is almost twice as rich in prenominal attributes with an epithetical function (total 17–18) and has a higher number of such attributes in the outer as opposed to the inner quatrains: seven in I ($_2$*full round*, $_2$*star-laden*, $_3$*loud*, $_3$*ever-singing*, $_4$*old and weary*) and seven in the earliest two versions of III (*1891* and *1892 Ind.*), whereas the number in *SL 1892* is reduced to six—$_2$*crumbling*, $_2$*white*, $_3$*loud*, $_3$*unquiet*, $_4$*old and weary*—by the replacement of the prenominal attribute *1891: angry* (*1892 Ind: warring*) *sparrows* by III $_1$*sparrows warring*. On the other hand, II contains only four prenominal attributes: $_1$*red mournful*, $_3$*labouring*, $_4$*myriad*.

One could say that the changes found in *SL 1925* are in line with such slogans as Marianne Moore's warning against the use of too many adjectives and adverbs, which is based upon the notion that "poetry is all nouns and verbs."[24] As Parkinson states, the revised text of the poem "reduces the number and sensuous reference of epithets."[25] Yeats himself acknowledges a tendency toward the exfoliation of his style.[26]

Postpositive Attributes

SL 1925 contains postpositive (semi-predicative) attributes only in the second distich of the inner quatrain. Of the three occurrences, two are past passive participles (II $_3$*Doomed,* $_4$*murdered*) and one is an adjective (II $_4$*proud*). The only postpositive attribute in *SL 1892* (II $_1$*sparrows* WARRING *in the eaves*) was absent in the two earliest variants (*1891, 1892 Ind.*).

Pronouns

1925

Only three pronouns occur in the poem. All three are attributive, and each of them—*his, that, all*—is repeated three times, giving a sum total of nine. *His* occupies the penultimate syllable of the last line in each quatrain and refers expressly to a masculine noun: I $_4$*his cry,* II $_4$*his peers,* III $_4$*his cry* (*man's* in I$_4$ and III$_4$; *Priam* in II$_4$). *That* appears in one odd line of each quatrain, as a demonstrative pronoun referring, in a rather high-flown manner, to abstracts in the outer quatrains (I $_3$*that . . . harmony,* III $_3$*that lamentation*) and as a relative pronoun referring to a feminine noun in the inner quatrain (II $_1$*a girl . . . that*)— in accordance with the subordinative structure of this stanza. *All* occurs only in the outer quatrains, two times in contiguous lines of the first and once in the third, in the combinations *and all the* (I$_2$), *And all that* (I$_3$, III$_3$), and refers to singular nouns of the overground level, I $_2$*sky,* I $_3$*harmony of leaves,* III $_3$*lamentation of the leaves.*

1892

The outer quatrains of *SL 1892* are devoid of pronouns, whereas the inner quatrain contains seven. In *SL 1925* Yeats "dropped the simulation of the structure of address,"[27] while all the early versions of SL twice make use of the personal pronoun *you* in the first distich, with reference to the female addressee of the poem, and then of *her* in the second distich, with reference to the *world,* which merges with the addressee: II$_1$*you came with . . .* $_2$*And with you came the whole of the world's tears.* All the lines of the inner quatrains are dominated by the *she*-gender, which is directly expressed in both lines of the second distich and clearly alluded to in the *you* and *world* of the first distich. In *SL 1925* the feminine pronoun of the first distich (the relative *that* of II$_1$) gives way to the masculine pronoun of the second distich (II $_4$*his*), and the division into two distichs contrasted in gender is supported by the distribution of feminine and masculine nouns (II $_1$*girl* and $_2$*world* vs. $_3$*Odysseus,* $_4$*Priam, peers*). Twice, in turn, the pronoun *all* opens the contiguous lines of the second distich in the inner quatrain of *SL 1892* (II $_{3,4}$*And all the* . . .), where it refers to nouns of the terrestrial level (II $_3$*sorrows,* $_4$*burdens*); in *SL 1925* this pronoun is found, on the contrary, in the outer quatrains (I$_3$, III $_3$*And all that* . . .), where it refers to the overground level. Finally, II $_1$*those,* in the context *you came with those red mournful lips,* reinforces the odic manner of direct address in the early version and makes the roles of both the addresser and the addressee more prominent.

Adverbs

Two adverbs, II $_1$*then and* III $_1$*now,* each preceded by the initial conjunction *And,* open the two sentences of the second and third quatrains of *SL 1892* (note also a third adverbial form in the first quatrain which is part of the complex adjective I $_3$*And . . . ever-singing*). All three disappear in *SL 1925.*

Articles

1925

The nine occurrences of *the* in the three quatrains form an arithmetical regression: 4—3—2. In the first half of the poem, three lines contain two definite articles each, and three have none, whereas the second half has three lines with one definite article in each, and three without any. In each quatrain of the poem, there are two lines with, and two without, definite articles.

	LINE: 1.	2.	3.	4.	TOTAL
I:	2 *the*	2 *the*	—	—	4
QUATRAIN: II:	—	2 *the*	1 *the*	—	3
III:	1 *the*	—	1 *the*		2
					9

Only one line in each quatrain, and in each case a different line, contains both the definite article and prenominal attributes: I$_2$, II$_3$,

III$_1$. Each quatrain has one line with the indefinite article *a* and/or *an,* which may be compared to the equal distribution of lines with the definite article (two lines per quatrain). The final line of each quatrain is completely devoid of articles.

The distribution of the articles is limited to the first two lines in the first quatrain and forms a rectangle. In the second and third quatrains the articles extend over the first three lines of each and form the figure of an oblique-angled quadrangle:

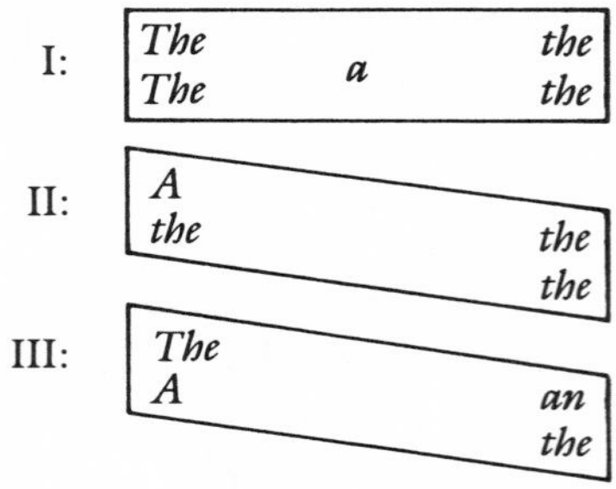

1892

Of the articles, *a* is totally absent from *SL 1892,* whereas the distribution of the definite articles—18 in the entire poem: seven in each of the outer quatrains and four in the inner one—corresponds strikingly to the identical pattern of prenominal attributes in the two earliest variants of the poem. It should be noted, finally, that in each quatrain of *SL 1892* only one line lacks the definite article: the final line of the outer quatrains, and the initial line of the inner quatrain.

Connectives

1925

The poem contains two equational conjunctions, both confined to the inner quatrain (II $_3$*like,* $_4$*as*), against nine copulative conjunctions, three instances of *and* in each quatrain. The other class of connectives, namely the prepositions (which here include *of, in, with, on,* and *upon*), like copulative conjunctions, numbers nine *in toto,* three per quatrain. The latter two classes of connectives taken together are attested nine times in each half of the poem (I_1—II_2 and II_3—III_4).

The distribution of these two categories (copulative conjunctions and prepositions) forms an identical chiasmus in the two distichs of each quatrain:

	CONJ.	+	PREP.	=	TOTAL
FIRST DISTICH:	1		2	=	3
SECOND DISTICH:	2	chiasmus	1	=	3
QUATRAIN	3		3	=	6

Thus in the transition from the first distich to the second each quatrain displays one and the same movement from government performed by the prepositions to grammatical agreement carried by the copulative conjunction *and*. This rule of transition from superposition to alignment may be juxtaposed to the consistent absence of masculine personal nouns in the first distichs of all three quatrains and the presence of such nouns in the final distich of each quatrain.

1892

Unlike *SL 1925*, the early version completely lacks equational conjunctions. As regards the copulative conjunctions and prepositions, their distribution in the two distichs of the first quatrain coincides with that of *SL 1925*. The tendency toward a higher number of prepositions in the first distich as opposed to the second is observable also in the other two quatrains of *SL 1892*, but the distribution is less regular than that of *SL 1925*, where the pattern established by the first quatrain was generalized throughout the poem. Thus, the distribution by distich exhibits the following pattern in *SL 1892* taken as a whole:

	CONJ.	+	PREP.	=	TOTAL
FIRST DISTICHS:	4		7	=	11
SECOND DISTICHS:	6		5	=	11
QUATRAINS:	10		12	=	22

In other words, the total number of all connectives throughout the early version of the poem is the same for its odd and even distichs. This equality is strengthened in *SL 1925* by the equal number of copulative conjunctions and prepositions in the poem as a whole and in each of its quatrains, and by the total number of such forms in each distich of the entire text.

Finite Verbs

1925

In the first half of the poem three lines without finites (I_{1-3}) are followed by three lines each containing one or more finites (I_4–II_2); in the second half of the poem the last line of each three-line group (II_3—III_2, III_{2-4}) contains a finite.

The number of finites is limited to six active forms referring to the third person. Three of these forms ($1 + 2$) appear in the outer quatrains, and three—in the first distich of the inner quatrain. The ratio of verbs to nouns is 1 : 3 in the inner and 1 : 8 in the two outer quatrains.

All three semantic types of verbs outlined by Jespersen[28]—verbs of action, of process, and of state—occur, each twice, among the six finite forms of *SL 1925*. The verbs of action are represented by two compound forms bound to the first hemistich of the last line in the outer quatrains (I $_4$*Had blotted out*, III $_4$*Could but compose*). The verbs of state are restricted to the first distich of the inner quatrain (II $_1$*had*, $_2$*And seemed*). The repeated verb of process occurs in the initial hemistich of the inner and last quatrains (II $_1$*arose*, III $_1$*Arose*). In *SL 1925* the verbs of action in their compound form each consist of four syllables, the verbs of process—two, and the verbs of state—of only one syllable.

The finites of the three quatrains exhibit a pervasive interplay. The initial and final predicates of the poem (I $_4$*Had blotted out*, III $_4$*Could but compose*), its only compound verbal forms and its only verbs of action, are dramatically played against one another. The auxiliary (I $_4$*Had* . . .) yields patently to the independent appearance of the same verb (II $_1$*had* . . . *lips*), which then pairs with the only other verb of status, II $_2$*And seemed*. . . . The only verb of process, arose, which heads the whole sentence of the inner quatrain (II $_1$*A girl arose* . . .), is repeated to introduce the third quatrain (III $_1$*Arose, and . . .*) and, finally, forms an internal rhyme with the last verb of the poem, III$_4$ . . . *compose.*

1892

SL 1925 contains a higher number of finites and, at the same time, exhibits a greater grammatical uniformity in their use than does the early version. The repertory of verbs in *SL 1892* is limited to four finites, two in the first distich of the inner quatrain and two in the last lines of the outer quatrains. The ratio of verbs to nouns is here 1 : 4 in the inner quatrain and 1 : 8 in the outer quatrain. The inner quatrain twice uses the same preterit, *came*, first in reference to the second person (II $_1$*you came with . . .*) and then in reference to the third person (II $_2$*with you came the whole . . .*). The compound finite forms of the outer quatrains, the sole verbs of action, differ in tense and voice (I $_4$*Had hid away*, III $_4$*Are shaken*).

In contradistinction to *SL 1925*, the early version lacks verbs of state. The verbs of action in the two versions are bound to the last line of the outer quatrains, whereas the first distich of the inner quatrain contains the verbs of process in *SL 1892* and the verbs of state in *SL 1925*. The verb of process occurs twice in both the early and final version, but in the former refers to different persons (second and third respectively) and in the latter qualifies as a genuine repetition (referring in both instances to II $_1$*A girl*). In *SL 1925* this verb of process pertains to the initial hemistich of the inner and final quatrains, while in *SL 1892* it is attached to the initial hemistich of the first and second line of the inner quatrain.

Despite these variations, the different semantic types of verbs follow the same mirror symmetry in both versions:

	1925	1892
Action	*Had blotted out*	*Had hid away*
Process	*arose*	*came*
State	*had*	
State	*seemed*	
Process	*Arose*	*came*
Action	*Could but compose*	*Are shaken*

231

Coordination and Subordination of Clauses

1925

The substantial difference between the inner quatrain and the two outer ones lies in their syntactic organization. The first and third quatrains are built on a coordination of four elliptical clauses: I(a) $_1$*The brawling* . . . (*Had blotted out* . . .); (b) $_2$*The brilliant moon (Had blotted out* . . .); (c) $_2$*and all the milky sky (Had blotted out* . . .); (d) $_3$*And* . . . *that harmony* . . . $_4$*Had blotted out man's image and his cry;* III (a)(*a girl*) $_1$*Arose;* (b) $_1$*and* . . . *eaves (Could but compose* . . .); (c) $_2$*A* . . . *moon* . . . (*Could but compose* . . .); (d) $_3$*And* . . . *that lamentation* . . . $_4$*Could but compose man's image and his cry.*

In the inner stanza, on the contrary, the syntactic division into four parts is based on grammatical subordination: II(a) $_1$*A girl arose;* (b) $_1$*that had* . . . $_2$*And seemed* . . . ; (c) $_3$*Doomed* . . . $_4$*And proud* . . .; (d) $_4$*murdered.* Each of the two inner parts of this quatrain—(b) and (c)— is in turn divided into two coordinate sections, each of which is bound together by the conjunction *and.*

1892

Each of the outer quatrains forms a sentence of four coordinated subjects bound elliptically with one and the same predicate: I(a) $_1$*The quarrel* . . . (*Had hid away* . . .); (b) $_2$*The* : . . *moon (Had hid away* . . .); (c) $_2$*and* . . . *the* . . . *sky (Had hid away* . . .); (d) $_3$*And the* . . . *song* . . . $_4$*Had hid away earth's old and weary cry;* III (a) $_1$*And now the sparrows* . . .; (b) $_2$*The* . . . *moon* . . .; (c) $_2$*the* . . . *stars* . . .; (d) $_3$*And the* . . . *chaunting* . . . $_4$*Are shaken with earth's old and weary cry.* In contradistinction to *SL 1925,* in the early version the inner quatrain also forms a coordinate sentence, which consists of a complete initial clause—(a) II $_1$*And then you came* . . .—followed by an elliptical combination of one predicate with three consequent subjects—(b) $_2$*And with you came the whole* . . .; (c) $_3$*And (with you came) all the sorrows* . . .; (d) $_4$(*with you came) all the burden.*

Thus in *SL 1892* coordination remains the constructive principle within each of the three quatrains, whereas *SL 1925* opposes the outer, coordinate quatrains to the inner quatrain, which is built on the principle of subordination.

Predication

1925

In the outer quatrains of both the early and final version, all the nominal subjects of the first three lines await their predicate in the fourth line. In the inner quatrain of *SL 1925* the main clause—II $_1$ *A girl arose*—takes up the initial hemistich of the first line, but the rest of the first distich is occupied by two collaterally subordinated clauses whose different predicates relate to the same antecedent subject, whereas in the outer quatrains different coordinated subjects relate to one and the same final predicate. In the final distich of this inner quatrain the two lines begin with semi-predicates of contracted collateral clauses (II $_3$ *Doomed*—$_4$ *And proud*) which are subordinated to an antecedent headword and followed in the final hemistich by a participial clause of lower syntactic rank (II $_4$ *murdered with his peers*).

1892

The basic structural difference between the inner quatrain of *SL 1892* and its outer quatrains lies in the progressive direction of the latter as opposed to the regressive orientation of the former.[29] Although the inner quatrain is composed, like the outer quatrains, of coordinated subjects with a joint predicate, there is an essential difference in the order of the primaries: in the outer quatrains the predicate is placed after the subject, whereas in the inner it appears before them (II $_2$ . . . *came the whole* . . .$_3$*And all the sorrows* . . .$_4$*And all the burden*). In the terms of *A Vision,* "these pairs of opposites [subject and predicate] whirl in contrary directions."[30] The same may be said of the distinctive criterion for the opposition of inner versus outer quatrains in *SL 1925,* that is, the principle of subordination as opposed to that of coordination.

Each of the two versions of *SL* contains one deviation from the opposition between the inner and outer quatrains established by the expression of subject and predicate. In *SL 1892* the first clause of the inner quatrain is the only one in the stanza which places the predicate after the subject (II $_1$ *And then you came* . . .). In *SL 1925* the initial, elliptical clause of the third quatrain, III $_1$ *Arose,* referring to the subject II $_1$ *A girl,* is the only among the elliptic clauses of the stanza which omits the subject rather than the predicate. It is significant that in both versions of *SL* the deviation occurs in regard to the only verb which is twice repeated and which signals the appearance of the heroine.

Sounds

According to Yeats' meditation of 1900, "all sounds, all colours, all forms, either because of their preordained energies or because of long association, evoke indefinable and yet precise emotions, or, as I prefer to think, call down among us certain disembodied powers, whose footsteps over our hearts we call emotions."[31]

The phonological association established in the early version of *SL* between the title of the lyric and the auditory imagery of its first quatrain is maintained in *SL 1925: Sorrow*—I $_1$*sparrow,* and *Love*—I $_3$*leaves.* Within the twelve lines of the poem the interplay of words allied in sound creates an affinity and contrast either between the components of the same line or between diverse lines within the same quatrain, and even within the same distichs, or, conversely, between correlative lines of two different quatrains. The appearance of expressive consonantal clusters through the use of tightly-knit word groups and of vocalic syncope furthers and widens the application of this poetic device.

Among other reasons for the textual changes in the final version of the outer quatrains, a pertinent role belongs to the paronomastic link established in these two stanzas between the auditory performance reported in their first lines and the visual phenomena referred to in their second lines. Moreover, especially in the first quatrain, a distinct alliteration binds these two vocables of the first distich, oriented respectively toward hearing and sight, with the predicate of the fourth line: I $_1$*brawling* /br.l/—$_2$*brilliant* /br.l/—$_4$*Had blotted* /bl/, and III $_1$*clamorous* /kl.m/—$_2$*climbing* /kl.m/—$_2$*empty* /mp/—$_3$*lamentation* /l.m/—$_4$*Could but compose* /k.mp/. The junctural cluster /db/ is common to both final predicates of the outer quatrains (I $_4$*Had blotted out*—III $_4$*Could but*). Note also the similar juncture /tk/ of III $_1$*instant clamorous*—III $_4$*but compose.* It is worth mentioning that none of the quoted words occurred in the early version.

Moon, the significant verbal image which in all variants of *SL* heads the second line of the two outer stanzas, finds no further support for its initial /m/ all through the first quatrain of the early version, and the only complementary instance of /m/ in the third quatrain—III

$_2$*crumbling moon* of *SL 1892*—was replaced in all editions from 1895 to 1924 by the nasal-less epithet *curd-pale*. Yet the latter form maintains the /k/, /r/, /l/ of its antecedent (which must have had an influence even on the sound shape and suffix of the corresponding attribute *climbing* in *SL 1925*). The chromatic and paronomastic correspondence to III $_2$*The curd-pale* /rd...l/ *lips* or *crumbling* /r.m.l/ *moon* was enclosed in the II $_1$*red mournful* /r.dm...l/ *lips* of the inner quatrain with three further enhancing occurrences of /m/: II$_1$, $_2$*came and* $_4$*myriad*. The focal innovation of *SL 1925* in its outer quatrains was the providing of $_2$*moon* with its vocalic, grammatical (*he*-gender), and semantic counterpart in the other even line of the same stanzas—I$_4$ and III $_4$*man's*.

In the outer quatrains of *SL 1925* the abstracts of the third, intermediate line—I $_3$*harmony* /m.n/ and III $_3$*lamentation* /m.n/—throw a paronomastic bridge between I, III $_2$*moon* and $_4$*man's;* at the same time they intensify the antithetic relation between the inner and outer stanzas, whereas in *SL 1892* the final distichs of the outer quatrains repeatedly confront I $_3$*the loud* /l.d/ *song* (or III $_3$*chaunting*) *of the* . . . *leaves* with I$_4$ and III $_4$*earth's old* /l.d/ *and weary cry*.

In *SL 1925* the even lines of the outer quatrains, in contradistinction to the odd lines, possess a clear-cut masculine break after the second downbeat of the iambic pentameter. In the outer quatrains the first hemistich of the second line finishes with *moon,* and the second hemistich of the fourth line begins with *man's*. The initial /m/ of the two alternants is symmetrically reinforced by the phonemic environment. In contradistinction to the only couple of grave (labial) nasals in *SL 1895* and subsequent editions before 1925 (I$_2$ and III $_2$*moon*), the outer quatrains of *SL 1925* number fourteen instances of this phoneme: within the initial quatrain /m/ appears twice in each of its even lines and in the intermediate line (I $_2$*moon* . . . *milky sky,* $_4$*man's image,* $_3$*famous harmony);* the final quatrain has one /m/ in each odd line and three in each even line (III $_1$*clamorous,* $_2$*climbing moon* . . . *empty sky,* $_3$*lamentation,* $_4$*compose man's image*). The double chain of the /m.n/ responses is most telling: I *moon—harmony—man's;* III *moon—lamentation—man's*. It is also significant that precisely the final picture of the lonesome lunar wanderer contains the greatest accumulation of nasals: III $_2$*A climbing moon upon an empty sky* (with seven nasals: three labial, three dental, and one velar).

In the initial simile of the inner quatrain the sounds of the "tenor," II$_1$*girl* /g.rl/, show twofold ties with the 'vehicle', II $_2$*greatness* /gr/ *of the world* /rl/. Let us mention in this connection that Marjorie Perloff was right in pointing out the "trilled r's" in the poet's recorded readings of his own poems;[32] the *r*-colored vowels of English include a postvocalic /r/ in Yeats' sound pattern, so that the vowel of *girl* and *world* is here really followed by a pair of liquid phonemes /rl/. The seven occurrences of a tautosyllabic /r/ distinctly detach the inner quatrain of *SL 1925* from the outer quatrains, where /r/, with one exception (I ₃*harmony*), regularly occupies a prevocalic position.

The only internal noun common to both versions of the second stanza—II₂*world*—is in both of them supplied with an antecedent analogous in its sonorant cluster /rl/: in *SL 1925* the preceding line of the same quatrain opens with the noun II ₁*girl,* whereas in *SL 1892* the corresponding line of the initial quatrain has two complex epithets each containing a cluster of these liquids—I ₂*full round* /lr/ . . . *star-laden* /rl/—echoed by /rl/ in II ₃*her lab(ou)ring.*

In the inner quatrain of *SL 1925,* two subordinate constructions, the first and last not only in this stanza but also in the poem as a whole, are bound together by their melancholy mood and form a complex paronomasia: II ₁*had red mournful* . . .—₄*murdered* /dr.dm.r—m.rd.rd/. It is curious that Parkinson[33] scorned the latter "major word" as prosaic, unordered, and unable to "participate in the alliterative pattern": II ₄*proud* /pr/—*Priam* /pr/—*peers* /p.r/. An alliterative pattern concludes each outer quatrain in *SL 1892* (I ₃*harmony*—₄*Had*—₄*his,* III ₄*Could*—*compose*—*cry),* along with a triple vocalic 'anlaut': I ₄*away earth's old* and III ₄*Are shaken with earth's old.* Furthermore, one observes that although it does not take part in the alliteration of the initial consonants, II ₄*murdered* in *SL 1925* is nevertheless tied to the words of the antecedent hemistich: *proud* /pr.d/—/rd.rd/ and *Priam* /pr.m/—/m.r/. The two marginal lines of the inner quatrain inspires Yeats from *SL 1892* on to seek a paronomastic bond in their somber imagery: II ₁*mournful* /m.r/ *lips*—₄*myriad* /m.r/ *years.* In *SL 1925* both of these lines are patently framed in their sound shape by the imagery of the surrounding distichs: I ₃*harmony of leaves* /rm.n...l/—II ₁*red mournful lips* /r.dm.rn..l/—II ₄*murdered* /m.rd.rd/—III ₁*clam(o)rous eaves* /l.mr/.

The only epithets taken over from the early version of the poem by *SL 1925* are those attached to the rhyme-words of the odd lines in the inner quatrain: II ₁*red mournful lips* and ₃*lab(ou)ring ships.* The latter attribute shared its sounds /l.br/ with II ₄*burden* /b.r/ of *SL 1892* and II

$_{3,4}$*trouble* /r.b.l/ of *SL 1895*. In *SL 1925* the inward antithesis (*a sparrow—the world*) of the outwardly similar lines I $_1$ and II $_2$ (*the . . . of . . . in . . .*) bursts into the utmost semantic contrast between the chirp of a single little bird and the heavy scend of Odysseus' ships: I $_1$*brawling*—II $_3$*lab(ou)ring,* tied together by the common suffix *-ing* and by their identical but differently ordered root consonants /br.l/—/l.br/. The same lines of these two quatrains were juxtaposed in *SL 1892* by the pun-like paronomasia I $_1$*of the sparrows*—II $_3$*the sorrows of.*

Verse Pattern

A detailed structural analysis of the masculine iambic pentameter in which *SL* is written would obviously require a careful examination of the poet's and his contemporaries' output in the same and cognate meters. Except for a few preliminary sketches by Dougherty and Bailey,[34] a systematic, linguistically-based inquiry into modern English versification has scarcely even begun, as compared to at least six decades of Slavic, especially Russian, investigation in the domain of metrics, with its historically and methodologically fruitful results in such questions as the rhythmical relevance of word boundaries and of higher syntactic units of varying rank.

For the main topic of our study—the comprehensive investigation of the basic oppositions which determine the relation, on the one hand, between the different parts of the poem in each version and, on the other, between *SL 1892* and *SL 1925*—the most illuminating aspect of the verse is the various patterning of the two fundamental prosodic types of words which fulfill the downbeats of the binary meter. These two types have been clearly distinguished both in the Russian tradition of metrical studies and in the most recent papers devoted to English versification. Thus Kiparsky singles out,[35] on the one hand, "members of lexical categories—nouns (including members of compounds), adjectives, verbs, and adverbs" and, on the other hand, "members of non-lexical categories (such as *his, the, and, with*)" which are in construction with the lexical members. (Russian tradition terms these two classes of units as "lexical" and "formal" respectively.) In *SL 1925*, for example, there is a significant difference between downbeats carrying the primary or only stress in the separate lexical constituents, I $_2$*milky sky,* with two primary stresses, as opposed to I $_3$*harmony,* with the primary stress on the first syllable, or I ₁*in the eaves,* with the primary stress on the third.

In *SL 1925* the outer quatrains display a clear regressive undulatory curve in the treatment of the downbeats: the three odd downbeats carry a greater percentage of primary stresses—and may thus be designated as "heavy" downbeats—than do the two even ("light") downbeats (see the figure below). In these two outer quatrains, as in all stanzas of *SL* irrespective of its version, the final downbeat of all lines is consistently allotted a primary stress. In the initial quatrain of *SL 1925* all three of the odd (heavy) downbeats receive a primary stress in all the lines, whereas the fourth and second downbeats carry a primary stress only in one and two lines respectively.

In the final quatrain the numerical superiority of primary stresses on odd downbeats over the even downbeats remains valid but is reduced throughout, thus slightly flattening out the undulatory curve exhibited in the initial quatrain: the first and third downbeats each carry three primary stresses, and the second and fourth have two.

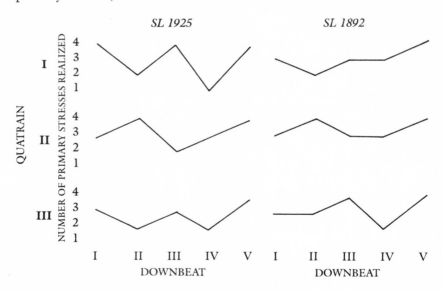

Frequency of primary stresses on the downbeats in the two versions

In opposition to the outer quatrains, with their sequence descent—ascent (4–2–4 and 3–2–3), the inner quatrain displays the reverse sequence (3–4–2), followed by a gradual ascent (3–4), so that it once again differs strikingly from the two outer quatrains. In *SL 1892,* as mentioned, the final downbeat of any line always carries a primary stress, but in the other four downbeats the undulatory curve is much less pronounced than in *SL 1925:* besides a sequence of descent and ascent, two neighboring downbeats may display an equal number of primary stresses. Thus there appears a mirror symmetry between the initial and final quatrain: descent—ascent—equality, and equality—ascent—descent, respectively. The sequence equality—ascent (3–3–4), which concludes the order of downbeats in the initial and inner quatrains, opens the final quatrain. In terms of this relation, the inner quatrain of *SL 1892* occupies an intermediary place between the two outer quatrains.

Within the line, monosyllabic lexical words occur on upbeats and are followed by downbeats under primary stress 10 times in *SL 1892,* four times in each outer quatrain (with a consistent lexical symmetry between I and III: *moon—star—loud—earth's*), and two times in the inner quatrain: I $_2$ *full round moon,* $_2$ *star-laden,* $_3$ *loud song,* $_4$ *earth's old;* II $_1$ *red mournful,* $_2$ *world's tears;* III $_2$ *curd-pale moon,* $_2$ *white stars,* $_3$ *loud chaunting,* $_4$ *earth's old.* Each quatrain of the final version preserves only one instance of the same phenomenon, literally repeating II $_1$ *red mournful,* and replacing the possessive *earth's* by I $_4$ and III $_4$ *man's.* The avoidance of filling inner upbeats with stressed monosyllabic words approaches a rule.

Only *SL 1925* contains instances of the standard use of stressed monosyllables in the initial upbeat (anacrusis): II $_3$ *Doomed like Odysseus,* III $_4$ *Could but compose.*

Constructive Principles

1925

SL 1925 displays an astounding symmetry in the distribution of the major grammatical categories among the three quatrains, a symmetry which is either lacking or muted in the early version. It may indeed be considered a persuasive example of the "geometrical symbolism" which was so vital a force both in the poet's subliminal imagery and in his abstract thought. The operative principle regulating the poem's symmetries is here the number 3 and its exponents (3^2, 3^3). When reflecting on the Great Wheel as the "principal symbol" of the universe, Yeats insisted that "each set of 3 is itself a wheel."[36] In his description of the 28 phases Yeats qualifies the first phase as "not being human,"[37] so that three to the third power (3^3) in fact exhausts the entire human realm.

There are 27 nouns in all (3^3), 9 per quatrain (3^2), which include 3 abstracts and 3 nouns with prepositions, each distributed one per quatrain. A total of three -*ing* forms are present, one per quatrain. Prenominal attributes and pronouns each total 9 (3^2), the former distributed symmetrically (3 per quatrain), the latter displaying only partial symmetry (three different pronouns, two of which appear once in each quatrain). The occurrences of the definite article also total 9. The connectives total 18, of which 9 (3^2) are copulative conjunctions and 9 (3^2)—prepositions, each appearing 3 times per quatrain. Only in the distribution of verbs does the principle of three find expression in a dichotomy of inner versus outer stanzas rather than in their symmetrical equivalence.

1892

The impressive symmetrical identity established between the quatrains of *SL 1925* by the distribution of grammatical categories is almost entirely lacking in *SL 1892*. Of the major categories, only the possessives are equally apportioned, one per stanza. Instead of the equivalence symmetry of *SL 1925*, one finds in *SL 1892* a dissimilatory use of grammatical means to distinguish the inner from the two outer quatrains.

In *SL 1892* the contrast between the three quatrains is conveyed either by the presence of certain grammatical categories in the inner quatrain, coupled with their absence in I and III, or by an equal distribution of certain categories in the two outer quatrains as opposed to their lower frequency in the inner, and here it is the number 7, rather than 3, which serves as the operative principle.

Thus, on the one hand, there are 7 pronouns in the inner quatrain, while the outer quatrains of *SL 1892* are completely devoid of this category. On the other hand, the inner quatrain has a lower number (4) of both prenominal attributes and definite articles than the outer quatrains, which each contain 7 such entities.

The inner quatrain of *SL 1892* also differs from the outer ones by the repetitive character of the initial part of the two lines within each distich (and their pronounced use of oxytones) and by the presence of redoubled grammatical words (the pronouns II $_{1,2}$*you*, $_{3,4}$*all*, $_{3,4}$*her* and the sociative prepositions $_{1,2}$*with*), which are lacking in the outer quatrains but are here strictly distributed by distich: II $_1$*And then YOU came WITH* . . .—$_2$*And WITH YOU came* . . .; $_{3,4}$*And ALL the* ($_3$*sorrows*, $_4$*burden*) *of HER*. . . . (In *SL 1895* and subsequent editions before 1925 the parallelism of the line beginnings in the second distich was complete: II $_{3,4}$*And all the trouble of her.*) The inner quatrain, moreover, is clearly dominated by the *she*-gender, which is merely hinted at in the last lines of the two outer quatrains.

Finally, the inner quatrain of *SL 1892*, although it follows the principle of coordination displayed by the two outer quatrains, is differentiated from them in terms of predication. Whereas the two outer quatrains are built on a progressive principle of four coordinated subjects bound elliptically to one and the same final verb, the inner quatrain opens with one complete "subject-predicate" clause, but then in the second line reverses the order of primaries into a sequence "predicate-subject."

It is worth noting that the two versions in several instances employ identical grammatical categories for opposite purposes. Generally, as is the case with prenominal attributes, articles and pronouns, the categories denoting equivalence of the quatrains in *SL 1925* designate contrast in *SL 1892*. The opposite case also holds: possessives, used in the early version as one of the sole means of establishing equivalence between quatrains, are, on the contrary, one of the sole means of contrasting the inner and outer quatrains in the late version.

1925

Despite the overwhelming preference of the final version for symmetries of equivalence rather than of contrast, the inner quatrain of *SL 1925* differs just as dramatically from the two outer quatrains as does that of *SL 1892*. In consecutive order each line of this quatrain breaks off manifestly from the pattern of the first stanza, which constitutes a separate sentence, detached in the final version from the rest of the text by the only full stop within the poem. As opposed to the outer quatrains, which are built entirely on the principle of coordination, it is based on subordination and contains the only two verbs of state to be found in the poem. The initial line of the inner quatrain is the only line in which one finds two finites; moreover, of these, one belongs to the main clause (II $_1$*arose*) and the other—to the first subordinate clause in the text (II $_1$*had*). The second line of this quatrain inaugurates a mirror-image sequence of diversified verbal types echoing the verbs of action, process and state which have appeared so far, but in reverse order. It also opens the set of three similes, which mark the metaphoric constitution of this quatrain as opposed to the metonymic structure of the two outer ones.

At the border between the two halves of the poem, the third line of the inner quatrain in *SL 1925* opens the distich II$_{3-4}$, the grammatical makeup of which diverges strikingly from all the other lines of the poem. This distich is the only to possess: (1) three personal nouns of the *he*-gender, namely two proper names (II $_3$*Odysseus,* $_4$*Priam*) and the appellative $_4$*peers;* (2) three postpositive semi-predicative attributes (II $_3$*Doomed,* $_4$*proud,* and *murdered*); (3) the only two equational conjunctions ($_3$*like,* $_4$*as*); and (4) the only sociative preposition in *SL 1925* ($_4$*with*). In contradistinction to this distich, the first distich of the same quatrain has three finites (II $_1$*arose, had,* $_2$*seemed*) and two nouns of the she-gender ($_1$*girl,* $_2$*world*). Thus a clear-cut set of features marks the borderline between the two halves of the poem.

The division of the poem into two halves of six lines each, further subdivided into two triplets, is also suggested by the distribution of certain grammatical categories. In the first half of the poem, three lines devoid of verbs are followed by three lines each containing at least one verb; in the second half, each of the two triplets has a verb in its last line. The definite article also displays a symmetrical distribution by halves and triplets: in the first half, a triplet containing two definite articles per line is followed by a triplet devoid of them; in the second half, a triplet containing one *the* per line alternates with a triplet again devoid of definite articles. Furthermore, the 18 copulative conjunctions and prepositions evenly divide into two sets of 9, one in each half of the poem.

Another division into two groups of six lines is clearly suggested by the subject matter. As mentioned above, in both versions six lines are devoted to the "overground" and six lines to the "terrestrial" (*SL 1892*) or "human" (*SL 1925*) level. This division is supported by the distribution of personal and non-personal nouns and pronouns: the personals are bound exclusively to the six 'terrestrial' or 'human' lines. The two versions differ, however, in the gender characterization of the personal nouns and pronouns of the terrestrial level. In *SL 1892* the four lines of the inner quatrain and the last line of each outer quatrain refer exclusively to the feminine gender. In *SL 1925*, however, the human lines are divided according to gender: those which belong to the second distichs of the quatrains are characterized as masculine (I_4, II_{3-4}, III_4); the others as feminine (III_{1-2}). The grammatical differentiation of the distichs finds consistent expression also in the relative distribution of copulative conjunctions and prepositions. The division of the quatrains into distichs is furthered by the alternating rhyme scheme (ABAB). It is significant that verbs appear in both versions only in the six lines referring to the terrestrial or human levels. The only exception to this rule is the bare repetitive transfer from the inner quatrain, III $_1$*Arose*, in *SL 1925*.

The external (marginal) and internal segments of the individual lines are mutually opposed by grammatical means. The line-ends in both versions are delimited by the fact that the rhyme-words are monosyllabic nouns and by the fact that plural nouns are proper in *SL 1925* only, and in *SL 1892* preponderantly, to the rhymes. In *SL 1925* any internal concrete noun enters into a metonymical relation with the following rhyme word, which in most instances specifies its framework: I $_1$*a sparrow in the eaves*, $_2$*The . . . moon and all the milky sky;* II $_2$*A girl . . . that had red mournful lips*, $_3$*Odysseus and the labouring ships*, $_4$*Priam murdered with his peers;* III $_2$*A . . . moon upon an empty sky.*

In *SL 1925* the final line of each quatrain is signaled grammatically by the presence of a noun of masculine human gender (I $_4$*man's*, II $_4$*Priam*, III $_4$*man's*) and of a corresponding possessive *his*, referring to these nouns and elsewhere absent, and by the lack of either articles or prenominal attributes.

The transition from one phase to another signaled in *SL 1892* by the pairs of adverbs, II $_1$*then* and III $_1$*now*, is obliterated in *SL 1925*. There, in agreement with *A Vision*, "every image is separate from every other, for if image were linked to image, the soul would awake from its immovable trance."[38] The focus upon time in *SL 1892* and its exclusion in *SL 1925* become particularly palpable when one opposes the six temporal indications of the early version—I $_3$*ever-* . . . , $_4$*old;* II $_1$*then*, $_4$*myriad years;* III $_1$*now*, $_4$*old*—to the total lack of such indications in the final version.

In both versions the properties common to the two outer quatrains are evident, whatever their relation (equivalence or contrast) to the inner. The equivalence of the two is semantically underlined, especially in *SL 1925*, where the first three lines in each portray a metonymic contiguity of overground images, visual in the even line, auditory in the odd lines, and thus correspond to the alternation of *man's* visible *image and his* audible *cry* in I_4, III_4. In *SL 1892* the terrestrial level referred to in the last line of each outer quatrain is described solely in auditory images (I_4, III_4 *earth's old and weary cry*).

The contrariety of the two outer quatrains finds a sharper grammatical expression in the early version, as in the differences of tense and voice in the verbs through the emergence of the present and passive (III $_4$*Are shaken*) and the confinement of prepositionless rhyme words to the first quatrain, whereas *SL 1925* has recourse chiefly to lexical means for contrasting the two outer quatrains. For example, an ironical turn inverts the syntactic hierarchy of the first two rhyme words: in I $_2$*sky* is a subject and I $_1$*eaves* an adverbial of place, while in the third quatrain the role of subject is assigned to III $_1$*eaves,* and $_2$*sky* is declassed to an adverbial of place.

The compound preterit forms of the predicate in the two outer quatrains of *SL 1925* are semantically opposed to each other: the initial one destructive and turned to the past, the final one constructive and prospective.

Semantic Correspondences

In the epithets of the manuscript version (*SL 1891*) there may be observed what the poet terms "an enforced attraction between Opposites";[39] III $_3$*The wearisome* [!] *loud chaunting of the leaves* suddenly reappears in III $_4$*shaken with earth's old and weary* [!] *cry.*

In comparison with *SL 1892*, the final version achieves a greater contrast between the two outer quatrains by impoverishing the image of the overground level in the third quatrain, and thus effectively pushes into the foreground the relation between the two opposite spheres. The characters that filled the overground lines of the first quatrain in *SL 1892* and *SL 1925* gradually diminish in number and their epithets become more subdued: I $_1$*a sparrow,* substituted in *SL 1925* for I $_1$ and III $_1$*the sparrows* of *SL 1892*, disappears behind the metonymy III $_1$*clamorous eaves* in the last stanza of the final version; the *famous harmony of leaves* which adorned I_3 gives way in III_3 to their plain *lamen-*

tation; I $_2$*the star-laden sky* and the *milky sky,* the grammatical subjects of the two versions, change in the final quatrain of *SL 1925* into a mere circumstantial modifier of place with a meager epithet, III $_2$*upon an empty sky.*

At the end of the two outer quatrains, the possessive *earth's* in *SL 1892* and *man's* in *SL 1925* designate the chief entity of the lower sphere. In the early version, I$_2$ and III$_2$ *sky* stood in direct opposition to the *earth's . . . cry* in the next even line of the same quatrains, whereas in the final version an analogous opposition embraces the initial nouns of the equivalent lines I$_2$ and III$_2$ *moon* in respect to I$_4$ and III$_4$ *man's.*

The threshold of the nineties was for Yeats marked by a "continual discovery of mystic truths."[40] The creation of *SL 1891* belongs to the period of his growing inclination toward esoteric research, with a faith in the correspondence between the human soul and body and the planets from Saturn to the Moon.[41]

The lunar body, as the main symbol in the poet's mythology, was promoted by Yeats with particular persistence in the first draft of his treatise *A Vision* (1925), which was prepared by the poet at the same time and with as much zeal as the final version of "The Sorrow of Love" (included by the author in another book of the same year, his *Early Poems and Stories*). In his note of 1925 to the latter collection, Yeats testifies that he is "now once more in *A Vision* busy with that thought, the antitheses of day and night and of moon and of sun"; he immediately turns to the cycle *The Rose* and relates that "upon reading these poems for the first time for several years" he realizes that their heroine has been imagined "as suffering with man and not as something pursued and seen from afar."[42]

Already in the early version of *SL* the contrasting images of I $_2$*The full round moon* and III $_2$*The crumbling* [*1891: withered*] *moon* were apparently related to the author's gradually maturing mystical doctrine later systematized in *A Vision.* This "philosophy of life and death" found its poetic embodiment in the phantasmagoria "The Phases of the Moon," first printed in 1919 and later included in the first edition of *A Vision.*[43] This poem[44] evokes the stage "When the moon's full" (lines 75ff), immediately followed by "the crumbling of the moon" (lines 87ff) and focuses on the diverse effects of these phases "Upon the body and upon the soul" (line 93). It is significant that from 1895 on, *crumbling* was replaced in *SL* by the trope *curd-pale,* and that in the final version of the poem these two telling epithets were supplanted by more remote allusions: I $_2$*The brilliant moon* and III $_2$*A climbing moon,* the latter ambiguous (climbing toward the zenith or rather toward the next phase?) and the former, *brilliant,* according to the author's own acknowledgement, for its "numbness and dullness," so "that all might seem, as it were, remembered with indifference, except some one vivid image."[45] That "one vivid image" must have been the dominant noun *moon* itself, the central visual motif common to the two pictures of the overground level in *SL 1925.*

"The full moon is Phase 15," Yeats writes, and "as we approach Phase 15, personal beauty increases and at Phase 14 and Phase 16 the greatest human beauty becomes possible."[46] While the inner quatrain of SL alludes to Phase 15, the two outer quatrains reflect its adjacent phases.

> Under the frenzy of the fourteenth moon,
> The soul begins to tremble into stillness,
> To die into the labyrinth of itself![47]

"Man's image and his cry," blotted out according to the initial quatrain of *SL 1925,* corresponds to the song of Robartes in "The Phases of the Moon" and to its further lines announcing the full moon:

> All thought becomes an image and the soul
> Becomes a body.[48]

—or in the terms of *SL 1925,* II $_1$ *A girl arose.*

> And after that the crumbling of the moon.
> The soul remembering its loneliness
> Shudders in many cradles; all is changed.[49]

As explained in *A Vision,* "there is always an element of frenzy," but "Phase 16 is in contrast to Phase 14, in spite of their resemblance of extreme subjectivity . . . It has found its antithesis, and therefore self-knowledge and self-mastery."[50] Briefly, it is the phase in which all the physical illusions of Phase 14 *Could but compose man's image and his cry.*

The inner quatrain lacks such pairs of opposites as *sky* and *earth* of *SL 1892* or *moon* and *man* of *SL 1925.* Yet at the same time, the *moon* of the two outer stanzas displays a particular correspondence to the heroine of the adjacent inner quatrain. In *SL 1892* the juxtaposed portrayals of I $_2$*The full round moon* and II $_1$*those red mournful lips* exhibit a multiple correspondence in the morphological and phonological makeup of the two phrases: *full—. . . ful* and /r.ndm.n/—/r.dm.rn/.

"My love sorrow [!]," says Yeats, "was my obsession, never leaving by day or night,"[51] and a passage in the first draft of his *Autobiography*, with a more than free paraphrase of Leonardo da Vinci's *Notebooks*, throws light on the image of the III $_2$*climbing moon* and its counterpart, the "arising" II $_2$*girl . . . that had red mournful lips* of *SL 1925*: "At last she came to me in I think January of my thirtieth year . . . I could not give her the love that was her beauty's right . . . All our lives long, as da Vinci says, we long, thinking it is but the moon that we long [for], for our destruction, and how, when we meet [it] in the shape of a most fair woman, can we do less than leave all others for her? Do we not seek our dissolution upon her lips?"[52] These lines may be confronted with an earlier paragraph of the same *Memoirs* (p. 72), the poet's confession of his twenty-seventh (3^3) year: "I think my love seemed almost hopeless . . . I had never since childhood kissed a woman's lips."

The outline of Phase 15 in *A Vision* adds that "now contemplation and desire, united into one, inhabit a world where every beloved image has bodily form, and every bodily form is loved. This love knows nothing of desire, for desire implies effort . . . As all effort has ceased, all thought has become image, because no thought could exist if it were not carried to its own extinction."[53] The motto to the poet's reflections on the Fifteenth Phase of the Moon reads: "No description except that this is a phase of complete beauty."[54] In *SL 1892* the inner quatrain, centered around this particular phase, strikingly differs from the outer stanzas grammatically and compositionally. Each of the two distichs is built on a widely pleonastic scheme. The first two lines display a pun-like juxtaposition of two identical sociative prepositions, one synecdochic (II $_1$*you came with those . . . lips*) and the other purely metonymic (II $_2$*with you came the whole of the world's tears*). In *SL 1895* the second distich achieved a heptasyllabic tautology, II $_{3-4}$*And all the trouble of her . . .* , with a salient sound figure, /r.b.l/—/l.b.r/ (*labouring*)—/r.b.l/.

The relative isolation of the second stanza with respect to the other quatrains of *SL 1892* is to a certain extent counterbalanced by the equivalent correspondences between the early version of this inner quatrain and a few of the surrounding poems of the cycle entitled *The Rose*. Writing on the birth of "those women who are most touching in their beauty," Yeats states in *A Vision* that Helen was of Phase 14.[55] The reference to Troy, later openly disclosed in *SL 1925*, remains rather obscure in the early version, but is clearly revealed in a poem which neighbors on *SL* in *The Rose* cycle, "The Rose of the World":

Who dreamed that beauty passes like a dream?
For *these red lips, with all their mournful pride,*
Mournful that no new wonder may betide,
Troy passed away in one high funeral gleam,
And Usna's children died.[56]

Not only phraseological but also versificational features reveal the affinity between the inner quatrain of *SL 1892* and the other lyrics of the same cycle. The repeated *arose* in II$_1$ and III$_1$ of *SL 1925* prompts one critic, John Unterecker, to see a double vision of "a girl arose" and "a girl, a rose."[57] The line II$_1$ is the only one in the poem with all the first three downbeats followed by a word boundary—*A girl/ arose/ that had/ red* . . . (cf. in *SL 1892* the corresponding line—II $_1$*And then/ you came/ with those/ red* . . . , and in *SL 1925* such initial oxytones in the same quatrain as II $_2$*And seemed/,* $_4$*And proud/*); it is interesting to note that the poem "The Rose" (1892), which opens the cycle of the same name, has the identical rhythm in its first line—*"Red Rose,/ proud Rose,/ sad Rose/* . . ."—literally repeated at the end of the poem (line 24), as well as in the initial line of the second twelve-line stanza—$_{13}$*"Come near,/ come near,/ come near/*."[58]

We are looking for correspondences between "The Sorrow of Love" and the adjacent poems of *The Rose,* but there is another tempting question, that of key words, abundant in the surrounding verses, which were passed over in silence in *SL.* Together with *SL* the poem "When You Are Old" is addressed to Maud Gonne[59] and is the only other text of *The Rose* cycle composed in three quatrains of iambic pentameter. It is hardly by chance that in this poem, which is placed in the edition of 1892 just before, and in editions from 1895 on immediately after, "The Sorrow of Love," the vocable *love,* confined to the title of *SL,* occurs six times, four times as a verb in the second quatrain (II $_1$*How many loved* . . . , $_2$*And loved your beauty,* $_3$*But one man loved* . . . , $_4$*And loved the sorrows* . . .) and twice as a substantive (II $_2$*with love false or true,* III $_2$ . . . *how Love fled*). In *SL* both love and Helen remain unnamed.

As to Helen's fate, "is it not because she desires so little, gives so little that men will die and murder in her service?"[60] According to the inner quatrain of *SL 1892,* she is accompanied by *the whole of the world's tears,* while in the ultimate version of this stanza, it is the *world in tears,* the second dramatis persona, which emerges as one of her metaphoric incarnations. Her further embodiments, the men who "die and murder" within the scene of the following distich, complete the list of personal nouns, and their subordinative pyramid pointedly distinguishes the inner stanza of *SL 1925* from the surrounding constructs, a dissimilarity further enhanced by the fact that the third central downbeat, which is the heaviest in the two outer quatrains, is the lightest downbeat in the inner stanza.

The world, incidentally, is the general character assigned in *A Vision* to the Phases 14, 15, 16 of the Great Wheel, with the subsequent inference *Sorrow,*[61] and it was under the title "The Sorrow of the World" that *SL 1892 Ind* appeared.

While the similarity association guides the patterning of the inner quatrain of *SL 1925,* in the early version of the poem the leading role belongs to relations of contiguity. The complete lack of human nouns (versus four in the same stanza of *SL 1925*), the surplus of pronouns (seven versus two in the final version), and especially the reiterated *you* of *SL 1892,* corresponding to *A girl* of *SL 1925,* all testify to the deictic function which underlies the inner quatrain of the early version. Quantifiers, as II ₂*the whole of the world's tears* and II ₄*myriad years,* are akin to the vocabulary of external relationship. The stanza devoted to Phase 15 either indicates (*SL 1892*) or names (*SL 1925*), but in either case restrains "description."

The critics may argue about which of the two versions is more "defective" and which of them requires more "indulgence." Nevertheless, the exacting selection and arrangement of verbal symbols summoned in "The Sorrow of Love" to build a harmonious system of rich semantic correlations and, in Yeats' own terms, "too much woven into the fabric of [his] work for [him] to give a detailed account of them one by one"[62] indeed warrant the poet's assertion: *And words obey my call.*

CHAPTER 14

Subliminal Verbal Patterning in Poetry

Que le critique d'une part, et que le versificateur d'autre
part, le veuille ou non.
Ferdinand de Saussure

Whenever and wherever I discuss the phonological and grammatical texture of poetry, and whatever the language and epoch of the poems examined, one question constantly arises among the readers or listeners: are the designs disclosed by linguistic analysis deliberately and rationally planned in the creative work of the poet and is he really aware of them?

A calculus of probability as well as an accurate comparison of poetic texts with other kinds of verbal messages demonstrates that the striking particularities in the poetic selection, accumulation, juxtaposition, distribution, and exclusion of diverse phonological and grammatical classes cannot be viewed as negligible accidentals governed by the rule of chance. Any significant poetic composition, whether it is an improvisation or the fruit of long and painstaking labor, implies a goal-oriented choice of verbal material.

In particular, when comparing the extant variants of a poem, one realizes the relevance of the phonemic, morphological, and syntactical framework for the author. What the pivots of this network are may and quite frequently does remain outside of his awareness, but even without being able to single out the pertinent expedients, the poet and his receptive reader nevertheless spontaneously apprehend the artistic advantage of a context endowed with those components over a similar one devoid of them.

The poet is more accustomed to abstract those verbal patterns and, especially, those rules of versification which he assumes to be compulsory, whereas a facultative, variational device does not lend itself so easily to a separate interpretation and definition. Obviously, a conscious deliberation may occur and assume a beneficial role in poetic creation, as Baudelaire emphasized with reference to Edgar Allan Poe. There remains, however, an open question: whether in certain cases intuitive verbal latency does not precede and underlie even such a conscious consideration. The rational account (*prise de conscience*) of the very framework may arise in the author ex post facto or never at all. Schiller's and Goethe's exchange of well-grounded assertions cannot be dogmatically dismissed. According to Schiller's experience (*Erfahrung*), depicted in his letter of March 27, 1801, the poet begins *nur mit dem Bewusstlosen* (merely with the unconscious). In his reply of April 3, Goethe states that he goes even farther (*ich gehe noch weiter*). He claims that genuine creation of a genuine poet *unbewusst geschehe* (happens unconsciously), while everything done rationally *nach gepflogner Überlegung* (after well-cultivated reasoning) occurs *nur so nebenbei* (only casually). Goethe does not believe that a poet's supplementary reflection would be capable of amending and improving his work.

Velimir Xlebnikov (1885–1922), when recollecting after several years his succinct poem "The Grasshopper," composed around 1908, suddenly realized that throughout its first, crucial sentence—*ot točki do točki* (between two full stops)—each of the sounds *k, r, l,* and *u* occurs five times "without any wish of the one who wrote this nonsense" (*pomimo želanija napisavšego ètot vzdor*), as he himself confessed in his essays of 1912–13, and thus joined all those poets who acknowledged that a complex verbal design may be inherent in their work irrespective of their apprehension and volition (*que . . . le versificateur . . . le veuille ou non*), or—to use William Blake's testimony—"without Premeditation and even against my Will." Yet also in his posterior reasonings Xlebnikov failed to recognize the much wider range of those regular phonological recurrences. Actually, all the consonants and vowels which pertain to the trisyllabic stem of the initial, picturesque neologism *krylyškúja,* derived from *krýlyško* (little wing), display the same "fivefold structuration," so that this sentence, divided by the poet now into three, now into four lines, comprises 5 /k/, 5 vibrants /r/ and /r'/, 5 /l/, 5 hushing (/ž/, /š/) and 5 hissing continuants (/z/, /s'/), 5 /u/, and within each of the two clauses 5 /i/ in both different, front and back, contextual variants of the given phoneme:

> Krylyškúja zolotopis'móm tončájšix žíl,
> Kuznéčik v kúzov púza uložíl
> Pribréžnyx mnógo tráv i vér.[1]

> Winging with the gold script of finest veins,
> The grasshopper filled the hollow of his belly
> With many offshore weeds and faiths.

The cited tristich, presenting a continuity of 16 duple, basically trochaic, feet, provides each of its three lines with four stressed syllables. Of the stressed phonemes, five flat (rounded) vowels, 3 /ú/ plus 2 /ó/, are opposed to their five nonflat (unrounded) correlates, 2 /í/ plus 3 /é/; and, on the other hand, these ten noncompact phonemes are divided into five diffuse (high) vowels, 3 /ú/ plus 2 /í/, and their five nondiffuse (middle) correlates, 2 /ó/ plus 3 /é/. The two compact /á/ occupy the same, second from the end position among the stressed vowels of the first and last lines and are both preceded by an /ó/: *pis' mÓm tončÁjšix— mnÓgo trÁv*. The five oxytones of the tristich, all five ending in a closed syllable, complete its pentamerous pattern.

The chain of quintets which dominate the phonological structuration of this passage can be neither fortuitous nor poetically indifferent. Not only the poet himself, originally unaware of the underlying contrivance, but also his responsive readers spontaneously perceive the astonishing integrity of the cited lines without unearthing their foundations.

While discussing examples of "self-contained speech" (*samovitaja reč'*) which show a predilection for a "five-ray structure" (*pjatilučevoe stroenie*), Xlebnikov detected this bent in the capital sentence of his earlier "Grasshopper" (written at the same time as Saussure's daring studies on poetic anagrams) but did not pay attention to the guiding role played in this connection by the gerund *Krylyškúja,* the initial neologism of the poem. Only when returning again to the same lines in a later essay (1914),[2] their author was charmed by the anagram hidden in the gerund: according to Xlebnikov, the word *uškúj* (pirate ship, metonymically pirate) sits in the poem "as if in the Trojan horse": *KRYLyŠKÚJA* 'winging' *sKRÝL uŠKÚJA derevjánnyj kón'* (the wooden horse concealed the pirate). The title hero *KUzNéčIK*, in turn, is paronomastically associated with *uŠKÚjNIK* (pirate), and the dialectal designation of the grasshopper, *konëk* (little horse), must have supported Xlebnikov's analogy with the Trojan horse. The lively ties of cognate words *kuznéčik* (literally little smith), *kuznéc* (smith), *kózni* (crafty designs), *kovát', kujú* (to forge), and *kovárnyj* (crafty) strengthen the imagery, and such a latent mainspring of Xlebnikov's creations as poetic etymology brings together *kuznéčik* with *kúzov* (basket, hollow), filled with many offshore weeds and faiths or perhaps varied foreign intruders. The swan evoked in the concluding neology of the same poem, *"Ó lebedívo—Ó ozarí!"* (send light!), seems to be a further hint of the Homeric subsoil of its ambiguous imagery: a prayer to the divine swan who begot Helen of Troy. *Lebed-ívo* is modeled upon *ogn-ívo* (strike-a-light), since the metamorphosis of Zeus into a flaming swan calls to mind the change of flint into fire. The form *ljúbedi* occurring in the primary sketch of "The Grasshopper" was a suggestive blend of *lébedi* (swans) with the root *ljub-* (love), a favorite root of Xlebnikov's word coinages. *Krylyškúja*, the key word of the poem, must have spontaneously, "in pure folly" (*v čistom nerazumii*), inspired and directed its whole composition.

The poet's metalanguage may lag far behind his poetic language, and Xlebnikov proves it not only by the substantial gaps in his observations concerning the quintuple pattern of the discussed tristich, but even more when in the next sentence of the same essay he deplores the lack of such arrangement in his militant quatrain—*Búd'te grózny kak OstrÁnica,‖ PlÁtov i BaklÁnov,‖ Pólno vam klÁnjat'sja‖ Róže basurmÁnov*—and thus surprisingly loses sight of its six quintets: five *a* under stress and downbeat; five flat (rounded) vowels, /ó/, /ú/, and unstressed /u/; five labial, all five initial, stops, /b/, /p/; five velar stops, /g/, /k/; five dental stops, /t/, /t'/; five hissing sibilants, /z/, /s/, /c/. Thus nearly one half of this string of phonemes takes part in the "five-ray" pattern; and, in addition to the cited vowels and obstruents, the lingual sonorants exhibit a chiseled symmetry—/rnrn'‖lln‖lnln'‖rrn/—and all the sonorants of the quatrain are divided evenly into eight liquids and eight nasals.

In the preface of 1919 to his planned collected writings,[3] Xlebnikov viewed the short "Grasshopper" as "a minute entrance of the fiery god" (*malyj vyxod boga ognja*). The line between the initial tristich and the terminal prayer, *Pin'-pin' tararáxnul* (originally *Tararapin'pín' knul*) *zinzivér*, astounds one in its combination of the violent, thunder-like stroke *tararax-* with the feeble peep *pin'* and the assignment of the oxymoron to the subject *zinzivér*, which, like other dialectal variants *zenzevér, zenzevél', zenzevéj*, is a loanword cognate with English ginger but means "mallow" in Russian. Incited by Xlebnikov's double reading of *krylyškúja*, one could suspect a similar paronomastic association be-tween *zinzivér* and thunderous *Zevés* (Zeus): /Z'InZ'IVÉr/—/Z'IVÉs/.

When the propensity to frequent quintuple sound repetitions in po-etry, particularly in its free, supraconscious (*zaumnye*) varieties, was observed and studied by Xlebnikov, this phenomenon prompted his comparisons with the five fingers or toes and with the similar makeup of starfish and honeycombs.[4] How fascinated the late poet and eternal seeker of far-reaching analogies would be to learn that the puzzling question of prevalently fivefold symmetries in flowers and human ex-tremities gave rise to recent scientific discussions, and according to Victor Weisskopf's synthesizing paper,[5] "a statistical study of the shape of bubbles in froth has revealed that the polygons that are formed on each bubble by the lines of contact with adjacent bubbles, are mostly pentagons or hexagons. In fact, the average number of corners of these polygons is 5.17. An assembly of cells should have a similar structure and it is suggestive that points of contact may give rise to special growth processes which may reflect the symmetry of the arrangement of these points."

Folklore provides us with particularly eloquent examples of a verbal structure heavily loaded and highly efficient despite its habitual free-dom from any control of abstract reasoning. Even such compulsory constituents as the number of syllables in a syllabic line, the constant position of the break or the regular distribution of prosodic features are not educed and recognized per se by a carrier of oral tradition. When he is faced with two versions of a line, one of which disregards the metrical standard, this narrator or listener may qualify the deviat-ing variant as less suitable or totally unacceptable, but he usually shows no capacity for defining the crux of a given deviation.

A few specimens picked up among the short forms of Russian folk-lore show us tight figures of sound and grammar in close unity with a definitely subliminal method of patterning.

Šlá svin'já iz Pítera,	A pig was coming from Petersburg,
vsjá spiná istýkana.	[its] back is pierced all over.

Napërstok (thimble) is the answer which is required by this folk riddle and is prompted by perspicuous semantic cues: this article comes to the country from the industrial metropolis and has a rough, pitted surface like the skin of a pig. Strict phonological symmetry closely connects both heptasyllabic lines: the distribution of word boundaries and stresses is exactly alike (-/⌣-/⌣-⌣⌣); at least six of the seven successive vowels are identical (/áiáií.a/); apart from the glide /j/ in /sv'in'já/, the number of consonantal phonemes before each of the seven vowels is equal in both sequences (2.2.1., 2.1.1.) with numerous features shared by the parallel segments: initial preconsonantal continuants /s/ and /v/; two pairs of preconsonantal /s/ (/sv'i/—/sp'í/ and /sp'i/—/stí/); two pairs of voiceless stops around /i/ (/p'ít'/—/tík/); two sonorants, /r/ and /n/, before the final /a/. Grammatical correspondences: feminines *šlá*—*vsjá;* feminine nouns as subjects, *svin'já*—*spiná;* preposition and prefix *iz.* The initial clusters of the two alliterating subjects are repeated in the other line: /sp'/ in *spiná* and *iz Pítera* and /sv'/—/vs'/ in *svin'já* and *vsjá* with a metathesis of consonants and constancy of sharpness (palatalization) in the second, prevocalic consonant.

The answer word is anagrammatized in the text of the riddle. Each hemistich of its second line ends with a syllable similar to the prefix /na-/ of the answer: /sp'iná/ and /istíkana/. The root /p'órst-/ and the last hemistich of the first line of the riddle /isp'ít'ira/ display an equivalent set of consonants with an inverted order: (A) 1 2 3 4; (B) 3 1 4 2 (the first two phonemes of the set A correspond to the even phonemes of the set B and the last two phonemes of A to the odd phonemes of B). The last hemistich of the riddle /istíkana/ echoes the consonantal sequence contained in the final syllable of the answer /-stak/. Obviously, *Piter* was chosen among the other appropriate city names just for its anagrammatic value. Such anagrams are familiar to folk riddles: *čërnyj kón'‖ prýgaet v ogón'* (the black horse jumps into fire). As O. M. Brik pointed out in his historic essay on the sound texture of Russian poetry,[6] all three syllables of the answer *kočergá* (poker) show up with the due automatic alternations of the stressed varieties /kó/, /čór/, /gá/ and their unstressed counterparts. Furthermore, the prevocalic phonemes of all four stressed syllables of the riddle prompt the four consonantal phonemes of the answer: /čó/—/kó/—/rí/—/gó/.

The dense phonological and grammatical texture of folk riddles is, in general, quite impressive. Two grammatically and prosodically parallel and rhyming trisyllables (-/⌣-)—*kón' stal'nój,‖ xvóst l'njanój* (a horse of steel, a tail of flax: a needle with a thread)—each count three identical vowels /óaó/ at least in that preponderant variety of Russian which preserves the pretonic /a/ in such forms as /l'n'anój/; in the other dialects the equivalence of both unstressed vowels is maintained merely on the morphophonemic level. Both lines begin with a voiceless velar. The interval between the two stressed vowels is filled in each line by five identical consonantal phonemes: /n'st.l'n/ (123.45)—/stl'n'.n/ (2341.5). The position of /n'/ makes the only sequential divergence between the two series. A typical syntactic feature frequent in Russian riddles and proverbs is the lack of verbs, a lack which effaces the difference between predicatives with zero copula and attributes.

Another riddle with the same topic and a similar metaphoric contrast of the animal's body and tail displays two pairs of rhyming disyllables—*Zverók s veršók, ‖ a xvóst sem' vërst* (A little beast of some two inches and a tail of seven versts). These four colons vary a sequence of /v/ or /v'/ plus /o/ or an unstressed /e/ and a postvocalic /r/ after a prevocalic /v'/; under stress this series is concluded with the cluster /st/, while in an unstressed syllable it begins with a hissing continuant: /zv'er/—/sv'er/—/vóst/—/v'órst/.

All these riddles replace the inanimate noun of the answer word by an animate noun of the opposite gender: masc. *napërstok* (thimble) by fem. *svin'já* (pig) and, inversely, fem. *iglá* (needle) by masc. *kón'* (horse) or *zverók* (little beast) and likewise fem. *nít'* (thread) by masc. *xvóst* (tail), a synecdoche relating to an animate. Compare fem. *grúd'* (bosom) represented by *lébed'* (swan), an animate of masculine gender, at the beginning of the riddle—*Bélyj lébed' na bljúde né byl* (the white swan has not been on a dish)—with a systematic commutation of sharp and plain /b/ and /l/: /b'.l/—/l'.b'.d'/—/n.bl'.d'./—/n'.b.l/. In this sentence all twelve occurrences of its four consonantal constituents display a network of symmetrical relations: six (4 + 2) occurrences of two sonorants and six (4 + 2) of two obstruents; three of these four archiphonemes occur each in the same number of sharp (palatalized) and of plain varieties: 2 /l'/ and 2 /l/; 1 /n'/ and 1 /n/; 2 /b'/ and 2 /b/, while the acute (dental) stop appears only in its sharp variety—once voiced /d'/ and once with a contextual loss of its morphophonemic voicing (*lébed'*).

No propounder or unriddler of folk enigmas identifies such devices as the presence of all three syllables of the answer in the three initial words of the poker riddle itself (2 1 3) or its binary meter with two border stresses in either line of this distich, its three /ó/ with three subsequent dental nasals (1 2 4), and the prevocalic velar stop in each of the three words concluding the entire puzzle (2 3 4). But everyone would feel that the replacement of *čërnyj kon'* by the synonymous *vóron kón'* or by *žéléznyj kón'* (iron horse) could only impair the epigrammatic vigor of this poetic locution. A semblance of prosodic symmetries, sound repetitions, and a verbal substratum—*les mots sous les mots* (Starobinski's felicitous expression)—transpire without being supported by some speculative insight into the methods of procedure involved.

Proverbs compete with riddles in their pungent brevity and verbal skill: *Serebró v bórodu, bés v rebró* ([When] silver—a metaphor for gray hair which in turn is a metonymy for old age—enters into the beard, a devil [concupiscence] enters into the rib—an allusion to the biblical connection between Adam's rib and the emerging woman). The two nominal pairs form a tenacious grammatical parallelism: corresponding cases in similar syntactical functions. Against this background, contrasting genders become particularly conspicuous: the animate masculine *bés* against the inanimate neuter *serebró* and, in turn, the inanimate neuter *rebró* against the inanimate feminine *bórodu*, and these genders come into a whimsical collision with the virile connotation of *bórodu*, and with the female symbolism of *bés*. The entire terse adage is a paronomastic chain: compare the rhyme words *serebró—rebró*, the latter encompassed in the former; the entire permutation of similar phonemes which connects the beginning of the proverb *serebró v* with its end *bes v rebró*; within the initial clause the correspondence between the end of its first and the beginning of its second noun: *serebró—bórodu*. The exquisite prosodic form of the proverb is based on a double contrast between its two clauses: the first one surrounds two contiguous stressed syllables by two pairs of unstressed syllables, whereas the second clause surrounds one single unstressed syllable by two single stressed syllables, and thus exhibits an antisymmetrical submultiple of the former clause. The presence of two accents is the metrical constant of both clauses:

‿‿⏤⏤‿‿/‿⏤‿

The noted Polish anthropologist K. Moszyński admires "the great formal condensation" of the humorous Russian proverb:[7]

Tabák da bánja,	Tobacco and bathhouse,
kabák da bába—	pub and female—
odná zabáva.	the only fun.

(If, however, a stronger accent falls on *odná* or *zabáva* rather than there being equal accents on the two words of the final line, the meaning acquired by this line is "same fun" in the former case, and "nothing but fun" in the latter.)

A rigorous cohesion of the entire tristich is achieved through various means. Its persistently uniform rhythmical pattern, $3 \cdot (\breve{} \text{-} \breve{} \text{-} \breve{})$, comprises fifteen pervasive /a/ alternately unstressed and stressed (notice the South Russian vocalism /adná/!). The onset of the three lines differs from all of their following syllables: the last line begins with a vowel, whereas the other 14 vowels of the tristich are preceded by a consonant; both anterior lines begin with voiceless consonants which appear to be the only two unvoiced segments among the 32 phonemes of the proverb (note the regular voicing of /k/ before /d/!). The only two continuants of its 17 consonants occur in the unstressed syllables of the terminal, predicative noun. The restricted grammatical inventory of this opus, its confinement to five nouns and one pronoun, all six in the nominative, and one reiterated conjunction, is a telling example of the elaborate syntactic style proper to proverbs and glimpsed in an observant sketch by P. Glagolevskij but never investigated since.[8] The central line carries the two culminant nouns—first *kabák,* an intrinsic palindrome, and afterwards *bába,* with its doubled syllable /ba/; *kabák* rhymes with the antecedent *tabák,* while *bába* forms an approximate rhyme with the final *zabáva* and shares its /bá/ with all the nouns of the proverb: five /bá/ on the whole. Reiterations and slight variations of the other consonants run jointly with the same vowel throughout the entire tristich:

$$_1/\text{ta}/-/\text{da}/-_2/\text{da}/-_3/\text{ad}/-/\text{za}/; \;\; _1/\text{ák}/-_2/\text{ka}/-/\text{ák}/; \text{ and } _1/\text{n'a}/-_3/\text{ná}/.$$

All these repetitive, pervasive features tie the four enumerated delights together and frame the chiastic disposition of their two pairs: tools of enjoyment, *tabák* and *bába,* juxtaposed with places of amusement, *kabák* and *bánja.* The metonymic character of these nouns, substituted for direct designations of enjoyments, is set off by the contrastive, intralinear neighborhood of locational and instrumental terms which is, moreover, underscored by the dissimilarity of masculine oxytones and feminine paroxytones.

While being distinct from the short sayings in the choice of devices, folksongs, in turn, reveal a subtle and manifold verbal structure. Two quatrains of a Polish song which belongs to the popular tradition of the countryseat will serve as an appropriate example:

Ty pójdziesz górą	You will go along the hill
a ja doliną,	and I along the valley,
ty zakwitniesz różą	You will blossom as a rose
a ja kaliną.	and I as a squashberry bush.
Ty będziesz panią	You will be a lady
we wielkim dworze,	in a great court,
a ja zakonnikiem	And I a monk
w ciemnym klasztorze.	in a dark monastery.

Excluding the third, hexasyllabic line of the quatrain, all the lines count five syllables, and the even lines rhyme with each other. Both stanzas reveal a rigorous selection of grammatical categories used. Every line ends with a noun in a marginal case, instrumental or locative, and these are the only nouns of our text. Each of its two only pronouns, one of the second and one of the first person, occurs three times and in contradistinction to the marginal cases and final position of the nouns all these pronouns are in the nominative and all of them appear at the beginning of the lines: *ty* (you) in the first syllable of the odd lines 1–3–5, *ja* (I), preceded regularly by the adversative conjunction *a*, occupies the second syllable of lines 2–4–7. The three verbs, all in the second person singular of the perfective present with a futural meaning, follow immediately after the pronoun *ty*, whereas their corresponding first person verbal form after the pronoun *ja* is deleted by ellipsis. In addition to the eight nouns (six in instrumental and two in locative), to the six occurrences of personal pronouns in nominative, to the three finites, and to the thrice repeated conjunction *a*, the text in its second quatrain contains two contextual variants of the preposition *in* ($_6$*we*, $_8$*w*) and two adjectival attributes to both locative forms of nouns.

An antithetic parallelism underlies three pairs of clauses: lines 1–2 and 3–4 within the first stanza and the two couplets within the second stanza. These three pairs, in turn, are interconnected by a close formal and semantic parallelism. All three antitheses confront the higher and brighter prospects for the addressee with the gloomier personal expectations of the addresser and employ the symbolic opposition of the hill and the valley first, then a metaphoric contrast between the rose and the squashberry. In the traditional imagery of Western Slavic folklore *kalina* (whose name goes back to Common Slavic *kalŭ,* mud) is linked ostensibly to marshy lands; compare the preambles of a Polish folk song:[9] "Czego, kalino, w dole stoisz? Czy ty się letniej suszy boisz?" (Why do you, squashberry bush, stand in a valley? Are you afraid of the summer drought?). The cognate Moravian song supplies the same motif with abundant sound figures:[10] *proč, kalino, v STrUZE STOJÍŠ? Snad se TUZE SUcha bOJÍŠ?* (Why do you, squashberry bush, stand in a stream? Are you greatly afraid of dryness?). The third antithesis predicts high stature for the addressee and a sombre future for the addresser; at the same time, personal nouns of feminine and masculine gender announce the sex of the two characters. The instrumental, used consistently in opposition to the invariable nominatives *ty* and *ja,* presents all these contrasted nouns as mere contingencies which will separate both ill-fated victims until their posthumous talks about the "disjointed love" (*niezłączona miłość*) resting in a joint grave.

The three pairs of antithetic clauses with their concluding instrumentals together form a thorough threefold parallelism of broad and complex grammatical constructions, and against the background of their congruent constituents, the significant functional dissimilarity of the three paired instrumentals becomes prominent. In the first couplet the so-called instrumentals of itinerary—*górą* and *doliną*—assume the function of adverbial adjuncts; in the second couplet the instrumentals of comparison—*różą* and *kaliną*—act as accessory predicatives, whereas in the second quatrain the instrumentals *panią* and *zakonnikiem,* in combination with the copula *będziesz* and with the elliptically omitted *będę,* form actual predicates: The weightiness of this case gradually increases with its transition from the two levels of metaphoric peregrination through a simile comparing both personae with flowers of unlike quality and unlike altitude to the factual placement of the two heroes on two distant steps of the social scale. However, the instrumental in all these three different applications preserves its constant semantic feature of bare marginality and becomes particularly palpable when contrasted with the adduced contextual variations. The medium through which the actor moves is defined as the instrumental of itinerary; the instrumental of comparison confines the validity of the simile to one single display of the subjects, namely, their blossoming in the context quoted. Finally, the predicative instrumental heeds one single, supposedly temporal aspect assumed by the subject; it anticipates the possibility of a further, though here a postmortem change which will draw the severed lovers together. When the last pair of instrumentals deprives this case of any adverbial connotation, both couplets of the second stanza provide the compound predicate with a new adverbial adjunct, namely, two limitative and static locatives of dwelling—*we wielkim dworze* (in a great court) and *w ciemnym klasztorze* (in a dark monastery)—which appear in manifest contradistinction to the dynamic instrumentals of itinerary evoked in the initial couplet.

The close interconnection between the first two of three parallelisms is marked by the supplementary assonance of lines 1 and 3 (*górą—różą*), faithful to the traditional Polish pattern of partial rhymes, namely rhymes juxtaposing voiced obstruents with sonorants and especially /ż/ with /r/ in view of the latter's alternations with /ż/ < /r̂/. The last two parallelisms are begun and concluded by corresponding groups of phonemes: ₃/zakv'itn'eš/—₇/zakon'ik'em/, and, with a metathesis: ₄*kaliną* /kal/—₈*klasztorze* /kla/ (cf. also the correspondence between ₆*wielkim* /lkim/ and ₈*ciemnym klasztorze* /imkl/).

The lines devoted to the dismal destiny of the first person differ patently from their cheerful counterparts. Under word stress the instrumentals carry a back vowel (₁,₃/u/, ₅/a/) in the lines concerned with the addressee but show only /i/ in the lines dealing with the apparently disparaged and belittled addresser: *doliną, kaliną, zakonnikiem*. All four nouns assigned to the maid are disyllabic—*górą, różą, panią dworze*—in contrast to the lengthy and bulkier nouns of the autobiographic lines—*doliną, kaliną, zakonnikiem, klasztorze*. Hence the second-person lines possess and the first-person lines lack a break before the penult.

Phonology and grammar of oral poetry offer a system of complex and elaborate correspondences which come into being, take effect, and are handed down through generations without anyone's cognizance of the rules governing this intricate network. The immediate and spontaneous grasp of effects without rational elicitation of the processes by which they are produced is not confined to the oral tradition and its transmitters. Intuition may act as the main or, not seldom, even sole designer of the complicated phonological and grammatical structures in the writings of individual poets. Such structures, particularly powerful on the subliminal level, can function without any assistance of logical judgment and patent knowledge both in the poet's creative work and in its perception by the sensitive reader of *Autorenleser* (author's reader), according to an apt coinage by that courageous inquirer into the sound shape of poetry, Eduard Sievers.

CHAPTER 15

Supraconscious Turgenev

In the memoirs of Count V. A. Sollogub (1813–1882) one finds a curious biographical episode recounted, apparently, directly by his guest Ivan Sergeevič Turgenev: "I like to amuse myself occasionally with a typically Russian word. I'll never forget a little incident that happened to me in London in this regard."[1] N. M. Žemčužnikov, the brother of the famous poet, who had settled in England, once invited Turgenev to dine "at one of the grandest clubs," where the writer was promptly "overcome by the frigidity of the overwhelming ceremoniousness." Around the two newcomers three butlers took up the solemn, ritualistic performance of their duties.

Here, in Sollogub's rendering, is the kernel of Turgenev's memorable "sketch" of the club: "I felt that I was beginning to get the creeps. The luxurious hall, gloomy despite being fully illuminated; the people, looking quite like shadows made of wood, scurrying about all round us; the whole ambience of the place began to exasperate me to the extreme." The apogee neared. "I was suddenly seized by some sort of frenzy. With all my might I banged my fist on the table and started screaming like a madman: *Réd'ka! Týkva! Kobýla! Répa! Bába! Káša!*

Káša! (Radish! Pumpkin! Mare! Turnip! Peasant Woman! Kasha! Kasha!)."

Turgenev's "outburst," as the journal version of Sollogub's memoirs christened it, is formed of seven exclamatory holophrases, consisting of seven nouns of feminine gender in the nominative singular, with the ending *a* and with stress on the penultimate syllable. Five inanimates—two initial, one central, and two final—are opposed directly on both sides of the central word by two animate nouns. The latter are distinguished by the voiced prevocalic /b/ of their stressed syllable, and both semantically convey sexual information: *Kobýla!* (mare), *Bába!* (peasant woman).

None of the seven words contains a rounded vowel. The central noun *Répa* (turnip) shares with the initial *Réd'ka* (radish) the same combination /ré/, whereas the intervening words repeat a stressed *y,* thus forming a kind of embracing rhyme /é-í-í-é/.

The entire verbal effusion numbers five velar consonants, to be more precise, five unvoiced plosive /k/, concentrated in the three initial and two final nouns. This same verbal chain is endowed with five labials, encompassing all the words from the second word, *Týkva!* (pumpkin) to the fifth, *Bába!* (peasant woman). Thus labial consonants gravitate toward the center of the cry, whereas velars are distributed along its borders. Five of the seven words begin with plosive consonants, as do five out of the seven stressed syllables.

It is appropriate in this context to recall the persistent testimony of Velimir Xlebnikov: "I studied models of selfsome speech (*samovitaja reč'*) and found that the number five is extremely significant for it, just as it is for the number of our fingers and toes."[2] It turns out, for example, that in the first four-line proposition of the poet's "Kuznečik" (The Grasshopper)—"apart from the desire of the one who wrote this nonsense, the sounds *u, k, l, r,* each repeat five times." Xlebnikov finds a parallel to this "law of freely flowing selfsome speech" in the "five-rayed makeup" of honeycombs and starfish.[3]

The structure of the peripheral three-word groups—the initial and the terminal—sharply differs. In distinction to the terminal word group, the initial is characterized by a variation in the number of syllables and in the stressed vowel, which is, moreover, consistently different from the unstressed vowel. On top of this, the initial three-word group displays a skilfully coordinated variety of consonants.

The three initial words contain three consonants, and the rest two each. The repertoire of consonantal classes, revealed in the first three words, in the words consisting of three consonants each, includes liquids (/r'/ and /l/), labials (/v/ and /b/), dentals (/t'/ and /t/), and velars (/k/).

The makeup and sequence in which the consonants of the various classes appear in the initial word (liquid—dental—velar) corresponds to the makeup and sequence of the same classes in the beginning of all three initial words (liquid—dental—velar). The makeup and sequence of the last word of the initial group (velar—labial—liquid) correspond to that of the same classes before the final vowel in all three initial words. The makeup and sequence of the consonants of the second word in the group (dental—velar—labial) correspond to that of the identical consonantal classes in the middle of all three initial words.

In short, between the position of all three consonants in the word and the position of the word in the structure of the initial three-word group, the strictest symmetry reigns. The initial and final consonant of the first word (liquid—velar) form a mirror symmetry with the initial and final consonant of the third word (velar—liquid). The velar occupies in the three initial words a position of mirror symmetry (3—2—1) in relation to the order of the words (1—2—3). In the limits of the word the velar may be preceded only by a dental and followed only by a labial. Thus the distribution of consonants in the three words of the initial group follows an unwavering scheme:

liquid—dental—velar
dental—velar—labial
velar—labial—liquid

The vocalism of unstressed vowels in all the words consistently amounts to the phoneme /a/: such, for example, are both unstressed vowels in the word *Kobýla!* In the three words of the terminal group the phoneme /a/ appears not only in the unstressed, but also in the stressed syllables, whereas, as we noted above, in the rest of the words the unstressed /a/ is opposed to a stressed /é/ or /í/. The terminal three-word series differs in general in its tendency toward homogeneity or, more precisely, in its repetition of words (*Káša! Káša!*), in its direct repetition of syllables (*Bába!*), and in the identity of the stressed and unstressed vowels throughout the sequence (/á-a-á-a-á-a/). The compactness of the stressed vowels in the whole terminal three-word unit and the compactness of both consonants (the velar and palatoalveolar) in the last, doubly repeated word create an apex of consonantal and vocalic compactness: *Bába! Káša! Káša!*

"I can't stand it any longer" (*moči moej net*) runs Turgenev's commentary to his incantatory improvisation as rendered by Sollogub: "I'm suffocating here, suffocating . . . I have to calm myself down with a few Russian words!" Thus the unexacting peasant woman with her kasha turns out to be victoriously opposed to the three majestic butlers and the pair of gentlemen of "an ever more lifeless appearance" eating in the hall. The feminine gender and sex in Turgenev's attack are contrasted to the masculine, stuck-up ambience of the club.

Turgenev's reply to the "religious rites" (*svjaščennodejstvija*—"no other word," he says, "could possibly be used for it") performed by the trinity of butlers, who seemed "more like members of the House of Lords than servants," was simple. He answered with a string of names for vegetables that developed into a craving for the peasant woman managing the estate and for kasha, the highest attainment of Russian folk cuisine. "The most imposing of the butlers," as if to emphasize the consumate ceremoniousness with which he was observing the ritual of the relentless diet poor Žemčužnikov's doctor had prescribed, served one identical dish after another in succession, majestically announcing: "First Cutlet! Second Cutlet! Third Cutlet!" As Ivan Sergeevič puts it, "there are no words in any human language" to express the irritation he experienced. Watching the ritualistic appearance of the invariable viands served on a silver plate covered by a silver bellglass, he experienced something, as it were, beyond words: the five velar consonants of his feverish tirade—concluding in the hypnotic catchword "Kasha! Kasha!"—alliteratively echo the overwhelmingly crushing, thrice-repeated announcement: "Cutlet!"

It is quite likely that latter embellishments by Turgenev crept into the narrative, as Sollogub hints, noting Ivan Sergeevič's "impeccable upbringing." One might well ask whether he actually spoke or merely thought up his seven-word table formula. It is possible, finally, that the memoirist himself is guilty of certain "exaggerations." Nevertheless, it is incredibly difficult to believe that this masterful experiment in creatively soldering together "disjointed Russian words" was not created by the courageous and mighty artist of the "free Russian tongue."

Frustration of anticipated *consummatum,* a characteristic motif of Turgenev's life and work—"Oh, why did I not answer her," and so on—makes itself felt in the writer's late peripheral activities: not only in the escapade at the London club but also in the grotesque little "fairytales" (*des choses bien invraisemblables*) which, on the threshold of the seventies and eighties, Claudie (1852–1914), the daughter of Pauline Viardot, received in the form of letters from Turgenev, "ton vieux qui t'adore" or "ton éperdument ahuri Iv. Tour."[4] In connection with the supraconscious symbolism of these tales, their Parisian editor quite correctly predicts their future inclusion in "anthologies of Surrealism."

The substitution, common to both Turgenev's tales and fables, of unrestrained scatology in place of elevated eroticism must have affected the young recipient of his epistolary *épanchements* with a force matching the fright of his London table companion (Turgenev relates: "He thought that I'd lost my mind."). Such, for example, is the narrative letter of September 3, 1882, in which "a pale young *au teint maladif*" utters an entreaty to his beloved German virgin. He contemplates suicide, hoping only that his beloved will allow him to share not her inaccessible bed but her private lavatory or, at the very least, her latrine "in the bosom of nature." This viscous motif is developed into a florid dialogue. One is tempted to compare it to the Indian taboo against a woman performing her natural needs in a place where a man has urinated.

In Turgenev's extravagant behavior at the London club as well as in the delirious phantasmagoria of his French epistles, the extreme shift toward the primitive is decked out in whimsical verbal figures that endow the text with a mad, unexpected, incontestable persuasiveness akin to the supraconscious "wisdom in a snare" (*mudrost' v silke*) that inspired Turgenev, half a century before Xlebnikov, in his "tale of the nightingales." In it, Turgenev renders the "summit" (*desjatoe koleno*) of the nightingale's art: "With a good throaty nightingale here's how it goes. First there's a 'tee-eé-wheet!', then there's a 'took!' They call that the 'knock.' Then again: 'tee-eé-wheet . . . took! took!' A double 'knock,' with a half stroke on the second—it's too much! Then, the third time around: 'tee-eé-wheet!' Damn, it scatters so fast in a tap or a peal, the son of a bitch, you can hardly stand on your feet, it burns so!"[5]

PART III

*Writer,
Biography,
Myth*

Vladimir Majakovskij's suicide in 1930 and Boris Pasternak's remarkable autobiography *The Safe Conduct* (1931) prompted Jakobson to rethink and approach anew the relation between the biography and creative work of a writer. This issue, which in the era of Romanticism had been termed *Dichtung und Wahrheit,* had been presented as a distinct cleavage between the "hard facts" of a writer's life and the "beautiful lies" advanced in his works. On the other hand, the positivistic tradition of the late nineteenth century insisted on a mechanistic causal relation between the two spheres, biography being viewed as the prime cause of a writer's output. A common denominator of these two approaches was the underlying dichotomy assumed between reality and mind. Such a separation, however, had been proclaimed erroneous by philosophers as early as Kant. The philosophical objections were confirmed by the psycho-physiological tests of the Gestalt psychologists at the turn of the century, who demonstrated that conscious sensations are not mere copies of the external world of real objects but instead *homologous constructs* of those objects.

In contrast to mechanistic attempts at approaching the problem of a writer's biography and his creative output, Jakobson's method proves to be both concrete and dialectical. He resolves the antinomies of cause/effect and reality/mind by pointing out their mutual relations. He insists that in the authentic life of the poet these two traditionally opposed realms merge in one indissoluble whole: the poet's own myth. On the one hand, a biographical fact may be interpreted by the poet in a way quite different from its perception by others; on the other, the poetic fact he himself creates can achieve in his life the status of a reality. For example, the verbal experiments of Velimir Xlebnikov, which were often created almost unconsciously, aroused in him physiologically palpable emotions. Similarly, Vladimir Majakovskij would bring into existence in his life situations that, previously or simultaneously, he had invented in his poems. The most striking instance of such a feedback system between literature and biography is Majakovskij's suicide: this leitmotif of his poetry was indeed "transformed into a literary-historical fact" when he shot himself on April 14, 1930. Myth enters the sphere of real life and, as Jakobson writes, it becomes "impossible to trace a limit between poetic mythology and the curriculum vitae of the author without committing terrible forgeries."

Similarly, in the case of Aleksandr Puškin it would be more appropriate to say that often the poet anticipated the course of his life in his work rather than the reverse. His myth of the destructive statue, which Jakobson ascertains as the thematic invariant of three works of different genres—a play, an epic poem, and a fairytale—predicts and anticipates certain events in his life. Puškin's unfortunate marriage brought on, instead of much desired peace and freedom, the poet's suicidal duel, prompted by the inert and deadly forces of the Petersburg establishment.

Czech Romanticism provided Jakobson with further material for revising dialectically the old antinomy of psychic reality and poetic intention. In "What is Poetry?" (1933) he examines the sensational personal diary of Karel Hynek Mácha (1810–1836) in relation to his poetics and reveals the Oedipal underpinnings of the "ruggedly beautiful improvisations" of the Slovak poet Janko Král' (1822–1876). The works of the conservative Czech Romantic K. J. Erben (1811–1887) inspired Jakobson to show how Romanticism adopted archaic mythological thinking, according to which myth is self-sufficient: it precedes history, is immortal, and alone presents reality fully. The ideological consequence of Erben's mythology is resignation to fate, since myth *is* fate in the poet's view.

Jakobson's article in memory of the Czech philologist and poet V. V. Hanka (1791–1861), written in 1931, casts further light on the importance of myth for the Romantic era. As Erben's friend, the philosopher K. B. Štorch, claimed, entire "nations and ages" have developed their cognition of reality primarily along the line of a mythological understanding of history, and this "effort has not lacked benefit for mankind." Hanka's forgeries of Old Czech epic poems, despite the scandal surrounding their unmasking, actually helped the Czechs in their quest for a national identity.

CHAPTER 16

On a Generation That Squandered Its Poets

Killed;—
Little matter
Whether I or he
Killed them.

Majakovskij's poetry—his imagery, his lyrical composition—I have written about these things and published some of my remarks. The idea of writing a monograph has never left me. Majakovskij's poetry is qualitatively different from everything in Russian verse before him, however intent one may be on establishing genetic links. This is what makes the subject particularly intriguing. The structure of his poetry is profoundly original and revolutionary. But how it is possible to write about Majakovskij's poetry now, when the paramount subject is not the rhythm but the death of the poet, when (if I may resort to Majakovskij's own poetic phrase) "sudden grief" is not yet ready to give in to "a clearly realized pain"?

During one of our meetings, Majakovskij, as was his custom, read me his latest poems. Considering his creative potential I could not help comparing them with what he might have produced. "Very good," I said, "but not as good as Majakovskij." Yet now the creative powers are canceled out, the inimitable stanzas can no longer be compared to anything else, the words "Majakovskij's last poems" have suddenly taken on a tragic meaning. Sheer grief at his absence has overshadowed the absent one. Now it is more painful, but still easier, to write not about the one we have lost but rather about our own loss and those of us who have suffered it.

It is our generation that has suffered the loss. Roughly, those of us who are now between thirty and forty-five years old. Those who, already fully matured, entered into the years of the Revolution not as unmolded clay but still not hardened, still capable of adapting to experience and change, still capable of taking a dynamic rather than a static view of our lives.

It has been said more than once that the first poetic love of our generation was Aleksandr Blok. Velimir Xlebnikov gave us a new epos, the first genuinely epic creations after many decades of drought. Even his briefer verses create the impression of epic fragments, and Xlebnikov easily combined them into narrative poems. Xlebnikov is epic in spite of our antiepic times, and therein lies one of the reasons he is somewhat alien to the average reader. Other poets brought his poetry closer to the reader; they drew upon Xlebnikov, pouring out his "word ocean" into many lyrical streamlets. In contrast to Xlebnikov, Majakovskij embodied the lyrical urges of this generation. "The broad epic canvas" is deeply alien to him and unacceptable. Even when he attempts "a bloody Iliad of the Revolution," or "an Odyssey of the famine years," what appears is not an epic but a heroic lyric on a grand scale, offered "at the top of his voice." There was a point when symbolist poetry was in its decline and it was still not clear which of the two new mutually antagonistic trends, Acmeism or Futurism, would prevail. Xlebnikov and Majakovskij gave to contemporary literary art its leitmotif. The name Gumilev marks a collateral branch of modern Russian poetry—its characteristic overtone. For Xlebnikov and for Majakovskij "the homeland of creative poetry is the future"; in contrast, Esenin is a lyrical glance backward. His verse expresses the weariness of a generation.

Modern Russian poetry after 1910 is largely defined by these names. The verse of Aseev and Sel'vinskij is bright indeed, but it is a reflected light. They do not announce but reflect the spirit of the times. Their magnitude is a derivative quantity. Pasternak's books and perhaps those of Mandel'štam are remarkable, but theirs is chamber verse:[1] new creation will not be kindled by it. The heart of a generation cannot take fire with such verses because they do not shatter the boundaries of the present.

Gumilev (1886–1921) was shot, after prolonged mental agony and in

274

great pain; Blok (1880–1921) died, amid cruel privations and under circumstances of inhuman suffering; Xlebnikov (1885–1922) passed away; after careful planning Esenin (1895–1925) and Majakovskij (1894–1930) killed themselves. And so it happened that during the third decade of this century, those who inspired a generation perished between the ages of thirty and forty, each of them sharing a sense of doom so vivid and sustained that it became unbearable.

This is true not only of those who were killed or killed themselves. Blok and Xlebnikov, when they took to their beds with disease, had also perished. Zamjatin wrote in his reminiscences: "We are all to blame for this . . . I remember that I could not stand it and I phoned Gor'kij: Blok is dead. We can't be forgiven for that." Šklovskij wrote in a tribute to Xlebnikov:

> Forgive us for yourself and for others whom we will kill. The state is not responsible for the destruction of people. When Christ lived and spoke the state did not understand his Aramaic, and it has never understood simple human speech. The Roman soldiers who pierced Christ's hands are no more to blame than the nails. Nevertheless, it is very painful for those whom they crucify.[2]

Blok the poet fell silent and died long before the man, but his younger contemporaries snatched verses even from death. ("Wherever I die I'll die singing," wrote Majakovskij.) Xlebnikov knew he was dying. His body decomposed while he lived. He asked for flowers in his room so that the stench would not be noticed, and he kept writing to the end. A day before his suicide Esenin wrote a masterful poem about his impending death. Majakovskij's farewell letter is full of poetry: we find the professional writer in every line of that document. He wrote it two nights before his death and in the interval there were to be conversations and conferences about the everyday business of literature; but in that letter we read: "Please don't gossip. The deceased hated gossip." We remember that Majakovskij's long-standing demand upon himself was that the poet must "hurry time forward." And here he is, already looking at his suicide note through the eyes of someone reading it the day after tomorrow. The letter, with its several literary motifs and with Majakovskij's own death in it, is so closely interrelated with his poetry that it can be understood only in the context of that poetry.

The poetry of Majakovskij from his first verses, in "A Slap in the Face of Public Taste," to his last lines is one and indivisible. It represents the dialectical development of a single theme. It is an extraordinarily unified symbolic system. A symbol once thrown out only as a kind of hint will later be developed and presented in a totally new perspective. He himself underlines these links in his verse by alluding to earlier works. In the poem "About That" ("Pro èto"), for instance, he recalls certain lines from the poem "Man" ("Čelovek"), written several years earlier, and in the latter poem he refers to lyrics of an even earlier period. An image at first offered humorously may later and in a different context lose its comic effect, or conversely, a motif developed solemnly may be repeated in a parodistic vein. Yet this does not mean that the beliefs of yesterday are necessarily held up to scorn; rather, we have here two levels, the tragic and the comic, of a single symbolic system, as in the medieval theater. A single clear purpose directs the system of symbols. "We shall thunder out a new myth upon the world."

A mythology of Majakovskij?

His first collection of poems was entitled *I*. Vladimir Majakovskij is not only the hero of his first play, but his name is the title of that tragedy, as well as of his last collection of poems. The author dedicates his verse "to his beloved self." When Majakovskij was working on the poem "Man" he said, "I want to depict simply man, man in general, not an abstraction, à la Andreev, but a genuine 'Ivan' who waves his arms, eats cabbage soup, and can be directly felt." But Majakovskij could directly feel only himself. This is said very well in Trotsky's article on him (an intelligent article, the poet said): "In order to raise man he elevates him to the level of Majakovskij. The Greeks were anthropomorphists, naively likening the forces of nature to themselves; our poet is a Majakomorphist, and he populates the squares, the streets, and the fields of the Revolution only with himself." Even when the hero of Majakovskij's poem appears as the 150-million-member collective, realized in one Ivan—a fantastic epic hero—the latter in turn assumes the familiar features of the poet's "ego." This ego asserts itself even more frankly in the rough drafts of the poem.[3]

Empirical reality neither exhausts nor fully takes in the various shapes of the poet's ego. Majakovskij passes before us in one of his "innumerable souls." "The unbending spirit of eternal rebellion" has poured itself into the poet's muscles, the irresponsible spirit without name or patronymic, "from future days, just a man." "And I feel that I am too small for myself. Someone obstinately bursts out of me." Weariness with fixed and narrow confines, the urge to transcend static boundaries—such is Majakovskij's infinitely varied theme. No lair in the world can contain the poet and the unruly horde of his desires. "Driven into the earthly pen I drag a daily yoke." "The accursed earth has me chained." The grief of Peter the Great is that of a "prisoner, held in chains in his own city." Hulks of districts wriggle out of the "zones marked off by the governor." The cage of the blockade in Majakovskij's verses turns into the world prison destroyed by a cosmic gust directed "beyond the radiant slits of sunsets." The poet's revolutionary call is directed at all of those "for whom life is cramped and unbearable," "who cry out because the nooses of noon are too tight." The ego of the poet is a battering ram, thudding into a forbidden Future; it is a mighty will "hurled over the last limit" toward the incarnation of the Future, toward an absolute fullness of being: "one must rip joy from the days yet to come."

Opposed to this creative urge toward a transformed future is the stabilizing force of an immutable present, overlaid, as this present is, by a stagnating slime, which stifles life in its tight, hard mold. The Russian name for this element is *byt*. It is curious that this word and its derivatives should have such a prominent place in the Russian language (from which it spread even to the Komi), while West European languages have no word that corresponds to it. Perhaps the reason is that in the European collective consciousness there is no concept of such a force as might oppose and break down the established norms of life. The revolt of the individual against the fixed forms of social convention presupposes the existence of such a force. The real antithesis of *byt* is a slippage of social norms that is immediately sensed by those involved in social life. In Russia this sense of an unstable foundation has been present for a very long time, and not just as a historical generalization but as a direct experience. We recall that in the early nineteenth century, during the time of Čaadaev, there was the sense of a "dead and stagnant life," but at the same time a feeling of instability and uncertainty: "Everything is slipping away, everything is passing," wrote Čaadaev. "In our own homes we are as it were in temporary quarters. In our family life we seem foreigners. In our cities we look like nomads." And as Majakovskij put it:

> . . . laws/ concepts/ faiths
> The granite blocks of cities
> And even the very sun's reliable glow—

> Everything had become as it were fluid,
> Seemed to be sliding a little—
> A little bit thinned and watered down.

But all these shifts, all this "leaking of the poet's room," are only a "hardly audible draft, which is probably only felt by the very tip of the soul." Inertia continues to reign. It is the poet's primordial enemy, and he never tires of returning to this theme. "Motionless *byt*." "Everything stands as it has been for ages. *Byt* is like a horse that can't be spurred and stands still." "Slits of *byt* are filled with fat and coagulate, quiet and wide." "The swamp of *byt* is covered over with slime and weeds." "Old little *byt* is moldy." "The giant *byt* crawls everywhere through the holes." "Force booming *byt* to sing!" "Put the question of *byt* on the agenda." "In fall,/ winter,/ spring,/ summer/ During the day/ during sleep/ I don't accept/ I hate this/ all./ All/ that in us/ is hammered in by past slavishness/ all/ that like the swarm of trifles/ was covering/ and covered with *byt*/ even our red-flagged ranks." Only in the poem "About That" is the poet's desperate struggle with *byt* fully laid bare. There it is not personified as it is elsewhere in his work. On the contrary, the poet hammers his verbal attack directly into that moribund *byt* which he despises. And *byt* reacts by executing the rebel "with all rifles and batteries, from every Mauser and Browning." Elsewhere in Majakovskij this phenomenon is, as we have said, personified—not however as a living person but rather, in the poet's own phrase, as an animated tendency. In "Man" the poet's enemy is very broadly generalized as "Ruler of all, my rival, my invincible enemy." But it is also possible to localize this enemy and give him a particular shape. One may call him "Wilson," domicile him in Chicago, and, in the language of fairytale hyperbole, outline his very portrait (as in "150,000,000"). But then the poet offers a "little footnote": "Those who draw the Wilsons, Lloyd Georges, and Clemenceaus sometimes show their mugs with moustaches, sometimes not; but that's beside the point since they're all one and the same thing." The enemy is a universal image. The forces of nature, people, metaphysical substances, are only its incidental aspects and disguises: "The same old bald fellow directs us unseen, the master of the earthly cancan. Sometimes in the shape of an idea, sometimes a kind of devil, or then again he glows as God, hidden behind a cloud." If we should try to translate the Majakovskian mythology into the language of speculative philosophy, the exact equivalent for this enmity would be the antinomy "I" versus "not-I." A better designation for Majakovskij's enemy could hardly be found.

Just as the creative ego of the poet is not coextensive with his actually existing self, so conversely the latter does not take in all of the former. In the faceless regiment of his acquaintances, all tangled in the "apartment-house spider web,"

> One of them/ I recognized
> As like as a twin
> Myself/ my very own self.

This terrible "double" of the poet is his conventional and commonplace "self," the purchaser and owner whom Xlebnikov once contrasted with the inventor and discoverer. That self has an emotional attachment to a securely selfish and stable life, to "*my* little place, and a household that's *mine*, with *my* little picture on the wall." The poet is oppressed by the specter of an unchangeable world order, a universal apartment-house *byt:* "No sound, the universe is asleep."

> Revolutions shake up violently the bodies of kingdoms,
> The human herd changes its herdsmen.
> But you/ uncrowned ruler of our hearts
> No rebellion ever touches.

Against this unbearable might of *byt* an uprising as yet unheard of and nameless must be contrived. The terms used in speaking of the class struggle are only conventional figures, only approximate symbols, only one of the levels: *the part for the whole.* Majakovskij, who has witnessed "the sudden reversals of fortune in battles not yet fought," must give new meaning to the habitual terminology. In the rough draft of the poem "150,000,000" we find the following definitions:

> To be a bourgeois does not mean to own capital or squander gold. It means to be the heel of a corpse on the throat of the young. It means a mouth stopped up with fat. To be a proletarian doesn't mean to have a dirty face and work in a factory: it means to be in love with the future that's going to explode the filth of the cellars—believe me.

The basic fusion of Majakovskij's poetry with the theme of the revolution has often been pointed out. But another indissoluble combination of motifs in the poet's work has not so far been noticed: revolution and the destruction of the poet. This idea is suggested even as early as the *Tragedy* (1913), and later this fact that the linkage of the two

279

is not accidental becomes "clear to the point of hallucination." No mercy will be shown to the army of zealots, or to the doomed volunteers in the struggle. The poet himself is an expiatory offering in the name of that universal and real resurrection that is to come; that was the theme of the poem "War and the Universe" ("Vojna i mir"). And in the poem "A Cloud in Trousers" ("Oblako v štanax") the poet promises that when a certain year comes "in the thorny crown" of revolutions, "For you/ I will tear out my soul/ and trample on it till it spreads out,/ and I'll give it to you,/ a bloody banner." In the poems written after the revolution the same idea is there, but in the past tense. The poet, mobilized by the revolution, has "stamped on the throat of his own song." (This line occurs in the last poem he published, an address to his "comrade-descendants" of the future, written in clear awareness of the coming end.) In the poem "About That" the poet is destroyed by *byt*. "The bloodletting is over. . . . Only high above the Kremlin the tatters of the poet shine in the wind—a little red flag." This image is plainly an echo of "A Cloud in Trousers."

The poet's hungry ear captures the music of the future, but he is not destined to enter the Promised Land. A vision of the future is present in all the most essential pages of Majakovskij's work. "And such a day dawned—Andersen's fairytales crawled about like little pups at his feet"; "You can't tell whether it's air, or a flower, or a bird. It sings, and it's fragrant, and it's brightly colored all at once"; "Call us Cain or call us Abel, it doesn't matter. The future is here." For Majakovskij the future is a dialectical synthesis. The removal of all contradictions finds its expression in the facetious image of Christ playing checkers with Cain, in the myth of the universe permeated by love, and in the proposition "The commune is a place where bureaucrats will disappear and there will be many poems and songs." The present disharmony, the contradiction between poetry and building, "the delicate business of the poet's place in the working ranks," is one of Majakovskij's most acute problems. "Why," he asked, "should literature occupy its own special little corner? Either it should appear in every newspaper, every day, on every page, or else it's totally useless. The kind of literature that's dished out as dessert can go to hell" (from the *Reminiscences* of D. Lebedev).

Majakovskij always regarded ironically talk of the insignificance and death of poetry (really nonsense, he would say, but useful for the purpose of revolutionizing art). He planned to pose the question of the future of art in the "Fifth International" ("Pjatyj internacional"), a poem that he worked on long and carefully but never finished. According to the outline of the work, the first stage of the revolution, a world-wide social transformation, has been completed, but humanity is bored. *Byt* still survives. So a new revolutionary act of world-shaking proportions is required: "A revolution of the spirit" in the name of a new organization of life, a new art, and a new science. The published introduction to the poem is an order to abolish the beauties of verse and to introduce into poetry the brevity and accuracy of mathematical formulas. He offers an example of a poetic structure built on the model of a logical problem. When I reacted skeptically to this poetic program—the exhortation in verse against verse—Majakovskij smiled: "But didn't you notice that the solution of my logical problem is a transrational solution?"

The remarkable poem "Homeward!" ("Domoj!") is devoted to the contradiction between the rational and the irrational. It is a dream about the fusion of the two elements, a kind of rationalization of the irrational:

> I feel/ like a Soviet factory
> Manufacturing happiness.
> I don't want/ to be plucked
> Like a flower/ after the day's work
> . . . . .
> I want/ the heart to be paid
> Its wage of love/ at the specialist's rate
> I want/ the factory committee
> To put a lock on my lips
> When the work is done
> I want/ the pen to be equal to the bayonet
> And I want Stalin/ to report in the name of the Politburo
> About the production of verse
> As he does about pig iron and steel.
> Thus, and so it is/ we've reached
> The topmost level/ up from the worker's hovels
> In the Union/ of Republics
> The appreciation of verse/ has exceeded the prewar level.

The idea of the acceptance of the irrational appears in Majakovskij's work in various guises, and each of the images he uses for this purpose tends to reappear in his poetry. The stars ("You know, if they light up the stars,/ that means, somebody needs them!"). The madness of spring ("Everything is clear concerning bread/ and concerning peace./ But the prime question,/ the question of spring/ must be/ elucidated"). And the heart that changes winter to spring and water to wine ("It's that I'm/ going to raise my heart like a flag,/ a marvelous twentieth-century miracle"). And that hostile answer of the enemy in the poem "Man": "If the heart is everything/ then why,/ why have I been gathering you, my dear money!/ How do they dare to sing?/ Who gave them the right?/ Who said the days could blossom into July?/ Lock the heavens in wires!/ Twist the earth into streets!"

But Majakovskij's central irrational theme is the theme of love. It is a theme that cruelly punishes those who dare to forget it, whose storms toss us about violently and push everything else out of our ken. And like poetry itself this theme is both inseparable from and in disharmony with our present life; it is "closely mingled with our jobs, our incomes, and all the rest." And love is crushed by *byt*:

> Omnipotent one
> You thought up a pair of hands
> Fixed it
> So that everyone has a head.
> Why couldn't you fix it
> So that without torment
> We could just kiss and kiss and kiss?

Eliminate the irrational? Majakovskij draws a bitterly satirical picture. On the one hand, the heavy boredom of certain rational revelations: the usefulness of the cooperative, the danger of liquor, political education, and on the other hand, an unashamed hooligan of planetary dimensions (in the poem "A Type" ["Tip"]). Here we have a satirical sharpening of the dialectical contradiction. Majakovskij says "yes" to the rationalization of production, technology, and the planned economy if as a result of all this "the partially opened eye of the future sparkles with real earthly love." But he rejects it all if it means only a selfish clutching at the present. If that's the case then grandiose technology becomes only a "highly perfected apparatus of parochialism and gossip on the worldwide scale" (from an essay "My Discovery of America"). Just such a planetary narrowness and parochialism permeates life in the year 1970, as shown in Majakovskij's play about the future, *The Bedbug* (*Klop*), where we see a rational organization without emotion, with no superfluous expenditure of energy, without dreams. A worldwide social revolution has been achieved, but the revolution of the spirit is still in the future. The play is a quiet protest against the spiritual inheritors of those languid judges who, in his early satirical poem "without knowing just why or wherefore, attacked Peru." Some of the characters in *The Bedbug* have a close affinity with the world of Zamjatin's *We*, although Majakovskij bitterly ridicules not only the rational utopian community but the rebellion against it in the name of alcohol, the irrational and unregulated individual happiness. Zamjatin, however, idealizes that rebellion.

Majakovskij has an unshakable faith that, beyond the mountain of suffering, beyond each rising plateau of revolutions, there does exist the "real heaven on earth," the only possible resolution of all contradictions. *Byt* is only a surrogate for the coming synthesis; it doesn't remove contradictions but only conceals them. The poet is unwilling to compromise with the dialectic; he rejects any mechanical softening of the contraditions. The objects of Majakovskij's unsparing sarcasm are the "compromisers" (as in the play *Mystery-Bouffe*). Among the gallery of "bureaucrat-compromisers" portrayed in his agitational pieces, we have in *The Bathhouse* (*Banja*) the Glavnačpups Pobedonosikov, whose very title is an acronym for "Chief Administrator for the Organizing of Compromises." Obstacles in the road to the future—such is the true nature of these "artificial people." The time machine will surely spew them out.

It seemed to him a criminal illusion to suppose that the essential and vital problem of building a worldwide "wonderful life" could be put aside for the sake of devising some kind of personal happiness. "It's early to rejoice," he wrote. The opening scenes of *The Bedbug* develop the idea that people are tired of a life full of struggle, tired of front-line equality, tired of military metaphors. "This is not 1919. People want to live." They build family nests for themselves: "Roses will bloom and be fragrant at the present juncture of time." "Such is the elegant fulfillment of our comrade's life of struggle." Oleg Bajan, the servant of beauty in *The Bedbug*, formulates this sentiment in the following words: "We have managed to compromise and control class and other contradictions, and in this a person armed with a Marxist eye, so to speak, can't help seeing, as in a single drop of water, the future happiness of mankind, which the common people call socialism." (In an earlier, lyrical context the same idea took this form: "There he is in a soft bed, fruit beside him and wine on the night table.") Majakovskij's sharply chiseled lines express unlimited contempt for all those who seek comfort and rest. All such people receive their answer from the mechanic in *The Bedbug:* "We'll never crawl out of our trenches with a white flag in our hands." And the poem "About That" develops the same theme in the form of an intimate personal experience. In that work Majakovskij begs for the advent of love, his savior: "Confiscate my pain—take it away!" And Majakovskij answers himself:

> Leave off./ Don't/ not a word/ no requests,
> What's the point/ that you/ alone/ should succeed?
> I'll wait/ and together with the whole unloved earth
> With the whole/ human mass/ we'll win it.
> Seven years I stood/ and I'll stand two hundred
> Nailed here/ waiting for it.
> On the bridge of years/ derided/ scorned
> A redeemer of earthly love/ I must stand
> Stand for all/ for everyone I'll atone
> For everyone I'll weep.

But Majakovskij knows very well that even if his youth should be renewed four times and he should four times grow old again, that would only mean a fourfold increase of his torment, a four times multiplied horror at the senseless daily grind and at premature celebrations of victory. In any case, he will never live to see the revelation all over the world of an absolute fullness of life, and the final count still stands: "I've not lived out my earthly lot; I've not lived through my earthly love." His destiny is to be an expiatory victim who never knew joy:

> A bullet for the rest
> For some a knife.
> But what about me?
> And when?

Majakovskij has now given us the final answer to that question.

The Russian Futurists believed in cutting themselves loose from the "classic generals," and yet they are vitally tied to the Russian literary tradition. It is interesting to note that famous line of Majakovskij's, so full of bravado (and at the same time a tactical slogan): "But why don't we attack Puškin?" It was followed not long after by those mournful lines addressed to the same Puškin: "You know I too will soon be dead and mute./And after my death/ we two will be quite close together." Majakovskij's dreams of the future that repeat the utopian visions of Dostoevskij's Veršilov in *A Raw Youth*, the poet's frequent hymns to the "man-god," the "thirteenth apostle's" fight against God, the ethical rejection of Him—all this is much closer to Russian literature of an earlier day than it is to official and regimented Soviet "godlessness." And Majakovskij's belief in personal immortality has nothing to do with the official catechism of Jaroslavskij's "godless" movement. The poet's vision of the coming resurrection of the dead is vitally linked with the materialistic mysticism of the Russian philosopher Fëdorov.

When in the spring of 1920 I returned to Moscow, which was tightly blockaded, I brought with me recent books and information about scientific developments in the West. Majakovskij made me repeat several times my somewhat confused remarks on the general theory of relativity and about the growing interest in that concept in Western Europe. The idea of the liberation of energy, the problem of the time dimension, and the idea that movement at the speed of light may actually be a reverse movement in time—all these things fascinated Majakovskij. I'd seldom seen him so interested and attentive. "Don't you think," he suddenly asked, "that we'll at last achieve immortality?" I was astonished, and I mumbled a skeptical comment. He thrust his jaw forward with that hypnotic insistence so familiar to anyone who knew Majakovskij well: "I'm absolutely convinced," he said, "that one day there will be no more death. And the dead will be resurrected. I've got to find some scientist who'll give me a precise account of what's in Einstein's books. It's out of the question that I shouldn't understand it. I'll see to it that this scientist receives an academician's ration." At that point I became aware of a Majakovskij that I'd never known before. The demand for victory over death had taken hold of him. He told me later that he was writing a poem called "The Fourth International" (he afterward changed it to "The Fifth International") that would deal with such things. "Einstein will be a member of that International. The poem will be much more important than '150,000,000.'" Majakovskij was at the time obsessed with the idea of sending Einstein a congratulatory telegram "from the art of the future to the science of the future." We never again returned to this matter in our conversations, and he never finished "The Fifth International." But in the epilogue to "About That" we find the lines: "I see it, I see it clearly to the last sharp detail . . . On the bright eminence of time, impervious to rot or destruction, the workshop of human resurrection."

The epilogue to "About That" carries the following heading: "A request addressed to . . . (Please, comrade chemist, fill in the name yourself)." I haven't the slightest doubt that for Majakovskij this was not just a literary device but a genuine and seriously offered request to some "quiet chemist with a domed forehead" living in the thirtieth century:

> Resurrect me!
> Even if only because I was a poet
> And waited for you.
> And put behind me prosaic nonsense.
> Resurrect me—
> Just for that!
> Do resurrect me—
> I want to live it all out.

The very same "Institute for Human Resurrections" reappears in the play *The Bedbug* but in a comic context. It is the insistent theme of Majakovskij's last writings. Consider the situation in *The Bathhouse:* "A phosphorescent woman out of the future, empowered to select the best people for the future age appears in the time machine: At the first signal we blast off, and smash through old decrepit time . . . Winged time will sweep away and cut loose the ballast, heavy with rubbish and ruined by lack of faith." Once again we see that the pledge of resurrection is faith. Moreover, the people of the future must transform not only their own future, but also the past: "The fence of time/ our feet will trample. . . . As it has been written by us,/ so will the world be/ on Wednesday,/ in the past/ and now/ and tomorrow/ and forever" (from "150,000,000"). The poem written in memory of Lenin offers the same idea, yet in disguised form:

> Death will never dare
> To touch him.
> He stands
> In the total sum of what's to be!
> The young attend
> to these verses on his death
> But their hearts know
> That he's deathless.

In Majakovskij's earliest writings personal immortality is achieved in spite of science. "You students," he says, "all the stuff we know and study is rubbish. Physics, astronomy, and chemistry are all nonsense" (from the poem "Man"). At that time he regarded science as an idle occupation involving only the extraction of square roots or a kind of inhuman collection of fossilized fragments of the summer before last.

His satirical "Hymn to the Scholar" became a genuine and fervent hymn only when he thought he had found the miraculous instrument of human resurrection in Einstein's "futuristic brain" and in the physics and chemistry of the future. "Like logs thrown into a boom we are thown at birth into the Volga of human time; we toss about as we float downstream. But from now on that great river shall be submissive to us. I'll make time stand still, move in another direction and at a new rate of speed. People will be able to get out of the day like passengers getting out of a bus."

Whatever the means of achieving immortality, the vision of it in Majakovskij's verse is unchangeable: there can be no resurrection of the spirit without the body, without the flesh itself. Immortality has nothing to with any other world; it is indissolubly tied to this one. "I'm all for the heart," he wrote in "Man," "but how can bodiless beings have a heart?/ . . . My eyes fixed earthward . . . / This herd of the bodiless,/ how they/ bore me!" "We want to live here on earth—/ no higher and no lower" (*Mystery-Bouffe*). "With the last measure of my heart/ I believe/ in this life,/ in this world,/ in all of it" ("About That"). Majakovskij's dream is of an everlasting earth, and this earth is placed in sharp opposition to all superterrestrial, fleshless abstractions. In his poetry and in Xlebnikov's the theme of earthly life is presented in a coarse, physical incarnation (they even talk about the "flesh" rather than the body). An extreme expression of this is the cult of tender feeling for the beast with his beastly wisdom.

"They will arise from the mounds of graves/ and their buried bones will grow flesh" ("War and the Universe"), wrote Majakovskij. And those lines are not just present simply as a poetic device that motivates the whimsical interweaving of two separate narrative levels. On the contrary—that vision is Majakovskij's most cherished poetic myth.

This constant infatuation with a wonderful future is linked in Majakovskij with a pronounced dislike of children, a fact that would seem at first sight to be hardly consonant with his fanatical belief in tomorrow. But just as we find in Dostoevskij an obtrusive and neurotic "father hatred" linked with great veneration for ancestors and reverence for tradition, so in Majakovskij's spiritual world an abstract faith in the coming transformation of the world is joined quite properly with hatred for the evil continuum of specific tomorrows that only prolong today ("the calendar is nothing but the calendar!") and with undying hostility to that "brood-hen" love that serves only to reproduce the present way of life. Majakovskij was indeed capable of giving full due to the creative mission of those "kids of the collective" in their unending quarrel with the old world, but at the same time he bristled whenever an actual "kid" ran into the room. Majakovskij never recognized his own myth of the future in any concrete child; these he regarded simply as new offshoots of the hydraheaded enemy. That is why we find in the marvelous movie scenario *How Are You? (Kak poživaete?)* childlike grotesques, which are the legitimate offspring of the Manilov pair Alcides and Themistoclus in Gogol''s *Dead Souls*. We recall that his youthful poem "A Few Words about Myself" ("Neskol'ko slov obo mne samom") begins with the line "I love to watch children dying." And in the same poem child-murder is elevated to a cosmic theme: "Sun!/ My father!/ At least you have pity and torment me not!/ That's my blood you shed flowing along this low road." And surrounded by that very aura of sunshine, the same "child complex" appears as both an immemorial and personal motif in the poem "War and the Universe":

> Listen—
> The sun just shed his first rays
> not yet knowing
> where he'll go when he's done his day's work;
> and that's me
> Majakovskij.
> Bringing as sacrifice to the idol's pedestal
> a beheaded infant.

There's no doubt that in Majakovskij the theme of child-murder and suicide are closely linked: these are simply two different ways of depriving the present of its immediate succession, of "tearing through decrepit time."

Majakovskij's conception of the poet's role is clearly bound up with his belief in the possibility of conquering time and breaking its steady, slow step. He did not regard poetry as a mechanical superstructure added to the ready-made base of existence (it is no accident that he was so close to the Formalist literary critics). A genuine poet is not one "who feeds in the calm pastures of everyday life; his mug is not pointed at the ground." "The weak ones simply beat time and wait for something to happen that they can echo; but the powerful rush far enough ahead so as to drag time along behind them!" Majakovskij's recurrent image of the poet is one who overtakes time, and we may say that this

288

is the actual likeness of Majakovskij himself. Xlebnikov and Majakovskij accurately forecast the Revolution (including the date); that is only a detail, but a rather important one. It would seem that never until our day has the writer's fate been laid bare with such pitiless candor in his own words. Impatient to know life, he recognizes it in his own story. The "God-seeker" Blok and the Marxist Majakovskij both understood clearly that verses are dictated to the poet by some primordial, mysterious force. "We know not whence comes the basic beat of rhythm." We don't even know where this rhythm is located: "outside of me or within me? But most likely within me." The poet himself senses the necessity of his own verse, and his contemporaries feel that the poet's destiny is no accident. Is there any one of us who doesn't share the impression that the poet's volumes are a kind of scenario in which he plays out the story of his life? The poet is the principal character, and subordinate parts are also included; but the performers for these later roles are recruited as the action develops and to the extent that the plot requires them. The plot has been laid out ahead of time right down to the details of the dénouement.

The motif of suicide, so alien to the thematics of the Futurist and "Left Front" groups, continually recurs in the work of Majakovskij, from his earliest writings, where madmen hang themselves in an unequal struggle with *byt* (the director, the "man with two kisses" in the *Tragedy*), to the scenario *How Are You?* in which a newspaper article about a girl's suicide induces horror in the poet. And when he tells about a young communist who committed suicide he adds, "How like me that is. Horrors!" He tries on, so to speak, all possible varieties of suicide: "Rejoice now! He'll execute himself . . . The locomotive's wheel will embrace my neck." "I'll run to the canal and there stick my head in the water's grinning mug . . ." "The heart bursts for a bullet, the throat raves for a razor . . . Beckons to the water, leads to the roof's slope . . . Druggist, give me the means to send my soul without any pain into the spacious beyond."

A simple résumé of Majakovskij's poetic autobiography would be the following: the poet nurtured in his heart the unparalleled anguish of the present generation. That is why his verse is charged with hatred for the strongholds of the established order, and in his own work he finds "the alphabet of coming ages." Majakovskij's earliest and most characteristic image is one in which he "goes out through the city leaving his soul on the spears of houses, shred by shred." The hopelessness of his lonely struggle with the daily routine became clearer to him at every turn. The brand of martyrdom is burned into him. There's no way to win an early victory. The poet is the doomed "outcast of the present."

> Mama!
> Tell my sisters, Ljuda and Olja,
> That there's no way out.

Gradually the idea that "there's no way out" lost its purely literary character. From the poetic passage it found its way into prose, and "there's no way out" turned up as an author's remark in the margin of the manuscript for "About That." And from that prose context the same idea made its way into the poet's life: in his suicide note he said: "Mama, sisters, comrades, forgive me. This is not a good method (I don't recommend it to others), but for me there's no other way out."

The act was long in preparation. Fifteen years earlier in a prologue to a collection of poems, he wrote:

> Often I think
> Hadn't I better just
> Let a bullet mark the period of my sentence.
> Anyway, today
> I'm giving my farewell concert.

As time went on the theme of suicide became more and more pressing. Majakovskij's most intense poems, "Man" (1916) and "About That" (1923), are dedicated to it. Each of these works is an ominous song of the victory of *byt* over the poet: their leitmotif is "Love's boat has smashed against the daily grind" (a line from his suicide note). The first poem is a detailed depiction of Majakovskij's suicide. In the second there is already a clear sense that the suicide theme transcends literature and is in the realm of "literature of fact." Once again—but even more disturbingly—the images of the first poem file past, the keenly observed stages of existence: the "half-death" in the vortex of the horrifyingly trivial, then the "final death"—"The lead in my heart! Not even a shudder!" This theme of suicide had become so real that it was out of the question to sketch the scene anymore. It had to be exorcised. Propaganda pieces were necessary in order to slow down the inexorable movement of that theme. "About That" already initiates this long cycle of exorcism. "I won't give them the satisfaction of seeing me dead of a bullet." "I want to live on and on, moving through the years." The lines to Sergej Esenin are the high point of this cycle. According to Majakovskij, the salubrious aim of the lines addressed to Esenin was to neutralize the impact of Esenin's death poem. But when you read them now, they sound even more sepulchral than Esenin's last lines. Esenin's lines equate life and death, but Majakovskij in his poem can only say about life that it's harder than death. This is the same sort of doubtful propaganda for life found in Majakovskij's earlier lines to the effect that only disquiet about the afterlife is a restraint upon the bullet. Such, too, are the farewell words in his suicide letter: "Stay happy here."

In spite of all this the obituary writers vie with one another: "One could expect anything of Majakovskij, but not that he would kill himself." (E. Adamovič). And Lunačarskij: "The idea of suicide is simply incompatible with our image of the poet." And Malkin: "His death cannot be reconciled with his whole life, which was that of a poet completely dedicated to the Revolution." And the newspaper *Pravda*: "His death is just as inconsistent with the life he led, as it is unmotivated by his poetry." And A. Xalatov: "Such a death was hardly proper for the Majakovskij we knew." Or Kol'cov: "It is not right for him. Can it be that none of us knew Majakovskij?" Petr Pil'skij: "He did not, of course, reveal any reason for us to expect such an end." And finally, the poet Demjan Bednyj: "Incredible! What could he have lacked?"

Could these men of letters have forgotten or so misunderstood *All That Majakovskij Composed*? Or was there a general conviction that all of it was only "composed," only invented? Sound literary criticism rejects any direct or immediate conclusions about the biography of a poet when these are based merely on the evidence of his works, but it does not at all follow from this that there is no connection whatsoever between the artist's biography and his art. Such an "antibiographical" position would be the equivalent, in reverse, of the simplistic biographical approach. Have we forgotten Majakovskij's admiration for the "genuine heroism and martyrdom" of Xlebnikov, his teacher? "His life," wrote Majakovskij, "matched his brilliant verbal constructs. That life is an example for poets and a reproach to poetizers." And it was Majakovskij who wrote that even a poet's style of dress, even his intimate conversations with his wife, should be determined by the whole of his poetic production. He understood very well the close connection between poetry and life.

After Esenin's suicide poem, said Majakovskij, his death became a literary fact. "It was clear at once that those powerful verses, just those verses, would bring to the bullet or the noose many who had been hesitating." And when he approached the writing of his own autobiography, Majakovskij remarked that the facts of a poet's life are interesting "only if they became fixed in the word." Who would dare assert that Majakovskij's suicide was not fixed in the word? "Don't gossip!" Majakovskij adjured us just before his death. Yet those who stubbornly mark out a strict boundary between the "purely personal" fate of the poet and his literary biography create an atmosphere of low-grade, highly personal gossip by means of those significant silences.

It is a historical fact that the people around Majakovskij simply did not believe in his lyrical monologues. "They listened, all smiling, to the eminent clown." They took his various masquerades for the true face of the man: first the pose of the fop ("It's good when the soul is shielded from inspection by a yellow blouse"); then the performance of an overeager journalist and agitator: "It's good when you're in the teeth of the gallows, to cry out: 'Drink Van Houten's cocoa'" ("A Cloud in Trousers"). But then when he carried out that slogan in practice in his advertising jingles ("Use the tea with the gold label!" "If you want good luck and good fortune buy a government lottery ticket!") his audience saw the rhymed advertisement but missed the teeth of the gallows. As it turns out, it was easier to believe in the benefits of a lottery loan or the excellent quality of the pacifiers sold in the state stores than it was to believe that the poet had reached an extreme of despair, that he was in a state of misery and near-death. "About That" is a long and hopeless cry to the ages, but Moscow doesn't believe in tears. They stamped and whistled at this routine Majakovskian artistic stunt, the latest of his "magnificent absurdities," but when the theatrical cranberry juice of the puppet show became real, genuine, thick blood, they were taken aback: Incredible! Inconsistent!

Majakovskij, as an act of self-preservation, often helped to spread illusions about himself. The record of a conversation we had in 1927 demonstrates this. I said, "The total sum of possible experience has been measured out to us. We might have predicted the early decline of our generation. But the symptoms of this are rapidly increasing in number. Take Aseev's line 'What about us, what about us, can it be we've lost our youth?' And consider Šklovskij's memorial service to himself!" Majakovskij answered: "Utter nonsense. Everything is ahead of me. If I ever thought that the best of me was in the past that would be the end for me." I reminded him of a recent poem of his in which the following lines occurred:

I was born/ increased in size
fed from the bottle—
I lived/ worked/ grew oldish
And life will pass
As the Azores Islands
Once passed into the distance.

"That's nothing," he said, "just a formal ending. An image only. I can make as many of them as you like. My poem 'Homeward' in the first version ended with the lines:

I want my country to understand me
But if not—so what:
I'll just pass my country by
Like a slanting rain in summer.

But you know, Brik told me to strike those lines out because they didn't go with the tone of the whole poem. So I struck them out."

The simplistic Formalist literary credo professed by the Russian Futurists inevitably propelled their poetry toward the antithesis of Formalism—toward the cultivation of the heart's "raw cry" and uninhibited frankness. Formalist literary theory placed the lyrical monologue in quotes and disguised the "ego" of the lyric poet under a pseudonym. But what unbounded horror results when suddenly you see through the pseudonym, and the phantoms of art invade reality, just as in Majakovskij's scenario *Bound in Film* a girl is kidnapped from a movie set by a mad artist and lands in "real life."

Toward the end of his life, the satire and the laudatory ode had completely overshadowed his elegiac verse, which, by the way, he identified with the lyric in general. In the West the existence of this basic core in Majakovskij's poetry was not even suspected. The West knew only the "drummer of the October Revolution." There are many explanations for this victory of agit-prop. In 1923 Majakovskij had reached the end of the road as far as the elegiac mode was concerned. In an artistic sense "About That" was a "repetition of the past," intensified and raised to perfection. His journalistic verse was a search for something new; it was an experiment in the production of new materials and in untested genres. To my skeptical comments about these poems

Majakovskij replied: "Later on you'll understand them." And when *The Bedbug* and *The Bathhouse* appeared it became clear that his most recent poems had been a huge laboratory experiment in language and theme, a labor masterfully exploited in his first efforts in the area of prose drama and offering a rich potential for future growth.

Finally, in connection with its social setting, the journalistic verse of Majakovskij represented a shift from an unrestrained frontal attack in the direction of an exhausting trench warfare. *Byt,* with its swarm of heartbreaking trivia, is still with him. And it is no longer "rubbish with its own proper face," but "petty, small, vulgar rubbish." You cannot resist the pressure of such rubbish by grandiloquent pronouncements "in general and in toto," or by theses on communism, or by pure poetic devices. "Now you have to see the enemy and take aim at him." You have to smash the "swarm of trivia" offered by *byt* "in a small way" and not grieve that the battle has been reduced to many minor engagements. The invention of strategies for describing "trifles that may also prove a sure step into the future"—this is how Majakovskij understood the immediate task of the poet.

Just as one must not reduce Majakovskij the propagandist to a single dimension, so, too, one-sided interpretations of the poet's death are shallow and opaque. "The preliminary investigation indicates that his act was prompted by motives of a purely personal character." But the poet had already provided an answer to that in the subtitle of "About That": "From personal motives, but about the general way of life."

Bela Kun preached to the late poet not to "subordinate the great cause to our own petty personal feelings." Majakovskij had entered his objection in good time:

> With this petty/ and personal theme
> That's been sung so many times
> I've trod the poetical treadmill
> And I'm going to tread it again.
> This theme/ right now
> Is a prayer to Buddha
> And sharpens a black man's knife for his master.
> If there's life on Mars/ and on it just one
> Human-hearted creature
> Then he too is writing now
> About that same thing.

The journalist Kol'cov hastened to explain: "Majakovskij himself was wholly absorbed in the business affairs of various literary groups and in political matters. Someone else fired that shot, some outsider who happened to be in control of a revolutionary poet's mind and will. It was the result of the temporary pressure of circumstances." And once again we recall the rebuke Majakovskij delivered long before the fact:

> Dreams are a harm
> And it's useless to fantasize.
> You've got to bear the burden of service.
> But sometimes—
> Life appears to you in a new light
> And through the mess of trifles
> You catch sight of something great and good.

"We condemn this senseless, unforgivable act. It was a stupid and cowardly death. We cannot but protest most vigorously against his departure from life, against his incongruous end." (Such was the pronouncement of the Moscow Soviet and others.) But Majakovskij had already parodied these very funeral speeches in *The Bedbug*: "Zoja Berëzkin's shot herself—Aha! She'll catch it for that at her party-section meeting." Says a doctor in the future world commune: "What is suicide? . . . You shot at yourself? . . . Was it an accident?" "No, it was from love." "Nonsense . . . Love makes you want to build bridges and have children . . . But you . . . Yes, yes, yes!"

In general life has been imitating Majakovskij's satirical lines with horrifying regularity. Pobedonosikov, the comic figure in *The Bathhouse*, who has many features that remind us of Lunačarskij, brags that "I have no time for boat rides . . . Such petty entertainments are for various secretaries: 'Float on, gondola mine!' I have no gondola but a ship of state." And now Lunačarskij himself faithfully echoes his comic double. At a meeting called in memory of the poet, the minister hastens to explain that the former's farewell lines about a "love-boat smashed on daily grind" have a pathetic sound: "We know very well that it was not on any love-boat that he sailed our stormy seas. He was the captain of a mighty ship of state." These efforts to forget the "purely personal" tragedy of Majakovskij sometimes take the form of conscious parody. A group of writers in a provincial town published a resolution in which they assure Soviet society that they will take very seriously the advice of the late poet not to follow his example.

It is very strange that on this occasion such terms as "accidental," "personal," and so forth are used precisely by those who have always preached a strict social determinism. But how can one speak of a private episode when the law of large numbers is at work, in view of the fact that in a few years' time the whole bloom of Russian poetry has been swept away?

In one of Majakovskij's longer poems, each of the world's countries brings its best gift to the man of the future; Russia brings him poetry. "The power of their voices is most resoundingly woven into song." Western Europe is enraptured with Russian art: the medieval icon and the modern film, the classical ballet and the latest theatrical experiment, yesterday's novel and the latest music. And yet that art which is probably Russia's greatest achievement, her poetry, has never really been an export item. It is intimately Russian and closely linked to the Russian language and would probably not survive the misfortunes of translation. Russian poetry has witnessed two periods of high flowering: the beginning of the nineteenth century and the present century. And the earlier period as well as the later had as its epilogue the untimely death of very many great poets. If you can imagine how slight the contributions of Schiller, Hoffmann, Heine, and especially Goethe would have been if they had all disappeared in their thirties, then you will understand the significance of the following Russian statistics: Ryleev was executed when he was thirty-one. Batjuškov went mad when he was thirty. Venevitinov died at the age of twenty-two, Del'vig at thirty-two. Griboedov was killed when he was thirty-four, Puškin when he was thirty-seven, Lermontov when he was twenty-six. Their fate has more than once been characterized as a form of suicide. Majakovskij himself compared his duel with *byt* to the fatal duels of Puškin and Lermontov. There is much in common in the reactions of society in both periods to these untimely losses. Once again, a feeling of sudden and profound emptiness overwhelms one, an oppressive sense of an evil destiny lying heavily on Russian intellectual life. But now as then other notes are louder and more insistent.

The Western mind can hardly comprehend the stupid, unrestrained abuse of the dead poets. A certain Kikin expressed great disappointment that Martynov, the killer of that "cowardly scoundrel Lermontov," had been arrested. And Tsar Nicholas I's final words on the same poet were: "He was a dog and he died a dog's death." And in the same spirit the emigré newspaper *The Rudder (Rul')* carried no obituary on the occasion of Majakovskij's death, but instead a cluster of abusive remarks leading up to the following conclusion: "Majakovskij's whole life gave off a bad smell. Is it possible that his tragic end could set all that right?" (Ofrosimov). But what of the Kikins and Ofrosimovs? They're but illiterate zeros who will be mentioned in the history of Russian culture, if at all, only for having defecated on the fresh graves of poets. It is incomparably more distressing to see slops of slander and lies poured on the dead poet by Xodasevič, who is privy to poetry. He certainly knows the value of things; he knows he is slanderously smearing one of the greatest Russian poets. When he caustically remarks that only some fifteen active years were allotted to Majakovskij—"the lifetime of a horse"—it is self-abuse, gallows humor, mockery of the tragic balance sheet of his own generation. If Majakovskij's final balance sheet was "life and I are quits," then Xodasevič's shabby little fate is "the most terrible of amortizations, the amortization of heart and soul."

The latter was written about emigré philistines. But the tradition of Puškin's days is repeated by the same philistines of Moscow stock who immediately try at all costs to replace the live image of the poet by a canonic saintlike mask. And even earlier . . . But of what went on earlier, Majakovskij himself related a few days before his death in a talk at a literary gathering: "So many dogs snipe at me and I'm accused of so many sins, both ones I have and ones I am innocent of, that at times it seems to me as if all I want to do is go away somewhere and sit still for a couple of years, if only to avoid listening to barking!" And this harrassment, framing the poet's demise, was precisely described in advance by Majakovskij:

> Yellow rag after yellow rag
>   of curses be raised!
> Gossip for your ears!
>   Gossip and bite!
> I'm like a cripple in the throes of love.
> Leave a tub of slops for your own.
> I'm not a hindrance.
>   But why all these insults?
> I'm only a verse
>   I'm only a soul.
> While below:
>   No!
>   You're our century-old foe.
> One such turned up—
>   A hussar!
> Have a sniff of powder,
>   a little pistol lead.

Fling open your shirt!
Don't celebrate the coward!

This is just another example of what they call the "incongruity" between Majakovskij's end and his life of yesterday.

Certain questions are particularly intriguing to journalists. Who was responsible for the war? Who was to blame for the poet's death? Biographers are amateur private detectives, and they will certainly take great pains to establish the immediate reason for the suicide. They will add other names to that variegated assemblage of poet-killers, the "son of a bitch D'Anthès" who killed Puškin, the "dashing Major Martynov" who killed Lermontov, and so forth. People who seek the explanation of various phenomena will, if they bear Russia a grudge, readily demonstrate, citing chapter, verse, and historical precedent, that it is dangerous to practice the trade of poet in Russia. And if their grudge is only against contemporary Russia, it will also be quite easy to defend such a thesis with weighty arguments. But I am of another mind. It seems to me that the one nearest the truth was the young Slovak poet Novomeský who said: "Do you imagine that such things happen only there, in Russia? Why that's what our world is like nowadays." This is in answer to those phrases, which have alas become truisms, concerning the deadly absence of fresh air, certainly a fatal condition for poets. There are some countries where men kiss women's hands, and others where they only say "I kiss your hand." There are countries where Marxist theory is answered by Leninist practice, and where the madness of the brave, the martyr's stake, and the poet's Golgotha are not just figurative expressions.

In the last analysis, what distinguishes Russia is not so much the fact that her great poets have ceased to be, but rather that not long ago she had so many of them. Since the time of the first Symbolists, Western Europe has had no great poetry.

The real question concerns not causes but consequences, however tempting it may be to protect oneself from a painful realization of what's happened by discussing the reasons for it.

It's a small thing to build a locomotive:
Wind up its wheels and off it goes.
But if a song doesn't fill the railway station—
Then why do we have alternating current?

Those lines are from Majakovskij's "Order to the Army of Art" ("Prikaz po armii iskusstv"). We are living in what is called the "recon-

struction period," and no doubt we will construct a great many loco-
motives and scientific hypotheses. But to our generation has been allotted the morose feat of building without song. And even if new
songs should ring out, they will belong to another generation and a
different curve of time. Yet it is unlikely that there will be new songs.
Russian poetry of our century is copying and it would seem outdoing
that of the nineteenth century: "the fateful forties are approaching,"
the years, in other words, of lethargic inertia among poets.

The relationships between the biographies of a generation and the
march of history are curious. Each age has its own inventory of requi-
sitions upon private holdings. Suddenly history finds a use for Beethoven's deafness and Cézanne's astigmatism. The age at which a generation's call to service in history's conscription comes, as well as the
length of its service, are different for different periods. History mobi-
lizes the youthful ardor of some generations and the tempered maturity or old wisdom of others. When their role is played out yesterday's
rulers of men's minds and hearts depart from the proscenium to the
backstage of history to live out their years in private, either on the
profits from their intellectual investments, or else as paupers. But
sometimes it happens otherwise. Our generation emerged at an extraordinarily young age: "We alone," as Majakovskij put it, "are the
face of our time. The trumpet of time blows for us." But up to the
present moment there are not any replacements, nor even any partial
reinforcements. Meanwhile the voice and the emotion of that generation have been cut short, and its allotted quota of feeling—joy and
sadness, sarcasm and rapture—have been used up. And yet, the par-
oxysm of an irreplaceable generation turned out to be no private fate,
but in fact the face of our time, the breathlessness of history.

We strained toward the future too impetuously and avidly to leave
any past behind us. The connection of one period with another was
broken. We lived too much for the future, thought about it, believed
in it; the news of the day—sufficient unto itself—no longer existed for
us. We lost a sense of the present. We were the witnesses of and participants in great social, scientific, and other cataclysms. *Byt* fell behind
us, just as in the young Majakovskij's splendid hyperbole: "One foot
has not yet reached the next street." We knew that the plans of our
fathers were already out of harmony with the facts of their lives. We
read harsh lines alleging that our fathers had taken the old and musty
way of life on a temporary lease. But our fathers still had left some
remnant of faith in the idea that that way of life was both comfortable

and compulsory for all. Their children had only a single-minded, naked hatred for the ever more threadbare, ever more alien rubbish offered by the established order of things. And now the "efforts to organize a personal life are like attempts to heat up ice cream."

As for the future, it doesn't belong to us either. In a few decades we shall be cruelly labeled as products of the past millennium. All we had were compelling songs of the future; and suddenly these songs are no longer part of the dynamic of history, but have been transformed into historico-literary facts. When singers have been killed and their song has been dragged into a museum and pinned to the wall of the past, the generation they represent is even more desolate, orphaned, and lost—impoverished in the most real sense of the word.

CHAPTER 17

Marginal Notes on the Prose of the Poet Pasternak

Textbook categories are comfortingly simple: prose is one thing, poetry another. Nevertheless, the difference between a poet's prose and that of a prose writer, or between the poems of a prose writer and those of a poet, is very striking. A mountaineer walking in the plains can find no foothold and stumbles over the level ground. He moves either with touching awkwardness or with overemphatic artistry; in either case it is not his natural gait, but involves obvious effort and looks too much like the steps of a dancer. It is easy to distinguish a language that has been learnt, however perfect its command, from one that has been naturally acquired. Cases of complete bilingualism are, of course, undeniable, and when we read the prose of Puškin or Mácha, of Lermontov or Heine, of Pasternak or Mallarmé, we cannot help being amazed at the command these writers have of the other language; but at the same time we are bound to pick out a foreign note, as it were, in the accent and inner form of their speech. Their achievements in this second language are brilliant sallies from the mountains of poetry into the plains of prose.

It is not only a poet's prose that has a particular stamp; there is also the prose peculiar to an age of poetry, the prose of a literary current oriented towards poetry, as distinct from those literary epochs and schools that are prose-oriented. The major achievements of Russian literature in the first decades of our century belong to poetry; it is poetry that is felt to be the pure canonical voice of literature, its perfect incarnation. Both Symbolism and the later literary fermentation often summed up under the heading of "Futurism" are almost exclusively represented by poets, and if many of these occasionally try an excursion into prose, it is a conscious deviation, an experimental digression by a virtuoso of verse. With but a few exceptions the standard literary prose of this period is a typical epigone product, a more or less successful reproduction of classic models: the interest of this hackwork lies either in its successful imitation of the old or in its grotesque brutalisation of the canon, or else its novelty consists in cunningly adapting new themes to traditional forms. In contrast to the great internal tension of the poetry of the time, this prose can claim to be distinguished only in the first place because Gogol' and after him Tolstoj have lifted the qualitative norm to such a high level, and in the second place because the requirements of modern reality are themselves so exacting. In the history of artistic prose this hundredth province of Russian classic realism has little evolutionary significance, whereas the prose of Brjusov, Belyj, Xlebnikov, Majakovskij and Pasternak—that remarkable colony of modern poets—opens up hidden paths to a revival of Russian prose. In the same way the prose of Puškin and Lermontov heralded the approach of the great festival of prose that was opened by Gogol'. Pasternak's prose is the characteristic prose of a poet in a great age of poetry.

The prose of a writer in a literary movement primarily concerned with poetry is very clearly defined both in those places where it is influenced by the dominant, that is, the poetic, element, and in those where it breaks free from that influence by an intense and conscious effort. No less essential is the general context of literary activity, its role in the whole concert of the arts. The hierarchy of artistic values changes for individual artists and artistic movements: for Classicism it is the plastic arts, for Romanticism music, and for Realism literature that is the highest, the most extreme and exemplary, expression of art possible. Romantic verse is required to sing and to merge into music; in the age of Realism, on the contrary, music—in musical drama and in program music—seeks to ally itself with literature. The Romantic's slogan of art gravitating toward music was adopted to a significant degree by Symbolism. The foundations of Symbolism first begin to be undermined in painting, and in the early days of Futurist art it is painting that holds the dominant positions. And then, as plastic art is stripped of its emblematic character, poetry becomes the model of artistic innovation. A tendency to identify art with poetry is manifested by all the poets of the Futurist generation. "Art as a whole, in other words—poetry," says Pasternak. But the origin of this hierarchy of values differs from poet to poet; different paths lead them to poetry, and they start from different points. Pasternak, a convinced pupil of "the art of Scrjabin, Blok, Kommissarževskaja and Belyj," that is, of the Symbolist school, comes to poetry from music, to which he is connected by a cult relationship characteristic of the Symbolists. Majakovskij's springboard to poetry is painting. For all the variety of the artistic tasks that Xlebnikov sets himself, the written word is his sole and unchanging material. We could say that, in the development of Russian post-Symbolist poetry, Majakovskij embodies the "Storm and Stress," Xlebnikov provides its most characteristic and remarkable achievement, while Pasternak's work is, as it were, the link between Symbolism and the school that follows it. And granted that Xlebnikov reached poetic maturity earlier than Majakovskij, and Majakovskij earlier than Pasternak, nonetheless it can be said that when the reader whose starting point is Symbolism comes to tackle Pasternak, he will inevitably stumble over Majakovskij and finally, after overcoming the latter, be faced with laying a long siege to the strongholds of Xlebnikov. However, any attempt to see writers of one and the same period as individual links in a chain of uniform literary development, and to establish the sequence of these links, is always conventionally one-sided. While in certain respects the individual poet continues a tradition, in many others he breaks away from it all the more decisively; the tradition is likewise never entirely negated; the elements of negation always appear only in conjunction with persisting traditional elements. Thus Pasternak, who conceives as his literary task the continuing of Symbolist tradition, is aware that out of his efforts to recreate and perpetuate the old a new art is always arising. The imitations turn out to be "more swift and fervent" than the model, and this quantitative difference evolves naturally into a qualitative one. According to the poet's own self-observation, "the new came into being not as a substitute for the old . . . on the contrary, it arose as an enraptured reproduction of the existing model." By contrast, Majakovskij is consciously out to abolish the old poetry: nevertheless Pasternak, with his acute awareness of Symbolism, senses in Majakovskij's "romantic manner," and the sense of life underlying it, the condensed heritage of the very school of poetry that the aggressive Futurist repudiates. What then is at issue? Pasternak's and Majakovskij's innovations are just as partial as is their connection with the literary past. Suppose we imagine two related languages which differ not only in their neologisms but also in their original vocabulary: what the one has retained from the common source, the other has often rejected, and vice versa. These two languages are the poetic worlds of Majakovskij and Pasternak respectively, while the common linguistic source is the poetic system of Symbolism. The theme of the remarks that follow is that unusual element in Pasternak's work which sets him apart from his predecessors, which is in part alien and in part strikingly akin to his contemporaries, and which is most clearly to be seen in the telltale awkwardness of his prose.

I

The textbooks confidently draw a firm line between lyric and epic poetry. If we reduce the question to a simple grammatical formula, we can say that the point of departure and the main theme are, for the lyric, invariably the first person of the present tense; for the epic, the third person of the past tense. Whatever subject matter the lyric narrative may have, it is never more than an appendage and accessory, a mere background to the first person; and if the past is involved, then the lyric past always presupposes a reminiscing first-person subject. In the epic, on the contrary, the present refers expressly back to the past, and if the "I" of the narrator does find expression, it is solely as one of the characters in the action. This objectified "I" thus appears as a variant of the third person; the poet is, as it were, looking at himself from outside. So that the first person may be emphasized as the point of reception but that point never fuses with the main subject of the epic poem itself; in other words, the poet as "subject of the lyric that looks at the world through the first person" is profoundly alien to the epic. Russian Symbolism is lyrical through and through; its excursions into the epic vein are typical attempts by lyric poets to masquerade as poets of epic. In post-Symbolist poetry the two genres diverge: while the persisting lyric strain clearly predominates, reaching its most extreme expression in the work of Majakovskij, the purely epic element finds an outlet, too, in the quite unparalleled poetry and prose of Xlebnikov. Pasternak's work is emphatically lyrical; his prose, especially, is the characteristic prose of a lyric poet, nor are his historical poems essentially different from his cycles of intimate lyric poetry.

Pasternak confesses that Xlebnikov's achievements are even now largely inaccessible to him and justifies himself with the declaration: "poetry in my view merges in history and in collaboration with real life." This reproach, with its implication that he had torn himself away from real life, would certainly have astonished Xlebnikov; for he had regarded his work as an affirmation of reality, unlike the negative literature of the preceding generations. Xlebnikov's symbolic world is so fully realized that for him every symbol, every created word, is endowed with a complete independent reality, and the question of its relations to any external object, indeed the very question of the existence of such an object, becomes entirely superfluous. For Xlebnikov, as for the little heroine in Pasternak's story, a name possesses the complete and comforting significance it has in childhood:

> She could not possibly define what was happening on the other shore, far, far away: it had no name, no distinct colour or precise outlines. . . . Ženya began to cry. . . . Her father's explanation was brief: 'It's *Motovilixa*.' . . . The little girl did not understand at all and, satisfied, swallowed a falling tear. For that was all that she needed: to know the name of the incomprehensible—*Motovilixa*.

When Ženya had grown out of childhood she was struck for the first time by the suspicion that there was something which appearances concealed or else revealed only to the elect. This attitude of childhood towards appearances corresponds perfectly to Pasternak's own. An epic attitude to his environment is naturally out of the question for a poet who is convinced that, in the world of prosaic fact, the elements of everyday existence fall dully, stupidly and with crippling effect upon the soul and "sink to the bottom, real, hardened and cold, like drowsy tin spoons," and that only the passion of the elect can transform this "depressingly conscientious truth" into poetry. Only feeling proves to be obviously and absolutely authentic. "Compared with this even the sunrise took on the character of urban rumor still needing to be verified." Pasternak bases his poetics on the personal, emotional experience—indeed appropriation—of reality. "In this form the events did not belong to me," and so on. Both his adjustment of the language of poetry to the purely expressive language of music, and the fact that this conception is based on the triumphing of passion, with its animating power, over the inevitable, show Pasternak to be continuing the romantic line of Symbolism; but as his work matures and attains individuality, so his initially romantic language of the emotions evolves gradually into a language about the emotions, and it is in his prose that this descriptive character finds its most extreme expression.

II

Whereas, despite the obvious echoes of Xlebnikov in Pasternak's work, these two poets are clearly distinguishable from each other, it is far more difficult to draw a line between Pasternak and Majakovskij. Both are lyric poets of the same generation, and Majakovskij, more than any other poet, deeply affected Pasternak in his youth and constantly won his admiration. A careful comparison of the respective tissue of metaphors of the two poets at once reveals remarkable similarities. "I was related to Majakovskij by the age and by common influences; certain things coincided in us," observes Pasternak. The metaphorical structure of Pasternak's poems reveals, too, direct traces of his enthusiasm for the author of "A Cloud in Trousers." In comparing the two poets' metaphors we must bear in mind that these have a quite different role to play in the work of each poet. In Majakovskij's poems the metaphor, sharpened by the tradition of Symbolism, is not only the most characteristic but also the most essential poetic trope, determining the structure and development of the lyric theme. In Pasternak's pertinent phrase, poetry here began "to speak in the language of sectarian parables." To define the problem: the poet's absolute commitment to metaphor is known; what remains to be determined is the thematic structure of his poetry. The lyrical impulse is, as we have said, provided by the poet's own self. Images of the external world in the metaphorical lyric are made to harmonize with this impulse, to shift it into different levels, to establish a network of correspondences and masterful assimilations amidst the diverse aspects of the cosmos, to merge the lyric hero into the multifariousness of Being and to dissolve the manifold planes of Being in the lyric hero. Metaphor works through creative association by similarity and contrast. The hero is confronted by the antithetical image of what is mortally inimical to him, protean like all the ingredients of a primarily metaphorical lyric poetry. Such poetry inevitably culminates in the theme of the hero's duel to the death. Held together by a firm and taut chain of metaphors, the heroic lyric fuses the poet's mythology and his being into an inseparable whole, and he, as Pasternak has perfectly understood, pays for its all-embracing symbolism with his life. In this way we have deduced from the semantic structure of Majakovskij's poetry both its actual libretto and the core of the poet's biography.

However rich and refined Pasternak's metaphors may be, they are not what determines and guides his lyric theme. It is the metonymical, not the metaphorical, passages that lend his work an "expression far from common." Pasternak's lyricism, both in poetry and in prose, is imbued with metonymy; in other words, it is association by contiguity that predominates. By comparison with Majakovskij's poetry, the first person is thrust into the background. But it is only an apparent relegation—here too the eternal hero of the lyric is present. It is merely a case of his being metonymically presented; in the same way, no railway train can be seen in Chaplin's *A Woman of Paris,* but we are aware of its arrival from the reactions of the people in front of the cameras—as if the invisible, transparent train were making its way between the screen and the audience. Similarly, in Pasternak's poetry, images of the surrounding world function as contiguous reflections, or metonymical expressions, of the poet's self. Now and then the author reveals his poetics clearly, but he egocentrically applies them to art in general. He does not believe that it is possible for art to adopt a truly epic attitude to the outside world; he is convinced that genuine works of art, while relating all sorts of things, are really telling of their own birth. "Reality arises in a kind of new category. This category seems to us to be its own condition, and not ours . . . We try to name it. The result is art." Thus Constantinople seemed to the pilgrim from old Russia to be an insatiable city because he never got tired of looking at it. It is the same with Pasternak's poems and, in particular, with his prose, where the anthropomorphism of the inanimate world emerges much more clearly: instead of the hero it is, as often as not, the surrounding objects that are thrown into turmoil; the immovable outlines of roofs grow inquisitive, a door swings shut with a silent reproach, the joy of a family reconciliation is expressed by a growing warmth, zeal and devotion on the part of the lamps, and when the poet is turned away by the girl he loves he finds that "the mountain had grown taller and thinner, the town was become lean and black." We have deliberately given simple examples; there is a wealth of much more involved imagery of this sort in Pasternak's work. The substitution of an adjacent object is the simplest form of association by contiguity. The poet has other metonymical devices as well; he can proceed from the whole to the part and vice versa, from the cause to the effect and vice versa, from spatial relations to temporal ones and vice versa, etc., etc. But perhaps what is most characteristic of Pasternak is his using an action instead of an actor, a man's condition, or one of his remarks or attributes, rather than the man himself, and the consequent separating off and objectifying of these abstractions. The philosopher Brentano, who steadfastly fought against the logically illegitimate objectification of such fictions based in language, would have discovered in Pasternak's poetry and prose a most abundant collection of such alleged *entia,* treated as creatures of flesh and blood. *Sestra moja—žizn'* (My Sister Life), the really untranslatable title and leitmotif of Pasternak's most relevant collection of poems ("life" is feminine in Russian), graphically exposes the linguistic roots of this mythology. This same being repeatedly appears in his prose too.

> Life lets very few people know what it is doing with them. It loves its job too much and while at work it speaks at most with those who wish it success and who love its workbench.

In *Safe Conduct* it reappears in a more complex metonymical setting:

> Suddenly I imagined, outside beneath the window, his life, which now belonged entirely to the past. It moved sideways away from the window in the form of some quiet street, bordered with trees . . . And the first to stand upon it, right beside the wall, was our State, our unprecedented, impossible State, rushing headlong into the ages and accepted among them for ever. It stood there below, and one could call to it and take it by the hand.

Pasternak's poetry is a realm of metonymies awakened to independent life. The footsteps of the tired hero, themselves longing for sleep as he is, continue to live and move behind him. On his steep path the poet's vision gently beats: "I am the vision." In his reminiscences the author relates how

> I often heard the whistling of a nostalgia that had not originated with me. Catching up with me from the rear, it frightened me and made me feel pity . . . My silence was travelling with me, I was

attached to its person for the journey, and wore its uniform, a uniform familiar to everyone from his own experience.

The sound uttered by an object assumes the latter's function:

> Somewhere nearby . . . a herd . . . was making music. . . . The music was sucked in by blue-bottles. Its skin was rippling to and fro spasmodically and surely.

Action and actor are objects in the same degree:

> Two rare diamonds were playing separately and independently in the deep nests of this half-dark bliss.

As an abstraction becomes objectified, it is overlaid with material accessories:

> Those were aerial ways, on which, like trains, the rectilinear thoughts of Liebknecht, Lenin and the few minds of their flight departed daily.

An abstraction is personified even at the cost of a catachresis:

> Midday quiet reigned. It communed with the quiet that was spread out below in the plain.

An abstraction becomes capable of independent actions, and these actions are objectified in their turn:

> Lacquered sounds of giggling from a disintegrating order of life winked at each other in the quiet.

Majakovskij, who had a predilection for continually surmounting obstacles, toyed for years with the thought of writing a novel. He even had ideas for a title—first *Two Sisters,* then *A Dozen Women.* It is no accident that the project was always postponed: Majakovskij's element is either the lyrical monologue or the dramatic dialogue; descriptive presentation is profoundly foreign to him, and he substitutes second-person for third-person themes. Everything that is not inseparably attached to the poet's self is felt by Majakovskij to be opposed and hostile to him, and he confronts his opponent face to face—challenges him to single combat, exposes, condemns, mocks and outlaws him. It is not surprising that the only undertaking he completed in the field of literary prose was the series of splendid stage plays written in the last years of his life. There is just as firm a logic about the path that Pasternak took toward narrative prose. There exist poems which are woven through and through with metonymies, while narrative prose may be studded with metaphors (a striking example is Belyj's prose), but in the main there is an undeniably closer relationship on the one hand between verse and metaphor, on the other between prose and metonymy. Verse relies upon association by similarity; the rhythmical similarity of the lines is an essential requirement for its reception, and this rhythmical parallelism is most strongly felt when it is accompanied by a similarity (or contrast) of images. An intentionally striking division into similar sections is foreign to prose. The basic impulse of narrative prose is association by contiguity, and the narrative moves from one object to an adjacent one on paths of space and time or of causality; to move from the whole to the part and vice versa is only a particular instance of this process. The more the prose is stripped of material content, the greater the independence achieved by these associations. For metaphor the line of least resistance is verse, and for metonymy it is a prose whose subject matter is either subdued or eliminated (Pasternak's short stories are an example of the first alternative, and his *Safe Conduct* of the second).

III

The essence of poetic figures of speech does not simply lie in their recording the manifold relationships between things, but also in the way they dislocate familiar relationships. The more strained the role of the metaphor in a given poetic structure, that much the more decisively are traditional categories overthrown; things are arranged anew in the light of newly introduced generic signs. Accordingly, the creative (or, as the foes of such novelty will say, the forced) metonymy changes the accustomed order of things. Association by contiguity, which in Pasternak's work becomes the artist's flexible tool, transforms spatial distribution and temporal succession. This emerges particularly clearly from the poet's prose ventures, outlined as it is against the background of a prose that seeks to communicate in the customary way. Pasternak grounds this dislocation in emotion, or else, if one's starting point is the expressive function of literature, he uses this dislocation to help express the emotions.

A poetic world governed by metonymy blurs the outline of things, as April, in Pasternak's story "The Childhood of Luvers," blurs the distinction between house and yard; similarly it turns two different aspects of one and the same object into independent objects, like the children in the same story who think that a street seen first from inside the house and then from outside it is two different streets. These two characteristic features—the mutual penetration of objects (the realization of metonymy in the strict sense of the word) and their decomposition (the realization of synecdoche)—bring Pasternak's work close to the endeavors of Cubist painters. The dimensions of things change:

> The gondola was, womanlike, gigantic, as everything is gigantic which is perfect in form and incommensurable with the place taken up by its body in space.

The distances between things change so that it becomes certain that a conversation about strangers has to be warmer than a conversation about kindred; and the vision of cosmic movement in the first part of *Safe Conduct* transforms inanimate objects into a distant, motionless horizon. A striking example of how settings are transformed:

> The lamps only accentuated the emptiness of the evening air. They did not give light, but swelled from within, like sick fruits, from the turbid and bright dropsy that puffed up their bloated shades. . . . The lamps came much less in contact with the rooms than with the spring sky which they seemed to be pushed close up to.

Pasternak himself compares, in passing, his dislocated space with the space of Gogol''s eschatology: "sudddenly it became possible to see far into the distance in all directions." Spatial relations are mingled with temporal ones, and the time sequence loses its strict regularity—objects "are jolted again and again from the past into the future, and from the future into the past, like sand in a frequently shaken hourglass." Any contiguity can be construed as a causal series. Pasternak is impressed by the terminology of the child who grasps the meaning of a sentence from the situation and says, "I did not understand it from the words but from the reason." The poet tends to identify the situation with the reason; he consciously prefers "the vicissitudes of guesswork to the eloquence of fact"; he proclaims that "time is permeated with the unity of a life's events," and builds bridges between them on just those prelogical "ridiculous grounds" which he openly opposes to the syllogisms of "adults." Thus it is no surprise when the chatter of Cohen's companions proves to be "uneven on account of the steplike construction of the Marburg pavements," and when the poet's numerous "therefores" not infrequently introduce clauses whose causal nature is a pure fiction.

The wider the range of the poetic figure of speech, the more thoroughly, to use Pasternak's language, "the accomplished" extinguishes "the subject of the accomplishment." A connection that has been created overshadows one that is still to be made, and governs it; "the fascination of autonomous meaning" takes on prominence, whilst material connectedness is subdued, sometimes to a mere glimmer. In this sense the metonymical connections which Pasternak establishes, no less than Majakovskij's metaphorical connections or the manifold ways of condensing speech—both internal and external—in the poetry of Xlebnikov, show a persistent tendency to dispense with the object, a tendency also characteristic of the other art forms of the period. A connection once created becomes an object in its own right. Pasternak does not tire of underlining the inessential, random nature of the thing to be connected:

> Each detail can be replaced by another . . . Any one of them, chosen at random, will serve to bear witness to the transposed condition by which the whole of reality has been seized . . . The parts of reality are mutually indifferent.

The poet defines art as the mutual interchangeability of images. Any images one cares to choose harbor more than similarity alone, and can consequently be mutual metaphors ("what cannot the sky be compared with?")—all images are in some way potentially contiguous. "Who has not something of dust, or home or a calm spring evening in him?" is Pasternak's apology for the all-embracing, metonymical elective affinity. The more unrecognizable this affinity and the more unusual the community that the poet creates, the more the juxtaposed images, and whole series of images, fall to pieces and lose their spellingbook clarity. Significantly, Pasternak consistently opposes "the meaning imported into objects" to their plasticity, for which he so delights in finding pejorative epithets—in Pasternak's world meaning is inevitably etiolating and plasticity deanimating.

IV

To define our problem: the absolute commitment of the poet to metonymy is known; what remains to be determined is the thematic structure of his poetry. The hero is as if concealed in a picture puzzle; he is broken down into a series of constituent and subsidiary parts; he is replaced by a chain of concretized situations and surrounding objects, both animate and inanimate. "Every small detail lived and arose, without regard to me . . . in its significance," Pasternak records in his early cycle of poems *Over the Barriers,* in which, as he has admitted, he had already found his own poetic system. The theme of the poem "Marburg" is the poet's rejected proposal of marriage, but the principal characters in the action are flagstone, paving-stone, wind, "innate instinct," "new sun," chicks, cricket and dragonfly, tile, midday, Marburger, sand, impending storm, sky, etc. One and a half decades later, in his book of reminiscences *Safe Conduct,* Pasternak mentions that he is intentionally characterizing his whole life at random, that he could increase the number of significant features or replace them by others, and that, in fact, the poet's life must be looked for under other people's names.

Show us your environment and I will tell you who you are. We learn what he lives on, this lyric hero outlined by metonymies, split up by synecdoches into individual attributes, reactions, and situations; we learn to what he is related, by what he is conditioned, and to what he is condemned. But the truly heroic element, the hero's activity, eludes our perception; action is replaced by topography. If in the case of Majakovskij the collision of two worlds inevitably culminates in a duel, the polished image of Pasternak's poems—the world is a mirror to the world—says over and over again that the collision is illusory: "The enormous garden stirs in the room, raises its fist against the mirror, runs to the swing, catches, hits with the ball, shakes—and doesn't break the glass." If Majakovskij unfolds his lyric theme in the form of a cycle of transformations undergone by the hero, the favorite transitional formula of Pasternak's lyric prose is a railway journey during which his excited hero experiences a change of locality in various ways and in enforced idleness. The active voice has been erased from Pasternak's poetic grammar. In his prose ventures he employs precisely that metonymy which substitutes the action for the actor: "a fully awake and vigorous man . . . waits for the decision to get up to come of its own accord, without his contributing anything." The *agens* is excluded from his thematic material. The heroine did not call, did not arrange anything—"it was all announced to her." The height of the heroine's activity, which conjures up the inevitability of the tragedy, is the mental

313

transformation of her surroundings; quite "fortuitously, uselessly and senselessly" she notices someone and in imagination she introduces him into her own life. Is man perhaps active in art? No, "in art," according to Pasternak's aesthetic, "man's lips are sealed"; that, indeed, is the distinctive feature of art. Is art itself active, then? No, it does not even invent metaphor, but merely reproduces it. And the poet will not present his reminiscences to the memory of the person who is their object. "On the contrary I myself received them from him as a gift." If the lyric "I" is in Pasternak's work a *patiens,* is some active third person then the real hero? No, the genuine agent has no place in Pasternak's poetic mythology; as a rule the individual has no idea of what "builds him up, tunes him and stitches him together," and the poet, too, is "perfectly indifferent as to the name of the power that has given him his book." The third person, as it appears in Pasternak's work, denotes the instrument rather than the agent. For example in "The Childhood of Luvers":

> Everything that came from the parents to the children came at the wrong moment, from one side, provoked not by them but by certain causes that had nothing to do with them.

The auxiliary, subordinate, marginal nature of the third person is often firmly underlined in Pasternak's themes:

> *Another* human being had entered her life, the third person, just anyone, without a name or with a random name which neither provoked hatred nor inspired love.

What is essential is solely his penetration into the life of the lyric self. Whatever is unrelated to this single hero is only "vague accumulations without names."

This strict body of semantic laws also determines the simple pattern of Pasternak's lyric narrative. The hero is either delighted or appalled at being governed by an external impulse; he is now branded by it, now suddenly loses contact with it, whereupon another impulse takes its place. *Safe Conduct* is an inspired account of how the author's enamoured admiration focuses in turn upon Rilke, Scrjabin, Cohen, a "dear beautiful girl," and Majakovskij, and how in this process he comes up against the "limits of his understanding" (a person's nonunderstanding is one of the most acute and compelling of Pasternak's lyric themes, just as a person's being misunderstood by others is one of Majakovskij's). Perplexed misunderstandings develop, and the inevitable passive solution follows—the hero goes off, leaving in the lurch, one after the other, music, philosophy, and romantic poetry. The hero's activity is outside Pasternak's sphere. When he does deal with action, he is banal and unoriginal, defending in theoretical digressions his right to triviality. Majakovskij, too, uses triviality as a part of his material, but with him, in contrast to Pasternak, it is used exclusively to characterize the hostile "Other." Pasternak's short stories are similarly empty of action. The most dramatic—*Aerial Ways*—is made up of the following "uncomplicated incidents": the former lover of the wife and friend of the husband is expected back from a sea voyage; all three are shattered by the disappearance of the child; the new arrival is shattered by the confession that the child is his son; fifteen years later he is shattered by the confirmation of this confession and then by the news of his son's death. Everything that in any way resembles action (the causes of the boy's disappearance, his rescue and the cause of his death) is left out of the picture. All that is recorded are the different stages of the emotional turmoil and their reflections.

We have tried to deduce the themes of Pasternak's and Majakovskij's work from the basic structural features of their poetics. Does that mean that the former are determined by the latter? Mechanistic Formalists would answer in the affirmative, supporting their case with Pasternak's claim that in his youth he had had formal affinities with Majakovskij which threatened to get out of hand, thus causing him radically to alter his poetic manner and, with it, the sense of life that lay at the base of it. The position of master of metaphor was filled, so the poet became master of metonymy and drew the appropriate ideological conclusions.

Others would try in their turn to prove the primacy of content. Mechanists of the psychoanalytical school would find the sources of Pasternak's thematic material in his confession that he had languished shamefully long "in the sphere of mistakes made by the childish imagination, boyish perversions, and the hungers of youth." From these assumptions they would infer not only the repeated theme of passive exaltation and the inevitable falls, not only the poet's agitated recourse to motifs of adolescent development, but also his metonymical deviations around every fixed object. Mechanistic materialists would note the author's witness to the apolitical nature of his environment, and would assert a socioeconomic basis for his obvious blindness to social problems—particularly to the social pathos of Majakovskij's poetry—

and for the mood of perplexed, inactive, elegiac distractedness which permeates both *Safe Conduct* and *Aerial Ways*.

It is legitimate to strive to find a correspondence between the different planes of reality, as it is also to try to infer facts about one of its planes from the corresponding facts about another—the method is one of projecting a multidimensional reality onto one surface. It would be a mistake, however, to confuse this projection with reality itself and to disregard both the characteristic structure and the autonomous movement of the individual planes, that is, their transformation into mechanical stratifications. From among the actual possibilities of formal development, a person or a particular milieu can choose those that correspond most closely to the given social, ideological, psychological, and other conditions; just as a cluster of artistic forms, come by the laws of their development to the point where they are available for use, seek out the appropriate milieu, or the creative personality, that will realize them. But this harmony of dimensions should not be made idyllically absolute; it must not be forgotten that dialectical tensions are possible between the different planes of reality. Conflicts such as these are essential to the progress of cultural history. If many individual characteristics of Pasternak's poetry are in accord with the characteristic features of his personality and his social environment, so, inevitably, there are also phenomena in his work which the contemporary poetic idiom forces upon every one of its poets, even if they contradict his own individual and social personality. (It is a question of the absolute axes of its total structure.) And if the poet rejects the demands of the idiom, he is automatically pushed off its tracks. The poet's artistic mission never penetrates his biography without a struggle, just as his biography is never entirely absorbed into his artistic mission. The hero of *Safe Conduct* is chronically unsuccessful, because Pasternak cannot do anything with the numerous successes that his original model actually achieved. (In the same way Casanova's book could not make anything of the failures that Casanova actually experienced.) The tendency which we have identified in the work of Pasternak and his contemporaries to make the sign radically independent of its object is the basic endeavor of the whole modern movement in art which has emerged as the antithesis of Naturalism. This tendency is inseparable from the progressive pathos of this movement and is to be found in all artists, independently of the details of their biography. The attempts of observers simply to attach this specific artistic phenomenon to a limited social sector or a particular ideology are typical mechanistic errors: to infer from the nonrepresentational nature of a man's art the unreality of his view of life is arbitrarily to suppress a fundamental antinomy. Rather it is the tendency of philosophy towards the concrete that corresponds most closely to the nonrepresentational tendency in art.

To belong to a compact collective group and to hold firmly to a particular direction are both repugnant to Pasternak, who is a passionate destroyer of customary affinities. He is at pains to convince Majakovskij of how splendid it would be if the latter would do away with Futurism for ever. He dislikes all "banal" affinities with his contemporaries, keeps himself separate from them, and advocates excursions off the common path. Nevertheless, despite the ideological confusion of the period, so variegated as to reach a point of mutual hatred and lack of comprehension, Pasternak's debt to his age comes out very strongly in his poetry. It is revealed both in his persistent creative annullment of the object and in his reconstruction of the grammar of art. This latter used to consist of past and present; in contrast to the simple past, the present was seen as a featureless "nonpast." It was, in fact, Futurism that wished to introduce the future into the poetic system by rubric, theory, and practice, and to introduce it as a decisive category. The poems and journalism of Xlebnikov and Majakovskij shout this tirelessly, and Pasternak's work is imbued with the same pathos, despite his profound inclination for "the deep horizon of recollection." In a new way, in the context of the new antithesis, he conceives the present as an independent category and understands that "the mere perceptibility of the present is already the future." It is not by chance that the high-flown hymn to Majakovskij which closes *Safe Conduct* ends with the words: "From his childhood he was spoiled by the future, which surrendered to him rather early and, obviously, without much difficulty." This "grammatical reform" fundamentally alters the very function of poetry in its relation to other social values.

CHAPTER 18

The Statue in Puškin's Poetic Mythology

Vladimir Majakovskij once remarked that the verse form of every really new and hence original poet can be mastered only if some of his basic intonation penetrates to the reader and takes hold of him. It then spreads and recurs, and the more the poet takes root, the more his admirers and adversaries become accustomed to the sound of his verse, the more difficult it is for them to abstract these original elements from his works. They are the essential, irreplaceable component of his poetry, just as intonation is the basic cement of our speech, and it is interesting that just such elements are the most difficult to analyze. If we move from the one aspect of poetry to the other, from sound to meaning, we encounter an analogous phenomenon. In the multiform symbolism of a poetic oeuvre we find certain constant organizing, cementing elements which are the vehicle of unity in the multiplicity of the poet's works and which stamp these works with the poet's individuality. These elements introduce the totality of a poet's individual *mythology* into the variegated tangle of often divergent and unrelated poetic motifs; they make poems by Puškin—Puškin's, those by Mácha—truly Mácha's, those by Baudelaire—Baudelaire's.

318

It is self-evident to every reader of a poet's work that certain elements constitute an irremovable, inseparable component of its dynamics, and this intuition on the part of the reader is trustworthy. The scholar's task is to follow this intuition and to extract these invariable components or constants directly from the poetic work by means of an internal, immanent analysis or, if it is a question of variable components, to ascertain what is consistent and stable in this dialectical movement, to determine the substratum of the variations. Whether it is a question of the rhythm, the melodics, or the semantics of a poetic work, the variable episodic, optional elements will differ substantially from its "invariants." There are verse components that vary from line to line and thus set off and individualize each line; there are other components that do not mark single lines but the verse of the whole poem or a poet's verse in general. They produce the verse design; they create the ideal metrical scheme without which the verse could not be perceived and the poem would disintegrate. In the same way, scattered symbols are in themselves mute; they can be understood fully only in their relation to a whole symbolic system. A fixed mythology, binding for a poetic cycle and often for a poet's entire oeuvre, operates in addition to the varying elements specific to individual poems.

In studying theater, one distinguishes the *emploi* from the *rôle;* the emplois (within the limits of a certain stage genre and style, of course) are fixed; for example, the emploi of the jeune-premier, of the intriguante, of the raisonneur does not depend on whether an officer or a poet is the jeune-premier in a given play or on whether he commits suicide or marries happily at the end. In linguistics we distinguish the *general meaning* of a grammatical form from single *partial meanings* conditioned by a given context or situation. In the combination *domogat'sja čego-libo* (to solicit something) the genitive designates the object to which the action is directed, whereas in the combination *storonit'sja čego-libo* (to avoid, to shun something) the same case designates the object away from which the action moves. This means that only the verb, on which the case depends, introduces the meaning of direction into the genitive; the case in itself does not have this meaning: the general meaning of the genitive, therefore, does not include the meaning of direction. If two contrary definitions are valid, and it can often happen that they are valid at one and the same time, it means that neither one of them really is valid, or more precisely, that both are insufficient. It means therefore, for example, that neither the acceptance of God's existence or of revolution nor their rejection is specific to Puškin's works. It is impossible to understand properly the partial meanings of a grammatical form and their mutual relationship if we do not pose the question of their general meaning. Likewise, if we wish to master a poet's symbolic pattern, we must first of all ascertain the symbolic constants which comprise the poet's mythology.

We must not, of course, artificially *isolate* a poet's symbol; rather we must start from its relationship to other symbols and to the whole system of the poet's work.

We must not, of course, succumb either to vulgar *biographism,* which takes a literary work for a reproduction of the situation from which it originated and infers an unknown situation from a work, or to vulgar *antibiographism,* which dogmatically denies any connection between the work and the situation. The analysis of poetic language can profit greatly from the important information provided by contemporary linguistics about the multiform interpenetration of the word and the situation, about their mutual tension and mutual influence. We do not wish mechanically to derive a work from a situation, but at the same time, in analyzing a poetic work, we should not overlook significant repeated correspondences between a situation and the work, especially a regular connection between certain common characteristics of a poet's several works and a common place or common dates; nor should we overlook the biographical preconditions of their origin if they are the same. The situation is a component of speech; the poetic function transforms it like every other component of speech, sometimes emphasizing it as an efficient formal device, sometimes, on the contrary, subduing it, but whether a work includes the situation positively or negatively, the work is never indifferent to it.

Of course, we must not assume that Puškin's mythology, which our description should comprehend, is *exclusively* his *own* poetic property. To what extent Puškin here conforms to contemporary Russian poetry, to say nothing of contemporary poetry in general and the whole of Russian poetry, is another question. Comparative linguistics eloquently instructs us that a fruitful comparison necessarily presupposes systematic descriptions.

Here I can offer only a small demonstration, only a contribution to the description of Puškin's symbolic pattern. It concerns one of the most striking images of his poetry—the image of the statue—and its meaning in the poet's work.[1]

320

As a rule the titles of Puškin's original poems, whether epic or dramatic, indicate the leading dramatis personae or the setting, if it is particularly specific to the plot and the whole subject. Compare *Ruslan and Ludmila, The Caucasian Captive, The Robber-Brothers, The Fiancé, Count Nulin, Angelo, Eugene Onegin, Boris Godunov, The Covetous Knight, Mozart and Salieri,* on the one hand, and *Poltava, The Little House in Kolomna, The Fountain of Baxčisaraj,* on the other. The "first person," as Puškin expressed it, can also be a collective body; it is not by chance that a poem about the Caucasians and an alien individual and their dramatic conflict is named after this individual, the "Caucasian captive," and that a later poem about the gypsies and an alien individual and their conflict is called *The Gypsies;* the center of gravity is located in a different place in each of them. The designation of the main character can be coupled with a specification of the poetic genre to which the work belongs: *The Song of Oleg the Seer; The Fairytale of Tsar Saltan and His Son, the Glorious and Mighty Hero Prince Guidon Saltanovič, and of the Beautiful Tsarevna Lebed'; The Fairytale of the Dead Tsarevna and the Seven Heroes; The Fairytale of the Fisherman and the Little Fish; The Fairytale of the Priest and His Workman Balda; The Comedy of Tsar Boris and Griška Otrep'ev* (the original title of *Godunov*).

In three of Puškin's outstanding poetic works, however, the title indicates not a living person but a statue, a plastic representation, and in each case an epithet defines the material of which the statue is made: the tragedy *The Stone Guest,* the narrative poem *The Bronze Horseman,* and *The Fairytale of the Golden Cockerel.* The hero of the tragedy, says a literary historian, is the "useless loafer" Don Juan.[2] Not at all, for the title proclaims the commander's statue as the main hero. A literary historian speaks about the "main dramatis persona of the narrative poem, Evgenij";[3] the poet, however, designates Falconet's monument of Peter the Great as the main character. And we can raise the same objection to the most outstanding study of Puškin's last fairytale:[4] "The famous Tsar Dadon," although his name crowns its first lines, is not its central character; the golden bird is the carrier of the action.

But the correspondence of these three works is not limited to the special character of the main hero. Similar, too, is the role of the statue in their action. In fact they have the same plot kernel:

I. *A man is weary, he settles down, he longs for rest, and this motif is intertwined with desire for a woman.* Don Juan speaks to Doña Anna at one and the same time about "weariness of conscience" and about his own rebirth: "Falling in love with you, I love virtue,/ And for the first time I humbly bend/ My trembling knees before it." Evgenij "is not Don Juan," as the poet explicitly points out in his sketches for *The Bronze Horseman:* no rebellion has preceded his settling down. Though deprived of the spirited romanticism of Don Juan's longings, Evgenij's dream before the dramatic dénouement is essentially the same: he wearily dreams of the alluring, peaceful life of happy idlers and of his impeded meeting with Paraša. Tsar Dadon "was terrible in his youth . . . / But in old age he wanted/ To rest . . . / And to secure peace for himself." It is precisely in this situation that he finds himself "charmed, fascinated" by the Tsaritsa of Šamaxan.

2. *The statue, more precisely the being which is inseparably connected with the statue, has a supernatural, unfathomable power over this desired woman.* The connection with a being transforms the statue into an idol, or rather—according to the nomenclature of modern Russian ethnology—a *lekan;* that is, the statue, understood as a pure "external representation," becomes an *ongon,* an incarnation of some spirit or demon.[5] The connection of the statue with such a being may be of diverse character. The titanism of the stone guest is the exclusive attribute of the statue (see Fig. 1):

> How he is represented here! Like a giant!
> What shoulders! What a Hercules! . . .
> But the deceased was himself short and puny
> . . . Like a dragonfly upon a pin.

In *The Bronze Horseman* this attribute of the statue merges with the titanism of the man represented, Peter the Great—"miracle-worker-giant" (*čudotvorec-ispolin*)—and of his symbolic partner, his steed (see Figs. 2 and 3). But in the fairytale, on the contrary, the statuette—"the cockerel on the spire"—is almost likened to a "dragonfly on a pin" (see Fig. 4). *Imitative magic,* according to Frazer's terminology, is replaced by *contagious magic,* or in other words: instead of the relationship of the representation to the object represented, the relationship of the property to the owner of the little golden bird, the old eunuch, moves to the foreground, although a certain hint of likeness is also present in the fairytale: the astrologer is compared to a bird, in particular to a swan.[6] But independent of all these variations, *evil magic* remains in force. In each case the power of the "ongon" over the woman is fatal; in each case life falls into the grasp of dead impotence: "A widow

1. Drawing by Puškin in manuscript of *The Stone Guest,* November 1830.

2. Monument to Peter I,
   by E.-M. Falconet.
   Gravure by G. I. Skorodumov.

3. Riderless horse on a cliff (after the
   Falconet monument). Drawing by
   Puškin in anticipation of *The Bronze
   Horseman,* 1829 or 1830.

4. Puškin's title page to *The Fairytale of the Golden Cockerel*, 1834.

should be faithful even to the grave," says Doña Anna. "A hundred years passed" emphasizes the introduction to *The Bronze Horseman:* a century separates Tsar Peter's life from Paraša's life, and if Doña Anna's past at least belongs to the commander, what did Peter have to do with Paraša or Paraša with Peter? "And what good is a girl to you?" Dadon sensibly asks the eunuch, but the latter persists in his preposterous claim on the Tsaritsa of Šamaxan.

3. *After a vain resistance the man perishes through the intervention of the statue, which has miraculously set itself into motion, and the woman vanishes.* Don Juan sees Doña Anna enslaved by the tomb statue of the commander, her slain husband, and wants to wrest her from the "fortunate dead man," "whose cold marble/ Is warmed by her heavenly breath." According to Don Juan's blasphemous proposal, the "marble spouse" is to stand guard during his love tryst with Doña Anna. She is favorably disposed toward her admirer, she will be his as soon as possible, but suddenly the tramp of the commander's footsteps is heard. The animated statue, which has left the monument, grips Don Juan's hand "heavily" in his "stone right hand"; Doña Anna vanishes from him; the man perishes. Evgenij loses his fiancée Paraša during the violent Petersburg flood. We do not find out anything about her demise; only tormenting questions without an answer are posed: ". . . Or is our whole/ Life nothing but an empty dream,/ Heaven's mockery of the earth?" And somewhat further on: "Well, what is it?" In his sudden madness Evgenij clairvoyantly perceives that the real culprit is the guardian of the city, the renowned Bronze Horseman, Tsar Peter (Figs. 2, 3), "by whose fateful will/ A city was founded under the sea." He threatens the statue: "Now then, miracle-working builder! . . . Just you wait! [*Užo tebe!*]." The animated statue leaves his pedestal and pursues Evgenij. The heavy tread (*tjaželyj topot*) of the Bronze Horse (see Fig. 2) corresponds to the firm grip (*tjaželoe požat'e*) of the commander's right hand and to the tramp of his footsteps. The man perishes. The golden cockerel serves Tsar Dadon as a "faithful guardian." His mysterious bearer, the castrated astrologer, does not want to renounce his ludicrous claim on the Tsaritsa of Šamaxan. The exasperated tsar punishes him with death. The golden bird leaves his spire and pursues Dadon. The light ringing of his flight (*legkij zvon*) echoes and simultaneously softens the Bronze Horseman's heavily ringing gallop (*tjaželo-zvonkoe skakanie*). Dadon perishes. "And the tsaritsa suddenly disappeared,/ As if she hadn't even existed." "I have dreamed the same

dream three times," Puškin could have repeated after his False Dmitrij (*Boris Godunov*). The deceased, as it were, has become incarnated in the statue—the commander in his monument, Peter in the Bronze Horseman, the astrologer in the golden cockerel—in order to punish a rebellious daredevil. Godunov's question—"Have you ever heard/ Of the dead rising from their graves?"—again receives an affirmative answer; however, in the tragedy of Tsar Boris the shade of the murdered Dmitrij had been incarnated in a living man—the Pretender. This fact had provided a more rational justification, on the one hand, and had intensified the ambiguity of the avenger's position, on the other; he is not only esteemed simultaneously as the tsarevich and as a "nameless vagabond," but he also affirms the dead Dmitrij in himself ("The shade of the Terrible One adopted me as his son") and at the same time repudiates him ("I don't want to share with a dead man/ The mistress who belongs to him"), whereas this role of a rival who is jealous of a dead man falls unambiguously to Don Juan in *The Stone Guest*.

In the drama, in the epic poem, and in the fairytale the image of the animated statue evokes the opposite image of *rigidified people*, whether it involves a mere comparison of them to a statue, an accidental situation, or actual dying and death. Here the boundary between life and immobile dead matter is deliberately obliterated. At the beginning of the drama Don Juan scornfully recalls the northern women: "To have relations with them is really a sin;/ There's no life in them, they're only waxen dolls." By way of contrast he shifts to a glorification not, as we might expect, of vigorous life, but of the lively charm in poor Inez's dying. The play ends with a direct transition from the "cold kiss" (*odin, xolodnyj, mirnyj*—single, cold, calm) that the subdued Don Juan gains from Doña Anna to the heavy grip of the commander's right hand. In Puškin's original version, moreover, there is, as in Mozart's opera, direct mention of the "cold grip" (*xolodnoe požat'e*), but later the poet struck out this too blatant "dissolve," as is said in today's film jargon. [7] The hero, longing for rest, inevitably makes his way toward the coldness and immobility of a statue. "Rule, lying down on your side!" reads the motto in *The Fairytale of the Golden Cockerel*. Before Peter's statue comes to life, Evgenij wastes away: "Neither one thing nor the other, neither an inhabitant/ Of this world nor a dead spectre." During his first encounter with the Bronze Horseman he grows stiff like a statue and merges with the marble lion onto which the flood has carried him, "as if he were riveted to the marble," whereas the lion "stands as if it were alive" (see Fig. 5). The rigidity of dead bodies stands out sharply against a background of intense love scenes: Don Juan with Laura near the corpse of Carlos ("Wait! . . . in the presence of the dead!");[8] Tsar Dadon who, in the presence of the Tsaritsa of Šamaxan, forgets the death of his two sons, whose bodies are lying nearby.[9]

The three works about destructive statues correspond in some secondary details as well. Thus, for example, each of them conspicuously emphasizes by different means the fact that a capital is the setting. Don Juan announces right at the beginning of the play: "Well, we have finally/ Reached the gates of Madrid!/ . . . If only/ I won't meet the king himself!" *The Bronze Horseman* begins with a hymn to Peter's capital city, and *The Fairytale of the Golden Cockerel* constantly mentions that the action takes place against the background of the capital (*v glazax u vsej stolicy,* in the eyes of the entire capital).

Someone may object that we are not dealing with completely independent themes—*The Golden Cockerel* is actually an elaboration of Irving's "Legend of the Arabian Astrologer"; *The Stone Guest* is a varia-

5. Triscorni, lions at entrance to building on the Neva Embankment, St. Petersburg, 1810.

tion on a traditional legend and borrows diverse details from Molière's *Festin de pierre* and the libretto of Mozart's *Don Giovanni*. In fact, however, a comparison of Puškin's poems with their foreign models clearly demonstrates the *originality* of his myth. From his models he selects only elements consistent with his own conception, and he transforms in his own way whatever contradicts it. We have pointed out the significance which the title of a poetic work has in Puškin: the choice of *The Stone Guest* from several traditional titles concerning Don Juan is therefore by no means fortuitous. Puškin contributed the triangle—the commander, Doña Anna, Don Juan; he also introduced the role of guard that Don Juan thrusts upon the statue, his settling down shortly before the dénouement, and the emphasis on the inevitability of the statue's intervention and Don Juan's death rather than on the appropriateness of the punishment, as is the case in Molière's play and Mozart's libretto. In *The Golden Cockerel* Puškin deliberately modifies Irving's tale and its title: he introduces the image of the tsar's dead sons, which emphasizes Dadon's desire for the Tsaritsa of Šamaxan, he intensifies the ludicrousness of the astrologer's claim on the tsaritsa by the fact of his castration, and most important he gives the fairytale a completely different dénouement—the statue's intervention and the tsar's death. In the model the astrologer tells the sovereign about a metal cockerel, but he makes him a "bronze horseman." Puškin read Irving's tale in 1833, and his first attempt at writing it in verse adjoins the first drafts of the Petersburg story about Evgenij in his manuscript. The figure of the bronze horseman became the main character of that poetic story, and only the cast cockerel remained for the tale, which was not realized until a year later. The combination "bronze tsar," not "bronze horseman," as one reads in Irving, appears in Mickiewicz's "Monument of Peter the Great," which inspired Puškin's description of Falconet's statue. Sometimes another author's work which is the starting point for one of Puškin's creations simultaneously provides a stimulus for another of his related works. Thus, Puškin essentially borrowed from Molière the scene in which Don Juan addresses the commander's statue, but Sganarelle's proposition "Ce serait être fou que d'aller parler à une statue" could have prompted the deranged Evgenij's conversation with the Bronze Horseman.

Autumn in the country, as the poet intimates, was most conducive to his intensive creative activity. Puškin retired to his Nižnij Novgorod estate, Boldino, three times during autumn—in 1830, in 1833, and again in 1834. "How charming the local countryside is," he wrote to his friend Pletnev from Boldino, "imagine: nothing but the steppe; no neighbors at all . . . you can write at home as much as you like, no one will bother you." *The Stone Guest* belongs to the rich harvest of the first Boldino autumn, *The Bronze Horseman* was the most outstanding product of the second autumn, and *The Fairytale of the Golden Cockerel* was the sole profit of the last and least fruitful of the Boldino autumns. These stays at Boldino occupy a truly unique place in the poet's life. The period into which they fall, the period beginning with the marriage proposal to Natalie Gončarova in the spring of 1829, is a wholly special stage in Puškin's life as well as in his literary activity, and the *myth of the destructive statue* belongs to it alone.

In the preceding period, beginning with the execution of the Decembrists and Puškin's return from exile, the source of horror in the poet's epic is the monstrous merging of different creatures (in Tat'jana's dream [1826]):

> Apparitions are sitting all round:
> Here one with horns and a dog's snout,
> There another with a cock's head,
> Here a hag with a goat's beard,
> Here a skeleton stiff and proud,
> There a dwarf with a little tail, and look:
> A half-crane, half-cat.
>
> Even stranger, even more bizarre:
> Look! A crab riding a spider,
> Look! A skull in a red cap
> Turns round on a goose's neck . . .

or a human face distorted by violent death (the hanged man in the fragment "Kakaja noč'" [What a Night] as well as in several of the poet's drawings, the drowned man in the ballad of the same name [1828]). In *Poltava*, written at the end of 1828, these two motifs merge in the deranged Marija's raving about the wolf's head of her executed father.[11]

At the point of transition from the horror of monsters to the horror of statues lies the story "The Solitary Little House on Vasil'evskij Island," which Puškin narrated in company at the turn of 1828 and 1829 and which the poet's acquaintance, V. P. Titov, wrote down and published under a pseudonym in the almanac *Northern Flowers* of 1829. It is a tale about the intrigues of an insidious devil who now enters—in the words of the narration—"with the same marble calm with which the commander's statue arrives at Don Juan's for dinner" and now turns once more into a mysterious coachman, and when a man strikes him with a stick, just as Dadon strikes the astrologer, the *ringing* sound of bones is heard; the coachman turns his head—here Xodasevič recalls the Bronze Horseman's analogous movement[12]—and a death's head appears instead of a face. Puškin's grotesque "The Coffinmaker," completed at Boldino two months before *The Stone Guest,* ridicules the outmoded horrific grotesque of hideous corpses and comically foreshadows the plot kernel of Don Juan's involvement with the stone guest.[13]

However, neither the myth of the destructive statue nor even the very *subject of the statue* occurs in Puškin's works of the twenties until the end of 1829, that is, with the exception of some insignificant allusions, which are entirely secondary and episodic, in the poem "Čern'" (The Mob, 1828), in the lyrical sketch "Kto znaet kraj" (Who knows the land, 1827), and earlier in the whimsical verses "Brovi car' naxmurja" (The Tsar frowned) and *Boris Godunov* (1825).

A scene in *Boris Godunov* depicts the ball at Duke Mniszek's. The ladies' gossip is recorded, and it provides a sharp contrast to reality. A statement is made about the Pretender: "And it is apparent that he is of royal blood," and it is said of Marina, whose wild obsession with passion Puškin admired, "a marble nymph:/ Eyes, lips without life." Here, then, is the usual opposition of a live man and his dead representation, complicated, on the one hand, by the fact that the second member of the opposition is metaphorically applied to the first and, on the other hand, by the fact that this application is in direct disagreement with reality.

In September 1829 Puškin arrived in Moscow on his way from the Caucasus, where he had witnessed the anti-Turkish campaign and the capture of Erzerum. Before his departure for the Caucasus he had asked for Natalie Gončarova's hand, but he had received an indefinite, evasive answer from her mother, and upon his return he was met with an ungracious welcome. His lack of piety and his invectives against Tsar Alexander especially repelled her,[14] and it was precisely during his Moscow stay (September 21, 1829) that the spurned Puškin concluded a caustic cycle of his poetic invectives against Alexander with the eight-line "K bjustu zavoevatelja" (For the Bust of the Conqueror) where he, so to speak, affirms his sharply negative attitude toward the late tsar by comparing his bust, sculpted by Thorwaldsen, and its ambiguity with the actual contradictoriness of its model, "A harlequin both in countenance and in life" (see Fig. 6). Aside from a contemporaneous occasional quatrain dedicated to Del'vig "upon the sending of the bronze Sphinx," this is the *first* of Puškin's poems of the twenties with a sculptural subject, and from the very beginning this subject is symptomatically coupled with the theme of the Petersburg tsardom. Here the classical form of inscriptions on statues is combined with an epigrammatic content. The traditional sublime tone of this form comes only later in Puškin.

By no means was the poet welcomed home cordially, for Nicholas confirmed the prohibition against publishing *Boris Godunov,* on which the author had staked so much, and reprimanded him through the chief of the All-Russian Gendarmerie, General Benkendorf, for his willful journeys. Freedom of movement was taken away from Puškin; his literary activity was retarded in every possible way. He realized that

6. Bust of Alexander I by B. Thorwaldsen. Executed in Warsaw, 1820.

the circle around him was constantly closing: "it is so precarious," he wrote to Benkendorf (March 24, 1830) about his situation, "that I see myself at every moment on the verge of a misfortune which I can neither foresee nor avoid." They were constantly demanding of him a more and more far-reaching *capitulation*.

I am speaking about the poet's gradual capitulation, not about his regeneration or reorientation, as this process is often called. Puškin, who had dreamed in the fiery verse of his youth that "we shall commune with the bloody chalice" of revolution (*krovavoj čašej pričastimsja*), was able to change his opinion about the road to liberation, was able to lose faith in its realizability and to declare the battle of liberation a premature and hence a madly hopeless delirium, was able in particular periods of his life to imagine a freedom of his dreams in completely different sociopolitical and philosophical contours, was able—from weariness and disappointment, from the impossibility of further battle, from the impossibility of escape to "foreign parts," and mainly perhaps from the impossibility of creative work without conforming to the oppressive contemporary conditions—to submit and even cleverly insinuate himself into his jailors' favor. Indeed, he himself repeatedly admits a hypocritical masking of his attitude ("I became clever, I play the hypocrite," *ja stal umen, ja licemerju*), and the local literary tradition furnished him with instructive models of such dissimulation, but he never forgot and, as a matter of fact, never obscured the fact that *a jail is a jail*. There is a well-known anecdote about a drummer who, when asked whether he would kill the tsar, objected: "But with what? With this drum?" Puškin's allegiance to the tsar was no deeper. What embarrasses the poet in the so-called "Radiščev crime"? The inadequacy of means that makes of his battle a "madman's act": "A petty official, a man without any power, without any support, dares to take up arms against the general order, against the autocracy, against Catherine."[16] Puškin condemns the Decembrists' rebellion for the same reasons. His capitulatory statement reads: "No matter what my political and religious views are, I keep them for myself alone, and I do not intend to madly oppose the established order and necessity."[17] Against the "young Jacobins" who were condemning the reasonings of Karamzin's history, which resounds to the advantage of autocracy, Puškin has the singular argument that "Karamzin published his *History* in Russia" and the tsar's patronage "imposed upon Karamzin the obligation of all the modesty and moderation imaginable".[18] These capitulatory slogans never completely dominated the poet: now he sought to wrest a greater independence from the regime, now he audaciously proceeded to the dividing line between legality and bellicose opposition, now he endeavored to deceive the tsar's censorship by means of a masterful tangle of allusions, hidden meanings, and allegories. But all of these fluctuations and deviations do not dispute the fact of the poet's painful capitulation, and the image of the "restrained siskin" (*nevol'nyj čižik nado mnoj*), which has forgotten the woods and freedom and whose only consolation is singing, is for the Puškin of the thirties at times closer than the captive eagle's once proud dream of freedom (the 1822 poem "Uznik" [The Prisoner]). Puškin's letters fully attest to the fact that his fateful marriage entirely accords with these capitulatory spirits, and his shrewder contemporaries comprehend this. The author Venelin, for example, writes in a letter of May 28, 1830: "A time comes . . . [when] one experiences a longing for a nest, [a longing] which bends the back of the proudest man before this law, and Puškin is the document and proof of this."

Toward the end of 1829 Puškin visited Tsarskoe Selo for the first time after years of exile. There everything reminded him of his youth at the lyceum, and the magnificent imperial gardens with their famous monuments in particular called to mind an image of the heroic period of the Petersburg monarchy.

> And I actually see before me
> The proud vestiges of bygone days.
> Still filled with the great woman [Catherine II],
>   Her beloved gardens
> Stand inhabited by palaces, gates,
> Columns, towers, idols of gods,
> And by the marble glory and the bronze praises
>   To Catherine's eagles.
>   Spectres of heroes alight
>   By the columns dedicated to them.

Thus, after his visit to Tsarskoe Selo, does Puškin modify by means of the same meter, the same stanzas and under the same title his "Vospominanija v Carskom sele" (Recollections at Tsarskoe Selo), written fifteen years earlier for his lyceum examinations and quite identically rendering homage to the "beautiful gardens of Tsarskoe Selo, to the sceptre of the great woman", to her glorious retinue and to the monuments celebrating victories, once more the Kagul Obelisk (see Fig. 7)

7. Kagul obelisk in Tsarskoe Selo, commemorating victory of Russian army over the Turks at Kagul River, Moldavia, July 21, 1770. Erected by the architect Antonio Rinaldi, 1771–72; reproduced here from watercolor by Giacomo Guarenghi.

8. Chesma column in Tsarskoe Selo, commemorating victory of Russian navy over the Turks, June 25–26, 1770. Erected in 1776 by the architect Rinaldi; reproduced here from engraved frontispiece to almanac *Tsarskoe selo* (St. Petersburg, 1829).

9. Morea column in Tsarskoe Selo, commemorating Russian victory of February 1770 over the Turks and surrender of Turkish fortress of Navarino to Brigadier Hannibal, Puškin's great-uncle. Erected in 1771.

and the Chesma Monument (see Fig. 8) and, moreover, the Morea Column (see Fig. 9), commemorating Puškin's great-uncle, the Brigadier Ivan Abramovič Hannibal, a hero of the victory at Navarino. This solemn official ode of the lyceum muse had soon given way to a fiery ode to freedom (1817), and likewise the "great woman" had soon received an entirely different evaluation from the young Puškin in 1822:

> But in the course of time history will assess the influence of her reign on morals, will reveal the cruel activities of her despotism under a mask of gentleness and patience, a people oppressed by vice-regents, a state treasury plundered by lovers, will show her momentous errors in political economy, her worthlessness in legislation, the repulsive hypocrisy in her relations with the philosophers of her century—and then the voice of the infatuated Voltaire will not save her glorious memory from the damnation of Russia.[19]

At this time the poet returns to an impassioned eulogy. He does not, however, stop at a repetitious, servile evocation of a glorious chapter in great-power history but at the same time recollects penitently the erring ways of his own youth and the mental gems frittered away in behalf of "inaccessible dreams." The date added to the manuscript of this unfinished poem—December 14, Saint Petersburg—the anniversary of the Decembrist rebellion—eloquently attests to what "inaccessible dreams" and what "prodigal sons" are at issue here. In the spring of the next year (April 5, 1830) Puškin recalls his sad, penitent spirits in a letter to his future mother-in-law, and, as a matter of fact, he recapitulates the content of the above-mentioned poem: "The errors of my first youth presented themselves to my imagination. They were only too violent, and calumny has aggravated them further; talk about them has become, unfortunately, widespread. You might have believed it; I dared not complain, but I was in despair." And at the same time he writes the identical thing to the tsar's confidant, Benkendorf: "Mme Gončarova is afraid to give her daughter to a man who has the misfortune of being in the Emperor's disfavor.—My happiness depends on a word of good will from Him towards whom my devotion and my gratitude are already pure and unbounded."

Aside from patriotic pride in the Russian victories, the poet's lyceum memories are the most passable road to a reconciliation with the court. Indeed, as early as October 1825 in the poem on the anniversary of the Lyceum, a "hurrah for the tsar," Puškin's sworn enemy, Alexander I,

335

resounds in this characteristic formulation: "Let us forgive him unjust persecution:/ He captured Paris, he founded the Lyceum." And when Puškin again celebrates the anniversary of the Lyceum in the last year of his life, October 19, 1836, he once again recalls the conquest of Paris, the Tsarina's palace (*čertog caricyn*), which the Lyceum had obtained from the tsar, and the imperial gardens. The memories of Tsarskoe Selo necessarily culminate in an evocation of its bloom—of Catherine's age and her monuments representing both the renowned martial victories and the magnificent conquests of Russia's young sculptural art. In the final chapter of *The Captain's Daughter*, which carries the same date, October 19, 1836, the Empress Catherine, while facing the Kagul Monument, "erected shortly before to honor the recent victories of Count Petr Aleksandrovič Rumjancev" (the "trans-Danubian giant"), decides to take mercy on a lad slanderously accused of having joined Pugačev's rebellion.

There is a characteristic association of statues with Catherine's age, in the poem "K vel′može" (To a Magnate, April 1830), which gained Puškin sharp rebukes, as if he had gone over to the side of the imperial dignitaries: "I am suddenly transported to Catherine's days./ The library, the idols and pictures." By strange chance the theme of the statue and Catherine had even crept into the poet's private life at this time. His marriage depended on a statue of the tsaritsa. His fiancée's mother did not want to consent to the marriage until her daughter had a luxurious trousseau. The family was bankrupt, however. Natalie Gončarova's grandfather was willing to sell on her behalf a gigantic bronze statue of Catherine which his grandfather had cast when he had wanted to erect a monument to the tsaritsa in front of his factory. Worries about the tsar's permission for the sale and about the sale itself rested on Puškin. The problem of converting the statue into money, however, dragged perilously, and Puškin's letters constantly refer half-jokingly, half-tragically to the "bronze grandmother".[20] "Except for the Emperor," he writes Benkendorf on May 29, 1830, "there is scarcely anyone except his late august Grandmother who could remove us from the difficulty." "What is the Grandmother of the factory doing, the bronze one, of course?" he asks his fiancée, and he returns to the "nasty Grandmother" (*la vilaine Grand'maman*) in almost every letter to her. "Seriously, I fear that it will delay our wedding" (July 30). "Do you know what [your Grandpapa] wrote to me? . . . It isn't worth the trouble of disturbing [Grand'maman] in her seclusion . . . Don't laugh

at me, for I am furious. Our wedding seems forever to flee before me
. . ." (September 1830). "What about grandfather with his bronze
grandmother? Both are alive and in good health, aren't they?" (October 11).

The letters from which the last two citations come were written
from Boldino where Puškin had retired in the autumn of 1830. In one
of these letters he passes from meditation upon the bronze tsaritsa to
a gloomy memory of his grandfather. At his grandfather's estate the
combination of a reminiscence of Catherine and a capitulatory mood
must have manifested itself to Puškin as an ancestral tradition, and in
the poem "Moja rodoslovnaja" ("My Pedigree," the end of 1830) the
author emphatically dates the submission of his rebellious family from
the imprisonment of his grandfather, who had resisted Catherine's palace revolution, just as his earlier ancestor, Fedor Puškin, had opposed
Peter I and had been executed at his command.

Puškin's Tsarskoe Selo reminiscences come to life in the very first
poems with sculptural subjects written at Boldino. There is, on the one
hand, the inscriptional tetrastich "Carskosel'skaja statuja" (The Statue
at Tsarskoe Selo, October 1, 1830)—see Fig. 10—and, on the other
hand, the unfinished tercets "At the beginning of life I recollect school"
("V načale žizni školu pomnju ja"), probably composed in the same
month. The atmosphere of this poem, it is true, smacks somewhat of
the Italian Middle Ages, but essentially it is another version, as it were,
of the "Vospominanija v Carskom sele" (Recollections at Tsarskoe
Selo) of the preceding year; it develops all the basic motifs of its model
but in a new scheme.[21]

Both poems are presented right from the beginning as a personal
remembrance. In both cases the kernel of this memory is the school
with its boisterous family of youthful schoolmates. The leading place
belongs to the majestic woman-protectress (*velikaja žena—veličavaja
žena*), who is Catherine in the poem of 1829, but who remains anonymous in the Boldino poem. Another common element of the two
poems is the speaker's dreamy wandering through the dusk of the
splendid gardens that are inhabited by marble statues and idols of
gods, the sense of self-oblivion that arises at the same time. But in the
poem "Recollections at Tsarskoe Selo" the Biblical image of the paternal home contrasts with the rememberer's delusions, with the "blaze
of fleeting raptures" and with the vain wooing of "inaccessible
dreams," and this image includes the school as well as the gardens and

10. "Carskosel'skaja statuja": fountain statue of
milkmaid with broken pitcher, sculpted by
P. P. Sokolov, c. 1810.

the remembrance of the majestic woman and the idols of the gods in
these gardens, whereas in the Boldino poem the gardens and their
idols, in contrast to the school and the majestic woman's "counsels and
reproaches," are linked directly to the conception of the wandering
dreams and the "dark hunger for unknown delights."

> Two other miraculous creations
> Attracted me with their enchanting beauty:
> They were the images of two devils.

> One young face (the Delphic idol)
> Was wrathful, full of terrible pride,
> And the whole of him breathed an unearthly force.

The other, of female shape, a voluptuous,
Questionable and false ideal—
A bewitching demon—false, but beautiful.

There are few of Puškin's images about which commentators could have pondered as much as about these two devils. It is enough to mention Merežkovskij who without firm grounds whatsoever imposes upon Puškin the Nietzschean antithesis of Apollo and Dionysius,[22] although here it is not at all a question of the opposition of the two devils and although the second devil is apparently Venus. As to Ermakov's vulgarized Freudianism, it leads him to consider the first image a dream about a father, the second a dream about a mother.[23] In the poet's youthful creation the image of titanism, of proud revolt is closely tied to the image of lustful service to Venus,[24] and the two are similarly linked in Puškin's penitent statements when he repudiates the dreams of his youth. The two closely associated images of the devils also appear in this very rôle in the poem "At the beginning of life I recollect school," which dates from October 1830. These were the days when Puškin was burying his amatory past—and, as a matter of fact, his love lyric in general—in farewell elegies: "Distant friend, receive/ My heart's farewell,/ As a widowed spouse." This was the month when Puškin burned the last canto of *Onegin,* his last overt poetic memory of the Decembrists' rebellion, and the date of this auto-da-fé is symptomatic—October 19, the anniversary day of the founding of the Tsarskoe Selo Lyceum, which Puškin always celebrated dutifully.

Surely the image of the ancient idol in the middle of the gardens, which had already appeared in a sketch of 1818, must have been tied to amatory associations. This apostrophe to Priapus reads as follows:

Mighty god of the gardens, I fall before you . . .
I have erected your ugly face with a prayer . . .
Not so that you would ward off capricious goats
And little birds from fruit that is both tender and unripe,
I have adorned you with a crown of wild roses
Accompanied by the dance of merry peasants.[26]

At this point the sketch breaks off, and likewise a fragment of the same period (1819), "Elegy" ("To the Kagul Monument"—see Fig. 7,) consists merely of an antithetical introduction of similar construction:

Haughty [var. mighty] monument of victory,
With veneration and anguish
I embrace your stern marble,

Which has been animated by memory.
Not the Russians' feat, not the Sultan
[var. Not the glory, gift to Catherine]
Not the trans-Danubian giant
Inflame me now.[27]

What was to have followed? Annenkov intimates that it concerned some amatory intrigue from the lyceum period. If this is the case,[28] this sketch would be an admission of the ambivalence of the Tsarskoe Selo sculptural monuments in the poet's symbolic pattern. One of the two conflicting conceptions is presented later in "Recollections at Tsarskoe Selo," the other in the poem "At the beginning of life." The negative content of the quoted "Elegy" becomes the positive content of "Recollections at Tsarskoe Selo." There are also some phraseological correspondences;[29] the same image of the Kagul monument appears here, and in both cases the first suggestion of the myth of the animated statue is linked directly to it: 1819—"marble . . . animated by memory"; 1829—"Spectres of heroes alight/ By the columns dedicated to them." "Kagul marble" reappeared also in a rough draft of "Lyrical Reminiscences on Lyceum Days" at the beginning of the eighth chapter of *Eugene Onegin* (late 1829–30).

In the poem "At the beginning of life" the fictive existence of statues, their sorcery and their alluring deception, are opposed to the austerity, calm, and truth of the guardianess's order. This poem, however, remained unfinished, and the parts were interchanged: the inexorable protector of order was embodied in the statue itself, and the "human, all too human" aspect of rebellious Don Juanism became its counterpart. Thus originated *The Stone Guest,* which was completed at Boldino on November 4, 1830.

We shall attempt to outline the biographical background against which this first version of Puškin's myth of the destructive statue took shape.

Puškin's longing for a wife and his weary resignation pervaded his entire Boldino life. But the dream is threatened: on the one hand, the buried past still lives on and oppresses the poet; on the other hand, the inflexible imperial power, which involuntarily calls to mind childhood memories of the Tsarskoe Selo monuments and statues, watches every move ("I see myself at each moment on the eve of a misfortune that I can neither foresee nor escape"), and finally absurd hindrances grow out of certain fictions—the poet's happiness depends on the "bronze

grandmother." The marriage is uncertain ("I left the door wide open
. . . Ha, that cursed thing, happiness!"), and in addition to this, "a
most charming personage," *cholera morbus,* playing havoc all around,
provokes an obtrusive thought about death, either his fiancée's or his
own; quarantines restrain him, shut him up in Boldino as on "an island
surrounded by rocks"; and in the days when Puškin is working on *The
Stone Guest* his father writes to him that his fiancée is lost to him. The
character of Don Juan in Puškin's play has already been interpreted
from an autobiographical point of view many times, and perhaps it
was precisely the too personal stamp of the drama that prevented the
author from having it published, just as the autobiographical element
in the first of the Boldino dramas, *The Covetous Knight,* caused the poet
to feign an anonymous translation from English.

If Don Juan's lyrical memories of the dead Inez are associated with
Puškin's graveyard lyric, and if the poet's longing for Gončarova,
which is interwoven with ardent poetic allusions to an unnamed mistress (or mistresses),[30] recalls the opposition of Doña Anna and Laura,
then everything irrational that stood between Puškin and his promised
one, whether it be the will of her family or of his own past or of
elemental obstacles, finds a meaningful equivalent in the power of the
stone commander. It is not just marriage that eludes the poet, however; at times the poet himself would like to escape marriage. He seeks
to precipitate it, and when Gončarova informs him that she is waiting
only for him, he replies: "Believe that I am happy only where you are,"
but the same day he notes in reference to her letter the proverb, "And
what will happen is that nothing will happen" (*A vot to i budet, čto
ničego ne budet*), and he writes to a friend: "You can't imagine how
delightful it is to run away from one's fiancée" (to Pletnev, September
9, 1830). He complains about the cholera that has closed the roads from
Boldino, and at the same time admits: "I couldn't have asked for better
than the plague." He confides to his friends: "I am becoming cool, I
am thinking about the cares of a married man and about the charm of
a bachelor's life" (to Pletnev, August 31, 1830); "I am getting married
without elation, without adolescent fascination. The future appears to
me not in roses, but in its severe nakedness. Sorrows will not surprise
me: they are registered in my domestic budget. Every joy will be a
surprise to me" (to N. I. Krivcov, February 10, 1831, the very week
before the wedding). He parts with his bachelorhood, as Hofman correctly remarks, as if he were actually parting with life.[32] The supersti-

tious Puškin recalls that a Moscow fortune-teller had predicted that his own wife would be the cause of his death.[33] The horror of the commander's visit would seem a warning dream.

Don Juan's success with Doña Anna provides the poet with another motivation for escape. It suffices to confront it with Puškin's previously cited letter to his fiancée's mother, in which this sentence occurs unexpectedly: "As the Lord is my witness, I am ready to die for her, but to be obliged to die in order to leave her a brilliant widow, free to choose a new husband tomorrow, this idea is hell itself."

During the first Boldino autumn the poet's work is saturated with the image of the statue. The Boldino drawings, as well as the poetic works, deal with sculptural images: a sketch of a pyramid with an

11. Egyptian colossus. Drawing by Puškin, October 1830.

12. J. A. Houdon's statue of
Voltaire. Drawing by Puš-
kin in notebook of March
10, 1832.

Egyptian colossus (October 1830—see Fig. 11) and with contrasting
arabesques of birds flying around it is akin to the adjacent drafts for
Puškin's poem "Autumn" ("Osen'"), where pyramids, as "slumbering
symbols of eternity," are confronted with the visionary's "lyrical
dreams"; and there is a classical bust (November 1830), painstakingly
and diligently drawn as part of a sketch of Puškin's study.[34] Puškin also
outlines the problem of sculpture in a theoretical essay drafted at Boldino ("On Drama").[35] It is possible that the poet's translation of the
beginning of Robert Southey's "Hymn to the Penates," which depicts
the escape of a tired soul to the redemptive idols, the givers of rest,
originated at this time, if not somewhat earlier.[36] After Puškin's return
from Boldino sculptural themes disappear from his poetic work for
three years until the second Boldino autumn, when he writes *The
Bronze Horseman*. A cursory sketch of Voltaire's statue, dated March
10, 1832, is the only drawing by Puškin with a sculptural topic during
this interval (see Fig. 12).

What circumstances accompanied the origin of this second version
of Puškin's myth of the destructive statue? Remembrance of the lonely

343

fiancé's tempestuous autumn in involuntary exile at Boldino, revived after three years by a repeated visit to his hereditary village. Mounting fear of the tsar, who was enslaving the poet and courting his wife, and indignation both at the whole imperial environment, which was wanton and seditious, and at the capital.[37] Ever more hopeless prospects for the future. Wistful and jealous letters to his wife from the road and from Boldino: "Without you I feel depressed . . ." (September 19, 1833); "What is the matter with you? . . . my heart sinks when I imagine . . . When I was approaching Boldino, I had the darkest forebodings." (October 2); "Don't flirt with the tsar." (October 11); "Here you have the whole secret of coquetry! *If only there is a trough, there will be pigs.*" (October 30). And once again the motif of anguish is tied to the motif of escape. When he is projecting his trip to Boldino, Puškin complains to a close friend: "My life in Petersburg is nothing at all [*ni to ni së;* in *The Bronze Horseman* he depicts the mad Evgenij's miserable life with the same words]. . . . I do not have time to myself, a free bachelor's life." (To P. V. Naščokin, c. February 25, 1833.) The bronze grandmother crowds the poet's Petersburg life, it depresses him, but it does not help him out of his financial predicament—hope for its sale founders. Mickiewicz's Petersburg satires (*Ustęp*), which the poet had just read and partially copied out, present sharply pointed images of the imperial metropolis.[38] The second tsarina erected a monument "to the first of the Tsars, who had worked wonders"; however, the inscription on Falconet's monument had already introduced the union of the two names: "To Peter I Catherine II," and Puškin's image of Peter's statue rising above a cliff and surrounded by the waves of a flood has features in common with the image of the monument of the Battle of Chesma (see Fig. 8), which the lyceum "Recollections at Tsarskoe Selo" depict.[39] Historical reminiscences and associations stand out much more distinctly in the initial drafts of *The Bronze Horseman* than in the subsequent version. On the one hand, the evocation of the glorious Decembrist rebellion, which had taken place near Peter's monument after Alexander's death and which creates the undertone of the "Petersburg tale,"[40] is accentuated more in the rough draft, for there the flood is directly depicted as the epilogue to Alexander's reign (*Tot samyj god/ Poslednim godom byl deržavstva Carja* [That very year was the last of the Tsar's rule]); on the other hand, there is an image of a similar flood which had burst forth during Catherine's reign (*Ekaterina Byla živa*

[Catherine was alive]) shortly after the Pugačev rebellion; it was just at this time that Puškin was working earnestly on a history of this "terrible period." And finally, in the initial drafts the role of Peter, the tamer of the rebellious nobility both during life and after death ("Peter's shade stood threateningly in the midst of the boyars"),[41] had prepared and motivated the bronze tsar's cruel intervention against the descendant of this rebellious nobility. In the process of further work on his poem Puškin removes the scaffolding of incidental motivations and thus makes the myth of the destructive statue independent of episodic stimuli.

The Petersburg tale differs markedly from the first version of Puškin's myth; long past is the period of Don Juan's youthful lack of restraint. Even his vigorous wooing of a last love has already been forgotten. The horror of her loss and of her partner's death supplants the preceding episodes. Originally Puškin's own deliberation about matrimony had passed over into *The Bronze Horseman* from the eighth chapter of *Eugene Onegin,* written during the first Boldino autumn and later destroyed (on the whole, the creation of the second autumn is connected to the harvest of the first.[42] "Other days, other dreams," the poet had meditated in this chapter,

> You have been humbled,
> Lofty visions of my spring;
> Now . . .
> My ideal is a housewife,
> My desires are rest
> And a pot of cabbage soup and me my own boss.

In *The Bronze Horseman* Evgenij had dreamed:

> Get married? What of it? Why not?
> In earnest. I'll fix up
> A modest nook for myself
> And set Paraša at ease in it.
> A bed, two chairs, a pot of cabbage soup
> And me my own boss; what more do I need?

But Puškin even robbed his hero of this very modest dream: he deleted these lines in the final edition. In *The Stone Guest* Don Juan had been individualized, and the commander had been depersonalized, almost anonymous. The exact opposite is true in *The Bronze Horseman.* The victim of the statue—Evgenij—has been depersonalized as much as possible:

345

> . . . a citizen of the capital,
> Such as you meet a lot of,
> And neither in countenance nor in intellect
> Does he differ from the others.

"He is like everyone" (*Kak vse on*), emphatically repeats another variant of the poem. ("There is no happiness," wrote Puškin about his own marriage, "except in the common ways . . . At thirty, people marry as a rule—I am acting just like other people, and probably I shall not regret this.")[43] On the other hand, the citizen's persecutor, the Bronze Horseman, is introduced, portrayed and delineated so concretely—despite every latitude of possible interpretations—that Tsar Nicholas made it impossible to publish the poem. In its first draft Puškin had still not impoverished Evgenij in this way; in fact the poet had defended his right to make him the hero of the tale, to pass over terrestrial idols (in his poem Puškin calls the bronze Peter an idol) in gloomy silence and to defy the establishment (*dlja tebja zakona net* [for you there is no law]). In the final edition there is not even a trace of the poet's pugnacity that had originally accompanied the appearance of Evgenij.

At the end of August 1834 Puškin left Petersburg so that he would not be forced to participate in the unveiling of Alexander's column (see Figs. 13–15). He notes this in his diary on November 28, and his aversion to the monument to Alexander I still reverberates a few lines later in the same note in his annoyed remark about the superfluousness and pointlessness of another, similar kind of monument, a column with an eagle, erected by Count S. P. Rumjancev at Tarutino in honor of the victory over Napoleon in the War of 1812.[44] Puškin went to Boldino; he wanted to get down to work there, but inspiration was lacking, and "verse [did] not come to mind."[45] Financial worries overcame him at the ruined estate, and he wrote to his wife: "I am sad, and when I am sad, I am drawn straight to you, as you cling to me when you are scared" (September 17, 1834). The third version of the myth of the destructive statue resulted from these moods, from Boldino reminiscences, from Irving's story, and from folk tale formulae. A derisive grotesque supplanted the tragic Petersburg tale; a castrated magician replaced Peter the Great, and a cockerel on a spire—probably an ironic allusion to the eagle on the Tarutino column (see Fig. 16) or the angel on Alexander's column—was substituted for the gigantic horseman above the cliff. The victim of the statue has grown old, and the poet's

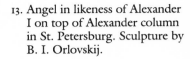

13. Angel in likeness of Alexander I on top of Alexander column in St. Petersburg. Sculpture by B. I. Orlovskij.

facetious complaint to his wife involuntarily comes to mind: "*Staram stala i umom ploxam!* [Became old and poor in spirit!]. I shall come and your youth will reanimate me, my angel." (October 21, 1833.) Don Juan had been conceived heroically; Evgenij, as a critic rightly points out, is indeed wretched but not even slightly farcical: "in spite of his external shabbiness he grows into a tragic hero, and his death arouses not disdainful pity but terror and compassion."[46] Dadon, on the contrary, is a ludicrous figure upon whom Puškin apparently confers particular attributes of his enemies: Axmatova points out that the caricatured traits of Alexander and Nicholas are combined in Dadon.[47]

The Fairytale of the Golden Cockerel exhausted the theme of the destructive statue in Puškin. It is noteworthy that three poetic genres in his verse creation died out along with this subject—*The Stone Guest* is the last of Puškin's original, completed dramas in verse, *The Bronze Horseman* is the last of his narrative poems, and *The Golden Cockerel* is his last fairytale. "Scenes from Chivalrous Times," it is true, came after the Boldino dramas, and another Petersburg tale, "The Queen of Spades," followed *The Bronze Horseman;* however, they are prose at-

14. Raising of Alexander column, 1832. Drawing by the architect
Auguste de Montferrant.

tempts, and Puškin rightly pointed out that there is "the devil of a
difference" (*d'javol'skaja raznica*) between the prosaic and versified varieties of one and the same literary genre (letter to Vjazemskij of November 4, 1823).

The whole set of sculptural themes in Puškin's work is neutralized
and gradually dies out with the myth of the destructive statue. It reappears only in 1836 in the epistle "Xudožniku" (To an Artist), dedicated
to the sculptor Orlovskij, and in the two four-line inscriptions to the
statues of players (see Fig. 17). The cycle of Puškin's poems about statues began and ended with inscriptions.

We can even speak directly about the overcoming of the sculptural
subject in the poet's work. Besides the parodistic tinge of *The Fairytale
of the Golden Cockerel,* which concludes the phantasmagoria of statues,
just as the story "The Coffinmaker" had previously ended the phantasmagoria of hideous corpses, and besides the episodic image of overthrown idols, which appears after *The Bronze Horseman* in the poet's
lyrical sketches and which every time is closely connected with the im-

348

15. Alexander column in St. Petersburg. Unveiled
August 30, 1834.

16. Monument celebrating Russian
victory of October 1812 over Napoleon in Tarutino, Kaluga Province. Unveiled June 24, 1834.

age of a moving crowd (December 9, 1833: "From step to step fly the
idols"; September [?] 1834: "From the toppled columns the idols fall"),
we may cite what Andrej Belyj has called "a very ambiguous and obscure passage"[48] in Puškin's letter of May 29, 1834, to his wife. The
writer speaks about his work on the history of Peter the Great: "I am
gathering materials—I am putting them in order—and suddenly I shall
cast a bronze monument which it will not be possible to drag from
one end of the city to the other, from square to square, from side street
to side street." Here it is indisputably a question of a verbal monument
which is independent of space in contrast to a statue. Puškin vigorously defined that dependence in his famous comments on Falconet's
horseman which Mickiewicz reproduced in his satire *Pomnik Piotra
Wielkiego* (The Monument of Peter the Great): "He sat on the bronze
back of the bucephalus and waited for a space into which he could
race." In these glosses Puškin also parodies V. G. Ruban's inscriptional
verses "K pamjatniku Petra I" (To the Monument of Peter I). The

eighteenth-century poet extols the miraculous monument above the Colossus of Rhodes and the pyramids, for its base is a true rock or, according to Ruban, rock not made by hand, but brought to Petersburg (*nerukotvornaja gora*). This Church Slavonic epithet *nerukotvornyj* (*acheiropoietos*) was used and reinterpreted by Puškin in his poem of August 21, 1836, "Exegi monumentum," for the delineation of his own monument, which had been created from the poetic word and whose unsubmissive head overshadows Alexander's Column, the highest such edifice in the world at that time. Thus *logos* (the word) overcomes *eidōlon* (the idol) and idolatry.

The fundamental request of the poet's call to his Muse is her freedom from any surroundings: "Do not require any wreath,/ And remain indifferent both to praise and to slander." Puškin's aversion toward the worship of crowned heads finds an eloquent expression in two of his self-portraits, captivatingly discussed in M. P. Alekseev's monograph on "Exegi monumentum."[49] The last of these drawings, made in 1835 or 1836 and inscribed *Il gran' Padre A. P.*, parodies the traditional medallions of Dante crowned by laurels (see Fig. 17). Puškin's earlier self-portrait of himself crowned by laurels (see Fig. 18) likewise "conveyed to his profile the character of a bust, with a sharp-angled cut-off at the breast typical of sculptural representations."[50] Mickiewicz's profile at the lower left hand side accompanies Puškin's, above, and the two parallel images of trees beneath them, apparently symbolizing the close ties between the two poets. Compare, on the one hand, Puškin's simile taken over from a Serbian folksong, "Not two oaks grew next to each other,/ But two brothers lived together," and, on the other hand, Mickiewicz's famous *Digression (Ustęp),* with its dialogue between the two poets beneath the monument to Peter the Great:[51]

Two youths stood deep in talk one rainy night,
Beneath one cloak, hand closely clasped in hand:
One was the pilgrim from a Western land,
An unknown victim of the tsar's grim might;
The other was the famous Russian bard,
Beloved through all the Northland for his song.
Although their friendship had not flourished long,
They were united by a great regard.
Their souls soared over earthly trials and woe,
Like twin crags jutting from an Alpine peak:
Though separated by a roaring creek,

17. Self-portrait by Puškin parodying traditional medallions of Dante, 1835–36.

18. Puškin, crowned with laurels, and Mickiewicz. Drawing by Puškin in drafts of *Tazit*, c. 1833.

> They scarcely hear the tumult of their foe,
> While each to each their towering summits lean.

The sketchy figures at the bottom of Puškin's drawing seem to refer to his work on the unfinished poem "Tazit." The pages to which this drawing belongs are covered with the draft of this poem and with a copy in Puškin's own hand of Mickiewicz's *Ustęp*. The Polish work reached Puškin toward 1833 and in his notes to *The Bronze Horseman* (October 1833) he refers to this *Digression* and particularly to the dialogue quoted above. Wacław Lednicki convincingly assigns Puškin's drawing of the two poets to 1833, against a surmised earlier date of 1829.[52] The conflict between human spiritual fraternity and tribal strife underlies the drafts of "Tazit," as well as the ties and tension between Puškin and Mickiewicz. Puškin, "the famous Russian bard," in Mickiewicz's terms, as Avram Èfros observes, "drew this apotheosis to himself and apparently was ashamed at such a self-glorification: having completed the drawing, he immediately struck out the characteristic part of the profile, as he used to do when he wanted, so to speak, to express a renunciation of or abdication from himself: the brow, the

351

nose, the lips, and the chin are completely struck out by thick, tightly placed strokes."[53] A laureate bust of oneself, the idea of which repeatedly repelled Puškin, is one of the significant facets of his obsessive sculptural demonology.

We have traced the image of the statue and particularly the myth of the destructive statue in the context of Puškin's work and life. But we are interested above all in the internal structure of this poetic image and poetic myth. The problem is all the more interesting in that it concerns the transposition of a work belonging to one kind of art into another artistic mode— into poetry. A statue, a poem—in brief, every artistic work—is a particular sign. Verse about a statue is accordingly a sign of a sign or an image of an image. In a poem about a statue a sign (signum) becomes a theme or a signified object (signatum). The conversion of a sign into a thematic component is a favorite formal device of Puškin's,[54] and this is usually accompanied by exposed and pointed internal conflicts (antinomies) which are the necessary, indispensable basis of any semiotic world. In Puškin's story "Egyptian Nights" a professional improvisator composes a poem on the prescribed theme "the poet himself chooses the subjects for his songs; the crowd is not entitled to guide his inspiration." Here, then, the nonprescriptive nature of the subject is the prescribed subject. The fundamental discrepancy between the two necessary components of linguistic expression— its theme and its situation, a discrepancy that turns into a flat contradiction in this case—is thus emphasized. In *The Stone Guest* Don Juan says that he suffers in silence. "And this is how you are silent?" Doña Anna asks him derisively and thereby reveals the contradiction between the first person as narrator and as topic of the narration.

"Rest eludes me" (*Pokoj menja bežit*), says Puškin in the poem "Vojna" (War), literally "runs away from me." This combination of words, directly contradicting one another, is made possible by the use of the verb *bežat'* (run) in the figurative sense. Here we have the union of two opposed semantic spheres—that of rest and that of movement, and this is one of the main motifs of Puškin's symbolic pattern in general. The equation movement-rest is presented in the poet's works now as a philosophical clash between external empiric data and a noumenon (cf. the poem "Dviženie . . ." [Movement]),[55] now as a contradiction between the material of a statue and its semantic aspect. A statue—in contrast to a painting—so approximates its model in its three-dimensionality that the inorganic world is nearly cancelled out of its themes: a sculptural still life would not suitably provide the distinct antinomy between the representation and the represented object that every artistic sign includes and cancels. Only the opposition of the *dead, immobile matter* from which a statue is shaped and the *mobile, animate being* which a statue represents provides a sufficient distance. Puškin's titles such as *The Stone Guest, The Bronze Horseman* and *The Golden Cockerel* pick up just this fundamental opposition, and it is just this basic antinomy of sculpture that has been most effectively captured and exploited in poetry. "You give thoughts to plaster," says Puškin to the sculptor ("To an Artist"), and in another poem he evokes the land where Canova's chisel brought obedient marble to life ("Who knows the land"). It is a traditional image: "He has brought me to life in stone," says Deržavin about the sculptor who molded his bust, and Daškov is constantly surprised in his inscriptions on statues that "Praxiteles' chisel has given stone sensibility and life" ("K istukanu Niovy" [To a Statue of Niobe]) and that "the hero breathes in metal" ("Izvajanie Aleksandra" [A Statue of Alexander]). "Divine bronze! It seems to come to life," proclaims an analogous inscription by Benitckij. For Baratynskij the mystery of sculpture is that the stone has revealed a nymph to the artist ("Skul'ptor" [The Sculptor]),[56] and in the idyll "Izobretenie vajanija" (The Invention of Sculpture), Del'vig announces a miracle: "I call you to the miracle: the image of Charis! Charis alive! Charis from clay!"—amorphous clay turns into a live image. The semantic aspect of the statue or the internal aspect of the sign cancels ("Charis alive!") its dead immobile nature, that is to say, the external aspect of the sign. The dualism of the sign, however, is its indispensable precondition, and as soon as the internal dualism of the sign is cancelled, the opposition between the sign and the object also disappears of necessity, and the sign becomes reified. The conventional space of the statue merges with the real space into which the statue has been placed, and despite its atemporal substance, an idea of something that has preceded the represented state and of something that should follow it comes of itself to mind: the statue is placed in temporal succession.[57]

> The youth took three steps forward, bent, and leaning one hand
> Against his knee, he raised the pointed bone.
> Look! He has already taken aim! Away! Make way, curious
>   people.
> Move aside; don't interfere with the bold Russian game.
> ("On the Statue of a Youth Playing Knucklebones"; see Fig. 19)

19. Statues of youth playing knucklebones, by N. S. Pimenov, and of young peg player, by A. V. Loganovskij. Both seen by Puškin at 1836 exhibition of the Academy of Art; cast in iron for entrance of Alexander's palace in Tsarskoe Selo, 1838.

Compare "A moment—and he will fly away! Such is the singer full of ecstasy" (1820). A statuesque Mercury, drawn by Puškin on the left side of a manuscript page, and a sketch of Mercury's legs in flight on the right side of the same page (see Fig. 20) symbolically separate from one another, on the one hand, Puškin's resignation from any service preventing his poetic work, a draft addressed to Count M. S. Voroncov through the latter's go-between, A. I. Kaznačeev, and on the other hand, the poet's verses prefacing Tat'jana's letter, which was to reach Onegin through her nanny's grandson as messenger.

A three-dimensional statue, of course, provides more suitable preconditions for inclusion in real space than a two-dimensional image. Nevertheless, Puškin's lyric poetry also offers such evidence as:

> When the great deed was accomplished,
> And Divinity was dying in torment upon the cross,
> There on either side of the life-giving wood
> . . . were standing two pale, weak women.
> . . . But at the foot of the holy cross . . .
> We see—standing in place of the holy women
> Two stern guards in shakos and at arms.

Here the boundary between the crucifixion in Brjulov's picture and the guards protecting the picture is intentionally obliterated.

The poetic transformation of semiotic antinomies is even more sharply obtruded in Puškin's inscription to the statue of the peg player. If we take into account the external material aspect, the statue appears to us as an immobile piece of live activity, but in Puškin's poem, on the contrary, the swift "action" of the statue (*bystraja igra*) is opposed to the immobility of a later, conjectured state (*posle igry otdyxat'*, rest after the game).

But what about the contrary case: cannot the empirical immobility of a statue triumph for the spectator over the motion that it represents? "They want to sculpt my bust here," wrote Puškin to his wife from Moscow on May 14, 1836, "but I don't want them to. Then my negroid ugliness will be delivered to eternity in all its *dead immobility*." Opposed to the "miracle" of the idea of motion overcoming the paralyzation of matter is the converse "miracle"—the immobility of matter overcoming the idea of motion. "Miracle!" says Puškin about the girl with the broken pitcher (see Fig. 10) in the inscription "The Statue at Tsarskoe Selo": "The girl sits eternally sad over the eternal stream." The internal dualism of the sign is cancelled: the immobility of the statue is perceived as the immobility of the girl, and inasmuch as the opposition of the sign and the thing vanishes, immobility is transferred into real time and appears as eternity.

We have therefore established two types of the poetic metamorphosis of a statue. How are they realized in lyrics? Subjectivity is the basis of all lyric poetry. It is a question, then, of the poet's subjective conception: the immobile statue of a mobile being is conceived either as a moving statue or as a statue of an immobile being. In the epic both of these transformations are objectified, they become a component of the plot: "Where are you galloping, proud steed,/ And where will you let your hooves fall?" The poet's reflection is the lyrical realization of a sculptural motif; this motif—the galloping of the horse—is temporally deployed in the poet's imagination, and the urgent question of what will then follow arises. The bronze horse is here conceived as mobile, and actual motion results from mobility—this is the epic realization of a sculptural motif: the Bronze Horseman gallops thunderously over the shaking pavement. On the other hand, the immobility of the horseman, rising with an arm outstretched over the furious waves, also becomes an element of the plot: it is the manifestation of a superhuman repose and of the bronze warrior's eternally unswerving power against the "impudent willfulness" of the savage elements and against every rebellion. Mickiewicz's "Monument of Peter the Great" had already presented the two antithetical motifs in their lyrical aspect: on the one hand—"Tsar Peter was giving his horse free rein,/ It is apparent that he was flying as he trampled on his way;/ All at once he jumped to the very edge of the cliff./ . . . You suppose that he will fall and burst into pieces"; on the other—"He has been standing for ages." The two motifs merge in the metaphorical image of the waterfall rushing down from the granite and solidified by frost. The two motifs are likewise connected in Vjazemskij's poem "Petersburg," the other model for *The Bronze Horseman*—Falconet's Peter is, on the one hand, the immobile, eternal guard who wards off enemies with his petrified appearance; on the other hand, he is ready to fall on them from the steep cliff.[58] The idea of life that is included in the meaning of a statue and the idea of duration that is furnished by its outer shape fuse into an image of continuing life.

The imperfective aspect of verbs carries this idea of pure duration in *The Bronze Horseman:* whether it concerns the historical or the bronze Peter, whether it concerns the immobile or the animated statue, not a

20. Drawing by Puškin, in manuscript, of the statue of Mercury (left) and of Mercury's legs in flight (right), May 1824.

single perfective verb is attached to him in the narration. This imperfectivity contrasts sharply with the perfective, limited character of the surrounding events, just as the morphological verbal categories—aspects, tenses, persons—are generally one of the most effective, most dramatic devices of actualization in Puškin. We hope to treat this question later.[59]

As we have already emphasized, the cancellation of the internal dualism of the sign obliterates the boundary between the world of the sign and the world of the objects. The equation between the "eternal sleep" of the deceased Peter and the eternal repose of his bronze double and the simultaneous contradiction between the ephemerality of his mortal remains and the steadfastness of his statue produce the notion of the life of the represented being continuing in its sculptural image, in the monument: "This is Peter, living on in eloquent bronze./ . . . He still rules the city that he created," reads Vjazemskij's poem. Thus for the threatening Evgenij, the Bronze Horseman really is the builder of Petersburg and the epithet "miracle-working" (*čudotvornyj*) acquires a purely Puškinian ambiguity in the madman's mouth: "creating miracles," as concerns Tsar Peter, and at the same time "having originated miraculously," as concerns his statue. "Miracle-worker" (*čudotvorec*)— Puškin calls Peter, "miraculous creations" (*čudesnye tvorenija*)—he says about idols.

The word *živoj* is polysemantic: it has the meaning "living," "being alive," the meaning "lively," the meaning "including the idea of life," "producing the impression of life"; all of these are, in fact, homonyms connected to one another by various semantic relationships. In poetry they are mutually independent variants—independent, equipollent expressions of a single general meaning: it is a question of a general meaning, for usually the etymological kinship of words is distinctly actualized in poetry; it is a question of independent variants, for poetry confers independence upon each lexical meaning. In poetic symbols he who lives in bronze or "in human hearts" has not a figurative but a real life. Deržavin renders this in an inscription of one word—a skillful abbreviation—on Peter's monument: "Živ" (Alive). In a significant scene of *The Stone Guest,* which prepares the way for the statue's active entrance into the plot, Leporello asks Don Juan how the commander—by which he half-jokingly means the tombstone statue—will look upon his amatory intrigue. Don Juan replies that the commander has settled down since the time of his death. Leporello doubts this and calls attention to the statue: "It seems to be looking at you and to be angry." Here (for the present in a humorous conversation, but later the tragic action will result from it) the commander's liveness is detached from his human life (it is possible that the deceased has settled down, it is possible that he has not), and the life of the statue, just as his human life, becomes, so to speak, a single segment of the commander's total existence.

> How he is represented here! Like a giant! . . .
> And the deceased himself was short and puny.
> Here, even if he were to stand on tiptoe,
> He wouldn't be able to reach his own nose with his hand.

It is hardly possible to express more drastically the simultaneous distinctness and identity of the representation and the object represented. Puškin was well aware of the uniqueness of the artistic sign, and at the time of work on *The Stone Guest* he wrote: "We still reiterate that *the beautiful* is an imitation of refined nature. . . . Why then do we like painted statues less than pure marble and bronze ones?" ("On Drama"). But the fundamental difference between the stone guest and Don Carlos, whom Don Juan had accidentally killed, necessarily presupposes the simultaneous identity of the two: the slain man's hand is to the same extent the commander's hand, just as the statue's nose is his own nose ("He wouldn't be able to reach his own nose with his hand"). And this very identity determines the ensuing action, as if the commander had become embodied in his statue.

The relationship of the sign to the object signified, and especially the relationship of the representation to the object represented, their simultaneous identity and difference, is one of the most dramatic semiotic antinomies. It was precisely this antinomy that led to the bitter fights around iconoclasm;[60] disputes about realistic art, which are constantly revived, are connected with precisely this antinomy, and poetic symbolism exploits it.

Facetious conversations are also the starting point in the story "The Coffinmaker," which wittily anticipates the plot of *The Stone Guest*. These conversations gradually expose the contradiction between the linguistic sign and the real object. The coffinmaker Adrian says: "If a living man does not have the means to buy shoes, . . . he goes barefoot, but if a dead man is poor, he takes a coffin for nothing." We are accustomed to identifying the grammatical subject of the action with the person acting; "a living man who goes barefoot" is actually such a person, but not "a dead man who takes a coffin." The syntactic parallelism of the two sentences increases even more the tension between the grammatical meaning and the objective relationship. In the cobbler's analogous utterance: "a living man will manage without shoes, but a dead man does not live without a coffin" the contradiction is sharpened by the opposition between the subject "a dead man" (*mërt-vyj*) and the basic meaning of the predicate verb "to live" (*žit'*) which has a transferred meaning in the given sentence: here "does not live" (*ne živët*) means "is not left [without . . .], does not exist" (*ne ostaëtsja, ne suščestvuet*). A client is the subject of the action; the dead are Adrian's clients. If the artisans drink to the health of their clients and if the coffinmaker is also called upon to drink to "the health of his dead," then the opposition of the word and reality is driven to its extreme and turns into its converse when the drunk Adrian invites his dead to a banquet and they accept his invitation. Thus in Doña Anna's words to Don Juan, "My husband torments you even in his grave," the husband is a purely figurative subject of the action, but later he turns into the real subject: "I have appeared at your call."

A statue is either an object of the discourse or a subject of the action. The confrontation of a statue with a living being is always the starting point of the discourse: the two schemes interpenetrate one another. A living being is likened to a statue (in *Boris Godunov,* in "The Solitary Little House"), or a statue is likened to a living being ("Takov i byl sej vlastelin" [Such was this ruler]). It becomes identified with a living being through the negation of dead matter (an emphatic variant of the fragment "Who knows the land": "Canova's lively chisel has brought the Paros marble alive");[61] the poem "The Mob": "It's by weight/ That you value the Belvedere idol/ . . . Yet this marble is really a god!" Or it is depicted ("is estranged," according to Šklovskij's terminology) as a living being. If the discourse about the statue is at the same time a discourse about the past, a reminiscence, then the immobile duration of the statue is opposed to the ephemerality of the living being, whether it is a question of an objective loss—"Recollections at Tsarskoe Selo" of 1814: "Everything has vanished, the great woman is no more"; the epistle "To the Artist" of 1836: "I walk sadly in a crowd of silent idols . . . Del'vig is no more"[62]—or a subjective loss (the poem "At the beginning of life I recollect school": the "magnificent woman" with her veracious pronouncements disappears from the youth who steals away to the immobile statues). What comes to the fore, then, is not the relationship of the representation to the object represented or a similarity (an imitative connection), but a contiguity (a contagious connection): the relationship of the deceased to the statue, a temporal or spatial continuity, the consecration of the statue to his memory. The representation can be replaced by a commemorative column, that is to say, by a statue of solely metonymic designation ("The spectres of heroes sit by the columns dedicated to them"). The statue as the subject of poetic (epic or dramatic) action includes and objectifies all of the elements that we have examined. The very opposition of the lasting statue and the vanishing man is thus projected into the action: the statue kills the man. The internal antithesis of the man's simultaneous longing for a woman and longing for rest (Don Juan's "cold kiss" is essentially an oxymoron) determines the woman's part in this action. It is symptomatic that Puškin's "myth of the destructive statue" is the *only* constant form in his oeuvre of the intervention of the statue in the poetic action.

The image of the statue—the maker of human destiny—does not remain isolated in Puškin's works; rather it is organically connected to his entire poetic mythology. Bicilli's study (one of the most insightful contributions to the literature on Puškin) emphasizes the dynamism of his poetry as the principle of its individuality:

> I do not know another poet who would use the image of running water as often as Puškin. His heavenly bodies are always moving. . . . He uses a wealth of epithets to characterize the dynamic properties of objects. . . . In his vocabulary 'life' and words of the same root occupy an exceptional place. . . . In Puškin everything breathes. . . . All objects are comprehended *sub specie* of motion, their origin or the potential rhythm included in them. . . . For him 'dead' nature is full of life. . . . Most often the idea of swift, vehement movements dominates him. . . . One of his favorite image-symbols is the ship, the embodiment of swift and, at the same time, light sliding motion. . . . In his poetry the stereotyped symbol of the road as the 'life path' acquires particular force and charge. . . . All life—cosmic, personal and social—is conceived as a continuous process. . . .[63]

In Puškin's system of symbols, therefore, rest–immobility is naturally a striking contrastive motif, and whether it appears in the form of *forced immobility*—here we can include the variously modified images of the prisoner "punished by the torture of rest," the enslaved people, the creature in a cage or the imprisoned stream—or in the form of *free rest* as an imagined, superhuman, and even supernatural state.[64] For the poet, time stops for a moment of amatory ecstasy ("Inscription on a Gazebo" ["Nadpis' k besedke," 1816 (?)]); the stream of his days becomes calm in momentary slumber and reflects the azure of the sky (from lyrical sketches, 1834); free rest, not happiness, is the poet's dream ("Pora, moj drug, pora" [It's time, my friend, it's time], 1834 [?]). Puškin connects the idea of solemn, undisturbed rest with the sanctity of miraculous beauty ("Krasavica," [The Beauty], 1832) and similarly extols the "joyful peace" and the "unbroken eternal sleep," the "solemn rest" of the last repose (the epitaph for N. S. Volkonskij, 1828; "Pered grobniceju svjatoj" [Before the holy tomb], 1831; "Kogda za gorodom, zadumčiv, ja brožu" [When, having grown pensive, I wander beyond the town], 1836), whereas human life is a vigorous manifestation of cosmic activity, and rest is only the negation of this life, only a deviation, only an anomaly. For a statue, on the contrary, rest is the natural, "unmarked" state, and the motion of a statue is a violation of the norm. To Puškin's myth-creating genius a statue, which always implies activity and movement[65] and which is at the same time immobile in itself, displays the pure embodiment of supernatural, free creative rest: in fact, a statue is "above all desires" and sleeps "with the sleep of force and peace,/ as the gods sleep in the deep heavens" (*The Covetous Knight*).

This reference to the gods in the mouth of a medieval knight sounds peculiar, but it is very characteristic of Puškin. For him the power of "immobile thought" has an undeniably pagan association. It is characteristic that the statues in his poems are usually designated as idols (*kumiry*), and Tsar Nicholas was particularly shocked by this designation in *The Bronze Horseman*.[66] Whether it concerns the nonbeliever Puškin,[67] the heretic Blok, or the anti-religious writings of Majakovskij, Russian poets have grown up in a world of Orthodox customs, and their work is unwittingly saturated with the symbolism of the Eastern Church. Precisely the Orthodox tradition, which severely condemned the art of sculpture, which did not admit it into churches, and which understood it as a pagan or diabolic vice (the two concepts were equivalent for the Church), suggested to Puškin the close association of statues with idolatry, with devilry, with sorcery. It is enough to read Gogol''s deliberations on sculpture for us to understand how inseparably plastic art was linked to the concept of paganism in the Russian view: "[Sculpture] was born along with a definitely formed pagan world, it expressed [this world] and died along with it. . . . It was as remote from Christianity as the pagan faith itself" ("Sculpture, Painting and Music," 1831). On Russian soil, sculpture was closely associated with whatever was unchristian, even antichristian, in the spirit of the Petersburg tsardom.[68] The discourse about statues in the poem "At the beginning of life . . ." is characteristic: "miraculous creations," "magic charm," "images of devils," "unearthly force," "bewitching demon." The pagan, demonic contour of the Bronze Horseman has inevitably manifested itself to interpreters as different as Merežkovskij, Brjusov, Xodasevič, and Mirskij.

Those scholars who associate Don Juan's invitation to the stone guest with the poet's evocation of the shade of a dead lover in the Boldino lyrics[69] and who see in the statue only the mask of a specter, which would have given the impression of an excessively mad raving without this veiling,[70] forget about the specific properties of the statue in Puškin's symbolic pattern: the animated statue, in contrast to a spectre, is an instrument of evil magic, it bears destruction, and it is never the embodiment of a woman.

Puškin's symbolism of the statue continues to affect Russian poetry to the present day, and it constantly points to its creator. Such is the case, for example, in the works of three outstanding Russian poets of this century. In the poem "The Steps of the Commander" Alexander Blok resumes the Puškinian conception of an adoring Don Juan, a Doña Anna who tantalizingly vanishes and the heavy steps "of old fate," and in the poems of the cycle *The City* he evokes the eternal life of a metallic Peter who vibrates between arrested sleep and dreadful activity ("Peter," "The Meeting"). In Velimir Xlebnikov's dramatic poem "Markiza Dèzes," which is linked to Puškin in various ways, people grow rigid and turn into statues, and things come to life; in his epic poem "The Crane" a boy flees—against a Neva background that is well known from *The Bronze Horseman*—from a destructive monster which has originated from animated iron chimneys, machines, and bridges, and which pursues him:

Life has yielded power
To the union of a corpse and a thing.
O, man, what insidious spirit,
Both a murderer and a counselor at the same time, whispered to
    you:

> Infuse the spirit of life into things! . . .
> Teachers and prophets
> Taught us to pray while speaking about invincible fate.

The punitive campaign of another Petersburg bronze horseman—the statue of Alexander III—is depicted in Xlebnikov's "The Monument"; his ringing gallop, however, is interrupted by the intervention of the police, who accuse him of devilry, and "it is once again narrow and cramped for the captive on the square." The motif of the forced, imprisoning immobility of a statue, polemically opposed to Puškin's myth of its sovereign rest, acquires particular vigor in Majakovskij. In his poetry an apostrophe to Puškin is inseparably connected with the theme of the statue. A poem inveighing in a revolutionary manner against the old art ("Radovat'sja rano" [It's Early to Rejoice]) associates Puškin with Alexandrian monuments and with the sculptor Rastrelli who immortalized Catherine. An epigram on Brjusov (1916) ends with the words: "What/ Could Puškin have against it?/ His fist/ is clad forever/ in bronze indifferent to insult." "Poslednjaja peterburgskaja skazka" (A Last Petersburg Tale) of the same year, which parodies *The Bronze Horseman,* leads into the lines "the anguish of Peter—/ a prisoner/ fettered in his own city." Life ignores the galloping tsar, whereas he, on the contrary, dreads coursing life. And likewise in the poem "Jubilee," where Majakovskij invites Puškin down from the pedestal of his monument, the statue's hand does not oppress the man; rather the man's hand oppresses the statue ("I squeezed too hard? It hurts?"), and the lyrical monologue ends with an expression of hatred for the posthumous, inert glory incarnated in the statue. This attack against bronze and marble still appears also in Majakovskij's farewell poem "At the Top of My Voice," which is obviously linked to Puškin's "Exegi monumentum."[71]

A. Èfros, a sensitive scholar and the author of a special study on Puškin and visual art, asserts in the previously cited book that the poet fulfilled only a worldly man's obligation to sculpture and took note of it to the extent which Onegin's commandment "du comme il faut" compelled him to find a place for it in his life. "Genius of form abandoned him here. For the most part he discerned only a literary *topic* in a work of plastic art . . ."[72] We have seen, however, how incisively Puškin's symbolic pattern engages the problems of sculpture and how deeply the symbolism of the statue is rooted in his work, in the poet's life, and in the tradition out of which he grew, and how vital it has turned out to be in the further development of Russian poetry. How, then, is this specialist's conclusion, which so flatly contradicts the facts, possible? Thus we return to our starting point: it is difficult to abstract from a work of art the elements most deeply rooted in it. We stop perceiving Falconet's statue in the Bronze Horseman; we experience it as the poet's surreal myth. We can paraphrase a French poet's aphorism about the flowers of a poetic work that do not grow in any garden.[73] The statues of Puškin's poems cannot be identified in any glyptotheca.

THE STATUE IN PUŠKIN'S WORKS

Year	In poems	In letters	In prose and in drawings
1814	"Vospominanija v Carskom sele" —strophes about monuments		
1815–1817	———		
1818–1819	Sketch "Moguščij bog sadov" Sketch "K Kagul'skomu pamjat-niku" ("Èlegija")		
1820–1823	———		
1824			Drawing of Mercury (V)
1825	*Boris Godunov*—mention of marble nymph "Brovi car' naxmurja"—mention of Peter's monument		
1826	———		
1827	"Kto znaet kraj"—mention of Canova		
1828	"Čern'"—mention of Apollo of Belvedere		"The Solitary Little House"—mention of commander
1829	"K bjustu zavoevatelja" (21.IX) "Zagadka"—apostrophe to the sphinx (XI.) "Vospominanija v Carskom sele" (14.XII)		Drawing of Falconet's horse
1830	Mention of Kragul in the drafts to Ch. 8 of *Eugene Onegin* "K vel'može"—mention of idols (23.IV)	about the "bronze grandmother" to Benkendorf (29.V) to A. N. Gončarov (7.VI) to Benkendorf (4.VII) to N. N. Gončarova (20-30.VII) to N. N. Gončarova (30.VII) to A. N. Gončarov (14.VIII) to N. N. Gončarova (30.IX)	

THE STATUE IN PUŠKIN'S WORKS

Year	In poems	In letters	In prose and in drawings
Boldino	"Carskosel'skaja statuja" (1.X) "V načale žizni" (X) *The Stone Guest* (finished 4.XI)	to N. N. Gončarova 11.X.	"The Shot"—mention of busts (14.X) Drawing of Egyptian colossus (X) Drawing of classical bust (XI)
1831		to A. N. Gončarov 24.II	
1832		to Benkendorf 8.VI	Drawing of statue of Voltaire (10.III)
1833		to Volkonskij 18.II	Drawing of Puškin and Mickiewicz in drafts of *Tazit*
Boldino	*The Bronze Horseman* (X) Sketch "Tolpa gluxaja"— about falling idols (9.XII)		
1834		to his wife about bronze monument to Peter (29.V)	
Boldino	"Vezuvij zev otkryl"— about falling idols (IX.?) *The Fairytale of the Golden Cockerel* (finished 20.IX)		
			Diary entry of 25.XI about Alexander's column and the Tarutino column
1835	——		
1836	"Xudožniku" (25.III) "Exegi monumentum" (21.VIII) Inscriptions to statues of players (X)	to his wife about his own bust (14.V)	Self-portrait of Puškin as laureate (toward 1836) Reference to Kagul at end of *The Captain's Daughter* (X)

CHAPTER 19

What Is Poetry?

"Harmony is the result of contrast," I said. "The whole
world is made up of opposing elements. And . . ." "And
poetry", he interjected, "true poetry—the more original
and alive its world, the more contradictory the contrasts
in which the secret kinship occurs."

Karel Sabina, biographer and close friend of Mácha

What is poetry? To define the term, we shall have to juxtapose
what poetry is to what it is not. But to determine even what poetry is
not is no longer simple.

The list of acceptable poetic themes during the Neoclassical or Romantic period was quite restricted. The traditional requisites—the
moon, a lake, a nightingale, a cliff, a rose, a castle, and the like—are
well known. Even the dreams of the Romantics were not allowed to
stray from the beaten path. "Today I dreamt I was standing among
ruins that came tumbling down around me," writes Mácha. "And in
the lake below I saw bathing nymphs . . . a lover going to the grave to
join his mistress. . . . And then piles and piles of bones came flying out
the windows of the old Gothic ruin." Gothic windows, preferably with
the light of the moon filtering through, were favored above all other
windows. Nowadays, the department-store mirror monstrosity and
the village inn's tiny fly-bespattered pane of glass are considered to be
of equal poetic worth. And just about anything can come flying out of
them. The Czech Surrealist Vítězslav Nezval writes:

I can be dazzled in mid-sentence by a garden
or a latrine it makes no difference
I no longer tell things apart by the charm
or plainness you have given them

For today's poet, as for Karamazov senior, "there is no such thing as an ugly woman." No nook or cranny, no activity, landscape, or thought stands outside the pale of poetic subject matter. In other words, the issue of poetic subject matter has no validity today.

Is it then possible to limit the range of poetic devices? Not in the least; the history of arts attests to their constant mutability. Nor does the *intent* of a device burden art with any strictures. We have only to recall how often the Dadaists and Surrealists let happenstance write their poetry. We have only to realize what pleasure Xlebnikov derived from typographical errors; the typographical error, he once said, is often a first-rate artist. During the Middle Ages, *ignorance* was responsible for the dismemberment of classical statues; today the sculptor does his *own* dismembering, but the result (visual synecdoche) is the same. How is the music of a Musorgskij and the painting of a Henri Rousseau to be interpreted? By the genius of their creators or by their creator's artistic illiteracy? What causes Nezval's grammatical errors? A lack of textbook knowledge or a conscious rejection of it? How would the norms of the Russian literary language ever have been relaxed had it not been for the Ukrainian Gogol' and his imperfect Russian? What would Lautréamont have written instead of his *Chants de Maldoror* had he been sane? Speculations like these belong to the category of anecdotal themes like the famous composition topic "How would Gretchen have responded to Faust had she been a man?"

But even if we succeed in isolating those devices that typify the poets of a given period, we have still to establish the line of demarcation between poetry and nonpoetry. The same alliterations and other types of euphonic devices are used by the rhetoric of the period; what is more, they even occur in everyday, colloquial language. Streetcar conversations are full of jokes based on the very figures found in the most subtle lyric poetry, and the composition of gossip often corresponds to the laws of composition followed by best-sellers, or at least last year's best-sellers (depending on the degree of the gossiper's intelligence).

The borderline dividing what is a work of poetry from what is not is less stable than the frontiers of the Chinese empire's territories. Novalis and Mallarmé regarded the alphabet as the greatest work of poetry. Russian poets have admired the poetic qualities of a wine list (Vjazemskij), an inventory of the tsar's clothes (Gogol'), a timetable (Pasternak), and even a laundry bill (Kručenyx). How many poets now claim that reportage is a more artistic genre than the novel or short story? Although "Pohorská vesnice" (A Mountain Village)—a story by one of the leading mid-nineteenth-century Czech prosaists, Božena Němcová (1820–1862)— can boast but few enthusiasts today, her intimate correspondence is for us a brilliant work of poetry.

A short anecdote is in order here. Once, when a world wrestling champion lost to an underdog, one of the spectators jumped up, charged that the bout had been fixed, challenged the victor, and defeated him. The next day a newspaper carried an article saying that the second as well as the first bout had been fixed. The spectator who had challenged the victor of the first bout then burst into the newspaper's offices and gave the editor responsible for the story a slap in the face. But both the newspaper article and the spectator's pique later turned out to be prearranged hoaxes.

Do not believe the poet who, in the name of truth, the real world, or anything else, renounces his past in poetry or art. Tolstoj tried in great exasperation to repudiate his works, but instead of ceasing to be a poet, he forged the way to new, unhackneyed forms of literature. As has rightly been noted: when an actor tears off his mask, makeup is sure to be forthcoming.

Do not believe the critic who rakes a poet over the coals in the name of the True and the Natural. All he has in fact done is to reject one poetic school, that is, one set of devices deforming material in the name of another poetic school, another set of deformational devices. The artist is playing no less a game when he announces that this time he is dealing with naked *Wahrheit* rather than *Dichtung* as when he assures his audience that a given work is sheer invention, that "poetry as a whole is one big lie, and the poet who fails to lie audaciously from the word go is worthless."

There are literary historians who know more about a poet than the poet himself or the aesthetician who analyzes the structure of his work or the psychologist who investigates the structure of the poet's psyche. With the certitude of a Sunday schoolteacher, these literary historians map out what in the poet's work is mere "human document" and what is "proof of artistic merit," what is "sincere" and "a natural outlook on

370

life" and what is "sham" and "a labored literary outlook," what "comes from the heart" and what is "affected." All the quotations given here come from the study "Hlaváček's Decadent Erotica," a chapter in a work by Fedor Soldán. Soldán describes the relationship between an erotic poem and a poet's erotic life as if he were dealing with static entries in an encyclopedia rather than a dialectical alliance with constant shifts, as if he regarded a sign and the object designated by it as monogamously and immutably bound to one another, as if he had never heard of the age-old psychological principle of the ambivalence of feelings—no feeling is so pure as to be free from contamination by its opposite feeling.

Numerous studies in the field of literary history still apply the dualistic scheme of "psychic reality versus poetic invention," seeking out relations of mechanistic causality between the two so that one cannot help recalling the problem that tortured the old French aristocrat, namely, is the tail attached to the dog or the dog to its tail?

As an example of how sterile these equations with two unknowns can be, let us look at Mácha's diary, an extremely instructive document, which to date has appeared only with considerable expurgations. Some literary historians concentrate entirely on the poet's published work, leaving aside all biographical problems; others try to reconstruct the poet's life in as much detail as possible. While conceding the merits of both these approaches, we very definitely reject the approach of those literary historians who replace genuine biography with official, schoolbook interpretation. Mácha's diary has been expurgated so that dreamy-eyed youths admiring his statute in Prague's Petřin Park will not be disillusioned. But as Puškin once said, literature (to say nothing of literary history) cannot take fifteen-year-old girls into account. And fifteen-year-old girls read much more dangerous things than Mácha's diary anyway.

The diary describes the author's physiological acts—both genital and anal—with epic tranquility. It records, in laborious code and with the inexorable accuracy of a bookkeeper, the manner and frequency of his sexual gratification with his mistress Lori. Karel Sabina (1813–1877) has written of Mácha that "the keen regard of darksome eyes, a sublime brow furrowed with deep thoughts, a pensive mien, which is so often marked by a pale complexion—these plus the feminine traits of refinement and fidelity are what endeared the fair sex to him above all else." And this is how feminine beauty appears in Mácha's poems and stories.

The detailed diary descriptions of his mistress's appearance, however, are more reminiscent of Josef Šima's surrealistic paintings of headless female torsos.[1]

Is it possible that the relationship between lyric poetry and the diary parallels the relationship between *Dichtung* and *Wahrheit?* Not at all. Both aspects are equally valid; they are merely different meanings or, in more scholarly terminology, different semantic levels of the same object, the same experience, or, as a filmmaker would put it, two different takes of a single scene. Mácha's diary is every bit as much a work of poetry as *Máj* (May, the narrative poem for which Mácha is best known) and "Marinka" (Marinka, a short story). It has no trace of utilitarianism; it is pure art for art's sake, poetry for the poet. Were Mácha alive today, he might well have set aside the lyrical poetry ("Little deer, little white deer, listen to my plea") for his own intimate use, and published the diary. He would consequently have been compared to Joyce and Lawrence, with whom he has many details in common, and a critic would write that these three authors "attempt to give a true picture of the type of man who has rid himself of all rules and regulations and now merely floats, drifts and rears up as pure animal instinct."

Puškin wrote a poem that begins

> I recall a wondrous moment:
> You appeared before me like a fleeting vision,
> Like a spirit of pure beauty.

Tolstoj in his old age waxed indignant over a bantering letter Puškin had written to a friend in which he referred to the woman of this poem in the following terms: "With God's help I had Anna Petrovna today."[2] But medieval farces like the Czech *Mastičkář* (*Unguentarius*) are far from blasphemy! The ode and the burlesque are equally valid; they are simply two poetic genres, two modes of expression for one theme.

A theme that never ceased to torture Mácha was the suspicion he was not Lori's first lover. In *May* this motif takes the following forms:

> Oh no, it is she! My angel!
> Why did she fall before I knew her?
> Why was my father her seducer?

and

My rival—my father! His murderer—his son!
He, the seducer of my mistress,
Unknown to me.

At one point in the diary Mácha describes how, after having Lori twice, he talked with her once more "about her having permitted someone else to take her. She wanted to die. 'O Gott,' she said, 'wie unglücklich bin ich!'" There follows another violent erotic scene, after which a detailed description is given of how the poet moved his bowels. The passage concludes: "God forgive her if she is deceiving me; I will not. If only she loves me. She seems to. Why, I would marry a whore if I knew she loved me."

Whoever claims that the diary version is a photographically perfect reproduction of reality and *May* a sheer fabrication on the part of the poet is simplifying the matter as much as the schoolbooks do. Perhaps *May* is even more revealing than the diary as a manifestation of psychic exhibitionism, intensified as it is by its Oedipal overtones ("My rival—my father").[3] The motif of suicide in the poetry of Majakovskij was once thought to be a mere literary trick. It might well be thought so today, had Majakovskij, like Mácha, died of pneumonia at the age of twenty-six.

Sabina writes that "Mácha's notes contain a fragmentary description of a person of the neoromantic ilk. That appears to be a faithful picture of the poet himself as well as the principal model he patterned his lovesick characters after." The hero of the fragment "slew himself at the feet of the girl whom he loved ardently and who returned his love even more ardently. Believing her to have been seduced, he tried to force the name of the seducer from her so that he might avenge her. She denied everything. He seethed with anger. She swore that nothing had happened. Then an idea struck him like a bolt of lightening: 'To avenge her I would have to kill him. My punishment would be death. Let him live. I cannot.'" And so he decides to commit suicide, firm in the conviction that his mistress "is a long-suffering angel, unwilling to bring sorrow even upon her seducer." Then, at the last minute, he realizes that "she has deceived him" and that "her angel face has turned into the face of a devil." Here is how Mácha describes his own tragic love affair in a letter to a trusted friend: "I once told you that one thing could drive me insane. It has come; eine Notzucht ist unterlaufen. The mother of my beloved died. A fearful vow was taken at midnight by

373

her coffin . . . and . . . it was not true—and I—ha ha ha!—Eduard, I did not go mad, but I did rant and rage."

And so we have three versions: murder and punishment, suicide, and ranting followed by resignation. Each of them was experienced by the poet; all are equally valid, regardless of which of the given possibilities were realized in the poet's private life and which in his oeuvre. Who can draw a line between suicide, the duel that led to Puškin's death, and Mácha's classically ludicrous end? [4]

The many-sided interplay between poetry and private life is reflected not only in the characteristically Máchovian heightened ability to communicate but in the intimate manner in which literary motifs intermingle with life. Moreover, the social function of Mácha's moods is as worthy of investigation as their individual psychological genesis. As Mácha's contemporary, the critic and playwright J. K. Tyl, pointed out in his brilliant pamphlet *Rozervanec* (The Malcontent), Mácha's words "My love has been deceived" are not his private concern; they signify a role, since the slogan of his literary school proclaims that "only pain can be the mother of true poetry." On the level of literary history (and only on that level), Tyl is correct in stating that it was all to Mácha's good to be able to say he was unhappy in love.

The seducer versus jealous lover theme is a fitting way of filling up an intermission, the period of exhaustion and melancholy following satisfied desire. A languorous feeling of distrust turns into a conventional motif thoroughly developed by poetic tradition. Mácha himself stresses the literary coloring of the motif in a letter to a friend: "Neither Victor Hugo nor Eugène Sue in their most terrifying novels had the ability to describe the sorts of things that have happened to me. And I was the one who experienced them, and—I am a poet." The question of whether Mácha's ruinous distrust had a basis in reality or—as Tyl implies—was born of free poetic invention is of importance to forensic medicine and forensic medicine alone.

Every verbal act in a certain sense stylizes and transforms the event it depicts. How it does so is determined by its slant, its emotional content, the audience it is addressed to, the preliminary "censorship" it undergoes, the supply of ready-made patterns it draws from. Because the poeticity of the verbal act makes it very clear that communication is not of prime importance, "censorship" here can be relaxed, toned down. Janko Král' (1822–1876), a truly gifted Slovak poet, a poet who in his ruggedly beautiful improvisations brilliantly obliterates the borderline between delirium and the folksong, and is even freer in his imagination, more spontaneous in his exquisite provincialism than Mácha—Janko Král' is along with Mácha a classic Oedipal case. Here, in a letter to a friend, is Božena Němcová's description of her first impressions of Král': "He is terribly eccentric, and his wife, though very young and nice, is terribly naive. He only keeps her as a servant girl, really. He said himself there was only one woman he ever loved, above all else, with all his soul—and that woman was his mother. He hated his father with the same passion: his father tormented his mother (just as he torments his wife). Since she died, he claims to have loved no one. As I see it, that man will end his days in an insane asylum!" But even though it frightened even the intrepid Božena Němcová with its overtones of madness, Král''s extraordinary brand of infantilism elicits no alarm whatsoever in his poems. Published in a collection entitled *Čitanie studujúcej mládeže* (Readings for Students), they seem little more than a mask. In fact, however, they reveal a mother-and-son love tragedy in such brutally straightforward terms as poetry has rarely known.

What are Král''s ballads and songs about? Ardent maternal love that "never could be shared"; the son's inevitable departure, in the firm belief—despite his "mother's counsel"—that "it was all in vain. Who can go against fate? Not I"; the impossibility of returning "home to mother from far-off lands." Mother searches desperately for son: "Throughout this world my mourning is of the grave, but no news have I of my son." Son searches desperately for mother: "Why go home to your brothers and father, why to your village, winged falcon? Your mother has gone out into the broad field." Fear—the physical fear of bizarre Janko sentenced to destruction—together with Janko's dream of his mother's womb recall the themes of present-day surrealist poets such as Nezval.

Here is an excerpt from Nezval's *Historie šesti prázdných domů* (A Story of Six Empty Houses):

> Mother
> Can you leave me forever down there
> In the empty room where there are never any guests
> I enjoy being your subtenant
> And it will be terrible when I am finally forced to go
> How many moves await me
> And the most terrible move of all

The move away to death.

And now an excerpt from Kráľ's "Zverbovaný" (The Recruit):

> Oh mother, if you really loved me,
> Why did you deliver me into the hands of fate?
> Don't you see you have put me out into this alien world
> Like a young flower discarded from a flower pot,
> A flower no one has ever sniffed.
> If they plan to pick it, why do they plant it?
> It is hard, so hard for a meadow to be without rain,
> But it is a hundred times harder for Janko to be tortured.

The inevitable antithesis of poetry's sudden flow into life is every bit as sudden as its ebb. Here again is Nezval, this time in the vein of poetism, a school he was instrumental in creating.

> I've never walked along this path
> Have I lost the egg who found it?
> A white egg of a black hen
> He's been in a fever three whole days
>
> The dog's been howling all night long
> The priest, the priest is coming
> He's blessing all the doors
> Like a peacock with his plumage
>
> There's a funeral, a funeral, it's snowing
> The egg is running around behind the coffin
> What a joke
> The devil is in the egg
>
> My bad conscience spoils me
> Then live without the egg
> Reader madman
> The egg was empty

Out-and-out advocates of a poetry of revolt were either so embarrassed by these poetistic games that they did their best to hush them up, or so annoyed by them that they spoke of Nezval's decline and betrayal of the cause. I am thoroughly convinced, however, that these childlike rhymes are as significant a breakthrough as the carefully thought-out, mercilessly logical exhibitionism of his antilyrics. They are an integral part of a united front, a united front to keep the word from being treated like a fetish. The latter half of the nineteenth century was a period of a sudden, violent inflation of linguistic signs. This thesis can be easily justified from the standpoint of sociology. The most

376

typical cultural phenomena of the time exhibit a determination to conceal this inflation at any cost and shore up faith in the paper word with all available means. Positivism and naive realism in philosophy, liberalism in politics, the neogrammarian school in linguistics, an assuasive illusionism in literature and on the stage (with illusions of both the naive naturalist and the solipsistic decadent varieties), the atomization of method in literary theory (and in scholarship and science as a whole)—such are the names of the various and sundry expedients that served to bolster the credit of the word and strengthen confidence in its value.

And today! Modern phenomenology is exposing one linguistic fiction after another. It has skillfully demonstrated the prime importance of the distinction between sign and designated object, between the meaning of a word and the content at which the meaning is directed. There is an analogous phenomenon in the sociopolitical field: the heated opposition to muddled, empty, harmfully abstract cant and phrasemongering, the ideocratic struggle against "humbug words," to use the picturesque expression. In art, it was motion pictures that revealed clearly and emphatically that language was only one of a number of possible sign systems, just as astronomy had revealed that the earth was only one of a number of planets and thus revolutionized man's view of the world. Columbus' voyage had essentially already marked the end of the myth of the Old World's exclusivity, but not until the recent rise of America did it receive its mortal blow. The film too was first regarded as no more than an exotic colony of art, and only as it developed, step by step, did it break asunder the ruling ideology that preceded it. Finally, the poetry of the poetists and poets belonging to related schools gave a sound guarantee of the autonomy of the word. Nezval's playful rhymes have therefore found effective allies.

It has been quite fashionable in critical circles to profess certain doubts about what is called the Formalist study of literature. The school, say its detractors, fails to grasp the relationship of art to real life; it calls for an "art for art's sake" approach; it is following in the footsteps of Kantian aesthetics. Critics with objections in this vein are so completely one-sided in their radicalism that, forgetting the existence of a third dimension, they view everything on a single plane. Neither Tynjanov nor Mukařovský nor Šklovskij nor I have ever proclaimed the self-sufficiency of art. What we have been trying to show is that art is an integral part of the social structure, a component that interacts with all the others and is itself mutable since both the domain of art and its relationship to the other constituents of the social structure are in constant dialectical flux. What we stand for is not the separatism of art but the autonomy of the aesthetic function.

As I have already pointed out, the content of the concept of *poetry* is unstable and temporally conditioned. But the poetic function, *poeticity*, is, as the "formalists" stressed, an element sui generis, one that cannot be mechanically reduced to other elements. It can be separated out and made independent, like the various devices in, say, a cubist painting. But this is a special case; from the standpoint of the dialectics of art it has its raison d'être, yet it remains a special case. For the most part poeticity is only a part of a complex structure, but it is a part that necessarily transforms the other elements and determines with them the nature of the whole. In the same way, oil is neither a complete dish in and of itself nor a chance addition to the meal, a mechanical component; it changes the taste of food and can sometimes be so penetrating that a fish packed in oil has begun to lose, as in Czech, its original genetic name, *sardinka* (sardine), and is being baptized anew as *olejovka* (*olej-*, oil- + *ovka,* a derivational suffix). Only when a verbal work acquires poeticity, a poetic function of determinative significance, can we speak of poetry.

But how does poeticity manifest itself? Poeticity is present when the word is felt as a word and not a mere representation of the object being named or an outburst of emotion, when words and their composition, their meaning, their external and inner form, acquire a weight and value of their own instead of referring indifferently to reality.

Why is all this necessary? Why is it necessary to make a special point of the fact that sign does not fall together with object? Because, besides the direct awareness of the identity between sign and object (A is A_1), there is a necessity for the direct awareness of the inadequacy of that identity (A is not A_1). The reason this antinomy is essential is that without contradiction there is no mobility of concepts, no mobility of signs, and the relationship between concept and sign becomes automatized. Activity comes to a halt, and the awareness of reality dies out.

CHAPTER 20

Notes on Myth in Erben's Work

Antonín Grund's *Karel Jaromír Erben* and his earlier specialized studies present abundant and varied preparatory material for a scholarly study of Erben's life and works.[1] This will certainly be the basis for new Erben research that confronts important tasks. Through a many-sided analysis of the poet's works, it has to place the great Czech Romantic in the overall development of domestic and world Romanticism, to establish Erben's place in Czech literary, cultural, and social history, and to define his simultaneous distance from and closeness to the present.

Grund's work does not, however, seek to be only a collection of materials for the study of Erben's life and works, for it also lays claim to being a scholarly interpretation of them. And if it does not produce desirable results in this respect, its methodological shakiness is the major reason. Lack of conceptual clarity is Grund's basic mistake. The author does not seek a scholarly precision in using words; he does not define his words epistemologically; he does not control their relationship to the reality designated; in short, he does not employ word-terms but words in their colloquial function, words with an indefinite semantic range, ambiguous and unsuitable for the tasks of formulation.

If the concepts of Classicism as a concrete historical artistic movement and of classicality as a general artistic perfection merge in Josef Jungmann's "On Classicality in Literature in General and in Czech Literature in Particular" ("O klasičnosti v literatuře vubec a zvláště české"), it is understandable for the ideologist of the Czech Classicism of the National Revival, but a modern literary historian is not entitled to conflate these two concepts. If we regard as classics "writers whose voice," according to Jungmann's formulation, "arbitrates and decrees in literature as the well-to-do citizens in Rome arbitrated and decreed in general affairs," we can speak about classics of Romantic or Realist literature, and we can deliberate about the classical utterances of literary schools directed against Classicism (for instance, about Mácha's *Maj* [May] as a classic work of Czech Romanticism). If we use the term "classicality" in this meaning, the thesis about Erben—a Czech classic—is indisputable. Grund comes close to such a conception of the term "classicality" but at the same time implies that he is concerned with the connection between Erben and Classicism and that classicality is not a mere evaluation but a well-defined movement. Only in this way can we understand his ruminations about a poet with classicizing predilections who intentionally cultivated Jungmann's Classicism and proved indeed that Czech classicality is justified. In his narrower definitions of "the poet's classicism," however, Grund cites elements which have nothing in common with Classicism—"a perfect fusion of content and form," "godliness," "national spirit," "reflection of real life," and so forth. These can be slogans of very different artistic trends, and such formulas even turn up in explicitly Romantic literary manifestos.

In no way do I wish to deny that a poetic work can fuse essential elements of two such opposed movements as Classicism and Romanticism. Goethe, Puškin, and Tjutčev are each in his own way splendid examples of such a fusion. But in Erben we seek in vain for traces of Classicism. Arne Novák has masterfully perceived elements of Classicism in the literature of the National Revival and has rightly emphasized that "the undisturbed and unlimited sway of Romanticism over Czech intellectual life was established only when personalities who had not already experienced a classicist preparation came to the fore of literary life. These are the two great poetic contemporaries and antipodes, Karel Jaromír Erben and Karel Hynek Mácha." But it is precisely the existence of the two antipodal faces of Romanticism, European and especially Czech, that Grund does not consider. He unjustifiably narrows Romanticism to the trend represented by Mácha's *May,* that is, to the "left" wing of Romanticism. Grund's conception therefore stems from erroneous definitions of Classicism and Romanticism. The author commits an obvious equivocation by simultaneously using the term "classical" in two meanings, and he is unaware that his conception of Romanticism is a typical synecdoche (*pars pro toto*).

Grund loses the key to the interpretation of Erben precisely because he does not consider the poet a genuine Romantic and artificially extracts his works from the context of universal Romantic problems. For this reason Grund also cannot treat the *myth* that is the central problem of any Erben study and the basic element of Romantic epistemology and poetics in general. The Romantic period conceives myth as a special, self-contained world. Myth is primary, that is, it cannot be derived from anything else or reduced to something else. It is a phantom and must not therefore be rationalized and interpreted allegorically. It is objective and obligatory. It is regulated by internal, immanent laws alone. It has its own criterion of genuineness, its own profundity. It precedes history and is immortal. Myth alone presents reality fully without shattering it; myth alone is an allusion to the inexpressible.

The philosopher Karel Boleslav Štorch, Erben's intimate friend and constant collaborator, was conceptually perhaps the person closest to him (the connection between Erben's and Štorch's views about national poetry, for example, has already been pointed out). Štorch sees in symbol and myth independent forms of cognition, that independence of subjective action (the power of the spirit) whereby "objectivity remains with still greater force and integrity" in symbol, while "the activity of the spirit, entirely above objectivity, performs its play with it" in myth. Štorch emphasizes the philogenetic and ontogenetic meaning of these forms: "A mere glance at history shows that entire nations and ages have developed their cognition primarily in these directions and that their effort has not lacked benefit for humanity. If we remember, we shall find that all of us have followed the same paths at a certain age. If we have not followed them, it certainly was not to the benefit of the overall development of our cognition," for "particular aspects of the world open up to us" through these forms.

The mythology of *A Bouquet of National Legends* (*Kytice z pověstí národních*) and Erben's mythological treatises are closely connected. Although Grund recognizes their connection with Romantic science and philosophy, he discusses them from the perspective of positivist science. Therefore the results of his analysis are limited to an obvious finding: Erben's dubious philological methods and fallacious etymologizing on the whole deprive his conclusions of truth, and his references to customs are more valuable than his mythological interpretations which have been superseded by the results of modern scholarship. However, it is precisely these interpretations that interest us in connection with *A Bouquet* and the period's whole way of looking at things, and we must, of course, judge them in light of those tasks which Erben's research pursued.

Erben ostentatiously takes his position against the views of the Enlightenment. He sharply condemns these views as an expression of a self-satisfied, affected, putative culture. In mythology he seeks "a fine and profound sense," a natural symbolism and folk philosophy, which for him is the essence of true philosophy and symbolism in general, just as the folksong is for him the source of all true poetry.

What are the poems of *A Bouquet* for Erben? *A resurrected myth*—a myth which "has returned and has been embodied." A mythological study is merely a commentary, merely a set of notes on this myth. If we reversed this relationship and conceived the symbolism of Erben's poems as a mere illustration, a mere reflection, of his investigations, we would lose our understanding of the poetic myth that is the relevant epistemological justification of his works of art. But Grund proceeds precisely in this way when, for example, he asserts that "a belief in fate *ensuing from a scholarly conviction* about the existence of the Slavic Witches or Fates *is reflected* in his poetry." If we desire to establish a hierarchy of values, it is the opposite in this case. A belief is embodied in the poetry, and the regularity of this embodiment, that is, of a given concrete set of symbols, seeks verification in scholarly conviction.

How Grund, who was familiar with Erben's mythological studies, could place them in a program of "national classicality" is a mystery. For Erben the mythologist the whole world is a chain of symbols. Even the tricolor of the Russian monarchy bears tinges of the three fates. In saying "good day" to someone, we are complying with the myth which attributes a creative power to the word. Every word is a manifold symbol. "Sea" (*moře*) is a word with three meanings: the image of liquidity necessarily gives rise to the second meaning, inevitability (South Slavic *morati*); as a consequence the third meaning, destruction (*mořiti*), then results. The word "night" (*noc*) symbolizes necessity (*nutnost*); the word "day" (*den*) means in fact fate.

> Eternity (*věčnost*) and age (*věk*) have the same relationship as fertility (*plodnost*) and fruit (*plod*). Eternity is the origin and cause of age, including in this way what pertains to time in one with the concept of the necessity of the sea and night. But this results in still another important consequence: age (*věk*) and world (*svět*), confined together as one thing, like a long day, must at length pass in this way, whereupon such a long eternal night will follow.

If this visionary's labyrinth of concepts, images, and puns is not the mysticism of an utter Romantic and if there is, for example, a pinch of Classicism in the Görresian tuning of the fantastic vision of the inevitable cosmic night, then the boundary between Boileau and Paracelsus has been erased.

Erben's interpretation of the symbolism of folksongs, "of these valuable pearls preserved in their undisguised purity coming down from ancient ancestors," provides valuable impulses for the analysis of the symbolism of his *Bouquet of National Legends,* whose task is precisely to revive in unclouded purity the mythological legacy of ancient ancestors.

Let me pause on the ballad "The Willow" ("Vrba"), which Grund places in "the peak period of the poet's Classicism."[2] The theme of "The Willow" is the reality of two inseparable planes. This legend seems important to the poet, among other reasons, because a man shares his life with another thing "so that one without the other, the man without that thing and the thing without that man, could not last long." Grund omits the passage about this impossibility in a citation from Erben's *Commentary* (*Poznamenání*) although the poet puts the main emphasis precisely on this inevitable, necessary two-planed nature. These problems of the poem "The Willow" correspond exactly to Štorch's contemporaneous (1853) philosophical deliberation:

> The unity of the universe, the possibility of life, consists only in the fact that there is nothing solely individual which is only itself alone, and not at the same time also something else, though in a subordinate sense. For precisely because nothing is solely individual, because everything has its opposite attached to itself and in itself, the very possibility of uniting with another and with the whole, of being a co-microcosm in the great macrocosm of the

universe, lies in everything. On this is based the greatness of the law of tripartiteness, which in its highest conception says nothing but whatever one takes must be not only itself, i.e. an individual, but its opposite as well, i.e. something else, being put together with it into an inseparable one.

The beginning of the ballad is intentionally de-folklorized or generalized. The hero is introduced as a third person without further definition, and it is not accidental if the reader perhaps erroneously, perhaps subconsciously identifies the hero directly with the poet (Erben, writes Grund, "does not send the mother but *goes himself* to the old woman for advice"). The hero "sits down to breakfast in the morning," and for the first time in two years of life together he reveals to his young wife his nocturnal anxiety by means of an importunate question and a suggestion of an artificial remedy. Whether the psychologizing reader solves the balladic abbreviation "at night the body lies dead" as the languor of unreturned passion, as the dread of nocturnal solitude imposed by the dead sleep of the "beloved wife," or as a painful sensation of the inevitable alienation in the most intimate relationship, the husband's anxiety is consistently the tragedy of an incomplete conception. Whatever does not belong to him in the life of his wife the hero wrongly identifies as death. Thus in the young Erben's awkward dream, anxiety from the notion that the beloved "Miss B." does not belong to him ("but she still is not Mrs. Erben") turns into a dreadful thought about her demise. A sheer graveyard metaphor—a voice "singing out a funeral song" to the poet's happiness—turns into a symbolic suggestion of painful loss—"the silence which now spreads out in a deadly manner."

The wife in "The Willow" exhorts her husband to be humble before "what is destined." We know how carefully Erben the mythologist traces in Slavic proverbs and songs this adjective in which he finds "in human nature itself precisely that realization in the face of an assigned inevitability." The husband resorts to the "potent word" with which he infallibly charges the elements, but the wife knows that "the human word does not undo what fate bids someone." Here, as in the line about the hollow sciences from the ballad "Christmas Day" ("Štědrý den"), the poet speaks directly "about the mysterious beings who penetrate everything with their power, who direct all changes in the world, themselves not being subject to anyone, by whom both heaven and earth have been created and are to expire, about these inexorable preparers of fate which no one can escape and to which even the gods themselves must be subject." According to Erben, these beings are even concealed in the Christian images of the legend of Christ and St. Peter. The wife's admonitory, humble speech about the fates is the wise but nevertheless fatefully powerless human word. "In vain are your words, lady; your husband has a different intention." Of course, his attempt to undo the mandate of fate is likewise predestined, for the command of inevitability is not unambiguous: fate directs all changes in the world, and the assignment of human destiny is, in fact, a dialectical process, as Romantic philosophy outlines it. In a note on "The Willow" the poet directly points out: "One [fate] says: *This* will become of him. The second says: Not so, *this* will become of him. The third then always decides."

In what seemed to be death the hero recognizes another being (*Anderssein*), which "transcends the limits of human understanding." The reality belonging to and intelligible to the husband is therefore, as the ballad says, "only a half-life." The husband, however, lays claim to an entire reality: "My wife shall live with me." The symbol of the other being, the willow with the white bark, miraculously linked to his wife's soul, has to be destroyed. The interpenetration of the two planes of reality is sharply emphasized. The man's exclamation "Let the willow rot in the ground" foretells murder in an anthropomorphic image. The demise of the willow is compared to the woman's demise: "He cut the willow off at the roots . . . it fell heavily . . . it murmured, it sighed as a mother passing away, as a dying mother looking around for her child." The same comparison announces the simultaneous death of the wife; however, what had been literal meaning has become metaphorical meaning and vice versa: "Your beloved wife died as if she had been slashed by a scythe . . . she fell like a tree being cut down; she sighed in dying, looking around for her child." Thus there are two shots, two equally valid aspects of the same indivisible reality. The destruction of one of the symbolic pair necessarily destroys the other symbol. The struggle for a complete life turns into murder. He who wished to gain full control over his wife's life is deprived of "a half-life." What before only apparently wished to molder now molders in earnest.

Is it a real death? "What the earth creates it again destroys. But nothing goes to waste." The third fate intervenes. "Number three is the arbitrator between the first two, whether for the good or the bad side; the fulfillment of perfection lies in three." The wife-willow lives on as the mother. And again, according to Erben's expression, "the farthest opposites—whiteness and blackness, life and death—meet in one."

What can be further from classical or classicizing art than this gravitation toward the laws of polarity and unity of constantly struggling antitheses, these invariable, capricious reversals of "the farthest opposites," this irrational union of an empirical reality with an unfathomable superreality, this symbolism investing metaphor with a claim to objective meaning? Every attempt at a rationalizing, classically unambiguous interpretation of a polysemic myth in Erben's *Bouquet* forcibly transforms the richness of the myth into the ordinariness of textbook instruction.

Grund finds in "The Willow" a celebration of motherhood and at the same time forgets that "in the word *mother* is brought together everything which romance has sought, desired, and for which it has longed," as the critic Baeumler puts it, and that "the celebration of motherhood" in this ballad is in fact a pure Romantic intensification of the unity of opposites. In the terms of Erben's mythology, the end is simultaneously a continuation—the mother dies, motherhood lives. In her mysterious nocturnal life, however, the heroine of "The Willow" is indifferent to her baby ("without that little one, bitterly crying, waking you up"). A living mother in Erben's poems destroys her child. Here we have another union of "the farthest opposites"—birth and murder or, in Erben's terms, a beginning and an end. "From its very beginning each creation has from its creator the embryo of its decay and destruction lodged within itself." Fate as the mother in labor merges with "fate as death incarnate, which again obliterates man from the world . . . again sends him back into the dark lap of the universal mother of inevitability from which he has come." Erben the mythologist recognizes fate in the Ukrainian song about the mother-snake who eats her children. Erben the poet depicts a mother who has killed her only child and in her own mother recognizes the source of her own destruction ("A Daughter's Curse" ["Dceřina kletba"]), a mother who in her exacting love for her child in fact destroys his life, like the evil mother-snake who jealously deprives her son of "the flower of life" and is cursed by him ("The Lily" ["Lilie"]), or the mother who does not let her daughter out of her sight and thus condemns her baby to death ("The Water Sprite" ["Vodník"]), and finally the mother who, for a while preoccupied with her own life, unconsciously causes the loss of

386

a child ("Pitch-Boil" ["Smolný var"], "The Treasure" ["Poklad"], "The Noon Spirit" ["Polednice"]). In brief, the life of a mother and the life of a child almost mutually exclude each other, which after all also occurs in the older mystical tradition.

The Karamazovian theme of a construction associated with the damnation of a child compelled Erben to write his study "A Sacrifice to the Earth" ("Obětování zemi"). When they walled up a child, "he was eating a roll and calling: 'Mommy, I still see you' and then later: 'Mommy, I still see a bit of you,' and when they inserted the last stone: 'Mommy, I do not see you anymore.'" For Erben the walling up is a manifestation of the unity of antitheses, "construction-destruction" or "love-ruin," and he does not require, as the poem "The Walled-Up One" ("Zazděná") attests, any closer and more rational justification.

Amorous love in Erben's poems is just as ambiguous as maternal love. It is always saturated with death. One of the two lovers is either an artificially revived dead man ("The Wedding Shirts" ["Svatební ko-šile"], the second marriage in "The Golden Spinning Wheel" ["Zlatý kolovrat"], "The Lily") or a murderer ("The Little Dove" ["Holou-bek"], the "mature sin" in "The Golden Spinning Wheel"). Hana's wedding in "Christmas Day" seems to be an exception, but it appears as a mere member of a parallelism, that is, the counterpart to Marie's death, and the conclusion of the ballad takes account only of her tragic part and forgets that in fact only Marie learned through prophecy the *awful* certainty, whereas Hana's vision and its realization were, on the contrary, joyful. Precisely in this way does Baeumler formulate it in his explication of Romantic mythology: "Den Hochzeitsjubel übertönt ewig die wehvoll ernste Totenklage" (the woefully serious dirge drowns out the wedding celebration). In "Christmas Day," which has a different compositional solution, a wedding shirt also merges with a shroud, the symbolism of marriage and birth with funeral symbolism.

How could it happen that a classical ideology was attributed to Erben's poems so that Grund proclaims even the identification of life and a dream in the *pointe* of "Christmas Day" ("A human life as a dream"), directly repeating Mácha's reflection, "Perhaps this life is sleeping," as a "classical image"? The scholar has forgotten, as it were, that besides the Romanticism of proud and destructive rebellion, besides the revolutionary Romanticism which Mácha and Janko Král' embody in Czechoslovak poetry, world literature also knows the antirevolutionary variation of the same artistic movement—the Romanticism of resignation—and Erben is precisely one of its most typical and most extreme representatives. We are the puppets of fate; everything is inexorably predestined, and "nowhere is there a remedy for what is destined at birth." Reconcile yourself to fate even if it seems that you have only a half-life. In vain can you seek a remedy. Do not even seek changes through prayer. Desires are illusory, and the return of the beloved and the abridgment of life—an apparent contradiction—are in reality identical. A longed-for world changes into its direct opposite—day is night and night is day; a garden in flower is a mere graveyard, and a desire turns into its opposite—into a prayer for warding off the beloved and the saving of life. A maiden "unworthily" complained about living a half-life and, now half-dead, longs only to be brought back into it again.[3] You live "in awkward uncertainty," and you do not even know whether you have taken as your wife a beloved maiden or a snake who has murdered her and is like her "as an eye to an eye in one head." An apparent identity is in reality a contradiction.

Grund speaks about Erben's "positive attitude toward life" as "a principle of Czech classicality"; however, deadly *fear* is the most intimate experience for Erben. The poet dreads knowledge of the awful certainty and prefers "to dream in false hope with sheer darkness before him."[4] The mythologist speaks as an expert about "the chilling fear which washes over the ordinary man" and about the vampirelike nightmare which manifests itself in "the crushing of a man in his sleep, as if a stone lay on his chest, and in weighty, troubled dreams." Weighty and troubled are "the dark dreams" of the consumptive Erben ("the air constricting the chest"), and when he wakes up, he notes: "Terror suffused me in chills." In "Accidental Phenomena" ("Úkazy náhodné") he constantly repeats: "A chill suffused my body," "terror gripped me again," and so forth. Záhoř's dream is of the same kind ("it grips me tightly, chokes me, and suffocates me; I stagger—I am already falling—there is no life in me"). Fear of gratifying a desire, shyness before a woman, permeates the dreams of the young Erben and suggests to him a myth entrusting to women the control of fate: "Everywhere human life hangs on their yarn."

Hněvkovský's letter to the twenty-five-year-old Erben is characteristic: "Ich muss es euch geradezu sagen, dass Ihr nicht zweimal einen Geliebten vorstellen kennet; denn Ihr sitzt und wieder sitzt und spielt Forte-Piano, ohne das verliebte Mädchen durch einen verliebten Blick,

Händedruck oder süssen Kuss etc. von der Gegenliebe zu überzeugen" (I must frankly say that you could not present yourself twice as a lover; for you sit and sit again and play "Forte-Piano," without convincing the infatuated girl of your own love through so much as a loving glance, a touch, or a sweet kiss). The dreams recorded by Erben are typical amatory dreams with a conventional suggestive landscape and other symbolic props of erotic visions ("a jumble like thick fog . . . in a narrow and deep gorge," "a deep gorge across which arches a narrow bridge," "some dark, narrow, and damp cave," steep mysterious rises and falls, a man "with long rods," a man "staggering around the sitting room with his head in his hand," and the like). A secret desire to escape the realization of love suggests to Erben numerous pretexts for escape. It seems to him that "some duty" urgently demands his presence elsewhere. Furthermore he is at a loss whether he should enter the bride's apartment "or postpone it to a more appropriate time" for the patently illogical reason that "in the morning the sky seemed cloudy." Then he finds that he is dressed only for the house in his shirt sleeves, and he dares not go further; then no one answers; therefore she is not at home; the longed-for maiden changes into her opposite; instead of a bride, two repulsive substitutes alternate, "strange female creatures . . . about forty years old," slovenly and with coarse voices. The ultimate and paramount justification of the impossibility of experiencing love arises: the substitutes make it understood that she has died.

The second of the dreams recorded by Erben must also have furnished him with reasons for concluding that "it isn't good to be here," or reasons for escape. Here too there is an ugly substitute for the poet's bride, "a woman about forty years old," who is already extremely pregnant; moreover, she even has a monstrous child, and yet she is a bride asking for a dowry (financial difficulties also impeded the poet's marriage). Here the gift likewise symbolizes an amatory gift. But Erben gets frightened and "quickly turns back." The same motif comprises the sole content of his "Accidental Phenomena" (a loathsome old woman with a face like death; he would gladly have given her a gift but, terror-stricken, he was not able to get near her, and so on). The pregnant beggarwoman is replaced by another one (there were also two substitutes in the first dream), and shyness about the gift is motivated by the fact that the woman "did not ask for anything." Another justification for denigrating the superfluousness of the attempt is that the woman remains indifferent, as if it were only a matter of "a broken nail." This metaphorical image immediately turns into another motif which in fact is only a variation of the theme of the two substitutes. Erben finds someone else's hat on the nail instead of his own, and while he calls in vain "Who has my hat?" this other person's hat is replaced by yet another, which is also someone else's and even worse: "a worn-out gray hat that moreover did not even fit my head." These intimate themes even penetrate Erben's ballad writing. In vain do you burn with love; in vain do you compete for the object of love; it does not belong to you; it is not yours—hence it is someone else's; it is not yours—hence it does not exist; it is dead, and what you have is only a deceptive substitute.

Why in fact does Erben object to Mácha (or rather to Mácha's *May,* for we must not forget Mácha the poet of *An Echo of Folksongs* [*Ohlas písní národních*])? He does not rebuke Czech Byronism for the theme of sorrow or the "dark, macabre, sepulchral images," since the critic's own work is full of them. What takes him aback is that the "splenetic malcontent" elaborates this set of themes "without a loftier aim," and thus he necessarily gets into conflicts with God, with himself, and with the whole world; that he laments sorrow without trying to understand its cause; and that he pursues "a lost idea." Modern research on irrational expressions discerns two tendencies in experiences of terror—one ontogenetic and the other philogenetic. In *May* Mácha proceeds in the first direction. He seeks to ward off "the power of terror" by means of an infantile dream ("far off his dream . . . mankind's lost paradise, the age of my childhood"); he pursues a lost idea; he excludes himself from the established order and enters into conflict with God, the world, and himself as a mature, regulated member of the given order and condemns everything that stands in the way of his dream as the nonsensical source of sorrow. Erben ironically replies with a folk ditty, "Whether it is thus or so, surely it will be one way or another: for one creature the world will not perish." Erben, like Štorch, considers "the self-ruling individuality of people" to be the negative pole of poetry, and to the rebellion of personality he opposes a "higher" philogenetic tendency, *a passive humility before a universally obligatory myth.* In *May* the superstition of common people is exploited as a mere intermezzo permeating the egocentric lyricism, but Erben even interprets the delirium of a woman in parturition, lying in a faint, philogenetically: "There would not have been that certain image always recurring in the same way if a firm belief in these creatures had not already prepared it in advance."

Souček's study, the most penetrating written on Erben, concludes that the first edition of the poem about Záhoř ("Záhoř I") "was supposed to be a triumphant intellectual and artistic contradiction, a palinode of *May*." In the spirit of rebellious European literature of the 1830s,[5] Mácha definitely sided with the son in the fatal father-son conflict. The leading stratum of Czech society, however, demanded through the most eminent critics that the patricide be condemned by the poet in an exemplary manner and that he surrender to God at least in his final hour, that "he breach his contract with eternal death and return to the source of eternal life." Erben attempted to comply with this "social demand" through the figure of Záhoř. Grund's objections to Souček's interpretations are not convincing. The ideological antithesis of the two contexts is indisputable. Opponents of *May* could not rebuke Mácha for the mildness of the punishment ("broken limb by limb," and such), but they could criticize him for the fact that the murderer and the poet siding with him do not admit their guilt and the justice of the punishment ("Whose guilt will the next day avenge?"). Záhoř, however, writhes in terror at the thought of his "guilt which neither a fierce flame can thwart, which neither the rain nor rivers of blood can wash away" and of the torments of hell about which there is not even a thought in *May*. "Vilém," emphasizes Grund, "is the poet's fiction; any more precise depiction does not matter; he only voices Mácha's subjective reflections, while Záhoř is a character of flesh and blood, an objective image of a robber." But precisely through this objectification Erben makes it impossible for the poet to merge with the hero, for which contemporary criticism reproached Mácha. Neither the friendly relations of the two antipodes, to which Grund refers, nor the obvious formal dependence of "Záhoř I" on *May* in any way, of course, rules out an attempt at a palinode, and Souček rightly states that the young poet in an effort to overcome *May* unconsciously yielded to its influence.

I believe that precisely for this reason "Záhoř I" remained unfinished, and only after several years of attempts did Erben realize his poetic protest against Mácha's epochal work. The monologues of "Záhoř I" about death and fate after death, pointed against Vilém's monologues, are gone in *Záhoř's Bed (Záhořova lože)*. The plot acquires more of an epic quality. The euphony of the final edition is much more sober and discreet, whereas "Záhoř I" accumulated in a Máchovian way repetitions of speech-sound groups, frequently colored by puns, sometimes associated with etymological figures.[6] But despite the conscious toning down of the connection with the model, the polemic between *Záhoř's Bed* and *May* remains obvious. "To the different periods of human life," to the tragedy of human passions, Mácha opposes the exultation of nature. Erben, however, rejects this contradiction—the autumnal whisper of the leaves on the oak tree corresponds to the tragedy of man's journey toward death, and for whoever understands it "there is nothing to laugh at," just as whoever heard Vilém's whisper before death never smiled again. In his depiction of the cycle of nature Erben imitates Mácha's abbreviations inspired by Horace's *annorum series et fuga temporum* (*May:* "Lovely May passed, the spring flower faded, and summer blazed; then the summer time passed, autumn and winter as well—and spring came again; until the flight of time had already carried away many years . . . Many a stormy vortex had transported me into a profound sorrow . . . It was again evening—the first of May." *Záhoř's Bed:* "Winter passed . . . Spring faded—summer . . . leaves are falling . . . Ninety years had flown by the world; in the meantime much had changed since that time . . . It is again spring"). But whereas the natural events in Mácha's poem are divested of any transcendental meaning ("Never—nowhere—no purpose"), the coming of spring in *Záhoř's Bed* heralds eternal life. As a symbol of unacceptable, nonsensical, never justifiable death, the scaffold towers menacingly above the landscape of *May* ("there a little hill stands, on it there is a tall stake, on the stake a wheel is looming"). Likewise a "little hill" lies over the landscape of *Záhoř's Bed,* but above it looms emblematically an image of Jesus Christ crucified, providently pointing with his left hand to the gates of hell, the just fate of damned souls.

The "awful lord of the woods," the perpetrator of unheard-of deeds, the robber Vilém killed his father and thereby "carried out a twofold revenge," for it was his father who had banished Vilém and seduced his love. The murderer should be executed, but he denies the legitimacy of this verdict and his own guilt, because he has been the mere administrator of his father's punishment ("Was I only enticed into the dream of life just to punish his guilt?"). This revenge and love are, in fact, the only meaning of life for him. Images of the cradle and the coffin, of his mother, of his beloved land, and of his mistress coalesce in Vilém's apostrophe before death. Vilém's destruction is suggested by the image "Into his mother, into his mother a son's blood flows upon her." There follows the hymn to beautiful infantile time and to an eternal tormenting love.

"The man of the woods," the robber Záhoř, a multiple murderer, has committed a crime which is not named ("Don't ask me anything") but which can be guessed from the most severe of the infernal punishments that Satan has meted out to him. Patricide is mentioned directly in "Záhoř I." Why then is the name of Záhoř's supreme crime suppressed in the final edition? Was the poet masking his model? Was he heeding the censorship of the 1850s which so scrupulously eliminated from literature the conflict between father and son that in the Prague production of *Kabale und Liebe,* for example, the father had to be replaced by the uncle? Or was the patricide disguised by Erben for reasons of internal censorship? The theme of the father's guilt and the apostrophe to the mother, essential elements of the final edition, were missing in "Záhoř I," and against their background the motif of patricide would have revealed the Oedipus complex too harshly.

The poet divested the crime of motivation and thereby made Záhoř worse. The malefactor's weighty guilt is therefore beyond doubt, and indisputably "just is the divine hand of revenge." Although Erben kept Mácha's theme of the father's guilt, he split Vilém: he let Záhoř have the role of the murderer, whereas he gave the pilgrim everything that arouses sympathy toward Vilém—the role of outlaw and the splenetic sorrow (*May:* "He whispering softly—softly and softly . . . In his heart a terrible grief . . . And a profound sorrow grips his heart; he sighs deeply—tear chases tear." *Záhoř's Bed:* "Perhaps sorrow is buried in your heart? . . . Now whispering something, shedding tears from his eyes, now he sighs again—heavily, from the bottom of his heart"). The son cursed by his father absolves the son who has cursed his father in the name of the Son condemned to torture by the Father. The image of the pilgrim ("Unknown pilgrim in the gloomy habit, with that cross in your hand on the long staff and with that rosary—who are you anyway, where are you now going toward evening? Where are you hurrying?") is certainly evoked by the conclusion of *May* ("Do you see a pilgrim, who is rushing to his destination across a long meadow before the red of the evening sky fades away?"). But whereas according to Mácha "your gaze will never more behold this pilgrim as he disappears behind that cliff on the horizon, never—oh never," Záhoř's anxiety about "whether the pilgrim will again return" is unfounded. Mácha recognizes in the disappearing pilgrim an image of his future life rushing toward death, but Erben's pilgrim brings Záhoř precisely a guarantee of a future life in heaven. In opposition to *May,* which pays tribute to eternally beautiful—in its transitoriness—earthly life, Erben preaches "kneel and wait." The pilgrim's slogan, "God's grace is endless," directly paraphrases *May*'s leitmotif, "Love is endless."

Erben takes pains to de-eroticize the images of *May*. He divests the description of vernal nature of Mácha's amatory symbolism. "It is again spring. A warm breeze blows, the fresh grass sways in the meadows; the nightingale once again tells his tales, and the violet once again gives off a new fragrance," whereas in *May*: "The soft moss whispered about love, the blooming tree lied about love's sorrow, the nightingale sang his love to the rose, a fragrant sigh revealed a rose." He downgrades Vilém's dreamed-of parting with the tearful girl to a purely metaphorical image of a youth's parting "from his dear maiden" to which he juxtaposes reality—the pilgrim's ardent kneeling before the crucifix.

If Mácha's poem about a patricide culminates in an apotheosis of childhood and love for the mother, the image of the mother making the child Záhoř's bed also turns up in Erben. According to Souček's subtle observation, this image replaced Záhoř's original dream about the bloody bed of his dying father calling to the murderer: "Are you the one, son? What do you want here?" Both images turn into visions of hell. In the final edition there is the dreadful image of Záhoř's infernal bed, much more terrible than the cruel breaking of bones and hence Vilém's analogous torture. This central chain of images, as the very title of the poem attests, is fine evidence of that "higher," philogenetic, mythological tendency which Erben found lacking in the dark images of *May*.[7]

Once again Erben tried to correct Mácha and to blunt his edge. In his "Prophecy for the Marriage of Franz Joseph I" ("Věštba ke sňatku Františka Josefa I," 1854), he "contents himself," as Grund observes, "with a simple tribute to the imperial couple without saying anything to the sovereign about his duty to the loyal Czech nation." But the obvious model for "Prophecy," Mácha's poem "On the King's Arrival" ("Na příchod krále," 1835), invests the speeches of the guardians of Prague and the Czech land with eloquent political allusions. Despite Grund's opinion that Erben "was miles from Mácha" as early as the forties, there is a clear connection—metrical, motivational, and textual—between the two poems.[8]

In his politically radical book *Our Men* (*Naši mužové*, 1862) Erben's contemporary Sojka rightly identifies what Grund calls "the principle of Czech classicality" in the poet's works as the typical lullabies of a legitimizing Romanticism. The closest and most eloquent analogue of Erben's world view is found in Štorch's essays of the fifties sharply condemning the Enlightenment and its heritage, the irreligious culture of the nineteenth century, which destroys understanding for authority ("Our time cannot tolerate anything outstanding, anything which could be obeyed, which could be worshipped with a genuine and profound respect"). Štorch warns against the serpent which a selfish modern culture "itself nourishes in its own home"; the proletariat, "until now only a domestic annoyance," is "now, if God does not foil it, a severe storm and a universal misfortune." Dread of conceited interferences, commotions, and collapse of order, a pious humility before the status quo, respect for any sort of censorship, a dreamy quietism obscuring reality—such is the concrete content of that "positive attitude toward life" which Grund finds in contrast to Mácha's "seditious tendency" ("And do not cry out that I am destroying your edifice") in *A Bouquet,* the most distinguished work of Czech poetry published (*habent sua fata libelli*) during the reactionary Bach period when there was, according to Erben's own journal entry, "everywhere only fear and apprehension." The same feeling resounds in the aphoristic abbreviation of a stern German observer of Prague at that time, August Schleicher: "Everyone is born in fear, lives in fear, and dies in fear."

Mácha and Erben are of course two great antipodes, but it is not the antithesis of Romanticism and Classicism, and it is not "the morals of insanity" overcome by a healthy and positive attitude toward life. On the contrary, they are opposite branches of the same literary movement: a Romanticism transforming reality as opposed to a passive Romantic escape from reality, an ecstasy of life ("How beautiful the world!") opposed to its ascetic negation. The revolutionary moods of the thirties provoked a reaction against themselves.

The political opportunism exhibited by Erben in the fifties is also certainly closely connected to this so-called positive attitude. It would be more timely to present a *sociological analysis* of the two extremes of Czechoslovak Romanticism and to verify on the basis of Erben's life and works the correctness of an opinion from Masaryk's *Havlíček*—"a reaction not only Bachovian but also in us ourselves"—than to continue in the tradition of commemorative biographies and to suppress in various ways those facts in a writer's life which cannot be educational models. Grund remarks that Erben stood aloof from Božena

Němcová for a longer time "not because she was under police surveillance but rather for emotional reasons." But why does the scholar not cite Erben's own admission from a letter to Šembera: "I cannot call on her . . . for I know that she is under strict surveillance and that attention is paid to everyone who goes near her"? Attempts at an apology for the poet's opportunism are even more peculiar. Grund relates how an external reversal in Erben's political opinions occurred in 1853 on account of oppressive public conditions, how the notorious Sacher-Masoch recommended him as a politically reliable man, how the poet had to buy back governmental trust, how he resigned from the board of the Committee for the Establishment of a Czech National Theater, how he dedicated books to the Emperor, to Bach, and to Thun, and how in general he strove by various deeds to evoke the impression of a completely progovernment citizen. And the scholar adds to his defense: "An official appointed to the municipal authorities only through the intercession of the government party, a writer whose possible deposing from office would have threatened all his plans so long deferred because of adversity, a man broken by illness . . . a father who had to count his money . . . if he were to send his wife and children on vacation to relatives in far-away Žebrák . . . he *could not risk and toy with the disfavor of the government*. But the official avowal of a loyal sentiment, which obliged him to nothing and which manifested itself primarily in a natural respect for the sovereign, restored to Erben the trust of the police."

I think that precisely in such cases a modern literary historian should carefully bear in mind Havlíček and Božena Němcová. After all, it is not by chance that attempts to solve the ideological quarrel over Mácha versus Erben in favor of the latter should occur just now, and that Erben's opportunism is painstakingly defended. But the barrenness of such attempts is equally typical.

CHAPTER 21

In Memory of V. V. Hanka

Seventy years ago Prague buried Václav Hanka (1791–1861). An unprecedented and unforgetable spectacle, the eyewitnesses unanimously exclaimed. The newspaper *National Pages* wrote:

> The funeral of Hanka, imposing and majestic, was indeed a national event in the literal sense of the word. The details are beyond description. Everything in Prague that personified culture, nobility, and patriotism appeared in uncountable, boundless crowds. Without exaggeration one can estimate the numbers of participants at forty to fifty thousand. Provincial towns and villages were represented by large delegations. Clergy, people in house windows, balconies filled beyond capacity, onlookers even on the rooftops! The coffin was decorated with an enormous laurel wreath, attached to the Slavic tricolor ribbons.

The cream of the nation gathered around the coffin: František Palacký, F. L. Rieger, J. V. Frietch, and others. There were Serbs in fezes, Poles in confederation caps. The pupils of Hanka carried a magnificent copy of the multilingual edition of the Královédvorský Manuscript on a velvet cushion crowned with laurels, next to which lay the Russian medals of the deceased.

> The Governor, the Rector heading the University professors, the
> learned societies, the schoolteachers, writers, artists, all the stu-
> dents of Prague, the city's inhabitants, an endless crowd, over four
> hundred torches and two hundred candles . . . The multilingual
> edition of the Královédvorský Manuscript was placed in the grave
> . . . What a magnificent procession! Czechs and Germans, aristo-
> crats and commoners, all who knew and honored Hanka marched
> abreast, united in brotherly fashion by the same noble impulse to
> pay final tribute to the departed son of the nation.

Soon after Hanka's death his biographer wrote: "Hanka is a man
who has a full right to take his place among the most meritorious and
popular representatives of the Czecho-Moravian nation. His name will
remain forever linked with that of the Královédvorský Manuscript,
which he revealed to the world." He did not foresee the ominous sense
that these words would soon take on. In the 1880s Czech scholarship
burst into an embittered debate over the two literary monuments that
had created Hanka's fame, the Královédvorský and Zelenohorský
Manuscripts. This dispute captivated not just scholarly circles, not just
the linguists and students of literature, the historians and sociologists;
it was carried out in the streets, engaged politicians and journalists,
and for a long time roused society as a whole. As a result of the years-
long polemics, accompanied by a thorough and multifaceted study of
both manuscripts, Hanka's so recently acquired and universal fame as
the discoverer of these incomparable pearls of Old Czech poetry was
forever destroyed. It was proven with irreversible certainty and finality
that the Královédvorský and Zelenohorský Manuscripts were skillful
forgeries fabricated at the beginning of the nineteenth century. It became clear that the main, if not the sole, perpetrator of the forgery was
none other than Václav Hanka. Enthusiastic panegyrics in Hanka's
honor were replaced by bitter pamphlets. If, earlier, all the imprudent
skeptics who had dared doubt the authenticity of the celebrated manuscripts suffered the most relentless criticism, now the target of defa-
mation became Hanka himself. Not long before people had claimed
that he was "a man of unusual straightforwardness, who practically did
not know the words for such vices of modern times as cunning, deception, tricks, and unscrupulousness" (*National Pages,* January 1861).
After the manuscripts were exposed as a forgery, he was depicted as
nothing less than an inveterate scoundrel, a dishonest dissembler and
intrigant. In vain did scholars of other Slavic countries (V. Jagić, V. A.
Francev) recall Hanka's indisputable merits; in vain did they insist that

a more objective attitude toward him should be taken. Their words went unheeded, just as during the years of the imperturbable fame of the manuscripts the Slovenian scholar B. Kopitar was ignored when he warned against a totally uncritical trust in Hanka and his discoveries.

Hanka was, without a doubt, one of the most outstanding representatives of the Czech National Revival. He was extraordinarily versatile in his activities. For his time he was a rare connoisseur of Old Czech literature, and he popularized it with skill and taste. His contributions to the reform of Czech orthography and to the creation and growth of the Czech Museum, with its incomparable manuscript and book collections, were significant. Hanka occupies an honored place in the history of Czech-Russian and Czech-Polish cultural relations. The newly born Slavic studies in Russia found in him one of its most devoted and gifted inspirers. But the most striking and richest fruits of Hanka's activities were doubtlessly the Královédvorský and Zelenohorský Manuscripts.

There is a great deal about the history of the manuscripts that remains to this day both puzzling and astonishing. Hanka's intuition was staggering. He was not a prominent scholar: his grammatical and literary-historical works are quite mediocre. Yet he was able to create the illusion of Old Czech and of Old Czech poetic form so convincingly and in such a refined way that it required many decades of intensive development in Czech philology, along with the meticulous work of such a great scholar as Jan Gebauer, before it was possible to clearly expose the manuscripts as forgeries. V. Flajšhans illustrates Hanka's refinement with a striking example. In the manuscript of the Old Czech legend of St. Prokop there is one page missing. In his edition of the legend, Hanka, guided by the corresponding Latin text, filled in this lacuna with verses of his own devising. For decades scholars took this interpolation for a genuine part of the legend. Misled by the skillfulness of the imitation, they even failed to notice the parentheses with which Hanka himself had bracketed his concoction! As Flajšhans notes, Hanka indeed knew many things better and more precisely than Palacký, Josef Fejfalík, and others. Indeed, in this respect he outstripped his time: so masterfully had the editor inserted the verses that even Hanka's teacher Josef Dobrovský had failed to distinguish his pupil's addition to the manuscript.

It is indeed difficult to say what is more astonishing: the artistic gift of the author of the Královédvorský Manuscript, his philological intuition, or finally the extraordinary skill with which he hid all traces of his forgery of the manuscripts. If one rejects the disputable deciphering of the cryptograms in the Zelenohorský Manuscript, one has to admit that, despite all the footwork of scholars, no one has succeeded in finding any *direct* evidence against Hanka. The history of the preparation of the manuscripts was hidden from the eyes of both Hanka's contemporaries and their curious descendants. One can only hazard a guess as to who participated in the "discovery" of the manuscripts, so totally successful was the conspiracy. And this happened in that same talkative Prague in which, as Mixail Bakunin wrote, any secret was known to everyone in an instant.

A grand old man of the Czech literary world, Antál Stašek, relates how Hanka, already advanced in years, once showed visiting Russian scholars the treasures of the Czech Museum. The guests examined with enthusiasm the Královédvorský Manuscript, and one of them was prompted to cry out indignantly: "Are there really such madmen who believe that you composed it? This kind of masterpiece would be beyond even your capacity." Eyewitnesses report that Hanka shuddered.

The poet Jiří Karásek ze L'vovic, one of the most gifted of the Czech Symbolists, wrote a witty article about the author of the Královédvorský Manuscript. He wondered why this great poet, who was destined to occupy a primary place on the Czech Parnassus of the nineteenth century, had sacrificed throughout his life his personal literary vanity with an almost ascetic humility, why he had voluntarily taken an oath of everlasting silence and had observed it so strictly. Some accused Hanka of being vain, but Karásek poses a psychologically legitimate question: how can we explain the fact that he did not unmask himself? He certainly could have spoken out at an appropriate time and declared: "Ladies and gentlemen, I am that genius to whom are due all the laurels of glorification. I thank you for the honor of designating me the lucky man who found these poetic treasures. But as a connoisseur of the Old Czech language, I made fools of you! And from now on I prefer that you honor me as a genuine poet who outgrew and overshadowed all of you. The only poetic works that you were capable of proved to be either nauseating syrup and sugar or unexperienced and clumsy naiveté, formless, rough-hewn logs . . . Only a genius is capable of preparing, in an epoch of literary gruel, a poetic dish so strong, an artistic meal so rich . . . And this genius is none other than myself, Václav Hanka, chevalier of the Russian order, a respectable scholar and patriotic versifier."

This monologue, however, was never to be spoken. Hanka was a zealous and faithful executor of social demands. When he appeared on the scene, what society needed was not so much new eminent literary figures as, first and foremost, new proofs of a great past. The direct testimonies of contemporaries about this "demand" are characteristic. These testimonies were collected by I. J. Hanuš, a renowned student of the manuscripts. Thus, for example, according to Palacký, Czech patriots complained that Czech literature lacked an epos comparable to that of the Russians or Serbs. The poet and philologist V. A. Svoboda, who presumably was one of Hanka's adherents, wrote: "In recent years, when noble national aspirations have awakened, when there appeared strong, inspired people who began to speak in Czech with the Czech nation, everyone was saddened by the absence of national poetry from the past. Such poetry, everyone thought, would be the necessary premise and basis for an entire new national culture." It is quite understandable that in such an epoch the scholarly work of Pavel Josef Šafařík, who was able to show the high cultural level and moral perfection of the Old Slavs, became a *social* event of the first importance.

Scholars of the Romantic period painted the national past in bright strokes. In "restoring" the picture of the ancient way of life, its customs and beliefs, they gave their fantasy free reign. A Middle Ages without bards or epic poetry seemed to them a contradiction in terms. If no epos had come down to us, it could mean only that the following centuries had wiped away all traces of it: the oral tradition had died out, the manuscripts had been destroyed. But one could reconstruct the hypothetical content and artistic form of such works by using the comparative method, and the plausibility of such reconstructions was not so inferior to the authenticity of the grammatical forms established by the Romantic linguists of the time. From the point of view of the scientific Weltanschauung of the period, it would be a grave error to conclude from the lack of preserved monuments that they simply did not exist: would it not be better to try to reconstruct these treasures that were lost by chance? Thus the line separating the quasi-scientific dreams and literary mystifications of the Romantics became obliterated in principle.

The nouveau riche who is quick to cover his walls with fabricated "portraits of ancestors" is repulsive. But is there any historian who would condemn a revolutionary for his forged residence permit? The Czech national movement was clearly of a revolutionary nature. Revolutionary tactics demanded that the right of the Czech folk heritage to national status be proved to the inert Czech philistine as well as to neighboring peoples. A heroic past was considered the essential feature of a nation, and the proof of that past was the heroic epic. The pressing task was to present to the world national legends from the remote past. It is not by chance that the first edition of the Královédvorský Manuscript (1818) was already supplied with a German translation; later a broad propaganda effort for the manuscripts was conducted abroad, both in Western Europe and in Russia, and became one of the primary goals of Hanka and his supporters.

At the beginning of the nineteenth century, the concepts of "native land" and "fatherland"—the country of one's fathers—were synonymous. The words of the philosopher about "countries of children," which exist alongside "fatherlands," had not yet been pronounced. Bohemia of the time was a typical "country of children": historical traditions were almost totally obliterated and lost; everything lay in the future. But what the ruling Weltanschauung of the epoch demanded in the meantime was a genealogy that could be traced to the remote darkness of past centuries.

There is a story about Pope Sixtus V. He had foreseen precisely the mood of his fellow cardinals: only a decrepit old man could count on being elected pope. From then on, no one saw him without a staff. He seemed less a man than a senile remnant of the past. Finally the election took place, and the staff was cast off: an old man's habits no longer served his purpose. His taking up of the staff and his casting it away were both gestures equally full of pathos. In the discovery and subsequent unmasking of the Královédvorský Manuscript there is just as much historical dramatism. The "discovery" of the manuscripts was evaluated as a triumph of historical justice: the great past of a people was revealed and proved, despite the accidental loss of covering vouchers. The manuscripts fulfilled their role, as did the mythology of historicism. But a new Weltanschauung fought its way onto the scene, and the annullment of the manuscripts proceeded in turn under the sign of triumphant truth.

The ideological function of the manuscripts is clear. No less interesting, however, is the literary-historical aspect of the question. Hanuš is right in stating that nothing in Czech poetry of the 1810s can be compared with the Královédvorský and Zelenohorský Manuscripts. One can even be so bold as to say that the manuscripts were the highest achievement of Czech verbal art during the first quarter of the nineteenth century. Particularly striking is a comparison of the manuscripts with the poems to which Hanka signed his name. Similar features point to a common authorship. But how pathetically poor is the literary level of these exercises in versification when placed next to the genuine poetry of the manuscripts! Why did the attempts of the time at original Czech poetry prove to be weak sophomoric exercises, while fabrications of ancient epics won general recognition? There is not a single work of Czech poetry of the nineteenth century that can compete with the manuscripts in the number of translations into foreign languages—all Slavic languages, almost all the languages of Western Europe, Goethe being among the translators. No other work inspired so many Czech composers and painters; no other work influenced so deeply the future development of the nation's poetry and literary language.

At the beginning of the nineteenth century, the emergence of modern Czech poetry was prevented by the fact that the stage preparatory to it had not yet been completed. It was still necessary to create a Czech literary language. The Czech tradition had been so deeply disrupted that it was difficult to utilize in a genuine way the treasure trove of the Old Czech language or its poetic forms. The abundance of archaisms met with a lack of understanding on the part of the reading public and with the protests of critics. Even so, it was only in the distant past that a model for a high poetic and linguistic culture could be found. For a Czech Romantic poet, archaisms were indispensable, but they had to be justified. Moreover, they had to be explained: a poetic work saturated with antiquated language required detailed commentaries, and the right to make such commentaries had in turn to be justified. Only under the cover of an archaic pseudonym, only under the mask of a medieval poet, was it possible at the beginning of the nineteenth century to imitate the great poetry of the Middle Ages. Such was the literary-historical raison d'être of Hanka's mystification. This mystification made it possible to forge a bridge between Old Czech verbal art and modern Czech poetry. The imprint of the Slavic past permitted the author of the manuscripts to use still another rich and kindred linguistic base, Russian vocabulary and stylistic devices, which Hanka resorted to extensively. There is an even closer connection between this linguistic base and an important event in the subsequent history of Czech literature, F. L. Čelakovský's *Echo of Russian Songs* (1829). Attempts at grafting Old Czech and Russian linguistic culture onto Czech language of the eighteenth century, which had been neglected and had run wild, was a necessary premise for the flourishing of the new Czech poetry that came in the 1830s (Mácha, Erben, and others).

The Enlightenment was of great importance for Czech culture. But by the time Hanka appeared on the scene, its historical role had been played out. Czech culture was confronted with new problems, which people of the previous generation were incapable of resolving because of their cast of mind and spiritual temperament. The fulfillment of these new tasks fell to the pioneers of Romanticism. It was the Romantics who reshaped the Enlightenment's approach to national studies: they transformed "chamber" scholarship into an ideology of belligerent nationalism, which was later to play an enormous and revolutionary role. They were the first to develop a political program for the Slavs. They boldly posed the question of the meaning of Czech history. Would the linguists of the Enlightenment have dared to introduce radical and well-planned reforms? The Romantics in fact created a new Czech literary language, and this was one of their most brilliant achievements. Would it have been possible for such masterpieces of late Romanticism as Mácha's poems and Erben's ballads to appear, had it not been for the Romantics of the older generation? For the latter had opposed to the narrow prosodic norms of the Enlightenment their own revolutionary manifestos of Czech verse.

The scholarly works of Šafařík and Palacký and their programmatic brochure *Fundamentals of Czech Poetry,* Jungmann's dictionary and Jan Kollár's journalism in versified and prose form, the Královédvorský Manuscript and Čelakovský's imitations of Russian and Czech folksongs—all are but individual manifestations of the same primordial force, the same historical impulse. Even if Dobrovský applied to Hanka the criteria of his own epoch, we have no right to repeat the same mistake today. The critical reason of Dobrovský and the unrestrained mythologizing of Hanka—it would be difficult to find more condensed expressions of these two strikingly constrasting epochs. The pupils clearly sensed a gap between themselves and their teachers.

In 1824 Svoboda, in his polemics with Dobrovský, demonstrated clearly the extent to which their attitudes toward literary mystification differed. The discussion centered on another gifted falsifier of medieval works, Thomas Chatterton, but it is clearly Hanka whom they both had in mind. "We would be happy," writes Svoboda, "if a second Chatterton appeared in our midst. We would not attach particular importance to the historical exactness of his works, and we would ask him to go on composing more and more such works . . . We are sincerely convinced that a genius like Chatterton is more beneficial for a culture than those who would devastate entire centuries with their excessive criticism." Svoboda condemns the severe sentence that Dobrovský had passed on the Zelenohorský Manuscript. In his opinion, even if a forgery had been committed, all the same, "the man who thus attempted to reproduce a medieval work does not merit such public censure. A real scholar would be satisfied simply to prove that it was not an ancient monument, but that the author nonetheless deserved recognition for his poetic talent and for his rare and praiseworthy knowledge of the Middle Ages. Any truly cultured man should acknowledge that fact."

PART IV

*Semiotic
Vistas*

Jakobson's semiotic studies begin with an examination of the nature of the linguistic sign. This is not simply because he was a linguist: rather, language has always been regarded as the primary semiotic system, and since antiquity any discussion of signs necessarily started with the word, the paramount means of communication and signification. Jakobson's work in semiotics continues his reassessment of the heritage of the founder of structural linguistics, Ferdinand de Saussure (1857–1913), whose insistence on the linearity of the signifier he had challenged with the introduction of distinctive features, more elementary units forming "bundles" termed phonemes. During his years in the United States, Jakobson turned for inspiration to the work of the American philosopher Charles Sanders Peirce (1839–1914) in analyzing not only the linguistic sign but also the relation of language to other signifying systems, such as music and painting, and the place of linguistics within the growing discipline of semiotics. The history of this field from the eighteenth to the twentieth centuries is sketched in Jakobson's magisterial "A Glance at the Development of Semiotics," which appropriately served as the keynote address at the First International Congress of Semiotics in Milan (1974).

"Quest for the Essence of Language" (1965) is Jakobson's most succinct formulation of the nature of the linguistic sign. Following Peirce's typology of signs into icon, index, and symbol, he acknowledges Saussure's definition of the word as a symbol, characterized by an arbitrary relation between *signans* and *signatum* (the word's sensuous aspect or sound and its intelligible aspect or meaning). That arbitrariness is not absolute, however: on many levels of language there is an inherent iconicity (or similarity) between sound and meaning. The most obvious case is the rather limited phenomenon of onomatopoeia, where the sound of a word imitates its source in nature. In grammar one finds numerous instances of more complex types of iconicity: for example, in the gradation of comparative forms such as *high–higher–highest,* the length of the morphological ending mirrors the meanings respectively of positive, comparative, and superlative. Moreover, paronomasia—a semantic linking of two words on the basis of their similarity in sound structure—is an essential aspect of the poetic function of language, whether manifested in puns, jokes, rhetoric, or poetry. Synesthesia, through which speakers associate color or size with certain phonemic oppositions, is a frequent experience of both children and poets. Indeed, the close ties between sound and meaning, which are maximally exploited in poetic texts, are the crux of the translator's difficulties, addressed by Jakobson in "On Linguistic Aspects of Translation" (1959). If words referred unequivocably to reality and were not caught up in the intrinsically linguistic patterning of the world, a universal language would be feasible and each individual natural language would be totally transparent and translatable. Jakobson answers Bertrand Russell's assertion that "no one can understand the word 'cheese' unless he has a nonlinguistic acquaintance with cheese" with the quip that "nobody has ever smelled or tasted the meaning of *cheese* or of *apple.*" The network of language, in particular its obligatory grammatical schema, places obvious constraints on the translator, who nevertheless is able to seek equivalents because "languages differ essentially in what they *must* convey and not in what they *can* convey."

Music is in certain respects the semiotic system closest to language: both utilize symbolic signs, unfold in time, and are primarily linear in nature. Jakobson's brief note on "Musicology and Linguistics" (1932) presents some of the parallels that can be drawn between phonology and the study of music. He insists on the concept of system, of a hierarchical relation of elements rather than their absolute values: only thus can musicology avoid the pitfalls faced by linguistics when it viewed the auditory phenomena of language as purely physical rather than as parts of a meaningful and purposive whole.

Jakobson's essay "Is the Film in Decline?" (1933) was written in the wake of debates over the introduction of sound into filmmaking. He considered sound, like the visual elements in film, a semiotic and not a mere imitative fact: "speech in film is a special kind of auditory object," used to convey information and not merely to reproduce real stimuli. With the advent of the sound film, even silence, the unmarked feature of the silent film, becomes a signifying device.

"On the Relation between Visual and Auditory Signs" (1964, 1967) offers Jakobson's fullest differentiation of signs that use space as a medium and are thus based on simultaneity, as opposed to those that unfold in time and rely on successivity. As the notorious unpopularity of abstract art testifies, vision is connected primarily with mimesis (iconicity and indexicality). In the auditory realm, symbolic signs such as music and speech prove to be superior to icons, mere imitations of natural sounds. These facts are correlated in turn with Jakobson's earlier work on aphasic disturbances (see "Two Aspects of Language," in Part I). The cardinal division between visual and auditory signs is in Jakobson's view linked to differences in the way the brain perceives and processes them.

An ingenious foray into man's expressive visual displays, "Motor Signs for 'Yes' and 'No'" (1970), demonstrates the interrelation of naturalness and conventionality in gestural signs; although expressed in opposite ways in different cultures, they share the same binary, antithetical character.

From his earliest days as a member of the Russian avant-garde, Jakobson was intrigued by the differences and common semiotic properties of auditory and visual signs in the arts. In his research of the 1960s and 1970s he constantly found striking analogies between the poetry of grammar and the grammar of poetry (see Part II) and the role of geometrical construction in pictorial art. In "On the Verbal Art of William Blake and Other Poet-Painters" (1970) Jakobson analyzes two cases of poems directly juxtaposed to pictures by their creators (Blake and Henri Rousseau) and a poem by Paul Klee that in its geometrical composition reflects his style as a painter. This work, which is on the cutting edge of current semiotic investigations, opens up new perspectives for a coherent study of visual and verbal art.

411

CHAPTER 22

Quest for the Essence of Language

Since "in human speech, different sounds have different meaning," Leonard Bloomfield's influential manual of 1933 concluded that "to study this coordination of certain sounds with certain meanings is to study language." And one century earlier Wilhelm von Humboldt taught that "there is an apparent connection between sound and meaning which, however, only seldom lends itself to an exact elucidation, is often only glimpsed, and most usually remains obscure." This connection and coordination have been an eternal crucial problem in the age-old science of language. How it was nonetheless temporarily forgotten by the linguists of the recent past may be illustrated by repeated praises for the amazing novelty of Ferdinand de Saussure's interpretation of the sign, in particular the verbal sign, as an indissoluble unity of two constituents—*signifiant* and *signifié*—although this conception was taken over entirely from ancient Stoic theory. This doctrine considered the sign (*sēmeion*) as an entity constituted by the relation of the signifier (*sēmainon*) and the signified (*sēmainomenon*). The former was defined as "perceptible" (*aisthēton*) and the latter as "intelligible" (*noēton*) or, to use a more linguistic designation, "translatable." In addition,

413

reference appeared to be clearly distinguished from meaning by the term *tynchanon*. St. Augustine's writings exhibit an adaptation and further development of the Stoic inquiry into the action of signs (*sē-meiōsis*), with Latinized terms, in particular *signum* comprising both *signans* and *signatum*. Incidentally, this pair of correlative concepts and labels was adopted by Saussure only at the middle of his last course in general linguistics, maybe through the medium of H. Gomperz's *Noologie* (1908). The outlined doctrine underlies the medieval philosophy of language in its magnificent growth, depth, and variety of approaches. The twofold character and the consequent "double cognition" of any sign, in Ockham's terms, were thoroughly assimilated by the scientific thought of the Middle Ages.

Perhaps the most inventive and versatile among American thinkers was Charles Sanders Peirce, so great that no university found a place for him. His first, perspicacious attempt at a classification of signs— "On a New List of Categories"—appeared in the *Proceedings of the American Academy of Arts and Sciences* in 1867, and forty years later, summing up his "life-long study of the nature of signs" the author stated: "I am, as far as I know, a pioneer, or rather a backwoodsman, in the work of clearing and opening up what I call *semiotic,* that is, the doctrine of the essential nature and fundamental varieties of possible semiosis; and I find the field too vast, the labor too great, for a first-comer." He keenly realized the inadequacy of general theoretical premises in the research of his contemporaries. The very name for his science of signs goes back to the antique *sēmeiōtikē;* Peirce praised and widely utilized the experience of the ancient and medieval logicians, "thinkers of the highest order," while condemning severely the usual "barbarous rage" against "the marvellous acuteness of the Schoolmen." In 1903 he expressed a firm belief that if the early "doctrine of signs" had not been sunk but pursued with zeal and genius, the twentieth century might have opened with such vitally important special sciences as, for instance, linguistics "in a decidedly more advanced condition than there is much promise that they will have reached at the end of 1950."

From the end of the last century, a similar discipline was fervently advocated by Saussure. Stimulated in turn by Greek impetus, he called it semiology and expected this new branch of learning to elucidate the essence and governing laws of signs. In his view, linguistics was to become but a part of this general science and would determine what properties made language a separate system in the totality of "semio-logical facts." It would be interesting to find out whether there is some genetic relation or merely a convergence between the efforts of both scholars toward this comparative investigation of sign systems. Half a century of Peirce's semiotic drafts are of epochal significance, and if they had not remained for the most part unpublished until the 1930s, or if at least the printed works had been known to linguists, they would certainly have exerted an unparalleled influence upon the inter-national development of linguistic theory.

Peirce likewise makes a clear-cut distinction between the "material qualities," the signans of any sign, and its "immediate interpretant," that is, the signatum. Signs (or *representamina* in Peirce's nomencla-ture) offer three basic varieties of semiosis, three distinct, "representa-tive qualities" based on different relationships between the signans and the signatum. This difference enables him to discern three cardinal types of signs.

(1) The *icon* acts chiefly by a factual similarity between its signans and signatum, between the picture of an animal and the animal pic-tured; the former stands for the latter "merely because it resembles it."

(2) The *index* acts chiefly by a factual, existential contiguity between its signans and signatum, and "psychologically, the action of indices depends upon association by contiguity." Smoke is an index of a fire, and the proverbial knowledge that "where there is smoke, there is fire" permits any interpreter of smoke to infer the existence of fire irrespec-tive of whether the fire was lighted intentionally in order to attract someone's attention. Robinson Crusoe found an index: its signans was a footprint in the sand, and its inferred signatum, the presence of some human creature on his island. The acceleration of pulse as a probable symptom of fever is, in Peirce's view, an index, and in such cases his semiotic actually merges with the medical inquiry into the symptoms of diseases labeled semeiotics, semeiology, or symptomatology.

(3) The *symbol* acts chiefly by imputed, learned contiguity between signans and signatum. This connection "consists in its being a rule" and does not depend on the presence or absence of any similarity or physical contiguity. The knowledge of this conventional rule is oblig-atory for the interpreter of any given symbol, and solely and simply because of this rule will the sign actually be interpreted. Originally the word *symbol* was used in a similar sense also by Saussure and his dis-ciples, yet later he objected to this term because it traditionally involves

some natural bond between signans and signatum (the symbol of jus-tice, a pair of scales), and in his notes the conventional signs pertaining to a conventional system were tentatively labeled *seme,* while Peirce had selected the term *seme* for a special, quite different purpose. It suffices to confront Peirce's use of the term *symbol* with the various meanings of *symbolism* to perceive the danger of annoying ambiguities; but the lack of a better substitute compels us for the time being to preserve the term introduced by Peirce.

The resumed semiotic deliberations revive the question, astutely dis-cussed in *Cratylus,* Plato's fascinating dialogue: does language attach form to content "by nature" (*physei*), as the title hero insists, or "by convention" (*thesei*), according to the counterarguments of Hermo-genes. The moderator Socrates in Plato's dialogue is prone to agree that representation by likeness is superior to the use of arbitrary signs, but despite the attractive force of likeness he feels obliged to accept a complementary factor—conventionality, custom, habit.

Among scholars who treated this question following in the foot-steps of Plato's Hermogenes, a significant place belongs to the Yale linguist Dwight Whitney (1827–1894), who exerted a deep influence on European linguistic thought by promoting the thesis of language as a social institution. In his fundamental books of the 1860s and 1870s, language was defined as a system of arbitrary and conventional signs (Plato's *epituchonta* and *synthēmata*). This doctrine was borrowed and expanded by Saussure, and it entered into the posthumous edition of his *Cours de linguistique générale,* adjusted by his disciples Charles Bally and Albert Sechehaye (1916). The teacher declares: "On the essential point it seems to us that the American linguist is right: language is a convention, and the nature of the sign that is agreed upon (*dont on est convenu*) remains indifferent." Arbitrariness is posited as the first of two basic principles for defining the nature of the verbal sign: "The bond uniting the signans with the signatum is arbitrary." The commentary points out that no one has controverted this principle, "but it is often easier to discover a truth than assign it to the appropriate place. The principle stated dominates all the science of language [*la langue* in the Saussurian sense of this term, that is, the verbal code] and its conse-quences are innumerable." In accord with Bally and Sechehaye, An-toine Meillet and Joseph Vendryes also emphasized the "absence of connection between meaning and sound," and Bloomfield echoed the same tenet: "The forms of language are arbitrary."

416

As a matter of fact, the agreement with the Saussurian dogma of the arbitrary sign was far from unanimous. In Otto Jespersen's opinion (1916), the role of arbitrariness in language was excessively overstated, and neither Whitney nor Saussure succeeded in solving the problem of the relationship between sound and meaning. J. Damourette and E. Pichon's and Dwight L. Bolinger's rejoinders were identically entitled: "Le Signe n'est pas arbitraire" (1927), "The Sign Is Not Arbitrary" (1949). Emile Benveniste in his timely essay "Nature du signe linguistique" (1939) brought out the crucial fact that only for a detached, alien onlooker is the bond between signans and signatum a mere contingence, whereas for the native user of the same language this relation is a necessity.

Saussure's fundamental demand for an intrinsic linguistic analysis of any idiosynchronic system obviously invalidates the reference to sound and meaning differences in space and time as an argument for the arbitrary connection between the two constituents of the verbal sign. The Swiss-German peasant woman who allegedly asked why cheese is called *fromage* by her French countrymen—"Käse ist doch viel natürlicher!"(But *Käse* is more natural!)—displayed a much more Saussurian attitude than those who assert that every word is an arbitrary sign instead of which any other could be used for the same purpose. But is this natural necessity due exclusively to pure habit? Do verbal signs— for they are symbols—act "by virtue only of there being a habit that associates" their signatum with their signans?

One of the most important features of Peirce's semiotic classification is his shrewd recognition that the difference among the three basic classes of signs is merely a difference in relative hierarchy. It is not the presence or absence of similarity or contiguity between signans and signatum, not the purely factual or purely imputed, habitual connection between the two constituents which underlies the division of signs into icons, indices, and symbols, but merely the predominance of one of these factors over the others. Thus the scholar refers to "icons in which the likeness is aided by conventional rules," and one may recollect the diverse techniques of perspective which the spectator must learn in order to apprehend paintings of dissimilar artistic schools; the differences in the size of figures have divergent meanings in the various pictorial codes; in certain medieval traditions of painting, villains are specifically and consistently represented in profile, and in ancient Egyptian art only en face. Peirce claims that "it would be difficult, if not impossible, to instance an absolutely pure index, or to find any sign absolutely devoid of the indexical quality." Such a typical index as a pointing finger carries dissimilar connotations in different cultures; for instance, in certain South African tribes the object pointed at is thus damned. On the other hand, "the symbol will involve a sort of index," and "without indices it is impossible to designate what one is talking about."

Peirce's concern with the different ranks of coassistance of the three functions in all three types of signs, and in particular his scrupulous attention to the indexical and iconic components of verbal symbols, is intimately linked with his thesis that "the most perfect of signs" are those in which the iconic, indexical, and symbolic characters "are blended as equally as possible." Conversely, Saussure's insistence on the conventionality of language is bound to his assertion that "the entirely arbitrary signs are the most appropriate to fulfill the optimum semiotic process."

The indexical elements of language have been discussed in my study "Shifters, Verbal Categories, and the Russian Verb." Now let us attempt to approach the linguistic pattern in its iconic aspect and to give an answer to Plato's question, by what kind of imitation (*mimēsis*) does language attach the signans to the signatum?

The chain of verbs—*veni, vidi, vici*—informs us about the order of Caesar's deeds first and foremost because the sequence of coordinate preterits is used to reproduce the succession of reported occurrences. The temporal order of speech events tends to mirror the order of narrated events in time or in rank. Such a sequence as "the President and the Secretary of State attended the meeting" is far more usual than the reverse, because the initial position in the clause reflects the priority in official standing.

The correspondence in order between signans and signatum finds its right place among the "fundamental varieties of possible semiosis" which were outlined by Peirce. He singled out two distinct subclasses of icons—*images* and *diagrams*. In images the signans represents the "simple qualities" of the signatum, whereas for diagrams the likeness between signans and signatum exists "only in respect to the relations of their parts." Peirce defined a diagram as "a *representamen* which is predominantly an icon of relation and is aided to be so by conventions." Such an "icon of intelligible relations" may be exemplified by two rectangles of different size which illustrate a quantitative comparison of steel production in the USA and the USSR. The relations in the signans correspond to the relations in the signatum. In such a typical diagram as statistical curves, the signans presents an iconic analogy with the signatum as to the relations of their parts. If a chronological diagram symbolizes the ratio of increase in population by a dotted line and mortality by a continuous line, these are, in Peirce's parlance, "symbolide features." Theory of diagrams occupies an important place in Peirce's semiotic research; he acknowledges their considerable merits, which spring from their being "veridically iconic, naturally analogous to the thing represented." The discussion of different sets of diagrams leads him to the ascertainment that "every algebraic equation is an icon, insofar as it exhibits by means of the algebraic signs (which are not themselves icons) the relations of the quantities concerned." Any algebraic formula appears to be an icon, "rendered such by the rules of commutation, association, and distribution of the symbols." Thus "algebra is but a sort of diagram," and "language is but a kind of algebra." Peirce vividly conceived that "the arrangement of the words in the sentence, for instance, must serve as *icons,* in order that the sentence may be understood."

When discussing the grammatical universals and near-universals detected by J. H. Greenberg, I noted that the order of meaningful elements by virtue of its palpably iconic character displays a particularly clear-cut universalistic propensity. Precisely, therefore, the precedence of the conditional clause with regard to the conclusion is the only admitted or primary, neutral, nonmarked order in the conditional sentences of all languages. If almost everywhere, again according to Greenberg's data, the only, or at least the predominant, basic order in declarative sentences with nominal subject and object is one in which the former precedes the latter, this grammatical process obviously reflects the hierarchy of the grammatical concepts. The subject on which the action is predicated is, in Edward Sapir's terms, "conceived of as the starting point, the 'doer' of the action" in contradistinction to "the end point, the 'object' of the action." The subject, the only independent term in the clause, singles out what the message is about. Whatever the actual rank of the agent, he is necessarily promoted to hero of the message as soon as he assumes the role of its subject: "The subordinate obeys the principal." Notwithstanding the table of ranks, attention is first of all focused on the subordinate as agent, turns thereupon to the undergoer, the "goal" of his action, the principal obeyed. If, however, instead of an action effected, the predicate outlines an action undergone, the role of subject is assigned to the patient: "The principal is obeyed by the subordinate." The impossibility of omitting the subject and the optional character of the object underscore the hierarchy discussed: "The subordinate obeys; the principal is obeyed." As centuries of grammatical and logical scrutiny have brought to light, predication is so cardinally different from all other semantic acts that the forced reasoning intended to level subject and object must be categorically rejected.

The investigation of diagrams has found further development in modern graph theory. When reading the stimulating book *Structural Models* (1965) by F. Harary, R. Z. Norman, and D. Cartwright, with its thorough description of manifold directed graphs, the linguist is struck by their conspicuous analogies with the grammatical patterns. The isomorphic composition of the signans and signatum displays in both semiotic fields very similar devices which facilitate an exact transposition of grammatical, especially syntactic, structures into graphs. Such linguistic properties as the connectedness of linguistic entities with each other and with the initial and final limit of the sequence, the immediate neighborhood and distance, the centrality and peripherality, the symmetrical relations, and the elliptic removal of single components find their close equivalents in the constitution of graphs. The literal translation of an entire syntactic system into a set of graphs permits us to detach the diagrammatic, iconic forms of relations from the strictly conventional, symbolic features of that system.

Not only the combination of words into syntactic groups but also the combination of morphemes into words exhibits a clear-cut diagrammatic character. Both in syntax and in morphology any relation of parts and wholes agrees with Peirce's definition of diagrams and their iconic nature. The substantial semantic contrast between roots as lexical and affixes as grammatical morphemes finds a graphic expression in their different position within the word; affixes, particularly inflectional suffixes, in languages where they exist, habitually differ from the other morphemes by a restricted and selected use of phonemes and their combinations. Thus the only consonants utilized in the productive inflectional suffixes of English are the dental continuant and stop, and their cluster -*st*. Of the 24 obstruents of the Russian consonantal pattern, only four phonemes, saliently opposed to each other, function in the inflectional suffixes.

Morphology is rich in examples of alternate signs which exhibit an equivalent relation between their signantia and signata. Thus, in various Indo-European languages, the positive, comparative, and superlative degrees of adjectives show a gradual increase in the number of phonemes, for example, *high-higher-highest, altus-altior-altissimus*. In this way the signantia reflect the gradation gamut of the signata.

There are languages where the plural forms are distinguished from the singular by an additional morpheme, whereas, according to Greenberg, there is no language in which this relation would be the reverse and, in contradistinction to the singular forms, the plural ones would be totally devoid of such an extra morpheme. The signans of the plural tends to echo the meaning of a numeral increment by an increased length of the form. Compare the finite verbal forms of the singular and the corresponding plural forms with longer endings: 1. *je finis—nous finissons*, 2. *tu finis—vous finissez*, 3. *il finit—ils finissent;* or in Polish: 1. *znam* (I know)—*znamy*, 2. *znasz—znacie*, 3. *zna—znają*. In the declension of Russian nouns the real (nonzero) endings are longer in the plural than in the singular form of the same grammatical case. When one traces the varied historical processes which persistently built up the diagram—longer plural/shorter singular forms—in diverse Slavic languages, these and many similar facts of linguistic experience prove to be at variance with the Saussurian averment that "in the sound structure of the signans there is nothing which would bear any resemblance to the value or meaning of the sign."

Saussure himself attenuated his "fundamental principle of arbitrariness" by making a distinction between the "radically" and "relatively" arbitrary elements of language. He assigned to the latter category those signs which may be dissociated on the syntagmatic axis into constituents identifiable on the paradigmatic axis. Yet also such forms as the French *berger* (from *berbicarius*, shepherd), in Saussure's view "completely unmotivated," could undergo a similar analysis, since *-er* is associated with the other specimens of this agentive suffix and occupies the same place in other words of the same paradigmatic series as *vacher* (cowboy), and so on. Furthermore, the search for the connection between the signans and signatum of the grammatical morphemes must involve not only the instances of their complete formal identity, but also such situations where different affixes share a certain grammatical function and one constant phonemic feature. Thus the Polish instrumental case in its various endings for the different genders, numbers, and parts of speech consistently contains the nasality feature in its last consonant or vowel. In Russian the phoneme *m* (represented by two automatic alternants, one with and the other without palatalization) occurs in the endings of marginal cases (instrumental, dative, locative), but never in other classes of grammatical cases. Hence separate phonemes or distinctive features within grammatical morphemes may serve as autonomous indicators of certain grammatical categories. Saussure's remark about "the role of relative motivation" may be applied to such performances of morphemic subunits: "The mind manages to introduce a principle of order and regularity in certain parts of the body of signs."

Saussure descried two drifts in language—the tendency to use the lexical tool, that is, the unmotivated sign, and the preference given to the grammatical instrument, in other words, to the constructional rule. Sanskrit appeared to him a specimen of an ultragrammatical, maximally motivated system, whereas in French as compared to Latin he found that "absolute arbitrariness which, in point of fact, is the proper condition of the verbal sign." It is noteworthy that Saussure's classification had recourse to morphological criteria only, while syntax was actually laid aside. This oversimplified bipolar sheme is substantially amended by Peirce's, Sapir's, and Whorf's insights into wider, syntactic problems. In particular, Benjamin Whorf, with his emphasis on "the algebraic nature of language," knew how to abstract from individual sentences the "designs of sentence structure" and argued that "the *patternment* aspect of language always overrides and controls the *lexation* or name-giving aspect." Thus the distinctly diagrammatic constituents in the system of verbal symbols are universally superimposed upon the vocabulary.

When abandoning grammar and approaching the strictly lexical problems of roots and further indissociable one-morpheme words (the lexicon's *stoicheia* and *prōta onomata,* as they are labeled in *Cratylus*), we must ask ourselves, as did the participants of Plato's dialogue, whether at this point it would be advisable to stop and abandon the discussion of the internal connection between signans and signatum or whether, without clever evasions, one must "play the game till the end and investigate these questions vigorously."

In French, *ennemi,* as stated by Saussure, "is not motivated by anything," yet in the expression *ami et ennemi* a Frenchman can hardly overlook the affinity of both juxtaposed rhyme words. *Father, mother,* and *brother* are indivisible into root and suffix, but the second syllable of these kinship terms is felt as a kind of phonemic allusion to their semantic proximity. There are no synchronic rules which would govern the etymological connection between *ten, -teen,* and *-ty,* as well as between *three, thirty,* and *third* or *two, twelve, twenty, twi-* and *twin,* but nevertheless an obvious paradigmatic relationship continues to bind these forms into serried families. However opaque is the vocable *eleven,* a slight connection with the sound shape of *twelve* supported by the immediate neighborhood of both numerals is still seizable.

A vulgarized application of information theory could prompt us to expect a tendency toward dissimilation of contiguous numerals, like the change of *zwei* (2) into *zwo* introduced by the Berlin telephone directory to avoid any confusion with *drei* (3). However, in various languages an opposite, assimilatory tendency prevails among adjacent cardinals. Thus Russian attests a gradual attraction within every pair of simple numerals: *sem'* (7)—*vosem'* (8), *devjat'* (9)—*desjat'* (10). The similarity of signantia enforces the junction of the paired numerals.

Coinages such as *slithy* from *slimy* and *lithe,* and multiform varieties of blends and portmanteaus, display a mutual adhesion of simple words resulting in a joint interaction of their signantia and signata.

Bolinger's paper cited above convincingly documents "the vast importance of cross influences" between sound and meaning and the "constellations of words having similar meanings tied to similar sounds" whatever the origin of such constellations may be (*bash, mash, smash, crash, dash, lash, hash, rash, brash, clash, trash, plash, splash,* and *flash*). Such vocables border upon onomatopoetic words where again the questions of origin are quite immaterial for synchronic analysis.

Paronomasia, a semantic confrontation of phonemically similar words irrespective of any etymological connection, plays a considerable role in the life of language. A vocalic apophony underlies the punning title of a magazine article "Multilateral Force or Farce?" In the Russian proverb "Síla solómu lómit" (power breaks straw) the connection between the predicate *lómit* and the object *solómu* is internalized by a quasi incorporation of the root *lóm-* into the root *solóm-*; the phoneme *l* adjacent to the stressed vowel pervades and unites the three parts of the sentence; both consonants of the subject *sila* are repeated in the same order by the object which, so to say, synthesizes the phonemic makeup of the initial and final word of the proverb. Yet on a plain, lexical level the interplay of sound and meaning has a latent and virtual character, whereas in syntax and morphology (both inflection and derivation) the intrinsic, diagrammatic correspondence between signans and signatum is patent and obligatory.

A partial similarity of two signata may be represented by a partial similarity of signantia, as in the instances discussed above, or by a total identity of signantia, as in the case of lexical tropes. *Star* means either a celestial body or a person—both of preeminent brightness. A hierarchy of two meanings—one primary, central, proper, context-free; and the other secondary, marginal, figurative, transferred, contextual— is a characteristic feature of such asymmetrical couples. The metaphor (or metonymy) is an assignment of a signans to a secondary signatum associated by similarity (or contiguity) with the primary signatum.

The grammatical alternations within the roots carry us again into the domain of regular morphological processes. The selection of alternating phonemes may be purely conventional, as for instance the use of front vowels in the Yiddish "umlaut" plurals quoted by Sapir: *tog* (day)—*teg* (days), *fus* (foot)—*fis* (feet), and so on. There are, however, specimens of analogous grammatical "diagrams" with a manifestly iconic value in the alternants themselves, as for instance the partial or entire reduplication of the root in the plural, iterative, durative or augmentative forms of various African and American languages. In Basque dialects palatalization which heightens the tonality of consonants brings about the concept of diminution. The replacement of grave vowels or consonants by acute, compact by diffuse, continuous consonants by discontinuous, and unchecked by checked (glottalized), which is used in a few American languages for "the addition to the meaning of the word of a diminutive idea," and the reverse substitutions in order to express an augmentative, intensive grade, are based on the latent synesthetic value inherent in certain phonemic oppositions. This value, easily detectable by tests and experiments in sound perception and particularly manifest in children's language, may build scales of "diminutivized" or "augmentativized" meanings as opposed to the neutral one. The presence of a grave or acute phoneme in the root of a Dakota or Chinookan word does not signal by itself a higher or lower degree of intensity, whereas the coexistence of two alternant sound forms of one and the same root creates a diagrammatic parallelism between the opposition of two tonal levels in the signantia and of two grading values in the respective signata.

Apart from these relatively rare instances of grammatical utilization, the autonomous iconic value of phonemic oppositions is damped down in purely cognitive messages but becomes particularly apparent in poetic language. Stéphane Mallarmé, amazingly sensitive to the sound texture of language, observed in his essay *Crise de vers* that the word *ombre* is actually shady, but *ténèbres* (with its acute vowels) suggests no darkness, and he felt deeply deceived by the perverse attribution of the meanings "day" to the word *jour* and "night" to the word *nuit* in spite of the obscure timbre of the former and the light one of the latter. Verse, however, as the poet claimed, "remunerates the defects of languages." A perusal of nocturnal and diurnal images in French poetry shows how *nuit* darkens and *jour* brightens when the former is surrounded by a context of grave and flat vowels, and when the latter dissolves in a sequence of acute phonemes. Even in usual speech a suitable phonemic environment, as the semanticist Stephen Ullmann remarked, can reinforce the expressive quality of a word. If the distribution of vowels between the Latin *dies* and *nox* or between the Czech *den* and *noc* fits the poetic chiaroscuro, French poetry drapes the "contradictory" vocables or replaces the imagery of daylight and nightly darkness by the contrast of heavy, stifling day and airy night, for this contrast is supported by another synesthetic connotation which associates the low tonality of the grave phonemes with heaviness and correspondingly the high tonality of the acute phonemes with light weight.

Poetic language reveals two effective causes in sound texture—the selection and constellation of phonemes and their components; the evocative power of these two factors, although concealed, is still implicit in our customary verbal behavior.

The final chapter of Jules Romains' novel *Les Amours enfantines* is entitled "Rumeur de la rue Réaumur." The name of this Paris street is said by the writer to resemble a song of wheels and walls and various other forms of urban trepidation, vibration, and rumbling. These motifs, tightly fused with the book's theme of flux and reflux, are embodied in the sound shape of *rue Réaumur.* Among the consonantal phonemes of this name there are only sonorants; the sequence consists of four sonorants (S) and four vowels (V): SVSV—VSVS, a mirror symmetry, with the group *ru* at the beginning and its reversal *ur* at the end. The initial and final syllables of the name are thrice echoed by the verbal environment: *rue Réaumur, ru-meur, roues* . . . *mur*ailles, trépidation d'im*meu*bles. The vowels of these corresponding syllables display three phonemic oppositions: 1) grave (back) versus acute (front);

2) flat (rounded) versus nonflat (unrounded); 3) diffuse (close) versus nondiffuse (open):

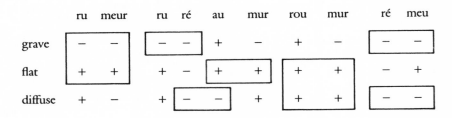

	ru	meur	ru	ré	au	mur	rou	mur	ré	meu
grave	–	–	–	–	+	–	+	–	–	–
flat	+	+	+	–	+	+	+	+	–	+
diffuse	+	–	+	–	–	+	+	+	–	–

The cunning intertexture of identical and contrasting features in this "song of wheels and walls," prompted by a hackneyed street sign, gives a decisive answer to Pope's claim: "The sound must be an echo to the sense."

When postulating two primordial linguistic characters—the arbitrariness of the sign and the linearity of the signans—Saussure attributed to both of them an equally fundamental importance. He was aware that if they are true, these laws would have "incalculable consequences" and determine "the whole mechanism of language." However, the "system of diagrammatization," patent and compulsory in the entire syntactic and morphological pattern of language, yet latent and virtual in its lexical aspect, invalidates Saussure's dogma of arbitrariness, while the other of his two "general principles"—the linearity of the signans—has been shaken by the dissociation of phonemes into distinctive features. With the removal of these fundamentals their corollaries in turn demand revision.

Thus Peirce's graphic and palpable idea that "a symbol may have an icon or [let us rewrite this conjunction in an up-to-date style: and/or] an index incorporated into it" opens new, urgent tasks and far-reaching vistas to the science of language. The precepts of this "backwoodsman in semiotic" are fraught with vital consequences for linguistic theory and praxis. The iconic and indexical constituents of verbal symbols have too often remained underestimated or even disregarded; on the other hand, the predominantly symbolic character of language and its consequent cardinal difference from the other, chiefly indexical or iconic, sets of signs likewise await due consideration in modern linguistic methodology.

The *Metalogicus* by John of Salisbury supplied Peirce with his favorite quotation: "Nominantur singularia, sed universalia significantur." How many futile and trivial polemics could have been avoided among students of language if they had mastered Peirce's *Speculative Grammar*, and particularly its thesis that "a genuine symbol is a symbol that has a general meaning" and that this meaning in turn "can only be a symbol," since "omne symbolum de symbolo." A symbol is not only incapable of indicating any particular thing and necessarily "denotes a kind of thing," but "it is itself a kind and not a single thing." A symbol, for instance a word, is a "general rule" which signifies only through the different instances of its application, namely the pronounced or written—thinglike—*replicas*. However varied these embodiments of the word, it remains in all these occurrences "one and the same word."

The prevalently symbolic signs are the only ones which through their possession of general meaning are able to form propositions, whereas "icons and indices assert nothing." One of Peirce's posthumous works, the book *Existential Graphs* with its eloquent subtitle "My chef d'œuvre," concludes the analysis and classification of signs with a succinct outlook toward the creative power (*energeia*) of language: "Thus the mode of being of the symbol is differnt from that of the icon and from that of the index. An icon has such being as belongs to past experience. It exists only as an image in the mind. An index has the being of present experience. The being of a symbol consists in the real fact that something surely will be experienced if certain conditions be satisfied. Namely, it will influence the thought and conduct of its interpreter. Every word is a symbol. Every sentence is a symbol. Every book is a symbol . . . The value of a symbol is that it serves to make thought and conduct rational and enables us to predict the future." This idea was repeatedly broached by the philosopher: to the indexical *hic et nunc* he persistently opposed the "general law" which underlies any symbol: "Whatever is truly general refers to the indefinite future, for the past contains only a certain collection of such cases that have occurred. The past is actual fact. But a general law cannot be fully realized. It is a potentiality; and its mode of being is *esse in futuro*." Here the thought of the American logician crosses paths with the vision of Velimir Xlebnikov, the most original poet of our century, in whose commentary of 1919 to his own works one reads: "I have realized that the homeland of creation lies in the future; thence wafts the wind from the gods of the word."

CHAPTER 23

On Linguistic Aspects of Translation

According to Bertrand Russell, "no one can understand the word 'cheese' unless he has a nonlinguistic acquaintance with cheese."[1] If, however, we follow Russell's fundamental precept and place our "emphasis upon the linguistic aspects of traditional philosophical problems," then we are obliged to state that no one can understand the word *cheese* unless he has an acquaintance with the meaning assigned to this word in the lexical code of English. Any representative of a cheese-less culinary culture will understand the English word *cheese* if he is aware that in this language it means "food made of pressed curds" and if he has at least a linguistic acquaintance with *curds*. We never consumed ambrosia or nectar and have only a linguistic acquaintance with the words *ambrosia, nectar,* and *gods*—the name of their mythical users; nonetheless, we understand these words and know in what contexts each of them may be used.

The meaning of the words *cheese, apple, nectar, acquaintance, but, mere,* and of any word or phrase whatsoever is definitely a linguistic or—to be more precise and less narrow—a semiotic fact. Against those who assign meaning (*signatum*) not to the sign but to the thing itself, the simplest and truest argument would be that nobody has ever smelled or tasted the meaning of *cheese* or of *apple*. There is no *signatum* without *signum*. The meaning of the word "cheese" cannot be inferred from a nonlinguistic acquaintance with cheddar or with camembert without the assistance of the verbal code. An array of linguistic signs is needed to introduce an unfamiliar word. Mere pointing will not teach us whether *cheese* is the name of the given specimen, or of any box of camembert, or of camembert in general, or of any cheese, any milk product, any food, any refreshment, or perhaps any box irrespective of contents. Finally, does a word simply name the thing in question, or does it imply a meaning such as offering, sale, prohibition, or malediction? (Pointing actually may mean malediction; in some cultures, particularly in Africa, it is an ominous gesture.)

For us, both as linguists and as ordinary word users, the meaning of any linguistic sign is its translation into some further, alternative sign, especially a sign "in which it is more fully developed," as Peirce, the deepest inquirer into the essence of signs, insistently stated.[2] The term "bachelor" may be converted into a more explicit designation, "unmarried man," whenever higher explicitness is required. We distinguish three ways of interpreting a verbal sign: it may be translated into other signs of the same language, into another language, or into another, nonverbal system of symbols. These three kinds of translation are to be differently labeled:

> (1) Intralingual translation or *rewording* is an interpretation of verbal signs by means of other signs of the same language.
> (2) Interlingual translation or *translation proper* is an interpretation of verbal signs by means of some other language.
> (3) Intersemiotic translation or *transmutation* is an interpretation of verbal signs by means of signs of nonverbal sign systems.

The intralingual translation of a word uses either another, more or less synonymous, word or resorts to a circumlocution. Yet synonymy, as a rule, is not complete equivalence: for example, "every celibate is a bachelor, but not every bachelor is a celibate." A word or an idiomatic phrase word, briefly a code unit of the highest level, may be fully interpreted only by means of an equivalent combination of code units, that is, a message referring to this code unit: "every bachelor is an unmarried man, and every unmarried man is a bachelor," or "every celibate is bound not to marry, and everyone who is bound not to marry is a celibate."

Likewise on the level of interlingual translation, there is ordinarily no full equivalence between code units, while messages may serve as adequate interpretations of alien code units or messages. The English word *cheese* cannot be completely identified with its standard Russian heteronym *syr* because cottage cheese is a cheese but not a *syr*. Russians say: *prinesi syru i tvorogu* (bring cheese and [sic] cottage cheese). In standard Russian, the food made of pressed curds is called *syr* only if ferment is used.

Most frequently, however, translation from one language into another substitutes messages in one language not for separate code units but for entire messages in some other language. Such a translation is a reported speech: the translator recodes and transmits a message received from another source. Thus translation involves two equivalent messages in two different codes.

Equivalence in difference is the cardinal problem of language and the pivotal concern of linguistics. Like any receiver of verbal messages, the linguist acts as their interpreter. No linguistic specimen may be interpreted by the science of language without a translation of its signs into other signs of the same system or into signs of another system. Any comparison of two languages implies an examination of their mutual translatability; the widespread practice of interlingual communication, particularly translating activities, must be kept under constant scrutiny by linguistic science. It is difficult to overestimate the urgent need for, and the theoretical and practical significance of, differential bilingual dictionaries with careful comparative definition of all the corresponding units in their intension and extension. Likewise differential bilingual grammars should define what unifies and what differentiates the two languages in their selection and delimitation of grammatical concepts.

Both the practice and the theory of translation abound with intricacies, and from time to time attempts are made to sever the Gordian knot by proclaiming the dogma of untranslatability. "Mr. Everyman, the natural logician," vividly imagined by Benjamin Whorf, is supposed to have arrived at the following bit of reasoning: "Facts are unlike to speakers whose language background provides for unlike formulation of them."[3] In the first years of the Russian revolution there were fanatic visionaries who argued in Soviet periodicals for a radical revision of traditional language and particularly for the weeding out of such misleading expressions as "sunrise" or "sunset." Yet we still use this Ptolemaic imagery without implying a rejection of Copernican doctrine, and we can easily transform our customary talk about the rising and setting sun into a picture of the earth's rotation simply because any sign is translatable into a sign in which it appears to us more fully developed and precise.

An ability to speak a given language implies an ability to talk about this language. Such a metalinguistic operation permits revision and redefinition of the vocabulary used. The complementarity of both levels—object language and metalanguage—was brought out by Niels Bohr: all well-defined experimental evidence must be expressed in ordinary language, "in which the practical use of every word stands in complementary relation to attempts at its strict definition."[4]

All cognitive experience and its classification is conveyable in any existing language. Whenever there is a deficiency, terminology can be qualified and amplified by loanwords or loan translations, by neologisms or semantic shifts, and, finally, by circumlocutions. Thus in the newborn literary language of the Northeast Siberian Chukchees, "screw" is rendered as "rotating nail," "steel" as "hard iron," "tin" as "thin iron," "chalk" as "writing soap," "watch" as "hammering heart." Even seemingly contradictory circumlocutions, like "electrical horse-car" (*èlektričeskaja konka*), the first Russian name of the horseless street-car, or "flying steamship" (*jeha paraqot*), the Koryak term for the airplane, simply designate the electrical analogue of the horsecar and the flying analogue of the steamer and do not impede communication, just as there is no semantic "noise" and disturbance in the double oxymoron—"cold beef-and-pork hot dog."

No lack of grammatical devices in the language translated into makes impossible a literal translation of the entire conceptual information contained in the original. The traditional conjunctions "and," "or" are now supplemented by a new connective—"and/or"—which was discussed a few years ago in the witty book *Federal Prose—How to Write in and/or for Washington.*[5] Of these three conjunctions, only the last occurs in one of the Samoyed languages.[6] Despite these differences in the inventory of conjunctions, all three varieties of messages observed in "federal prose" can be distinctly translated both into traditional English and into this Samoyed language. Federal prose: (1) John and Peter, (2) John or Peter, (3) John and/or Peter will come. Traditional English: (3) John and Peter or one of them will come. Samoyed: (1) John and/or Peter, both will come, (2) John and/or Peter, one of them will come.

If some grammatical category is absent in a given language, its meaning may be translated into this language by lexical means. Dual forms like Old Russian *brata* are translated with the help of the numeral: "two brothers." It is more difficult to remain faithful to the original when we translate into a language provided with a certain grammatical category from a language lacking such a category. When translating the English sentence *She has brothers* into a language which discriminates dual and plural, we are compelled either to make our own choice between two statements "She has two brothers"—"She has more than two" or to leave the decision to the listener and say: "She has either two or more than two brothers." Again, in translating from a language without grammatical number into English, one is obliged to select one of the two possibilities—*brother* or *brothers* or to confront the receiver of this message with a two-choice situation: *She has either one or more than one brother.*

As Franz Boas neatly observed, the grammatical pattern of a language (as opposed to its lexical stock) determines those aspects of each experience that must be expressed in the given language: "We have to choose between these aspects, and one or the other must be chosen."[7] In order to translate accurately the English sentence *I hired a worker,* a Russian needs supplementary information, whether this action was completed or not and whether the worker was a man or a woman, because he must make his choice between a verb of completive or non-completive aspect—*nanjal* or *nanimal*—and between a masculine and feminine noun—*rabotnika* or *rabotnicu.* If I ask the utterer of the English sentence whether the worker was male or female, my question may be judged irrelevant or indiscreet, whereas in the Russian version of this sentence an answer to this question is obligatory. On the other hand, whatever the choice of Russian grammatical forms to translate the quoted English message, the translation will give no answer to the question of whether I *hired* or *have hired* the worker, or whether he/she was an indefinite or definite worker (*a* or *the*). Because the information required by the English and Russian grammatical pattern is unlike, we face quite different sets of two-choice situations; therefore a chain of translations of one and the same isolated sentence from English into Russian and vice-versa could entirely deprive such a message of its initial content. The Geneva linguist S. I. Karcevskij used to compare such a gradual loss with a circular series of unfavorable currency transactions. But evidently the richer the context of a message, the smaller the loss of information.

Languages differ essentially in what they *must* convey and not in what they *can* convey. Each verb of a given language imperatively raises a set of specific yes-or-no questions, as for instance: is the narrated event conceived with or without reference to its completion? is the narrated event presented as prior to the speech event or not? Naturally the attention of native speakers and listeners will be constantly focused on such items as are compulsory in their verbal code.

In its cognitive function, language is minimally dependent on the grammatical pattern, because the definition of our experience stands in complementary relation to metalinguistic operations—the cognitive level of language not only admits but directly requires recoding interpretation, that is, translation. Any assumption of ineffable or untranslatable cognitive data would be a contradiction in terms. But in jest, in dreams, in magic, briefly, in what one would call everyday verbal mythology, and in poetry above all, the grammatical categories carry a high semantic import. Under these conditions, the question of translation becomes much more entangled and controversial.

Even such a category as grammatical gender, often cited as merely formal, plays a great role in the mythological attitudes of a speech community. In Russian the feminine cannot designate a male person, nor the masculine specify a female. Ways of personifying or metaphorically interpreting inanimate nouns are prompted by their gender. A test in the Moscow Psychological Institute (1915) showed that Russians, prone to personify the weekdays, consistently represented Monday, Tuesday, and Thursday as males and Wednesday, Friday, and Saturday as females, without realizing that this distribution was due to the masculine gender of the first three names (*ponedel'nik, vtornik, četverg*) as against the feminine gender of the others (*sreda, pjatnica, subbota*). The fact that the word for Friday is masculine in some Slavic languages and feminine in others is reflected in the folk traditions of the corresponding peoples, which differ in their Friday ritual. The widespread Russian superstition that a dropped knife presages a male guest and a dropped fork a female one is determined by the masculine gender of *nož* (knife) and the feminine of *vilka* (fork) in Russian. In Slavic and other languages where "day" is masculine and "night" feminine, day is represented by poets as the lover of night. The Russian painter Repin was baffled as to why Sin had been depicted as a woman by German artists: he did not realize that "sin" is feminine in German (*die Sünde*) but masculine in Russian (*grex*). Likewise a Russian child, while reading a translation of German tales, was astounded to find that Death, obviously a woman (Russian *smert'*, fem.), was pictured as an old man (German *der Tod*, masc.). *My Sister Life*, the title of a book of poems by Boris Pasternak, is quite natural in Russian, where "life" is feminine (*žizn'*), but was enough to reduce to despair the Czech poet Josef Hora in his attempt to translate these poems, since in Czech this noun is masculine (*život*).

What was the first problem which arose in Slavic literature at its very beginning? Curiously enough, the translator's difficulty in preserving the symbolism of genders, and the cognitive irrelevance of this difficulty, appears to be the main topic of the earliest Slavic original work, the preface to the first translation of the *Evangeliarium*, made in the early 860s by the founder of Slavic letters and liturgy, Constantine the Philosopher, and recently restored and interpreted by André Vaillant.[8] "Greek, when translated into another language, cannot always be reproduced identically, and that happens to each language being translated," the Slavic apostle states. "Masculine nouns like *potamos* (river) and *astēr* (star) in Greek, are feminine in another language like *rěka* and *zvězda* in Slavic." According to Vaillant's commentary, this divergence effaces the symbolic identification of the rivers with demons and of the stars with angels in the Slavic translation of two of Matthew's verses (7:25 and 2:9). But to this poetic obstacle Constantine resolutely opposes the precept of Dionysius the Areopagite, who called for chief attention to the cognitive values (*silě razumu*) and not to the words themselves.

In poetry, verbal equations become a constructive principle of the text. Syntactic and morphological categories, roots, and affixes, phonemes and their components (distinctive features)—in short, any constituents of the verbal code—are confronted, juxtaposed, brought into contiguous relation according to the principle of similarity and contrast and carry their own autonomous signification. Phonemic similarity is sensed as semantic relationship. The pun, or to use a more erudite and perhaps more precise term—paronomasia, reigns over poetic art, and whether its rule is absolute or limited, poetry by definition is untranslatable. Only creative transposition is possible: either intralingual transposition—from one poetic shape into another, or interlingual transposition—from one language into another, or finally intersemiotic transposition—from one system of signs into another (from verbal art into music, dance, cinema, or painting).

If we were to translate into English the traditional formula *Traduttore, traditore* as "the translator is a betrayer," we would deprive the Italian rhyming epigram of all its paronomastic value. Hence a cognitive attitude would compel us to change this aphorism into a more explicit statement and to answer the questions: translator of what messages? betrayer of what values?

CHAPTER 24

A Glance at the Development of Semiotics

Emile Benveniste in his "A Glance at the Development of Linguistics," the beautiful study whose heading I borrow for this presentation, brings to our attention that "linguistics has a double object: it is the science of language and the science of languages . . . It is on languages that the linguist works, and linguistics is first of all a theory of languages. But . . . the infinitely diverse problems of languages have the following in common: at a certain degree of generality, they always put language into question."[1] We deal with language as a universal invariant with respect to varied local languages which are variable in time and space. In the same order of things, semiotics is called upon to study the diverse systems of signs and to bring out the problems which result from a methodical comparison of these varied systems, that is to say, the general problem of the *sign:* sign as a generic notion with respect to the particular classes of signs.

The question of the sign and of signs was approached several times by the thinkers of Antiquity, of the Middle Ages and of the Renaissance. Around the end of the seventeenth century, John Locke's famous essay, in its final chapter on the tripartite division of the sciences, promoted this complex problem to the level of the last of the "three great provinces of the intellectual world" and proposed to call it "*sē-meiōtikē* or the 'Doctrine of signs,' the most usual whereof being words," given that "to communicate our thoughts for our own use, signs of our ideas are also necessary. Those which men have found most convenient, and therefore generally make use of, are articulate sounds."[2] It is to words, conceived of as "the great instruments of cognition," to their use and to their relation to ideas that Locke devotes the third book of his *Essay Concerning Human Understanding* (1690).

I

From the beginning of his scientific activities, Jean Henri Lambert took account of the *Essay* and, while working on the *Neues Organon* (1764),[3] which holds a pertinent spot in the development of phenomenological thought, he saw himself profoundly influenced by Locke's ideas, despite his taking a critical stance toward the sensualist doctrine of the English philosopher.[4] Each of the two volumes of the *Neues Organon* is divided into two parts and, among the four parts of this whole treatise, the third—*Semiotik oder Lehre von Bezeichnung der Gedanken und Dinge,* followed by the *Phänomenologie*—inaugurates the second volume (pp. 3–214) of the work and owes to Locke's thesis the term *semiotic* as well as the theme of research, "the investigation of the necessity of symbolic cognition in general and of language in particular" (paragraph 6), given that this symbolic cognition "is to us an indispensable adjunct to thought" (paragraph 12).

In the preface to his work, Lambert warns us that he is working on language in nine chapters of the *Semiotik* (2–10) but allows only one chapter to other types of signs, "because language is not only necessary in itself and extraordinarily diffuse, but occurs with all other types of signs." The author wishes to devote himself to language, "in order to get to know its structure more closely" (paragraph 70) and to approach "general linguistics, *Grammatica universalis,* which is still to be sought." He reminds us

> that in our language the arbitrary, the natural and the necessary are blended. The primer of general linguistics should then mainly discuss the natural and the necessary, and the arbitrary, as far as is

possible, sometimes on its own, sometimes in tight link with the natural and the necessary.

According to Lambert, the difference between these three elements which one finds in signs reveals a tight relationship with the decisive fact "that the first causes of language are in themselves already in human nature," and therefore this problem demands a meticulous examination (paragraph 13). The problem of algebra and of other systems of science's artificial languages with respect to natural languages (*wirkliche Sprachen*) is treated by Lambert (paragraphs 55ff) as a sort of double translation (*gedoppelte Übersetzung*).

The book studies the difference in the use of natural and arbitrary signs (paragraphs 47 and 48); the natural signs of affects (*natürliche Zeichen von Affekten*) are those that first attract attention (paragraph 19). Lambert takes into account the significant role played by gestures, for example, "in order to enlighten the concept, which is dark in the soul [mind] . . . or at least to give an indication of it to ourselves and to others," and he foresees the semiotic scope of *simulacra* (which reappear after a century in Peirce's list under the labels of *icons* or *likenesses*).[5] Lambert raises the question of signs whose internal structure is founded upon similarity relationships (*Ähnlichkeiten*) and, in interpreting signs of a metaphorical order, he evokes the effects of synesthesia (paragraph 18). Despite the summary character of his remarks on nonverbal communication, neither music, nor choreography, nor the blazon, nor the emblem, nor ceremonies escape the researcher's eye. The transformations of the signs (*Verwandlungen*) and the rules for their combination (*Verbindungskunst der Zeichen*) are placed on the agenda for further study.

II

It is because of Locke's and Lambert's creative initiative that the idea and the name of semiotics reappear at the beginning of the nineteenth century. In his early career, the young Joseph Marie Hoene-Wroński, familiar with Locke's work, sketched, among other speculative essays, a *Philosophie du language* which was not published until 1879.[6] The author, who is linked by his disciple Jerzy Braun to Husserl's phenomenology and who is presented as "the greatest of Polish thinkers,"[7] examines "the faculty of signation (*facultas signatrix*)." The

438

nature of signs (see p. 38) must be studied first of all with respect to the categories of existence, that is to say, to the *modality* (proper/improper signs) and to the *quality* (determined/undetermined signs), and secondly with respect to the categories of production, that is to say, to the *quantity* (simple/composite signs), to the *relation* (natural/artificial signs) and the *union* (mediate/immediate signs). Following Hoene-Wroński's program, it is the "perfection of signs" ("perfection of language" in Locke's terms, "*Vollkommenheit der Zeichen*" according to Lambert) which forms "the object of *séméiotique*" (p. 41). One should note that this theory reduces the field of "signation" to acts of cognition: "This signation is possible, whether for sensory form or for sensory or intelligible content, of the objects of our knowledge," while "the signation of acts of will and feeling" seems to be "impossible" (p. 38ff.).

III

The Prague philosopher, Bernard Bolzano, in his major work *The Theory of Science* (1837),[8] mainly in the last two of the four volumes, reserves much space for semiotics. The author frequently cites Locke's *Essay* and the *Neues Organon,* and discovers in Lambert's writings "on semiotics . . . many very estimable remarks," though these are of little use "for the development of the most general rules of scientific discourse," one of the aims Balzano sets himself (paragraph 698).

The same chapter of *The Theory of Science* bears two titles, one of which—*Semiotik*—appears in the table of contents (vol. IV, p. xvi), the other of which—*Zeichenlehre*—heads the beginning of the text (p. 500); paragraph 637, which follows, identifies both designations—the theory of signs or semiotics (*Zeichenlehre oder Semiotik*). If, in this chapter and in several other parts of the work, the author's attention is held above all by the testing of the relative perfection of signs (*Vollkommenheit oder Zweckmässigkeit*) and particularly of signs serving logical thought, then it is in the beginning of the third volume that Bolzano tries to introduce the reader to the fundamental notions of the theory of signs throughout paragraph 285 (pp. 67–84), which overflows with ideas and is titled "the designation of our representations" (*Bezeichnung unserer Vorstellungen*).

This paragraph begins with a bilateral definition of the sign: "An object . . . through whose conception we wish to know in a renewed fashion another conception connected therewith in a thinking being, is known to us as a *sign*." A whole chain of geminate concepts follows, some of which are very new, while others, referring back to their anterior sources, are newly specified and enlarged. Thus Bolzano's semiotic thoughts bring to the surface the difference between the meaning (*Bedeutung*) of a sign as such and the significance (*Sinn*) that this sign acquires in the context of the present circumstance, then the difference between the sign (1) produced by the addresser (*Urheber*) and (2) perceived by the addressee who, himself, oscillates between understanding and misunderstanding (*Verstehen und Missverstehen*). The author makes a distinction between the thought and expressed interpretation of the sign (*gedachte und sprachliche Auslegung*), between universal and particular signs, between natural and accidental signs (*natürlich und zufällig*), arbitrary and spontaneous (*willkürlich und unwillkürlich*), auditory and visual (*hörbar und sichtbar*), simple (*einzeln*) and composite (*zusammengesetzt*, which means "a whole whose parts are themselves signs"), between unisemic and polysemic, proper and figurative, metonymical and metaphorical, mediate and immediate signs; to this classification he adds lucid footnotes on the important distinction to be made between signs (*Zeichen*) and indices (*Kennzeichen*) which are devoid of an addresser, and finally on another pressing theme, the question of the relationship between interpersonal (*an Andere*) and internal (*Sprechen mit sich selbst*) communication.

IV

The young Edmund Husserl's study, "Zur Logik der Zeichen (Semiotik)," written in 1890, but not published until 1970,[9] is an attempt to organize the sign categories and to answer the question of knowing in which sense language, that is, our most important system of signs, "furthers and, on the other hand, once again inhibits thinking." Criticism of signs and their improvement are conceived of as an urgent task which confronts *logic*: "A deeper insight into the nature of signs and of arts will rather enable [logic] to devise additionally such symbolic procedural methods upon which the human mind has not yet come, that is, to lay down the rules for their invention." The 1890 manuscript contains a reference to the "*Semiotik*" chapter of *The Theory of Science* which is said to be *wichtig* (p. 530): in aiming at two targets in this essay, one structural and the other regulative, Husserl does in fact follow the example of Bolzano, whom he will later call one of the greatest logicians of all time. In the semiotic ideas of the *Logical Investigations* one can find "decisive instigations from Bolzano" as the phenomenologist acknowledges; and the second volume of the *Investigations,* with its important treatise on general semiotics set up as a system, exerted a profound influence on the beginnings of structural linguistics. As Elmar Holenstein indicates, Husserl made several notes in the margins of paragraph 285 in his own copy of Bolzano's *The Theory of Science III* and he underlined the term *Semiotik* and its definition in Locke's *Essay* in its German translation, *Über den menschlichen Verstand* (Leipzig, 1897).[10]

V

For Charles Sanders Peirce, the nature of signs remained a favorite subject of study since 1863 (cf. V.488 and VIII.376) and especially from the time of his magnificent profession of faith—"On a New List of Categories"—which was published in 1867 by the American Academy of Arts and Sciences (1.545–559); thereupon followed two ingenious contributions to the *Journal of Speculative Philosophy* in 1868 (cf. V.213–317), and finally, materials collected in 1909–10 for his unfinished volume *Essays on Meaning* (II.230–232; VIII.300).[11]

It is notable that, throughout the thinker's whole life, the conception which underlies his continual efforts to establish a science of signs gained in depth and in breadth, and simultaneously remained firm and unified. As for the "semiotic," "semeiotic," or "semeotic," it only surfaces in Peirce's manuscripts at the turn of the century; it is at this time that the theory "of the essential nature and fundamental varieties of possible semiosis" captures the attention of this great researcher (I.444; V. 488). His insertion of the Greek *sēmeiōtikē,* as well as the concise definition "doctrine of signs" (II.277)—puts us on the track of Locke, whose celebrated *Essay* was often referred to and cited by the doctrine's partisan. In spite of the marvelous profusion of original and salutary finds in Peirce's semiotics, the latter nonetheless remains tightly linked to his precursors—Lambert, "the greatest formal logician of those days" (II.346), whose *Neues Organon* is cited (IV.353), and Bolzano, whom he knows from the latter's "valuable contribution to the lucidity of human concepts" and his "work on logic in four volumes" (IV.651).

Still, Peirce declared rightly: "I am, as far as I know, a pioneer, or rather a backwoodsman, in the work of clearing and opening up what I call *semiotic* . . . and I find the field too vast, the labor too great, for a first-comer" (V.488). It is he who is "the most inventive and the most universal of American thinkers,"[12] who knew how to draw up conclusive arguments and to clear the ground in order to erect at his own risk the framework of the science which two centuries of European philosophical thought had anticipated and foreseen.

Peirce's semiotic edifice encloses the whole multiplicity of significative phenomena, whether a knock at the door, a footprint, a spontaneous cry, a painting or a musical score, a conversation, a silent meditation, a piece of writing, a syllogism, an algebraic equation, a geometric diagram, a weather vane, or a simple bookmark. The comparative study of several sign systems carried out by the researcher revealed the fundamental convergences and divergences which had as yet remained unnoticed. Peirce's works demonstrate a particular perspicacity when he deals with the categoric nature of language in the phonic, grammatical and lexical aspects of words as well as in their arrangement within clauses, and in the implementation of the clauses with respect to the utterances. At the same time, the author realizes that his research "must extend over the whole of general Semeiotic," and warns his epistolary interlocutor, Lady Welby: "Perhaps you are in danger of falling into some error in consequence of limiting your studies so much to Language."[13]

Unfortunately, most of Peirce's semiotic writings were only published during the fourth decade of our century, around twenty years after the author's death. Nearly a century was needed to print some of his texts; thus the amazing fragment of one of Peirce's courses given in 1866–67—"Consciousness and Language"—first appeared in 1958 (VII.579–96); let us note too that there remains in Peirce's heritage numerous unpublished pieces. The tardy publication of his works, which appeared dispersed and in fragments in the maze of the *Collected Papers of Charles Sanders Peirce,* vols. I–VIII, for a long time hampered a complete and exact understanding of his precepts and unfortunately delayed their effective influence on the science of language and the harmonious development of semiotics.

Readers and commentators of these works have often been mistaken about the fundamental terms introduced by Peirce, although they are indispensable to an understanding of his theory of signs and although these terms, even if forced occasionally, nonetheless receive a definition that is always very clear in the author's text. Thus the *interpreter* and the *interpretant* designations have given rise to an unfortunate confusion, in spite of the distinction Peirce makes between the term *interpreter,* which designates the receiver and decoder of a message, and *interpretant,* that is, the key which the receiver uses to understand the message he receives. According to popularizers, the sole role attributed to the *interpretant* in Peirce's doctrine consists in clarifying each sign by the mediating context, while in fact the brave "pioneer" of semiotics asks rather "to distinguish, in the first place, the Immediate Interpretant, which is the interpretant as it is revealed in the right understanding of the sign itself, and is ordinarily called the *meaning* of the sign" (IV.536). In other words, it is "all that is explicit in the sign itself, apart from its context and circumstances of utterance" (V.473); all signification is but the "translation of a sign into another system of signs" (IV.127). Peirce casts light upon the ability of every sign to be translatable into an infinite series of other signs which, in some regards, are always mutually equivalent (II.293).

According to this theory, the sign demands nothing more than the possibility of being interpreted, even in the absence of an addresser. The symptoms of illnesses are therefore also considered signs (VIII.185, 335) and at a certain point, medical semiology neighbors semiotics, the science of signs.

In spite of all the differences in the presentation's details, the bipartition of the sign into two conjoined facets and, in particular, the Stoic tradition, which conceives of the sign (*sēmeion*) as a referral on the part of the signans (*sēmainon*) to the signatum (*sēmainomenon*), remains strong in Peirce's doctrine. In conformity with his trichotomy of semiotic modes and with the rather vague names that he gives them, (1) the *index* is a referral from the signans to the signatum by virtue of an effective contiguity; (2) the *icon* is a referral from the signans to the signatum by virtue of an effective similarity; (3) the *symbol* is a referral from the signans to the signatum by virtue of an "imputed," conventional, habitual contiguity. Accordingly (cf. in particular II.249, 292ff, 301, and IV.447ff, 537), "the mode of being of the symbol is different from that of the icon and from that of the index." In contradistinction to these two categories, the symbol as such is not an object; it is nothing but a frame-rule which must clearly be distinguished from its functioning in the form of "replicas" or "instances," as Peirce tries to define them. The elucidation of the generic character which qualifies both the *signantia* and the *signata* in the code of language (each of these aspects "is a kind and not a single thing") has opened new perspectives on the semiotic study of language.

Now, the trichotomy in question has also given rise to erroneous views. Attempts have been made to attribute to Peirce the idea of the division of all human signs into three rigorously separate classes, while the author only considers three modes, one of which "is predominant over the others" and, in a given system, finds itself often linked to the other two modes or to either of them. For example,

> a symbol may have an icon or an index incorporated into it (IV.447). It is frequently desirable that a representamen should exercise one of those three functions to the exclusion of the other two, or two of them to the exclusion of the third; but the most perfect of signs are those in which the iconic, indicative, and symbolic characters are blended as equally as possible (IV.448). It would be difficult if not impossible, to instance an absolutely pure index, or to find any sign absolutely devoid of the indexical quality (II.306). A diagram, though it will ordinarily have Symbolide Features, as well as features approaching the nature of Indices, it is nevertheless in the main an Icon (IV.531).

In his successive attempts to establish a complete classification of semiotic phenomena, Peirce ended up outlining a table consisting of 66 divisions and subdivisions,[14] which embraces the action "of almost any kind of sign"—action known under the ancient name of *sēmeiōsis*. Ordinary language and the diverse types of formalized languages find their place in Peirce's semiotics which emphasizes not only the primacy of the symbolic relationship between the signans and the signatum in the linguistic data but at the same time, the co-presence of the iconic and indexical relationship.

VI

Ferdinand de Saussure's contribution to the progress of semiotic studies is evidently more modest and more restricted. His attitude toward the *science de signes* and the name *sémiologie* (or sporadically *signologie*),[15] which he imposed on it immediately, remains, it seems, completely outside of the current created by such names as Locke, Lambert, Bolzano, Peirce, and Husserl. One can surmise that he did not even know of their research in semiotics. Nonetheless, in his lessons he asks: "Why hasn't semiotics existed until now?" (1:52). The question of the precedent which might have inspired the program constructed by Saussure remains unanswered. His ideas on the science of signs have only come to us in the form of sparse notes, the oldest of which date back to the 1890s,[16] and in the last two of his three courses in general linguistics (1:33, 45–52, 153–55, 170ff).

From the end of the century, Saussure tried to get, according to his own terms, "a correct idea of what a semiological system is"[17] and to discover the traits "of language, as of the entire general semiologic system,"[18] while having in mind mainly systems of "conventional signs." The oldest of Saussure's remarks on the theory of signs try to apply it to the phonic level of language; with a clarity superior to the treatment of the same matter in his later teachings, these theses allow for the emergence of

> the relationship between sound and idea, the semiological value of the phenomenon [which] can and should be studied outside all historical preoccupations, [since] study of the state of language on the same level is perfectly justified (and even necessary, although neglected and poorly understood) insofar as we are dealing with semiologic facts.[19]

The equation *Phonème = Valeur sémiologique* is placed at the head of the *phonétique sémiologique*, the new discipline foreseen by Saussure at the beginning of his activities at the University of Geneva.[20]

The only mention of Saussure's semiological ideas that appeared during his lifetime is a brief summary which his relative and colleague, A. Naville, gives in a book in 1901.[21] The text of the *Cours de linguistique générale*, published in 1916 by Charles Bally and Albert Sechehaye from notes taken by members of Saussure's audience, is so reworked and touched up by the editors that it causes quite a number of errors in the master's teachings. At present, thanks to the beautiful critical edition by Rudolf Engler, we are able to compare the direct accounts of Saussure's students and to get a far truer and far more precise idea of the original text of his talks.

Unlike Peirce and Husserl, who were both conscious of having laid the foundations of semiotics, Saussure speaks of semiotics in the future only. According to the notes on Saussure's courses between 1908 and 1911 which were collected by several students, language is above all a system of signs, and therefore it must be classified as a science of signs

(1:47). This science has hardly developed. Saussure proposes to call it *sémiologie* (from the Greek *sēmeion,* sign). One cannot say what this science of signs will be, but it is our task to say that it is worthy of existence and that linguistics will occupy the principal compartment of this science: "this will be one particular case of the great semiological fact" (1:48). Linguists will have to distinguish the semiological characteristics of language in order to place it properly among systems of signs (1:49); the task of the new science will be to bring out the differences between these diverse systems as well as their common characteristics—"There will be general laws of semiology" (1:47).

Saussure underlines the fact that language is far from being the only system of signs. There are many others: writing, visual nautical signs, military trumpet signals, gestures of politeness, ceremonies, sets of rites (1:46ff); in the eyes of Saussure, "Customs have a semiological character" (1:154). The laws of transformation of the systems of signs will have completely topical analogies with language's laws of transformation; and, on the other hand, these laws will reveal enormous differences (1:45, 49). Saussure envisions certain dissimilarities in the nature of different signs and in their social value: the personal or impersonal factor, a thought-out act or an unconscious one, dependence or independence vis-à-vis the individual or social will, ubiquity or limitedness. If one compares the different systems of signs with language, one will witness, according to Saussure, the surfacing of aspects which one had not suspected; in studying rites or any other system separately, one will notice that all of these systems yield a common study—that of the specific life of signs, semiology (1:51).

According to the thesis Saussure maintained from the time of his preparation in 1894 of an unfinished study on William Dwight Whitney, "language is nothing more than one *particular case* of the Theory of Signs," and

> this will be the major reaction of the study of language in the theory of signs, this will be the ever new horizon which it will have opened—to have taught and revealed to the theory of signs *a whole other and new side of the sign,* that is to say that the sign does not begin to be really known until we have seen that it is not only a transmissible thing but by its very nature a thing *destined to be transmitted.*[22]

(Therefore, in Peirce's terms, the sign demands the participation of an "interpreter.")

Now, at the same time, Saussure puts the "particularly complex nature of the semiology of spoken language" in opposition to the other semiological systems. According to the Saussurean doctrine, these systems use signs which have at least a basic link of reference between the signatum and the signans, *icons* in Peirce's terminology, *symbols* as Saussure's *Course* will call them later: "The symbol is a sign, but not always completely arbitrary" (1:155). On the contrary, language is "a system of independent symbols." Thus, in 1894, purely conventional, and as such "arbitrary," signs are those which Peirce called *symbols* (or *legisigns*). "The independent symbols," according to the old notes of Saussure, "possess the particular major characteristic of not having any sort of perceivable connection with the object to be designated." The result is that "whoever sets foot on the terrain of language may say to himself that he is abandoned by all the analogies of heaven and earth."[23]

Although Saussure is inclined to see the primary concerns of semiology in "arbitrary systems," this science, he affirms, will always see its field grow, and it is difficult to predict where semiology will stop (1:153ff). The "grammar" of the game of chess, with the respective value of its pieces, authorizes Saussure to compare the game and language and to conclude that in these semiological systems "the notion of identity meshes with that of value, and vice versa" (1:249).

It is precisely questions linked to identities and values which, according to an astute note made by Saussure at the beginning of the century, appear to be decisive in mythical studies, as in the "parental domain of linguistics": on the level of semiology

> all the incongruities of thought stem from insufficient reflection about what *identity* is, or what the characteristics of identity are, when we talk about a nonexistent being, like a *word*, or a *mythic person*, or *a letter of the alphabet*, which are only different forms of the sign in a philosophical sense.

"These symbols, without realizing it, are subject to the same vicissitudes and to the same laws as are all the other series of symbols . . . They are all part of semiology."[24] The idea of this semiological being which does not exist *in itself*, "at any time" (*à nul moment*) (2:277) is adopted by Saussure in his 1908–09 course where he proclaims "the reciprocal determination of values by their very coexistence," while adding that there are no isolated semiological beings, and that such a determination can occur only on a synchronic level, "for a system of values cannot stay astride a succession of epochs" (2:304).

Saussure's semiotic principles during the last twenty years of his life demonstrate his striking tenacity. The 1894 sketches, cited above, open with an inflexible assertion:

> The object that serves as sign is never "the same" (*le même*) twice: one immediately needs an examination or an initial convention to know within what limits and in the name of what we have the right to call it the same; therein lies its fundamental difference from an ordinary object.

These notes insist on the decisive role of the "plexus of eternally negative differences," the ultimate principle of non-coincidence in the world of semiological values. In approaching semiological systems, Saussure tries to "take exception to what preceded," and as of 1894 he gladly refers to comparisons between the synchronic states in language and the chessboard. The question of the "antihistoric character of language" will even serve as title to Saussure's last notes in 1894 (2:282), and, one could add, to all of his thoughts on the semiological aspects of language and of all the *créations symboliques*.[25] These are the two intertwined principles of Saussurean linguistics—*l'arbitraire du signe* and the obstinately "static" conception of the system—which nearly blocked the development of the *sémiologie générale* that the master had foreseen and hoped for (cf. Saussure, 1:170ff).

Now, the vital idea of semiological invariance which remains valid throughout all of its circumstantial and individual variations is clarified by Saussure thanks to a felicitous comparison of language to the symphony: the musical work is a reality existing independently of the variety of performances made of it; "the performances do not attain the status of the work itself." "The execution of a sign is not its essential characteristic," as Saussure points out; "the performance of a Beethoven sonata is not the sonata itself" (1:50, 53ff). We are dealing with the relationship between *langue* and *parole* and with the analogous link between the "univocality" (*univocité*) of the work and the multiplicity of its individual interpretations. Mistakenly, in the text arranged by Bally and Sechehaye, these interpretations are represented as "errors that [the performers] might commit."

Saussure must have thought that in semiology the "arbitrary" signs were going to occupy a fundamental place, but it would be useless to look in his students' notes for the assertion that the Bally-Sechehaye text gives, that is: "signs that are entirely arbitrary actualize the ideal of semiological process better than other signs" (1:154).

In his expansionist view of the science in the process of becoming (*science en devenir*) Saussure goes as far as to admit that "everything comprising forms must enter into semiology" (*loc. cit.*). This suggestion seems to anticipate the current idea of the topologist René Thom, who wonders if one must not immediately attempt to develop a "general theory of forms, independent of the specific nature of substratum space."[26]

VII

The relationship of the science of language and languages with that of the sign and of different signs was defined briefly and explicitly by the philosopher Ernst Cassirer in his address to the New York Linguistic Circle, pointing out that "linguistics is a part of semiotics."[27]

There is no doubt that signs belong to a field which is distinguishable in certain respects from all the other facets of our environment. All of the sectors of this field need to be explored, taking into account the generic characteristics and the convergences and divergences among the various types of signs. Any attempt to tighten the limits of semiotic research and to exclude from it certain types of signs threatens to divide the science of signs into two homonymous disciplines, namely *semiotics* in its largest sense and another province, identically named, but taken in its narrower sense. For example, one might want to promote to a specific science the study of signs we call "arbitrary," such as those of language (so it is presumed), even though linguistic symbols, as Peirce demonstrated, can easily be related to the *icon* and to the *index*.

Those who consider the system of language signs as the only set worthy of being the object of the science of signs engage in circular reasoning (*petitio principii*). The egocentrism of linguists who insist on excluding from the sphere of semiotics signs which are organized in a different manner than those of language, in fact reduces semiotics to a simple synonym for linguistics. However, the efforts to restrict the breadth of semiotics sometimes go even further.

At all levels and in all aspects of language, the reciprocal relationship between the two facets of the sign, the signans and the signatum, remains strong, but it is evident that the character of the signatum and the structuring of the signans change according to the level of linguistic phenomenon. The privileged role of the right ear (and, more properly, that of the left hemisphere of the brain) solely in the perception of language sounds is a primary manifestation of their semiotic value, and all the phonic components (whether they are distinctive features, or demarcational, or stylistic, or even strictly redundant elements) function as pertinent signs, each equipped with its own signatum. Each higher level brings new particularities of meaning: they change substantially by climbing the ladder which leads from the phoneme to the morpheme and from there to words (with all their grammatical and lexical hierarchy), then go through various levels of syntactic structures to the sentence, then to the groupings of sentences into the utterance and finally to the sequences of utterances in dialogue. *Each one* of these successive stages is characterized by its own clear and specific properties and by its own degree of submission to the rules of the code and to the requirements of the context. At the same time, each part participates, to the extent possible, in the meaning of the whole. The question of knowing what a morpheme means, or what a word, a sentence, or a given utterance means, is equally valid for all of these units. The relative complexity of signs such as a syntactic period, a monologue, or an interlocution does not change the fact that in any phenomenon of language everything is a sign. The distinctive features or the whole of a discourse, the linguistic entities, in spite of the structural differences in function and in breadth, all are subject to one common science, the science of signs.

The comparative study of natural and formalized languages, and above all those of logic and mathematics, also belongs to semiotics. Here the analysis of the various relationships between code and context has already opened broad perspectives. In addition, the confrontation of language with "secondary modeling sytems" and with mythology in particular points to a rich harvest and calls upon able minds to undertake an analogous type of work which attempts to embrace the semiotics of culture.

In semiotic reseach touching upon the question of language, one will have to guard against the imprudent application of the special characteristics of language to other semiotic systems. At the same time, one must avoid denying to semiotics the study of systems of signs which have little resemblance to language and following this ostracizing activity to the point of revealing a presumably "nonsemiotic" layer in language itself.

VIII

Art has long escaped semiotic analysis. Still there is no doubt that all of the arts, whether essentially temporal like music or poetry, or basically spatial like painting or sculpture, or syncretic, spatio-temporal, like theater or circus performances or film showings, are linked to the sign. To speak of the "grammar" of an art is not to employ a useless metaphor: the point is that all art implies an organization of polar and significant categories that are based on the opposition of marked and unmarked terms. All art is linked to a set of artistic conventions. Some are general: for example, let us say that we may take the number of coordinates which serve as a basis for plastic arts and create a consequential distinction between a painting and a piece of statuary. Other conventions, influential ones or even mandatory ones for the artist and for the immediate receivers of his work, are imposed by the style of the nation and of the time. The originality of the work finds itself restricted by the artistic code which dominates during a given epoch and in a given society. The artist's revolt, no less than his faithfulness to certain required rules, is conceived of by contemporaries with respect to the code that the innovator wants to shatter.

The attempted confrontation between arts and language may fail if this comparative study relates to ordinary language and not directly to verbal art, which is a transformed system of the former.

The signs of a given art can carry the imprint of each of the three semiotic modes described by Peirce; thus, they can come near to the symbol, to the icon, and to the index, but it is obviously above all in their artistic character that their significance (*sēmeiōsis*) is lodged. What does this particular character consist of? The clearest answer to this question was given in 1885 by a young college student, Gerard Manley Hopkins: "The artificial part of poetry, perhaps we shall be right to say all artifice, reduces itself to the principle of parallelism. The structure of poetry is that of continuous parallelism."[28]

The "artifice" is to be added to the triad of semiotic modes established by Peirce. This triad is based on two binary oppositions: contiguous/similar and factual/imputed. The contiguity of the two components of the sign is factual in the *index* but imputed in the *symbol*. Now, the factual similarity which typifies *icon* finds its logically foreseeable correlative in the imputed similarity which specifies the *artifice,* and it is precisely for this reason that the latter fits into the whole which is now forever a four-part entity of semiotic modes.

Each and every sign is a referral (*renvoi*) (following the famous *aliquid stat pro aliquo*). The parallelism alluded to by the master and theoretician of poetry, Gerard Manley Hopkins, is a referral from one sign to a similar one in its totality or at least in one of its two facets (the signans or the signatum). One of the two "correspective" signs, as Saussure designates them,[29] refers back to another, present or implied in the same context, as we can see in the case of a metaphor where only the "vehicle" is *in presentia*. Saussure's only finished writing during his professorship in Geneva, a clairvoyant work on the concern for repetition in ancient literatures, would have innovated the world-wide science of poetics, but it was unduly hidden, and even today the notebooks, which are quite old, are only known to us through Jean Starobinski's fascinating quotations. This work brings out "the 'coupling,' that is, the repetition in even numbers" in Indo-European poetry, which allows for the analysis of "the phonic substance of words whether to construct an acoustical series (e.g. a vowel which requires its 'counter-vowel'), or to make of them a significative series."[30] In trying hard to couple signs which "find themselves naturally evoking each other,"[31] poets had to control the traditional "skeleton of the code," namely, first the strict rules of approved similarity, including accepted license (or, as Saussure puts it, the "transaction" on certain variables), then the laws prescribed for the even (*paire*) distribution of corresponding units throughout the text and, finally, the order (*consecutivité* or *non-consecutivité*) imposed on reiterative elements with respect to the march of time.[32]

"Parallelism" as a characteristic feature of all artifice is the referral of a semiotic fact to an equivalent fact inside the same context, including the case where the aim of the referral is only an elliptic implication. This infallible belonging of the two parallels to the same context allows us to complement the system of times which Peirce includes in his semiotic triad: "An icon has such being as belongs to past experience . . . An index has the being of present experience. The being of a symbol . . . is *esse in futuro*" (IV.447; II.148). The artifice retains the *atemporal* interconnection of the two parallels within their common context.

Stravinsky never tired of repeating that "music is dominated by the principle of similarity."[33] In the musical art the correspondences of elements that are recognized, in a given convention, as mutually equivalent or in opposition to each other, constitute the principal, if not the only, semiotic value—"intramusical embodied meaning," according to the description by the musicologist Leonard Meyer:

> Within the context of a particular musical style one tone or group of tones indicates—leads the practiced listener to expect—that another tone or group of tones will be forthcoming at some more or less specified point in the musical continuum.[34]

The referral to what follows is felt by composers as the essence of the musical sign. In the eyes of Arnold Schönberg, "to compose is to cast a glance upon the theme's future."[35] The three fundamental operations of the musical "artifice"—anticipation, retrospection, and integration—remind us of the fact that it is the study of melodic phrase undertaken in 1890 by Ehrenfels, which suggested to him not only the notion of Gestalt but also of a precise introduction to the analysis of musical signs: "In temporal formal qualities only *one* element can, logically, be given in [acts of] perceptual representations, while the rest are available as images of memory (or as images of expectation projected into the future)."[36] If in music the questions of intrinsic relationships prevail over the tendencies of an iconic order and are capable of reducing them to nothingness, the representational function, on the other hand, easily comes to the fore in the history of the necessarily spatial visual arts.[37] Nonetheless, the existence and the great successes of abstract painting are incontrovertible facts. The "responsions" between the various chromatic and geometric categories which, it goes without saying, play a non-prescriptive role in representational painting, become the only semiotic value in abstract painting. The laws of opposition and equivalence which govern the system of the spatial categories that are at work in a painting offer an eloquent example of similarities imputed by the code of the school, of the epoch, of the nation. Now here, clearly, as is the case in all semiotic systems, the convention is founded on the use and the choice of universally perceptible potentialities.

Instead of the temporal succession which inspires the anticipations and retrospections of the listener of musical phrases, abstract painting makes us aware of a simultaneity of conjoined and intertwined "correspectives." The musical referral which leads us from the present tone to the anticipated or remembered tone is replaced in abstract painting by a reciprocal referral of the factors in question. Here the relationship of the parts and the whole acquires a particular significance, although the idea of the entire work is emphasized in all arts. The manner of being of the parts reveals their solidarity with the whole, and it is according to this whole that each of its component parts emerge. This interdependence between the whole and the parts creates a patent referral from the parts to the whole and vice-versa. One might recognize in this reciprocal referral a synecdochic procedure, following the traditional definitions of the trope, like that of Isidorus Hispalensis: "Synecdoche est conceptio, cum a parte totum vel a toto pars intellegitur."[38] In short, significance underlies all the manifestations of the "artifice."

IX

By way of concluding, we can propose a tautological formula: Semiotics or, put otherwise, *la science du signe et des signes,* the science of signs, *Zeichenlehre,* has the right and the duty to study the structure of all of the types and systems of signs and to elucidate their various hierarchical relationships, the network of their functions, and the common or differing properties of *all* systems. The diversity of the relationships between the code and the message, or between the signans and the signatum, in no way justifies arbitrary and individual attempts to exclude certain classes of signs from semiotic study, as for example nonarbitrary signs as well as those which, having avoided "the test of socialization," remain individual to a certain degree. Semiotics, by virtue of the fact that it is the science of signs, is called upon to encompass *all* the varieties of the signum.

CHAPTER 25

Musicology and Linguistics

The address recently delivered by G. Becking, professor of musicology at the German University of Prague, to the Prague Linguistic Circle is one of the most significant recent events in Prague's scholarly world. At the phonetic congress that took place in July of this year in Amsterdam, Becking, in his lecture on musical aspects of Serbo-Croatian popular epics,[1] and the chairman of the congress, J. van Ginneken, in his introductory remarks, both spoke about the striking parallels between the fundamental problems of phonology and musicology. Becking's lecture at the Circle revealed the importance of these relationships. Clearly, and with many examples intelligible even to laymen, he formulated a compelling comparative analysis between musicology and phonology.

An African native plays a melody on a bamboo flute. A European musician will have great difficulty in reproducing the melody accurately, but when he is finally successful in establishing the pitches, he is convinced that he reproduces the African piece exactly. But the native does not agree, since the European has not taken sufficient notice of the tone color of the notes. Now the native repeats the same melody on another flute. The European thinks it is another melody, since as a result of the different construction of the new instrument, the pitches have completely changed, but the native swears it is the same piece. The difference is that for the African the tone color is the essential point, whereas for the European it is the pitches. What is important in music is not the physically given reality. It is not those tones that are realized, but rather those that *are meant*. The native and the European hear the same sound and mean by it totally different things, since they comprehend it in terms of two different musical systems: musical sound functions as an element of a system. The realizations can be diverse, as the acoustician can precisely confirm, but what is musically essential is that musical pieces be *recognized as identical*. There is, consequently, exactly the same relationship between a musical value and its realizations as there is in language between a phoneme and the articulated sounds which represent this phoneme in speech.

The difference between medieval neumes and modern notes is not one of mere notation, but rather reflects an essential difference between two musical systems: Gregorian chant, contrary to more recent European music, is concerned not with pitch but with sonic motion. The close connection between the phonological construction of a language and its corresponding written form (which has been addressed especially in the articles of N. S. Trubetzkoy and A. Artymovych in the Prague Circle) provides a close parallel.

Becking attempts to construct a typology of musical systems. He distinguishes "one-dimensional systems," where only the number of steps in the scale is relevant; "two-dimensional systems," which affirm the principle of inner relationships within the sonic material; "three-dimensional systems," which are characterized by functional simultaneities; and finally "four-dimensional systems," in which a single tone also represents the function of its harmony as part of a tonal harmonic system. The structural regularity of the system is reminiscent of the typology of a phonological system. To illustrate, for the first type the scholar cited music of the Montenegrin Guslars, for the second an ensemble piece from Bali, for the third a fourteenth-century English church composition, and for the fourth a Venetian Baroque composition. With some vivid examples Becking pointed out the error of scholars who impose the attitudes of one musical system onto another: for example, in construing a one-dimensional system as a "badly played" chromatic scale.

456

The principles of development of a musical system are, as the lecture showed, also related to phonological language transformations. Either a (previously) irrelevant distinction assumes pertinence, or the reverse. Usually the losses and gains of relevant distinctions are mutually linked.

In conclusion, Becking outlined the fundamental difference between music and language. Indeed, there are in music history cases where certain musical formula become unambiguously associated with certain specific expressions (in Italian opera, in Wagner, and so on). It is noteworthy that the most highly organized elements of a given system often have a mystical significance. In general, though, in music as opposed to language it is the tone system itself that bears meaning, and this system is indissolubly linked to a world view.

Becking's remarks are of the greatest importance not only for music scholars but also for linguists. He postulates a new principle for fruitful comparisons: in both music and speech the relationship of sound values and their realizations as well as the relationship between these values and their notation create the basis of mutation.

Musicology teaches us that neighboring peoples and tribes often form singular "musical bonds." So, for example, people of the Far East according to Becking share a particular musical system, distinguished by the use of an unusual number of small intervals. It is highly interesting that the same people create a "phonological alliance," characterized by tonal inflections in the phonological system. It is necessary to compare the boundaries and distinctive traits of each musical and phonological alliance. The structural laws of music and those of the sound structure of poetry are especially fruitful material for comparative study. In linguistic terms, the individuality of music, as opposed to poetry, lies in the fact that its totality of conventions (*langue,* after Saussure's terminology) is restricted to the phonological system, without any distribution of phonemes according to the etymology and therefore without a vocal.

Musicology must take advantage of phonology's achievements: the structural approach, the notion of a system, and so on. Thus, for example, the fact that (according to phonological theory) the difference between two correlated values always emerges as the opposition between a *marked* and an *unmarked* value could be of significance for musical scholarship as well.

CHAPTER 26

Is the Film in Decline?

"We are lazy and uninquisitive." The poet's pronouncement still holds.[1]

We are witnessing the rise of a new art. It is growing by leaps and bounds, detaching itself from the influence of the older arts and even beginning to influence them itself. It creates its own norms, its own laws, and then confidently rejects them. It is becoming a powerful instrument of propaganda and education, a daily and omnipresent social fact; in this respect it is leaving all the other arts behind.

Art studies, however, seem to remain completely unaware of the emergence of this new art. The collector of paintings and other rare objects is interested only in the old masters. Why preoccupy oneself with the rise and self-determination of the cinema, when one can simply remain content with dreamy hypotheses about the origin of theater or about the syncretic nature of prehistoric art? The fewer the traces preserved, the more thrilling the reconstruction of the development of aesthetic forms. The scholar finds the history of the cinema too banal; it is virtually vivisection, whereas his hobby is hunting for antiques. Still it is clear that the search into the early heritage of film will soon be a task worthy of the archaeologist. The first decades of the cinema have already become an "age of fragments." For example, of French films prior to 1907, there remains almost nothing except the Lumière Brothers' first productions, as the specialists report.

However, is the cinema an autonomous art? Where is its specific hero to be found? What kind of material does this art transform? The creator of the Soviet film, Lev Kulešov, correctly states that it is real things that serve as cinematographic material.[2] And the creator of the French film, Louis Delluc, has perfectly grasped that in film even man is "a mere detail, a mere bit *de la matière du monde.*"[3] On the other hand, signs are the material of every art. The semiotic essence of cinematic elements is clear to filmmakers. "The shot must operate as a sign, a kind of letter," emphasizes Kulešov. For this reason essays on cinema always speak in a metaphorical way about the language of the film and even introduce the notion of film sentences, with subject and predicate, and of film subordinate clauses (Boris Èjxenbaum),[4] or look for verbal and nominal elements in film (André Beucler). Is there a conflict between these two theses? According to one of them, film operates with things; according to the other, with signs. There are observers who answer this question affirmatively: rejecting the second thesis and bearing in mind the semiotic nature of art, they refuse to recognize the cinema as art. However, the incompatibility of the two above-mentioned theses was actually eliminated already by St. Augustine. This great thinker of the fifth century, who aptly distinguished between the object meant (*res*) and the sign (*signum*), taught that besides signs whose essential task is to signify something, there exist objects that may be used in the function of signs. It is precisely things (visual and auditory), transformed into signs, that are the specific material of cinematic art.

We can say about the same person: "hunchback," "big-nose," or "big-nosed hunchback." In all three cases the object of our talk is identical, whereas the signs are different. Likewise, in a film we can shoot such a person from behind (his hump will be seen), then *en face* (his nose will be shown), or in profile (both will be seen). In these three shots we have three things functioning as signs of the same object. Now let us demonstrate the synecdochic nature of language by referring to our ugly fellow simply as "the hump" or "the nose." The analogous method in cinema: the camera sees only the hump or only the nose. *Pars pro toto* is a fundamental method of filmic conversion of things into signs. Scenario terminology with its "mid-long shots," "closeups," and "mid-closeups" is sufficiently instructive in this respect. Film works with manifold fragments of objects which differ in magnitude, and also with fragments of time and space likewise varied. It changes their proportions and juxtaposes them in terms of contiguity or similarity and contrast; that is, it takes the path of *metonymy* or *metaphor* (two fundamental kinds of cinematic structure). The treatment of the functions of light in Delluc's *Photogénie* and the analysis of filmic time and motion in Jurij Tynjanov's penetrating study[5] clearly show that each phenomenon of the exterior world changes into a *sign* on the screen.

A dog does not recognize a painted dog, since a painting is wholly a sign—the painter's perspective is a conventional device. A dog barks at dogs on film because the material of the cinema is a real thing, but he remains blind to the montage, to the semiotic interrelation of things he sees on the screen. The theoretician who disclaims cinema as art perceives the film as a mere moving photograph; he does not notice the montage, nor does he want to acknowledge the fact that here a specific sign system is involved—this is the attitude of a reader of poetry for whom the words of the poem make no sense.

The number of those who absolutely reject the cinema is steadily declining. They are being replaced by the critics of sound film. Current slogans state: "Sound film marks the decline of cinema," "it considerably limits the artistic potentialities of cinema," "the style of the film is in inherent contradiction to speech," and so on.

Criticism of sound film is particularly rich in premature generalizations. It does not take into consideration the temporarily limited history and narrow character of certain phenomena in the cinema. Theoreticians have hastily assumed that silence is one of the cinema's structural properties, and now they are offended that its venture into sound makes it deviate from their biased formulas. If the facts do not correspond to their theory, they accuse the facts instead of recognizing the fallacy of the theory.

They have hurriedly assumed that the features of today's films are the only ones that cinema will devise. They forget that the first of the sound films cannot be compared with the last of the silent ones. The sound film is absorbed today with new technical achievements (it's good enough if one can hear well . . .) and preoccupied with the search for new forms to utilize them. We are in a period analogous to that of the prewar silent film, whereas the most recent silent films have already achieved a standard, have created classical works, and perhaps just this realization of a classical canon contained its own demise and the necessity of a fundamental reform.

It has been stated that sound film has brought cinema dangerously close to the theater. Certainly it has again brought the two closer together, as they were at the dawn of the century, during the years of the "electric theaters"; and it was this new bringing together that prepared the way for a new liberation. For, in principle, speech on the screen and speech on the stage are two profoundly different phenomena. As long as the film was silent, its only material was the visual object; today it uses both visual and auditory objects. Human behavior is the material of the theater. Speech in film is a special kind of auditory object, along with the buzzing of a fly or the babbling of a brook, the clamor of machines, and so forth. Speech on the stage is simply one of the manifestations of human behavior. Talking about theater and cinema, Jean Epstein once said that the very essence of their respective expressive methods is different.[6] This thesis remains valid for the sound film as well. Why are asides and soliloquies possible on the stage, yet not on the screen? Precisely because inner speech is an instance of human behavior and not an auditory object. On the same grounds that film speech is an auditory object, the stage whisper in the theater, which is heard by the audience but by none of the dramatis personae, is impossible in film.

A characteristic peculiarity of speech on screen, as opposed to speech on stage, is also its optional nature. The critic Emile Vuillermoz condemns this freedom of selection: "The convulsive and irregular way in which speech is sometimes imposed upon and sometimes eliminated from an art consistently silent in the past has destroyed the laws of the spectacle and assigned an arbitrariness to the silent segments."[7] This rebuke is erroneous.

If on the screen we *see* people speaking, we simultaneously *hear* either their words or music. Music, but not silence. Silence in the cinema is valued as an actual absence of sounds; consequently, it becomes an auditory object, just like speech, a cough, or street noises. In a sound film we perceive silence as a sign of real silence. It is sufficient to recall how the classroom grows quiet in a scene of L. Vančura's film *Before Graduation* (1932). In cinema it is not silence but music that announces the exclusion of the auditory object. Music in cinema serves

461

this end because musical art operates with signs which do not relate to any objects. Auditorily a silent film is entirely "nonrepresentational" and for that very reason demands continual musical accompaniment. Observers unwittingly struck upon this neutralizing function of music in the cinema when they remarked that "we instantly notice the absence of music, but we pay no attention to its presence, so that any music whatever is appropriate for virtually any scene" (Bela Balázs),[8] "music in the cinema is destined not to be listened to" (Paul Ramain), "its only aim is that one's ears be occupied while complete attention is concentrated on seeing" (Frank Martin).

The frequent alternation of speech with music in the sound film must not be seen as an unartistic chaos. Just as the innovation of Edwin Porter, and later D. W. Griffith, involved rejection of the use of an immobile camera in relation to the object and brought a variety of shots into film (the alternation of long shots, mid-shots, closeups, and so on), similarly the sound film with its new diversity replaces the inertness of the previous approach, which consistently discarded sound from the realm of film objects. In a sound film visual and auditory reality can be given either jointly or, on the contrary, separately from one another: the visual object is shown without the particular sound to which it is normally connected, or else the sound is severed from the visual object (we still hear a man speaking, but instead of his mouth we see other details of the given scene or perhaps an entirely different scene). Thus there arise new possibilities for filmic synecdoches. At the same time, the number of methods of joining shots increases (a purely auditory or verbal transition, a clash between sound and image, and so forth).

Titles in silent films were an important means of montage, frequently functioning as a link between shots. In his *Attempt at an Introduction to the Theory and Aesthetics of the Cinema* (1926), Semen Timošenko even sees this as their primary function.[9] Thus the film maintained elements of purely literary composition. For this reason some silent-film directors made attempts to rid film of titles, but these attempts either necessitated the simplification of the plot or considerably retarded the film's tempo. Only in the sound film has the elimination of titles actually been accomplished. Between today's uninterrupted film and yesterday's film interlaced with titles, there is essentially the same difference as between opera and musical vaudeville. Laws of purely cinematic shot linkage at present are obtaining a monopoly.

If someone in a film shows up in one place and then we see him in another place noncontiguous to the first, a time segment must have lapsed between the two situations during which the person is absent from the screen. In the process we are shown either the one place after the person has already departed, or the other place before his arrival, or finally a "crosscut": some other scene appears in which the person does not take part. This principle occurred already in silent films, but there, of course, it was enough to connect such scenes with titles in the vein of: "And when he came home . . ." Only now is the above-mentioned law consistently realized. It can be dispensed with only when two scenes are not joined by contiguity but by similarity or contrast (the person occupies the same position in both scenes), as well as when the intent is especially to stress the rapidity of the jump from one situation to another, or the interruption, the break between the two scenes. Similarly unacceptable within a scene are unmotivated jumps of the camera from one object to another, noncontiguous one. If such a jump nevertheless occurs, it cannot but emphasize and semantically overload the second object and its sudden interference in the action.

After an event, only a succeeding, not a preceding or simultaneous, event can be shown in today's film. A return to the past can be performed only as a reminiscence or a story narrated by one of the participants. This principle has an exact analogy in Homeric poetics (in the same way as the Homeric *horror vacui* corresponds to filmic crosscuts). Simultaneous actions are presented in Homer, as Tadeusz Zieliński points out, either as if they were consecutive events or by the omission of one of the two parallel events, and a palpable gap results if an event is not delineated in advance so that we may easily anticipate its course.[10] Surprisingly enough, the montage of sound film coincides exactly with these principles of ancient epic poetics. An obvious tendency toward the "linear" character of cinematic time already appeared in silent film, but titles allowed for exceptions. On the one hand, announcements such as "And meanwhile . . ." introduced simultaneous actions, and, on the other hand, titles like "NN spent his youth in the village" made possible jumps into the past.

Just as the above-mentioned "law of chronological incompatibility" belongs to the Homeric age, not to narrative poetry in general, so in turn we do not want to generalize hastily upon the laws of contemporary cinema. The theoretician of art who attempts to include the future development of art in his formulas too often resembles Baron Munchausen lifting himself by his own hair. But perhaps one can pick out certain points of departure from which more definite tendencies might develop.

As soon as an inventory of poetic devices takes root and a model canon is established so thoroughly that the literacy of epigones can be taken for granted, then, as a rule, a striving toward prosaization usually develops. The *pictorial* aspect of film has been minutely elaborated by the present time. And just for this reason filmmakers are suddenly calling for sober, epically oriented reportage and there is an increasing aversion to filmic metaphor, to self-contained play with details. In a parallel way, interest in plot construction, which until recently was almost ostentatiously neglected, is increasing. Let us recollect, for instance, Eisenstein's famous, almost plotless films; or Chaplin's *City Lights,* which in fact echoes the scenario of *A Doctor's Love,* a primitive film by Gaumont from the beginning of the century: a blind woman is treated by an ugly hunchbacked doctor, who falls in love with her but does not dare tell her; he says that she can remove the bandage from her eyes the next day because the treatment is over and she will see. He leaves, suffers, convinced that she will despise him for his ugliness; however she throws herself upon his neck: "I love you, for you cured me." A kiss. The end.

As a reaction against an overdone sophistication, against a technique reeking of ornamentation, there arises a purposeful looseness, an intentional rawness, sketchiness as a device (*L'Âge d'or* of the cinematic genius Buñuel). Dilettantism is beginning to delight. In current vocabulary, the words "dilettantism" and "illiteracy" sound despairingly pejorative. Yet there are periods not only in the history of art but even in the history of culture when these factors undoubtedly have a positive, dynamic role. Examples? Rousseau—Henri or Jean-Jacques.

After an abundant harvest, a field needs to lie fallow. The center of film culture has already changed several times. Where the tradition of silent film is strong, sound film has particular difficulties in breaking a new path. Only now is Czech film going through a period similar to the modest Czech debuts at the threshold of the eighteenth and nineteenth centuries for a new national literature. In the Czech silent film, little of significant interest was done. Now, since speech has penetrated the cinema, Czech films worth seeing have appeared. It is highly probable that precisely the lack of a burdensome tradition facilitates experimentation. Real virtue arises from necessity. The ability of Czech artists to profit from the weakness of their native tradition is almost traditional in the history of Czech culture. The fresh, provincial originality of Mácha's romanticism would hardly have been possible if Czech poetry had been burdened with a mature classical norm. And is there a more difficult task for contemporary literature than the discovery of new forms of humor? Soviet humorists imitate Gogol', Čexov, and so on; Kästner's poems echo the sarcasm of Heine; present-day French and English humoresques largely recall centos (poems composed from quotations). *The Good Soldier Švejk* could emerge only because the Czech nineteenth century did not generate a canonical humor.

CHAPTER 27

On the Relation between Visual and Auditory Signs

It is impossible to analyze exhaustively a single system of signs without constant reference to the general problems of semiotics, and in the context of this new and rapidly developing science the question of the relation between the various systems of signs is one of the fundamental and burning questions. We face the task of constructing an overall model of sign production and sign perception and separate models for different types of signs.

The structural and perceptual relation between visual and auditory signs is one of the questions that figures prominently on today's semiotic agenda. I returned to this problem after reading newspaper reports about Nikita Xruščev's recent declarations on modern art, his sharp and dictatorial protests against nonrepresentational, abstract painting. It was clear that he really has a violent aversion to this kind of picture, and the question inevitably arises in our mind, why do we so often meet this outraged reaction, this superstitious fear and inability to grasp and accept nonobjective painting? An official Moscow handbook has summarized this attitude of repugnance: "We do not like abstract art for the simple reason that it takes us away from reality, from labor and beauty, from joy and sorrow, from the very throb of life, into an illusory and spectral world, into the futility of so-called self-expression." But why does the same tirade lose all sense when applied to musical art? In the entire history of the world quite rarely have people grieved and asked, "What facet of reality does Mozart's or Chopin's sonata such-and-such represent? Why does it take us away from the very throb of life and labor into the futility of so-called self-expression?" The question of mimesis, of imitation, of objective representation seems, however, to be natural and even compulsory for the great majority of human beings as soon as we enter into the field of painting or sculpture.

The late M. I. Aronson, a gifted observer who had studied first in Vienna with N. S. Trubetzkoy, then in Leningrad with B. M. Èjxenbaum, wrote in 1929 an instructive report on the experiments conducted by him and several other research workers at Radio Leningrad in order to improve and develop radio dramas.[1] Attempts were made to introduce into the montage of the scripts verisimilar reproductions of various natural noises. Yet, as the experiment disclosed, "only an insignificant part of the noises that surround us is perceived by our consciousness and connected to a concrete phenomenon." The radio station carefully recorded noises of railroad stations and trains, streets, harbors, sea, wind, rain, and various other noise producers, but people were incapable of discriminating different noises and assigning them to their sources. It was unclear to the listeners whether they were hearing thunder or trains or breakers. They knew only that it was noise and nothing more. The conclusion drawn in Aronson's study from these very interesting data was, however, inaccurate. He supposed that vision plays a much greater role than audition. It is enough to recall that radio deals solely with audition of speech and music. Thus the essence of the problem lies not in the degree of importance but in a functional difference between vision and audition.

I have mentioned one puzzling question, namely, why does nonobjective, nonrepresentational abstract painting or sculpture still meet with violent attacks, contempt, jeers, vituperation, bewilderment, sometimes even prohibition, whereas calls for imitations of external reality are rare exceptions in the perennial history of music?

This question is paralleled by another notorious puzzle: Why is audible speech the only universal, autonomous, and fundamental vehicle of communication? All human beings except those with pathological conditions speak. Speechlessness (*aphasia universalis*) is a pathological state. On the other hand, illiteracy is a widespread, in some ethnic groups even general, social condition.[2] Why is it that visual sign patterns are either confined to a merely concomitant, subsidiary role, such as gestures and facial expressions, or—as with letters and glyphs—these semiotic sets constitute, in John Lotz's terminology, parasitic formations, optional superstructures imposed upon spoken language and implying its earlier acquisition?[3] In Edward Sapir's succinct formulation, "phonetic language takes precedence over all other kinds of communicative symbolism, all of which are, by comparison, either substitutive, like writing, or excessively supplementary, like the gesture accompanying speech."[4] These facts demand elucidation.

Using C. S. Peirce's division of signs into indexes, icons, and symbols, one may say that for the interpreter an index is associated with its object by a factual, existential contiguity and an icon by a factual similarity, whereas there is no compulsory existential connection between symbols and the objects they refer to. A symbol acts "by virtue of a law." Conventional rules underlie the relations between the diverse symbols of one and the same system. The connection between the sensuous signans of a symbol and its intelligible (translatable) signatum is based on a learned, agreed upon, customary contiguity. Thus the structure of symbols and indexes implies a relation of contiguity (artificial in the former case, physical in the latter), while the essence of icons consists in similarity. On the other hand, the index, in contradistinction to the icon and symbol, is the only sign which necessarily involves the actual copresence of its object. Strictly speaking, the main difference among the three types of signs is rather in the hierarchy of their properties than in the properties themselves. Thus any painting, according to Peirce, "is largely conventional in its mode of representation," and as long as "likeness is aided by conventional rules," such a sign may be viewed as a *symbolic icon*.[5] On the other hand, the pertinent role played in language by *iconic* and *indexical symbols* still awaits a thorough examination.

In our everyday experience the discriminability of visual indexes is much higher, and their use much wider, than the discernment and utilization of auditory indexes. Likewise, auditory icons, imitations of natural sounds, are poorly recognized and scarcely utilized. On the other hand, the universality of music, the fundamental role of speech in human culture, and, finally, a mere reference to the predominance of word and music in radio suffice to prove that Aronson's conclusion as to the supremacy of sight over hearing in our cultural life is valid only for indexes or icons and not for symbols.

We observe a strong and conspicuous tendency to reify visual signs, to connect them with objects, to ascribe mimesis to such signs, and to view them as elements of an "imitative art." Painters of all periods have splashed blotches or spots of ink or color and tried to visualize them as faces, landscapes, or still lifes. How often broken twigs, furrows in stones or other natural bends, crooks and patches are taken for representations of things or beings. This universal, innate tendency explains why a naive spectator when looking at an abstract painting subconsciously assumes it to be a kind of puzzle picture and then loses his temper when unable to discover what this work "is supposed to represent" and concludes that "this is just a mess!"

Both visual and auditory perception obviously occur in space and time, but the spatial dimension takes priority for visual signs and the temporal one for auditory signs. A complex visual sign involves a series of simultaneous constituents, while a complex auditory sign consists, as a rule, of serial successive constituents. Chords, polyphony, and orchestration are manifestations of simultaneity in music, while the dominant role is assumed by the sequence. The primacy of successivity in language has sometimes been misinterpreted as linearity. Yet phonemes, simultaneous bundles of distinctive features, reveal the second axis of any verbal sequence. Moreover, it is the linearity dogma which prompts its adherents to associate such a sequence with a Markov chain and to overlook the hierarchical arrangement of any syntactic construction.

There is a striking difference between a primarily spatial, simultaneously visible picture and a musical or verbal flow which proceeds in time and successively excites our audition. Even a motion picture continually calls for simultaneous perception of its spatial composition. The verbal or musical sequence, if it is to be produced, followed, and remembered, fulfills two fundamental requirements—it exhibits a consistently hierarchical structure and is resolvable into ultimate, discrete, strictly patterned components designed ad hoc. This is precisely the case with the distinctive features in language, and it is likewise exact about notes as members within any type of musical scale. The same idea was clearly formulated by Thomas Aquinas. When defining the characteristic traits presented by the phonic components of language,

469

he stated that they are *significantia artificialiter*. They act as significant units in an artifical arrangement. Such a system of compulsory hierarchical structures does not exist in painting. There is no obligatory superposition or stratification, as we find in language and in music. When discussing problems of visual perception at a scientific meeting, Walter Rosenblith, well acquainted with the linguistic investigation of distinctive features, aptly observed: "What a pity that in our visual experience we find no correlates to distinctive features. How much easier it would be to dissect and describe the visual percepts." It is not a fortuitous difference but a cardinal and specific property inherent in the temporal, sequential, auditory systems of signs.

Cinema offers a very fruitful field for semiotic studies, and some initial steps in this direction have been made by international research workers. In connection with this discussion of spatial and temporal signs let me share with you my personal experience with abstract films. Although I have always been an ardent and active adherent of abstract painting from the time of the first Russian steps in this direction (Kandinskij, Larionov, Malevič, Bajdin, Romanovič, Rodčenko), I feel completely exhausted after five or ten minutes of watching such films, and I have heard many similar testimonies from other people. George MacKay uses a good expression—"visual noise"—which renders perfectly my response to these stimuli. The chasm between the intention of the artist and the reaction of an unsophisticated decoder to a non-representational visual sequence is a noteworthy psychological fact.

If we continue to discuss problems of simultaneity and successivity, we must refer to the instructive views on this matter expressed in the modern literature about aphasia. Especially the Moscow expert in language pathology, A. R. Luria, insisted on the substantial difference between two basic types of disturbances which I have termed "the similarity disorder" and "the contiguity disorder." Luria convincingly demonstrates the distinct characteristics in the topography of the cortex which correspond to these two kinds of impairments. Together with the contiguity disorders, similarity disturbances also play a considerable role in the pathology of language. When we say "similarity" we mean not only deficiencies in operating with "chords" of concurrent components such as the distinctive-feature bundles (phonemes) but also all the impairments affecting the selectional axis of language, impairments in the choice of grammatical or lexical forms which can occupy the same place in the sequence and thus constitute a commutative (or permutative) set within our verbal pattern. The whole field of transformational grammar evidently belongs to the same area.

In his book on the *Human Brain and Mental Processes* (1963),[6] Luria shows that it was wrong to connect all the disturbances in the visual perception of such objects as paintings solely with the so-called visual centers at the back of the cortex. He discloses that its frontal, pre-motor part is also responsible for certain distortions, and he has analyzed the essence of these impairments. In our perception of a painting, we first employ step-by-step efforts, progressing from certain selected details, from parts to the whole, and for the contemplator of a painting integration follows as a further phase, as a goal. Luria observed that certain pre-motor impairments affect precisely this process of passing from one stage to the next in such preliminary perception, and he refers to I. M. Sečenov's pioneering studies of the 1870s.[7] In connection with speech and similar activities, this great neurologist and psychologist of the last century outlined two distinct, cardinal types of synthesis, one sequential and the other simultaneous. Both varieties participate not only in verbal behavior but also in visual experience. While simultaneous synthesis proves to be the determinant of visual perception, this final stage, as stressed by Luria, is preceded by a chain of successive search processes. With regard to speech, simultaneous synthesis is a transposition of a sequential event into a synchronous structure, whereas in the perception of paintings such a synthesis is the nearest phenomenal approximation to the picture under contemplation.

Simultaneous synthesis, both in verbal behavior and in visual experience, is affected by dorsolateral lesions (see also Luria's paper of 1959 on disorders of simultaneous perception).[8] On the other hand, successive synthesis, particularly the "dynamics of visual perception" and the construction of integrated speech sequences, is impaired by lesions of the mediobasal cortical sections. When Luria's patient suffering from a mediobasal brain injury "was faced with a complex picture, one isolated component could be grasped immediately and only afterward did the other components begin to emerge, little by little."

The problem of the two types of synthesis plays a very great role in linguistics. The interrelation of contiguity and similarity in speech and language has been vividly discussed by linguists of our century, but certain paramount aspects of the same problem were sagaciously approached already in the Old Indic science of language. In the fifth

471

century Bhartrihari, the great master of Indic linguistic theory, distinguished three stages in the speech event. The first is the conceptualization by the speaker which implies no time sequence; the message as a whole may be simultaneously present in the mind of the speaker. What follows is the performance itself which, according to this scholar's treatise, has two faces—production and audition. Both of these activities are naturally sequential. This stage yields to the third one, namely the stage of comprehension, where the sequence appears to be changed into a concurrence. The sequence must be seized and experienced by the interpreter at one and the same time. This conception is akin to the modern psychological problem of "immediate memory," astutely examined by George Miller,[9] or in other words, of "short-term memory." At this stage the whole sequence, whether it be a word, a sentence, or a group of sentences, emerges as a simultaneously present totality which is decoded by means of "simultaneous synthesis."

These vital questions reappear again and again in world literature, and similar principles have been applied repeatedly to verbal art. Two centuries ago a fascinating discussion took place in Germany, where the famous master and theoretician of literature, G. E. Lessing, tried to fix a rigid boundary between verbal art and the fine arts. He taught that painting is an art based on simultaneity (*räumliches Nebeneinander*), whereas poetry operates solely with time sequence (*zeitliches Nacheinander*). Another remarkable German writer and thinker, J. G. Herder, answered Lessing that the idea of a mere literary succession is fictitious, and an art based on mere *Zeitfolge* is impossible. In order to comprehend and evaluate a poetic work, we must have, according to Herder, a synchronic insight into its whole, and he gives the Greek name *energeia* to the simultaneous synthesis which enables us to comprehend the entirety of a verbal flow.

It is clear that between visual, spatial signs, particularly painting, and on the other hand verbal art and music, which deal primarily with time, there are not only a number of significant differences but also many common traits. Both these divergences and convergences must be carefully taken into account, and whatever the import of simultaneous synthesis, nonetheless there exists a profound dissimilarity between the spatial and temporal arts, and between spatial and temporal systems of signs in general. When the observer arrives at the simultaneous synthesis of a contemplated painting, the painting as a whole remains before his eyes, it is still present; but when the listener reaches a synthesis of what he has heard, the phonemes have in fact already vanished. They survive as mere afterimages, somewhat abridged reminiscences, and this creates an essential difference between the two types of perception and percepts.[10]

At the end I would like to add that my remarks should by no means be interpreted as a common front with the antagonists of abstract art. The fact that it is a superstructure and does not follow the line of least resistance with regard to our perceptual habits stands in no contradiction to the legitimate and autonomous existence of nonrepresentational painting or sculpture and of representational bents in music. The transmutative character of the abstract art which forcefully infringes the border between music and the fine arts cannot be branded as decadent, perverse, or degenerate (*entartet*). From the fact that writing is socially and territorially limited, whereas oral speech is universal, one would hardly draw the conclusion that literacy is harmful or futile. The same principle is to be applied to nonobjective art. It is clear that both of these designs—written language and abstract painting—are superstructures, secondary patterns, epiphenomena; but it is not an argument against their prosperous development and diffusion, even if at some loss to oral communication and tradition or to the strictly figurative arts.

CHAPTER 28

Motor Signs for "Yes" and "No"

Since the domain of certain conventional gestures and head motions often encompasses a wider area than linguistic isoglosses, a naive notion about the universality of certain meaningful gestures and movements of the head and facial muscles arises very easily.[1] When Filippo Tommaso Marinetti visited Moscow in the beginning of 1914, the painter Mixail Fëdorovič Larionov, who had at first greeted the Italian Futurist with hostility, soon struck up friendly relations with him, although at the time Larionov did not know a single foreign language and his new friend did not understand a single word of Russian. Larionov treated his guest alternately to paintings done by himself and other members of his team and to Russian vodka. Once Mixail Fëdorovič was impatiently awaiting the end of the debates in French between Marinetti and Russian writers at a meeting of the Moscow Literary-Artistic Circle, and suddenly took the Italian by surprise, coming up close to him and twice flicking himself on the neck above the collar with his finger. When the attempt to remind the foreigner in this way that it was time to go drinking—or, speaking metonymically, "to pour [a drink] behind the collar"[2]—turned out to be manifestly unsuccessful, Larionov remarked acidly, "A real jerk! Even *that* he cannot understand!"

Russian soldiers who had been in Bulgaria in 1877–78 during the war with Turkey could not forget the striking diametrical opposition between their own head motions for indicating "yes" and "no" and those of the Bulgarians. The reverse assignment of signs to meanings threw the parties into a conversation off the track and occasionally led to annoying misunderstandings. Although facial expressions and head motions are less subject to control than speech, the Russians could, without great effort, switch over to the Bulgarian style for the signs of affirmation and negation; but the main difficulty was contained in the uncertainty of the Bulgarians over whether a given Russian in a given instance was using his own code of head motions or theirs.

Such juxtaposition of two opposite systems of motions signifying "yes" and "no" easily leads to a new false generalization, namely the conviction that the distribution of the two semantically opposed head motions is a purely arbitrary convention. A careful analysis, however, reveals a latent imagery—"iconicity," to use C. S. Peirce's terminology[3]—underlying these symbols, seemingly entirely devoid of any connection or similarity between their outward form and their meaning. "Our" binary system of signs for affirmation and negation belongs to the code of head motions used by the vast majority of European peoples, including among others the Germanic peoples, the East and West Slavs (in particular, the Russians, Poles, and Czechs), the French and most of the Romance peoples. Moreover, similar signs in the same function are in general widespread, though by no means universal, among various peoples of all parts of the world. A nod of the head serves here as an expression of agreement, in other words, as a synonym for the word "yes."

Like certain forms of affirmative hand motions, this head motion has a close analogue in the particular welcoming ritual which is used in the same ethnic environment.[4] The movement of the head forward and down is an obvious visual representation of bowing before the demand, wish, suggestion, or opinion of the other participant in the conversation, and it symbolizes obedient readiness for an affirmative answer to a positively worded question.[5] The direct opposite of bending the head forward as a sign of obedience ought to be throwing the head back as a sign of disagreement, dissent, refusal—in short, as a sign of a negative attitude. However, such a straightforward opposition of two motions of the head is obstructed by the need for insistent emphatic repetition of both the affirmative and the negative head motions: the vocal repetitions "yes, yes, yes!" and "no, no, no!"[6] The corresponding chain of head motions in the first case would be the alternation "forward-backward-forward-backward-forward-backward", and in the second case the reverse set "backward-forward-backward-forward-backward-forward," or two similar series; the entire difference between them comes down to the initial movement forward or backward and easily slips by the addressee, remaining beyond the threshold of his perception.

The semantically opposite signs of affirmation and negation required perceptibly contrasting forms of head motions. The forward-bending movement used in an affirmative nod found its clear-cut opposite in the sideward-turning movement which is characteristic of the head motion synonymous with the word "no." This latter sign, the outward form of which was undoubtedly constructed by contrast to the affirmative head motion, is in turn not devoid of iconicity. Turning the face to the side, away from the addressee (first, apparently, usually to the left),[7] symbolizes, as it were, alienation, refusal, the termination of direct face-to-face contact.[8]

If in the system of head motions for "yes" and "no" under discussion the sign for affirmation appears to be the point of departure, then in the Bulgarian code, which also has parallels among a few ethnic groups in the Balkan Peninsula and the Near East, it is rather the sign for negation which serves as the point of departure for the system. The Bulgarian head motion for "no," appearing at first glance visually identical to the Russian head motion for "yes," under close observation displays a significant point of difference. The Russian single affirmative nod is delimited by a bending motion of the head forward and its return to the usual vertical position. In the Bulgarian system, a single negative sign consists of throwing the head *back* and the consequent return to the vertical position. However, emphatic intensification makes the return to the normal position into a slight bending of the head backward in our "yes" or forward in the Bulgarian "no." Frequently, because of emphasis, the same head motion undergoes immediate repetition—once or many times—and such repetition, as already noted above, more or less obscures the difference between our sign for affirmation and the Bulgarian sign for negation.

In the pure form of the Bulgarian negation, the head—thrown back, away from the addressee—bespeaks departure, disagreement, discord, a rejected suggestion, refusal of a positive answer to a given question, while the Bulgarian sign for affirmation—turning the head from side to side—represents an obviously secondary form, a derivative from its negative antonym. In keeping with Saussure's formula,[9] observations of the structure of the Bulgarian head motion for "yes" and of its basic core of inalienable properties should reveal even in this visual sign a certain degree of iconicity. With the initial turn of the head—usually to the right—and with each further turn, the addressor of this affirmative cue offers his ear to the addressee, displaying in this way heightened attention well-disposed to his words; compare such Bulgarian figures of speech as "Az s″m celijat v uši" (I'm all ears); "davam uxo/nadavam uxo" (I give [you my] ear, lend me your ears).

Systems of head motions for affirmation and negation are represented in Europe by both types considered above—"ours" and the "Bulgarian" type, as I label them—and also by a third type, occurring in certain parts of the Mediterranean area, consisting of bending the head forward for affirmation and backward for negation. I have observed that this kind of opposition is consistently used by the Greeks in Athens, and the same system is preserved in certain regions of southern Italy, for example among the Neapolitans and Calabrians.[10] Nevertheless, the fact that it is difficult to perceive the difference between the two sets of repeated noddings of the head—forward and backward—is completely corroborated, even in the present case. Both of these head motions are in fact accompanied by two mutually contrasting movements of the pupils, eyeballs, and eyebrows—downward as a sign of agreement and upward as a sign of negation. But even these movements, just like the aforementioned movements of the head, turn out to be nothing more than concomitant, redundant phenomena, while the role of the autonomous, distinctive signal in this case is played by the furrow between the eyebrows and the cheekbones, especially the right eyebrow and cheekbone; this furrow is narrowed as a sign of affirmation and is, in contradistinction to this, widened as a sign of negation.[11]

The work of the facial musculature, causing the movement of the eyebrow either toward or away from the cheekbone, creates a kind of synecdoche: the lowered or raised eyebrow becomes a meaningful, valid substitute for the submissively-bent-down or obstinately-thrown-back head. Another signal for specifying the head motion for negation—used, for example, among those Arabic tribes which have a similar opposition built around bending the head forward or backward—

is a click sound, which accompanies the basic movement of the negative sign, i.e. the initial bending of the head backwards.

Several other motions of the head and face are connected in form and meaning with the signs for "yes" and "no" of "our" type. A question is contrasted to an affirmative nod in which the head is thrown back by having the chin thrust forward and up. The head either remains set in this position or the questioner moves it slightly from side to side. In addition, opening the eyes wide signals a puzzled question, while squinting is characteristic of an encouraging attitude on the part of the questioner. As has been already noted above in another connection, the key role here is played by the widened or narrowed space between the eyebrows and the cheekbones.

Amazement, as if removing the capability of an unambiguous reply ("neither yes nor no"), is expressed by rocking the head from side to side, usually from left to right. An inclined movement of the head relates this sign to the head motion for "yes," and the direction from side to side relates it to the motion for "no." Shrugging the shoulders signifies doubt ("perhaps yes, perhaps no"). Reducing the angle between the head and the shoulders brings together the signs of surprise and doubt; but in the case of the former, the head is bent toward the shoulders, which remain stationary, and in the case of the latter the head remains stationary while the shoulders are raised toward it.

It is necessary to subject the formal makeup and semantics of various systems of motions to thorough analysis, eliciting the invariants of the sign within each of them. The ethnological and geographical distribution of individual systems, as well as the role assigned to them in the processes of communication (the hierarchical significance of gesture, motion, facial expression, and speech, and the degree of their interconnection) are subject to investigation. In such an investigation the linguist ought to take into account the highly instructive indigenous terminology, both nominal and verbal, used for referring to the customary gestures, head motions, and facial expressions.

The exciting questions about the interrelation of naturalness and conventionality in these motor signs, about the binary, "antithetical" principle of their construction, and, finally, about the ethnic variations and universal invariants—for example, in signs for affirmation and negation—raised long ago in Darwin's searching study *The Expression of the Emotions in Man and Animals* (1872)—demand a comprehensive and systematic examination.[12]

CHAPTER 29

On the Verbal Art of William Blake and Other Poet-Painters

I. One of the Songs of Experience

Not a line is drawn without intention . . .
as Poetry admits not a Letter that is
Insignificant so Painting admits not a
Grain of Sand or a Blade of Grass
Insignificant much less an Insignificant
Blur or Mark.

   Blake, "A Vision of the Last Judgment"

The spelling and punctuation of "Infant Sorrow" presented be-
low strictly follow the text which was engraved by William Blake in his
Songs of Experience (1794) and which is entirely uniform both in all the
early copies owned by the Houghton and Widener libraries of Harvard
University and in the facsimile edition of the *Songs of Innocence and of
Experience* published by Trianon Press in London and Beccles.

  ₁My mother groand! my father wept.
  ₂Into the dangerous world I leapt:
  ₃Helpless, naked, piping loud:
  ₄Like a fiend hid in a cloud.

~5~Struggling in my fathers hands:
~6~Striving against my swadling bands:
~7~Bound and weary I thought best
~8~To sulk upon my mothers breast.

The two quatrains of the poem are divided into four clear-cut couplets. In particular, the two lines of each couplet are bound by a rhyme, and the odd couplets of the poem differ from the even ones in the structure of their rhymes. Both rhyming words of any odd couplet belong to the same morphological category, end with the identical consonantal inflectional suffix, and are devoid of agreement in their prevocalic phonemes: ~1~*wep-t:* ~2~*leap-t,* ~5~*hand-s:* ~6~*band-s*. The similar formal makeup of the two odd rhymes underscores the divergent semantic orientation of the two quatrains, that is, the conceptual contrast between the inaugural preterits and the inanimates looming over the second quatrain which are, *nota bene,* the sole plurals of the poem. The grammatical rhyme is combined with the deep parallelism of the rhyming lines. The third couplet consists of two strictly symmetrical clauses: ~5~*Struggling in my fathers hands:* ~6~*Striving against my swadling bands.* In the first couplet two coordinate clauses of the initial line, the only parallel hemistichs within the poem—~1~*My mother groand! my father wept*—find their response in the third coordinate clause: ~2~*I leapt.* In contradistinction to the odd couplets, the even rhymes confront grammatically dissimilar words; namely, in both cases an adjectival adjunct rhymes with an inanimate noun. The entire phonetic makeup of the former word appears to be included in the second member of the rhyming pair: ~3~*loud:* ~4~*cloud,* ~7~*best:* ~8~*breast.*

Thus the even rhymes, nongrammatical by themselves, are patently grammatical in their juxtaposition. In particular, they assert the kinship of the two terminal images—~4~*a cloud* as a metaphor of placenta and ~8~*breast*—two successive links between the infant and his mother.

The eight lines of the poem build an array of close and telling grammatical correspondences. The four couplets of the octastich are divided into two pairs in three different ways similar to the three types of rhymes within a quatrain. Both successive pairs of couplets—the two *anterior* couplets (I–II) of the first quatrain (lines 1–4) and the two *posterior* couplets (III–IV) of the second quatrain (lines 5–8) are comparable to the two paired (or plain) rhymes *aabb* within a quatrain. The relation between the two *odd* couplets (I, III: lines 1–2 and 5–6) and the two *even* couplets (II, IV: lines 3–4 and 7–8) is analogous to

480

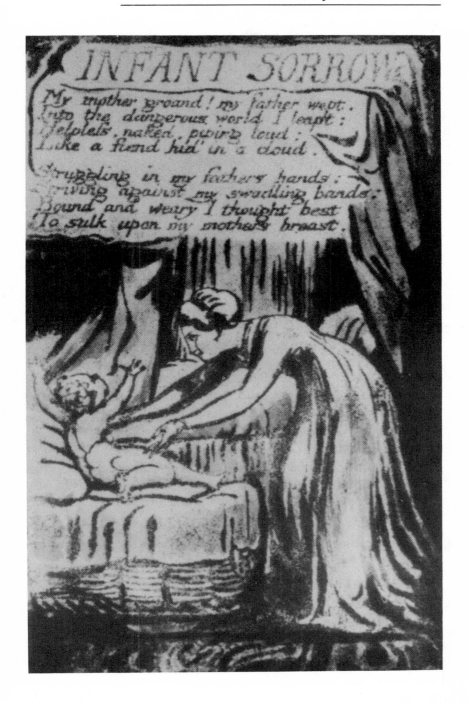

the alternate rhymes *abab*. Finally, the contraposition of the *outer* couplets (I, IV: lines 1–2, 7–8) and the *inner* couplets (II, III: lines 3–6) is tantamount to the embracing rhymes *abba*. These three types of grammatical correspondences are distinctly interconnected in "Infant Sorrow." An isomerism, i.e., an equal number of equivalent components, underlies the correlation of the couplets and presents two significant varieties. A *global* symmetry equating both couplets of one class with both couplets of the opposite class, namely I + II = III + IV or I + III = II + IV or I + IV = II + III, differs from a *sectional* symmetry which builds an equation between the couplets within each of the two opposite classes, namely I = III and II = IV or I = IV and II = III.

Here in each instance of global symmetry between the anterior and posterior couplets, one of the two further correspondences—outer/inner or odd/even—is also global and supports the equilibrium of the quatrains: it assigns the same total number of similar grammatical units to the two pairs of opposites (to the entire pairs of odd and even or of outer and inner couplets), whereas the other displays a sectional symmetry and assigns a like number of similar grammatical entities to both couplets of one and the same pair.

In addition to the leading constructive role assumed by the entire couplets, the autonomous part played by the single lines within the quatrain must also be taken into account. Thus, the two outer, marginal lines of each quatrain and also of the whole octastich appear to present particular correspondences.

Blake's reminder that both Invention and Identity "are Objects of Intuition" provides a paramount clue to the poetic network of his words. Each of the two quatrains contains five nouns and five verbal forms. These five nouns are distributed in an equal manner among the four lines of each quatrain:

1. mother, father	=	*2*	=	*fathers hands*	*5.*
2. world	=	*1*	=	*bands*	*6.*
3.	=	#	=		*7.*
4. fiend, cloud	=	*2*	=	*mothers breast*	*8.*

In the disposition of nouns all three compositional correlations of the couplets prove to be involved.

I. 3   3   III.
II. 2   2   IV.

The global symmetry between the anterior and posterior couplets (I + II = III + IV = 5) is accompanied by a similar global symmetry between the outer and inner couplets (I + IV = II + III = 5) and by a sectional symmetry of the odd and even couplets (I = III = 3; II = IV = 2). This sectional symmetry is not confined to the entire couplets but applies also to their constituent lines: there are (1) two nouns in the first and one in the second line of the odd couplets, (2) no nouns in the first and two in the second line of the even couplets. In this way the homogeneity of the odd couplets and that of their even opposites as well as the contrast of these two classes are outlined. In contradistinction to all other lines of the poem, the marginal lines of both quatrains differ from all other lines of the octastich: each of the four marginal lines contains one pair of nouns: $_1$*mother, father;* $_4$*fiend, cloud;* $_5$*fathers hands,* $_8$*mothers breast.*

The ten nouns of the poem are divided evenly into five animates and five inanimates. The five animates are confined to the four marginal lines of the two quatrains. The distribution of animates and inanimates among the two anterior couplets of the first quatrain and the two posterior couplets of the second quatrain and, moreover, among the outer and inner couplets, follows the principle of antisymmetry:

Anterior couplets:	3 animates,	2 inanimates	
Outer couplets:	3 "	2 "	
Posterior couplets:	2 "	3 "	
Inner couplets:	2 "	3 "	

A manifestly spatial treatment opposes inanimates to animates. The inanimates are constantly bound with locative prepositions, whereas, of the five animates, four are used without any preposition, and one with an equational preposition ($_4$*Like a fiend*).

Two epithets emerge in the poem. Both are attached to the second line of the quatrains and pertain to similar syntactic constructions: $_2$*Into the dangerous world I leapt;* $_6$*Striving against my swadling bands.* Jointly with all other prepositive attributes—possessive forms of nouns and pronouns, definite and indefinite articles—these epithets form a conspicuously symmetrical design in the poem. Such attributes occur twice in each line of both quatrains with the exception of their penultimate line: $_1$*My, my;* $_2$*the dangerous;* $_3$*#;* $_4$*a, a;* $_5$*my fathers;* $_6$*my swadling;* $_7$*#;* $_8$*my mothers.* Six of these attributes belong to the first, and six to the second quatrain; correspondingly, an equal number pertain to

483

the outer and inner couplets of the poem. The odd couplets oppose four (2 + 2) prepositive attributes to two (# + 2) in the even couplets.

As compared with the ten nouns, the ten verbal forms present significant similarities and divergences in their distribution among the four couplets:

I. 3   2   III.
II. 2   3   IV.

We are faced with the same global symmetry between the anterior and posterior couplets (I + II = III + IV = 5), but the treatment of the correlations outer/inner and odd/even is diametrically opposite in the nominal and verbal sets. The disposition of verbal forms exhibits a global symmetry between the odd and even couplets (I + III = II + IV = 5), and a sectional symmetry of the outer and inner couplets (I = IV = 3; II = III = 2). This symmetry applies both to the couplets and to their lines. The first line of the outer couplets contains two verbal forms ($_1$*groand, wept;* $_7$*bound, thought*), the second line contains one ($_2$*leapt;* $_8$*to sulk*); and each line of the inner couplets contains one verbal form ($_3$*piping,* $_4$*hid;* $_5$*struggling,* $_6$*striving*).

There is a sensible difference between a global symmetry of outer/inner and odd/even constituents: the former suggests a closed configuration, and the latter, an open-ended chain. Blake's poem associates the former with nouns and the latter with verbs, and one ought to recall Edward Sapir's semantic definition of nouns as "existents" and of verbs as "occurrents."

The passive participle appears once in each even couplet ($_4$*hid,* $_7$*bound*). No transitives occur among the active verbal forms. In the active voice the first quatrain counts three finite and one nonfinite form, while the second quatrain displays an antisymmetrical relation of one finite and three nonfinite forms. All four finites are preterits. A sharp contrast arises between the inner couplets, with their three gerunds as the sole verbal forms, and the outer couplets, which possess no gerunds but have five verbs proper (four finites and one infinitive). In both quatrains the inner couplet is subordinate to the contiguous line of the outer couplet: lines (3, 4) to the second line of the octastich, and lines (5, 6) to the second line from its end.

Prepositions parallel the verbs in the global symmetry of their distribution. Among the six prepositions in the poem, three belong to the anterior couplets (₂*into,* ₄*like, in*) and three to the posterior couplets (₅*in,* ₆*against,* ₈*upon*) and, correspondingly, three to the odd and three to the even couplets, whereas any outer couplet uses one preposition and any inner couplet, two.

The impressive grammatical balance between the correlative parts of the poem frames and sets off the dramatic development. The only four independent clauses with the only four finite predicates and the only four grammatical subjects—two of them pronominal and two, nominal—are all confined to the outer couplets. While the pronominal clause with the first person subject occurs in both quatrains—in the next to the first and next to the last line of the octastich (₂*I leapt;* ₇*I thought*)—the two nominal subjects detach the first line from the rest of the poem, and Blake concludes this line with a period. *Infant,* the title hero, and the two other dramatis personae are presented with reference to the addresser of the message: *I, my mother, my father.* Both nouns along with their determiners reappear in the second quatrain, however, with significant syntactic and semantic shifts. Grammatical subjects are transformed into possessive attributes of indirect objects, which are governed by subordinate verbal forms. The two matching parts of the inaugural octosyllable become disjointed. The initial line of the second quatrain concludes with the same paternal evocation as the corresponding line of the first quatrain: ₁*my father wept;* ₅*my fathers hands.* The original vision of the weeping parent yields to the twofold image of strife against *fathers hands* and *swadling bands,* the hostile forces which befall the infant at his leap *into the dangerous world.*

The opening words of the poem—₁*My mother*—reappear once more at its end—₈*my mothers*—and, jointly with the subject *I* of the second and seventh lines, they display a mirror symmetry. The first of these two pronouns is followed by the pair of semipredicates ₃*Helpless, naked,* while the second *I* is preceded by a syntactically analogous pair: ₇*Bound and weary.* The placement and chiastic structure of this pair retain the principle of mirror symmetry. The participle *Bound* supersedes the antonym *naked,* and the primordial helplessness turns into exhaustion. The loud piping of the infant, which supplanted the deep moan of the mother, yields to an urge for silence: ₇*I thought best* ₈*To sulk upon my mothers breast.* The exodus from the mother portends the return to her, a new maternal screen for shelter and protection (₄*hid in*—₈*To sulk upon*).

The author's drafts of a longer poem were reduced to its first eight lines for his *Songs of Experience*.[1] The inquiry into the verbal texture of these two quatrains corroborates and strengthens the intuitive grasp expressed astutely by Jacob Bronowski: "The whole progression lies coiled in the first helplessness."[2] A scrutiny of the chiselled octastich with its far-flung grammatical framework may illustrate and specify another pertinent conclusion of the same author: "Blake's was an imagination of pictures, astonishing in its geometrical insight."[3]

In this connection it seems to me suitable to restate the "remarkable analogy between the role of grammar in poetry and the painter's composition based on a latent or patent geometrical order or on a revulsion against geometrical arrangements."[4] In particular, the headwords, the principal clauses, and the prominent motifs which fill the diverging outer couplets stand out against accessory and subordinate contents of the contiguous inner couplets, quite similar to the converging lines of the background in a pictorial perspective.

The firm and plastic relational geometricity of Blake's verbal art assures a startling dynamism in the development of the tragic theme. The coupled antisymmetrical operations outlined above and the categorial contrast of the two parallel grammatical rhymes underscore the tension between the nativity and the ensuing worldly experience. In linguistic terms, the tension is between the initial supremacy of animate subjects with finite verbs of action and the subsequent prevalence of concrete, material inanimates used as indirect objects of gerunds, mere verbals derived from verbs of action and subordinate to the only finite $_7thought,$ in its narrowed meaning of a wish conceived.

The peculiar feature of Blake's punctuation is his use of colons. The colons of "Infant Sorrow" signal the division of the inner couplets into their constituent lines and dissociate the inner couplets from the outer ones. Each of the inner lines containing a gerundial construction ends in a colon and is separated by a colon from the antecedent clause of the same sentence.

The growing motif of weary resignation finds its gripping embodiment also in the rhythmical course of the poem. Its initial octosyllable is the most symmetrical of the eight lines. It consists of two tetrasyllabic coordinate clauses with an expressive pause between them, rendered in Blake's text by means of an exclamation point. An optional secondary pause emerges between the subject and predicate of both juxtaposed clauses. The consequent of these contrastive pauses precedes the final syllable of the line: $_1$ *My mother groand! my father wept.*

In the next line, which concludes the first odd couplet, the internal syntactic pause arises before the second to the last syllable (6 + 2), and with each line the interval between the final and the internal pause becomes one syllable longer, until the last line of the second odd couplet fixes the internal pause after the second syllable of the line: 2 + 6. Thus the widest swing which the verse takes (₂*Into the dangerous world / I leapt*) changes gradually into the shortest, bated, constrained span: ₆*Striving / against my swadling bands*.

Each quatrain includes two iambic octosyllables and two trochaic heptasyllables. One observes the iambic design in the two marginal lines of the octastich, both of them with the evocation *my mother,* and in the final line of both odd couplets, each of them characterized by an oppositive impetus—in the first case toward, and in the second away from, the "dangerous" environment. The similar length of these two correlative lines lends a particular cogency to the double contrast of their rhythmical phrasing and semantic orientation. The thought of salvation *upon my mothers breast* as a retort to the image of hateful *swadling bands* reinforces the association between the two even lines of the second quatrain by their rhythmical identity: ₆*Striving / against my swadling bands* and ₈*To sulk / upon my mothers breast*. The intermediate line which opens the last even couplet shares, as mentioned above, several structural features with the initial line of the first even couplet and duplicates its trochaic measure with a medial pause (4 + 3).

In the iambic lines the main or only pause always falls before an upbeat. In the trochaic lines the pause occurs before the downbeat or, exceptionally, before an upbeat fulfilled by a stressed syllable (₄*Like a fiend / hid in a cloud*). The distribution of pauses in Blake's octastich illustrates its stunning symmetry. In the diagram below, numerals followed by a dot show the order of the eight lines; the subsequent vertical indicates the beginning, and the oblong vertical at the right of the table, the end of the line. The syllables of the line from its end toward its beginning are designated by the upper horizontal row of numerals. The vertical between the two limits of each line renders its inner pause, while the secondary, optional inner pause is represented by a dotted vertical. A slant marks the increasingly regressive tendency displayed by the disposition of the interlinear and then, in the last couplet, prelinear pauses.

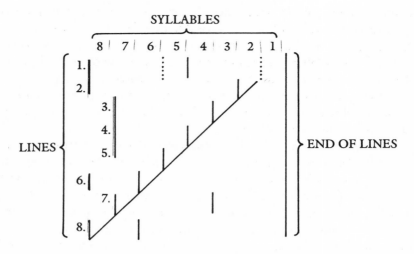

As the poet himself asserts in the foreword to "Jerusalem," he has indeed attained "a variety in every line, both of cadences & number of syllables" within its segments.

The initial heptasyllabic line of each even couplet is linked with the octosyllabic end of the foregoing odd couplet by means of an alliteration of the two final words ($_2$*Leapt*—$_3$*Loud*, $_6$*Bands*—$_7$*Best*), and by a paronomastic affinity between the final and initial word of both successive lines ($_2$LEAP*t*—$_3$*h*ELP*less*, $_6$B*a*NDs—$_7$B*ou*ND). Within a couplet the lines are parisyllabic in the first quatrain, imparisyllabic in the second. Two words alliterate in the former case, three in the latter: $_1$*Wept*—$_2$*World*, $_3$*Loud*—$_4$*Like*; $_7$*Bound*—*Best*—$_8$*Breast*. In the first, parallelistic couplet of the second quatrain, the alliteration develops into a paronomastic blend of two subsequent words in the antecedent member of a triple chain: $_5$STR*ugg*LING—$_6$STR*iv*ING—*swad*LING. The similarity of clusters counterbalances the dissimilar distribution of downbeats and upbeats in both confronted gerunds, one of which begins a trochaic ($_5$*Struggling in*) and the other an iambic line ($_6$*Striving against*).

At the limit of both quatrains the parisyllabic contiguous lines of the two inner couplets, one even and the next odd, display a manifold propinquity in their sound texture: $_4$F*ie*ND—H*i*D IN—$_5$IN *my* F*a*ther*s* H*a*NDS. No sooner has the fourth line, the only simile of the poem, introduced a mythicized hero, than the adverse image of the father's fettering hands, in a kind of filmic dissolve, appears slightly under the first shot, whereupon the salient metamorphosis comes into being: the would-be supernatural hero (₄*Like a fiend hid in a cloud*) is victimized (₅*Struggling in my fathers hands*).

The eight lines of "Infant Sorrow" are remarkably rich in what Gerard Manley Hopkins infers by "figures of grammar" and "figures of sound," and it is to their eloquent symmetry and palpable interplay imbued with diaphanous symbolism that this succinct, ingenuous story owes most of its mythological power and suggestiveness.

The Douanier Rousseau has been compared with Blake and said to be close to him.⁵ An octastich of the French painter will be our next topic.

II. Henri Rousseau's Poetic Appendix to His Last Painting

I have kept my naïveté . . . I will not now be able to change my manner which I have acquired by stubborn application.

Rousseau to André Dupont, April 1, 1910

Shortly before the artist's death (September 2, 1910), he exhibited one single painting, *The Dream,* at the Salon des Indépendants (March 18–May 1 of the same year) and wrote to Guillaume Apollinaire: "I have sent my large picture; everyone finds it pleasing; I think that you will deploy your literary talent and avenge me for all the insults and affronts I have received" (March 11, 1910).⁶ Apollinaire's commemorative paper "Le Douanier" recounts that Rousseau had never forgotten his early, Polish love, Yadwigha (Jadwiga), "who inspired *The Dream,* his masterpiece," and among a few instances of the painter's poetic activities ("gentils morceaux de poésie") his "Inscription pour Le Rêve" supplements Apollinaire's essay.⁷

₁Yadwigha dans un beau rêve
₂S'étant endormie doucement
₃Entendait les sons d'une musette
₄Dont jouait un charmeur bien pensant.
₅Pendant que la lune reflète
₆Sur les fleuves, les arbres verdoyants,
₇Les fauves serpents prêtent l'oreille
₈Aux airs gais de l'instrument.

A nearly literal English translation reads as follows:

Yadwigha in a beautiful dream
Having fallen asleep peacefully
Was hearing the sound of a reed
Upon which a well-meaning charmer was playing.
While the moon casts a reflection
Of the greening trees on the rivers,
The savage serpents lend their ear
To the gay tunes of the instrument.

This octastich was written by the painter on a little gilded plate as an "explanation" of this painting, because, according to Arsène Alexandre's report on his visit to the artist published in *Comœdia,* March 19, 1910, Rousseau declared that paintings need to have an explanation: "People don't always understand what they see . . . it's always better with a few verses."[8] In the *Catalogue de la 26 Exposition* of the *Société des Artistes Indépendants* (Paris, 1910, p. 294) the reference to Henri Rousseau's "*4468 Le Rêve*" is accompanied by the same verses, printed, however, with gross errors and distortions, e.g., *Yadurgha,* so that Apollinaire's version and the identical text in W. Uhde's *Henri Rousseau* (Paris, 1911) still appear to be the most reliable.

The four even, "masculine" lines of the poem end in one and the same nasal vowel, whereas the four odd, "feminine" lines end in a closed syllable with a short or long variety of $[\varepsilon]$ as its nucleus. Among the approximate rhymes displayed by these two sets of lines, those which tie together the two inner couplets (lines 3–4 with 5–6) and, in turn, the rhymes of the two outer couplets (1–2 with 7–8) exhibit a supplementary similarity between the rhyming words in comparison with the rhymes within the quatrains: in the outer couplets the complete identity of syllabic vowels is reinforced by a supporting prevocalic consonant ($_1$Rêve— $_7$OREille; $_2$douceMENT— $_8$instruMENT) and in the inner couplets a similar vocalic identity is seconded by the postvocalic consonant of the feminine rhymes ($_3$musETTE— $_5$reflÈTE) or by the salient grammatical sameness of the words sharing the masculine rhyme ($_4$pensant— $_6$verdoyants,* the only two participial forms in the poem).

As the rhymes underscore, the octastich presents a clear-cut division into outer (I, IV) and inner couplets (II, III). Each of these two pairs of couplets contains an equal number of six nouns with the same bifurcation into four masculines and two feminines. The initial as well as the final line within each of these two pairs of couplets contains two nouns: one feminine and one masculine in the initial line ($_1$*Yadwigha, rêve;* $_3$*sons, musette*), two masculines in the final ($_8$*airs, instrument;* $_6$*fleuves, arbres*). The global symmetry displayed by the nouns of the outer and inner couplets finds no support in the distribution between odd and even or anterior and posterior couplets, but both inner couplets comprise one and the same number of three nouns in mirror symmetry (II: $_3$*sons, musette,* $_4$*charmeur;* III: $_5$*lune,* $_6$*fleuves, arbres*), and, consequently, the relation between nouns of the even and odd couplets—seven to five—is precisely the same as the relation between nouns of the posterior and anterior couplets.

Each of the two quatrains comprises one sentence with two subjects and two finite predicates. Every couplet of the octastich contains one subject, while in the distribution of the finites—three to one—the even couplets have the same relation to the odd ones as the inner to the outer couplets.

The subjects of the outer couplets pertain to the two main clauses of the poem, whereas both subjects of the inner couplets form a part of subordinate clauses. The main subjects begin the line ($_1$*Yadwigha dans un beau rêve;* $_7$*Les fauves serpents*) in contradistinction to the non-initial position of the subordinate subjects ($_4$Dont jouait *un charmeur;* $_5$Pendant que *la lune*). The feminine subjects emerge in the odd couplets of the octastich, and the masculine subjects in its even couplets. Thus in each quatrain the first subject is feminine and the second, masculine: $_1$*Yadwigha,* $_4$*charmeur;* $_5$*lune,* $_7$*serpents.* Consequently, both anterior couplets (the first quatrain of the poem), with the feminine gender of their main subject *Yadwigha* and the masculine of their subordinate subject *charmeur,* are diametrically opposed to the posterior couplets (second quatrain), where the main subject *serpents* is masculine and the subordinate subject *lune* is feminine. The personal (human) gender distinguishes the grammatical subjects of the anterior couplets ($_1$*Yadwigha,* $_4$*charmeur*) from the nonpersonal subjects of the posterior couplets ($_5$*lune,* $_7$*serpents*).

These data may be summarized in a table with italic inscriptions indicating the placement of the four subjects in the composition of the octastich and with roman type denoting their grammatical properties.

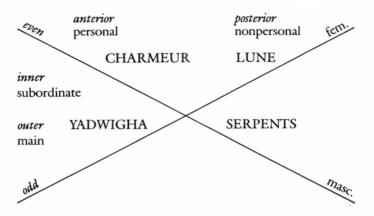

This distribution of the four grammatical subjects proves to correspond to the *relative* disposition of their pictorial referents on Rousseau's canvas.[9]

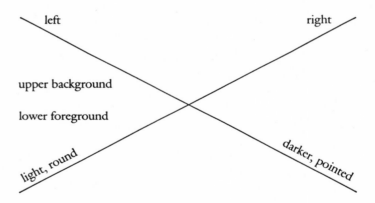

The pictorial figures of the foreground areas are rendered in the poem by the main subjects' placement in the diverging, outer couplets, whereas the background figures which have been moved upwards and shortened in the painting produce subordinate subjects assigned to the converging, inner couplets of the octastich. Tristan Tzara's suggestive essay, published as a preface to the exhibition of Rousseau's paintings in the Sidney Janis Gallery (New York, 1951), discusses "The Role of Time and Space in his Work" and points out the relevance and peculiarity of "perspective as Rousseau conceived it" and, in particular, a

Henri Rousseau, *The Dream*, 1910 (Collection, The Museum of Modern Art, New York)

significant trait of his great compositions: a series of movements split up "into individual elements, veritable slices of Time bound together by a sort of arithmetical operation."[10]

While the charmer and the full moon face the spectator, the profile figures of Yadwigha and the snake are turned toward each other; the snake's windings parallel the curve of the woman's hip and leg, and the vertical green ferns jut out under both of these curves and point to Yadwigha's hip and to the upper curve of the reptile. In fact, this bright and slim snake emerges against the background of another, thicker, black, and hardly discernible serpent; the latter mirrors the skin of the charmer while the former corresponds to the color of a stripe in his variegated belt. The blue and violet flowers rise above Yadwigha and the two snakes. In the poem two parallel constructions connect the heroine with the reptiles: $_3$*Entendait les sons d'une musette* and $_7$*prêtent l'oreille $_8$Aux airs gais de l'instrument.*

Some challenging questions of grammatical gender arise in this connection. To the two feminine subjects of the poem the painting responds with two salient features characteristic of Yadwigha and the moon, their diverse paleness in comparison with the deeper colors of the environment and especially of the charmer and reptiles, and the similar roundness of the full moon and of the female's breast in comparison with the pointed body of the bright snake and the charmer's reed. The *sexuisemblance* (sexual likeness) of the feminine and masculine genders experienced by any member of the French speech community was scrutinized lucidly and exhaustively by J. Damourette and E. Pichon in the first volume of their historic accomplishment, *Des mots à la pensée—Essai de grammaire de la langue française* (Paris 1911–1927), chap. 4:

All of the nominal substantives in French are masculine or feminine: this is a fact that is both incontestable and uncontested. The national imagination has reached the point where it can no longer conceive of nominal substances except as they contain an analogy with one of the sexes; so much so that "sexual likeness" has become a mode for classifying these substances generally [§302] ... It has in the speech and thought of every French person an omnipresent role [§306] ... This assessment is obviously not of a purely intellectual nature. It is something in the realm of affect ... "Sexual likeness" is so clearly a comparison with sex that feminine vocables in French cannot be figuratively compared to anything but women [§307] . . . The classification of "sexual likeness" is the mode of expression for the personification of things [§309].

It is noteworthy that the four feminines of Rousseau's poem are tied to its four odd lines. They inaugurate the line when functioning as grammatical subjects in the odd couplets, and they terminate the line when they act as modifiers in the even couplets.

The mandatory association of the feminine gender with odd, or feminine, lines demands an interpretation. The tendency to differentiate feminine and masculine forms by the closed and open end of the word[11] creates an association between the final syllable of the line, closed or open, and the gender, feminine or masculine. Also the term "feminine rhymes," popular even in French elementary textbooks, may have favored the distribution of feminine nouns among those lines.

In Rousseau's verses the distribution of genders is submitted to a dissimilative principle. The closest object of the verb belongs to the gender opposite to that of the subject of the given clause, and if there is a further governed modifier, be it adverbial or adnominal, it retains the gender of the subject; in this way the role of genders in the poem becomes particularly accentuated: $_1$*Yadwigha* (f.) . . . $_3$*entendait les sons* (m.) *d'une musette* (f.); $_4$*Dont* [referring to *musette* (f.)] *jouait un charmeur* (m.); $_5$*la lune* (f.) *reflète* $_6$ . . . *les arbres* (m.); $_7$*Les fauves serpents* (m.) *prêtent l'oreille* (f.) $_8$*Aux airs gais* (m.).

The foreground of Rousseau's painting and poem belongs to Yadwigha and the snakes; one is prompted to recall *Eve,* his somewhat earlier picture, with its stupendous duet of two profiles, the naked woman and the serpent.[12] This hierarchy of the dramatis personae was overlooked, however, by critics. Thus Apollinaire's eulogy of March 18, 1910, "De ce tableau se dégage de la beauté,"[13] saw the nude woman on a sofa, tropical vegetation around her with monkeys and birds of paradise, a lion, a lioness, and a fluting Negro, "a figure of mystery." But the snakes and the moon remained unmentioned. Jean Bouret[14] also confines his discussion of the compositional order in *The Dream* to the flute player, the tiger(?), the bird, and the reclining woman. These observers stop at the left, larger section of the painting without shifting to the minor right part, the topic of the second quatrain. The initial stage of inspection of the picture is, naturally, its left side: "this woman sleeping on this sofa" who dreams that she has been transported "into the middle of this forest, hearing the notes of the charmer's pipe," according to the painter's explanation of his own picture.[15]

From Yadwigha and the mysterious charmer the focus shifts to the second fold of the diptych, separated from the first one by a blue flower on a long stem, which parallels a similar plant on the left side of the heroine. The narrative order and successive cognition and synthesis of the canvas *Dream*[16] find their terse correspondence in the transition from the first quatrain with its two parallel imperfects—or present preterits, in L. Tesnière's terminology[17]—($_3$*entend*AIT—$_4$*jou*AIT) to the two rhyming presents of the second quatrain ($_5$*refl*ÈTE—$_7$*pr*ÊTE*nt*) and in the substitution of mere definite articles ($_5$*la lune,* $_6$*les fleuves, les arbres,* $_7$*les serpents, l'oreille,* $_8$*aux airs, l'instrument*) for the indefinite articles, which, with the sole exception of $_3$*les sons,* dominate the preceding quatrain ($_1$*un rêve,* $_3$*une musette,* $_4$*un charmeur*).

In Rousseau's poetic as well as pictorial composition, the dramatic action is borne by the four subjects of the poem and their visual referents on the canvas. As outlined above, all of them are interconnected by three binary contrasts, glaringly expressed by the poet-painter and transforming this unusual quartet into six opposite pairs which determine and diversify the verbal and graphic plot. In the "Inscription" each of the four subjects is endowed with a further categorial feature which contrasts it with the three other correspondents: *Yadwigha* is the only proper name in the poem; *un charmeur,* its sole personal appellative; *les serpents,* its only animate plural; and *la lune* is the one inanimate among the four subjects. This diversity is accompanied by a difference of articles—the zero article which signals the proper name, the indefinite *un,* followed by the plural *les* and the feminine *la* of the definite article.

A multifarious interplay of concurrent similarities and divergences underlies and vivifies the written and painted *Dream* in all its facets: the silence of the moonlit night interrupted by the tunes of a swarthy charmer; the enchantment of moonshine and musical charms; the female's moonlight dream; two auditors of the magic tunes, the woman and the serpent, both alien and alluring to each other; the serpent as the legendary tempter of the woman and the inveterate target of the snake charmer and, on the other hand, the maximal contrast and mysterious affinity between the pallid Yadwigha on her old-fashioned sofa and the well-meaning tropical flutist amid his virgin forest; and, after all this, in the eyes of the inhabitant of *2 bis, rue Perrel* the equally exotic and attractive tinge of the African magician and the Polish enchantress with her intricate name.

496

As to the lion escorted by a lioness and omitted in the poem, in the picture it belongs to the fluteplayer's triangle and, as Bouret[18] has observed, builds its "apex" pointing downwards. This front face seems to be a double of the superposed charmer and in a similar way the bright half-faced bird over Yadwigha looks like her double. Yet in the iconographic comparison of Rousseau's canvas and poem, our attention has been focused upon their common denominator, easily extractable despite their different props, such as the rivers reflecting the trees in the verse or the zoological abundance in the painting.

Like Blake's "Infant Sorrow," Rousseau's octastich, in order to ensure the cohesion of its expressly differentiated couplets, connects them with tight phonological bonds between the even and the subsequent odd lines: / $_2$setā tādɔrmi dusmāt $_3$ātādɛ/; / $_4$pāsā $_5$pādā/. Moreover, the last two couplets are tied together by a palpable sound texture: $_6$les FLEUVES—$_7$Les FAUVES (with two corresponding rounded vowels); $_6$SUR . . . les ARBRES—$_7$SERPents PRêtent (where the phoneme /R/ alternates with hissing continuants and labial stops).

In my natural conclusion I am following Vratislav Effenberger when this Czech expert on Henri Rousseau's work defines it as "a sign of rising symbiosis between painting and poetry."[19] A similar appraisal of Paul Klee by Carola Gledion-Welcker[20]—in this artist "ist der Dichter mit dem Maler eng verknüpft" (poet and painter are tightly bound)—impels us to go on to Klee's poetic remains.

III. Paul Klee's Octastich

Senseless talk . . . Does inspiration have eyes, or does it sleepwalk?
The work of art as an act: the division of the toes into three groups: 1 + 3 + 1.

From Klee's diaries of 1901 (nos. 183, 310)

The painter's poem of 1903 about beasts, gods, and men, written down, according to the author's custom, without any vertical arrangement of verses, displays nonetheless a clear-cut rhythmical division into eight lines of two hemistichs; the second hemistich in the first and third lines carries three, and each of the other hemistichs bears two strong word stresses. Actually the author himself separates the verses of this poem by spacing the intervals between them, especially when these verses are not divided from one another by a punctuation mark.[21]

₁Zwei Bérge gíbt es / auf dénen es héll ist und klár,
₂den Bérg der Tíere / und den Bérg der Götter.
₃Dazwíschen aber líegt / das dämmerige Tál der Ménschen.
₄Wenn éiner éinmal / nach óben síeht,
₅erfásst ihn áhnend / eine únstillbare Séhnsucht,
₆íhn, der wéiss, / dass ér nicht wéiss
₇nach íhnen die nicht wíssen, / dass síe nicht wíssen
₈únd nach íhnen, / die wíssen dass sie wíssen.

A literal translation:

There are two mountains on which it is bright and clear,
the mountain of beasts and the mountain of gods.
But in between there lies the dusky valley of men.
When once someone looks upwards,
an unquenchable longing seizes him forebodingly,
him who knows that he doesn't know
after them who don't know that they don't know
and after them who know that they know.

Klee's punctuation in his autograph of this poem reveals a significant difference between the rhythmical phrasing of syntactic constructions in the two final lines: ₇*nach ihnen die nicht wissen, dass sie nicht wissen* and, on the other hand, ₈*und nach ihnen, die wissen dass sie wissen*. The comma indicates the different place of the boundary between the hemistichs in these two lines. Thus the reading *únd nach íhnen, / die wíssen dass sie wíssen* with an emphatic stress on the antithetical conjunction appears to be the only correct one.

The transcription of this poem in Felix Klee's edition of his father's diaries and poems[22] unfortunately reshapes the artist's punctuation according to the orthographic norm. Of these two publications the former prints the octastich like prose, while in the latter it is artificially broken into twelve lines; namely, some of the hemistichs are treated as separate lines, and, moreover, the inaugural proclitic of the second hemistich is assigned to the end of the first hemistich:

Dazwischen aber liegt das
dämmerige Tal der Menschen.

With the exception of the second, solemn amphibrachic hemistich of the first line—*auf dénen es héll ist und klár*—the verses of the poem display a duple, predominantly iambic rhythm. The first hemistich, dipodic in six and tripodic in two lines, looses the initial upbeat in two instances: ₆*íhn, der wéiss;* ₈*únd nach íhnen*. The second hemistich of

498

two, three, or four duple feet begins with an upbeat after a masculine caesura (lines 3 and 6) while after a feminine caesura it begins either with a downbeat, thus preserving the metrical uniformity of the entire line (₂*den Bérg der Tiere / und den Bérg der Götter;* ₅*erfásst ihn áhnend / eine únstillbare Séhnsucht*), or it begins with an upbeat, and thus achieves its own autonomous iambic pattern (₄*Wenn éiner éinmal / nach óben sieht;* cf. lines 7 and 8).

Three genitive plurals, the only animate nouns of the poem—₂*der Tiere, der Götter,* ₃*der Menschen*—point to its triadic heroes. The ternary principle, partly connected with this thematic trichotomy and partly autonomous, runs throughout the entire octastich. The poem encompasses three sentences (1–2; 3; 4–8) which, in turn, comprise three independent clauses with three finites: ₁*gibt,* ₃*liegt,* ₅*erfasst,* all three of which are placed before the subject in contradistinction to the predicates of the dependent clauses. The accusative plural ₁*Berge* is followed by the double apposition ₂*Berg . . . Berg,* and the relative pronoun ₁*denen* by the cognate articles ₂*den . . . den.* Three neuters with three finite predicates—₁*gibt es, es hell ist,* ₃*liegt das*—begin the poem. The domiciles of the threefold heroes—₂*Berg der Tiere, Berg der Götter,* and ₃*Tal der Menschen*—are associated with three adjectives: ₁*hell, klar,* ₃*dämmerige,* and the contrasting images which end the first two sentences are underlined by paronomastic contrivances: ₂*Berg der Götter* (erg-erg); ₃*dämmerige . . . der Menschen* (dem.r-derm). The third sentence, too, is permeated by ternary repetitions; ₄*einer, einmal,* ₅*eine;* ₄*nach,* ₇*nach,* ₈*nach;* ₆*ihn, der weiss, dass er* nicht *weiss*—₇*ihnen die* nicht *wissen, dass sie* nicht *wissen*—₈*ihnen, die wissen dass sie wissen*—with the triple negative *nicht* thoughtfully distributed in the sixth and seventh lines. The thrice occurring conjunction ₁, ₂, ₈ *und* is connected with a correspondence between the first and last sentences: the accusative ₁*Berge,* followed by an apposition of the two pleonastic accusatives interlinked by *und,* is parallelled by the accusative ₅*ihn* and its pleonastic apposition ₆*ihn* with two subsequent datives ₇*nach ihnen . . .*₈*und nach ihnen.*

A purely metaphorical, spatial design of biblical stamp underlies the whole poem. The valley is the only abode of the unsolvable antinomy between the two contraries, the awareness of one's own unawareness, which perhaps alludes to its likewise antinomic reversal, the tragic unawareness of one's own awareness.

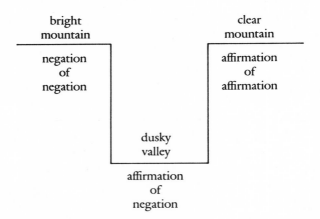

The thematic tripartition of the octastich superposes a symmetrical pattern upon its syntactic division into three uneven sentences of two, one, and five lines. The first three lines of the poem depict the permanent quasi-material status of its heroes; the outer, initial couplet (lines 1 and 2) is devoted to beasts and gods, while the third line deals with men. Correspondingly, the last three lines of the poem characterize the permanent mental status of its heroes, and the outer, final couplet (lines 7–8) contemplates the beasts and gods, whereas the third line from the end (6) is consecrated to men. The central of the three sections (lines 4–5) may be defined as dynamic and is concerned with active processes which occur—once again with permanence—in "the dusky valley of men." Each of these three sections is signaled by a stressed monosyllable at the end of its initial line ($_1$*klar*, $_4$*sieht*, and $_6$*weiss*), whereas the other five lines of the poem are closed with a paroxytone.

Since the two-line central section (4, 5) jointly with the two adjacent lines (3 and 6) focuses on men, all four inner lines may be treated in a certain regard as a whole opposed to the towering theme of the two outer couplets. The borderlines (3 and 6) are evoked by a stressed monosyllable at the end of their first hemistich (two parallel verbal forms $_3$*liegt*, $_6$*weiss*), while the two pairs of lines surrounding each of these borderlines display a feminine caesura.

In their grammatical shape, lines three and six occupy an obviously transitional position; each of them is basically akin to the contiguous outer couplet, but at the same time they share certain formal features with the two central lines.

This central distich, the most dramatic part of the poem, is endowed with verbs of process ($_4$*nach oben sieht,* $_5$*erfasst*), in contradistinction to the verbs of state in (1–3) and to the *verba sciendi* in (6–8). The abstract noun $_5$*Sehnsucht* differs from the six concrete substantives of the three preceding lines and from the total absence of nouns in the next three lines. The components of *Sehnsucht* are related, one with the verb *sehnen,* and the other, through folk etymology, with the verb *suchen.* The entire line displays an ostensibly verbal leaning, and besides the transitive verb *erfasst* with the direct object *ihn,* it contains a gerund *ahnend* and a deverbative adjective *unstillbare.* The temporal adverbial clause ($_4$*Wenn . . .*), as compared with the relative clauses in the other two sections, underlies the primacy of the verb in the central lines. The verb-oriented hexapodic line which concludes the central distich— $_5$*erfásst ihn áhnend / eine únstillbare Séhnsucht*—contrasts in particular with the terminal, purely nominal pentapody of the initial distich— $_2$*den Bérg der Tíere / und den Bérg der Götter*—the only two integrally iambic lines with feminine endings in both hemistichs. The indefinite triplet $_4$*einer-einmal-*$_5$*eine* contrasts with two chains of "determinates": $_1$*denen-*$_2$*den-der-den-der-*$_3$*dazwischen-das-der* (including the alliterative *dämmerige*) in the first section and $_6$*der-dass-*$_7$*die-dass-*$_8$*die-dass* in the final tercet. The vocalic onset of the thrice repeated *ein-* is reinforced by the similar initials of the surrounding words—$_4$*einer einmal . . . oben . . .*$_5$*erfasst ihn ahnend eine unstillbare . . .* —while the final words of this distich produce a triple alliteration of hissing continuants: $_4$*sieht-Sehnsucht.*

With the antecedent transitional line, the central distich shares the only nominal subjects and the only epithets in the octastich; by the way, these two tetrasyllabic attributes in the unique tetrapodic hemistichs—$_3$*dämmerige* and $_5$*unstillbare*—are the lengthiest vocables of the entire text. These sole nouns in the nominative case together with their adjectival modifiers refer indirectly to men and are contraposed to the three nominal accusatives of the initial distich, which points to beasts and gods. Furthermore, the gender opposes the obscure $_3$*Tal,* the only neuter noun of the poem, and especially its only feminine, the affective $_5$*Sehnsucht,* to the five masculine nouns of the initial distich, as if this difference were to confirm the peerlessness of human whereabouts and troubles. In general, oppositions of contraries and of contradictories are much more typical of Klee's grammatical texture than the numerical correspondences between its different sections.

With the subsequent transitional line the central distich shares the only singular forms of masculine pronouns (₄*einer;* ₅*ihn;* ₆*ihn, der, er*) and the absence of plurals, against the numerous nominal, pronominal, and verbal plurals of the other lines.

This singular loneliness, graphically delineated in the acme of Klee's poem, finds a kindred preamble in the immediately preceding lines of his diary (no. 538): "to reduce oneself completely to oneself, to prepare oneself for the greatest solitude. Distaste for procreation (ethical supersensitivity)."

The three final, strictly relational and cogitative lines manifesting three varieties of a double hypotaxis and consisting of nine pronouns, six forms of the verb "to know," three times with and three times without the negative *nicht,* and of six conjunctions and prepositions, put an end to the metaphorical network of the two prior sections with their conventionally figurative inanimates and verbs. The reader is called upon to proceed from spatial visions to stringent spiritual abstractions.

In agreement with the longing of the terminal distich for the inhabitants of the mountains, *auf denen es hell ist und klar,* or perhaps in agreement rather with the terminal striving for the heights of abstract meditation, seven full stresses of the two final lines fall on the acute and diffuse vowel /i/—₇*nach ihnen die nicht wissen, dass sie nicht wissen* ₈*únd nach ihnen, die wissen dass sie wissen.* Also in the three lines of the initial section, it is /i/ that carries the last stress of the first hemistich. Among the thirty-four strong stresses of the octastich, twenty-three fall on front (viz. acute) vowels, and, in particular, thirteen fall on /i/. The four diphthongs /ai/ with their acute termination in turn reinforce the "bright" tinge of Klee's poem, which manifestly avoids back rounded vowels under stress and tolerates merely two /u/ and one /o/.

An astounding union of radiant transparence and masterful simplicity with multiform intricacy enables Klee the painter and the poet to deploy a harmonious disposition of unusually varied devices either on a strip of canvas or in a few lines of a notebook. The appended scheme may summarize those concurrent binary and ternary arrangements of subject matter and grammatical expedients which lent depth and monumentality to the artist's verbal miniature and which appear to exemplify Klee's dialectic of artistic markedness with his acute sense for cor-

1st sentence	Beasts and gods	1. Initial 2. distich	I Externalized status	
2nd sentence	Men — Seclusion — doom	3.		Imagery
3rd sentence: men in relation to beasts and gods		4. Central distich 5. 6.	II Motion	
	Beasts and gods	7. Terminal distich 8.	Internal status	Abstraction

relations of dynamic and static, of bright and deep, of intensive and extensive, of grammatical and geometrical concepts, and, finally, of rule and overruling, all of which he intimated in his diary of 1908 (no. 832):

> Let action be the exception, not the rule. Action is in the aorist tense; it must be contrasted with a static situation. If I want to act light, the static situation must be laid on a dark base. If I want to act dark, we need a light base for our static situation. The effectiveness of the action is greater when its intensity is strong and the quantity of space occupied by it is small, but with slight situational intensity and great situational extension. Never give up the all-important extension of the static element! On a medium-toned static ground, however, a double action is possible, depending on whether one considers it from the point of view of lightness or that of darkness.

Notes

In referring to works by Roman Jakobson included in his *Selected Writings* (Berlin–New York–Amsterdam: Mouton Publishers, 7 vols., 1962–1985), we use the abbreviation *SW*, followed by volume and page number. The set contains: I. *Phonological Studies* (1962; 2nd ed. 1971, to which we refer); II. *Word and Language* (1971); III. *Poetry of Grammar and Grammar of Poetry* (1981); IV. *Slavic Epic Studies* (1966); V. *On Verse, Its Masters and Explorers* (1979); VI. *Early Slavic Paths and Crossroads* (1985): Pt. 1, *Comparative Slavic Studies: The Cyrillo-Methodian Tradition,* and Pt. 2, *Medieval Slavic Studies;* VII. *Contributions to Comparative Mythology: Studies in Linguistics and Philology, 1972–1982* (1985). For further bibliographical data, including listings of all of Jakobson's works now available in English translation, see *Roman Jakobson: A Complete Bibliography of His Writings, 1912–1982,* ed. Stephen Rudy (Berlin–New York–Amsterdam: Mouton, 1988).

Introduction
1. Roman Jakobson, *Verbal Art, Verbal Sign, Verbal Time,* ed. Krystyna Pomorska and Stephen Rudy (Minneapolis, 1985).

2. Roman Jakobson and Krystyna Pomorska, *Dialogues* (Cambridge, Mass., 1983), p. 7.

3. Jakobson, *SW* II, vi.

4. Jakobson, *SW* I, 631–632.

5. *Dialogues,* pp. 102–103.

6. Ibid., pp. 106–107.

7. Jakobson, *SW* IV, 643–644.

8. Claude Lévi-Strauss, "Roman, mon ami," *Le Nouvel Observateur,* February 1, 1985, pp. 54–55.

9. Hayden White, *Metahistory: The Historical Imagination in Nineteenth-Century Europe* (Baltimore, 1973).

10. *Dialogues,* pp. 62–64.

11. Reprinted in Jakobson, *SW* V, 227–236.

12. Vjačeslav V. Ivanov, "Roman Jakobson: The Future," in *A Tribute to Roman Jakobson, 1896–1982* (Berlin–New York–Amsterdam, 1983), pp. 56–57.

1. On Realism in Art

Originally published in Czech in 1921. The translation from the original Russian manuscript (see *SW* III, 723–731) by Karol Magassy reprinted here first appeared in *Readings in Russian Poetics: Formalist and Structuralist Views,* ed. Ladislav Matejka and Krystyna Pomorska (Cambridge, Mass.: MIT Press, 1971).

2. Futurism

Originally published in the Moscow journal *Iskusstvo* 7 (August 2, 1919). The English translation by Stephen Rudy appears here for the first time, with notes added by the editors.

1. Albert Gleizes and Jean Metzinger, *Du cubisme* (Paris, 1912).

2. Carl Stumpf, *Über den psychologischen Ursprung der Raumvorstellung* (Berlin, 1873), pp. 112–113.

3. The Russian term *ustanovka* (orientation, set) is a calque for German *Einstellung,* a philosophical term designating apperception, the viewpoint or mental set crucial in the perceiver's constituting an object.

4. Umberto Boccioni, Carlo Carrà, Luigi Russolo, Giacomo Balla, and Gino Severini, "Futurist Painting: Technical Manifesto 1910," in U. Apollonio, ed., *Futurist Manifestos* (New York, 1973), pp. 27–29.

5. Carlo Carrà, "The Painting of Sounds, Noises, and Smells" (1913), in Apollonio, *Futurist Manifestos,* p. 113.

6. Gleizes and Metzinger, *Du cubisme.* The quotation from Leonardo is from Ms. 2038 Bib. Nat. 28r.

7. Aristotle, *Poetics* 1448b, in Kenneth A. Telford's translation (Chicago, 1961), pp. 6–7.

3. Dada

Originally published in the Moscow journal *Vestnik teatra* 82 (February 8, 1921). The English translation by Stephen Rudy appears here for the first time, with notes added by the editors.

1. *Byta ne ostalos'* (there is no established order of things left). The heavily loaded Russian term *byt* suggests "mores," "convention," "daily grind." See Jakobson's discussion of this term in relation to Majakovskij in "On a Generation That Squandered Its Poets," included in this volume (pp. 277–290).

2. Velimir Xlebnikov, "Razgovor dvux osob," in his *Sobranie proizvedenij,* ed. N. Stepanov and Ju. Tynjanov (Leningrad, 1933), V, 183.

3. Most of Jakobson's quotations from the Dadaists are taken from *Dada Almanach,* ed. Richard Huelsenbeck (Berlin, 1920).

4. The reference is to Prince V. F. Odoevskij's story "The Improvvissatore" (1833), later included in his collection *Russian Nights* (1844).

5. A reference to the decorations made for the first anniversary of the October Revolution by various avant-garde artists. The artist Lentulov painted the trees and grass outside the Bolshoi Theater and the Alexander Gardens in shades of light blue and red.

6. "Self-valuable words": in Russian *samovitye slova,* a term coined by the Futurists for neologistic, autonomous language.

4. The Dominant

From the unpublished Czech text of lectures on the Russian Formalist school delivered at Masaryk University in Brno in the spring of 1935. The translation by Herbert Eagle reprinted here first appeared in *Readings in Russian Poetics: Formalist and Structuralist Views,* ed. Ladislav Matejka and Krystyna Pomorska (Cambridge, Mass.: MIT Press, 1971).

5. Problems in the Study of Language and Literature

Written in Russian during Jurij Tynjanov's visit to Prague in the winter of 1928 (see *SW* V, 560–568) and first published, under the title "Problemy izučenija literatury i jazyka," in *Novyj Lef* 12 (1928). The translation by Herbert Eagle reprinted here first appeared in *Readings in Russian Poetics: Formalist and Structuralist Views,* ed. Ladislav Matejka and Krystyna Pomorska (Cambridge, Mass.: MIT Press, 1971).

6. Language in Operation

Written in English in Hunter, New York, in 1949 as an introductory chapter to the planned book *Sound and Meaning;* first published in *Mélanges Alexandre Koyré,* 1: *L'Aventure de l'esprit* (Paris: Hermann, 1964).

1. Quotations followed by page references are from Poe's "The Philosophy of Composition," *The Works of Edgar Allan Poe,* ed. E. C. Stedman and G. E. Woodberry (Chicago, 1895), VI, 31–46. Quotations from "The Raven" are given in italics.

2. *The Letters of Edgar Allan Poe,* ed. J. W. Ostrom (Cambridge, Mass., 1948), II, 287.

3. "Marginalia," sec. 10, *The Works of the Late Edgar Allan Poe* (New York, 1855), III, 492.

4. Winston Churchill, *My Early Life* (London, 1930), p. 84.

5. O. H. Mowrer, *Learning Theory and Personality Dynamics* (New York, 1950), pp. 688–689.

6. See Poe, *The Raven and Other Poems,* reproduced in facsimile from the L. Graham copy of the 1845 edition, with Poe's corrections (New York, 1942), p. 2.

7. "Marginalia," sec. 16, p. 495.

8. D. Lagache, *Les Hallucinations verbales et la parole* (Paris, 1934).

9. See F. M. Dostoevskij, "Tri rasskaza Èdgara Poè," *Vremja* (1861); *Polnoe sobranie xudožestvennyx proizvedenij,* ed. B. V. Tomaševskij and K. I. Xalabaev (Moscow, 1930), XIII, 523–524.

10. R. G. Kent, "Assimilation and Dissimilation," *Language* 12 (1936), 252–253.

11. *Works,* X, 156.

12. "Marginalia," sec. 10, p. 492.

13. *Letters,* II, 329.

14. "Marginalia," sec. 72, p. 521.

15. D. Marion, *La Méthode intellectuelle d'Edgar Poe* (Paris, 1952), pp. 97–99.

16. Letter of January 4, 1848, in *Letters,* II, 356.

17. Edward Sapir, "Communication," *Selected Writings* (Berkeley, 1949), p. 108.

18. "Marginalia," sec. 10, 493.

19. A. Taylor, "Locutions for Never," *Romance Philology* 2 (1948–49), 103–134.

20. *Baudelaire on Poe,* ed. L. and F. Hyslop (State College, Pa., 1952), p. 156.

7. Linguistics and Poetics

Originally presented at a conference on style held at Indiana University in the spring of 1958, then revised and published in *Style in Language,* ed. Thomas A. Sebeok (Cambridge, Mass.: MIT Press, 1960).

1. Carl F. Voegelin, "Casual and Noncasual Utterances within Unified Structures," in *Style in Language,* ed. Thomas A. Sebeok (Cambridge, Mass., 1960), p. 57.

2. Edward Sapir, *Language* (New York, 1921), p. 40.

3. Martin Joos, "Description of Language Design," *Journal of the Acoustical Society of America* 22 (1950), 701–708.

4. Anton Marty, *Untersuchungen zur Grundlegung der allgemeinen Grammatik und Sprachphilosophie,* I (Halle, 1908).

5. Sol Saporta, "The Application of Linguistics to the Study of Poetic Language," in *Style in Language,* p. 88.

6. Karl Bühler, "Die Axiomatik der Sprachwissenschaft," *Kant-Studien* 38 (Berlin, 1933), 19–20.

7. V. J. Mansikka, *Litauische Zaubersprüche (Folklore Fellows Communications* 87, 1929), p. 69.

8. P. N. Rybnikov, *Pesni* (Moscow, 1910), III, 217–218.

9. Bronislaw Malinowski, "The Problem of Meaning in Primitive Languages," in C. K. Ogden and I. A. Richards, eds., *The Meaning of Meaning* (New York and London, 9th ed., 1953), pp. 296–336.

10. Term introduced by Alfred Tarski, *Pojęcie prawdy w językach nauk dedukcyjnych* (Warsaw, 1933), and "Der Wahrheitsbegriff in den formalisierten Sprachen," *Studia Philosophica* 1 (1936).

11. Dell H. Hymes, "Phonological Aspects of Style: Some English Sonnets," in *Style in Language*, pp. 123–126.

12. T. Maretić, *Metrika narodnih naših pjesama* (Zagreb, 1907), secs. 81–83.

13. G. M. Hopkins, *Journals and Papers*, ed. Humphry House and Graham Storey (London, 1959), p. 289.

14. John Lotz, "Metric Typology," in *Style in Language*, p. 137.

15. A. Levi, "Della versificazione italiana," *Archivum Romanicum* 14 (1930), secs. 8–9.

16. G. M. Hopkins, *Poems*, ed. W. H. Gardner and N. H. Mackenzie (London, 1967, 4th ed.), p. 45.

17. William K. Wimsatt and Monroe C. Beardsley, "The Concept of Meter: An Exercise in Abstraction," *PMLA* 74 (1959), 592.

18. Jakobson, *O češskom stixe preimuščestvenno v sopostavlenii s russkim* (Berlin and Moscow, 1923); reprinted in *SW* V, 3–130.

19. J. L. Bishop, "Prosodic Elements in T'ang Poetry," *Indiana University Conference on Oriental-Western Literary Relations* (Chapel Hill, 1955), pp. 49–63.

20. E. D. Polivanov, "O metričeskom xaraktere kitajskogo stixosloženija," *Izbrannye raboty: stat'i po obščemu jazykoznaniju* (Moscow, 1968), pp. 310–13.

21. Wang Li, *Han-yü Shih-lü-hsüeh* (Versification in Chinese; Shanghai, 1958). See also Jakobson, "The Modular Design of Chinese Regulated Verse," *SW* V, 215–223.

22. See his "Survey of African Prosodic Systems," *Culture in History: Essays in Honor of Paul Radin*, ed. Stanley Diamond (New York, 1960), pp. 927–978. The prosodic pun and rhyme correspondences between query and response in the diverse varieties of African tone-riddles or between the parts of a simile in analogous proverbial forms must be, the closer we view them, carefully differentiated from questions of versification patterns. See also Kenneth L. Pike, "Tone Puns in Mixteco," *International Journal of American Linguistics* 11 (1945) and 12 (1946).

23. D. C. Simmons, "Specimens of Efik Folklore," *Folk-lore* 66 (1955), p. 228. See also his articles: "Cultural Functions of the Efik Tone-Riddle," *Journal of American Folklore* 71 (1958); "Erotic Ibibio Tone-Riddles," *Man* 61 (1956).

24. Kiril Taranovsky, *Ruski dvodelni ritmovi* (Belgrade, 1955). Cf. John Bailey, "Some Recent Developments in the Study of Russian Versification," *Language and Style* 5:3 (1972).

25. E. Colin Cherry, *On Human Communication* (New York, 1957).

26. Poe, "Marginalia," *Works* (New York, 1855), V, 492.

27. Otto Jespersen, "Cause psychologique de quelques phénomènes de métrique germanique," *Psychologie du langage* (Paris, 1933), and "Notes on Metre," *Linguistica* (London, 1933).

28. Jakobson, "Slavic Epic Verse: Studies in Comparative Metrics," *SW* IV, 414–63. See also "Über den Versbau der serbokroatischen Volksepen," *SW* IV, 51–60.

29. Seymour Chatman, "Comparing Metrical Styles," *Style in Language*, p. 158.

30. S. I. Karcevskij, "Sur la phonologie de la phrase," *Travaux du Cercle Linguistique de Prague* 4 (1931).

31. B. M. Ejxenbaum, *Melodika russkogo liričeskogo stixa* (1922), reprinted in *O poèzii* (Leningrad, 1969), pp. 327–511, and V. M. Žirmunskij, *Voprosy teorii literatury* (Leningrad, 1928).

32. Wimsatt and Beardsley, "The Concept of Meter," p. 587.

33. Archibald A. Hill, review in *Language* 29 (1953).

34. Hopkins, *Journals and Papers,* p. 276.

35. Hopkins, *Poems,* p. 46.

36. Eduard Sievers, "Ziele und Wege der Schallanalyse," *Stand und Aufgaben der Sprachwissenschaft: Festschrift für W. Streitberg* (Heidelberg, 1924).

37. Paul Valéry, *The Art of Poetry,* in *Collected Works,* VII (New York, 1958).

38. Hopkins, *Journals and Papers,* p. 286.

39. Ibid., p. 286.

40. William K. Wimsatt, Jr., "On the Relation of Rhyme to Reason," *The Verbal Icon* (Lexington, 1954), pp. 152–166.

41. Hopkins, *Journals and Papers,* p. 85.

42. Ibid., p. 106.

43. Thomas A. Sebeok, "Decoding a Text: Levels and Aspects in a Cheremis Sonnet," in *Style in Language,* pp. 221–235.

44. Robert Austerlitz, *Ob-Ugric Metrics (Folklore Fellows Communications* 174, 1958), and Wolfgang Steinitz, *Der Parallelismus in der finnisch-karelischen Volksdichtung (Folklore Fellows Communications* 115, 1934).

45. John Crowe Ransom, *The New Criticism* (Norfolk, Conn., 1941), p. 295.

46. See *Style in Language,* p. 205.

47. See A. A. Potebnja, *Ob''jasnenija malorusskix i srodnyx narodnyx pesen',* I (Warsaw, 1883), pp. 160–161, 179–180, and II (1887).

48. William Empson, *Seven Types of Ambiguity* (New York, 1947).

49. W. Giese, "Sind Märchen Lügen?", *Cahiers S. Puşcariu* (1952).

50. Valéry, *The Art of Poetry,* p. 319.

51. Hymes, "Phonological Aspects of Style."

52. Edgar Allan Poe, "The Philosophy of Composition," *Works,* ed. E. C. Stedman and G. E. Woodberry (Chicago, 1895), VI, 46.

53. Stéphane Mallarmé, *Divagations* (Paris, 1899).

54. Benjamin Lee Whorf, *Language, Thought, and Reality,* ed. John B. Carroll (New York, 1956), pp. 276–277.

55. Kazimierz Nitsch, "Z historii polskich rymów," *Wybór pism polonistycznych* 1 (Wroclaw, 1954), 33–77.

56. G. Herzog, "Some Linguistic Aspects of American Indian Poetry," *Word* 2 (1946), 82.

57. Leonid Arbusow, *Colores rhetorici* (Göttingen, 1948).

58. Charles Sanders Peirce, *Collected Papers* (Cambridge, Mass., 1931), I, 171.

59. Hopkins, *Journals and Papers,* pp. 267, 107.

60. Vladimir Propp, *Morphology of the Folktale* (Bloomington, 1958).

61. Claude Lévi-Strauss, "Analyse morphologique des contes russes," *International Journal of Slavic Linguistics and Poetics* 3 (1960); *La Geste d'Asdival* (École Pratique des Hautes Études, Paris, 1958); and "The Structural Study of Myth," in Thomas A. Sebeok, ed., *Myth: A Symposium* (Philadelphia, 1955), pp. 50–66.

62. Jakobson, "The Metaphoric and Metonymic Poles," *SW* II, 254–259 [included in this volume, Chapter 8].

63. "Results of a Joint Conference of Anthropologists and Linguists," *SW* II, 555.

64. John Crowe Ransom, *The World's Body* (New York, 1938), p. 235.

65. Paul Valéry, "De l'enseignement de la poétique au Collège de France," *Variété,* 5 (1945), 289.

66. John Hollander, "The Metrical Emblem," *Kenyon Review* 21 (1959), 295.

8. *Two Aspects of Language and Two Types of Aphasic Disturbances*

Originally published as Part II of *Fundamentals of Language,* written in collaboration with Morris Halle (The Hague: Mouton, 1956).

1. Hughlings Jackson, "Papers on Affections of Speech (Reprinted and Commented by H. Head)," *Brain* 38 (1915).

2. Edward Sapir, *Language* (New York, 1921), chap. 7: "Language as a Historical Product; Drift."

3. See e.g. the discussion on aphasia in the Nederlandsche Vereeniging voor Phonetische Wetenschappen, with papers by the linguist J. van Ginneken and by two psychiatrists, F. Grewel and V. W. D. Schenk, *Psychiatrische en Neurologische Bladen* 45 (1941); also F. Grewel, "Aphasie en linguistiek," *Nederlandsche Tijdschrift voor Geneeskunde* 93 (1949), 726ff.

4. Alexander Luria, *Travmatičeskaja afazija* (Moscow, 1947); Kurt Goldstein, *Language and Language Disturbances* (New York, 1948); André Ombredane, *L'Aphasie et l'élaboration de la pensée explicite* (Paris, 1951).

5. H. Myklebust, *Auditory Disorders in Children* (New York, 1954).

6. The aphasic impoverishment of the sound pattern has been observed and discussed by the linguist Marguerite Durand together with the psychopathologists T. Alajouanine and A. Ombredane, in their joint work *Le Syndrome de désintégration phonétique dans l'aphasie* (Paris, 1939), and by Jakobson, *SW* I, 328–401.

7. A joint inquiry into certain grammatical disturbances was undertaken at the Bonn University Clinic by the linguist G. Kandler and the physicians F. Panse and A. Leischner: see their report, *Klinische und sprachwissenschaftliche Untersuchungen zum Agrammatismus* (Stuttgart, 1952).

8. Donald M. MacKay, "In Search of Basic Symbols," *Cybernetics, Transactions of the Eighth Conference* (New York, 1952), p. 183.

9. Lewis Carroll, *Alice's Adventures in Wonderland,* chap. 6.

10. Ferdinand de Saussure, *Cours de linguistique générale,* 2nd ed. (Paris, 1922), pp. 68f., 170f.

11. Charles Sanders Peirce, *Collected Papers,* II and IV (Cambridge, Mass., 1932, 1934).

12. Henry Head, *Aphasia and Kindred Disorders of Speech* (New York, 1926), I, 412.

13. Cf. Leonard Bloomfield, *Language* (New York, 1933), chap. 15: "Substitution."

14. Sigmund Freud, *On Aphasia* (London, 1953), p. 22.

15. Franz Lotmar, "Zur Pathophysiologie der erschwerten Wortfindung bei Aphasischen," *Schweiz: Archiv für Neurologie und Psychiatrie* 35 (1933), 104.

16. Peirce, "The Icon, Index and Symbol," *Collected Papers,* II (1932).

17. Rudolf Carnap, *Meaning and Necessity* (Chicago, 1947), p. 4.

18. See the remarkable studies of A. Gvozdev: "Nabljudenija nad jazykom malen'kix detej," *Russkij jazyk v sovetskoj škole* (1929); *Usvoenie rebenkom zvukovoj storony russkogo jazyka* (Moscow, 1948); and *Formirovanie u rebenka grammatičeskogo stroja russkogo jazyka* (Moscow, 1949).

19. "Results of the Conference of Anthropologists and Linguists," *Indiana University Publications in Anthropology and Linguistics* 8 (1953), 15 (*SW* II, 554–567).

20. R. E. Hemphil and E. Stengel, "Pure Word Deafness," *Journal of Neurology and Psychiatry* 3 (1940), 251–262.

21. Hughlings Jackson, "Notes on the Physiology and Pathology of the Nervous System" (1868), *Brain* 38 (1915), pp. 65–71.

22. Jackson, "On Affections of Speech from Disease of the Brain" (1879), ibid., pp. 107–29.

23. Jackson, "Notes on the Physiology and Pathology of Language" (1866), ibid., pp. 48–58.

24. Edward Sapir, "The Psychological Reality of Phonemes," *Selected Writings* (Berkeley and Los Angeles, 1949).

25. I ventured a few sketchy remarks on the metonymical turn in verbal art ("Pro realizm u mystectvi," *Vaplite* 2 [Kharkov, 1927] and "Ranbemerkungen zur Prosa des Dichters Pasternak," *Slavische Rundschau* 7 [1935]), in painting ("Futurizm," *Iskusstvo,* August 2, 1919), and in motion pictures ("Úpadek filmu," *Listy pro uměni a kritiku* 1 [1933]), but the crucial problem of the two polar processes awaits a detailed investigation. [Cf. Jakobson's "On Realism in Art," "Marginal Notes on the Prose of the Poet Pasternak," "Futurism," and "Is the Film in Decline?" included in this volume.—*Eds.*]

26. Cf. his striking essay "Dickens, Griffith, and We": Sergej Eisenstein, *Izbrannye stat'i* (Moscow, 1950).

27. Cf. Bela Balazs, *Theory of the Film* (London, 1952).

28. For the psychological and sociological aspects of this dichotomy, see Gregory Bateson's views on progressional and selective integration and Talcott Parsons on the conjunction-disjunction dichotomy in child development: J. Ruesch and G. Bateson, *Communication, the Social Matrix of Psychiatry* (New York, 1951); T. Parsons and R. F. Bales, *Family, Socialization and Interaction Process* (Glencoe, 1955).

29. A Kamegulov, *Stil' Gleba Uspenskogo* (Leningrad, 1930), pp. 65, 145. One of such disintegrated portraits cited in the monograph: "From underneath an ancient straw cap, with a black spot on its visor, peeked two braids resembling the tusks of a wild boar; a chin, grown fat and pendulous, had spread definitively over the greasy collar of the calico dicky and lay in a thick layer on the coarse collar of the canvas coat, firmly buttoned at the neck. From underneath this coat to the eyes of the observer protruded massive hands with a ring which had eaten into the fat finger, a cane with a copper top, a significant bulge of the stomach, and the presence of very broad pants, almost of muslin quality, in the wide bottoms of which hid the toes of the boots."

30. James G. Frazer, *The Golden Bough: A Study in Magic and Religion,* part 1, 3rd ed. (Vienna, 1950), chap. 3.

31. C. F. P. Stutterheim, *Het begrip metaphor* (Amsterdam, 1941).

9. Poetry of Grammar and Grammar of Poetry

Address to the International Conference for Poetics in Warsaw, 1960, and published in the proceedings of the conference in Russian as "Poèzija grammatiki i grammatika poèzii" (*Poetics Poetyka Poètika,* Warsaw, 1961). The text offered here is a collation of Jakobson's abbreviated English version, first published in *Lingua* in 1968, with Stephen Rudy's translation of sections 2 and 4 of the Russian version, on Puškin; as such it represents the first full-length English version of the article.

1. Jakobson, "Na okraj lyrických básní Puškinových," in *Vybraně spisy A. S. Puškina*, ed. Alfred Bem and Roman Jakobson, vol. 1 (Prague, 1936), p. 263; English translation, "Marginal Notes on Puškin's Lyrical Poetry," in *SW* V, 284.

2. Jakobson, "Socha v symbolice Puškinově," *Slovo a slovesnost* 2 (1937), p. 20; English translation included in this volume, "The Statue in Puškin's Poetic Mythology." See also "The Kernel of Comparative Slavic Literature," *SW* VI, 14ff.

3. Edward Sapir, *Language* (New York, 1921), p. 89.

4. See Donald Davie, *Articulate Energy: An Inquiry into the Syntax of English Poetry* (London, 1955), p. 144.

5. Sapir, *Language*, p. 125.

6. See Edward Sapir, *Totality* (Language Monographs, no. 6, Linguistic Society of America, Baltimore, 1930), p. 3.

7. Jeremy Bentham, *Theory of Fictions*, ed. C. K. Ogden (London, 1932), pp. 73, 15.

8. Ibid., pp. 38, 15, 12.

9. Sapir, *Language*, p. 104.

10. F. F. Fortunatov, *Izbrannye trudy* (Moscow, 1956), I, 124.

11. Bentham, *Theory of Fictions*, p. 18.

12. See E. Faral, *Les Arts poétiques du XIIe et XIIIe siècle* (Paris, 1958), pp. 195, 227.

13. G. M. Hopkins, *Journals and Papers*, ed. Humphry House and Graham Storey (London, 1959), p. 289.

14. Jan Gonda, *Stylistic Repetition in the Veda* (Amsterdam, 1959).

15. Louis J. Newman and William Popper, *Studies in Biblical Parallelism* (Berkeley, 1918, 1923); Tschang Tscheng-ming, *Le Parallélisme dans le vers du Chen King* (Paris, 1937).

16. Wolfgang Steinitz, *Der Parallelismus in der finnisch-karelischen Volksdichtung* (*Folklore Fellows Communications* 115, 1934); Jakobson, "Aktuelle Aufgaben der Bylinenforschung," *Prager Presse*, April 26, 1936, p. 10; Robert Austerlitz, *Ob-Ugric Metrics: The Metrical Structure of Ostyak and Vogul Folkpoetry* (Helsinki, 1958); Nikolaus Poppe, *Der Parallelismus in der epischen Dichtung der Mongolen* (*Ural-Altaische Jahrbuch* 30, 1958).

17. On the present state of international research on parallelistic foundations of written and oral poetry, see Jakobson, "Grammatical Parallelism and Its Russian Facet" (included in this volume).

18. Steinitz, *Der Parllelismus*.

19. See N. Xaruzin, *Russkie lopari* (*Izvestija Imp. Obščestva Ljubitelej Estestvoznanija, Antropologii i Ètnografii, sostojaščego pri Imp. Moskovskom Universitete* 66, 1890), esp. pp. 342–394.

20. See the instructive surveys of three stories: N. Aristov, "Povest' o Fome i Ereme," *Drevnjaja i novaja Rossija* 1:4 (1876), 359–368, and V. P. Adrianova-Peretc, *Russkaja demokratičeskaja satira XVII v.* (Moscow-Leningrad, 1954), pp. 43–45, as well as their careful examination by Petr Bogatyrev, "Improvizacija i normy xudožestvennyx priemov na materiale povestej XVIII v., nadpisej na lubočnyx kartinkax, skazok i pesen o Ereme i Fome," *To Honor Roman Jakobson* (The Hague, 1967), I, 318–334.

21. See particularly its variants published by A. I. Sobolevskij, *Velikorusskie narodnye pesni*, I (St. Petersburg, 1895), nos. 82–88, and A. M. Astaxova, *Byliny severa*, II (Moscow-Leningrad, 1951), nos. 118, 120, 127, 146, 176, 708–711.

22. See Christine Brooke-Rose, *A Grammar of Metaphor* (London, 1958).

23. Hopkins, *Journals and Papers*, p. 106.

24. Francis Berry, *Poets' Grammar: Person, Time and Mood in Poetry* (London, 1958).

25. See Jakobson, "Linguistics and Poetics" (included in this volume).

26. See Jakobson, "Ktož jsú boži bojovníci," in *SW* III, 215–231.

27. Analyzed in a mimeographed supplement to a Warsaw lecture of 1960, in *SW* VII, 341–348.

28. R. Spottiswoode, *Film and Its Technique* (Berkeley, 1951), p. 417.

29. V. V. Veresaev, "Zapiski dlja sebja," *Novij mir* 1 (1960), 156.

30. T. G. Cjavlovskaja, "Dnevnik A. A. Oleninoj," *Puškin. Issledovanija i materialy* 11 (1958), 289–292.

31. See Jakobson, "'Przeszłość' Cypriana Norwida," in *SW* III, 499–507.

32. [The instrumental, like the dative, is a peripheral case, which further intensifies the ties between the forms *vam* (you) and *drugim* (another).—Eds.] See A. A. Šaxmatov, *Sintaksis russkogo jazyka* (Leningrad, 1941), sec. 445; Jakobson, "Morfologičeskie nabljudenija nad slavjanskim skloneniem," in *SW* II, 158 [cf. the English translation, "Morphological Observations on Slavic Declension," in Jakobson, *Russian and Slavic Grammar: Studies, 1931–1981*, ed. L. R. Waugh and M. Halle (Berlin–New York–Amsterdam, 1984), p. 109].

33. A. Slonimskij, *Masterstvo Puškina* (Moscow, 1959), p. 119.

34. Otto Jespersen, *The Philosophy of Grammar* (London–New York, 1924), ch. 24.

35. Julian Tuwim, *Z rosyjskiego* (Warsaw, 1954), I, 198.

36. C. Bragdon, *The Beautiful Necessity* (Rochester, 1910).

37. Cf. Jakobson, "Boas' View of Grammatical Meaning," in *SW* II, 489–496.

38. See G. Wallerand, *Les Oeuvres de Siger de Courtrai* (Louvain, 1913), p. 46.

39. Benjamin Lee Whorf, *Language, Thought and Reality: Selected Writings,* ed. John B. Carroll (New York, 1956), pp. 253, 257.

40. Iosif Stalin, *Marksizm i voprosy jazykoznanija* (Moscow, 1950), p. 20. As V. A. Zvegincev brought to my attention, Stalin's confrontation of grammar with geometry was prompted by the views of V. Bogorodickij, an outstanding disciple of the young Baudouin de Courtenay and M. Kruszewski.

41. See e.g. A. Zareckij, "O mestoimenii," *Russkij jazyk v škole* 6 (1960), 16–22.

42. See *SW* III, 215–231, esp. the graphs on 226–231.

43. Erwin Panofsky, *Gothic Architecture and Scholasticism* (New York, 1957), p. 31.

44. Quoted in Panofsky, p. 38.

45. Hopkins, *Journals and Papers*, p. 106.

46. Šaxmatov, *Sintaksis*, secs. 393–394.

47. Bentham, *Theory of Fictions*, p. 62.

10. Grammatical Parallelism and Its Russian Facet

First published in English in *Language* 40 (1966), with the note: "Thanks for help are due to Professors F. M. Cross, Morris Halle, James R. Hightower, Alexander Schenker, and Kiril Taranovsky, and to my assistant, Alice Iverson."

1. G. M. Hopkins, "Poetic Diction," *Journals and Papers,* ed. Humphry House and Graham Storey (London, 1959), p. 84.

2. Robert Lowth, *Isaiah* (London, 1799, 2nd ed.) x–xi. See also his *De sacra poesia hebraeorum* (Oxford, 1753). Lowth's doctrine inspired not only further research but also poetry. Christopher Smart's parallelistic poem of 1759–1763 "represents an attempt to adapt to English verse some of the principles of Hebrew verse expounded by Bishop Robert Lowth," as William H. Bond points out in his edition of Smart's *Jubilate agno* (London, 1954), p. 20.

3. Louis I. Newman and William Popper, *Studies in Biblical Parallelism* (Berkeley, 1918).

4. See esp. Harold L. Ginsberg, "The Rebellion and Death of Ba'lu," *Orientalia* 5:2 (1936), and "The Legend of King Keret," *Bulletin of the American Schools of Oriental Research,* Supplementary Studies, nos. 2–3 (1946); William F. Albright, "The Old Testament and the Canaanite Language and Literature," *Catholic Biblical Quarterly* 7 (1945); idem, "A Catalogue of Early Hebrew Lyric Poems (Psalm 68)," *The Hebrew Union College Annual* 23:1 (1950–51); idem, "The Psalm of Habakkuk," *Studies in Old Testament Prophecy Presented to Theodore H. Robinson* (Edinburgh, 1950); Frank M. Cross and David N. Freedman, "The Blessing of Moses," *Journal of Biblical Literature* 47:3 (1948); idem, "Notes on a Canaanite Psalm in the Old Testament," *Bulletin of the American Schools of Oriental Research* 117 (1950); Stanley Gevirtz, *Patterns in the Early Poetry of Israel* (Chicago, 1963).

5. John Francis Davis, "Poeseos Sinensis Comentarii," *Transactions of the Royal Asiatic Society of Great Britain and Ireland* (1830), II, 410–419.

6. Lowth also brought to notice the fact that in those biblical pairs of lines which are neither equivalent nor opposite in terms, "there is a parallelism equally apparent, and almost as striking, which arises from the similar form and equality of the lines, from the correspondence of the members and the construction" (xxv).

7. See e.g. M. J. L. Hervay-Saint-Denis, *Poésies de l'époque Thang* (Paris, 1862); Gustave Schlegel, *La Loi du parallélisme en style chinois démontrée par la préface du "Si-yü-ki"* (Leiden, 1896); B. Tchang Tcheng-Ming, *Le Parallélisme dans les vers du Chen King* (Shanghai-Paris, 1937).

8. James R. Hightower, "Some Characteristics of Parallel Prose," *Studia Serica Bernhard Karlgren* (Copenhagen, 1959).

9. Professor Hightower has graciously provided me with a detailed English summary of Kūkai's list.

10. Cf. Heinrich Lausberg, *Handbuch der literarischen Rhetorik,* I, sec. 750: "similitudo" (Munich, 1960).

11. Peter A. Boodberg, "On Crypto-Parallelism in Chinese Poetry" and "Syntactical Metaplasia in Stereoscopic Parallelism," *Cedules from a Berkeley Workshop in Asiatic Philology,* nos. 001–540701 and 017–541210 (Berkeley, 1954–55).

12. Johann Gottfried Herder, *Vom Geist der hebräischen Poesie* (Dessau, 1782), p. 23.

13. Eduard Norden, *Die antike Kunstprosa* (Darmstadt, 1958), II, 816–817.

14. Janusz Chmielewski, "Notes on Early Chinese Logic," *Rocznik Orientalistyczny* 28:2 (1965), 87–111.

15. Witold Jabłoński, *Les 'Siao-ha(i-eu)l-yu' de Pékin: Un Essai sur la poésie populaire en Chine* (Cracow, 1935), pp. 20–21.

16. Cf. Jakobson and Halle, *The Fundamentals of Language* (The Hague, 1956); *SW* II, 254ff.

17. Jan Gonda, *Stylistic Repetition in the Veda* (Amsterdam, 1959).

18. See W. L. Steinhart, *Niassche teksten* (Bandung, 1937).

19. Wolfgang Steinitz, *Der Parallelismus in der finnisch-karelischen Volksdichtung* (*Folklore Fellows Communications* 115, 1934), sec. 4.

20. Erik Cajanus, *Linguarum ebraeae et finnicae convenientia* (Abo, 1697), pp. 12–13; Daniel Juslenius, "Oratio de convenientia linguae Fennicae cum Hebraea et Graeca," *Schwedische Bibliothek* (1728), I, 163: "Inprimis notabilis est Hebraicorum et Fennorum carminum consistens qua poësin in Periodi cujusvis divisione in duo Hemistichia, quorum posterius variata phrasi, sensum cum priori continet eundem, vel etiam *emphatikoteron.* Si vero contingit plura poni membra, aut partium est enumeratio, aut gradatio orationis." These observations were further developed by Henrik Gabriel Porthan, *De poesi fennica* (Helsinki, 1766–1768).

21. August Ahlqvist, *Suomalainen runousoppi kielelliseltä kannalta* (Helsinki, 1863); a revised and improved version, "Suomalainen runo-oppi," was included in the author's *Suomen kielen rakennus,* I (Helsinki, 1877).

22. Steinitz, *Der Parallelismus* and *Ostjakische Volksdichtung und Erzählungen aus zwei Dialekten,* I (Tartu, 1939), II, no. 1 (Stockholm, 1941).

23. Robert Austerlitz, *Ob-Ugric Metrics* (*Folklore Fellows Communications* 174, 1958), p. 8. Cf. the reviewer's "procedural query" against the eschewing of semantic criteria in the analysis of structural recurrence and parallelism: John L. Fischer, *Journal of American Folklore* 72 (1960), 339.

24. Dell H. Hymes, *Anthropos* 60 (1960), 575.

25. John Lotz, "Kamassian Verse," *Journal of American Folklore* 67 (1954), 374–376.

26. Tadeusz Kowalski, "Ze studjów nad formą poezji ludów tureckich," *Mémoires de la Commission orientale de l'Académie polonaise des sciences et des lettres* 5 (Cracow, 1921); V. M. Žirmunskij, "Ritmiko-sintaksičeskij parallelizm kak osnova drevnetjurkskogo narodnogo èpičeskogo stixa," *Voprosy jazykoznanija* 13:4 (1964), and a German version of the latter: Viktor Schirmunski, "Syntaktischer Parallelismus und rhythmische Bindung im alttürkischen epischen Vers," *Beiträge zur Sprachwissenschaft, Volkskunde und Literaturforschung, Steinitz Festschrift* (Berlin, 1965).

27. V. M. Žirmunskij, "Oguzskij geroičeskij èpos i 'Kniga Korkuta'," *Kniga moego deda Korkuta: oguzskij geroičeskij èpos,* ed. Žirmunskij and A. N. Kononov (Moscow-Leningrad, 1962).

28. Nikolaus Poppe, "Der Parallelismus in der epischen Dichtung der Mongolen," *Ural-Altaische Jahrbücher* 30 (1958), 195–228.

29. In the folklore of other Slavic peoples, parallelism occupies a much more restricted place, notwithstanding its relevance in certain poetic genres such as Ukrainian *dumy* or South Slavic lyric songs. See Herbert Peukert, *Serbokroatische und makedonische Volkslyrik* (Berlin, 1961), pp. 146–158.

30. "Kalevala, finskaja jazyčeskaja èpopeja," *Biblioteka dlja čtenija* 55:7 (1842), 33–65. In surveying the content of Finnish folksongs and noting the difficulty of translating them, the Petersburg article, as Dagmar Kiparsky kindly brought to our attention, reproduces Xavier Marmier's outline, "De la poésie finlandaise," *Revue des deux mondes* 32 (1842), 68–96. But Marmier gives no comparative study of parallelism and confines his observations on this Finnish device to the following brief remark: "Ces vers sont, en outre, composés en grande partie par un procédé

de parallélisme, c'est-à-dire que le second vers de chaque strophe répète en d'autres termes ou représente avec d'autres nuances la pensée ou l'image tracée dans le premier, et il y a parfois dans ces deux vers, qui sont comme le double écho d'un même sentiment, qui se fortifient l'un par l'autre, et s'en vont sur la même ligne sans se confrondre, un charme indéfinissable et impossible à rendre" (p. 96).

31. The Scandinavian analogue cited apparently concerns alliteration only.

32. A. A. Olesnickij, "Rifm i metr v vetxozavetnoj poèzii," *Trudy Kievskoj duxovnoj akademii* 3 (1872), 564–566.

33. S. N. Šafranov, "O sklade narodno-russkoj pesennoj reči, rassmatrivaemoj v svjazi s napevami," *Žurnal ministerstva narodnogo prosveščenija* 199–205:2 (1878–79).

34. M. P. Štokmar, *Issledovanija v oblasti russkogo stixosloženija* (Moscow, 1952), p. 116.

35. V. M. Žirmunskij, *Rifma, ee istorija i teorija* (Petersburg, 1923), pp. 263–296.

36. "Linguistics and Poetics," *SW* III, 40–41 [included in this volume]. See also "Poèzija grammatiki i grammatika poèzii," *SW* III 67–69, 91–92, which discusses a Russian folk parody of the parallelistic style ("Foma and Erëma") and the promotion of antithetic parallelism into a constituent of the balladic plot ("Vasilij and Sofija") [included in this volume].

37. Anastasija P. Evgen'eva, *Očerki po jazyku russkoj ustnoj poèzii v zapisjax XVII–XX vv.* (Leningrad, 1963), pp. 277–281.

38. A. P. Evgen'eva and B. N. Putilov, eds., *Drevnie rossijskie stixotvorenija sobrannye Kiršeju Danilovym* (Leningrad, 1958), pp. 256, 474. See the editors' commentaries on this collection and its only preserved copy, dating from the end of the eighteenth century, on pp. 514–565, 575–586.

39. See P. K. Simoni, *Povest' o Gore i Zločastii* (*Sbornik Otd. rus. jaz. i slov. I. Akad. Nauk*, 83:1, 1907). My quotations refer to the text restored on pp. 74–88.

40. V. F. Ržiga, "Povest' o Gore i Zločastii i pesni o Gore," *Slavia* 10 (1931).

41. V. I. Dal', *Tolkovyj slovar' živogo velikorusskogo jazyka* (Moscow, 1882), IV, 276.

42. There is a substantial difference between the pervasive, canonical parallelism in the Russian oral tradition and the optional parallelistic constructions that occur in Old Russian literature, partly under the influence of the Psalter. See D. S. Lixačev, "Stilističeskaja simmetrija v drevnerusskoj literature," *Problemy sovremennoj filologii* (Moscow, 1964).

43. Samuel R. Driver, *An Introduction to the Literature of the Old Testament* (New York, 1922), p. 364.

44. About Grief as "a mythological creature" in the *Povest'* and in songs, see N. I. Kostomarov, "O mifičeskom značenii Gorja-Zločastija," *Sovremennik* 59 (1856), 113–24, and William Harkins, "The Mythic Element in the tale of Gore-Zločastie," in *For Roman Jakobson* (The Hague, 1956), pp. 201–212. The two synonyms *góre* (grief) and *zločastie* (misfortune) are bound by the conjunction *i* (and) in the title of the *Povest'* merely to reinforce the meaning of the pair (*292: A mne, górju i zločastiju, ne v puste že žit'*). See Evgen'eva, p. 271. The second synonym is in apposition to the former (*273: podslušalo góre-zločastie; 394: utéšil on góre-zločastie*), changeable into an epithet (*378, 438, 463: góre zločástnoe*) or inversely (*351: zločástie gorinskoe*) or into a simple adjective (*298, 315: Ino ZLo to góre IZLukavilos'* and *432: a čtó ZLOe góre napered' ZašLO*). On the other hand, coupled synonyms split easily into two independent personae (*280: i já ix, góre, peremúdrilo, 281: učinisja im zlo-*

částie velikoe; or *288: i já ot nix, góre, minoválosja, 289: a zločastie na ix v* [sic] *mogile ostálosja*).

45. Austerlitz, *Ob-Ugric Metrics,* p. 80, outlines an "important sub-class" of un-paired lines "which contain the etymological figure."

46. See A. B. Nikitina, "Iz vospominanij Anatolija Mariengofa," *Russkaja lite-ratura* 7:4 (1964), 158.

47. Their difference with regard to Chinese has been aptly discussed by Janusz Chimelewski, "Język starochiński jako narzędzie rozumowania," *Sprawozdania z prac naukowych Wydziału I PAN* (1964). Cf. Tchang Tcheng-Ming, *Le parallélisme,* pp. 78–83.

48. Both Lowth, in application to the Proverbs of Solomon (xx) and following him Davis, with regard to Chinese maxims (p. 412), observed that antithetic par-allelism "is peculiarly adapted . . . to adages, aphorisms, and detached sentences." Their "elegance, acuteness, and force," according to Lowth, "arise in a great mea-sure from the Antithetic form, the opposition of diction and sentiment."

49. See Heinrich Lausberg, *Handbuch der literarischen Rhetorik,* I (Munich, 1960), secs. 259, 586–588; Gonda, pp. 93ff.

50. Cf. in Kirša's bylina on Vol'x Vseslav'evič: *A vtápory knjaginja ponós poneslá— ponós ponesla i ditjá rodilá.* Šafranov compares this construction to a link of a chain which is in contract with both the foregoing and the following ring (p. 85).

51. Another paronomastic association—linking three odd hemistichs—may be suspected here: 2/A*v*GÓR*'e/* ~ 3/*n*AGÓmu/ ~ 5/GR*'ivna/*. In this connection Saussure's precept might be recalled: "Mais si ce doute peut à tout instant s'élever, de ce qui est le mot-thème et de ce qui est le groupe répondant, c'est la meilleure preuve que tout se répond d'une manière ou d'une autre dans les vers." See Jean Starobinski, "Les Anagrammes de Ferdinand de Saussure," *Mercure de France* 255 (1964).

52. Herman Weyl, *Symmetry* (Princeton, 1952), p. 43, defines this device as "re-flexive congruence."

53. The older form in *Povest' 409, / d'et'at'i/,* must have belonged to the original version of this line.

54. *Opredelenie attributivno-predikativnoe,* in terms of A. A. Šaxmatov, *Sintaksis russkogo jazyka* (Leningrad, 1941), pp. 393–394.

55. A. M. Peškovskij, *Russkij sintaksis v naučnom osveščenii* (Moscow, 1956), pp. 381–382, would ascribe to the infinitive clauses in lines 2–3 "a connotation of sub-jective necessity" and in 6–11 "a connotation of objective necessity."

56. See Jakobson, *SW* I, 535.

57. V. I. Varencov, *Sbornik russkix duxovnyx stixov* (St. Petersburg, 1860), p. 131.

58. A. I. Sobolevskij, *Velikorusskie narodnye pesni* (St. Petersburg, 1895), I, 533, 536.

59. F. M. Istomin and G. O. Djutš, *Pesni russkogo naroda* (St. Petersburg, 1894), p. 60.

60. A. B. Šapiro, *Očerki po sintaksisu russkix narodnyx govorov* (Moscow, 1953), p. 71.

61. Another possible conjecture is *a góre préžde ⟨da v⟩ vék zašël* (and grief came beforehand and forever); then the parallelism of the hemistiches would rest on the two temporal adverbs *préžde* and *vvék (vovék? navék?).* Cf. the corresponding expression in the *Povest' 437: ne na čás ja k tebe góre zločastnoe privjazálosja,* and in the lyrical-epic song of the grief cycle recorded by A. F. Hilferding, *Onežskie byliny,*

II (St. Petersburg, 1896), no. 177: *i ne na čas ja k tebe góre privjazálosi* and *a ja tut navek góre rosstaválosi.*

62. Cf. the allusion in *Povest' 181:* at the feast the lad was seated *ne v ból'šee mesto, ne v mén'šee.*

63. Robert Austerlitz, "Parallelismus," *Poetics Poetyka Poètika* (Warsaw, 1961), states: "Die Spannung, welche zwischen synonymen oder antonymen Parallelwörtern herrscht, verleiht dem Text eine Art von semantischen Rhythmus" (p. 441). The tension between paralleled synonyms *and* antonyms plays in turn an effective part.

64. Cf. Jakobson, *SW* IV, 434ff.

65. See A. M. Seliščev, *Dialektologičeskij očerk Sibiri* (Irkutsk, 1920), p. 137: *róstit',* etc., and S. P. Obnorskij, *Imennoe sklonenie v sovremennom russkom jazyke* (Leningrad, 1927), I, 244: *kónja, kónju.* A dialectal stress on the desinence is most probable in *močalámi* (line 14); cf. Obnorskij (Leningrad, 1931), II, 384ff.

66. Cf. Jakobson, *SW* IV, 425ff.

67. Franz Miklosich, "Die Darstellung im slavischen Volksepos," *Denkschriften der K. Akademie der Wissenschaften in Wien,* 38:3 (1890), 7–8.

68. See e.g. Marcel Jousse, *Études de psychologie linguistique, le style oral rythmique et mnémotechnique chez les verbo-moteurs,* chaps. 10, 12, 15–18 (Paris, 1925); Gevirtz, *Patterns in the Early Poetry of Israel,* p. 10.

69. See Claude Lévi-Strauss, *La Pensée sauvage* (Paris, 1962).

70. A. N. Veselovskij, "Psixologičeskij parallelizm i ego formy v otraženijax poètičeskogo stilja," in his *Poètika* (St. Petersburg, 1913), I, 130–225.

71. V. Ja. Propp, *Morfologija skazki* (Leningrad, 1928); in English: *Morphology of the Folktale* (Bloomington, 1958).

72. Alfred Bertholet, "Zur Stelle Hohes Lied 4⁸," *Beihefte zur Zeitschrift für die alttestamentliche Wissenschaft* 33:18, pp. 47–53.

73. Albright, "The Psalm of Habakkuk," p. 7.

74. Cf. Jakobson, "Linguistics and Poetics," *SW* III, 23: "Orientation toward the ADRESSEE, the CONATIVE function, finds its purest grammatical expression in the vocative and imperative" [p. 67 above].

75. P. V. Šejn, *Velikorus v svoix pesnjax, obrjadax, obyčajax, verovanijax, skazkax, legendax, i t.p.* (St. Petersburg, 1900), no. 1659.

76. See Lausberg, *Handbuch,* sec. 737: an isocolon modeled upon the scheme $q(a^1b^1/a^2b^2)$ where q designates "den klammerartigen gemeinsamen Satzteil."

77. Jakobson, "Signe zéro," *SW* II, 211–212.

78. Driver, *An Introduction,* p. 363. "Climactic" parallelism, as Driver defines it, appears to be a mere combination of the repetitive form with the above-cited form which in the second line "completes" the first one. Thus in the example he quotes from Psalm 29:8, "The voice of the Lord shaketh the wilderness: / The Lord shaketh the wilderness of Kadesh," the initial part of the second line catches up the end part of the first line and adds "of Kadesh." The repetitive device may be confined either to an anadiplosis, as in the above example, or to an anaphora, as in the other instances of climactic parallelism adduced by Driver.

79. B. M. and Ju. M. Sokolov, *Skazki i pesni belozerskogo kraja,* no. 73 (Moscow, 1915).

80. Jakobson, *O češskom stixe* (Berlin-Moscow, 1923), p. 105; *SW* V, 108.

81. Cf. "Lettres de Ferdinand de Saussure à Antoine Meillet," ed. Emile Benven-

iste, *Cahiers Ferdinand de Saussure*, no. 21 (1964), p. 110: "Il est d'emblée accordé que l'on peut se rattraper pour un couple sur le vers suivant, et même sur l'espace de plusieurs vers."

11. Charles Baudelaire's "Les Chats"

Originally published in French in *L'Homme* 2 (1962). The translation by Katie Furness-Lane appears here in a revised version corrected by Jakobson and published in the second edition of *Introduction to Structuralism*, ed. Michael Lane (New York: Basic Books, 1973).

1. Maurice Grammont, *Petit traité de versification française* (Paris, 1908), p. 86.

2. Maurice Grammont, *Traité de phonétique* (Paris, 1930), p. 384.

3. Ibid., p. 388.

4. Marguerite Durand, "La Spécificité du phonème. Application au cas de R/L," *Journal de psychologie* 62 (1960), 405–419.

5. Cf. *L'Intermédiaire des chercheurs et des curieux* 67, cols. 338, 509.

6. Emile Benveniste, who was kind enough to read this essay in manuscript, pointed out to us that between *les amoureux fervents* and *les savants austères, la mûre saison* also plays the role of intermediary: it is, in effect, in *leur mûre saison* that they reunite to identify themselves *également* with the cats. For, continues Benveniste, to remain *amoureux fervents* in *leur mûre saison* already signifies that one is outside the common fold, as are *les savants austères* by their vocation. The initial situation of the sonnet is that of a life outside this world (nevertheless life in the underworld is rejected) and, transferred to the cats, this situation develops from chilly seclusion to vast starry solitudes where *science et volupté* are a dream without end. In support of these comments, we would cite another poem in *Les Fleurs du mal:* "Le savant amour . . . fruit d'automne aux saveurs souveraines" ("L'Amour du mensonge").

7. Baudelaire, *Oeuvres* (Paris, 1961), II, 243ff.

8. Baudelaire, ed. *Les Fleurs du mal,* J. Crépet and G. Blin (Paris, 1942), p. 413.

9. Michel Butor, *Histoire extraordinaire, essai sur un rêve de Baudelaire* (Paris, 1961), p. 85.

10. In L. Rudrauf's study, *Rime et sexe* (Tartu, 1936), the exposition of "a theory of the alternation of masculine and feminine rhymes in French poetry" is followed by a "controversy" with Maurice Grammont (pp. 47ff). According to Grammont, "for alternation as established in the 16th century based upon the presence or absence of an unstressed *e* at the end of the word, we have availed ourselves of the terms 'feminine' and 'masculine' because the unstressed *e* at the end of a word was, in the majority of cases, indicative of the feminine gender: *un petit chat/ une petite chatte,* or rather one could say that the specific termination of the feminine, in contradistinction to the masculine, always contained an unstressed *e*." However, Rudrauf expressed certain doubts: "But was it purely the grammatical consideration that guided the poets of the 16th century in their establishment of this rule of alternation and in their choice of the epithets 'masculine' and 'feminine' to designate the two kinds of rhymes? Let us not forget that the poets of the Pleiade wrote their stanzas with an eye to song, and that song underscores, much more than does the spoken word, the alternation of a strong (masculine) syllable and of a weak (feminine) syllable. Consciously or unconsciously, the musical point of view

and the sexual point of view must have played a role along with the grammatical analogy" (p. 49).

Inasmuch as this alternation of rhymes based upon the presence or absence of an unstressed *e* at the ends of lines is no longer realized, in Grammont's view it has been replaced by an alternation of rhymes ending either with a consonant or with a stressed vowel. While fully prepared to acknowledge that "the final syllables ending with a vowel are all masculine" (p. 46), Rudrauf is at the same time tempted to establish a scale of 24 degrees for the consonantal rhymes, "ranging from the most brusque and virile end syllables to the most feminiely suave" (pp. 12ff). The rhymes with a voiceless stop at their end form the extreme masculine pole (1°) and the rhymes with a voiced spirant are viewed as the feminine pole (24°) on Rudrauf's scale. If one applies this tentative classification to the consonantal rhymes of "Les Chats," one is conscious of a gradual movement toward the masculine pole, which results in an attenuation of the contrast between the two kinds of rhymes: $_1$*austères*—$_4$*sédentaires* (liquid: 19°); $_6$*ténèbres*—$_7$*funèbres* (voiced stop followed by a liquid: 15°); $_9$*attitudes*—$_{10}$*solitudes* (voiced stop: 13°); $_{12}$*magiques*—$_{14}$*mystiques* (voiceless stop: 1°).

12. Shakespeare's Verbal Art in "Th' Expence of Spirit"

Originally published as a separate brochure by Mouton (The Hague–Paris, 1970).

1. H. Kökeritz, *Shakespeare's Pronunciation* (New Haven, 1953), pp. 126–127, 164, 175.

2. George Wyndham, ed., *The Poems of Shakespeare* (London, 1898).

3. Charles Sanders Peirce and J. B. Noyes, "Shakespearian Pronunciation," *North American Review* 98:202 (1864), 343.

4. Kökeritz, *Shakespeare's Pronunciation;* M. M. Mahood, *Shakespeare's Wordplay* (London, 1957).

5. Sister Miriam Joseph, *Shakespeare's Use of the Arts of Language* (New York, 1947).

6. Kökeritz, *Shakespeare's Pronunciation,* pp. 58–59.

7. Hilton Landry, *Interpretations in Shakespeare's Sonnets* (Berkeley, 1964).

8. G. Puttenham, *The Arte of English Poesie* (repr. London, 1869), p. 175.

9. Douglas Bush and Alfred Harbage, eds., *Shakespeare's Sonnets* (Baltimore, 1961), p. 18; Laura Riding and Robert Graves, "William Shakespeare and E. E. Cummings," in their *A Survey of Modernist Poetry* (New York, 1928), p. 80.

10. Cf. V. H. Yngve, "The Depth Hypothesis," *Proceedings of Symposia in Applied Mathematics* 12 (American Mathematical Society, 1961); M. A. K. Halliday, "Class in Relation to the Axes of Chain and Choice in Language," *Linguistics* 2 (1963).

11. Otto Jespersen, "Notes on Metre," in his *Linguistica* (Copenhagen, 1933).

12. Joseph, *Shakespeare's Use of the Arts of Language,* p. 296.

13. Barbara Strang, *Modern English Structure* (New York, 1968), p. 67.

14. See e.g. Barbara H. Smith, ed., *William Shakespeare: Sonnets* (New York, 1969), p. 183.

15. See P. Christophersen, *The Articles: A Study of their Theory and Use in English* (Copenhagen, 1939), pp. 30–31, 77.

16. See Strang, *Modern English Structure,* p. 125f.

17. Edward Sapir, *Totality,* Linguistic Society of America, Language Monographs 6 (Baltimore, 1930).

18. C. L. Barber, "An Essay on the Sonnets," in *The Sonnets of Shakespeare,* ed. F. Fergusson (New York, 1960).

19. H. E. Rollins, ed., *A New Variorum Edition of Shakespeare: The Sonnets* (Philadelphia, 1944), I, 331.

20. Jeremy Bentham, *Theory of Fictions,* ed. C. K. Ogden (London, 1932); Franz Brentano, "Anhang," in his *Psychologie vom empirischen Standpunkt,* II (Hamburg, 1959).

21. Puttenham, *The Arte of English Poesie,* p. 92.

22. Kökeritz, *Shakespeare's Pronunciation,* pp. 122, 232.

23. Ibid., p. 177.

24. Ibid., pp. 153–154.

25. See A. C. Partridge, *Orthography in Shakespeare and Elizabethan Drama* (London, 1964), p. 25.

26. John Crowe Ransom, "Shakespeare at Sonnets," *Southern Review* 3 (1938), 535.

27. J. M. Robertson, *The Problems of Shakespeare's Sonnets* (London, 1926), p. 219.

28. Edward Hubler, *The Sense of Shakespeare's Sonnets* (Princeton, 1952), p. 35; Hubler, ed., *Shakespeare's Songs and Poems* (New York, 1959), p. 72.

29. C. W. M. Johnson, "Shakespeare's Sonnet 129," *Explicator* 7:6 (1949), 41.

30. Richard Levin, "Sonnet 129 as a 'Dramatic' Poem," *Shakespeare Quarterly* 16 (1965), 179.

31. Riding and Graves, *Survey,* p. 72.

13. Yeats' "Sorrow of Love" through the Years

Originally published as a separate brochure by Peter de Ridder Press (Lisse, 1977).

1. Paul Valéry, "Poésie et pensée abstraite," in his *Variété* (Paris, 1945), V, 141.

2. Ibid., p. 319.

3. W. B. Yeats, *Memoirs: Autobiography—First Draft, Journal,* ed. Denis Donoghue (New York, 1973), pp. 283–284.

4. Benjamin Lee Whorf, *Language, Mind, and Reality* (Cambridge, Mass., 1956), p. 258.

5. *The Variorum Edition of the Poems of William Butler Yeats,* ed. Peter Allt and Russell K. Alspach (New York, 1957), p. 846.

6. Ibid., p. 778.

7. Ibid., p. 848.

8. Ibid., p. 842.

9. For an exhaustive survey of the text's history, see Yeats, *Variorum Edition,* pp. 119–120, George Monteiro, "Unrecorded Variants in Two Yeats Poems," *Papers of the Bibliographical Society of America* 60:3 (1966), 367–368, and Richard Ellmann, *The Identity of Yeats* (New York, 1954), pp. 122, 317n.

10. Yves Bonnefoy, "Le Chagrin de l'amour," *Argile* 1 (1973), p. 65; Richard Exner, "Trübsal der Liebe," in W. B. Yeats, *Werke,* vol. 1, ed. W. Vordtriede (Neuwied, 1960).

11. Samuel H. Parrish, *A Concordance to the Poetry of W. B. Yeats* (Ithaca, 1963), p. 159.

12. W. B. Yeats, *A Vision* (New York, 1965), p. 249.

13. Yeats, *Variorum Edition*, pp. 842, 855.

14. Ibid., p. 855.

15. See Raymond Cowell, *W. B. Yeats* (New York, 1969), p. 144.

16. Louis MacNeice, *The Poetry of W. B. Yeats* (London, 1941), p. 71.

17. Joseph Hone, *W. B. Yeats* (New York, 1943), p. 126.

18. G. B. Saul, *Prolegomena to the Study of Yeats's Poems* (Philadelphia, 1957), p. 56.

19. Barbara Strang, *The Structure of English Grammar* (London, 1968), p. 175.

20. Otto Jespersen, *The Philosophy of Grammar* (London, 1924), p. 237.

21. Yeats, *Variorum Edition*, p. 65, line 18, and p. 126, line 4.

22. Thomas Parkinson, *W. B. Yeats, Self-Critic* (Berkeley, 1951), p. 168.

23. Yeats, *Variorum Edition*, p. 301, line 9, and p. 304, variant to line 41.

24. Marianne Moore, quoted in *New York Times,* March 22, 1961, p. 31.

25. Parkinson, *Yeats,* p. 172.

26. Yeats, *A Vision,* p. 291.

27. Parkinson, *Yeats,* p. 168.

28. Jespersen, *The Philosophy of Grammar,* p. 86.

29. On these terms see M. A. K. Halliday, "Class in Relation to the Axes of Chain and Choice in Language," *Linguistics* 2 (1963), 5–15, and V. H. Yngve, "The Depth Hypothesis," *Proceedings of Symposia in Applied Mathematics* 12 (1961), 130–138.

30. Yeats, *A Vision,* p. 74.

31. W. B. Yeats, "The Symbolism of Poetry," in *Essays and Introductions* (New York, 1968), pp. 156–157.

32. Marjorie Perloff, *Rhyme and Meaning in the Poetry of Yeats* (The Hague, 1970), p. 29.

33. Parkinson, *Yeats,* p. 169.

34. Adelyn Dougherty, *A Study of Rhythmic Structure in the Verse of William Butler Yeats* (The Hague, 1973); James Bailey, "Linguistic Givens and their Metrical Realization in a Poem by Yeats," *Language and Style* 8:1 (1975), 21–33.

35. Paul Kiparsky, "Stress, Syntax, and Meter," *Language* 51:3 (1975), 581.

36. Yeats, *A Vision,* pp. 82–83.

37. Ibid., p. 105.

38. Ibid., p. 136.

39. Ibid., p. 93.

40. Yeats, *Memoirs,* p. 30.

41. Ibid., p. 23.

42. Yeats, *Variorum Edition,* p. 842.

43. Ibid., p. 821.

44. Ibid., p. 375.

45. W. B. Yeats, *Autobiography* (New York, 1965), p. 291.

46. Yeats, *A Vision,* pp. 78, 131.

47. Yeats, *Variorum Edition,* p. 374, lines 53–55.

48. Ibid., p. 374, lines 58–59.

49. Ibid., p. 375, lines 87–89.

50. Yeats, *A Vision,* p. 137f.

51. Yeats, *Memoirs*, p. 74.

52. Ibid., p. 88.

53. Yeats, *A Vision*, p. 136.

54. Ibid., p. 135.

55. Ibid., p. 132.

56. Yeats, *Variorum Edition*, p. 111.

57. John Unterecker, *A Reader's Guide to William Butler Yeats* (New York, 1959), p. 159.

58. 1893; cf. *Variorum Edition*, pp. 100–101.

59. See Curtis Bradford, "Yeats and Maude Gonne," *Texas Studies in Language and Literature* 3 (1961–62), 454.

60. Yeats, *A Vision*, p. 133.

61. Ibid., p. 102.

62. Yeats, *Variorum Edition*, p. 843.

14. Subliminal Verbal Patterning in Poetry

Originally published in *Studies in General and Oriental Linguistics, presented to Shiro Hattori* (Tokyo: TEC, 1970). The expanded version published here first appeared in *SW* II, 136–147.

1. See esp. Velimir Xlebnikov, *Sobranie proizvedenij*, ed. N. Stepanov and Ju. Tynjanov (Leningrad, 1933), V, 191.

2. Ibid., p. 194.

3. Xlebnikov, "Svojasi," *Sobranie proizvedenij* (Leningrad, 1928), II, 8.

4. Xlebnikov, *Sobranie proizvedenij*, V, 187, 185.

5. Victor Weisskopf, "The Role of Symmetry in Nuclear, Atomic, and Complex Structures," contribution to Nobel Symposium, August 26, 1968.

6. Osip Brik, "Zvukovye povtory," *Poètika* (Petrograd, 1919), p. 59.

7. Kazimierz Moszyński, *Kultura ludowa Słowian* 2:2 (Cracow, 1939), 1384.

8. P. Glagolevskij, "Sintaksis jazyka russkix poslovic," *Žurnal ministerstva narodnogo prosveščenija*, 7 (1871), 1–45.

· 9. See Moszyński, *Kultura*, p. 1402.

10. See F. Sušil, *Moravské národni pisně* (Prague, 1951), no. 807.

15. Supraconscious Turgenev

Written in Russian in 1979 for the Edward Stankiewicz Festschrift (*International Journal of Slavic Linguistics and Poetics*, 25–26, 1982) and first published in *SW* III, 707–711. Translated into English by Stephen Rudy. [The title adjective, *zaumnij* (supraconscious), alludes to the particular form of experimental poetry practiced by the Russian Futurists, which in its most extreme instances verges on verbal delirium. The literal meaning of the term is "beyond the mind," "trans-sense." The title might thus be rendered in colloquial English as "Turgenev Leaves His Senses."—Translator's note.]

1. V. A. Sollogub, *Vospominanija*, ed. S. P. Šesterikov (Moscow–Leningrad, 1931), pp. 445–448 (a critical edition of the memoirs prepared before the author's death, first published in the journal *Istoričeskij vestnik* in 1886 and as a book in 1887).

3. Velimir Xlebnikov, *Sobranie proizvedenij* (Leningrad, 1933), V, 185, 187, 191.

[*Samovitaja reč'*, a neologism coined by Xlebnikov, has been translated variously as "self-centered," "self-moving," "self-sufficient," or "autotelic" speech. I render it by an analogous English neologism, "selfsome."—Translator's note.]

4. Cf. my analysis of Xlebnikov's poem "The Grasshopper" in "Subliminal Verbal Patterning in Poetry," in *SW* III, 137ff [included in this volume].

5. Ivan Turgenev, *Nouvelle correspondance inédité*, ed. Alexandre Zviguilsky (Paris, 1971), I, xliii–lii, 278–280, 310–312.

6. Ivan Turgenev, *Sočinenija* (Moscow–Leningrad, 1967), XIV, 174; V. Xlebnikov, "Mudrost' v silke," *Pervyj žurnal russkix futuristov* (1914).

16. On a Generation That Squandered Its Poets

First published in Russian under the title "O pokolenii, rastrativšem svoix poètov" in Jakobson and D. S. Svjatopol'-Mirskij, *Smert' Vladimira Majakovskogo* (Berlin: Petropolis, 1931). The translation by Edward J. Brown reprinted here first appeared in his anthology *Major Soviet Writers* (New York: Oxford University Press, 1973).

1. When we say "chamber" (*kamernaja*) we certainly do not intend to detract from the value of their work as poetic craftsmanship. The poetry of Evgenij Baratynskij or of Innokentij Annenskij, for instance, might be called thus.

2. Xlebnikov himself describes his own [alter ego's] death using suicide imagery: "What? Zangezi's dead!/ Not only that, he slit his own throat./ What a sad piece of news!/ What sorrowful news!/ He left a short note:/ 'Razor, have my throat!'/ The wide iron sedge/ Slit the waters of his life,/ He's no more."

3. "New name,/ tear off!/ fly/ into the space of the world dwelling/ thousand-year-old/ low sky,/ vanish, you blue-ass!/ It is I./ I, I/ I/ I/ I/ the inspired sewage-disposal man of the earth."

17. Marginal Notes on the Prose of the Poet Pasternak

Originally published in German under the title "Randbemerkungen zur Prosa des Dichters Pasternak" in *Slavische Rundschau* 6 (1935). The translation by Angela Livingstone reprinted here first appeared in *Pasternak: Modern Judgements,* ed. Donald Davie and Angela Livingstone (London: Macmillan, 1969).

18. The Statue in Puškin's Poetic Mythology

Originally published in Czech under the title "Socha v symbolice Puškinově" in *Slovo a slovesnost* 3 (1937). The translation by John Burbank reprinted here was extensively revised by Jakobson, who also added the illustrations, for publication in *Puškin and His Sculptural Myth*, ed. John Burbank (The Hague-Paris: Mouton, 1975). The editors have made certain revisions in this volume for the sake of continuity, including, in some cases, removal of the original Russian quotations from Puškin; readers with a knowledge of Russian may wish to consult the version in *Puškin and His Sculptural Myth*.

1. Unless otherwise noted, quotations from Puškin are from *Polnoe sobranie sočinenij,* 3rd ed. (hereafter abbreviated PSS), 10 vols. (Moscow-Leningrad, 1962–1966). Citations from Puškin's letters are to the following editions: A. Hofman

and S. Lifar', eds., *Pis'ma Puškina k N. N. Gončarovoj* (Paris, 1937); B. and L. Modzalevskij, eds., *Pis'ma Puškina*, 3 vols. (Moscow-Leningrad, 1926–1935); V. Saitov, ed., *Sočinenija Puškina: Perepiska*, III (St. Petersburg, 1911).

2. D. Darskij, *Malen'kie tragedii Puškina* (Moscow, 1915), p. 53.

3. B. V. Tomaševskij, "'Cygany' i 'Mednyj vsadnik' A. S. Puškina," foreword to the edition of both poems (Leningrad, 1936), p. 6.

4. Anna Axmatova, "Poslednjaja skazka Puškina," *Zvezda* 1 (1933), 175ff; this article has been reprinted in Axmatova, *Sočinenija* (Munich, 1968), II, 197–222.

5. See D. K. Zelenin, *Kul't ongonov v Sibiri* (Moscow–Leningrad, 1936), pp. 6–7.

6. Perhaps the very difference between the metonymic relationship of the golden cockerel to the astrologer and the metaphoric relationship of the monuments to Peter and the commander prevented scholars from seeing the affinity of the fairy tale to *The Bronze Horseman* and *The Stone Guest,* when they were pointing out single points of contact between those two works in passing (V. Ja. Brjusov, *Moj Puškin* [Moscow, 1929], p. 87; V. F. Xodasevič, *Stat'i o russkoj poèzii* [Petersburg, 1922], p. 94; Wacław Lednicki, *Jeździec miedziany* [Warsaw, n.d.], pp. 47–48). By the way, in *The Stone Guest* it is a question of a tombstone monument, so that an association according to contiguity accompanies the main association according to similarity. Puškin consciously calls attention to it and suggests its irrationality: "O, let me die right now at your feet,/ Let them bury my poor remains here/ . . . So that you might touch my stone / With your light foot or your dress." To which Doña Anna replies: "You aren't in your right senses."

7. Puškin, *PSS* VII, 568–569.

8. Cf. the following scene with Doña Anna, which develops similarly: "Here, near this grave?!/ Go away!"

9. Cf. the poem "At the beginning of life I recall school" ("V načale žizni školu pomnju ja," discussed below), where a youth is "paralyzed" and dumb in the presence of statues.

10. For a characterization of the first Boldino autumn see D. D. Blagoj, *Sociologija tvorčestva Puškina* (Moscow, 1929), pp. 156ff, and Alfred Bém, *O Puškine* (Užhorod, 1937), pp. 64ff.

11. The monstrous tree of death in the poem "The Upas Tree" ("Ančar," 1828) can also be included with these ghastly monsters.

12. Xodasevič, *Stat'i*, p. 84.

13. See Iskoz-Dolinin in Puškin, *Sočinenija,* ed. S. Vengerov, 6 vols. (St. Petersburg, 1907–1915), IV, 19–20.

14. S. N. Gončarov's account recorded by P. Bartenev in *Russkij arxiv* 15:2 (1877), 98ff.

15. *PSS* III, 113.

16. *PSS* VII, 353.

17. From a letter to Žukovskij, March 7, 1826.

18. *PSS* VIII, 368.

19. *PSS* VIII, 128.

20. Cf. *Pis'ma* 2 (1928), 439–440, and 3 (1935), 502ff. A list of pertinent literature can also be found there.

21. Cf. Innokentij Annenskij, *Puškin i Carskoe selo* (Petrograd, 1921), p. 18.

22. Dmitrij S. Merežkovskij, *Večnye sputniki,* 3rd ed. (St. Petersburg, 1906), p. 313.

23. I. D. Ermakov, *Ètjudy po psixologii tvorčestva A. S. Puškina* (Moscow, 1933), p. 169.

24. See e.g. the poem to V. V. Engel'gardt, extolling "the happy lawless one, the lazy citizen of Pindus . . . the devoted worshipper of Venus and the sovereign of delights" and aimed against the celestial and terrestrial tsar.

25. From the poem "Farewell" ("Proščanie"). Puškin did not return to the love lyric again; the "mysterious melody" of its verse is renounced and cursed in the poem "When in my embraces" ("Kogda v ob"jatija moi," 1831). Moreover, either he provided expressions of an intimate lyric from the first Boldino autumn with bogus earlier dates ("Farewell"—with the year 1829; "Conjury" ["Zaklinanie"] and "For the shores of your distant country" ["Dlja beregov otčizny dal'noj"]—with the year 1828) and still did not publish them, or he made himself out to be a mere translator ("The Gypsies" ["Cygany"]).

26. Cf. Puškin, *Sočinenija* (St. Petersburg, 1905), II, 139–140.

27. "The trans-Danubian giant" is a reference to Count P. A. Rumjancev, leader of the Russian victory in July 1770 over the Turkish army at Kagul, a tributary of the Danube. The final text as given in *PSS* I, 380, reads somewhat differently: "Intoxicated with reminiscence/ With veneration and anguish/ I embrace your stern marble,/ Kagul's haughty monument./ Not the Russians' bold feat,/ Not the glory given to Catherine,/ Not the trans-Danubian giant/ Are what inflame me now." For variants see *Polnoe sobranie sočinenij* (Moscow, 1947), II.1, 552–553.

28. Cf. *Sočinenija* (1905), II, 31, 80–81.

29. "Embarrassed by memories, filled with sweet anguish" (1829). Cf. the initial lines of the earliest reading of the 1819 "Elegy": "Haughty monument of victory . . . Embarrassed by reminiscence," with the initial line of 1829: "Embarrassed by memories," and the same variant in both poems: "Intoxicated with reminiscence," as well as the second line of 1829: "Filled with sweet anguish," and a variant of 1819: "with both delight and anguish."

30. "On the hills of Georgia lies a nocturnal haze" ("Na xolmax Gruzii ležit nočnaja mgla"), May 1829; "I loved you . . ." ("Ja vas ljubil: ljubov' ešče, byt' možet"), 1829; "What is there for you in my name?" ("Čto v imeni tebe moem?"), January 19, 1830 (?); "The Page or the Fifteenth Year" ("Paž ili Pjatnadcatyj god"), October 7, 1830. If we are to believe Puškin's admission, not even the poem "Madonna," which is dedicated to Gončarova, was inspired by her (see *Pis'ma* II [1928], 397).

31. From a letter to Pletnev, September 9, 1830.

32. *Pis'ma . . . Gončarovoj*, p. 116.

33. *Russkij arxiv* 50:3 (1912), 300.

34. Abram Èfros, *Risunki poèta* (Moscow, 1932), pp. 432–439.

35. In *PSS* this essay will be found under the title "O narodnoj drame i drame *Marfa Posadnica*."

36. See Blagoj, *Sociologija*, p. 352; see *PSS* III, 157, for Puškin's translation.

37. Andrej Belyj has understood the poet's mood very well in his book *Ritm kak dialektika i "Mednyj vsadnik"* (Moscow, 1929).

38. See Jerzy Tretiak, *Mickiewicz i Puszkin* (Warsaw, 1906); Lednicki, *Jeździec*; M. Cjavlovskij, L. Modzalevskij, and T. Zenger, eds., *Rukoju Puškina* (Leningrad, 1935), pp. 353–536.

39. "*He looks:* surrounded by *waves,/ Above* a solid, mossy *crag/* The monument

rose . . . Around its pedestal, resounding, *grey billows* / subsided in the glistening *foam.*"

40. See G. Vernadskij, "'Mednyj vsadnik' v tvorčestve Puškina," *Slavia* 2 (1923–24), 645–654; Blagoj, *Sociologija,* pp. 263–264; Belyj, *Ritm.* The combination and opposition of a storm and Peter's monument in direct proximity with mention of the cruel executioner's law, however, occurs in Puškin's stock of poetic images even before the Decembrist rebellion—the poet's somewhat enigmatic, derisive couplets "The Tsar, wrinkling his brow" ("Brovi car naxmurja"), written two or three months before the rebellion, acquired shortly thereafter a tragic fulfillment that may have provided at least one of the impulses for the poet's later "sad story." Perhaps there is a similar relationship between the fragment "The terrible hour will come" ("Pridet užasnyj čas") and "Conjury" ("Zaklinanie"): following a draft of a poem about a lover's death (1823) comes a lover's death (1825) and later, in Boldino, a poem about her death (1830).

41. *PSS* IV, 534.

42. See Blagoj, *Sociologija,* pp. 283ff, 347–348.

43. From a letter to N. I. Krivcov, February 10, 1831.

44. See D. Jakubovič in *Puškin, 1834 god* (Leningrad, 1834), p. 45.

45. From a letter to his wife, September 20–25, 1834.

46. D. S. Mirskij, "Problema Puškina," *Literaturnoe nasledstvo* 16–18 (1934), 103.

47. "Poslednjaja skazka," pp. 171–172; cf. Puškin, *Sočinenija,* ed. B. V. Tomaševskij (Leningrad, 1935), p. 845.

48. Belyj, *Ritm,* 71.

49. M. P. Alekseev, *Stixotvorenie Puškina "Ja pamjatnik sebe vozdvig"* (Leningrad, 1967).

50. Abram Èfros, *Avtoportrety Puškina* (Moscow, 1945), p. 139.

51. Given here in the English translation edited by George R. Noyes (New York, 1944).

52. Wacław Lednicki, *Bits of Table-Talk on Pushkin, Mickiewicz, etc.* (The Hague, 1956), pp. 195–196.

53. Èfros, *Avtoportrety,* p. 139.

54. See esp. Jurij Tynjanov, *Arxaisty i novatory* (Leningrad, 1929), pp. 241–242.

55. "Dvižen'ja net, skazal mudrec bradatyj" (There is no movement, said the bearded wiseman), *PSS* II, 279.

56. Cf. Camille Mauclair, *Auguste Rodin, l'homme et l'oeuvre* (Paris, 1918): "J'ai dit un jour à Rodin: 'On dirait que vous savez qu'il y a une figure dans ce bloc, et que vous vous bornez à casser tout autour la gangue qui nous la cache.' Il m'a repondu que c'était absolument son impression en travaillant" (p. 51).

57. Auguste Rodin eloquently testifies how a sculptor strives intentionally to master time: "Dans son oeuvre, on discerne encore une partie de ce qui fut et l'on découvre en partie ce qui va être" (*L'Art* [Paris, 1911], p. 77).

58. "Gotovyj past' na nix s otvažnoj krutizny." There is an intentional play on the two meanings of Russian *past'*: (1) to fall; (2) to descend upon, to attack.

59. See "Poetry of Grammar and Grammar of Poetry" [included in this volume].

60. See O. Ostrogorskij, "Gnoseologičeskie osnovy vizantijskogo spora o sv. ikonax," *Seminarium Kondakovianum* II, 47–48.

61. Puškin's dearest friend and faithful admirer, author of the idyll "The Invention of Sculpture."

62. "Poèzija Puškina" in his *Ètjudy po russkoy poèzii* (Prague, 1926), pp. 65–224, esp. 129ff.

63. Cf. Mixail D. Geršenzon, *Mudrost' Puškina* (Moscow, 1919), pp. 14ff.

64. Rodin, *L'Art,* p. 72.

65. Cf. T. Zenger, "Nikolaj I, redaktor Puškina," *Literaturnoe nasledstvo* 16–18 (1934), 522.

66. Cf. V. F. Xodasevič's interesting article "Koščunstva Puškina," *Sovremennye zapiski* 19 (1924), 405–413, and E. G. Kislicyna's mass of material in "K voprosu ob otnošenii Puškina k religii," *Puškinskij sbornik pamjati professora Semena Afanas'eviča Vengerova* (Moscow–Petrograd, 1923), pp. 233–269.

67. The Russian Old Believer tradition very sharply opposed the statue as a pagan feature, and it is noteworthy that according to one of the original sketches for *The Bronze Horseman,* Evgenij's ancestor fought against Peter on the side of the Old Believers.

68. Bém, *O Puškine,* p. 80.

69. See Geršenzon in *Iskusstvo* 1 (1923), 137.

70. "Mne naplevat' na bronzy mnogopud'e, mne naplevat' na mramornuju sliz' . . ." (I spit on the tons of bronze, I spit on the marble slime).

71. "Je dis: une fleur! et, hors de l'oubli où ma voix relègue aucun contour, en tant que quelque chose d'autre que les calices sus, musicalement se lève, idée même et suave, l'absente de tous bouquets." Stéphane Mallarmé, "Crise de vers," *Oeuvres complètes* (Paris, 1945), p. 368.

19. What Is Poetry?

First delivered as a lecture in Czech to the artists' society Mánes, Prague, and published under the title "Co je poezie?" in *Volné směry* 30 (1933–34). The translation by Michael Heim reprinted here first appeared in *Semiotics of Art: Prague School Contributions,* ed. Ladislav Matejka and Irwin Titunik (Cambridge, Mass.: MIT Press, 1976).

1. *Poems:* "Your blue eyes. Raspberry lips. Golden hair. The hour that robbed her of everything had inscribed a fascinating sorrow and melancholy on her mouth, eyes, and brow." *Prose:* "Marinka": "Black hair fell artlessly in heavy curls around her pale, gaunt face, which bore the tokens of great beauty, and down upon a pure white dress, which, buttoned up to her neck and reaching down to her tiny feet, revealed a tall, slender frame. A black sash contained her frail body, and a black hairpin spanned her beautiful, high, white brow. But nothing could touch the beauty of her fiery, black, deeply set eyes. No pen can describe that expression of melancholy and yearning." "Cikáni" (The Gypsies): "Her black curls heightened the beautiful pallor of her tender face, and her black eyes, which smiled for the first time today, had not yet lain aside their long enduring melancholy." *The diary:* "I lifted up her skirt and inspected her from the front, the sides, and the back . . . What a fabulous ass . . . She had beautifully white thighs . . . I played with her foot, and she took off a stocking and sat down on the couch," and so on.

2. The original has a coarser ring to it.

3. See also "The Gypsies": "My father! My father seduced my mother—no, he murdered my mother—he used my mother—he did not use my mother to seduce

my beloved—he seduced my father's beloved—my mother—and my father murdered my father!"

4. Here is how Mácha describes his febrile state three days before his death: "When I read that Lori had been out, I flew into a rage that could have been the death of me. I've been looking very bad ever since. I have smashed everything here to pieces. My first thought was that I had to leave and that she could do what she pleased. I knew why I didn't even want her to leave the house." He threatens her in iambs: "Bei meinem Leben schwor ich Dir, Du sichst mich niemals wieder."

20. Notes on Myth in Erben's Work

Part One of "Poznámky k dílu Erbenovu," *Slovo a slovesnost* 1 (Prague, 1935). The translation by John Burbank appears here for the first time.

1. Antonín Grund, *Karel Jaromír Erben* (Prague, 1935); *Národopisný věstník československý* (1932–33), *Listy filologické* (1933), *Časopis Českého muzea* (1934).

2. I am leaving aside the tempting question of the characteristic differences between the mythology of "The Willow" and that of its indisputable model—here I am in agreement with Otakar Fischer—Božena Němcová's story "Viktorka."

3. According to Erben's note on "The Wedding Shirts," the "healthy, strong spirit of the people" manifests itself in this triumph over "immoderate love."

4. Cf. "When a weighty time falls on you, then I bring you a branch of hope."

5. See K. Wais, *Das Vater-Sohn Motiv in der Dichtung, 1880–1930* (Berlin–Leipzig, 1931).

6. "*Že přes to tělo* i *přes to čelo*—mnohé jaro, *léto* již *přeletělo*" (this word is a "euphonic contamination" of the words *léto* and *tělo*); "*A povsta*ne znovu *v posta*vě jiné"; "*ha, co to h*ulákáš *h*oloto, po lese?"; "*tě*la mého *k*os*ti* zach*rastí*ly m*raz*em"; "zuby mi jek*taly a vstávaly vlasy*"; "na *sta—zás*tup ros*te*"; "*A peklo? Ha peklo!*—Kdo se *leká pekla!* Já se *nelekám!* Vrah se *peklu* směje" (cf. the polyptoton, likewise intensifying the play of the consonants *k-l*, in *May:* "U *kolo* vpleteno nad *ků*lem v *kol*e pnělo, i hlava nad *kol*em").

7. The image of the mother in connection with the theme of hell also appears in a dream recorded by the poet and belonging to the period close to the writing of "Záhoř I." In this poem Erben obviously drew from the records of his dreams. The entry in question concurs with "Záhoř I" motivationally, compositionally, and textually. In both cases there are descriptions of a sudden awakening from a horrifying dream and the transition to a new dream introduced by the same remark: "I again fell asleep." Both here and there we find a cave associated with hell, infernal creatures, and yells, and the image of the father flashes momentarily. Erben's dream is a typical ambivalent dream. A red blaze, fed by odd things and ringing with the harmonious music of unknown instruments with pleasing voices, appears as a symbol of something seductive, but at the same time it frightens Erben with the coarse and squealing singing of the Prince of Hell, and that song underscores the ambivalent character of the entire plot with its prophecy: "You the first—the last on this earth." "And as I was standing here, contemplating, fearing, its devilish meaning, I suddenly saw standing beside me my mother who seemed to be ordering me to do something very sternly; on the other hand, I then urgently entreated her to let me stay here for a while." The content of the mother's command is unknown; hence it admits an ambiguous interpretation. The son asks his mother

to let him stay in the proximity of the seductive flame; however, the mother dreads the destructiveness of that longing or, on the contrary, draws him toward the ominous fire, while the son is horrified by Lucifer's menacing singing. When he wakes up, he has in mind an association with the folk ballad about the maiden whom the black men drag to hell, while she begs that they leave her: "When I sing to you, I will call my father." This association already reflects Erben's attempt to supplant an infantile dream by a dream.

8. [A lengthy juxtaposition of passages from Erben's "Prophesy" and Mácha's "On the King's Arrival" is omitted, since it depends on nuances of Czech inaccessible to most English readers.]

21. In Memory of V. V. Hanka

Originally published in Russian under the title "Pamjati V. V. Ganki" in *Central'naja Evropa* 4 (1931). The translation by Krystyna Pomorska and Stephen Rudy appears here for the first time.

22. Quest for the Essence of Language

Address to the American Academy of Arts and Sciences, February 10, 1965; originally published in *Diogenes* 51 (1966).

23. On Linguistic Aspects of Translation

Originally published in *On Translation,* ed. Reuben A. Brower (Cambridge: Harvard University Press, 1959).

1. Bertrand Russell, "Logical Positivism," *Revue internationale de philosophie* 4 (1950), 18; cf. p. 3.

2. John Dewey, "Peirce's Theory of Linguistic Signs, Thought, and Meaning," *Journal of Philosophy* 43 (1946), 91.

3. Benjamin Lee Whorf, *Language, Thought, and Reality* (Cambridge, Mass., 1956), p. 235.

4. Niels Bohr, "On the Notions of Causality and Complementarity," *Dialectica* 1 (1948), 317ff.

5. James R. Masterson and Wendell Brooks Phillips, *Federal Prose* (Chapel Hill, 1948), pp. 40–41.

6. Cf. Knut Bergsland, "Finsk-ugrisk og almen språkvitenskap," *Nordsk Tidsskrift for Sprogvidenskap* 15 (1949), 374–375.

7. Franz Boas, "Language," *General Anthropology* (Boston, 1938), pp. 132–133.

8. André Vaillant, "La Préface de l'Évangéliaire vieux-slave," *Revue des études slaves* 24 (1948), 5–6.

24. A Glance at the Development of Semiotics

Opening address to the First International Congress of Semiotics, Milan, June 2, 1974; first published, in French, by Indiana University Press under the title *Coup d'oeil sur le développement de la sémiotique* (Bloomington, 1975). The translation by

Patricia Baudoin reprinted here first appeared in Jakobson's *The Framework of Language* (Ann Arbor: University of Michigan, 1980).

1. Emile Benveniste, *Coup d'oeil sur le développement de la linguistique* (Paris: Academie des inscriptions et belles-lettres, 1963).

2. John Locke, *Essay Concerning Human Understanding* (1694), book IV, ch. 21, sec. 4.

3. Jean Henri Lambert, *Neues Organon, oder Gedanken über die Erforschung und Bezeichnung des Wahren und dessen Unterscheidung vom Irrthum und Schein* 1–2 (Leipzig, 1764). Reprint: *Philosophische Schriften* 1–2, ed. Hans-Werner Arndt (Hildesheim, 1965).

4. Cf. Max E. Eisenring, *Johann Heinrich Lambert und die wissenschaftliche Philosophie der Gegenwart* (Zürich, 1942), pp. 7, 12, 48, 82.

5. Charles Sanders Peirce, *Collected Papers,* I (Cambridge, Mass., 1933), p. 588. Further references to this edition, vols. I–VIII (1931–1958), are given in text with volume and page number in parentheses.

6. J. M. Hoene-Wroński, "Philosophie du langage," *Septs manuscrits inédits écrits de 1803 à 1806* (Paris, 1897).

7. Jerzy Bronisław Brau, *Aperçu de la philosophie de Wroński* (Rome, 1969).

8. Bernard Bolzano, *Wissenschaftslehre. Versuch einer ausführlichen und grösstentheils neuen Darstellung der Logik mit steter Rücksicht auf deren bisherige Bearbeiten* 1–4 (Sulzbach, 1837; reprint ed. Wolfgang Schultz, Leipzig, 1930–31).

9. Edmund Husserl, "Zur Logik der Zeichen (Semiotik)," *Gesammelte Werke* 12 (The Hague, 1970).

10. Elmar Holenstein, *Linguistik, Semiotik, Hermeneutik: Plädoyers für eine strukturale Phänomenologie* (Frankfurt, 1976), p. 206, n. 9.

11. Cf. Irwin C. Lieb, ed., *Charles S. Peirce's Letters to Lady Welby* (New Haven, 1953), p. 40.

12. Jakobson, "Quest for the Essence of Language," *SW* II, 345ff [included in this volume].

13. Lieb, *Peirce's Letters,* p. 39.

14. Ibid., pp. 51–53.

15. See Ferdinand de Saussure, *Cours de linguistique générale,* ed. Rudolf Engler (Wiesbaden, 1974), II, 47ff. Further references to this edition (I, 1967; II, 1974) are given in text with volume and page number in parentheses.

16. Robert Godel, *Les Sources manuscrites du "Cours de linguistique générale" de F. de Saussure* (Geneva, 1957), p. 275.

17. Ibid., p. 49.

18. "Notes inédites," *Cahiers Ferdinand de Saussure* 12 (1954), 71.

19. Cited in Jakobson, "World Response to Whitney's Principles of Linguistic Science," *SW* VII, 228ff.

20. Ibid.

21. Adrien Naville, *Nouvelle classification des sciences. Étude philosophique* (Paris, 1901), chap. 5.

22. Cited in Jakobson, "World Response," *SW* VII, 228.

23. Ibid.

24. Cf. Jean Starobinski, *Les Mots sous le mots: Les Anagrammes de Ferdinand de Saussure* (Paris, 1971), p. 15.

25. Cf. his notes published by D'Arco Silvio Avalle, "Noto sul 'segno,'" *Stru-*

menti critici 19 (1972), 28–38; cf. D. S. Avalle, "La Sémiologie de la narrativité chez Saussure," in *Essais de la théorie du texte*, ed. C. Bouazis (Paris, 1973).

26. René Thom, "La Linguistique, discipline morphologique exemplaire," *Critique* 30 (1974), 244ff.

27. Ernst Cassirer, "Structuralism in Modern Linguistics," *Word* 1 (1945), 115.

28. Gerard Manley Hopkins, "Poetic Diction" (1865), in *Journals and Papers* (London, 1959), p. 84.

29. Starobinski, *Les Mots*, p. 34.

30. Ibid., pp. 21, 31ff.

31. Ibid., p. 55.

32. Ibid., p. 47.

33. Igor Stravinsky, *Poetics of Music in the Form of Six Lessons* (Cambridge, Mass., 1942).

34. Leonard B. Meyer, *Music, the Arts, and Ideas* (Chicago, 1967), pp. 6ff.

35. Jan Maegaard, *Studien zur Entwicklung des dodekaphonen Satzes bei Arnold Schönberg* (Copenhagen, 1974).

36. Christian von Ehrenfels, "Über 'Gestaltqualitäten,'" *Vierteljahrsschrift für wissenschaftliche Philosophie* 14:3 (1890), 263ff.

37. Cf. Jakobson, "On Visual and Auditory Signs" and "About the Relation between Visual and Auditory Signs," *SW* II, 334–344. [A combined version of these two essays appears in this volume as Chapter 27.]

38. Cf. Heinrich Lausberg, *Handbuch der literarischen Rhetorik* (Munich, 1960), pgh. 572.

25. Musicology and Linguistics

First published in *Prager Presse*, December 7, 1932, under the title "Musikwissenschaft und Linguistik." The translation by Anne Chatoney Shreffler reprinted here first appeared in *Sonus: A Journal of Investigations into Global Musical Possibilities* 3:2 (Spring 1983).

1. G. Becking, "Der musikalische Bau des Montenegrischen Volksepos," *Proceedings of the First International Congress of Phonetic Sciences, Amsterdam, July 3–8, 1932* (*Archives Néerlandaises de phonétique expérimentale* 8–9, 1933), pp. 144, 153.

26. Is the Film in Decline?

Originally published under the title "Úpadek filmu?" in *Listy pro umění a kritiku* 1 (Prague, 1933), 45–49. The translation by Elena Sokol reprinted here was revised by Jakobson for publication in *Semiotics of Art: Prague School Contributions*, ed. Ladislav Matejka and I. Titunik (Cambridge, Mass.: MIT Press, 1976).

1. Puškin, *Journey to Erzerum*.

2. See Lev Kulešov, *Repeticionnyj metod v kino* (Moscow, 1922).

3. See Louis Delluc, *Photogénie* (Paris, 1920).

4. See Boris Èjxenbaum, "Problemy kinostilistiki," in *Poètika kino* (Moscow, 1927).

5. Jurij Tynjanov, "Ob osnovax kino," in *Poètika kino* (Moscow, 1927). [French translation: "Fondements du cinéma," *Cahiers du cinéma*, 1970.]

6. See Jean Epstein, *Bonjour cinéma* (Paris, 1921).

7. Emile Vuillermoz, "La Musique des images," in *L'Art cinématographique,* III (Paris, 1927).

8. *Der sichtbare Mensche oder die Kultur des Films* (Vienna–Leipzig, 1924), p. 143.

9. *Iskusstvo kino i montaž fil'ma: Opyt vvedenija v teoriju i èstetiku kino* (Leningrad, 1926), p. 71.

10. "Die Behandlung gleichzeitiger Ereignisse im Antiken Epos," *Philologus,* suppl. 8:3 (1901), 422.

27. On the Relation Between Visual and Auditory Signs

This text combines two papers: "On Visual and Auditory Signs," *Phonetica* 11 (1964), and "About the Relation between Visual and Auditory Signs," concluding remarks at the Symposium on Models for the Perception of Speech and Visual Form, Boston, October 1964, published in the proceedings of the symposium (1967); see *SW* II, 334–337, 338–344. Jakobson's montage of the two papers, which he made for the second volume of his *Essais de linguistique générale* (Paris: Les Editions de Minuit, 1973), appears here in English for the first time.

1. M. I. Aronson, "Radiofilme," *Slavische Rundschau* 1 (1929), 539ff.

2. Around 43–45 percent of the world's population is totally illiterate, and 65–70 percent functionally illiterate, according to the UNESCO statistical survey *L'Analphabétisme dans le monde au milieu du XXe siècle* (1957). According to the results of more recent research published in the *Harvard Educational Review* (1970), more than half of the population of the United States over the age of twenty-five does not possess the level of literacy necessary to master such common documents as street signs, newspapers, and job applications.

3. John Lotz, "Natural and Scientific Language," *Proceedings of the American Academy of Arts and Sciences* 80 (1951), 87–88.

4. Edward Sapir, "Language," *Selected Writings of Edward Sapir in Language, Culture, and Personality,* ed. David G. Mandelbaum (Berkeley, 1949), p. 7.

5. Charles Sanders Peirce, "Speculative Grammar," *Collected Papers* (Cambridge, Mass., 1932), II, 129–130.

6. Alexander Luria, *Mozg čeloveka i psixičeskie processy* (Moscow, 1963).

7. I. M. Sečenov, *Èlementy mysli* (Moscow, 1959).

8. Alexander Luria, "Disorders of Simulantaneous Perception in a Case of Bilateral Occipito-parietal Brain Injury," *Brain* 82 (1950), 437–438.

9. George A. Miller, "The Magical Number Seven, Plus-or-minus Two, or, Some Limits on Our Capacity for Processing Information," *Psychological Review,* 63 (1959).

10. Alvin M. Liberman and F. S. Cooper, "Some Observations on a Model for Speech Percpetion," *Proceedings of the AFCRL Symposium on Models for the Perception of Speech and Visual Form,* ed. W. Watten-Dun (Cambridge, Mass., 1967).

28. Motor Signs for "Yes" and "No"

The original Russian version of this paper, "'Da' i 'net' v mimike," was published in *Jazyk i čelovek,* a memorial volume for P. S. Kuznecov (Moscow: University of Moscow, 1970). Jakobson's English version of the essay, reprinted here, first appeared in *Language in Society* 1:1 (1971).

1. Giuseppe Cocchiara, in his interesting book *Il Linguaggio del gesto* (Turin, 1932), poses the question: "Il linguaggio del gesto è un linguaggio universale?" (p. 20).

2. A common colloquial metonymic expression in Russian meaning "to have a drink"—cf. English "to down a few."

3. Charles Sanders Peirce, "Speculative Grammar," *Collected Papers,* II (Cambridge, Mass., 1932). D. Efron uses the term "pictorialism," in *Gesture and Environment* (New York, 1941).

4. Arnold H. Landor remarks that for affirmation and negation the Ainu do not use head motions, but only hand gestures: "Both hands are gracefully brought up to the chest and prettily waved downwards—palms upwards—in sign of affirmation. In other words, their affirmation is a simpler form of their salute, just the same as with us the nodding of the head is similarly used both ways" (*Alone with the Hairy Apes,* London, 1893, p. 234).

5. The analysis of affirmative and negative hand gestures does not enter into the present analysis. A copious but rather mechanical and unsystematic compendium was made by Garrick Mallery: "Sign Language among North American Indians," *Bureau of Ethnology, Annual Report* 1 (1881), 263–552. In connection with the numerous examples of the hand—with the fingers held touching each other—moving forward and downward as a sign of agreement, the author refers to sources interpreting the hand in the yes-gesture of the Dakota and Iroquois Indians as a metaphor for an affirmative nod of the head (p. 455). Cf. W. Tomkins, *Universal Indian Sign Language* (San Diego, 1926), p. 58.

6. "Puede reforzarse por la iteración simple o mútiple," as G. Meo-Zilio puts it: "El lenguaje de los gestos, en el Uruguay," *Boletín de Filología* 13 (1961), 129. Cf. G. Meo-Zilio, *El Lenguaje de los gestos en el Rió de la Plata* (Montevideo, 1960), p. 100.

7. This kind of negative movement of the head specifically to the left has been observed, e.g. among the Indians of Terra del Fuego (see M. Gusinde, "Die Yamana: vom Leben und Denken der Wasser-nomaden am Kap Hoorn," *Die Feuerland-Indianer,* Vienna, 1937, II, 1447) and among the Persians (D. C. Phillott, "A Note on Sign, Gesture, and Secret Language amongst the Persians," *Journal and Proceedings of the Asiatic Society of Bengal,* 3.9 (1892), 619–622.

8. Among many peoples in both hemispheres, the iconic gesture accompanying or replacing the head motion for "no" consists of raising the palms—open and with fingers extended—in front of the addressee, as if in a sign of rebuff or defense. The hands in this gesture move either forward and back, as if parrying the other party, or from side to side, as if shutting oneself off from him, brushing him aside or pushing away from him. These two variants can be compared to two variants of the gesture of threatening, which are related to them in both form and meaning: the movement of the raised index finger perpendicular to the line of the shoulders in Eastern Europe or parallel to the shoulders in the Central European region.

9. Ferdinand de Saussure, *Cours de linguistique générale* (Paris, 1916), chap. 1, sec. 2.

10. As Mallery states, "The ancient Greeks, followed by the modern Turks and rustic Italians, threw the head back, instead of shaking it, for 'no'" ("Sign Language among North American Indians," p. 441). It is interesting that in the cases of occurrence of both forms of negation—vertical and horizontal—the selection

of the first of these two gesticulatory synonyms in southern Italy is interpreted in the same way as a look meekly directed upward in avoidance of a bold, unseemly, categorical denial or of an impolite, point-blank refusal.

11. A similar correlation has been observed among the Persians (see Phillott) and the Polynesians (A. Métraux, *Ethnology of Easter Islands,* Honolulu, 1940, p. 33).

12. I would like to thank Claude Lévi-Strauss for the valuable bibliographical references he so kindly provided.

29. On the Verbal Art of William Blake and Other Poet-Painters

Originally published in *Linguistic Inquiry* 1:1 (1970), dedicated to Meyer Schapiro.

1. See *The Poetry and Prose of William Blake,* ed. D. V. Erdman (New York, 1965), pp. 719–721.

2. Jacob Bronowski, *William Blake and the Age of Revolution* (New York, 1965), p. 161.

3. Ibid., p. 139.

4. Jakobson, "Poetry of Grammar and Grammar of Poetry," in *SW* III, 94 [included in this volume].

5. See Northrop Frye, *Fearful Symmetry: A Study of William Blake* (New York, 1965), p. 105.

6. See Guillaume Apollinaire, "Le Douanier," in *Les Soirées de Paris* 3:20 (January 15, 1913, actually 1914), 56.

7. Ibid., pp. 11, 65.

8. See Dora Vallier, *Tout l'oeuvre peint de Henri Rousseau* (Paris, 1970), p. 10.

9. Thanks are due to the Museum of Modern Art in New York for the reproduction of *The Dream* and for their kind permission to use it as an illustration in this essay.

10. Cf. Tristan Tzara, "Le Rôle du temps et de l'espace dans l'oeuvre du Douanier Rousseau," *Art de France* 2 (1962).

11. Damourette and Pichon, *Des mots à la pensée,* sec. 272.

12. Vallier, "Tout l'oeuvre peint de Henri Rousseau, pl. 25.

13. See Guillaume Apollinaire, *Chroniques d'art* (Paris, 1960), p. 76.

14. Jean Bouret, *Henri Rousseau* (Neuchatel, 1961), p. 50.

15. See Apollinaire, "Le Douanier," p. 57.

16. Cf. Alexander Luria, *Higher Cortical Functions in Man and Their Disturbances in Local Brain Lesions* (Moscow, 1962).

17. Lucien Tesnière, *Éléments de syntaxe structurale* (Paris, 1966).

18. Bouret, *Henri Rousseau,* p. 50.

19. Vratislav Effenberger, *Henri Rousseau* (Prague, 1963).

20. C. Gledion-Welcker, *Anthologie der Abseitigen* (Bern, 1946).

21. See the autograph reproduced in *Gedichte von Paul Klee,* edited by the painter's son, Felix Klee (Zurich, 1960), p. 56.

22. *Tagebücher von Paul Klee, 1898–1918* (Cologne, 1957), no. 539; *Gedichte,* p. 56.

INDEX